Comparative Politics
of Latin America

This new edition brings Daniel C. Hellinger's brilliantly succinct and accessible introduction to Latin America up to date for a new generation of educators. In crisp detail, Hellinger gives a panoramic overview of the continent and offers a unique balance of comparative politics theory and interdisciplinary country-specific context, of a thematic organization and in-depth country case studies, of culture and economics, of scholarship and pedagogy. Insightful historical background in early chapters provides students with ways to think about how the past influences the present. However, while history plays a part in this text, comparative politics is the primary focus, explaining through fully integrated, detailed case studies and carefully paced analysis. Country-specific narratives are integrated with concepts and theories from comparative politics, leading to a richer understanding of both.

Updates to this new edition include:

- Revisiting contemporary populism and the global emergence of right-wing populism.
- The pros and cons of extractivism; the impact of Chinese investment and trade.
- Contemporary crisis in Venezuela; expanded treatment of Colombia and Peru.
- The role of the military; LGBTQ+ issues; corruption; violence; identity issues.
- New sections on social media, artificial intelligence, and big data cyber technologies.
- Examination of post-Castro Cuba; Costa Rica's exceptionalism.
- Broader study of environmental movements; how governments relate to social movements.
- Examination of personalist parties; refugee and asylum rights.
- Interventionist policies of the current U.S. administration.
- Early impact of the COVID-19 pandemic.

Comparative Politics of Latin America is a thoughtful, ambitious, and thorough introductory textbook for students beginning Latin American Studies at the undergraduate level.

Daniel C. Hellinger is Professor Emeritus of International Relations, Webster University. His other books include *Venezuela: Tarnished Democracy* (1991); *Venezuelan Politics in the Chávez Era* (2001), and *Bolivarian Democracy in Venezuela* (2011). He has held Fulbright awards at the Universidad Católica de Valparaíso, Chile, and the Autonomous University of Madrid and has been a visiting scholar at St. Antony's College, Oxford, the Central University of Venezuela, and Shanghai Institute for Finance and Economics.

"Like no other, Hellinger's book incisively analyzes the complexities of Latin American politics and development. It allows students to develop the analytical and critical thinking skills, as well as the empathy, needed to comprehend the region today. This third edition will continue to be an essential tool for students and practitioners at all levels."

Angelo Rivero Santos, *Center for Latin American Studies,*
Georgetown University

"The organization of this book around the contemporary themes of democracy, inclusion, social justice and development, both motivates and fits perfectly with the learning needs of students in global studies and international development programs. This is my go-to textbook."

Paul A. Haslam, *University of Ottawa*

"I highly recommend this text for undergraduate Latin American politics classes. The conversational style is attractive and accessible to students. The thematic approach, with country illustrations, identifies the important challenges and progress, while keeping students from getting bogged down in a country-by-country approach. The comparative approach and the highlighting of competing scholarly views helps to develop student analytical skills. Updated to 2020, it even includes the pandemic crisis."

Jennifer McCoy, *Professor of Political Science,*
Georgia State University

"This Third Edition of Dan Hellinger's *Comparative Politics of Latin America* is a great introductory text for students interested in Latin American politics. The focus of the text is on questions that are specific to Comparative Politics but it does not neglect the role of history, culture, socio-economic, and international issues which all contribute to the diversity of Latin American politics. This new edition gives particular attention to questions related to understanding how the political and economic crises have contributed to deep and immediate challenges to democracy in the region."

Tony Spanakos, *Monclair State University*

"This new edition takes an already outstanding textbook and advances it in a timely and meaningful way. In the last decade, Latin America has changed in ways that have forced scholars and policymakers to rethink how critical aspects of democracy and development work (or don't) in the region. Hellinger has ably recast the entire text in light of the growing awareness of shortcomings and opportunities in dominant political and economic models, and this book helps us see the region in a fresh, and insightful, perspective."

Matthew Carnes, *Associate Professor of Government,*
Georgetown University

Comparative Politics of Latin America

Democracy at Last?

Third Edition

Daniel C. Hellinger

Routledge
Taylor & Francis Group

NEW YORK AND LONDON

Third edition published 2021
by Routledge
52 Vanderbilt Avenue, New York, NY 10017

and by Routledge
2 Park Square, Milton Park, Abingdon, Oxon, OX14 4RN

Routledge is an imprint of the Taylor & Francis Group, an informa business

© 2021 Taylor & Francis

First edition published by Routledge 2011

Second edition published by Routledge 2014

Library of Congress Cataloging-in-Publication Data
Names: Hellinger, Daniel, author.
Title: Comparative politics of Latin America : democracy at last? / Daniel C. Hellinger.
Description: Third edition. | New York, NY : Routledge, 2021. | Includes bibliographical references and index.
Identifiers: LCCN 2020026535 (print) | LCCN 2020026536 (ebook) | ISBN 9780367898953 (hardback) | ISBN 9780367898915 (paperback) | ISBN 9781003021865 (ebook) | ISBN 9781000220612 (adobe pdf) | ISBN 9781000220636 (mobi) | ISBN 9781000220650 (epub)
Subjects: LCSH: Latin America—Politics and government. | Comparative government—Latin America.
Classification: LCC JL960 .H45 2021 (print) | LCC JL960 (ebook) | DDC 320.3098—dc23
LC record available at https://lccn.loc.gov/2020026535
LC ebook record available at https://lccn.loc.gov/2020026536

ISBN: 978-0-367-89895-3 (hbk)
ISBN: 978-0-367-89891-5 (pbk)
ISBN: 978-1-003-02186-5 (ebk)

Typeset in Minion Pro
by Apex CoVantage, LLC

Visit the companion website: www.routledge.com/cw/hellinger

Dedication

To the late Dr. Benjamin Barber, indefatigable advocate for strong democracy.

Contents

Punto de Vista Feature Boxes

Figures

Tables

Preface

When I did the revisions for the second edition (2013) of this text, I optimistically wrote, "Neither liberal nor Marxist orthodoxy has much appeal to most people in the region today, and perhaps that explains why Latin America has been a hothouse for democratic experimentation." Now, six years later, the first part of that sentence remains true; the second part seems, well, myopic.

The retreat from experiments with more egalitarian and participatory democracy is undeniable as the 2020s loom. Some of the responsibility rests with the failures of leadership among the leaders who presided over the most ambitious projects in Venezuela, Brazil, Ecuador, and Bolivia, but they often faced disloyal oppositions supported by U.S. money and power. I hope that the students, teachers, and other readers who take the time to read this book will find that there remains much to admire and to learn from these experiments. Political solutions to the Latin American and global problems lie in the more egalitarian and participatory conception of democracy that Latin Americans have tried to develop.

Readers might note that the subtitle of the third edition has shifted from "Democracy at Last?" to "Can Democracy Last?" Some of my colleagues and collaborators in academic projects will disagree with the conclusion in the Afterword that dissatisfying as it may be, liberal democracy is the one we've got for now. It is endangered and worth defending.

My own agenda for democracy puts me somewhere on the left of the political spectrum, but I hope readers will feel this text has fairly represented arguments drawn from the liberal tradition of democracy and the orthodox pluralist views that dominate American political science. I would like comparative political scientists, whose work reflects different views on democracy, to feel that this book is passionate, is intellectually honest, and avoids polemics. As in the first two editions, this volume uses a thematic framework rather than a country-by-country approach. I feel it is the best method to help students organize the massive amount of information typically provided in courses of this nature.

Latin Americans have contributed in the last 30 years to the quest for more perfect democracy. The worldwide human rights movement began in Latin America during its last transition from military rule to electoral democracy. The region's social movements continue to reconceptualize the relationship among the state, civil society, and the market, seeking to tame both the centralized power of states and the tyranny of market forces. Brazilians started experimenting 25 years ago with participatory budgeting, a practice now spreading to other parts of the globe. Andean Indigenous peoples have gone further than anyone in promoting responsible stewardship of the earth on a world stage, insisting that we can have the good life (*buen vivir*) without the materialism and consumption of unbridled capitalism. Venezuelans have provided the world with its first constitution written in gender-neutral language. Cubans wrestle with how to open their economy and politics without losing the values of solidarity, facing the challenge of a transition from the old Leninist model of the state. It is much more common to find women in executive positions in Latin America, even in the presidency, than in North America.

We in the North should learn from their successes, not just their shortcomings.

Changes From the Second to the Third Edition

I have thoroughly updated the second edition. In addition, a few changes in how chapters are organized and features enhanced are worth noting.

- The two chapters on, respectively, democratic breakdowns and transitions now belong more in Part III, dealing with historical legacies. Some of the discussion of the military in politics has been relocated to chapter 10, which otherwise is mostly new and explores military influence in politics today.
- Largely thanks to the suggestions of perceptive reviewers, I have introduced new material on social media and on new cyber and communication technologies. Some of the political implications for political campaigning, protest politics, and state surveillance can be found in chapter 12; implications for Latin American dependency and the quest for development are included in chapter 15, on globalization.
- I have significantly expanded coverage of three Andean countries—Peru, Colombia, and Ecuador. More space has been given to themes not previously treated in sufficient depth in earlier editions, including LGBTQ+ struggles, femicide, and, of course, health, given the impact that the coronavirus has had. The idea of "precarity," which has become a major theme in the literature on populism, has been integrated into several sections of the book, including those examining COVID-19 and the social class structure. Besides integrating this theme into discussion of Latin America's informal sector, I have provided tables and discussion that demonstrate how it influences middle-class politics.
- Chapter 16 in the second edition took the viewpoint that U.S. hegemony in the region was weakening and that new diplomatic organizations excluding Washington showed promise. The waning of this promise and the policies of the Trump administration means that I have returned to giving more weight to U.S./Latin America relations. However, chapter 15 on globalization reflects a counter trend to U.S. influence, as Asia (especially China) has expanded trade and investment in the region.

Learning Aids in This Edition

In response to feedback from instructors, some new pedagogy was introduced in the second edition. Here there is little new, but all these features have been retained, updated, and revised to reflect new and changed material. Thumbnail "locator" maps are strategically placed throughout the text to help geographically challenged students develop familiarity with the location of countries. "Democracy Snapshots" from the 2018 Latinobarómetro poll on attitudes toward democracy for various Latin American countries are also included where each country is discussed in depth. These "snapshots" provide instructors with an interesting talking point in class. I would urge instructors and students to examine results from 2019 and subsequent years as they become available (free). The "Punto de Vista" debate boxes appear in every chapter and ask students to debate issues facing citizens in Latin American countries, including affirmative action programs in Brazil, Ecuador's regulation of the media, Uruguay's amnesty for human rights abuses, and which of Venezuela's two claimants to the presidency in 2019 had the better case. The glossary of key terms has been updated.

Companion Website

Routledge hosts a companion website that includes a number of useful resources for both students and instructors. Students looking for extra study aids will find chapter summaries, country profiles from Europa World, and web links to online resources. We are fortunate to be able to partner with Europa because they have a wealth of information available on the countries of Latin America. The inclusion of select Europa World content enables teachers to combine the thematic approach of this book with assignments to help provide students with a coherent narrative of the history, the social and economic features, and the recent development of individual nations in the region. It is also a good resource for students to have on hand if they are not familiar with the region or if they are researching a country-specific topic for the course. To help instructors with classroom preparation, the companion website includes PowerPoint lecture slides, suggestions for exam questions, suggestions for classroom activities, and more. The accompanying website has been thoroughly updated and revised. The companion website can be found at https://routledgetextbooks.com/textbooks/_author/hellinger/.

Acknowledgments

In addition to all of those who helped with the first and second editions, I especially want to thank several people whose work has helped enormously in this third edition. I always must start with my love and life-partner, Joann Eng-Hellinger, whose patience and support is invaluable. Once again I want to thank especially commissioning editor Michael Kerns at Routledge for his faith in the first edition. Also deserving of my thanks is Phil Meeks for taking on development of a website that I hope teachers and students will find to be an invaluable resource. When Sawyer Judge, a high school junior, approached me about helping do research for this book, I was skeptical that she would have the background and skills at such a young age. I put her to work finding new entries for "Resources for Further Study," and she did a fine job. Jake Seifert helped me compile the glossary and references for the second edition, read every chapter carefully with the eye of a student, identifying unclear and confusing passages in need of redrafting, and culled many of the mistakes in the penultimate draft of the book. This time I benefited from the sharp eye of Mackenzie Long-Sánchez, a Webster University student. Rebecca Pearce, the textbook development manager at Routledge at the time the second edition was prepared, deserves credit for the idea of creating the "Puntos de Vista." Two members of my family, Gabrielle Serang-Hellinger and Michael Hellinger, drew original graphical representations of supply chains to enhance chapter 15. Thanks to Natalja Mortenson and Charlie Baker for their faith in this text and their help and patience. Thanks also to Kate Fornadel, whose copy-editing caught so many errors and made the book just so much better written overall. (I learned from another publisher the hard way just how necessary a good editor is.) A special thank you to the reviewers, anonymous and otherwise, whose insights and recommendations have helped to improve this edition. Any shortcomings or mistakes in this text are ultimately my responsibility.

Introduction

Latin American Studies and the Comparative Study of Democracy

Focus Questions

▶ Why should we focus on democracy as the theme for an introduction to Latin America, a region long associated with political instability, military coups, and dictatorships?

▶ What do opinion polls tell us about support for democracy in Latin America today?

▶ Why does the study of Latin America fall into the field called "comparative politics"?

TWENTY YEARS AGO, most political scientists believed that a "third wave" of democratization had enveloped the world. The only debatable question seemed to be how long before the laggards in the world community would join the rising tide. In Latin America, the rising tide took on a rosy hue, with the rise of leftist parties and movements eager to embark on experiments in participatory democracy and more equal economic relationships, especially on the South American continent. Leftist governments came to power through electoral processes in Venezuela, Bolivia, Brazil, Argentina, Chile, Nicaragua, El Salvador, and Uruguay. In other countries, most notably Mexico, leftist parties or movements were not governing but exercised significant influence. Cuba too, though still a one-party state, seemed ready to liberalize as it faced a future without Fidel and Raúl Castro. The fact that the United States, by far the dominant power—the **hegemon**—in the hemisphere, had elected Barack Obama as its first **Afro-descendent** president reinforced the idea that at least in this hemisphere, democracy would not only be lasting, but broader and deeper.

Today, most Latin Americans younger than 40 do not have a direct memory of the period between 1973 and 1990, when democracy barely existed. All the countries of the **Southern Cone** of the continent were under harsh military rule. (You can find definitions of terms in bold in the glossary.) Central America was wracked by three civil wars involving leftist insurgencies against brutal military regimes. Venezuela, Colombia, and Costa Rica remained liberal democracies but did not entirely escape the weakening of their political systems. Peru endured a civilian dictator who allied with the military to fight a vicious war against an equally vicious insurgency, the Maoist Shining Path. Mexico and Cuba had civilian governments, but in Mexico the ruling party clung to power through electoral fraud, and Cuba remained constitutionally a one-party state.

But by 2000, the military had retreated from presidential palaces to the barracks. Students, often on the front lines of protest movements, were studying; rebels were laying down their arms and founding political parties; poverty rates were falling. Although optimism was tempered, comparative political scientists—i.e., those who specialize in studying politics in **nation-states** outside their home country—had few doubts that the outlook for democracy was positive overall. As evidence, they could point to the rising percentage of Latin Americans expressing confidence in democracy in surveys. Latinobarómetro, an annual poll of more than 20,000 Latin Americans in 18 countries, found in 2011 that 58 percent agreed that "democracy is preferable to any other form of government." (You can see the full results, by country, in the online material that accompanies this text.)

Jorge Castañeda, a prominent Mexican intellectual who had once identified with revolutionary movements, seemed optimistically prophetic in his widely read (1993) book, *Utopia Unarmed*. He wrote that Latin American leftists no longer sought to emulate Fidel Castro's revolution in Cuba and were abandoning armed insurrection for elections and other peaceful strategies for seeking power. They now wanted reform, not revolution. In 2011, Michael Shifter of the Washington-based Inter-American Dialogue argued that Latin America had experienced a "surge" in the pragmatic center, with both leftist and right-wing politicians moving toward more moderate positions.

In the 2000s, the left seemed to be following the electoral path into presidential palaces in all but a handful of Latin American countries. This tendency came to be called the "**Pink Tide**." "Pink" acknowledges that these leftist leaders and parties did not think of themselves as "Reds," at least in the sense that they had little interest in communism as it was practiced in the Soviet Union in the twentieth century. This had always been the perspective of moderate social democrats, such as Chile's Michelle Bachelet, but even more radical leaders who sympathized with Cuban communism, such as Venezuela's Hugo Chávez, were drawn philosophically toward a less centralized, party-driven system of "twenty-first-century socialism." None of the new leftist leaders, though friendly to Cuba, said that they wanted to replicate the Cuban model.

Castañeda (2006) and Shifter (2011) had a different view of leftists like Chávez, Bolivia's Evo Morales, Ecuador's Rafael Correa, and Nicaragua's Daniel Ortega, who though elected tended toward "autocratic concentration of vast power into the hands of a single person." These leaders, said Castañeda (2006), were men "born of the great tradition of Latin American **populism** [that] is nationalist, strident, and close-minded." These leaders did go down that path, although to different degrees. Their legacies, we will see, are mixed.

Steve Ellner (2012), an American historian who has lived in Venezuela for over 40 years, argues that what separates the more radical leaders from the moderates is the attempts to address more aggressively Latin America's highly unequal economic order and their experimentation with new participatory institutions. For Ellner, this is not a return to stale populism or an authoritarian tendency but a commitment to construction of a more profound form of democracy better suited to Latin America's needs. Furthermore, he argued, there were not just two lefts, as Castañeda asserted; left populism differs from country to country. The two leftist presidents, Luiz Inácio da Silva (Lula) and Dilma Rousseff, who governed Brazil from 2003 to 2016, do not fit neatly fit into either the moderate social democratic or the populist types as Castañeda defined them.

United States policy, during the administrations of both the George W. Bush and the Obama presidencies (2000–2016), made little secret of their preference for the Bachelet style.

Democrats and Republicans alike provided support for promoting democracy as practiced in the U.S. and other wealthy capitalist countries, through agencies like the taxpayer-funded National Endowment for Democracy (NED) and the State Department's Office of Transition Assistance. (See chapter 16.) The Argentine political scientist Atilio Borón (2005) objected that the United States should not be preaching about democracy to Latin America, given its own problems conducting clean elections. Already one U.S. president (Bush) had lost the popular vote but entered the White House through the Electoral College. Unlike Venezuela, Borón pointed out, the United States does not permit its people to vote by referendum on important national issues or to recall a president. As for human rights, the U.S. repeatedly violated those of prisoners held at its base in Guantánamo Bay. For Borón, the brand of democracy promoted by the United States seeks to instruct Latin Americans to "accept meekly our ineluctable neocolonial destiny under the dominion of the American Rome."

Today, Latin Americans could see many more reasons why "los estadounidenses" (citizens of the U.S.) had little moral authority to export their democracy. Again, a president, Donald J. Trump, had been "elected" with fewer votes than his opponent had. For many Latin Americans, Trump's self-confessed assaults on women, conflicts of interest between policies and financial interests, association with shady lawyers and business partners, threats against news media and his macho *bravado* were not unlike what many Latin Americans have seen in their own politicians (see Green 2012). His slurs against Mexicans hardly enhanced the U.S. image. A Pew Research Center survey in early 2017 found that fewer than 20 percent of people in eight different Latin American countries—and fewer than 5 percent in Mexico—expressed confidence in the new American president.

In *How Democracies Die*, political scientists Steven Levitsky (who happens also to be a Latin America expert) and Daniel Ziblatt (2018) argued that the "guardrails" were coming off U.S. democracy. Constitutions may provide a set of formal "rules of the game" for democracy, but they are full of ambiguities, ideals, and contradictions. These can only be worked out when citizens, and especially elites, they say, respect "norms" and informal procedures that ensure consensus and respect for democratic institutions. A surge of publishing in this vein by academics and journalists has reinforced this thesis. Former Secretary of State Madeleine Albright's (2018) book perhaps expresses the warning most stridently in its title, *Fascism: A Warning*.

By 2010, there were already doubts about just how broadly and deeply democracy had been consolidated throughout the region. New social movements were raising questions about the appropriateness of liberal democratic institutions for dealing with economic inequality and persistent social problems. Much of the significant progress in reducing economic inequality began to erode, first after the global financial crisis of 2008 and then by falling prices of Latin America's economic engines of growth: oil, mining, and agricultural (notably, soybeans) exports. Political storm clouds began to gather over a few countries as several presidents extended their terms by constitutionally dubious methods and other presidents were removed in the same way. The latter was the case for the region's most influential country, Brazil.

Popular discontent began to erupt against poverty and inequality. Mass protests, sometimes violent, erupted twice (in 2006 and 2019) in Chile, challenging what seemed to be a model of success for combining a market economy with liberal democracy. Venezuela's future lay in doubt as the country relapsed into polarized conflict and economic catastrophe, one year after the death (in March 2013) of President Chávez. Brazil, the region's great economic "success story," experienced mass protests against its Pink Tide government over lavish spending to host soccer's World Cup and the Olympic Games. New revelations of corruption in hacked documents known as the "Panama Papers" reverberated against both left- and right-wing governments. Mexico's government was losing control of swaths of territory to drug gangs or vigilantes finding them.

These were only a few of the reasons that the subtitle of this introduction to Latin American politics changed from "Democracy at Last?" in earlier editions to "Can Democracy Last?" for this one. In this introduction to the politics of Latin America, we take a closer look at the strengths and weaknesses of democracy in Latin America in the post-**Cold War** (1948–1991) era. To accomplish this task, we draw not just upon political science but also upon many other academic disciplines. Some questions we address will include:

- Did the shift to more market-friendly economic policies and free trade in the final 20 years of the last century encourage or discourage democracy?
- Have popular demands for more influence of common people, economic justice, and defense of human rights strained or enriched the practice of democracy and its institutions?
- Have the left given up armed insurgency and the right given up coup making, both committed now to contesting politics through constitutional processes?
- Has globalization weakened or strengthened democratic institutions?
- What kind of democratic regime, liberal or some alternative, best suits Latin America's people today?

But if we are to address whether democracy has arrived there "at last," we need to think about what democracy means to us and also what it means to Latin Americans.

For Review

What changes in Latin America made Castañeda and Shifter initially optimistic about democracy? Why is the Pink Tide called "Pink"? How do Castañeda and Shifter differ from Ellner and Borón in their views about the Pink Tide's more radical leftist presidents?

What Is Democracy?

So where do I come down on these questions? I prefer to let my answer unfold as we go through the chapters, and I hope to offer you a fair summary of the contrasting views. However, it is customary in such introductions for authors to reveal their own values so that the reader may be aware of biases that influence their work. Just about every political scientist will profess allegiance to democracy, but that usually takes the form of expressing a commitment to liberal or representative democracy. By that I do not mean "liberal" as commonly used in the United States, where a "liberal" refers to someone who typically favors welfare programs, more regulation of markets, expansion of civil rights protections, etc. I mean "liberal" as a democratic regime with (1) regularly scheduled elections, (2) a constitutionally defined boundary between the state and society (often called "civil society"), (3) respect for minority and individual rights, (4) equality before the law, (5) constitutional **checks and balances** on the power of different branches of government, (6) defense of private property, especially ownership of a society's productive and financial capital, and (7) reliance primarily on market forces to direct the economy.

Although I too believe in the first five of these democratic principles, I have some issues with the last two. Is a capitalist economic system a prerequisite for democracy? Or, on the contrary, does democracy seem to be compatible with other kinds of economic systems? If people have the right to participate but do not, can the political system still be called "democratic"? If many people lack economic resources to exercise or defend their rights (e.g., have a qualified lawyer when accused of a crime; can access media to express their views), do we still have "rule of law"? Should markets drive how societies function, or should markets be subordinate to social needs?

Here I offer my preferred definition: *Democracy is a system whereby ordinary people in a society have the ability to participate as equals in the major decisions that shape the future of their nation and communities.* Among *necessary* conditions for democracy is that people have the ability to periodically hold government accountable for its policies through periodic elections and that there exist protections of civil liberties (i.e., freedom of speech and association) that guarantee the ability of loyal opposition to contest incumbents. But this is not a *sufficient* condition for democracy because extreme inequalities in wealth and income translate into great differences in real power in a society. Besides social class, inequalities arising from racial, ethnic, religious, and gender prejudices also hinder democracy. Real equality in a democracy involves more than just legal equality and voting. Many fundamental decisions about the future of a society take place beyond the reach of elected governments, most importantly in the age of globalization under the influence of enormous, transnational corporations.

I hope that this book allows you to think through your own position by exposing you to issues of democracy in Latin America, and not just the ones consistent with my particular democratic values. With that in mind, I recommend that we evaluate the quality of democracy, and not just in Latin America, by three criteria: choice, participation, and equality. Liberal democracies, which today are sometimes called **polyarchies** (defined and explained in chapter 1), generally score well on "choice," meaning that elections, reinforced by civil liberties, offer channels for citizens to choose who governs them. But countries also vary on participation and equality, which researchers and media pundits usually ignore when discussing the condition of democracy.

"Participation" here refers to more than just voting. Participation can also mean extension of democracy into social and economic life—for example, encouraging more forms of direct democracy (referendums, citizen meetings to decide directly on public spending, worker control over factories and farms). Many Latin American countries have been experimenting with participatory democracy, with mixed results. Grassroots social movements in Latin America have been pressing for more democracy not only in affairs of state but also in family, social, and economic life, which is where we live and work. "Equality" is not just a condition or outcome for political democracy; it is an essential part of democracy itself. Latin America is notorious for corruption and egregious economic inequality, so it should not surprise us when masses of people mobilize for redistribution of wealth, not just for elections, when they take to the streets to demand democracy.

▊ What Latin Americans Tell Pollsters About Democracy

Let us shift our attention from what intellectuals think about democracy in Latin America to the attitudes of the people in the region. In its 2013 report, based on its poll of over 20,000 Latin Americans, Latinobarómetro, based in Santiago, Chile, found that there were "two Latin Americas, one which enjoys the benefits of economic growth and one which watches while the other enjoys." It went on to warn, "We are seeing more and more protests as an expression of citizens' awareness of the deficiencies of the economic, political and social system. There is demand for more democracy".

Six years later, María Lagos (2019: 1), Latinobarómetro's director, offered a devastating indictment of the state of democracy in the region, calling 2018 an *"annus horribilis"* and lamenting that we find ourselves to be "spectators at the end of the third wave of democracy." The "horrible year" had seen electoral victories by authoritarian-leaning candidates; widespread corruption in business and politics; presidents jailed on corruption charges; and massive migrations away from regions with deteriorating political and social conditions—the highest in the region's history. All of this took place in a global context where authoritarian leaders had come to power not, as in the past, as a result of military coups, but as a result of elections. And Lagos was writing more than a year before the global coronavirus pandemic struck in early 2020.

Figure 0.1 compares levels of support for democracy to levels of satisfaction with democracy registered for 2018 in Latin America. You can see that satisfaction varies greatly from country to country, but Uruguay is the country where satisfaction (the striped of the two bars) really seems to be highest. In only four other countries does it hover near 50 percent; very worrisome is the low score for the countries with the largest populations. In Mexico, which has the largest Spanish-speaking population in the world, only 16 percent expressed satisfaction. In Brazil, things were not much better at 25 percent.

Although satisfaction scores may be low in most places, the responses of Latin Americans to another question are a little more encouraging. Seventy-nine percent told Latinobarómetro, "democracy may have its problems but is preferable to any other form of government" (see top bar in Figure 0.2). However, as you can see from the striped bars in Figure 0.2, in response to a question about whether they think their country is a democracy, a democracy with major problems, or not a democracy, almost half of Latin Americans in the survey said that their country "is not a democracy" or "has major problems." If we were to break out only the results (not shown in Figure 0.2) for those who say their country is "not a democracy," Nicaragua and Venezuela stand out as the countries where people are most troubled about the state of democracy. More than one third of respondents say their country is not a democracy in those countries. In the rest of Latin America, no more than 25 percent of respondents said their country was not a democracy. Remember, these responses are from the 2018 survey (published in 2019). The following two years have provided little reason for optimism, as Lagos (the Latinbarómetro director) indicated, and the Covid-19 crisis had yet to strike the region.

This raises a question: Why is satisfaction so much lower than support for democracy? We might expect something of a gap, but in Figure 0.2, several countries that have long been regarded as bastions of democracy (Costa Rica, Uruguay, Chile) have more than one third of the population seeing either major problems or saying outright that the country is not a democracy. Several answers are possible. Perhaps people are discontented with social and

FIGURE 0.1   Support and Satisfaction With Democracy 2018

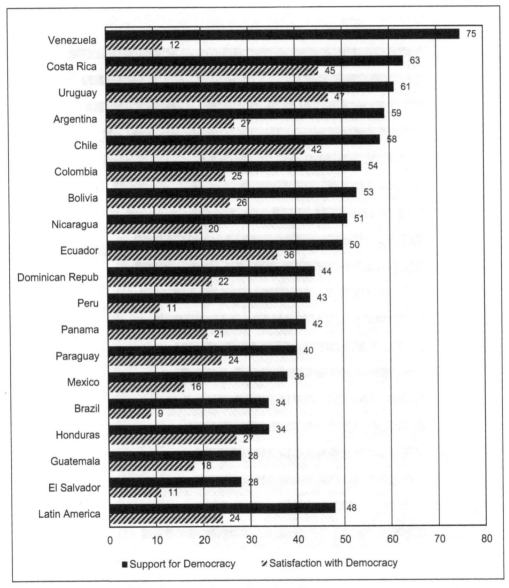

Source: Latinobarómetro 2018.

Support: Answer to "With which of the following do you most agree?" (1) Democracy is superior to any other form of government. (2) In some situations an authoritarian government is preferable to a democracy. (3) For people like me, there's no difference between a democratic and a non-democratic regime. Here, percentage is those choosing answer (1).

Satisfaction: Answer to "In general, would you say you are (1) Satisfied, (2) More or less satisfied, (3) Not very or not at all satisfied with the functioning of democracy in [country]?" Here, reported answer is (1).

FIGURE 0.2   Percent Respondents Agreeing With Churchillian View of Democracy; Evaluations of Democratic Condition

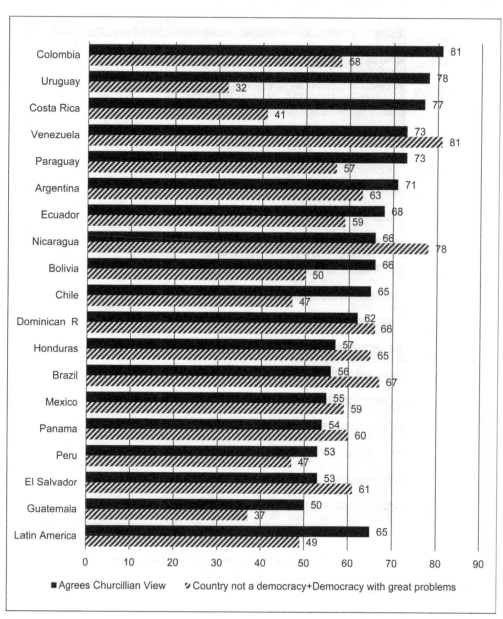

Source: Latinobarómetro 2018.

Dark Bar: Percent answering "agree" or "strongly agree" with claim, "Democracy may have its problems, but it's the best system of government." Other options were "disagree" and "strongly disagree."

Striped bar: Refer to percent answering, "A democracy with great problems" (striped) or "Not a democracy" to question: "How do you evaluate democracy in your country?" Respondent could also choose "Democracy with small problems" or "Full democracy."

economic conditions and think that the best answer is more democracy or restoration of a democracy that has deteriorated. Consistent with this theory is the case of Venezuela, where only 19 percent of respondents expressed satisfaction with democracy, but where support for democracy far exceeds the average for Latin America, topping all the other countries. The country is highly polarized, and a year after this survey was published, violent clashes between predominantly middle-class citizens and the government broke out, with many of the protestors calling for the resignation of President Nicolás Maduro, the successor to the deceased Hugo Chávez. The Latinobarómetro report for 2018 finds that both poor and middle-class Venezuelans differ little in their answers, but we might also consider that they differ in their reasons. That is, there may be a significant gap between what the middle class expects of democracy and what the poorer classes expect. There also may be a gap between how they conceive of democracy—in this case, how the country's oil wealth should be distributed. We will look more closely at these hypotheses in chapter 8.

We might also take note of the percentage for Bolivia. In November 2018, Bolivia's President Evo Morales had been ousted and forced to flee the country by a military coup after a week of violent protests by his opposition, which claimed fraud in the 2019 election. Morales's supporters had a quite different view, of course. By the time this book is published and distributed, Latinobarómetro will be preparing to publish its 2020 survey. Most of the polling in Bolivia will have been completed before the coup, but it will be interesting to see if public opinion had changed much in the run-up. The 2018 Latinobarómetro survey included a question, "Would you say that [your country] is being governed in the interest of all or by powerful groups that govern in their own interest?" Bolivia had the highest percentage (33) that chose "in the interest of all." The next highest percentage came from Uruguayans, at 27 percent, and the percentage overall in Latin America was only 17 percent. We will probably have to wait until 2020 (if surveys can even be conducted during the Covid crisis) to see what Bolivians think of the state of democracy in the post-coup era. (We look more closely at Evo Morales and Bolivia in chapter 3.)

Making sweeping generalizations about the results of Latinobarómetro surveys of Latin Americans risks overlooking the considerable variation from country to country. For example, only 24 percent of Guatemalans and Salvadorans said that democracy was preferable to all other kinds of government, in contrast to the 75 percent of Venezuelans. Here, history helps us understand why there might be such divergence. Guatemalans and Salvadorans live in small countries that experience acute civil wars, and no more than a small handful of the population has ever come anywhere close to rising out of poverty. By contrast, from 1922 to 1980, Venezuela, as a result of its oil exports, saw a dramatic increase in living conditions, lifting 80 to 90 percent of the population out of acute poverty. The country lived through a social and economic crisis for nearly all of the 1980s and 1990s, only to see better economic times again in the period from 2000 to 2014, when the oil prices crashed again. Since 1958 the country has had electoral democracy, so even if they have seen democracy deteriorate recently, their experience with democracy and economic conditions has had ups and downs—not chronic failure to deliver positive change.

Lagos's analysis of Latinobarómetro's polling over time suggests that the third wave saw a **broadening of democracy** but a more limited **deepening of democracy**, that is, little political empowerment of citizens beyond elections. Deepening democracy requires citizens to be meaningfully involved in discourse and debate about the important issues facing their society (see Almojuela 2012). Critics point out, however, that liberal democracies have some intrinsic tendencies that hinder such deepening. Most are constitutionally constructed to wall off many issues from democratic decision-making. For example, liberal democracies all allow market forces ("the invisible hand") to determine the distribution of society's income and wealth, or they require super majorities of votes (typically 60 to 67 percent) to make certain decisions. Even in the United States, we can see this at work. The U.S. Constitution of 1787 was the product of negotiation by elites—planters, bankers, and merchants. They were eager to lay the basis for a republic with some democratic features but also, in a context of political unrest and a high percentage of enslaved people, to limit popular power. Perhaps the most important undemocratic compromise they made was the attempt to wall off from democracy the issue of the emancipation of enslaved people. We live with the pact they made behind closed doors in Philadelphia to this day.

In Latin America, just about all liberal democracies in the region were institutionalized as part of a transition from military rule or civil war to democracy. These were negotiated by elites under the pressure of popular movements for democracy. Lagos highlights negotiated **pacts** as one of the main reasons that leaders in Latin America are often caught off guard when apparently stable democracies are suddenly wracked by mass protests, sometimes violent, as happened in several countries in the late 1980s and most recently in late 2019. A few months after she made this observation, her own home country, Chile, was wracked by massive rioting that was set off when the government tried to increase transportation fares. The increases were part of a negotiated austerity agreement with the International Monetary Fund (IMF), leading to demands for the resignation of the elected president. As she points out, this unanticipated social explosion should not have been so surprising. Latinobarómetro surveys had been showing for years that support and satisfaction with democracy had been falling pretty steadily since 2010.

Throughout this book, we have inserted "Democracy Snapshots" for each country in Latin America. These snapshots give you a quick thumbnail reference to the degree of support and satisfaction with democracy for each country in the region, taken from Latinobarómetro reports. Results are given in each snapshot for three different pairs of questions. The first pair (Support) deals with the percentage of respondents to a question measuring support for democracy as a system of government; the second pair (Satisfaction) shows the percentage who express satisfaction for how democracy is working in their country; and the third (Powerful govern for own interests) shows the percentage who agree with a statement that those governing the country are only acting in their own interests, not those of the country as a whole. Unlike the first two pairs, a high percentage on this third question can be interpreted as a poor reflection on the democratic condition. For each pair of bars, the top bar shows results for 2018. The second, lighter bar shows the results for the year that "Support" (top bar) was highest since the year 2000.

For example, Figure 0.3 is a large version of the snapshot for Panama. You will see three pairs of bars. For each pair of bars, the top (darker) one is for 2018—the same for all the other snapshots you will see. The highest percentage of support for democracy in Panama was recorded in the 2009 survey, so the lower bar presents the percentage of Panamanians who expressed support for democracy in that year. The data for all three of the lighter bars is taken from that same 2009 survey. Reading the Panama snapshot we see that in 2018 only 42 percent of Panamanians surveyed by Latinobarómetro said that they agreed, "Democracy is preferable to any other kind of government," a big drop-off from 64 percent nine years earlier. In each year, other respondents said that one of two other responses was closer to their

FIGURE 0.3   Democracy Snapshot Panama, 2018, 2009

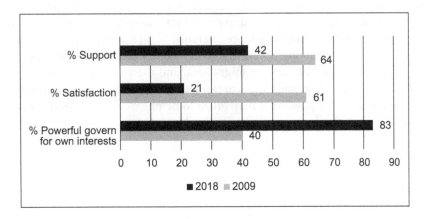

opinion. These options were, "Under some circumstances, an authoritarian government can be preferable to a democratic one" or "For people like me, it doesn't matter whether we have a democratic or non-democratic regime."

Looking at the rest of the snapshot, we can see that satisfaction with democracy also fell, and drastically—from 61 to 21 percent between 2009 and 2018. The specific question asked was, "In general, are you satisfied, somewhat satisfied, not very satisfied, or not at all satisfied with the working of democracy in Panama?" The percentages were those who answered either "satisfied" or "somewhat satisfied." Finally, the last pair of bars shows that in 2018, 83 percent of Panamanians said they thought the country is "governed by a number of powerful groups in their own interest rather for the good of the people." Only 40 percent thought so in 2009. Unfortunately, as Figures 0.1 and 0.2 showed, the pattern for Panama is seems to fit many other countries in the region.

Survey results are always subject to interpretation. The snapshots are provided for each country in a section where you are provided some background, and you may want to come back to these snapshots and the figures in this Introduction to make your own interpretations of the democratic condition in each country. And these numbers can change quickly. Bolivia, for example, had an elected, popular leftist president in 2018, but in 2019 he was ousted in a coup. Certainly, we may see very different attitudes registered the next time Bolivians are surveyed.

You will notice that Cuba is not included in the Latinobarómetro reports, as the island's government has restricted polling by outside, Western agencies. Cuba's leaders insist that Cuba's political system is truer to democracy than are others in the hemisphere. We look more closely at its system in chapter 9.

One last caveat about polling. There are limits to what it tells us and what it predicts about citizen attitudes about democracy and authoritarianism. Few academic or media analysts predicted the rise of right-wing populist movements in the United States; polling data might provide danger signs, but bursts of popular anger and rebellion have erupted in many places, and these events themselves impact popular consciousness and political culture, as they have in Chile against a country long regarded as a stable democracy.

Mabel Berezin, in her book about the rise of "illiberal politics" in Europe, argues that individual and collective experiences influence how people see the possibilities of the future. If you have lived under military dictatorship or civil war, accepting the limitations, the constraints of liberal democracy might be more tolerable. If, on the other hand, you have lived through an era like the recent one, where liberal democracy seems helpless to deal with the challenges of global inequality, massive migrations, and the erosion of economic security, you may be more inclined than polls tell us to feel dissatisfied by democracy. It is just possible that the coronavirus global pandemic may prove to be one of those collective experiences that reshape politics radically and not very predictably.

For Review

Looking at Figures 0.1 and 0.2, what does the Latinobarómetro poll indicate regarding popular support for democracy in Latin America? For which countries does support seem weakest, and for which does it seem strongest? If you were writing a paper about support for democracy, how would you define the difference between "broad" versus "deep" support for democracy?

Comparative Politics and Latin American Area Studies

So far, we have been considering how to evaluate democracy in Latin America without thinking about what method is best to evaluate it. As the title of this book implies, our approach must be "comparative," and in political science there exists a subfield called "**comparative politics**." If you are a political science major, you probably are expected to have a course not only in comparative politics but also in international relations, political philosophy (or theory), and American politics. The boundaries separating these subjects as "subfields" in political science are blurry, to say the least.

Comparative politics has a name that implies it is about a method of studying politics, but more likely you would take a course in Latin American politics because you have an interest in this part of the world. Some students may not even have much interest in political science at all but want to understand the region better because they are interested in its history or culture. You are in the right place; comparative politics tends to attract students and academics with an interest in or love of a particular area of the world. As a methodology, "comparative" refers to a way to test theories about politics by comparing cases to one another; inevitably we will be doing this, comparing countries to one another. We already started in the first half of this Introduction. Many books and articles in "comparative politics" are not, strictly speaking, "comparative." They frequently are "case studies" of a particular country. But even these studies usually attempt to test ideas and theories about politics in general against observation.

The U.S. government adapted this approach during World War II (1939–1945), when the U.S. military and diplomatic establishment competed for the loyalty and support of people all over the world against the Axis powers—Germany, Italy, and Japan. This project carried over into the Cold War, when the United States and the Soviet Union competed to integrate other parts of the world into the capitalist or communist bloc of nations. Funds went to foundations and universities to fill in the gap in expertise about the rest of the world. There appeared **area studies** centers, an investment by American taxpayers in better understanding the cultures and languages of other regions of the world, including Latin America (Lewis and Wigen 1997: 163–167, 181–182).

Comparativists who specialize in area studies draw not only on political science but also other disciplines—such as anthropology, history, economics, and sociology—in the study of politics. Sometimes getting a Ph.D. in political science requires foreign language study, which is often considered a formality or merely an option, but **comparativists** would agree that competence in the language of a region is essential to qualify as an area expert. Increasingly, comparativists rely as well on quantitative methods, usually statistical analysis of data, something especially important to studying "transnational themes." This is the most common (but not only) form of what we call "cross-national studies," the other branch of comparative politics. Since the collapse of communism in Eastern Europe (1989–2001), funding for comparative political studies began to move from area studies to "cross-national" studies that attempt to understand the causes of corruption, roots of terrorism, effectiveness of courts, human rights, and so on. One of the main themes is "democratization"—transitions from authoritarian systems to democracy, a theme of great importance to the study of Latin America. Researchers usually assume that "democracy" is primarily "liberal" or "representative" democracy.

PUNTO DE VISTA: WHAT COUNTRIES SHOULD BE INCLUDED IN LATIN AMERICAN AREA STUDIES?

Geography simply will not cooperate in establishing boundaries for Latin American area studies. Belize lies on the Caribbean coast of Central America and until 1981 was the colony of British Honduras. On the South American continent, on the Caribbean coast, one finds the occupied territory of French Guiana, still under the sovereignty of France, as well as Guyana (a former British colony) and Suriname (formally a Dutch colony). Colonial powers brought not only slaves but also large numbers of indentured East Asians to work the mines and plantations, and today descendants of East Indians outnumber any other ethnic group, including Afro-descendant inhabitants, the next largest ethnic group in the region.

It may not be a burning issue, but for comparativists who choose to specialize in the politics of a particular area of the world, sooner or later we come up against the question, what countries should we include

under our specialization? It normally comes up as a practical matter. What languages should be required to get a graduate degree? Is it enough just to know Portuguese or Spanish? What about major Indigenous languages, such as Aymara, Quechua, or Nahuatl? Would a Ph.D. dissertation about Jamaica qualify a person as an expert on Latin America?

There exists a Caribbean Studies Association, separate from the Latin American Studies Association. The small island nations of the Caribbean all are voting members of the Organization of American States (OAS), as are Belize, Guyana, and Suriname. All share the legacies of colonialism and slavery with Spanish and Portuguese America. Some countries typically studied as "Latin American" are in the Caribbean Sea. You will find coverage of Cuba and the Dominican Republic, as well as some attention to Puerto Rico and Haiti. In Haiti, the dominant language is Creole, which is significantly influenced by French. Why include Haiti? Haiti had a significant impact on the hemisphere during its revolution of 1791–1804. Puerto Rico is a "commonwealth" subordinated to the United States, so does it properly belong?

Cuba, Hispaniola (the island shared by the Dominican Republic and Haiti), Puerto Rico, Jamaica (which provided Simón Bolívar refuge from Spanish forces for a while during wars for independence from Spain), and the Cayman Islands are an archipelago that make up the Greater Antilles. The Lesser Antilles include two strings of islands, one including Aruba, Barbados, Curacao, and the Venezuelan state of Margarita, which are stretched out along the coast just north of Venezuela and the Guyanas (French Guiana, Guyana, and Surname); the other are an archipelago of smaller islands that run like pearls along the mapmakers' boundary between the Atlantic Ocean and Caribbean Sea. Some are independent (e.g., Grenada, invaded by U.S. forces in 1982), and a few still remain colonies of France, the United Kingdom, Holland, and the United States. A case could be made for the Bahamas as well, which is properly in the Atlantic but shares much history and common problems with others in the area.

What are some of the commonalities and differences that might make a case for inclusion or exclusion from the same area studies rubric?

- The entire hemisphere was once populated by Amerindian peoples, and this leaves come common genetic and linguistic markers on the people and culture of the Americas. However, no significant Amerindian populations survive in the islands. The native Caribs and Arawaks were wiped out by conquest and disease.
- Like most of the Americas, all the countries and territories in the Caribbean region were integrated into the global capitalism as colonies exporting primary goods (especially sugar) to the wealthier, more powerful European and (later) North American nations. This pattern of economic dependency and **underdevelopment** persists today.
- Many of the islands are microstates and are highly threatened by changes in water levels, stronger hurricanes, and tides. Almost all today are highly dependent on tourism. While countries like Brazil and the United States have seen far right leaders (Jair Bolsonaro, Donald Trump) denying the threat of global warming come to power in the 2000s, it is hard to conceive that any of the Caribbean area governments could politically do the same. They too elect conservatives, but no one can ignore how the waters have grown around them.
- The colonial social and economic legacies certainly mean that Caribbean countries share with Latin America reasons to identify and cooperate with the Global South, or the Third World, as it is alternatively called. To some degree, one difference from other parts of the Global South is that they live under the shadow of the global hegemon, which sees all of the Caribbean and Central America as its "backyard." They too have suffered intervention and sometimes direct military invasion.
- Politically, the non-Spanish Caribbean largely has political constitutions that reflect the influence of European parliamentary democracy. Instead of directly elected presidents, as in Latin America, most countries and territories have prime ministers. This influences other political structures, such as party systems and the media, in different ways.
- The linguistic differences between the Caribbean nations and others in the Americas have given rise to cultural expression (art, books, film, music, and so on) that transcends regional differences in colonial backgrounds. The themes are also familiar to most Latin Americans—diaspora, the colonial legacy, the slave era, racial experience, and creolization. But the Caribbean experience,

climate, and geography (especially the sea itself) have left a distinctive mark and foster regional identity.

- In the academic world, there exist both a Latin American Studies Association and Caribbean Studies Association, suggesting that in the world of area experts there seems to be agreement that some specialization is useful. However, the most important United Nations organ with a focus on the hemisphere south of the United States is the U.N. Economic Commission on Latin America *and the Caribbean* (my emphasis).
- In the world of diplomacy, the OAS includes the entire hemisphere, but it is often viewed externally as a Latin American institution—though critics point out that the United States wields its hegemonic power in decisive ways within the organization. In 1973 a number of Caribbean nations—Antigua and Barbuda, the Bahamas, Barbados, Belize, Dominica, Grenada, Guyana, Haiti, Jamaica, Montserrat, Saint Kitts and Nevis, Saint Lucia, Saint Vincent and the Grenadines, Suriname, and Trinidad and Tobago—formed the Caribbean Community Market (CARICOM), with the intention of promoting regional integration.

For Discussion

So the question for you is, should this text and your class feature more coverage of the Caribbean region? Even at the expense of less coverage of some countries more commonly understood to be included in Latin American area studies?

For More Information and Perspectives

The Caribbean Studies Association's website can be found at www.caribbeanstudiesassociation .org. A fine regional history is Laurent Dubois and Richard Turits's *Freedom Roots: Histories From the Caribbean* (Chapel Hill, University of North Carolina, 2019). A Caribbean voice that continues to echo through the region is that of Walter Rodney, including his *The Groundings With My Brothers* in a new annotated edition (London: Verso 2001), which includes the quote, "I have sat on a little oil drum, rusty and in the midst of garbage, and some black brothers and I have grounded together," a reference to how his life of political activism began.

This book embraces both transnational and area studies. I assume that there are some constants in politics across cultures, but I also believe that an adequate understanding of politics must take into account cultural diversity, historical inheritances, and the specific challenges that confront particular societies. Transnational specialists lacking background in the history and culture of a particular region are usually less familiar with its political peculiarities than are area studies specialists. They risk choosing and interpreting cases in a manner that fits preconceived ideas. How does this affect understanding? For example, many comparativists who study democratization date the transition process in Nicaragua from the defeat of the Sandinistas (FSLN), who came to power, through a revolution in 1979, in the 1990 presidential elections. On the other hand, the Latin American Studies Association (LASA 1984) observed the election of 1984, won by the FSLN, and generally found it free and fair.

Area studies specialists are sometimes too focused on the particular region or country to see broader global forces at work or to take into account the commonalities in politics that cut across cultures. Consider, for another example, the question of whether Cuba will remain a socialist regime with only one legal political party. Cuba, by virtue of its language, colonial past, and so on, clearly belongs to the family of Latin American nations. On the other hand, its political system echoes characteristics of communism as it emerged in Eastern Europe and Asia. In assessing Cuba's political future, would we not profit from studying the successes and failures of the post-communist era in Eastern Europe? In recent years, the government has seemed more open to economic liberalization (introduction of more room for market forces), Asian style. So we might want to compare Cuba's economic reform measures to those implemented in Vietnam or China.

As we noted earlier, a spate of books in the United States have argued that the rise of Trump to the presidency in 2016 signaled concern that "it can happen here"—the "it" being some form of fascism. Consider how we might address whether fascism is taking hold. First, we have to consider just what is and is not a "fascist" state. That means looking at the regimes by that name that arose in the 1930s in Germany, Italy, Spain, Portugal, and (maybe) Japan. Then we would have to assess why and how fascist leaders and government ascended to power, but at the same time recognize that these historical regimes were somewhat different from each other. The global conditions of the 1930s resemble in some ways those of today, but there are major differences as well. Yet it would be foolish to think that history has no lessons or that the human condition varies so much from one culture to another that we can learn nothing by comparing the experiences of different countries to one another.

Area and People

As is customary, we must begin our study of Latin American politics by surveying the major features of its land and people. How much commonality is there among countries in the region? If we know that, we can better assess what kinds of comparisons are best for addressing which questions.

South of the Rio Grande, not all Latin Americans regard Spanish or Portuguese as their native tongue. Many Latin Americans—a majority in some regions—speak an Indigenous language. Wherever the European conquerors established plantation agriculture (sugar, cotton, cacao, etc.), people are predominantly descendants of enslaved Africans. The late nineteenth and the twentieth century saw important immigrations to South America from places such as Japan, China, Palestine, Germany, and other parts of the world. Some countries (Belize, Jamaica, Haiti, the Guyanas, etc.) often included in "Latin America and Caribbean Studies" were colonized by the British, Dutch, and French and not by the Iberians. Are these people "Latin"?

The idea of "Latin America" was conjured up by the government of France, under the dictator Louis Napoleon III around 1865. Napoleon III had designs to incorporate parts of the region into a new French empire. Aware of growing British and U.S. influence, the emperor enlisted French geographers to propagate the idea that these Spanish- and Portuguese-speaking countries had more in common culturally with his French-speaking country than with North America and Britain, the "Anglo" countries. The French designation stuck as universities created area studies programs that baptized the region "Latin America" (see Figure 0.4).

For our purposes, we will consider Latin America to embrace the continent of South America; Mesoamerica, that is, the isthmus between the continents (beginning at Colombia's

FIGURE 0.4 Map of Latin America

border with Panama and ending at the border with the United States); and those islands in the Caribbean that were part of the Spanish Empire in the centuries following Columbus's voyages and the conquest. We will find it useful at times to refer as well to countries such as Haiti, Belize, the three Guyanas, and Jamaica that share some history and culture with the former Portuguese and Spanish colonies in the hemisphere. We consider Puerto Rico, though ruled by the United States, to be part of Latin America. As a practical matter, we will not include areas of the United States with significant Hispanic populations as part of Latin America, but residents can easily "journey" to Latin America in many parts of the U.S. by simply taking a bus to another part of town.

Scholars will never agree whether "geography is destiny," but most area experts agree that some formidable natural features have influenced the political map and development in

Latin America. The Andes are not the highest mountains in the world, but they are the dens-est, with several parallel ranges. They run like a spine down the back of the continent, toward the Pacific side, making travel and communication difficult not only between east and west but also between north and south. Today one can travel by good highways and air routes, but rarely by good trains, from one capital to another. To travel from one major city to another as recently as 100 years ago meant several days. Most of the population lives in highland areas, especially in the tropics, so it might be necessary to descend from your home, perhaps in Mérida in the Venezuelan Andes, by some combination of mules and river traffic, to catch a steamer from Maracaibo, which would then take you to La Guaira, the Caribbean port for Caracas. Caracas lies only a few miles inland—but on the other side of a mountain, Ávila, which rises approximately 9,000 feet straight out of the sea. So you would go by horse and carriage (until the late 1800s, when rail became available) to reach the capital of your country.

Travel by river? In Argentina, yes, but Spanish colonial authorities actually blocked much trade to the Atlantic to keep trade flowing north through the mountains instead. In the Amazonian region this is somewhat possible, but the rivers were also barriers because of the incredible volume of water they channeled. The Amazon River is not as long as the Nile, but it carries by far the most water of any river in the world. It empties over 200,000 cubic meters of water per second on average into the Atlantic Ocean; the Nile empties only a little more than 5,000, the Mississippi a little over 1,600. Several of the Amazon's tributaries them-selves are among the 25 longest rivers in the world. Other rivers in South America among this group are the Orinoco (Venezuela), Paraná (Brazil), and three other Brazilian rivers. All carry vast amounts of water compared to rivers in North America. The continent boasts the highest waterfall (Angel Falls, in Venezuela), the driest desert (the Atacama, in northern Chile), the largest rainforest (mostly in Brazil), the highest capital city (La Paz, in Bolivia), and the highest lake that is navigated for commerce (Titicaca, in Peru).

The climate varies enormously because the region is aligned more on a north-south than an east-west axis. The equator runs through Ecuador, Colombia, and northern Brazil. However, the climate can be quite pleasant and spring-like all year round in the highland regions. In the **Southern Cone** region of Argentina, Chile, Uruguay, Paraguay, and southern Brazil, the climate is temperate, excellent for growing many different kinds of grains, soy, and grass for livestock. Most people in this region experience winter, though it is generally mild. However, in the far south—toward an area revealingly named Tierra del Fuego (land of fire)—the cold becomes increasingly more forbidding.

The Central American region, Mexico's Yucatán Peninsula, and the Caribbean islands are all in the tropics, but Mexico's topography and climate vary as one moves from Chiapas, on the southern border, north to the capital city, the largest metropolitan area in the world, with more than 20 million inhabitants. As one moves farther north, the area becomes drier, with desert bordering much of the frontier with the United States.

Latin Americans live in societies where ethnicity, race, gender, and social class interact in ways that generate both conflict and pride in diversity. We can divide the population very broadly and imprecisely into an Indigenous population that is most numerous in the high-land areas and almost extinct in the Caribbean; Afro-descendant people who were enslaved and transported from Africa; and descendants of European people, not just ancestors from Portugal and Spain, the colonial powers, but also immigrants from other regions from just about every part of Europe. For example, a province in Chile is named O'Higgins after Ber-nardo O'Higgins, son of an Irish employee of Spain's colonial administration. Many more

Europeans came after 1850 when governments of the day sought to "whiten" their popula-tions, believing this would spur economic development (see chapter 4). Asian and Middle Eastern immigrants have populated some regions—though it seems other Latin Americans often lump them together as, respectively, "Chinos" (Chinese) or "Turcos" (Turks), regard-less of their origins.

The largest sectors of the population have a genealogy and cultural heritage that is a mixture of all these different groups. These Latin Americans are often called "*mestizos*" (if they or their ancestors have Indigenous physical characteristics) or "mulattos" (for those with some African ancestry). But there are many other terms (e.g., "*pardos*," in Venezuela) for differentiating race and ethnic composition, varying with the country and the mixture.

Social and economic conditions vary tremendously among countries and often within countries. We focus on poverty and inequality in chapters 2 and 11. The Socio-Economic Database for Latin America and the Caribbean (SEDLAC) data for 2013 (see the "Resources for Further Study" section at the end of this chapter) indicated that the prior 20 years saw a significant fall in poverty. In 1992, 45 of 100 Latin Americans lived on $4 per day (even taking different purchasing power into account); in 2013 that ratio was 25 of every 100. The United Nations Economic Commission for Latin America and the Caribbean (ECLAC 2012) estimated a slightly higher rate of poverty and expressed concern that the rate by which it has fallen has slackened in recent years. The global financial crisis of 2008 eventually took its toll six years later, after China too slowed its economic growth. As the growth slackened, economic inequality and poverty rates began to rise again. Still, Brazil, Chile, Colombia, Chile, Uru-guay, Mexico, and Argentina are all generally considered middle-income countries, though all are afflicted with some of the world's highest rates of inequality. Bolivia (though one of the few countries to have continued to make progress), Honduras, and Nicaragua are among the poorest countries. Venezuela's economy collapsed in 2014 under the combined weight of economic mismanagement, tumbling oil prices, and (later) punishing sanctions by the U.S.

We would be remiss if we did not recognize the remarkable contributions by Latin Americans to global culture in the form of vibrant music, modern art, philosophy (e.g., the Indigenous conception of *buen vivir*, "the good life"), and award-winning novels. The region is often known in the North American media for "coups, Castro, and catastrophe," but that stereotype belies the vibrant culture and diversity of the region.

For Review

What is the difference between a transnational approach and an area studies approach in comparative politics? What advantages and disadvantages does each approach offer for studying democracy in Latin America? If you wanted to ask whether Cuba will "liberalize," what countries would you choose for comparison?

How did the name "Latin America" come about? Why is it not clear that the name adequately describes what countries do or do not lie within the region?

Why might some people wonder if "Latin America" really is "Latin"?

Preview of the Chapters

One of the challenges of introducing this subject matter to students is how to make a text engaging and thematic on the one hand, but a useful reference and guide to the field on the other. The first task requires a lively style; the other demands the dry and passionless prose of an encyclopedia. Addressing the question of whether democracy is finally taking root in Latin America permits us, I hope, to avoid draining the lifeblood out of politics while providing the comprehensive coverage one needs in a text.

In chapter 1 we take up how political scientists typically define "democracy" and offer readers alternative ways of thinking about how to evaluate the condition of democracy. Chapter 2 argues that inequality is one of the key features influencing Latin American politics. We put inequality in the context of social, personal, and family relationships, and we explore how economic inequality intersects with gender and racial divides in the region.

Part II takes up the historical context of Latin American politics. In chapters 3 and 4, one of our goals is to understand "legacy" as a story about the past. These stories give modern citizens a sense of who they are and what binds them together, at least in their imaginations, as a nation. But not everyone shares the same meaning for these stories. Colonialism has left a legacy of deep divisions and issues—social cleavages—that democracy, like any other form of state, must mediate. The history of "Latin America" begins well before Columbus, and colonialism established a pattern in which race or ethnicity became strongly correlated with economic, social, and political exclusion.

Chapter 3 looks at the pre-colonial and colonial eras, and chapter 4 picks up the story with the theme of how economic dependency in Latin America persisted beyond colonialism. In both chapters I try to weave the present into the past. For example, we do not just refer to Indigenous culture as though it exists in a history museum but as a vital force in Latin America today. Its legacies for the present most interest us in a necessarily brief overview. In chapter 5, the main theme is how populism in the twentieth century first brought democracy to the forefront in the form of mass politics. Chapter 6 explores different theories about development and underdevelopment, especially two major schools of thought, modernization and dependency theory.

Part III introduces the theme of "regimes" and "regime transitions." Chapter 7 explores the quarter century that begins with a coup in Brazil in 1964. In this period, harsh dictatorships emerged in all but a few countries—after what most political scientists characterize as a "breakdown of democracy." The chapter examines the era of military rule that resulted and then the subsequent "transitions to democracy." The repressive years created the context for a return to economic development policies that were more market oriented and export oriented—more "neo" liberal (a new version of the market- and export-oriented policies of the nineteenth century), which in turn gave rise to a new era of populism and the "Pink Tide." These topics are critical to any assessment of whether the current era of left- and right-wing populism has weakened prospects for democracy today, the main theme of the last part of chapter 7, which looks mainly at the Southern Cone countries, and most closely at Brazil, Argentina, and Chile. Chapter 8 examines other transitions that occurred in Mexico and Venezuela, two of the few countries to escape military rule in the earlier period. Chapter 9 examines revolutions and regime change, focusing mainly on Cuba and Central America.

Finishing out this section, chapter 10 looks at how despite civilian government and the outer trappings of democracy, military and other security forces still have influence, paying closer attention to the Andean region, especially Colombia.

Part IV, "Civil Society, Institutions, Human Rights," looks with some detail at the formal constitutional rules of the game, the influences of social and economic power, and issues of human rights. Chapter 11 returns to the theme of economic inequality and how social class forces are ever present—something not unique to Latin America, but a theme that has much to do with the surge of movement politics in the region. Chapter 12 examines political parties and what the notion of "left" and "right" means in Latin America today. Here again we look more closely at populism, but in its leftist and rightist variants. Chapter 13 examines constitutions and institutions. What interests us here is not just how countries are governed but also how constitutions seem to have limited staying power in the region. Many social movements have adopted the idea of "constituent power" as the right of people in a democracy society to reshape, or reconstitute, their governing structures through constituent assemblies. Chapter 14 broadens the theme of human rights beyond civil rights. It also looks at the idea of "rule of law" and how declining satisfaction with democracy is linked to the idea of impunity, violence, and corruption in public life.

Part V consists of two chapters. The first, chapter 15, examines how Latin America's place in the world has evolved under globalization, with emphasis on how its export-based economies rely on extraction of natural resources and labor to integrate into the "global assembly line." We also examine how China's dramatic economic expansion has reached into Latin America and simultaneously reinforced some and disrupted other ways the region is integrated into the world economy. Chapter 16 examines Latin America's difficult and complex history with the United States, but also how Latin Americans have struggled to economically and politically cooperate with one another to address global problems.

An Invitation

This book is an invitation to students not only to learn about the politics, history, and culture of a fascinating part of the world, but also to reflect on what democracy ought to mean. It is an invitation to study issues of social justice in a world where nations have in recent decades yielded some part of their sovereignty to the forces of globalization. My own encounter with Latin America has caused me to examine the values and motives behind U.S. foreign policy. I also wonder whether democracy at home would be durable if we faced the economic challenges and social inequalities that characterize Latin America. To have a global perspective requires not only understanding others but also understanding ourselves.

Throughout this book, you will find "Puntos de Vista." These short sections introduce you to the kinds of issues that Latin Americans themselves are debating. For example, there is a "Punto" about Brazil's use of quotas for university admissions for people of African descent, a response to the legacy of slavery. This is an issue in the United States as well. I hope you will find in taking a position yourself that you can on the one hand clarify your own values about some important issues, but on the other hand simultaneously put yourself in the shoes of people living in another part of the world, for whom the question might have some different meaning or consequences.

I finished the manuscript for this third edition of *Comparative Politics of Latin America* as the COVID-19 pandemic was reaching its peak in the United States but had not yet reached that point in Latin America. How the governments respond to this challenge will undoubtedly have implications for the future of democracy. By the time this book reaches print, we will know more. Routledge hosts a companion website that includes useful resources for both students and instructors. The companion website can be found at https://routledgetextbooks.com/textbooks/_author/hellinger/. I plan to add commentary and update developments there.

Discussion Questions

1. Why do you think that to study politics we rely so much on comparing countries to one another?
2. What are your initial ideas about whether democracy can exist in Latin America (or anywhere) alongside high levels of poverty and inequality?
3. Rather than a question, I have a suggestion for those of you who have to or want to write a paper. Pick a country to study. Next, find the snapshot for it in this text. Think about whether the country seems to fit the general pattern in the region. Use the index to read sections of the text that deal with this country. You can find a snapshot for every country somewhere in this text. Use the resources at the end of this chapter and others to get an update on how things have gone since 2018. You can easily obtain a copy of Latinobarómetro, in English or Spanish, from its website, where you can also find lots of other opinion data. Do all of this and consult other sources in your library to write a paper that evaluates overall support for democracy, how it compares to other countries in the region, and why it has fallen, risen, or stayed about the same since 2000.

Resources for Further Study

For Basic Information: Do you need a primer on Latin America's geography—capitals, rivers, mountains, and so on? Sheppard Software has a briefing page consisting of map games that are easy to play and will bring you up to speed quickly: www.sheppardsoftware. com/South_America_Geography.htm. Help Teaching provides a good self-quiz at www.helpteaching.com/questions/South_American_Geography.

Several sources are available for basic demographic and geographic facts about Latin America. The Socio-Economic Database, http://www.cedlas.econo.unlp.edu.ar/wp/en/ estadisticas/sedlac/, provides information gathered about the region by the World Bank and Universidad de La Plata.

Reading: Few Latin American politics courses are required, so presumably you chose to study this topic because you already have an interest. To feed your mind when it's done, you can do no better than the *NACLA Report on the Americas*, which comes out six times per year and, though it draws heavily on academic specialists, is written for a general audience. *Latin American Research Review* is the most prestigious area-study journal. Among many other good journals, *Latin American Perspectives* differs in dedicating itself more to Latin American views, particularly radical ones. Other good journals include *Latin American Politics and Society* and the *Journal of Latin American Politics* (published in Great Britain).

Video and Film: A list of hundreds of Latin American films with English translation can be found at Steve Volk's resource page: www.oberlin.edu/faculty/svolk/latinam.htm. A recent look, sympathetic to more radical leftist leaders, is *South of the Border*, Oliver Stone's 2009–2010 documentary. Icarus Films is a repository of hundreds of documentaries; for Latin America, you can find them listed at www.icarusfilms.com/subjects/latin_am.html. Another source of good documentary material is www.journeymantv.com, which seems to add five or six high-quality videos of varying length every week and which can be streamed for free (and sometimes downloaded for free).

On the Internet: The portal *Zona Latina* (www.zonalatina.com/) contains innumerable resources, systematically listed by type and then broken into country or region, and in various languages, including English. The Library of Congress offers the *Handbook of Latin American Studies* (HLAS) online, providing the titles and annotations of all sorts of articles and books concerning the region. Using the website's search engine, a student can find citations of documents for further study on any specific topic found in this textbook. The main page is located at http://lcweb2.loc.gov/hlas/hlashome.html. Steve Volk maintains a varied and useful site at www2.oberlin.edu/faculty/svolk/latinam.htm

Following News: The Center for Economic Policy Research (CEPR), a Washington-based think tank, provides a valuable compilation three to five days per week of English-language news. You can sign up to receive the digest (links to articles divided by region) via e-mail at the organization's website, www.cepr.net. A great source on Brazil, available in Portuguese and English, is Brazil de Fado, available at www.brasildefato.com.br/2018/05/14/brazil-130-years-of-an-unfinished-abolition-of-slavery.

PART I

Comparative Politics, Democratic Theory, and Latin American Area Studies

1 Conceptions of Democracy

Focus Questions

▶ When we speak of a "third wave of democracy," what do we mean?

▶ What is "polyarchy" as a model of democracy? How does it compare to other conceptions of democracy?

▶ Should we consider social and economic equality to be a measure, an outcome, or a precondition of democracy?

▶ What are some alternative views on liberal democracy and polyarchy in Latin America?

IN THIS CHAPTER we will delve more deeply into some of the themes explored in the Introduction, where I suggested that there are some alternative ways of thinking about democracy, and where I briefly argued for including social and economic equality as well as participation in assessing the democratic condition. I also suggested that Latin Americans might not always share the notion that the only brand of democracy that would work best for them is liberal democracy. First, however, we will review the more orthodox conception of democracy that prevails in the field of comparative politics. You may very well find your own view closer to it than to my own.

One common term that comparativists use to describe a modern liberal democratic state is "**polyarchy**." Rarely do you see this term in everyday speech or in the news. But over the last 50 years, "polyarchy" has migrated from academia to the world of policy. In the late 1970s, beginning with the formal commitment of President Jimmy Carter (1977–1980) to the promotion of human rights, and then the creation of a federally funded **National Endowment for Democracy** (**NED**) by President Ronald Reagan (1981–1988), the United States made defense of democracy the goal of its foreign policy—or at least so it professed. During this same period, most of Latin America was emerging from harsh military dictatorship, and the transition to civilian rule was welcome but still fragile. Then, the years 1989 to 1991 saw the collapse of the Berlin Wall and the Soviet Union. Liberal democracy and capitalism seemed triumphant.

In 1994, at the Summit of the Americas in Miami, all countries in the hemisphere (except Cuba, which was not invited) proclaimed themselves committed to liberal democracy, also commonly called "representative democracy." The summit's Statement of Principles (1994; emphasis added) stated,

> [R]epresentative democracy . . . [is] the sole political system which guarantees respect for human rights and the rule of law; it safeguards cultural diversity, **pluralism**, respect for the rights of minorities, and peace within and among nations. Democracy is based, among other fundamentals, on free and transparent elections and includes the right of all citizens to participate in government.

This political model was tied explicitly to an economic model, capitalism, and more specifically neoliberal capitalism based on a reduced role for government and an expanded role for the market, both nationally and internationally.

> A key to prosperity is trade without barriers, without subsidies, without unfair practices, and with an increasing stream of productive investments. Eliminating impediments to market access for goods and services among our countries will foster our economic growth. . . . Free trade and increased economic integration are key factors for raising standards of living, improving the working conditions of people in the Americas and better protecting the environment.
>   We, therefore, resolve to begin immediately to construct the "**Free Trade Area of the Americas**" (**FTAA**), in which barriers to trade and investment will be progressively eliminated. . . . [We] are committed to create strengthened mechanisms that promote and protect the flow of productive investment in the Hemisphere, and to promote the development and progressive integration of capital markets.

In late 2001, the governments (again, not including Cuba) of the hemisphere formally adopted the Inter-American Democratic Charter, stating, "Essential elements of representative democracy are the holding of free and fair elections as an expression of popular sovereignty, access to power through constitutional means, a pluralist system of political parties and organizations, and respect for human rights and fundamental freedoms." Take note of "**pluralist**," a term closely connected to polyarchy. Most importantly, the charter states, "any unconstitutional alteration or interruption of the democratic order in a state of the Hemisphere constitutes an insurmountable obstacle to the participation of that state's government in the Summits of the Americas process." It went on to note the agreement of all signing governments to develop

> a mechanism for collective action in the case of a sudden or irregular interruption of the democratic political institutional process or of the legitimate exercise of power by the democratically-elected government in any of the Organization's member states, thereby fulfilling a long-standing aspiration of the Hemisphere to be able to respond rapidly and collectively in defense of democracy.

Many Latin Americans have questioned the "Washington Consensus," as these agreements came to be known. Even as the ink was drying on the Democratic Charter, social movements, some having grown out of demands for an end to military rule, were already challenging its emphasis on representative democracy and free-market capitalism. They began to stress vesting decision-making not just in the institutions of government but also in many other places—communities, the workplace, ethnic groupings, and so forth. Latin America did experience economic growth, but this growth accentuated inequality and failed to alleviate poverty sufficiently. After 1990, a bottom-up process had begun to press for a democracy of greater participation, social equality, and inclusion. Social movements sought to transfer more power and control over decisions to women, people living in poverty, Indigenous and Afro-descendent peoples, and others who benefited little from economic growth. Buoyed by social movements, the region experienced an electoral swing toward the left—the **Pink Tide**, first evident in the election of President Hugo Chávez in Venezuela in 1998.

Social movements and Pink Tide leaders questioned not only the adequacy of liberal democracy, but also the type of socialism practiced in the Soviet Union. The Latin American left remained supportive of Cuba's defense of its sovereignty; the collapse of Eastern European communism and the island's struggles to maintain the social and economic accomplishments of the 1959 revolution also encouraged this rethinking about socialism.

Liberal Democracy in the Real World of Latin America

In the United States, we often associate the term "liberal" with politicians who favor government regulation of the economy and welfare rights, but in its original form **liberalism** refers to a political ideology that sees individual choice as the essence of freedom. Liberal democracies assume the following:

- The individual takes priority over the community and the state; the foundation of society and the state is a decision taken by individuals to form associations. As far back as ancient Greece, other political philosophers have questioned this kind of individualism and contended that an individual is a product of human society—of the family and group-life that naturally make up a political community.
- The market is preferred over government planning or other forms of allocating economic resources and resolving economic conflicts. Government action is reserved for exceptional circumstances—severe economic crisis, megaprojects that only the state can afford, threats to national security, and key areas of human welfare (such as education and health). Most modern-day liberals have come to advocate government regulation and welfare to ameliorate market shortcomings, but they continue to regard such political action as an artificial interference of the "invisible" hand of the market. Market life is natural to humans; political life was created by artificial convention.
- The right to private property is a "natural right"; that is, property, including wealth, is accumulated mostly as a result of some combination of hard work, creativity, and risk on the part of individuals. Property rights are seen as individual human rights.
- Liberals seek to limit the power of the state through constitutions that (1) keep many social and economic questions off-limits to government and (2) divide the powers of government into branches that compete against one another—"checks and balances."

Is it possible for a government to be "liberal" without being democratic? The Canadian political philosopher C. B. MacPherson (1972) pointed out the historical fact that liberal democracies established limited government, individual property rights, and a market economy *before* all citizens had obtained the right to vote or enjoyed equal rights before the law. For example, Jefferson, Washington, and other founders were Liberals but tolerated slavery, barred women from voting, and limited the vote to landowners in some states until the

1830s. In Europe, liberalism and **capitalism** existed well before workers achieved the right to vote. In Latin America, economic policies were imposed by factions of landowning elites who created "liberal" parties (see chapter 4). Nearly 100 years later, some of the region's fiercest dictatorships (e.g., in Chile between 1973 and 1989) adopted liberal (market-oriented) economic policies.

This latter-day emphasis on laissez-faire capitalism came to be known as **neoliberalism**, "neo" meaning "new form of." Instead of monarchs and blue-blooded aristocrats, the target of neoliberal plans in Latin America was a shift away from active state policies to promote economic development by protecting and subsidizing industrialization and toward reliance of the private sector, foreign investment, and free-trade policies as the main forces for economic development (see chapter 6).

For Review

What does the term "liberal" signify in "liberal democracy"? What does "neoliberal" signify?

Liberalism, Pluralism, and Polyarchy

Perhaps the political scientist who most influenced how we think about democracy following World War II was Robert Dahl. Dahl tried to develop a concept of democracy that was real, as opposed to "ideal." He coined the term "**polyarchy**" to describe his vision of "real democracy."

Dahl (1971: 7–8) defined polyarchy as a political regime in which elites, by which he meant leaders drawn from different sectors (labor, business, education, religion, etc.) of society, compete with one another for influence in a system characterized by liberal freedoms (freedom of expression, right to assembly, fair elections) and extension of citizenship, especially the right to vote, to everyone. Dahl derived his views from the **pluralist** school of thought in American sociology. Pluralists argue that the real "stuff" of politics is found in group life, where citizens band together to promote their points of view. The result is a sphere of politics separated from the state, called "**civil society**." Groups and elites in civil society compete for power to advance their interests. Some may become established and lose contact with their members, but this does not matter as long as new groups can be formed freely. Civil society is kind of a political marketplace, where ideas and policies compete for acceptance from politically equal citizens who can influence the outcome by their participation, especially by voting.

Pluralists generally think that most people really cannot or do not wish to be that involved in politics. Dahl and other pluralists were more concerned with developing a democratic theory that could respond to a school of thought that argued that any political organization, even those that started out as highly democratic, inevitably would give way to a concentration of power in the hands of a few leaders. The most famous theory is Robert Michels's (1915) "iron law of oligarchy"—"He who says organization says oligarchy." After World War II, sociologists such as C. Wright Mills (1956) and G. William Domhoff (1967) argued that the United States is not really a democracy because powerful networks of decision makers—elites, both in government and in society—are the real "invisible government" in the country, a theme that echoes in American politics today. As mentioned earlier, Latin American social movements that oppose neoliberalism also use the term "civil society," and they question the idea that the state and civil society are or ought to be separate from one another. Civil society is not just a place where citizens pressure representatives; it is also a place where people can directly participate in governing.

Democracy must be, says Dahl (1971: 1), "a regime in which the opponents of the government [can] openly and legally organize into political parties to oppose the government in free and fair elections." When such conditions are met, the decision makers—that is, the elites of a society—must compete with one another for political power, and competition forces them to be responsive to public opinion. Perfect democracy may be unattainable, given that power is unequally distributed in all societies. However, the combination of elections and political rights gives people a chance to air grievances and hold elites, and government, responsible.

The result of liberal rules of the political game create what Dahl called *polyarchy*. Instead of one unified elite ruling class, polyarchies have a ruling class composed of many ("poly" means "many") elite actors relying on a variety of organized groups and political parties to compete for influence. Pluralism is the theory; polyarchy refers to the political system. Elitism, pluralism, and polyarchy are represented graphically in Figure 1.1, "Models of Democracy."

The elitist model sees all states as inherently oligarchic, most famously expressed in sociologist Robert Michels's "iron law of oligarchy": "He who says organization says oligarchy." True democracy of government by equals is impossible.

FIGURE 1.1   Models of Democracy, Relations Between Mass and Elite

Elitist Model: Mass, not Civil Society

- "Iron Law of Oligarchy"
- Policy is result of decisions made by political elites
- Elites have little accountability to masses

Pluralist Theory of Group Politics

- Emphasis on competition between groups of citizens
- Policy is the result of interest group competition

Pluralist Model of Democracy: Polyarchy, or "Democratic Elitism"

- Blending of Elite and Pluralist models
- Policy is the result of competition and bargaining among group elites

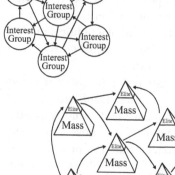

The pluralist school sees democracy emerging from the interaction and political competition of interest groups that form to influence government decision-making. This is what happens in a representative democracy.

Robert Dahl says Michels is right: Power tends to concentrate, but elites rarely can impose a single outlook on society. In a representative democracy built on consent and political equality, elites must compete with each other for support to influence decision makers. Democratic states are "poly"archies, not "olig"archies.

In a polyarchy, democracy consists of governing elites responding "to the preferences of its citizens, considered as political equals." All citizens should have "unimpaired opportunities" to formulate their preferences, signify them, and have them weighted equally in the conduct of government (1971: 1–2). Dahl believes that no actual, existing political system will ever fully measure up to this ideal, but neither does any political system ever really reach its opposite, **totalitarianism**. To Dahl, all systems fall somewhere between these two polar opposites: at one end, airtight dictatorship by an oligarchy, and at the other, fully participatory democracy. Even under highly dictatorial systems, such as the Soviet Union under Stalin and Germany under Hitler, elites competed with one another for influence, and government had to pay some attention to the demands of citizens. This is worth our attention, since Cuba is often described as a "totalitarian" society. Indeed, Cuba's only legal party is the Communist Party, but there are significant differences within the party elite, and there are elections and other institutions (e.g., local assemblies) that allow popular influence (how much is debated) over policies.

For Review

On what basis do pluralists maintain that democracy is possible, even though they allow that elites will always have more power than ordinary people have? How do the concepts of "oligarchy" and "polyarchy" differ? Why might pluralists reject terming Cuba a "totalitarian" society? Why would they also reject calling it a "democracy"?

■ Latin America and the "Third Wave" of Liberal Democracy

Three waves have occurred in the spread of **liberal democracy** worldwide, the latest "third wave" having occurred after 1970. The prior waves occurred in the early 1800s after the American and French revolutions and after World War II in places such as Germany and Japan. Figure 1.2 reproduces the way two political sociologists, Ronald Inglehart and Christian Welzel (2005), chart the wave that occurred in the second half of the twentieth century. Notice the spike between 1987 and 1996, when nations in Eastern Europe cast off communism and also when several Latin American countries held elections after years of military dictatorship. In the minds of some Western intellectuals, the third wave was a step toward liberal democracy becoming the world's only form of state (Fukuyama 1992; Huntington 1991).

Between 1964 and 1980, stable governments in Latin America chosen by opposition-contested, popular elections were rare—found only Colombia, Costa Rica, and Venezuela.

FIGURE 1.2   Number of Nations Shifting Toward Democracy

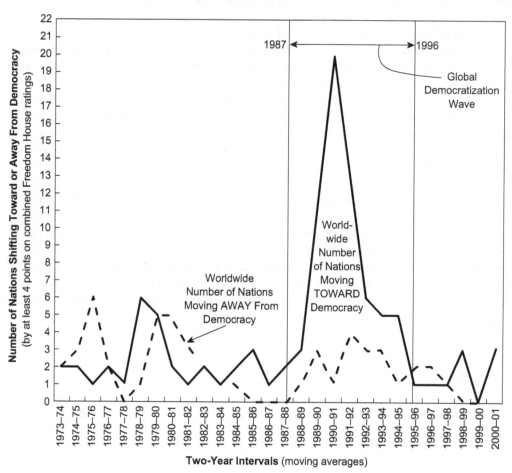

Source: Inglehart and Welzel (2005: 176).

In Latin America, the third wave took place in the 1980s and 1990s, following a long, dark period of military rule on the continent. In Central America, the transition was encouraged by the U.S. as the political side of its military intervention against revolutionary forces in the region, though domestic factors were also important. In Mexico, the Institutional Revolutionary Party, which had governed the country since 1928, began liberalizing in 1982 and accepted electoral defeat in 2000. This ushered in a new era of multiparty competition. By 1990, only Cuba remained outside the club of liberal democratic nations.

Neoliberalism became inextricably tied to the third wave in what came to be called "the Washington Consensus." The term was coined by John Williamson (2002), a British economist, who said in a retrospective essay, "The three big ideas here are **macroeconomic** discipline, a market economy, and openness to the world (at least in respect of trade and FDI [foreign direct investment])." Williamson says that by "macroeconomic discipline" he meant balancing exports and imports with fiscal responsibility in budgeting. He insists that he did not mean cuts in programs that defend human welfare. Perhaps, but "macroeconomic discipline" came to be enforced by the **International Monetary Fund** (**IMF**) upon Latin America as a condition for much needed loans, and it proved to be highly painful to Latin America's poorest sectors. The Inter-American Democratic Charter does not specifically link market-friendly economic policies to liberal democracy, but it tends toward very broad statements of support for "human rights" in accord with equal political rights.

In Latin America, most political leaders and many intellectuals fell in step with the trend to see liberal democracy as the inevitable and sole legitimate form of government. To give some examples, Mario Vargas Llosa made his reputation with brilliant novels criticizing the race and class system of his native Peru, but he turned to politics in the 1980s espousing free-market capitalism. Mexico's Jorge Castañeda, whom we met in the Introduction, started political life as a communist but in his popular book *Utopia Unarmed* (1993), he pronounced the traditional left in Latin America as "utopian." He ultimately became foreign minister in the government of President Vicente Fox (2000–2006). Venezuela's Teodoro Petkoff was a Marxist guerrilla in the 1960s and then founded the Movement to Socialism (MAS) party to advance revolutionary goals in a more democratic way. However, as the minister of planning from 1993 to 1998, he backed privatizing state-owned companies and cutting back social security and unemployment benefits. Joaquín Villalobos, the most important leader of the Salvadoran guerrillas in the civil war of the 1980s, later took up residence at Oxford University in England. He endorsed the U.S. proposal for the Free Trade Area of the Americas, which had it been approved would have committed all member countries to open their markets to global competition. Fernando Henrique Cardoso, once a leading academic critic of capitalism, eventually entered politics in Brazil with a different agenda. As minister of finance and then as president (1995–2002), he implemented economic policies designed to put Brazil in step with capitalist globalization. Although Cardoso has denied saying it, he was reported to have told a group of Brazilian businesspeople, "Forget what I wrote" (Kane 2005).

We should not exaggerate and say that these prominent Latin Americans became right-wing advocates of unrestricted markets. Most endorsed a welfare safety net and criticized some of the neoliberal **structural adjustment** economic policies that governments adopted under pressure of the **IMF** (see chapters 6 and 15). Williamson himself argued for increased spending on health and education for the poor. Still, the Washington Consensus said at the time that democracy could only be liberal and flourish with a free-market system. Hernando De Soto (1989), a Peruvian entrepreneur and head of the Instituto Libertad y Democracia, introduced a version of neoliberalism contending that the huge sector of "informal" workers (itinerant vendors, sidewalk merchants, day workers, unlicensed repair shops, etc.) would spur economic development if only they had more secure property rights and legal status. Less government regulation, he said, would unleash the entrepreneurial energies of this stratum of the population.

Few leftists would agree. They see competition from global corporations (e.g., Walmart and McDonald's) squeezing out street vendors and small stores. Smaller enterprises have a difficult time competing with big companies' modern technology, marketing power, and ability to sell cheap long enough to drive out competitors. However, there is some common ground here between left and right on the desirability of strengthening the legal security for the homes and small businesses (microenterprises) of workers in the informal sector.

Neoliberalism did have a political impact, but in a way that neither detractors nor supporters fully expected. Free-trade policies and globalization attracted more scrutiny of human rights conditions. Fiscal austerity caused hardship but also reduced the patronage resources available to politicians to reward friends and punish enemies. So, in certain ways, liberal policies widened spaces for political participation that had been limited in an earlier era (roughly 1930–1970) of electoral democracy, before the years of harsh military rule. Many new social movements, including those of Indigenous peoples, women, Afro-descendant peoples, landless peasants, democratic unions, among many others, recognized the opening and arose to demand more inclusion in social and economic life. They began to pose alternatives to neoliberal economic policies and more participation in governing themselves.

The economic policies associated with neoliberalism lost their luster in part because of the growth of inequality during the 1990s, despite the decade being one of economic growth. The privatization (selling off of government-owned businesses and services to private investors) of the 1980s and 1990s was rife with corruption that allowed a handful of businesspeople to make huge profits. For example, Mexico's Carlos Slim benefited from the privatization of communications and media companies to become an overnight billionaire. Implementation of laissez-faire policy, called "**structural adjustment**," resulted in higher unemployment, difficulties for small farmers, and reductions in social services. Critics began to see representative democracy—something that Latin Americans had won in bitter struggles to send military regimes back to the barracks—as a façade masking a corrupt process of transferring public resources to private control and exposing the poor to the rapaciousness of the wealthy. In the face of mounting hardships, especially those felt in the family, where women bore the brunt of the costs of "adjustment," social movements began to exert themselves in a way suggesting a different conception of civil society, one less wedded to the liberal conception as a sphere of life separate from the state.

As an alternative, many Latin Americans want to build a civil society that stands between the market and the state. As Carlos Vilas (1993: 38) puts it,

> The concept of civil society refers to a sphere of collective action distinct from both the market and "political society"—parties, legislatures, courts, state agencies. Civil society is not independent of politics, but clearly, when people identify themselves as "civil society," they are seeking to carve out a relatively autonomous sphere for organization and action.

The political left, on the defensive for most of the period between 1970 and 2000, took advantage of the popular discontent with neoliberal economic policies and scored a wave of electoral successes that became the **Pink Tide**. The tide rose along with social movements that were wary of being captured or manipulated by any politicians, leftist or otherwise. This has created some tensions because, as we'll see in Part IV, the perspective of those in government is not always in harmony with the perspective of the movements.

The pushback in Latin America has not been limited to the left. Norberto Ceresole, a right-wing Argentine nationalist, contended that the "third wave" of democracy is little more than an attempt to reinforce the subordination of underdeveloped countries of the periphery to wealthy ones. By "countries of the **periphery**," we mean those parts of the world that in both political and economic terms have relatively little power compared with wealthy **core nations**, such as the United States, Europe, and Japan. For Ceresole (1999), liberal democracy in Latin America and the poorer countries of the world reinforces rule by an elite who function as subordinate partners of their counterparts in the wealthy countries, especially the United States. He urged resistance to economic globalization and the liberalism associated with the third wave of democracy.

Twenty years later, little attention has been paid to Ceresole's critique, but today some political scientists see that a surge of authoritarian populism seems to be taking place not only in Latin America but also in other parts of the world. This so-called third wave of autocratization refers to the emergence of elected but autocratic leaders in places like Bolivia, Brazil, Burundi, Hungary, the Philippines, India, Russia, Serbia, Venezuela, and Turkey. Most now include the United States under Trump on a list of endangered democratic species. The trend also goes by the term "militarized democracies." Once again, the concept of "polyarchy" is being invoked to assess the level of threat to democracy. As two Swedish theorists (Lührmann and Lindberg 2019) put it, "Our notion of democracy is based on Dahl's famous conceptualization of electoral democracy as 'polyarchy', namely clean elections, freedom of association, universal suffrage, an elected executive, as well as freedom of expression and alternative sources of information."

For Review

What were the Washington Consensus and the Summit of the Americas? To what kind of economic policies did they commit Latin Americans? To what kind of political system did they commit them? What is the Pink Tide, and why is it seen sometimes as a reaction to the Washington Consensus?

Polyarchy and Alternative Democracy in Latin America

In the past 30 years, comparative political scientists have used a pluralist framework to analyze phases in Latin America's recent political evolution, especially the **breakdown of democracy** and **transition to democracy**. The "breakdown of democratic regimes" refers to the economic crises, violence, and political polarization that afflicted Latin America beginning in the mid-1960s (starting with a coup in Brazil in 1964); transition refers to the return of civilian government and retreat of the military back to the barracks. Until recently, many anticipated a new phase of consolidation or deepening to democracy, but more recently attention has shifted to a concern with "autocratization." In all of three of these processes, it is Dahl's notion of polyarchy that conceptually defines "democracy."

Although Latin America has a long history of military intervention, the period after breakdown was marked by especially harsh repression. Similar events had transpired in a number of Mediterranean countries, attracting the attention of an international team of comparative political scientists. With support from several large foundations, they began to search for common causes. Although they identified multiple causes of crisis and breakdown, they placed greatest emphasis on the inability of elites to continue to respect each other's vital interests within the framework of constitutional democracy (Linz and Stepan 1978).

By the mid-1980s, Latin Americans had endured 20 years of brutal military rule. Communism in Eastern Europe and the **apartheid** regime in South Africa were under pressure to democratize. The U.S. was at least formally committed to promoting human rights, if for no other reason than to hasten communism's demise. In Nicaragua (1979) and Iran (1978), two dictatorships long supported by Washington had fallen. Latin America's resistance movements were placing pressure on the generals to return to the barracks. These protestors often braved imprisonment, torture, and death squads in the process. The persistence and growth of this movement, along with the changed international climate, induced politicians and business elites to negotiate a transition to democracy through elections, before popular pressure assumed revolutionary proportions.

Pluralists tend to see regime transitions as a kind of game in which the elites negotiate with one another to arrive at a pact about the future after the civilians return and elections are allowed to go forth. The pact is an agreement among political, business, military, and economic elites to make sure that the vital interests of each group will not be at risk in the new democracy. Pluralists see this process as a way of building a political consensus and preventing conflict from destroying a new, fragile democracy. The people in the streets are a reminder to the negotiators that failure to reach agreement risks a more radical outcome or a new round of repression.

In the most influential study of this type, the authors defined democracy as "the right to be treated by fellow human beings as equal with respect to the making of collective choices and the obligation of those implementing such choices to be equally accountable and accessible to all members of the polity" (O'Donnell et al. 1986: 7). However, in negotiating a pact, elites seek to limit what can be changed. Think, for example, of the U.S. Constitution. Some of the limits to prevent "tyranny of the majority" protected the institution of slavery. A key issue was thus taken out of the realm of democracy, eventually being resolved through civil war 75 years later.

Most of the "transitions" literature gave way to studies about a new wave, the consolidation or **deepening of democracy**. One prominent school of thought, **institutionalism**, emphasizes the importance of institution building (Linz and Stepan 1996; Linz and Valenzuela 1994; Mainwaring and Scully 1995; Mainwaring and Shugart 1997). This approach stresses the importance of developing the **rule of law**—that is, ensuring that all citizens are procedurally treated the same and can rely on the state to guarantee justice and security for both persons and property. More optimistic scholars now see hope for the establishment of stable democratic institutions in what they perceive to be an abandonment of extraconstitutional, violent challenges from both the political left (Castañeda 1993) and the right (Chalmers et al. 1992). More pessimistic scholars worry that social inequality and/or tendencies toward **personalism** remain too strong to inspire confidence in democratic stability. We look more closely at institutions and rule of law in Latin America in chapters 13 and 14.

Transitional pacts have often included immunity from prosecution for human rights violators, severe limits on the ability of the government to tax wealth, limits on the rights of labor, and systems of representation guaranteeing conservative parties votes in the legislature in excess of their share of the electoral vote. Perhaps the best-known case where all these elements were present was that of Chile, where General Augusto Pinochet, dictator between 1973 and 1989, incorporated limits on democracy into the country's present constitution, which dates from 1980. After Pinochet was forced out of the presidency, his constitution functioned just as he had designed it—posing severe obstacles to any attempt to legislate changes in the social and economic direction he had set in motion. Some of these limits have been lifted since 2000, but many Chileans have been disappointed that a return to democracy did not bring much change in the inherited economic model or cause rapid progress on human rights issues.

Although the scholars responsible for most of the literature on the "breakdown, transition, and consolidation" of democracy were guarded in their conclusions, there was a general tone of optimism in their work consistent with Huntington's (1991) third-wave thesis. For example, in his review of debates and recent research on democratic politics in Latin America for the *Annual Review of Political Science*, Gerardo L. Munck (2004) writes,

> Latin American politics has recently undergone a fundamental transformation. For many decades prior to the 1990s, most elected leaders could not discount the possibility of military coups, and most authoritarian rulers could not ignore the actions of antiauthoritarian movements. Now, in contrast, elections are held regularly, winners take office and make legally binding decisions, and losers and new players prepare for the next election. Latin America has made a clear break with its past.

As we saw in the Introduction, this optimism has waned in the last few years. Political scientist George Philip (1996: 34–35) recognized one underlying weakness early on. "The point is simply that Latin American elites have so far been more successful at holding elections than at creating state institutions which work well. This situation holds out the permanent threat of state failure." Philip saw the threat emanating from three sources: (1) capitalism and globalization, which have accentuated inequalities; (2) the resentfulness of those losing out; and (3) a society that remains weak and "patrimonially structured." With this last phrase, Philip refers to a state in which "who you know" rather than your merit determines how social benefits—jobs, university scholarships, construction contracts, etc.—are distributed.

Fareed Zakaria (1997), an influential journalist, coined the phrase "**illiberal democracy**" to refer to situations where concentration of executive power is combined with more serious abuses of human rights or limitations on civil freedoms. His article cited strongmen of the time, such as Argentina's president Carlos Menem and Peru's president Alberto Fujimori, along with a number of presidents of Eastern and Central European countries, as examples of this phenomenon. Critics of deceased Venezuelan President Hugo Chávez (1999–2013) said that he made Venezuela into an illiberal democracy; in contrast, his defenders said that he tried to breathe life into a moribund democracy by offering poor Venezuelans a new sense of empowerment. We will look more closely at this debate in upcoming chapters.

O'Donnell (1994: 164) fears that Latin Americans have a predilection for rule by a strongman. **Delegative democracies**, as he calls them,

> rest on the premise that whoever wins election to the presidency is thereby entitled to govern as he or she sees fit, constrained only by the hard facts of existing power relations and by a constitutionally limited term of office. The president is taken to be the embodiment of the nation and the main custodian and definer of its interests. Governmental policies need bear no resemblance to campaign promises.

Some comparative political scientists use yet another term, "**hybrid regimes**," to describe some political systems that have emerged recently in Eastern Europe, the Middle East, and Latin America. This concept recognizes that these regimes mix hallmarks of electoral democracy with autocracy. Originally, "hybrid regimes" were seen as transitional, moving toward democracy, but many comparativists now see them as a type of state, relatively stable and persistent over time.

Several **nongovernmental organizations** offer "democracy rankings" of countries around the world. All utilize the polyarchy model, but variations exist. Some, such the **libertarian** Freedom House, use a "thin" conception of democracy, assigning a score by evaluating countries largely based on free elections and civil liberties, but it does use 25 different measures, each with a scale of 1 (democratic) to 7 to make its evaluation. Another organization, the Polity Project (see Center for Systemic Peace 2019), uses an even "thinner" notion of democracy. It evaluates countries by first scoring them from 0 to 10 (highly democratic) on only three criteria: elections, constraints on the power of executives, and civil liberties. Then, its evaluators score countries on a measure of autocracy, based on their evaluation of how much "competitive political participation" among both elites and the general population is repressed. The final score subtracts the autocracy score from the democracy score. The Economist Intelligence Unit (EIU), which is linked to the British weekly *The Economist*, uses similar methodology but seeks to go beyond Dahl's "polyarchy" model by measuring a "thicker" concept of democracy. It uses five measures: electoral process and pluralism, civil liberties, the functioning of government, political participation, and political culture. Countries are ranked from 10 (high) to 0. The idea is to better measure how substantive democracy is. It is worth noting that all three of these evaluation systems consider some form of "economic freedom" based on protections of property rights and ability to found and run a business.

What we see here is an attempt to use comparative politics methodology to produce something useful for the study of democracy not only in academic circles, but for the general public as well. All three of these widely cited measures of democracy (including EIU's) follow Dahl's conception of democracy as polyarchy. They depend upon evaluations by experts—of specific regions of the world and political scientists. These experts may disagree with one another about how they rate countries on each of dozens of questions about politics in the countries evaluated, but they overwhelming share "polyarchy" as the lens through which they judge democracy. To be fair to the evaluators, we should acknowledge that all expressly say that the resulting rankings of countries need to be accompanied by more qualitative, close-up evaluations of the actual democratic conditions in each one.

My conception of democracy is even thicker than that of the EIU's. I would considerably broaden the participation index and include economic equality in any measure of democracy. Maldistribution of wealth and income directly translates into more political power for some individuals and groups. Large transnational corporations are largely immune from influence by anyone but the billionaire owners or the largest shareholders. They exercise more power than many governments in the world. However, this is not to say that the liberal criteria used in these evaluations are without value. Whether or not we are satisfied with capitalism, most of us would prefer to live, I think, in a capitalist democracy than in a capitalist dictatorship. In the next chapter, we will factor inequality into the discussion of democracy and Latin American politics. In this first look at the state of democracy overall in Latin America, I will simply present to you the rankings for 2018 by the EIU, which offers the broadest criteria (see Table 1.1). Notice that besides the actual scores, each country is classified by the EIU into four categories: full democracies, flawed democracies, hybrid regimes, and authoritarian regimes. I have listed all the Latin American and most of the Caribbean countries, and added a few others (Norway, Canada, the United States, North Korea, Spain, and Portugal).

TABLE 1.1   Economist Intelligence Unit Democracy Index, 2018, Latin America, Caribbean, Others

	Rank	Overall Score	Electoral Process and Pluralism	Functioning of Government	Political Participation	Political Culture	Civil Liberties
"FULL DEMOCRACIES"							
Norway	1	9.87	10.00	9.64	10.00	10.00	9.71
Canada	6	9.15	9.58	9.64	7.78	8.75	10.00
Uruguay	15	8.38	10.00	8.57	6.11	7.50	9.71
Spain	19	8.08	9.17	7.14	7.78	7.50	8.82
Costa Rica	20	8.07	9.58	7.50	6.67	7.50	9.12
"FLAWED DEMOCRACIES"							
Chile	23	7.97	9.58	8.57	4.44	8.13	9.12
United States	25	7.96	9.17	7.14	7.78	7.50	8.24
Portugal	27	7.84	9.98	7.50	6.11	6.88	9.12
Trinidad & Tobago	43	7.16	9.58	7.14	6.11	5.63	7.35
Panama	45	7.05	9.58	6.06	6.67	5.00	7.94
Argentina	47	7.02	9.17	5.36	6.11	6.25	8.24
Jamaica	47	7.02	8.75	7.14	4.44	6.25	8.53
Suriname	49	6.98	9.17	6.43	6.67	5.00	7.65
Brazil	50	6.97	9.58	5.36	6.67	5.00	8.24
Colombia	51	6.96	9.17	6.79	5.00	5.63	8.24
Guyana	54	6.57	9.17	5.71	6.11	5.00	7.35
Peru	59	6.60	9.17	5.00	5.56	5.63	7.65
Dominican Republic	61	6.54	9.17	5.36	6.11	5.00	7.06
Ecuador	68	6.27	8.75	5.36	6.11	4.38	6.76
Paraguay	70	6.24	8.75	5.71	5.00	4.38	7.35
Mexico	71	6.19	8.33	6.07	3.13	3.13	6.18
"HYBRID REGIMES"							
El Salvador	77	5.96	9.17	4.29	5.56	3.75	7.06
Bolivia	83	5.70	7.50	4.64	5.56	3.75	7.06
Honduras	85	5.63	8.50	4.64	4.44	4.38	6.18
Guatemala	87	5.60	7.92	5.36	3.89	4.38	6.47
Haiti	102	4.91	5.58	2.93	3.89	6.25	5.88
"AUTHORITARIAN" REGIMES							
Nicaragua	122	3.63	2.67	1.86	3.89	5.63	4.12
Venezuela	134	3.16	1.67	1.79	4.44	4.38	3.53
Cuba	142	3.00	1.08	3.57	3.33	4.38	2.65
Syria	166	1.43	0.00	0.00	2.78	4.38	0.00
North Korea	167	1.08	0.00	2.50	1.67	1.25	0.00

Source: Democracy Intelligence Index, 2019, www.eiu.com/topic/democracy-index

I would urge you to look at Table 1.1 before going on. Are you surprised by any of the findings? What do you think of the ranking of the United States relative to other countries? If you wish to look more closely at the criteria used in these rankings, you can use the URL provided at the end of this chapter; I have also placed a link on the website that accompanies this book.

Perhaps what strikes you is that Uruguay and Costa Rica are both categorized as full democracies and score significantly higher than does the United States; Chile also placed just ahead of the U.S. among the "flawed democracies." Costa Rica stands out as well among Central American countries, three of which are hybrid regimes, and one, Nicaragua, is classified as authoritarian. Notice that Haiti, the poorest country in the region, is predictably ranked low, but notice how much higher it ranks on "political culture"—higher than Brazil, Colombia, Mexico, and other Latin American countries. EIU does not provide direct access to the score for each component of political culture (and the other four variables), but the criteria used (which is provided) seem to emphasize popular support for democracy. Keep in mind that 2019 has been, like 2018, a year of political convulsion, with Chile and Bolivia joining the list of countries in the region experiencing significant mass protest, both peaceful and violent. Acute political polarization and increased military involvement are evident in politics. In future rankings, several countries, including the United States, may have slipped in the evaluations.

For Review

When we study democracy, what do we mean by "breakdown," "transition," and "consolidation" or "deepening"? According to pluralists, what role does a "pact" play in the transition to democracy? What might be some limits? Why do comparativists sometimes refer to some regimes as "hybrid," "delegative," or "illiberal" democracies?

▪ Political Culture in Latin America

George Philip is just one of many political scientists who see an obstacle to democracy in Latin American culture, which they see as more traditional and personalist than in developed, wealthier countries. In a modern culture, the argument goes, favoritism toward relatives or friends may occur, but it is regarded as an abuse of authority and source of corruption. In traditional cultures, such behavior is much more a norm—that is, not deviant. One example is the persistence of *compadrazgo*, which refers to the special relationship between a godparent and godchild in Catholic cultures. Latin Americanists use the term more broadly to refer to the importance of family ties. Such a culture, some argue, favors the formation of a **patrimonial state**, referring to a type of political system where personalism and patronage prevail. Within such a system, politics mostly involves leaders (patrons) who offer resources provided by the state—anything from a water pump for a poor village to multimillion-dollar construction contracts—in exchange for political support (e.g., votes). This practice is known as **clientelism**—and when practiced to an extreme, including outright corruption, it sometimes is called "crony capitalism."

Political culture is best conceived as habitual practices and common beliefs that have their roots in history and are intimately connected with the social and economic structures of society. We have to take care to avoid stereotypes and a tendency to see culture as immutable, simple, and determinate in shaping politics. Culture is also dynamic and changeable. In the United States, we Americans tend to think that individual effort and hard work always pays off in success, but in some time periods and circumstances we are disposed to using the power of government to level the playing field. Similarly, Latin Americans are said to be more family oriented and to have less of a predilection toward racism, i.e., to be more disposed to racial mixing. These generalizations are not without some foundation, but they also are somewhat mythical, as we shall see.

Howard Wiarda (1981) believes that Latin America inclines toward "**corporatism**." While pluralists tend to see competition as the essence of democracy, corporatists see it as an alternative ideology promoting harmonization, amelioration of the worst characteristics of capitalism, and a common effort toward economic development. Corporatists see a need for the state to take responsibility for regulating the formation of interest groups—whereas pluralists believe that individuals should freely form groups to advocate and defend their interests. Take labor relations, for example. For the pluralists, workers should have the right to form unions to bargain with employers. Corporatists go further; by law, workers are required to join state-approved unions, usually grouped into higher-level federations in predefined branches of the economy, and employers are required to join "syndicates" of companies in the same economic sector. When it is time to negotiate a contract, union federations and syndicates sit at the table with a third actor, the state, representing the larger interest of society.

Wiarda (1981) and others see corporatism not as a perversion of pluralism but as a theory more consonant with Latin American tradition, with its emphasis on family and solidarity and the practice of *compadrazgo*, a tendency to favor ties of kinship and friendship over more neutral criteria, such as expertise. Also, corporatists believe that economic development requires that the nation put aside conflicts that weaken the interest of the nation, a "family" of a sort, as a whole. But many political scientists see corporatism as a negative tendency in pluralist systems, generally not viewing it as favorably as Wiarda does. They see it undermining pluralism when organizations gain an advantage over rivals that later emerge because they already have won privileged access to the state (Schmitter 1974). And this can degenerate into corruption.

In Mexico, until recently almost all peasants belonged to a single Confederación Nacional de Campesinos (CNC; National Confederation of Peasants) formally linked to the Partido Revolucionario Institucional (PRI; Institutional Revolutionary Party). The PRI controlled the presidency and monopolized Mexican politics from 1928 to 2000. The CNC's access to the state bureaucracy made it a privileged channel for distributing benefits critical to the well-being of peasants—land, credit, subsidies, transportation, water projects, and so on. Peasants received a piece of the economic pie, but they had little real influence over the leaders and groups representing them. They depended on the CNC more than the CNC depended on them. The leaders of the federation kept their jobs because they faithfully protected the interests of the PRI and not because they defended the interests of the peasants.

In Latin America, it has been quite common for unions to receive subsidies and be allocated some power in management (e.g., the right to fill some percentage of jobs), and to benefit from laws requiring membership and facilitating collection of dues. Usually, there are strings attached. Officially or unofficially, they can lead to unions putting political priorities ahead of the interest of workers (Collier 1995). If a rival organization arises, the politically well-connected union confederation can rely on the labor ministry to maintain the status quo. A rival labor union may find its petitions dismissed on technical grounds or tiny discrepancies. To quell a rebellion of the rank and file, the ministry will work with employers to negotiate a highly favorable contract just before a crucial vote.

I witnessed an example of union co-optation while doing research on labor unions in Ciudad Guayana, in eastern Venezuela. In 1984, the workers of Hornos Eléctricos de Venezuela (HEVENSA), which processed ores for the nearby steel industry, voted to replace its union leadership. The workers were unhappy with the conditions in the plant, where they worked with hazardous materials in 125°(F) heat. The management then hired a powerful old-guard local labor leader as its personnel director. He proceeded to fire the new labor leaders, provoking a strike, which in turn resulted in more firings. The National Confederation of Venezuelan Workers, closely associated with Venezuela's most important party, Acción Democrática (AD; Democratic Action), invited a few of the rebel workers to Caracas to be "trained" to become union leaders. Some accepted, dividing the strikers. After one year of struggle, workers settled the dispute, were reemployed, and received back pay. A victory? Only 30 of the original 108 workers made it through the long struggle and benefited from the settlement (Hellinger 1991: 184–188).

In Brazil, a huge movement of landless workers, the Movimento dos Trabalhadores Sem Terra (MST; Landless Workers' Movement), has demanded land reform, with some success. In doing so, however, it has worked with the Workers' Party, which was a key force behind Brazil's transition to democracy in the 1980s. The MST determines who settles on redistributed land and administers financial resources to make new settlements viable—50 million dollars by one account (Mark 2001). So far, the MST has done relatively well in balancing autonomy versus cooperation, but there is an evident danger of the MST evolving into the kind of corporatist, organization that emerged in Mexico during the PRI era.

After 1968, the military government in Brazil implemented a corporatist measure by abolishing all the old political parties and permitting only two parties to contest elections and hold offices. One was an official party of government (the Alliance for National Renovation, ARENA) and the other an official party of opposition (Brazilian Democratic Movement, MDB). Ultimately, however, the generals eventually gave up and under pressure permitted parties to form freely again in a "transition to democracy" after 1982 (see chapter 7).

Juan Perón, president of Argentina from 1946 to 1955, championed an ideology that he called *justicialismo*. Perón condemned both free-market capitalism and socialism. He repressed the Communist Party, a competitor with Peronism for control of the unions, but his appeal, and that of his wife, Eva Perón, was to working class and poor Argentines. *Justicialismo*'s cardinal principles were to be "social justice, economic independence, and political sovereignty." He defined "the just state as one in which each class or element [like the human body] exercises its functions and its special abilities for the benefit of all" (Perón 1950).

In Venezuela, Hugo Chávez (who died in 2013) instituted a number of programs to funnel super-profits from the country's oil industry to people through local communal councils. These councils were often led by ordinary residents, most often women, in poor neighborhoods. Fearing that Chávez's opponents would terminate these programs, local leaders often felt obligated to support candidates of Chávez's United Socialist Party of Venezuela (PSUV), which included many career politicians (García-Guadilla 2011; Schiller 2011). This tendency led critics, including many from within the PSUV, to conclude that old patterns of top-down control were reasserting themselves.

Corporatism is commonly found in papal encyclicals and other religion-based theories of justice that urge the state to defend society's weaker members, relevant here because Catholic social doctrines have been influential in Latin America. An encyclical from Pope Leo XIII, *Rerum Novarum*, in 1891, issued to respond to the influence of Marxist thought at the time, acknowledged that social class conflict exists but also made an argument very typical of corporatist thought. Keep in mind that the word "corporatism" is derived from the Latin world "corpus," meaning "body."

> Just as the symmetry of the human frame is the result of the suitable arrangement of the different parts of the body, so in a State is it ordained by nature that these two classes should dwell in harmony and agreement, so as to maintain the balance of the body politic. Each needs the other: capital cannot do without labor, nor labor without capital. Mutual agreement results in the beauty of good order.

Leo's social doctrines became influential through the emergence in the twentieth century of Christian democratic parties in many parts of Latin America. John Paul II, a native of Poland and pope from 1978 until 2005, was stridently anticommunist, and many were surprised that he lashed out at neoliberal economics as unbridled "savage capitalism" on a visit to Cuba in 1994. But what he said was consistent with what he wrote in 1981, while still a bishop in Poland.

> Each person is fully entitled to consider himself a part-owner of the great workbench at which he is working with everyone else. A way towards that goal could be found by associating labor with the ownership of capital, as far as possible, and by producing a wide range of intermediate bodies with economic, social and cultural purposes. They would be bodies enjoying real autonomy with regard to the public powers, pursuing their specific aims in honest collaboration with each other and in subordination to the demands of the common good, and they would be living communities both in form and in substance, in the sense that the members of each body would be looked upon and treated as persons and encouraged to take an active part in the life of the body.
> (Quoted in Perone 2000)

Pope Francis, an Argentine and the first pope from Latin America, has even more assertively criticized inequality, arguing in his 2014 encyclical, *Evangelii Gaudium* (2013),

> As long as the problems of the poor are not radically resolved by rejecting the absolute autonomy of markets and financial speculation and by attacking the structural causes of inequality, no solution will be found for the world's problems or, for that matter, to any problems. Inequality is the root of social ills.

Francis added a corporatist rationale for action on inequality and poverty—"its urgency for the good order of society."

For Review

How does a corporatist image of the role of the state differ from one typical of a liberal democratic or pluralist perspective? Why do some Latin Americans think corporatism is stronger in
Latin America than in the United States? Why might there be a tension between corporatism and
participatory social movements?

Caudillism

Distraught about the blatant theft of an election by President Alberto Fujimori in Peru (in
2000) and alleging that his own country's president (Chávez) was embarked on a similar
route, the Venezuelan political scientist Aníbal Romero (1999) once complained,

> We are dealing, in truth, with toy democracies, attached as we are to the erroneous
> belief according to which the temporary support of the masses justifies for the *cau-
> dillo* practically anything he wants to do, violating most of time judicial procedures
> and making a mockery of any notion of a state of law. . . . They are poor imitations
> of another reality, of true liberal democracies that protect the rights of minorities,
> maintain inviolable the sphere of individual rights, administer justice impartially, and
> balance powers.

The term **caudillo** literally means "man on horseback," an allusion to the strongmen,
sometimes illiterate, who assumed regional or national leadership as a result of their fighting
ability and leadership skills during the violent, anarchic nineteenth century (see chapter 4).
The ability to fight on horseback with great skill and courage could inspire the loyalty of poor
peasants, ranch hands, and other men (sometimes women) desperate for land. With firearms
or machetes, they banded into irregular armies behind the *caudillos* who fought each other
for control of territories. In the nineteenth century, after independence, the national armies
of the new states were not sufficiently armed and trained to suppress regional rebellions.
In many countries even large landowners were deeply in debt to banks and trading houses
operating out of the ports. In times of natural catastrophe or falling prices for their export
goods, revolts against elites in the capital and larger cities were common. Times of turmoil
were also opportunities to settle scores over past grievances, often about land ownership. Just
as gun culture has roots in the United States in the settlement of the West and removal of
Indigenous peoples, so too can we trace caudillism in Latin America to historical forces and
the myths that form around them.

Not everyone views caudillism negatively. An Argentine sociologist, Norberto Ceresole,
admired Juan Perón as a charismatic leader who forged a unity between popular aspirations
and the military (Ceresole 1999). In 1919, a Venezuelan intellectual made a similar argument to justify the harsh, personal dictatorship (1908 to 1935) of Juan Vicente Gómez, which
he called "democratic caesarism" (Lanz 1919). More recently, Diane Raby (2006), a British
political scientist who otherwise would find little in common with Ceresole, portrayed Hugo
Chávez as a popular leader, a model to undermine the power of oligarchies, challenge the
hegemony of the United States, and enable new forms of mass participation to arise.

An elected *caudillo* seems to fit O'Donnell's idea of "delegative democracy," and recent experiences (Venezuela, Bolivia, among others) with this type of democracy have revealed its vulnerability to degeneration toward autocracy or collapse because of its dependence on a charismatic leader, rather than on institutions. However, there is some evidence that populist leaders in Latin America have overcome institutionalized obstacles to the inclusion of people who have previously been politically and economically excluded. In "More Inclusion, Less Liberalism in Bolivia," an article published three years before Morales was forced to step down and flee the country in 2019, political scientist Santiago Anria took note that discontent with centralization of power, erosion of rights, and politicization of the courts were eroding the president's popularity despite his success managing the economy, redistributing wealth, and raising the cultural and political status of Indigenous people (two-thirds of Bolivians have Indigenous ancestry). But those who were already calling Bolivia "nondemocratic" were wrong, he said, preferring for his part "democracy with an adjective," in this "delegative."

The coup that drove President Morales out of office and the country was organized by Bolivian elites deeply imbued with prejudices against the Indigenous population and unwilling to accept the redistributive economic policies of the president and the way that MAS was transforming Bolivia as a nation-state. As a result of mobilization of Indigenous Bolivians by Morales and his Movimiento al Socialismo party (MAS; Movement Toward Socialism—but very different from the Venezuelan party by the same name), Anria wrote, "Inclusiveness of Bolivian politics is real, even if checks and balances are weak. Larger numbers of Bolivians do enjoy effective rights of citizenship and greater input into decision making" (2016: 103). This was taking place in several settings, including popular assemblies, something cropping up more often as a democratic device in Latin America. Membership in the national legislature no longer was limited to elites, as is evidenced by the occupations of representatives who had entered Congress. For 2010–2014, the largest contingent came from "workers, artisans, and the primary sector" (the latter being mining and agriculture), up from 4 percent in 1993–1997 to 26 percent. Anria's research showed that MAS's recruitment of candidates deserved a lot of the credit—which suggests that while Morales's leadership might have much to do with the new inclusion, so did his party. The MAS was bringing women and peasants into politics in an unprecedented way. With Morales in exile and signs of persecution of the MAS in late 2019, the future of democracy in Bolivia seemed dark, but the polls were showing that the MAS was likely to win the election scheduled for May. Whether the elites who seized power would allow a fair election and accept a MAS victory, with or without Morales, was not clear.

More typically, political scientists see caudillism as an obstacle to democracy, even when the caudillo's power is ratified through elections. Zakaria (1997: 22) put it this way in the influential magazine *Foreign Affairs*:

> Democratically elected regimes, often ones that have been reelected or reaffirmed through referenda, are routinely ignoring constitutional limits on their power and depriving their citizens of basic rights and freedoms. From Peru to the Palestinian Authority, from Sierra Leone to Slovakia, from Pakistan to the Philippines, we see the rise of a disturbing phenomenon in international life—illiberal democracy.

The tendency toward personalism reinforces a style of politics known as "populism." **Populism** here means the practice of appealing for mass support by championing the causes of ordinary people against powerful elites. We will look more closely at populism in Latin America in chapters 5 and 12. For now, I will only note that the *caudillo* often practices populism in the ascent to power and sometimes to hold onto it, but often populists are co-opted by the elites they initially challenged. However, this tendency may not play out the same way in the Bolivian case.

For Review

Why is personalism in Latin America often called "caudillism"? How did Latin America's history after independence encourage it as a tendency? Why do some regard caudillism as unhealthy for democracy? Can you explain how, on the other hand, some argue that populist leadership can be democratic?

Clientelism and Corruption

The tendency toward personalism and corporatism in Latin America is reinforced by the strong ties that often develop between leaders with resources and those who need these resources. The result is **clientelism**, an unequal exchange between public officials with patronage to dispense and those who need those resources. The benefit might be anything from a multimillion dollar subsidy for an industrialist or a subsidized license for a trader to import millions of chickens or bottles of milk for desperate mothers or a bag of cement for a barrio neighborhood trying to repair the steps down to the water pump. In return, the person enjoying this benefit offers political support, often in the form of votes or financial contributions.

To some extent, these practices are rooted in the very nature of politics. Everywhere in the world, winners of elections reward those who have worked on campaigns or provided money with appointments, access, or funds. The practice does seem more pervasive in Latin America, in part because government employees are not as well protected by law and courts from losing their jobs. Often, the political appointee seems unqualified for a position. For example, someone who cannot type might get a job requiring the ability to enter data on a computer keyboard.

Clientelism is not corruption, but it can easily become just that. Often it seems that in Latin America even the most ordinary and routine service requires political pull, that is, *palanca* (leverage). Perhaps the person in charge of processing applications for unemployment looks favorably only on applicants who carry the same party ID card. Renewing a passport can be a nightmare. The company dispatcher who schedules a phone or cable installation simply cannot find a free crew until you make it worth her while. The worker in the highway tollbooth feels entitled by his low salary to keep some of the receipts—provided he passes along a percentage to his superior. A job as a policeman is also a license to collect little bribes from drivers (the *mordita*, or "little bite," as Mexicans call it). A permit to operate a taxi might require a bribe to a bureaucrat. All these acts of petty corruption are sustained in part because further up the social pyramid more lucrative and serious corrupt practices are tolerated, such as kickbacks on construction projects.

Clientelism, this exchange of material benefits for political loyalty, might not be all bad. It ensures that at least some economic benefits trickle down to the masses. Still, clientelism reduces the capacity of citizens to exercise effective control over public officials and to run local affairs in their best interests. **Patronage** politics take precedence over debate about policies and programs. It frustrates those who want to make positive change. Politicians have long exploited the needs of the poor—and of other people—by delivering something the community needs in return for the loyalty of its leaders and their ability to deliver votes. It may be providing cement to build concrete steps to replace the muddy, winding paths leading high up into a poor *barrio*(neighborhood). Grateful residents are appropriately grateful and reward parties with votes, but often the relationship goes further. After the "right" election outcome, the neighborhood expects to receive benefits. Is this corruption or clientelism?

In Venezuela, two parties dominated politics until 1998 and competed fiercely with one another for votes, giving the appearance of a well-institutionalized polyarchy. Winning an election meant access to a trove of state funds generated by the country's bountiful oil exports. The parties, AD and its rival, the Social Christian Party (COPEI), would put aside competition and cooperate at the polling tables to steal votes from smaller parties (Buxton 2001), threatening their joint monopoly over politics. Conversely, they might slough a few votes off to one another rather than allow more a troublesome opponent to get a foot in the door—and a hand in the oil.

Journalist Alma Guillermoprieto (2000: 30), while covering Mexico's July 2000 election for the *New Yorker*, described how Mexico's PRI exercised "prestidigitation" to make up electoral deficits. Such efforts included

the *ratón loco*, or crazy mouse, in which a group of hired voters was sent to one polling station after another to cast ballots for the PRI; the *urna embarazada*, or pregnant urn, in which a ballot box lost its way on the road to the counting station and was found again, mysteriously fuller of PRI votes than when it started out; and the *voto comprometido*, in which even before voting day the Party was able to tally millions of votes that had been promised—sometimes in writing—by labor and peasant unions, small businesses, street vendors, and the garbage pickers of every town.

Álvaro García Linera, once vice president of Bolivia, told an interviewer of the challenges posed by clientelism to Evo Morales, Bolivia's first Indigenous president (2006–2019), and his party, Movimiento al Socialismo:

People believe that if they have worked for the party, they deserve something in return—a job or access to certain privileges. Evo has said repeatedly to social-movement leaders that they should not expect anything from the government, and this often provokes disgruntlement and questioning. He insists that they need to deepen their commitment to the process of social changes without seeking personal gain. This is hard for many to accept because that is not the way things have ever been done here. So of course corruption and clientelism continue, and addressing it repeatedly takes up an enormous amount of our time and energy. We have no choice but to stay on top of it all the time.

(Farthing 2010: 32)

Evo was very successful in managing Bolivia's economy, reinforcing the advances made by the country's Indigenous movements, and raising standards of living of the poorest sectors. But he too seemed to embrace the "elective affinity" toward caudillism that has asserted itself many times in the region. Morales, despite his Indigenous Aymara roots, had come to portray himself as the country's indispensable leader. He first tried and failed to win a referendum for a constitutional change to permit him to run for a third term; then he used his influence over the Electoral Court to rule that banning him from running was a violation of his human rights. This weakened his capacity to respond to mass protests, many violent and organized by the extreme right, in reaction to claims that his victory in the first round of the election of November 2019 was fraudulent. Anti-Indigenous racism reared its head. The army and police withdrew their support, and Morales and many other members of his party left for exile in Mexico vowing to return. (We look more closely at his political career in chapter 3.)

For Review

Can you explain how the practice of clientelism is different from corruption—or do you think there is no difference? How might clientelism and corruption erode popular confidence in democracy? How does the leadership of Morales fit or not fit the idea of populist caudillism?

Latin American Experiments With Popular Democracy

You are likely to find a broad range of views about the meaning of democracy among Latin Americanists. Most political scientists equate polyarchy with democracy. Some others believe that only revolution and some radical alternative to capitalism and liberal democracy can ever truly bring justice to the region. Many Latin America area specialists think that polyarchy is a conception of democracy too much in the service of U.S. **hegemony**—that is, that polyarchy is "exported" to Latin America and keeps the region in a **neocolonial** status, ensuring that only ruling elites acceptable to American corporate and political interests hold power. William Robinson calls polyarchy "low-intensity democracy"; it limits popular participation and weakens the state, so that Latin America remains business-friendly for **transnational corporations** (big businesses that operate across national boundaries). According to Robinson (1996: 6), the United States promotes polyarchy "to achieve the underlying objective of maintaining essentially undemocratic societies inserted into an unjust international system."

C. B. MacPherson (1972: 24–25) argued that liberal democracy and its economic companion, market capitalism, have been less appealing to cultures that rate community and equality more highly than individual freedom. MacPherson noted that the communists claimed to be democrats too. Communists interpreted the "common people" to mean the working class, or **proletariat**, whose "dictatorship" was democratic because workers were, presumably, the majority. The idea of a proletariat as used by Karl Marx does not apply very well to Latin America. Unlike Europe, Japan, and North America, Latin America has never been through an era when most workers were employed in manufacturing or mining.

There still are a few places in Latin America where peasants work not for wages but on large, landed estates (*haciendas* or *latifundia*) in exchange for access to their own small plots of land (*minifundios*). Today most Latin Americans live in urban areas, but the cities are heavily populated with people who are unemployed or barely eking out a living on the streets (Stavenhagen 1966–1967, 1974).

MacPherson points out that from China and Vietnam to Cuba and Chile, Marxists and others on the left have broadened the idea of the "oppressed class"—the "demos" in democracy—to mean a coalition of social classes from the poor, the peasantry, the working class, and even, sometimes, the middle class. Rather than a "working class," leftist politicians often refer to the "popular sector," vaguely defined to include all people favoring egalitarian development and opposition to imperialism. Closely related to this is the idea of *el pueblo*, "the people," best understood as a term suggesting that the "common people" or "masses" are in a power struggle with an elite that rules, usually in support of imperialists from other countries.

In colonized Africa, Asia, the Middle East, and the Caribbean, the twentieth-century struggle for independence required not just political sovereignty but something larger, called "national liberation." In these countries, the struggle to wrest control over the nation's destiny from colonial powers and foreign economic interests required national unity. Of course, most of Latin America had achieved political sovereignty a hundred years earlier, but the theme of "national liberation" also ran through the great social revolutions in Latin America in Mexico (1910), Cuba (1959), and Nicaragua (1979). These revolutions gave rise, for at least some time, to governments dominated by a single party whose main goal was to unite the country for economic and social advancement and for "liberation" from foreign domination. All proclaimed themselves "democratic," but liberal critics claimed that they failed a key test—the possibility for an opposition to win a fair election.

Most critics of polyarchy often now speak of "popular democracy" to refer to alternative ways of constituting a democratic state, or most modestly, enhancing representative democracy. Robinson (1996) is among those who pose the notion of popular democracy as an alternative to polyarchy. The concept is vague, but several Latin American governments have experimented with the idea. After the 1979 revolution, which expelled the 35-year, U.S.-supported dictatorship of the Somoza family, the Sandinistas of Nicaragua attempted in the early years to set up a system allowing direct representation of social groups (women, unions, small farmers, etc.) in the legislature. Sergio Ramírez, then vice president, said at the time,

> For us, the efficiency of a political model depends on its capacity to resolve the problems of democracy and justice. Effective democracy, like we intend to practice in Nicaragua, consists of ample popular participation—a permanent dynamic of the people's participation in a variety of political and social tasks . . . For us democracy is not merely a formal model but a continual process capable of giving people that elect and participate in it the real possibility of transforming their living conditions, a democracy which establishes justice and ends exploitation.
>
> (quoted in Ruchwarger 1985: 4)

The Sandinistas (FSLN) encouraged all citizens to join and become actively involved in mass organizations representing businesspeople, women, students, workers, small ranchers and farmers, peasants, and others. The mass organizations, in turn, would be represented in the Council of State, where important decisions would be made. Most of the leaders would coordinate their work through the FSLN, just as they had worked together to overthrow the dictatorship.

In 1984, the Sandinistas abandoned the Council of State and replaced it with a more typical legislature chosen directly by elections. Threatened by the U.S.-armed and -trained *contras*, the Sandinistas hoped that a more typically democratic system would help them attract international support. Instead, Robinson argues, the Sandinistas' shift toward polyarchy made them vulnerable to intervention by the United States. The Sandinistas themselves abused power and made mistakes, but their problems were made worse when the United States continued to support armed rebels (the *contras*) after the 1984 election was judged fair by all observers except those sent by the U.S. State Department. By Robinson's estimate, the U.S. spent US$18.7 million openly and even more clandestinely to influence the outcome of the 1990 elections (Robinson 1992: 136). The Sandinistas had made a Faustian bargain—that is, had sold their souls. To gain international **legitimacy**, they had accepted the precepts of polyarchy, but by doing so they also undermined the participatory and egalitarian goals of the revolutionary agenda.

The Sandinista experiment in some ways resembled the original, Aristotelian conception of democracy as rule by the ordinary people, by the poor. For all of its serious flaws and vulnerability, the Sandinistas made a serious attempt in the first years of the revolution to build a democratic alternative to polyarchy, but without rejecting some of its key principles, such as legal opposition and civic freedoms (see La Ramée and Polakoff 1997; Prevost and Vanden 1997).

The notion of popular democracy presents its own problems. To participate, citizens must join and be active, but constant involvement in politics can take its toll. How much time can people devote to democracy in their day-to-day lives—especially poor people who often must worry simply about survival? In the Cuban and Nicaraguan cases, people are expected to participate in **mass organizations** that are represented in government and that become their main channels of access to government. More recently, President Chávez and his followers began an experiment with participatory democracy in the **Bolivarian** Republic of Venezuela. In Venezuela, Chávez hoped that networks of grassroots communal councils would be engines of direct popular participation in government. That experiment too has nearly collapsed as a result of both domestic failures in Venezuela and persistent efforts by Washington to bring it down.

Fidel Castro, who served first as premier (head of government) after 1959 and then as president of Cuba from 1976 until 2008, always rejected the claim that he was a dictator. He insisted that Cuba, which constitutionally is a single-party state, is a democracy suited to the country's needs, one committed to "national liberation." In an interview with Nicaragua's Tomás Borge (1992) in which Fidel was asked to define what democracy meant to him, he replied,

> Democracy, as Lincoln defined it, is the government of the people, by the people, and for the people. To me democracy entails the defense of all the rights of citizens, including the rights to independence, freedom, national dignity, and honor. To me democracy is the brotherhood of men.

He went on to say that Cuba's democratic character had allowed it to resist U.S. economic, military, and economic threats, as well as to survive the disappearance of the Soviet Union, its economic benefactor during the Cold War. He also said that Cuba could not afford idealism about democracy to risk "the independence and security of the country." (These and other quotes on democracy from Fidel Castro can be found in the leftist newspaper *Workers World*, archived at www.workers.org.)

Groups such as Amnesty International and the Watch Committees have repeatedly reported that dissidents in Cuba are harassed, often with short-term detention and intimidation. Challenged by American reporter Robert MacNeil (1985) to defend his record on freedom of speech and the press, Castro argued that public (state) ownership of the media is a more democratic arrangement than one where wealthy private owners of the media have the last word. Cubans have a high level of knowledge about the world, in contrast to the U.S. where

> an astonishingly high number of people do not know where Nicaragua is, where the countries of Latin America are. They don't know what countries belong to Africa, what countries belong to Asia. There is an incredible ignorance, astonishing. That does not happen here.

In Cuba, candidates are nominated at grassroots assemblies, are not allowed to campaign but are also not allowed to be supported by or to be identified with a party (including the Communist Party, the only legal one in the country), and are then elected by secret balloting by all citizens. No one needs to raise or spend money on the campaign. Certainly, for many Cubans, both on the island and in exile, this argument is insufficient. But one of Dahl's points is that democracy is an ideal, and the label "totalitarian" is its dystopian equivalent. Cuba habitually falls into the bottom ranks of democracy ratings, but concerning equality and participation, there are ways that Cuba may rank higher than another "flawed democracy," the United States.

Revolutionary leaders, such as Fidel Castro, Evo Morales, and Hugo Chávez, tend to see themselves as entrusted with a mission to transform a society, but this attitude can encourage the formation of a new elite that sees itself as guardians of the process. Transformation of political culture is a long, difficult process. How should revolutionary leaders react when the people themselves threaten to betray the democratic principles of the revolution? **Machismo**, racism, economic exploitation, violence, and myriad other social problems are hard to overcome, and even harder to overcome when a powerful neighbor wants you to fail.

As MacPherson (1972: 19) put it,

> If you believe, as the makers of all these revolutions have believed, that the very structure of the society, the dominant power relations in it, have made people less than fully human, have warped them into inability to realize or even to see their full human potentiality, what are you to do? How can the debasing society be changed by those who have themselves been debased by it? . . . The debased people are, by definition, incapable of reforming themselves *en masse*. They cannot be expected to pull themselves up by their own bootstraps.

This dilemma will not be resolved in this book. If it is ever overcome, it probably will be through continued experimentation by the world's people and not through classroom discussion or on the pages of a book. As for myself, as stated in the Introduction, I believe democracy is a system whereby ordinary people in a society participate as equals in the major decisions that shape the future of their nation and communities.

PUNTO DE VISTA: THE ZAPATISTAS AND THE QUESTION OF POWER

The history of the state of Chiapas (see Figure 1.3) in Mexico has been punctuated by rebellion on the part of Indigenous people, and the revolution did little to address the underlying causes of the persistent unrest. After the 1910 Revolution, the new *mestizo* elite acquired 4.5 million acres of Chiapas land; it avoided the revolutionary land reforms of the 1930s because landowners switched sides early and avoided confrontation with the new regime. Zapata became the namesake of the Chiapas movement not because he fought there but because of his reputation as an almost saintly and humble peasant leader who picked up arms only

after being called to leadership by his people (Womack 1968).

The Zapatistas, heavily Mayan, made their entry onto the world stage in dramatic fashion on January 1, 1994, when they seized San Cristóbal de las Casas, the capital of the state. In Mexico City, the new President Salinas and the elite around him were celebrating the New Year and the launch of the North American Free Trade Agreement (NAFTA), a treaty between Mexico, Canada, and the United States. The peasants in Chiapas were in no mood to celebrate. They were already being pushed off the land by the expansion of ranching and export-oriented crops, such as

FIGURE 1.3   Map of Chiapas in Mexico

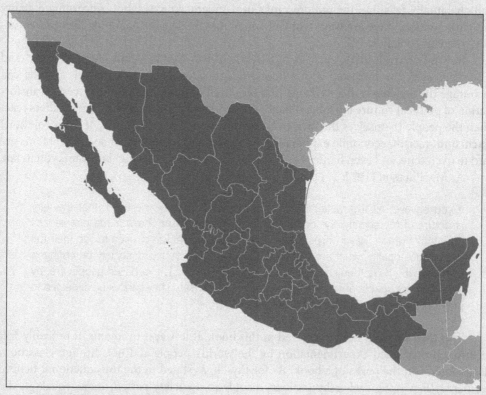

Source: © iStockphoto.com/rambo182

sugar and cotton. A birth rate spiraling out of control (3.35 per woman) increased pressure on the land. Expansion of export agriculture and the influx of displaced peasants in search of new land had greatly reduced the Lacandon rainforest, located in Chiapas. "Modernization" was destroying the ecology that sustained many of the state's inhabitants. Out of 1,000 live births, 66 infants would not survive their first year because of disease and malnutrition. Over half the population could not read or write. Worst affected were 200,000 descendants of the original Mayan population. All these were in a state that was Mexico's leading source of electric power (Tangeman 1995: 4–7).

The Catholic Church, though it did not endorse the Zapatistas (Ejército Zapatista de Liberación Nacional, EZLN), was sympathetic to the demands of peasants. San Cristóbal de las Casas had once been the diocese governed by Bartolomé de las Casas, the sixteenth-century bishop who had battled the local colonial landholding elite and successfully urged the Spanish Crown to abolish the *encomienda* system (see chapter 3). His Dominican order subsequently abandoned these ideals, but 415 years later, another progressive bishop, Samuel Ruiz, assumed office in the diocese (January 1960). Only one year before, Pope John XXIII had launched his important initiative to modernize the Catholic Church and make it more sensitive to the needs of the poor. This would culminate in the Second Vatican Council of 1962–1965, which laid the basis for some theologians to develop the idea of a **preferential option for the poor**. Bishop Ruiz became an outspoken critic of social injustice and defender of human rights, without endorsing or joining the Zapatistas. This distance from the EZLN allowed him to play a role as mediator between the rebels and the national government.

The conflict in Chiapas cannot be reduced to a simple confrontation between humble Christian peasants and the elite. It is complicated by the growth of Protestant evangelical churches. In some parts of Latin America, politically conservative Protestants have sometimes been backed by the U.S. government and the CIA, especially in areas where Indigenous people are facing incursions by big mining and oil companies (see Lewis 1989). However, the evangelical movement in Latin America is complex and not easily stereotyped as conservative. The Zapatistas face the challenge of bridging the gap between Protestant poor and Catholic poor if they are to resist the Mexican army's attempts to isolate them from their social base.

One might question whether the Zapatistas really qualify as a revolutionary organization or whether they are more accurately a social movement (see chapter 11). The Zapatistas differ from other guerrilla movements because they do not aim to take immediate control of national government. Marcos (said to be Rafael Sebastián Guillén Vicente by the government) and his followers see their struggle as an extension of centuries of Indigenous resistance to a state that has always reflected a form of politics alien to Indigenous interests and traditions. The Zapatistas have said that they conceive of their struggle as one that will take generations to achieve.

Marcos has spoken of making change "without taking power." However, the existence of the Mexican state is a fact that the EZLN cannot ignore. Hence, the movement has sought to extend its influence with other movements seeking social justice and a more democratic state. A convention that gathered social movements from the length and breadth of Mexico in the town of Aguascalientes, where forces of the Mexican Revolution mapped out the future of the country in 1914, was among several actions in which the Zapatistas have both supported and inspired grassroots democratization efforts in Mexico. Like these movements, the EZLN identifies with leftist politics, but it has avoided aligning itself with any political party, arguing that none of them represent a fundamental break with the style and substance of the present regime.

The Zapatistas have attracted attention and solidarity worldwide. Still, they remain far from achieving their goals, and the Mexican army remains poised to ratchet up counter-insurgency efforts. Frustrated by the lack of progress in negotiations on autonomy, and accusing President Vicente Fox (2000–2006) of breaking promises to withdraw the army and negotiate seriously on autonomy, the Zapatistas declared certain villages and adjacent areas autonomous liberated zones (*caracoles*, "snails"). Presidents Fox and Felipe Calderón (2006–2012) were restrained from sending the military against the rebels by world sympathy for the Zapatistas and the prospect of major bloodletting if the army were to be turned loose in Chiapas. Such an operation might generate mass revulsion and anger throughout the country.

In 2003 Comandante Marcos, the Zapatista leader, wrote a letter to a Basque (Spain) nationalist organization that had urged the group to create a more centralized leadership capable of moving more clearly and quickly to its goals. He wrote,

> Our weapons are not used to impose ideas or ways of life, rather to defend a way of thinking and a way of seeing the world and relating to it, something that, even though it can learn a lot from other thoughts and ways of life, also has a lot to teach . . . Our struggle has a code of honor, inherited from our guerilla ancestors and it contains, among other things: respect of civilian lives (even though they may occupy government positions that oppress us); we don't use crime to get resources for ourselves (we don't rob, not even a snack store); we don't respond to words with fire (even though many hurt us or lie to us). One could think that to renounce these traditionally "revolutionary" methods is renouncing the advancement of our struggle. But, in the faint light of our history it seems that we have advanced more than those that resort to such arguments . . . Our enemies (who are not just a few nor just in Mexico) want us to resort to these methods.
>
> P.S. P.S. Before I forget . . . in respect to your final "¡Viva Chiapas Libre!" [Long Live a Free Chiapas!] . . . We don't want to make ourselves independent from Mexico. We want to be a part of it, but without leaving who we are: Indigenous . . . We struggle for . . . all the men and women of Mexico no matter if they are Indian or not.

Point/Counterpoint

For all the passion and eloquence of Marcos's letter, is his very leadership proof that for a revolutionary group like the Zapatistas, some kind of leadership is not only needed but also inevitable? Robert Michels's "iron law of oligarchy" would seem to point toward the futility of attempting to create the kind of democracy that the Zapatistas want to build. So, is the Zapatista project really utopian, impossible to achieve?

If you answer "yes," how do you respond to the way that Marcos and the Zapatistas have so far, even as the 2020s dawn, avoided betraying their philosophy of trying to make revolution without taking power?

If you answer "no," how can you reconcile Zapatista's ideals with the way Marcos had become the visible spokesperson for the Zapatistas?

For More Information

On leadership and revolution, see MacPherson (1972) in the bibliography. On the Zapatistas, there is an extensive literature. For more about the Zapatista movement, see Tom Hayden (ed.), *The Zapatista Reader* (New York: Nation Books, 2002).

Many Latin Americans living today experienced life under military regimes that literally terrorized major parts of the population and stripped citizens of all the protections from arbitrary repression that are associated with liberal democracy. And if capitalism has not fulfilled its promises, few Latin Americans see twentieth-century socialism as a viable or desirable alternative. If nothing else, in this minimal way liberal democracy retains some appeal.

For Review

What do politicians and analysts mean by the "popular sector" in Latin America? How is this idea different from the idea of the "proletariat," or "working class"? What is the difference between "national liberation" and simply fighting for independence from colonialism? How might a "popular democracy" differ from a polyarchy? Why might a popular democracy end up producing a new elite rather than the intended goal of more power in the hands of people?

PHOTO 1.1 In Cuba, only one party exists legally, but candidates need not be communists. They run for office as independents and cannot campaign beyond making their backgrounds and views known, as you see here in a local community office. In other countries, candidates run with the support of one or more parties. As in the United States, they need to raise and spend lots of money to have a chance to win. What do you think of Cuba's claim to have a more democratic system?
Source: STR/AFP via Getty Images.

Not Taking Democracy for Granted

As we examine Latin American politics, I urge you not to take democracy for granted. However much it seems that everyone agrees today that it is the *only* legitimate form of government, remember that this contemporary notion of universal appeal of democracy is historically unprecedented. And with the worldwide surge of nationalist populism, what was once taken for granted about democracy's bright future is now in doubt.

Furthermore, the pluralist idea of democracy as polyarchy is subject to debate. Most political scientists embrace it overall. They criticize unconstrained capitalism and globalization, but most public intellectuals, the pundits and academic experts we see and hear in the news cycles, speak of "free markets and democracy" as though they are inextricably connected. This text seeks to incorporate the ways that Latin Americans are debating and experiencing democracy into our understanding of the region's politics. I hope that you, like me, will find the comparative study of the democratic condition in Latin America a rich and rewarding path to reflection on our own systems of government.

Discussion Questions

1. Do you think that democracy is mainly a matter of elections, of making sure that a government holds fair elections, respects civil rights, and applies laws impartially? Do you think that democracy can function in conditions of social and economic inequality?
2. Increasingly, in this age of globalization, it seems that democracy is becoming the only form of government that is accepted as legitimate. Do you think this is a good trend—or should we accept that there are other legitimate forms of state that are not democratic?
3. At this point in your readings, and presumably your class experience, if you were evaluating the condition of democracy for each country of the world, would you focus, as many indices do, on factors that affect "choice," such as elections, civil rights, and free markets, or would you include some attention to participation (e.g., rates of voting, extension of democracy to social and economic spheres of life) and to socioeconomic equality (e.g., wealth and income equality)? Gapminder, at gapminder.org, is a good place to find comparative data, and it comes with an easy-to-use interface to compare countries of the world on animated graphs.

Resources for Further Study

Reading: Robert Dahl's most accessible work for newcomers to the pluralist approach is the hard-to-find *Pluralist Democracy in the United States: Conflict and Consent* (Chicago: Rand-McNally, 1968), a textbook on U.S. politics, but a good overall introduction to his ideas. Easier to find but a more challenging read is his *Polyarchy: Participation and Opposition* (New Haven: Yale University Press, 1972). C. B. MacPherson's very readable *Real World of Democracy* (CBC Enterprises, 1965) argues that liberal democracy is but one form of democracy. It is a good explanation of liberalism, and it is online at http://books.google.com/books.

Video and Film: Political philosopher Benjamin Barber and host Thomas Watson produced *The Struggle for Democracy*, a 10-part series produced for PBS and CBS in 1998, exploring the idea from the ancient Greeks until modern times. You can find a debate that took place at an Australian University on the topic, "Is Democracy Not for Everyone?" at http://fora.tv/2009/10/04/Is_Democracy_Not_For_Everyone.

On the Internet: See the AmericasBarometer Insight Series of the Latin America Public Opinion Project (LAPOP), located at Vanderbilt University: www.vanderbilt.edu/lapop/insights.php. Several different nongovernmental organizations rank the world's countries on democracy using liberal criteria. See, for example, Democratic Audit at www.democraticaudit.com/our-work/audits-worldwide, and Freedom House, which is partly funded by the U.S. government, at www.freedomhouse.org. One of the few rankings to include social and economic criteria is at http://democracyranking.org. Upside-Down World, at http://upsidedownworld.org, carries news reports from a social movement perspective. As just mentioned, http://gapminder.org is a great place to go for comparative data and historical trends about economic and social progress in countries of the world.

2

The Few and the Many: Inequality in Latin American Politics

Focus Questions

▶ How much inequality is there in Latin America, and what are the social and historical roots of inequality in the region?

▶ How does inequality in Latin America relate to democratic conditions?

▶ What is social "exclusion"? Why has it become an issue in the region in recent decades?

L ONG BEFORE KARL Marx expressed skepticism about liberal democracy, Aristotle thought democracy was best defined in terms of the distribution of power between the wealthy and ordinary people. He did not really think much of democracy, thinking it, like oligarchy, a perverted form of rule and not in the best interest of the whole society. But he thought that the difference between oligarchy and democracy was a question of which social class holds power:

> The real ground of the difference between oligarchy and democracy is poverty and riches. It is inevitable that any constitution should be an oligarchy if the rulers under it are rulers in virtue of riches, whether they are few or many; and it is equally inevitable that a constitution under which the poor rule should be a democracy.
>
> (quoted in Barker 1962: 116)

Aristotle, of course, was writing primarily about the "constitution" of Athens, Sparta, and the other city-states of ancient Greece, where the "constitution" referred not just to the rules of the political game or structures of government but also to how the community was "constituted" according to its economy (for example, farming versus fishing) and the social structure. Aristotle used the term "the people" (*demos* in Greek) not so differently from how populist politicians in Latin America use it today—referring not to all citizens but to those who usually made up the majority: the poorer parts of the body politic. He was not at all enthusiastic about democracy, which could easily, in his view, degenerate into mob rule. Nor did he advocate levelling everyone to the same economic status. What is relevant to this chapter, however, is that he did not just think of inequality as a social condition that might affect democracy or be affected by democracy; he recognized that economic equality was part of political equality.

In those countries that suffered dictatorships and civil wars, Latin Americans might reasonably have expected a return to democracy to bring about a more egalitarian society. But though the record here is mixed, I think we can safely say that many Latin Americans were disappointed with the weak record of liberal democracy in dealing with inequality and, to some degree, poverty too. Some progress was registered in the 2000s, but poverty and inequality remain issues throughout the region, and in some ways have gotten worse since the global financial crisis of 2008, followed by a slowdown in China's (up until then) phenomenal economic growth rate. Latin American economies are still highly dependent upon the export of mining, agriculture, and hydrocarbons, and as these shifts in the global economy took hold, they hit the poor, the working class, and most of the middle class.

In this chapter we will examine how social and economic inequality have shaped issues, political culture, and social structures. The last quarter of the twentieth century saw not only a wave of democratization in the form of elected civilian governments replacing military regimes but also a sharp increase in inequality and poverty, especially in the 1990s. In addition to social class, we need to examine inequalities rooted in gender and ethnicity—in particular, how all these inequalities intersect with one another. We begin with income inequality, and then widen our lens to inequalities in wealth. A policy brief by the United Nations in July 2020 anticipated that Covid-19 would increase the number of poor by 45 million (to a total of 230 million) and extreme poor by 45 million (to 96 million overall), increasing inequality, exclusion and negatively impacting human rights and democracy. We will update the impact on the companion website to this text (See www.un.org/sites/un2. un.org/files/sg_policy_brief_covid_lac.pdf).

Precarious Nature of Being Human

Have you ever lost your passport or your wallet? How did it feel? That is **precarity**—the psychological state of feeling that your very life, your ability to "make a living" or "support your family," is precarious. Most of us experience precarity to some degree, and a few readers many have experienced it in a major way, for example, similar to someone who lives in a refugee camp, or, as is not uncommon in Latin America, someone whose birth was not officially recorded and has no state-issued proof of citizenship. Precarity in the United States is magnified for middle-class residents of rural communities and small towns who live several hours from the closest hospital or have no doctor at all within hours. One might "learn to live with" this condition, but it is hardly conducive to social trust and a sense that one is an equal citizen in a democratic society. Therefore, in chapters 1 and 2, I argue for considering equality not just as a condition or outcome of democracy, but as an intrinsic quality that should be factored into evaluating democracy comparatively.

Before the era of modern globalization, that is, from about 1980 onward as new technologies were deployed to change the shape of the workforce all over the world, political economists would conceive of the "working class" as wage or salary earners mainly in manufacturing, transportation, construction, and other industries. After World War II, in the "developed countries" a large portion of these workers belonged to unions and benefited from health and safety regulations, pensions and social security, and other forms of welfare. These "blue-collar workers" were "manual" workers, though some clerical jobs might also have qualified, some more skilled than others. The "middle class," on the other hand, consisted of those who occupied jobs, usually were salaried (paid by the week or month; not having to "punch a clock"), and were paid highly enough to participate in higher levels of consumption than workers. Both lived in the cities, which were growing as agriculture became more scientific and industrialized. Towns and small cities as a result were shrinking and populations decreased, a tendency that would ultimately accelerate the decline of rural middle-class farmers and local businesses (grocers, druggists, department stores, etc.).

These two urban classes in the core, wealthier nations seemed to have attained a high level of social security in the prosperous years between the end of World War II and 1980. For those members of these classes born after the war, the risk had receded that everything solid in their lives might suddenly melt away. This contrasts with what befell many middle- and working-class households in the Great Depression of the late 1920s and 1930s. And unlike workers and employees of the nineteenth and early twentieth centuries, the era of rapid industrialization, the threat of falling into impoverished urban squalor, seemed to have receded. The Marxist idea that a "lumpen-proletariat" provided capitalists with leverage to force down wages and to discipline the working class proletariat seemed obsolete.

But precarious living has become much more common in the gig economy of the globalization era. In this era, the world become "richer" by traditional economic measures, but the wealth is spread unevenly. Even those not in poverty have experienced growing insecurity in their lives, not just in terms of crime but in terms of achieving happiness and well-being—what some Indigenous groups in Latin America call "*buen vivir*." This idea was inserted under Indigenous pressure into the constitution of Ecuador, an Andean country with a large population whose ancestors were incorporated in the Inca Empire. The clause reads, "We . . . hereby decide to build a new form of public coexistence, in diversity and in harmony with nature, to achieve the good way of living."

Large parts of the population in the U.S. and other wealthy countries now feel "excluded" from circuits of social and economic life. Those who find themselves excluded experience diminished hope for a lifelong career, wonder how they will make ends meet from week to week, and suffer a sense of the precariousness of life on a day-to-day basis, which wears on their psychological welfare. This is one reason why opioid and other forms of drug abuse have become social crises. The coronavirus pandemic heightened this reawakening to the precarious nature of being human. Some of the readers of this book may already know from personal experience that their personal security is much diminished.

Lack of access to health care, the costs of communication and recreation, increasing indebtedness, a sense of vulnerability to crime (magnified by news reporting), concerns about health, and the impact of a financial meltdown in 2008 and the coronavirus pandemic of 2020 have introduced everyone to what sociologists such as Judith Butler (2011) and Isabel Lorey (2015) label "precarity." Their argument about the nature of politics starts from the assumption that all human life is precarious, in the sense that biologically we are always vulnerable because we depend upon one another for survival.

Even the world's one-percenters and billionaires feel precarity, which partly explains why so many of them have invested in creating luxury bunkers to survive a nuclear war or some other Armageddon (CNN, August 7, 2019). But it should come as no surprise that life is more precarious for those living in poverty. Psychologically it also falls heavily on those who have once attained or who saw within reach a more socially secure status, if not for themselves, then for their children. It is difficult to establish a causal relationship, but there is evidence to support a long-considered theory that social explosions often follow a period of substantial improvement in economic conditions (as in the post-World War era) and "rising expectations," followed by dashed expectations (see Gurr 1970). That may very well be one of the factors driving the unrest we have seen in recent years in many places around the globe, including Latin America.

Hyperurbanization in Latin America

Latin America was a much less urbanized place at the beginning of the twentieth century than it was at the end. Urban dwellers live in a very different environment than do rural people. Highly concentrated landownership meant that most of the peasantry lived off low-paying, seasonable work, often on export plantations or *haciendas*. Slightly better off were peasants allowed to work a small plot either on the landowner's domain or on a tiny plot of land insufficient by itself to support a family. While there were periods in which the countryside seethed with unrest, in more normal times a kind of semi-feudal dependency of peasant families on landowners prevailed. This is one root of the clientelism and personalism discussed in chapter 1.

In the twentieth century, most Latin American countries sought to achieve higher levels of development, and in that era "development" was almost synonymous with "industrialization." In chapter 6 we will look more closely at various theories and experiences with development; here we need mainly to understand that development in Latin America has been a process, often heavily influenced by government, to invest publicly and to create incentives for local and foreign capitalists to industrialize. This almost always meant favoring the cities over the countryside.

The result was a massive demographic revolution throughout Latin America, as rural poor migrated to cities all over Latin America, places where the jobs, health facilities, and schools were concentrated. Table 2.1 shows how dramatically the urban core grew in the

TABLE 2.1 Population Growth, Latin America's Largest Cities

City	1900	1950	1960	1970	1990	2019
Bogotá	125,429	647,429	1,682,228	2,892,668	4,851,000	10,779,376
Buenos Aires	1,251,000	4,622,959	6,739,045	8,314,341	10,886,163	13,381,800
Caracas	90,000	683,659	1,346,708	2,174,759	2,989,601	2,900,000*
Lima	140,000	645,172	1,845,910	3,302,523	6,422,875	10,674,100
Mexico City	349,721	3,145,351	5,173,540	8,900,513	15,047,685	20,976,700
Rio de Janeiro	926,585	2,885,165	4,392,067	6,685,703	9,600,528	12,460,200
Santiago	269,886	1,509,169	2,133,252	2,871,060	4,676,174	6,723,516
São Paulo	240,200	2,333,346	4,005,631	7,866,659	15,183,612	20,847,500

* Caracas estimated on assumption that United Nations' estimate of a 13 percent decline, if applied to Caracas, assuming a modest rate of growth from 1990 to 2015, would mean the city's population today would have fallen back to approximately 2.9 million.

Source: For 1900, figures cited *The 1911 Edition Encyclopedia* (of Britannica), accessed July 9, 2002, at www.1911.encyclopedia.org. For other years, national census figures cited by Alan Gilbert, *The Mega-City in Latin America* (New York: United Nations Press), accessed July 9, 2019, at www.unu.edu/unupress/unupbooks/uu23me/uu23me00.htm#Contents.

twentieth century. Demographers call this **hyperurbanization**—growth of the population of the cities well out of proportion to their infrastructure (sewers, electricity, telephones, etc.). Although many Latin American countries experienced economic growth and industrialization in the populist era, the opportunities and benefits generated (jobs, education, health care, housing, etc.) did not keep pace with the growth of cities.

The Southern Cone countries already had two large cities (Rio de Janeiro and Buenos Aires) approaching more than one million people in 1900, but they nonetheless experienced explosive growth. Countries farther north saw the emergence of "megacities" for the first time after 1900. Mexico City went from 350,000 to 3.1 million people between 1900 and 1950; by 1990, it held 15.2 million people. Caracas was a sleepy capital of 90,000 at the turn of the century. By 1950, it had grown to 684,000, and then it exploded to near three million (6.4 million if the whole metropolitan area is counted) over the next 40 years. São Paulo doubled in size in the first 50 years of the century and then exploded from 2.3 to 15 million people in the next 40 years.

The new factories fostered by state subsidies and protection from foreign competition did produce employment and other benefits for many, but this industrialization could not absorb the entire flood of migrants. Nor did it lift workers completely to "First World" standards of living or generate the dynamic increases in productivity characteristic of industrialization in the Global North. Latin America's factories relied on imported machinery that was often obsolete in the countries of origin, putting them at a competitive disadvantage that was offset by using cheaper labor. More jobs were generated than might have been created using the most up-to-date technology, but at the same time the available technology meant that Latin America's factories required less labor than that generated in the early stages of industrialization in Europe and the United States. Hence, Latin Americans had good reasons to migrate to the cities from the very precarious conditions of life in rural areas, but the pace of social and economic development was less rapid than in earlier comparable eras of rural to urban migration in the Global North.

This raises an important issue in development theory. Is the urban poverty experienced in Latin America merely a phase through which all industrializing countries passed at an earlier time? Or have late industrialization and continued dependence on exports and foreign capital made hyperurbanization chronic in Latin America? We have seen cases, such as China, Korea, and Japan, where countries industrialized using imported, older technologies, but at some point, they showed a capacity to innovate on their own. In general, that did not happen in Latin America.

There have always been urban poor in Latin America, but side by side with the middle class and formally employed workers reside millions of people living in makeshift houses, often perched perilously on hillsides. Sociologists often refer to these residents as "**marginal**" because they typically live outside the networks of services (sanitation, electricity, water, etc.) necessary to live a dignified life in the city. They typically work in the **informal sector** of the economy—that is, they are not employed in wage-paying jobs that are covered by labor laws (e.g., occupational safety, minimum wage standards) or that come with benefits, such as health care and social security. More recently, the term "excluded" has come into use to signify that the deprivation these people experience is not chosen and to indicate that the goal of economic development ought to be *inclusion*—political, social, and economic inclusion—of the poor.

During the middle decades of the twentieth century, roughly from 1930 to 1960, in most Latin American countries the "many"—that is, the peasants, workers, and urban poor—became "incorporated" into the social, economic, and political fabric of most of Latin America. This was an earlier era of populism (see chapter 5), preceding the surge of populism after 2000. In this first populist era, in most countries (with exceptions—e.g., parts of Central America) large numbers of ordinary Latin Americans gained not only political rights but also important social rights and benefits, such as unemployment and retirement insurance, access to social welfare (education, affordable food, etc.), and union rights.

During the years of military rule of the 1970s and 1980s (the "lost decade"), many workers were forced out of formal employment to join the ranks of millions of others working on their own account. An International Labour Organization (ILO) study (Van der Hoeven 2000) estimated that the percentage of Latin Americans who were self-employed in activities (e.g., selling toys, cosmetics, lottery tickets, and smuggled clothing on sidewalks) outside the formal labor force rose from 51.6 percent to 57.7 percent. Some were recent migrants from rural areas; others were (and are) the children or grandchildren of those who left earlier, but many others were working and middle-class people who fell into their ranks. The Organization of American States (OAS) estimates conservatively that 39 percent of all households in Latin America and the Caribbean were poverty-stricken in the mid-1990s, up from 35 percent found 15 years earlier (see Lustig 1998).

The period between 1970 and 1990, then, saw many of these people "de-incorporated." The military regimes in most of the region smashed unions, outlawed political parties, and took away many of the social and economic rights achieved under populism. Employees who had once belonged to unions, built up pensions, held protections from health and safety laws, received unemployment compensation if discharged, been protected from arbitrary firings, and so on now found themselves working on their own account or unemployed with little hope of finding new work. Residents of poor neighborhoods and sometimes of middle-class areas saw services like regular garbage collection, access to health care, and schooling shrink. The 1990s were years of recovery, but the benefits of growth were concentrated in just a few parts of the population, even though every country except Cuba had a liberal democratic constitution. Academic experts and social actors began to speak of "**exclusion**" as an emerging issue for democracy.

The **excluded sectors** continue today to scratch out a living as petty vendors, "guarding" parked cars, domestic workers, waiters, temporary laborers, and even as clerks. The poorest, the ones suffering "extreme poverty," scavenge garbage dumps to survive. Some eventually find jobs in small enterprises, but because of their size, these companies are usually exempted from complying with labor laws, including unionization. In the countryside, economic well-being depended on a personal connection with a landowner; in the city, the poor often depend on a similar connection but with a different kind of *patron* (boss). Knowing a relative or a friend or developing a personal relationship with a well-connected person could be the key to making it in the new environment. The more personalist, clientelist culture of the countryside, including *compadrazgo* (traditions associated with the Catholic practice of godparenting), was transplanted into the city to some degree. But here it should be noted that clientelism is not just a cultural proclivity; the client has a more precarious existence than does the patron, be it an employer, a landlord, the head of drug syndicate, or a politician.

The overcrowded districts where the migrants arrived took on various names: *favelas* in Brazil and *barrios* in many parts of Spanish America. The term *callampas*, meaning "mushrooms," used in Chile, is an especially apt description of how these poor neighborhoods sprung up on vacant land. In most of Latin America, persons occupying unused lands for ten years have established a right to ownership of the property. This leads to conflict when squatters seize abandoned or unused parcels of land. Municipal authorities usually evict the newcomers, but many times they return, determined to begin their new life with little more than cardboard, wooden slats, and corrugated tin or zinc roofs. Next come bricks, electricity tapped from a nearby power line, and maybe a bus or jitney route to carry residents into the city center and, they hope, to a job. This social mix created conditions for populist politics when political leaders and grassroots activists mobilized the urban poor and peasants and began to demand greater inclusion in social and economic life. We explore the consequences more fully in later chapters, but the political crises that arose out of populism were significant reason why from the late 1960s to 1990 most Latin Americans lived under military rule.

The overall growth rate of cities in Latin America continued apace, as we can see by comparing the population figures (in Table 2.1) for each city in 1970 (when the economic growth was notably slowing) with those for 1990 (when growth began to pick up again) and 2019 (after a period of slow growth). The one exception is Caracas, the capital of Venezuela, a country that has been mired in a severe economic and political crisis since 2014—so severe that the United Nations estimates that more than 13 percent of the country has fled abroad. This is a unique case; not even has the surge of migration in Central America produced such a mass exodus from cities. The Venezuela exodus is rooted in a perfect storm, generated by the combination of a collapse of oil prices in 2014 (from $130/barrel in mid-2014 to less than $50), the failure by the Chávez government to prepare for an inevitable end of the boom, and then economic sanctions imposed by the United States in an effort to topple Chávez's successor, President Nicolás Maduro (see chapter 8 for a fuller explanation).

So why has the urban population continued to grow in the rest of Latin America, even as so much of the cities' workforce continues to eke out a living in the informal sector? Part of the answer lies in the overall birthrate, which has declined in Latin America and the Caribbean from 20 live births to 16.6 live births per 1,000 inhabitants. In the United States, the rate is less than 12 per 1,000 live births. But as Figure 2.1 shows, there continues to be a push

FIGURE 2.1 Urban vs. Rural Poverty, Percentage of Households

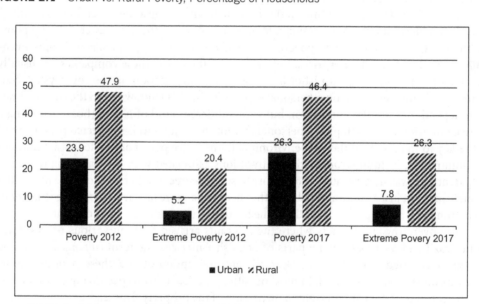

Source: ECLAC, *Social Panorama of Latin America, 2018.*

factor in the countryside, reflected in a significantly higher rate of poverty in rural areas compared to urban areas. Especially alarming is that nearly half the households in rural areas in Latin America remained impoverished in 2017, despite the fact that poverty levels in 2012, the base year in Figure 2.1, had significantly declined overall from levels in 1990. In fact, extreme poverty in rural areas actually ticked up six percentage points. We should add here that these figures, compiled by the United Nations Economic Commission on Latin America (ECLAC), reflect not just income levels but the overall ability of household income in different countries and regions of countries to buy and consume at a minimum level, a level that ECLAC sets quite low. Note also that the data used here does not include Venezuela, whose social crisis is so acute that the government has failed to collect and publish information on social conditions. But we know from independent study that a severe deterioration in living conditions continued to afflict the majority of the population as the 2010s came to a close.

We can see from Figure 2.2 that the overall poverty rate in Latin America significantly declined between 2002 and 2015, reflecting in part robust growth fueled mainly by raw material exports and the policies of Pink Tide governments in most of the region. Overall poverty was cut in half in this period. It remains today below 2012 levels, when approximately 4.5 out of every ten households in Latin America were below the poverty line. But 2016 surveys showed a substantial jump in poverty, coinciding with a precipitous drop in export prices of raw materials and agricultural goods. These prices had persisted at relatively high levels despite the global financial crisis largely because of demand for these commodities by China. But China's overall growth slacked in 2014, ultimately showing the vulnerability inherent in

FIGURE 2.2   Poverty, Extreme Poverty, Percentages

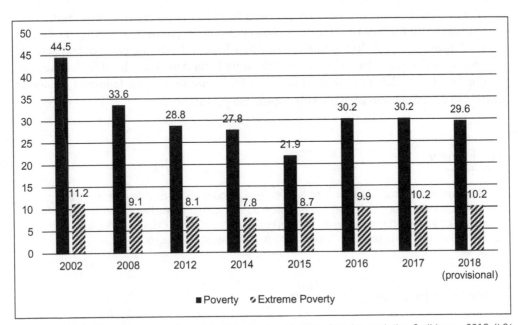

Source: ECLAC, *Preliminary Overview of the Economies of Latin America and the Caribbean, 2018* (LC/PUB.2019/1-P), Santiago, 2019.

FIGURE 2.3   Poverty and Extreme Poverty; Millions of Persons

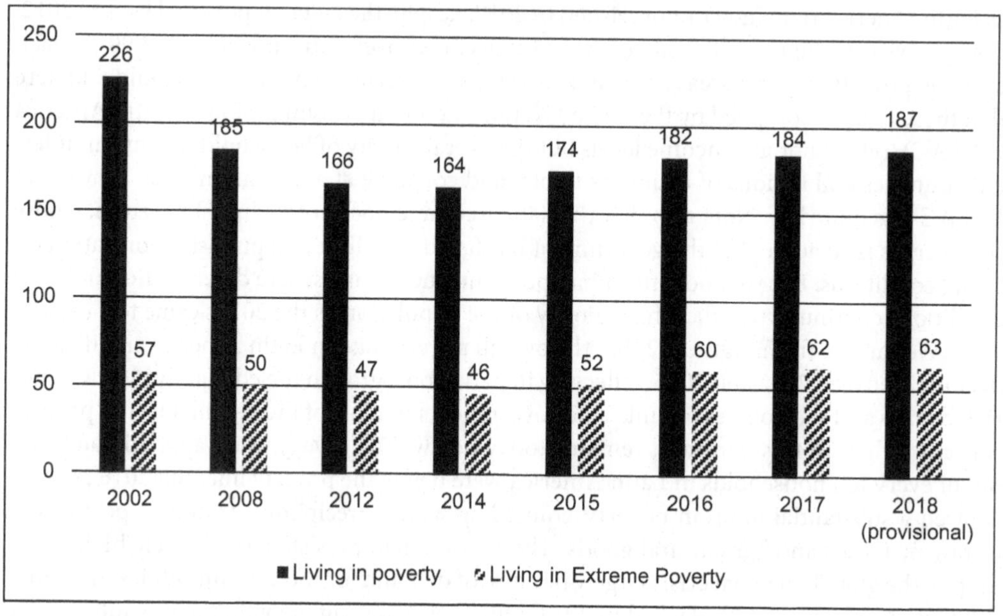

Source: ECLAC, Social Panorama of Latin America, 2018.

Latin America's dependence upon *extraction*, i.e., the export of oil, gas, minerals, and agricultural products (especially soybeans).

Poverty levels remained significantly lower in 2018 than they were early in the decade, but the record for the last three years showed that progress toward meeting the United Nations Millennium goals had virtually come to a halt, and extreme poverty had actually worsened over that time. Twenty-three million more Latin Americans lived under the poverty line (see Figure 2.3) in 2018 than did in 2014, a reflection of the failure of economic growth and distribution to keep up with population growth.

For Review

What is "hyperurbanization"? How does it differ from "urbanization" as it developed in the wealthier capitalist countries? What is the relationship between hyperurbanization and poverty? How have conditions in rural areas contributed to hyperurbanization? How much progress toward reducing poverty has Latin America made in the twenty-first century?

Income Inequality

As we have just seen, overall Latin America remains a region where inequality is high by many measures and where progress toward reducing poverty has been substantial but

TABLE 2.2 Economic Growth and Real Wages in Latin America

	1981–1990	1991–1997	1998–2002	2003–2010	1980–2010	2011–2018	1980–2018
% Change in GDP	14.4	26.2	8.9	35.6	113.2	14.7	129.8
% Change in real wages	−37.5	14.9	3.1	14.3	−15.3	10.6	−6.6

Source: ECLAC, *Social Panorama of Latin America*, various years.

halting over the last few decades. Conservative economists often argue that the best remedy for inequality is economic growth, but there is nothing automatic about how the benefits of growth are distributed. In Latin America, as in several other parts of the world (including the United States), there is evidence that the benefits of economic growth have been highly concentrated. Table 2.2 shows side by side the evolution of two economic measures that illustrate this tendency. One is the rate of growth (or contraction) of gross domestic product (GDP), which attempts to account for the total value of goods and services produced in a country's domestic economy in a given year. (Take note that we are not looking at GDP per capita, which would measure whether growth takes place with changes in the size of the population.) The other variable in Table 2.2 is the change in real wages (that is, we take inflation into account) for the employed workforce. So we are not looking here at the large number of people who work in the **informal sector**—that is, sidewalk merchants, day laborers, domestic servants, and others. Nor are we taking into account other sources of income, such as returns on investment or savings, and (more importantly) money transferred by people who have emigrated (legally or illegally) to places (including the United States) where they attempt to find employment to earn money to send back home. The latter is crucial to many Latin Americans near or below the poverty line, but this in turn is partly related to the matter of whether the benefits of overall GDP growth are being reflected in workers' wages. We show these two variables in periods of different lengths, chosen to highlight when the economy was in recession and when it was growing. We ask, "Has economic growth in the region benefited the workers fairly?"

We can see in the column for 1980 to 2010 that real wages in 2010 were still 15 percent lower than they were in 1980, even though the economy had grown by 113 percent. The 14 percent growth in the first column might seem impressive, but it covers the entire decade of the 1980s. This period is often called the "lost decade," as almost all of the **Third World** became mired in debt. If you were working in Latin America in 1980 for about $100 per week (actually, this is higher than the typical level for workers), ten years later your real wages would have fallen to where you were making only $65. Thirty years later, real wages still had not caught up with their 1980 level. During this period in most Latin American countries, you would have also lived through a "transition" from an authoritarian system to a democracy. Many Latin Americans expected this transition would bring some economic benefit, not just relief from rule by the military or some other kind of autocracy. Indeed, real wages did rise some, but they lagged far behind overall economic growth.

Table 2.3 shows the overall distribution of income in 18 Latin American countries, along with the number of billionaires (for those countries that have them). The table divides the total income into five parts, with the richest quintile subdivided in tenths

TABLE 2.3   Percentage of Income by Quintiles (poorest to richest fifth); Deciles; Number of Billionaires

Country	Year	Billionaires	Poorest ↔ Richest					
			Quintile 1	Quintile 2	Quintile 3	Quintile 4	Quintile 5	
							Decile 9	Decile 10
Argentina	2017		10	16	17	22	14	21
Bolivia	2015		5	12	18	25	16	25
Brazil	2017	43	5	10	12	20	15	38
Chile	2017	12	8	12	15	20	14	31
Colombia	2017	3	5	11	15	21	15	33
Costa Rica	2017		5	10	15	22	17	31
Dominican R	2016		7	11	16	21	15	30
Ecuador	2017		7	12	17	23	15	27
El Salvador	2017		8	13	18	23	15	24
Guatemala	2014		5	10	14	20	16	35
Honduras	2016		5	10	15	22	16	31
Mexico	2016	15	6	11	15	21	15	33
Nicaragua	2014		5	10	16	21	14	34
Panama	2017		5	10	16	22	15	32
Paraguay	2017		5	10	15	21	14	35
Peru	2017	5	5	11	17	24	16	27
Uruguay	2017		10	14	17	22	14	23
Venezuela	2014	2	8	14	19	23	14	22
Latin America	2017	90*	6	11	16	22	15	30
United States	2018	585	3.1	8.3	14.1	22.6	52	

* Total for Latin America and Caribbean would rise to 92 with two additional for St. Kitts & Nevis.

Source: ECLAC, *Social Panorama of Latin America, 2018*. Washington DC 2010 (2015 for Venezuela). Billionaire count from *Forbes Magazine*, 2019 list, compiled by Wikipedia, *The World's Billionaires*. https://en.wikipedia.org/wiki/The_World%27s_Billionaires (accessed December 5, 2019).

(deciles). We have also included the figures for the United States for comparison. Keep in mind that typical income varies greatly from the poorest country in the region (Nicaragua at around $5,700 per capita PPP) to the two richest (Panama and Chile, around $28,000 per capita PPP). "PPP" here refers to "purchasing power parity," expressed in dollars and adjusted to reflect what a dollar would actually purchase in each country. To use a widely used example, a "Big Mac" hamburger might cost much more in a Scandinavian country and much less in Brazil, so just using the standard exchange rate from each country's currency to the dollar is somewhat inaccurate. In Table 2.3, we include the number of billionaires and divide the fifth quintile into two deciles because the concentration of income at the very top has a strong impact on income and wealth inequality. In the next table (2.4), we will be using a statistic, the **Gini coefficient**, that provides an overall summary of inequality, and as ECLAC noted in its press release accompanying its annual socioeconomic round-up,

> If the Gini index is corrected utilizing other sources of information, which are better able to capture the income of the wealthiest 1%, it can be seen that inequality is higher and the downward trend is attenuated when compared with the estimate made on the basis of household surveys alone.
>
> (ECLAC 2019a)

The distribution in Table 2.3 reveals a long-standing pattern of inequality. Brazil has by far the largest number of billionaires in the region, but it is also the largest and most populous country in the region by far. Still, Brazil's highest decile (10 percent) of earners takes in the largest share (53 percent) of total income. The top quintile in the United States, at 52 percent, actually absorbs a higher percentage of income than Guatemala, the second highest in Latin America at 51 percent. Chile often is seen as a highly unequal society, but in this way of dividing the pie, it is simply more like others in Latin America. What is notable is that Chile counts 12 billionaires in such a relatively small population. Brazil, with 215.6 million people in 2019, is more than 11 times more populous than Chile.

Evidence that points to Latin America as the most unequal region on the globe (sub-Saharan Africa would be next) comes from a common statistic used to compare countries on inequality: the Gini coefficient. Figure 2.4 provides a graph of what a Gini coefficient

FIGURE 2.4 The Lorenz Curve, Used to Calculate the Gini Coefficient

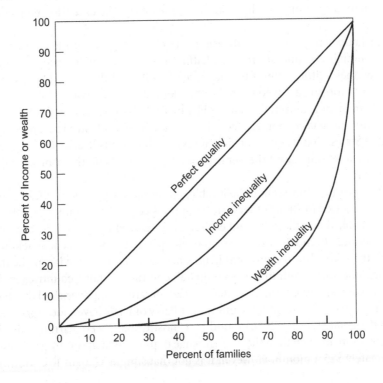

represents. It shows a geometrical representation, called a "Lorenz curve," that is mathe-matically expressed by the Gini coefficient. Each curve in the graph plots cumulatively the percentage of households (not people) against the cumulative percentage of income (vertical axis) each receives in a given year. Each of the two curves begins at 0,0 and gradually bulges out and then in toward the diagonal line until each reaches the upper-right corner, where they converge at 100,100. The bigger the area under each curve, the greater the degree of inequality. This is summarized as a decimal—the Gini coefficient.

The Gini is used to measure not only equality of income distribution but also the degree of equality of distribution of wealth. Wealth is a household's or individual's total accumulated value of savings, real estate, stocks and bonds, and other kinds of property. If every house-hold had exactly the same income or wealth, there would be no curved line at all, because the plotted line would fall right on the diagonal. So a score of 0 is perfect equality. A score of 1 is just the opposite, a situation in which all of the income was gobbled up by a single household. Income is typically what each household earns in a single year. We should keep in mind that Gini is not a perfect instrument for measuring inequality; it underestimates inequality the more concentrated income or wealth is toward the top 1 percent, which is exactly what has been happening globally over the past 50 years.

Table 2.4 gives us a look at the Gini coefficients for income and wealth for the coun-tries as they were ranked and scored in the *Economist* evaluations of democracy, which we reviewed in chapter 1 (Table 1.1). As is generally the case throughout the world, wealth inequality coefficients are significantly larger. One factor of importance here is that wealth is a form of capital that more often than not generates income beyond labor. Also, unlike income, much wealth is inherited. Even Norway, which ranked first among "full democ-racies," has a very high Gini on wealth distribution, but its score on income distribution is much better than just about any other country in the table—the exception being Cuba (more on that later).

Within Latin America, Costa Rica is relatively average on both wealth and income distribution, though it is one of only two Latin American countries rated as a full democ-racy. Uruguay does a little better. But take note of Chile and the United States, two "flawed democracies" not too far removed from the "full democracy" category. Chile scores relatively high on the Gini income and trails only slightly behind Haiti on wealth. Perhaps in no coun-try in Latin America has economic inequality been a more explosive issue than in Chile. As for the United States, that its Gini coefficient on wealth exceeds Brazil's (the highest in Latin America) says something about the hemisphere's hegemon. Note the contrast with Canada, especially on income.

Cuba's score of 22 may seem unbelievable, given that it suggests a radically reduced rate of inequality compared to all the others. The country is certainly an outlier, and the indication is much less reliable than others, but not entirely without usefulness for purposes of compari-son. The last serious attempt to measure income inequality by the Gini coefficient was in 1999 (as shown in the table), but the problem here is not so much the time lag as the difficulty in measuring income and wealth in a way comparable to the capitalist countries in the region. Many Cuban exiles and other critics say that the Cubans are so impoverished that the low Gini simply means that no one except top Communist Party officials have much income. A survey by the *Miami Herald* (July 12, 2016) found that most Cubans were earning anywhere from $300 to $2,000 more in 2016 than the average wage in pesos, which was by government statis-tics approximately $25 a month. However, it is not that simple. Cubans live within a socialist

TABLE 2.4   Democracy Rank and Index; Income, Wealth Inequality

Country	Rank	Index	Gini Income	Gini Wealth
Full Democracies				
Norway	1	9.87	25.8	79.8
Canada	6	9.15	32.1	72.8
Uruguay	15	8.38	41.6	72.1
Spain	19	8.08	35.9	69.4
Costa Rica	20	8.07	48.5	75.0
Flawed Democracies				
Chile	23	7.97	50.5	79.8
United States	25	7.96	45.0	85.2
Portugal	27	7.84	33.9	69.2
Trinidad & Tobago	43	7.16	N/A	73.2
Panama	45	7.05	50.7	78.0
Argentina	47	7.02	41.7	76.8
Jamaica	47	7.02	35.0	77.5
Suriname	49	6.98	N/A	N/A
Brazil	50	6.97	49.0	84.9
Colombia	51	6.96	51.1	77.0
Guyana	54	6.57	44.6	73.4
Peru	59	6.60	45.3	78.8
Dominican Republic	61	6.54	47.1	N/A
Ecuador	68	6.27	45.9	75.9
Paraguay	70	6.24	51.7	76.8
Mexico	71	6.19	48.2	77.7
Hybrid Regimes				
El Salvador	77	5.96	36.0	74.3
Bolivia	83	5.70	47.0	76.4
Honduras	85	5.63	47.1	N/A
Guatemala	87	5.60	53.0	N/A
Haiti	102	4.91	N/A	80.1
Authoritarian Regimes				
Nicaragua	122	3.63	47.1	75.9
Venezuela	134	3.16	39.0	74.3
Cuba	142	3.00	22.0*	N/A

*Estimated.

Sources: United Nations Development Project. (2019); CIA, *The World Factbook* (www.cia.gov/library/publications/the-world-factbook/ (accessed April 2020). For Cuba: Monreal (1999) "Sea Changes: the New Cuban Economy." *NACLA Report on the Americas* 32, 5: 21–29. Gini estimate from *Global Finance Magazine*. (2018). *Wealth Distribution and Income Inequality, 2018* (www.gfmag.com/global-data/economic-data/wealth-distribution-income-inequality).

system that has provided free high-quality health care, high levels of education, and security from violent crime without a large number of armed police on the street. Also, most basic household necessities are sold in minimum quantities in pesos at highly subsidized prices. As far as wealth, rather than income, is concerned, periodically there are indications that some top officials of the Communist Party have managed to accumulate some foreign currency and channel it out of the country, but so far at least, no Cuban on the island has appeared in the leaks (for example, in the Panama Papers; see chapter 14) of major fortunes stashed in outside wealth havens. In any event, except for some important assets (mostly hotels) in the tourism industry, the economic property remains overwhelmingly in state hands.

But there likely has been some fluctuation in income and wealth accrual in Cuba in the last 20 years. Until 2016, Cuba was experiencing a tourist boom as a result of the restoration of relations between the island and the United States during the administration of President Barack Obama. The Trump administration has returned to a hostile policy of enforcing U.S. sanctions on Cuba, including on tourism. The tightening of sanctions comes as Cuba faces the impact of declining cheap oil provided by Venezuela.

By many accounts, including those of many Cuban sociologists and economists that I have met, the economic reforms allowing small private businesses to form and the tourist boom that followed Obama's loosening of the "embargo" contributed to the creation of a new middle class. However, at the same time the gap increased between those in a position to obtain dollars and those trying to live on Cuban pesos alone. With the more recent contraction of the economy since 2016, it is likely that the income inequality has lessened, but there is little doubt that times are harder for most Cubans today than they were five years ago. Signs of poverty on the outer edges of Havana and the appearance of poor people searching garbage are indications that Havana is experiencing some of the distress found in other large Latin American cities.

Intersections of Class, Race, and Gender

Just as Europeans and North Americans often regard Latin cultures as inferior, so also have many in the Latin American ruling class and middle class viewed Indigenous people and the descendants of slaves as less than equal. Under Spanish and Portuguese colonialism, Indigenous and enslaved African peoples were often regarded as children to be baptized and brought into the Christian family, all the while, of course, providing labor for their masters. After independence, for decades many Latin American countries retained laws reserving important positions in government, the military, and the Catholic Church for people who could prove their blood was "pure"—that is, "uncontaminated" with Indigenous or African ancestry. Intellectuals and government officials later in the century promoted European immigration to "improve" the genetic stock and to overcome the presumed cultural deficiencies inherent to the tropical climates.

Simply put, lighter-skinned descendants of Europeans have long tended to occupy the ranks of the upper class; Indigenous and descendants of African slaves have tended to occupy the bottom rungs; and mixed-race people have tended to be in the middle. But we must caution here that the relationship is not one to one, and in several ways race relations have been less bitter and more flexible in Latin America than in the United States, for reasons we explore more closely in chapter 3.

PHOTO 2.1   Latin Americans, especially those with darker skin, have experienced racism in the United States and Europe. Many recent immigrants are excluded from legal rights by their undocumented status, and the poorest among them are more likely to be of African or Indigenous descent. Here, Venezuela's President Hugo Chávez.

Source: Sven Creutzmann/Mambo Photo/Getty Images.

Regardless of how racial classification is done, the results are consistent with what we would expect from the long history of colonialism and ethnic purification that marks the history of the Americas and other places in the world that Europeans established settler colonies. Judith Morrison (2007) estimates that nearly 78 percent of Brazil's 80 million Afro-descendants were living below the poverty line, compared, she says, "to 40 percent for whites." The 80 million count is well above that used by the World Bank in Figure 2.5, which seeks to estimate the percentage who live in "chronic poverty," provided by the World Bank for the years 2012 to 2015, shown in Figure 2.5. This finding is consistent with that of Morrison's study.

ECLAC compares poverty rates for Indigenous people to rates for the "Non-Indigenous and Non-Afro-Descendant Population" in nine different Latin American countries (see Figure 2.6). Non-Afro-descendant people, we should realize by now, will almost certainly include not only those who have a mainly European genealogy and appearance but also many people who might be considered in one of the mixed race categories. Figure 2.6 shows the kind of gap we would expect, with poverty rates higher for Indigenous people. The poverty rates show that little changed between 2012 and 2017. To the extent the gap has closed at all, it is because the rate of extreme poverty for the "Nons" has risen (from 7.3 to 9.9 percent).

FIGURE 2.5   Chronic Poverty, Percent of Afro-Descendant and Non-Afro-Descendant Households, 2012–2015

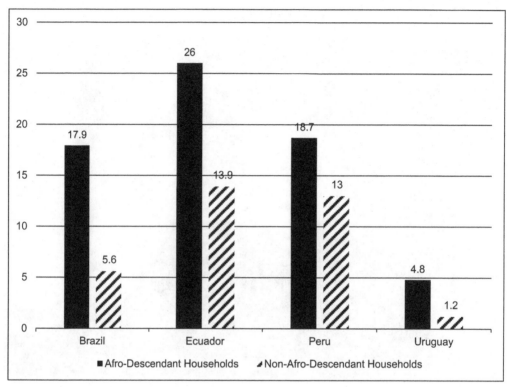

Source: The World Bank. 2018. Afro-Descendants in Latin America: Toward a Framework of Inclusion. Washington, DC

This finding is reinforced by what we saw in Figure 2.1, which showed that poverty rates in rural areas are much higher in urban areas. In countries with the largest Indigenous populations, large parts of the countryside are predominately Indigenous. As noted earlier, "push factors" related to poverty are motivating migration to the cities, but in the cities, Indigenous peoples face discrimination and prejudice (United Nations 2008). Some Latin Americans use "Indio" as a slur.

The World Bank study examines chronic poverty over a four-year period, which is likely to be lower than the poverty rate for any one year. But the measurements of the poverty difference between white and non-white populations in Brazil and three other countries certainly support the conclusion that Afro-descendants as a group remain economically disadvantaged (as, of course, they are in North America too). Take note that Figure 2.6 includes comparisons for Ecuador and Peru, two countries with large Indigenous populations, so the gap between Afro-descendant peoples, who tend to live on the Pacific coast of those two countries, and the Euro-descendant population is probably closer to that for Brazil.

FIGURE 2.6   Percent Households in Poverty and Extreme Poverty, 2012, 2017, Indigenous vs. Non-Indigenous*

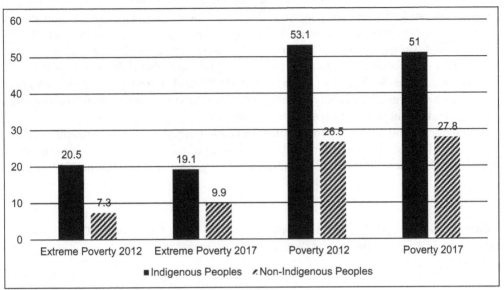

Source: ECLAC, *Social Panorama of Latin America, 2018.*

*Household survey data collected from Brazil, Chile, Ecuador, Guatemala, Mexico, Panama, Peru, Bolivia, and Uruguay.

Women, Gender, and Exclusion

Democracy is "gendered" in several senses. Although there have been notable advances in recent decades—including in Latin America, which has seen the rise of several women to presidencies—women remain less wealthy and powerful than men in proportion to their numbers in the population. As those most often responsible for care of families, women disproportionately bear the costs of economic deprivation and inequality. As in other cultures, men often tend to regard women as more emotional and less rational—certainly ironic, given that outside the region both Latin men and women are often stereotyped as more "fiery" and emotional.

As is typical in patriarchal societies (like ours), for many men a woman's "proper" domain of influence is often defined to be "domestic." This does not mean, however, that Latin Americans are uniformly more sexist than are most people of most other cultures. For example, Latin Americans are more likely to elect women to their legislatures than are most of the rest of the world (United Nations 1999: 142–145). In 2013, Brazil, Chile, and Argentina had already elected women to be president—whereas in the United States only in 2016 was a woman even nominated by a major political party.

According to the Gender Equality Observatory of the United Nations Economic Commission on Latin America and the Caribbean, in 2019 women held 28.5 percent of positions in presidential cabinets and 31.6 percent of seats in the national legislative body. And there was tremendous variation. In Brazil, for example, women held only 9 percent of seats;

the three highest percentages were for Cuba (53 percent), Bolivia (53 percent), and Mexico (49 percent). The same source reported in 2012 that although rates of poverty and indigence had fallen overall in Latin America and the Caribbean, the proportion of women living in such conditions had risen. Although many more women than men have no independent wage or salaries of their own, women in the seven countries studied actually worked more than men did. The gap went from 8 hours more per week in Brazil to 23 hours more per week in Uruguay—the latter regarded as having one of the most liberal democratic cultures in Latin America (Gender Equality Observatory 2019). Note also that Cuba, which prides itself on strides toward gender equality since the 1959 Revolution, shows women working many more hours without pay than men do (see Figure 2.7).

Figure 2.8 and Table 2.5 provide some indication of the economic inequalities related to gender. The first provides a look at the percentage of men and women (and both combined) earning below the national minimum wage, by gender and age, around 2016. In every

FIGURE 2.7 Hours per Week of Paid, Unpaid Work Time[3], Women and Men, for Brazil, Cuba, Spanish South America[1], Mexico, and Central America + Dominican Republic[2]

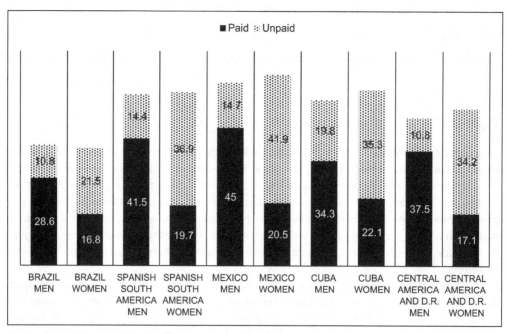

Source: Gender Equality Observatory for Latin America and the Caribbean (oig.cepal.org, accessed December 13, 2019).

1 Unweighted average for Argentina, Chile, Colombia, Ecuador, Paraguay, Peru, Uruguay
2 Unweighted average for Costa Rica, El Salvador, Guatemala, Honduras, Panama, Dominican Republic
3 Total work time is the sum of paid work time and unpaid work time. Paid work refers to work done for the production of goods or services for the market and is calculated as the sum of time devoted to employment, job search and commuting. Unpaid work refers to work done without payment and develops mainly in the private sphere. It is measured by quantifying the time a person spent on self consumption work, unpaid domestic work and unpaid care for their own home or to support other household work (quoted from source web page).

FIGURE 2.8 Approximate Percent Employed Persons With Average Earning Below the National Minimum Wage, by Gender and Age, Around 2016

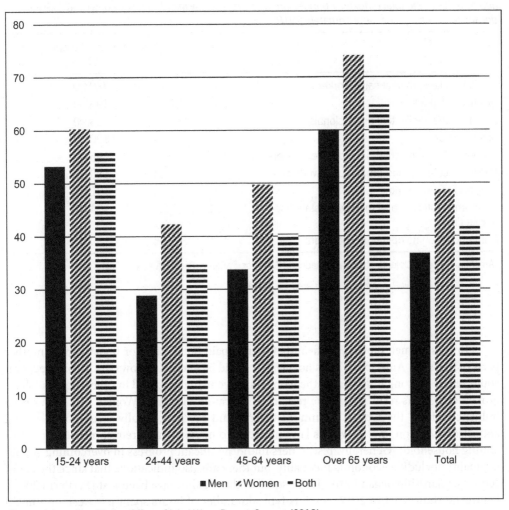

Source: International Labor Office. *Global Wage Report*. Geneva (2018).

age category a significantly higher percentage women earned below the minimum, which over the course of a lifetime has a cumulative negative impact on the quality of older women's lives. Table 2.5 shows how women and men are distributed in the paid labor force in different Latin American countries, and the percentage by which women's wages fall beneath those of men. The gap is lowest (5 to 5.5 percent) for those who work as farmers and skilled workers in agriculture and fishing and for unskilled workers in general. These, as well as service and market sales positions, are generally very low-paying jobs. The gap reaches 20 percent in several categories, including "unskilled" labor. However, the gap in pay is not radically different from the United States, where the Organization of Economically Development States estimates it as approximately 18 percent overall.

TABLE 2.5   Gender Pay Gap in Latin America

Latin America (averages for nine countries* weighted for population). Distribution (percent) of males and females of the total employed population, and the dollar wage of females compared to each 100 dollars earned by males, approximately 2018.

	% Male	*% Female*	*Female pay per each $100 paid to males*
Service workers, market sales workers	13.1	29.5	$80.20
Unskilled workers	18.9	26.0	$95.50
Scientific and intellectual professionals	6.9	11.5	$83.90
Office workers	5.3	9.1	$90.40
Farmers, skilled agricultural, and fisheries workers	13.7	7.2	$95.00
Mid-level technical and professional workers	7.3	7.1	$88.10
Craft and related workers	17.7	5.6	$91.10
Government officials and managers, state and private firms	2.9	2.3	$84.80
Plant and machine operators and fitters	13.9	1.6	$80.50

*Argentina, Bolivia, Chile, Costa Rica, Ecuador, El Salvador, Panama, Peru, Uruguay

Source: ECLAC. *Social Panorama for Latin America, 2018.*

Brazil's women report significantly fewer unpaid hours of labor than women in other parts of the Latin America. Why is not clear; it could be a result of how data is collected, or it could reflect a strong influence of the women's movement compared to other regions. I have broken out Cuba's results from the rest. The Federation of Cuban Women exercises strong influence within the Cuban Communist Party and has successfully championed strong anti-discrimination laws as well as laws intended to make men more responsible for maintaining households. Generally, researchers found significant progress in overcoming gender inequality, including economic inequality, but there are also indications that since the era of economic hardship began in the 1990s some of those gains have been lost (Pertierra 2008). Figure 2.7 shows that in 2019 women's typical number of hours spent per week on unpaid labor is not radically different than the rest of Spanish-speaking South and Central America.

The Precarious Latin American Middle Class

The phrase "popular sectors" is deliberately ambiguous, used mostly by leftist politicians in Latin America to build a majority, anti-elitist bloc of supporters against the upper class and, often, foreign "imperialists." It is useful because the middle class has long been regarded as a swing constituency. Since Aristotle, some political scientists have seen the middle class as a bulwark of constitutional democracy (for such a perspective on Latin America, see Johnson 1958). But for some Latin American political scientists (see Nun 1967), the middle class is an unreliable ally of peasants, workers, and the urban poor, likely to support military intervention against the threat of revolutionary change.

The ambiguous status—neither secure nor precarious—of the middle sectors makes them a shifting factor in class conflict. Their participation in many of the popular uprisings of the late 2010s reflects their discontent with political and economic elites but not necessarily support for radical political change. On the one hand, they are more "included" economically and socially than are the informal sectors of the cities, but a closer examination of income and wealth distribution in Latin America reveals that most people above the official poverty line, including much of the middle class, experience highly precarious lives.

Figure 2.9 breaks down the incomes per day of the Latin American population. Keep in mind that in this figure the amounts are in purchasing power parity dollars, so the amounts are comparable to what a dollar in the United States would typically be. Even allowing that this measure may still underestimate how much one needs to live in Latin America, we can say that in 2017, 63 percent of Latin Americans (corresponding to the striped vertical bar in the figure) are attempting to live on about $20 per day (about $7,300 per year). The preparers of the report, published by the McKinsey Global Institute, a large and prestigious corporate consulting firm, used $5 as the breaking point for absolute poverty. Usually, when researchers refer to the "middle sectors" (as opposed to "middle class"), everyone at $5 per day and above, up to those somewhere around the 95th percentile, are included in this "sector." Those living on between $5 and $10 per day are considered "vulnerable." The "middle class" consists of those whose per capita income is between $11 and $110. McKinsey's estimate would locate only about 1.5 percent of the population living above $100 per day. This count may be a little low, as the ECLAC annual *Social Panorama of Latin America* for 2019 put the "high-income strata" in Latin America in the range of 2.2 to 3 percent.

The "vulnerable" sector (earning $4–$5 to $10) per day is clearly precarious, as it is most prone to fall into poverty, but precarity extends much farther up through the class system.

FIGURE 2.9   Precarious Incomes for 63 Percent of Latin Americans

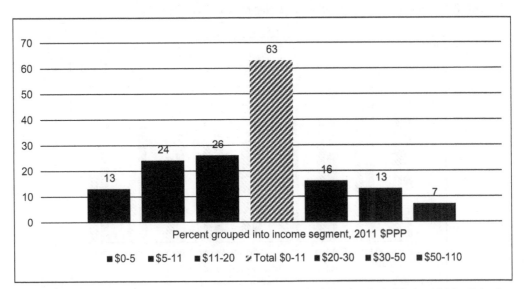

Source: World Data Lab data in McKinsey Global Institute Analysis. *Latin America's Missing Middle: Rebooting Inclusive Growth.* Available at www.mckinsey.com, accessed December 13, 2019.

Looking at Figure 2.10, which examines the middle class in seven South American countries and Mexico, we can see that the infant mortality and percentage living in homes lacking indoor plumbing both steadily rise as one moves from the "high" middle class (making over $50 per day, about $7,250) to the low middle class (making $10 or more). Figure 2.11 looks at "labor informality," defined as "middle level households with no contributor to social insurance." The rates for the "middle class" are markedly higher for those earning $10 to $50 per day.

FIGURE 2.10   The Precarious Middle Class in Eight Latin American Countries*

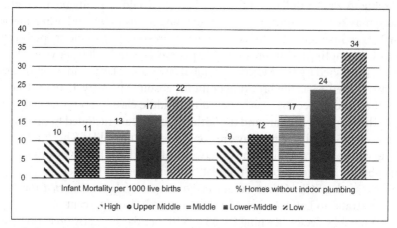

Source: Economic Commission for Latin America and the Caribbean (ECLAC). *Panorama de Desarrollo Territorial en América Latina y el Caribe, 2015.*

*Countries: Argentina, Brazil, Chile, Colombia, Ecuador, Mexico, Peru, and Bolivia.

FIGURE 2.11   Informality: Vulnerable, Vulnerable Middle Class Circa 2015

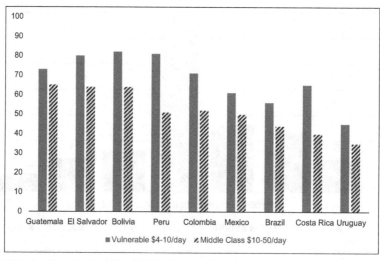

Source: Angel Melguizo, Nora Lustig, "How Middle Class Are Middle-Income Households in Latin America?" OEDC (www.oecd.org/dev/development-posts-how-middle-class-are-middle-income.htm, accessed December 2, 2019).

Figure 2.12 shows that the degree of inequality, poverty, and precarity can vary quite a bit from country to country in Latin America and the Caribbean. And the poverty rate can rise very quickly if international economic factors turn negative or if natural or personal disasters intervene. Given low levels of income, few households accumulate many assets (wealth) that they can draw upon. Public welfare systems are usually inadequate in terms of benefits. In many cases, large sectors of the population are excluded from coverage. Even in Chile and Uruguay, where poverty and extreme poverty rates are very low, very high

FIGURE 2.12   Percent Responses About Distribution of Wealth; by and for Whom the Country Is Governed

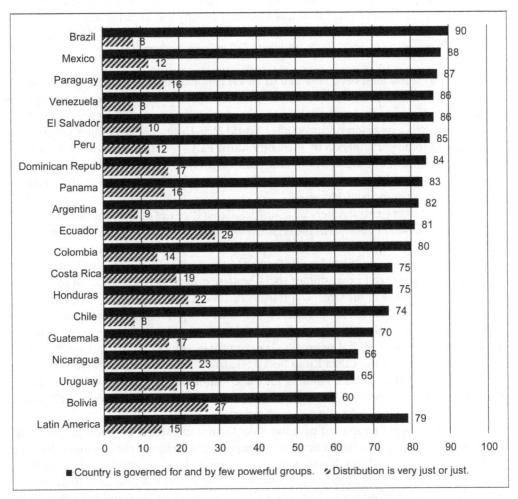

Source: Latinobarómetro 2018.

Question: Generally, would you say that (country) is governed by a few powerful groups for their own benefit or is governed for the good of all? Here, percent saying "few powerful groups for their own benefit."

Question: How just is the distribution of income in (country)? Very just, just, unjust, or very unjust? Here, very just + just.

percentages of households have below $10,000 in net assets (homes, automobiles, land, savings, etc., on the positive side; debts of various sorts on the negative side). A serious illness to the main income earner, unemployment, natural disaster (e.g., floods, earthquakes, mudslides, hurricanes), and accidents all threaten to cast them back into poverty.

Latin American economies are highly dependent on extraction and export of natural resources. Some, especially in Central America and parts of Mexico and the Caribbean, depend heavily on "remittances," money sent home from workers living legally or illegally in other countries. Any interruption of export earnings or remittances can deepen and expand poverty rates. In a news release to accompany *Social Panorama of Latin America for 2019* ECLAC (29) warned,

> Continuing the upward trend that has been recorded since 2015 in Latin America, 30.1% of the region's population was below the poverty line in 2018, while 10.7% lived in situations of extreme poverty—rates which are seen rising to 30.8% and 11.5%, respectively, in 2019, according to ECLAC's projections.

Costa Rica has long been regarded as an exceptional country in the region as, along with Cuba, it is one of two states whose government-funded social security programs (health, retirement, etc.) are universal; that is, they cover all citizens. Some programs go back to the 1900s, and expansion occurred after World War II, first by a coalition government that included some participation by the Communist Party, and then again after the victory over this government by a social democratic political party after a brief civil war in 1948. The victors, the National Liberation Party, led by Pepe Figueres, expanded and institutionalized these programs over the next 30 years.

First, like other Central American countries, Costa Rica was poor and **underdeveloped**, but compared to other countries in the region it long enjoyed a more egalitarian distribution of land than did its neighbors. Second, Figueres had the support of the United States, which sought to expel the communists from influence in the region. In this era, the United States had also just experienced expansion of social welfare programs (the New Deal of Franklin Roosevelt) in the wake of the Great Depression and World War II.

Costa Rica was able to sustain reduced inequality and poverty in part because Figueres's programs were **institutionalized** as universal rights, not just limited to the poor or distributed through partisan political networks. The country established a national health service, an Insurance Institute, the Costa Rican Social Security Institute, and the National Institute for Housing and Urban Affairs. Funding for these institutions was aided by the abolition of the national military after the 1948 revolution—though the country maintains a well-funded and well-armed national police force (see chapter 10).

Costa Rica is not a capitalist paradise. Like the rest of Latin America, it has faced difficult choices as low prices for its agricultural exports put strain on the economy. Tourism, including an influx of retiring North Americans attracted by its relatively low cost of living and personal security, has filled the gap somewhat, but it also has generated high levels of income inequality as land prices have risen (straining small farmers' ability to stay on the land) and budget deficits have risen. Still, its poverty rates are remarkably low compared to the rest of Central America. Institutionalized and universal welfare policies may not have created a capitalist paradise; it remains to be seen whether they can survive the pressures that were created by the "lost decade," weak prices for its exports, and pressure from global financial institutions to reduce its deficits. But the country managed to escape the wave of repressive military dictatorships of the 1970s and 1980s, as well as the devastating civil wars that wracked the rest of Central America in that period.

The Poverty of Democracy in Latin America

Africa may have recently surpassed Latin America as the most unequal region in the world, but the latter's levels of income and wealth inequality remain among the highest in the world. In some parts of the hemisphere, poverty approaches levels of the poorest region, sub-Saharan Africa. How this relates to the condition of democracy is less clear. Costa Rica and Uruguay are among the few places that had not experienced mass unrest or some irregular transfer of power or a coup, and they are, in relative terms, places where levels of inequality and poverty are lowest. Mexico has experienced a lot of violent crime and remains among the most unequal countries, but it has escaped widespread political violence and carried out an election in 2019 that saw power transferred from a very conservative political party to one led by a left populist.

Latinobarómetro surveys give some indication of the interaction between inequality and democracy. As we can see from Figure 2.12, only about 15 percent of Latin Americans believe that income distribution is "very fair" or "fair" in their country, and nearly four of every five Latin Americans think their country is governed by a few powerful groups in their own interest. A bad sign for Costa Rica's "exceptionalism" is that 75 percent of those polled

PHOTOS 2.2 & 2.3   Both photos are taken in San Miguel de Allende, Mexico. Do you think that their lives are in any way connected to each other?

Source: © Shutterstock.

in that country in 2018 agreed. Latinobarómetro polls have shown a steady increase over the last ten years in the percentage who believe their country is governed by the powerful few for themselves, a definition that closely fits the classical definition of "oligarchy." Those agreeing with that statement increased from 61 percent in 2008 to 79 percent in 2018. These findings cut across ideology. Evo Morales's Bolivia comes out relatively well, but only in comparison to other countries in the region. Brazil, where the presidency has been controlled by the political right since August 2016, displays the worst results of all. Venezuela is highly polarized, but the percentages suggest that discontent is not limited to opponents of the government of Nicolás Maduro, which has tried to portray itself as defending "the people" and Hugo Chávez's "Bolivarian Revolution."

The argument of this chapter is to treat economic equality not simply as a precondition or outcome of political democracy but as one of the criteria by which we should measure or evaluate the democratic condition of a country. Guillermo O'Donnell (1999: 196), an Argentine who was among the most influential comparative political scientists of his generation, wrote, "Extensive poverty and deep social inequality are characteristics of Latin America that go back to the colonial period. We have not overcome these conditions; we have aggravated them." He connected this condition to a weakness in democracy.

> This weakness opens ample opportunity for manifold tactics of co-optation, selective repression, and political isolation. Democracy makes a difference, in that the poor may use their votes to support parties that are seriously committed to improving their lot. But, if elected, these parties face severe economic constraints. In addition they must take into account that determined pro-poor policies will mobilize concerns not only among the privileged but also among important segments of the middle class who, after their own sufferings through economic crises and adjustments, feel that it is they who deserve preferential treatment.
>
> (O'Donnell 1999: 197)

There are widely divergent views among comparativists on how inequality and cultural traditions relate to democracy. By now you should realize that many of the inequalities are rooted in history, especially the legacy of the colonial era. In the next chapter, we will examine how this occurred, and then in chapter 4 we will ask why the achievement of political independence failed to impact most of the economic and social legacies of colonialism. Therefore, we now turn to examining how "existing" democracy has evolved over the region, including how pre-Columbian patterns and colonialism have left their mark on the region's contemporary culture, class structure, and politics.

Discussion Questions

1. Should we treat the degree of inequality among social classes, men and women, and different ethnic groups as a test of how democratic a nation is? Or should we limit the idea of democracy to procedures and the form of government, looking at equality as something that might be an outcome of democracy?
2. Do you find it surprising that Latin America, often stereotyped for its **machismo**, has produced several women presidents, whereas the United States has yet to produce one?

3.   What are the most important ways we might measure the extent to which someone, not only in Latin America but wherever they may live, is part of those "excluded," as we have used the term here?

4.   Has anything in this chapter about equality and political culture changed your thinking or reinforced your earlier response to the question of how much we should take equality into account in evaluating the democratic condition of Latin American countries?

Resources for Further Study

Reading: The World Bank publishes the annual *World Development Report* with an appendix filled with comparative economic statistics, including measures of inequality. *Clientelism in Everyday Latin American Politics*, edited by Tina Hilgers (London: Palgrave MacMillan 2012), gives well-supported insight into the relationship between democracy and clientelism.

Video and Film: *In Women's Hands*, in the Americas series, explores the role of women in politics through the tumultuous years of revolution, dictatorship, and re-democratization in Chile. *Las Madres: Mothers of the Plaza de Mayo* (1986) exemplifies the powerful influence of women in the human rights movement. *Black Orpheus* (1959) is a classic, a great film about the life of African descendants in the *favelas* of Rio de Janeiro. On the same subject, a more recent film is *City of God* (2002). See also *The Maid* (2002). *Romero* (1989) is a powerful biography of the Salvadoran archbishop.

On the Internet: The United Nations Development Project has a page devoted to the Millennium Project, which has much information on trends regarding poverty. See www.undp.org/mdg. The emergence of Indigenous and Afro-descendant identity is very evident on the Indigenous Cultures page of the Latin American Network Information Center portal (http://lanic.utexas.edu/la/region/indigenous) and the African Diaspora page at the same site (http://lanic.utexas.edu/la/region/african). A wiki page with extensive information on class in Latin America can be found at https://en.wikipedia.org/wiki/Wealth_inequality_in_Latin_America, accessed March 27, 2020.

PART II

Historical Legacies, Mass Politics, and Democracy

3 Historical Legacies of the Pre-Colombian and Colonial Eras

Focus Questions

▶ How do the legacies of the pre-Columbian and colonial eras exert influence over Latin American politics today?

▶ How did colonialism shape ethnic diversity and national identity in Latin America?

▶ What kinds of issues about national identity, sovereignty, and rights are still contested politically and pose challenges for democracy in Latin America today?

▶ How did colonialism influence the role that Latin America came to play in the global economy?

▶ How do attitudes about race in Latin America compare to those in the United States? How do race and social class relate to each other in the region?

LIKE OTHER PEOPLES, Latin Americans can and do frame the past in a way that influences the present. For example, their schoolbooks, movies and TV programs, holiday rituals, and statues memorialize the past and tell stories. Who tells the stories and how they tell them differ in ways that reflect ideology and political perspectives. In the United States, we have seen this play out in political conflicts over how to deal with public statues that praise Confederate Civil War generals, most of whom were slaveholders. Human culture and rituals romanticize heroes and vilify those "on the wrong side of history." Latin Americans are no different in this regard. For this reason, this chapter is less a chronology than a broad, interpretative account of Latin America's history, leavened with commentary about the relevance of this account to the present.

I do not want to merely provide "historical background" but historical legacies. This chapter and the next address the legacies left by colonialism and the tumultuous first century after independence. Colonialism drastically impacted the social and economic structures of the people who were in the Americas before Columbus, but the history of Latin America does not begin with the Portuguese and Spanish conquest. In various ways, the way of life of Indigenous peoples continues to resonate in Latin American society and politics. The impact is felt more where they are found in greater numbers, but it persists even in places (like the Caribbean) where they disappeared in the face of the forces of biology and conquest. Indigenous peoples, enslaved Africans, and immigrants (covered more in the next two chapters) shaped a Latin American identity as well as national identities that vary from country to country. This story cannot be told without taking gender relationships, especially the role of women, into account. We cannot understand how issues of identity influence Latin American politics without understanding pre-Columbian and colonial history. Colonialism left its mark on the social class structures of Latin American societies and also on how social class intersects with gender, racial, and ethnic differences in the region. It shaped the way that Latin Americans relate to the present-day global economic and political order.

Before and After 1492: Diversity and Change

The climate and populations of the areas where Europeans imposed themselves in Latin America differed significantly before 1492, as they do today for that matter. Northern Latin America resides in tropical latitudes; the Southern Cone has a temperate climate. Geography and climate influenced how colonial economies and social structures evolved over more than 300 years of (mostly) Iberian dominance. Perhaps the greatest differentiating factors were the degree to which Indigenous cultures survived and the extent to which immigrants and African slaves followed the Iberian conquerors into the region. Indigenous people were more numerous in the highland regions than in lowlands. Indian wars comparable with those fought in North America were common until the late 1800s in the temperate Southern Cone. Some cultures in remote regions, such as the Amazon, survived relatively intact until the twenty-first century—though we are learning that European diseases may have decimated populations in these parts of the South American continent as well as in more populated areas. Slavery was more prevalent in tropical regions. These are only a handful of the factors that have shaped cultural diversity in the region.

The region's largest country, Brazil, which borders on every other South American country except Ecuador and Chile, was colonized by Portugal, which along with Spain makes up the Iberian Peninsula in Europe. As a result, Portuguese became Brazil's main language, whereas Spanish has been the native tongue of most other Latin Americans. Also, Brazil's path to independence in the 1800s was quite different (see chapter 4) from that of most of the Spanish colonial empire. Portugal's American empire did not fracture into smaller nation-states, and for several decades of the nineteenth century, it was a monarchy.

For many historians, the colonial era (roughly from 1500 to 1810) "signifies economic backwardness; political arbitrariness, corruption, and nepotism; a hierarchical social order and attitudes of condescension and contempt on the part of elites toward the masses" (Keen and Haynes 2000: 2). For most Indigenous peoples, the period signifies conquest and the subordination of their way of life to European overlords. Neither Indigenous people nor descendants of African slaves see much to celebrate in colonial history, unless it is the struggle of ordinary people, sometimes thrust into leadership of mass resistance, to overcome autocratic traditions, to replace hierarchical structures with democratic practices, and to achieve economic development, providing inspiration to democratic movements today.

In large parts of the Andes and **Mesoamerica**, which includes Central America and Mexico, the conquistadors encountered settled populations with great cities and impressive accomplishments in art, architecture, science, and so on. Central Mexico was more densely populated than was Europe at the time. Pre-Columbian populations were very dense in the Yucatán Peninsula and surrounding regions, as well as in the Mexican highlands. Indigenous populations were also dense in the Andean highlands, which include large parts of present-day Peru, Bolivia, Ecuador, Colombia, western Venezuela, and northern Chile. Most of the Southern Cone (Chile, Argentina, Paraguay, Uruguay, and part of Brazil) has a more temperate climate, and in several respects the history of Indigenous peoples in this region is more like those found in North America.

In the Caribbean, the Amazonian region, and other tropical regions at low elevations, it was once thought that the Indigenous peoples were primarily fishers, hunters, and gatherers. Recent anthropological evidence (Mann 2005) suggests that their societies were much more complex, populous, and sophisticated than once thought. When Europeans finally explored these regions, in many cases not until after 1800, they may have found these societies in a "primitive" condition not because they lacked technology or complexity but because the ravages of disease, including smallpox brought by Columbus and early conquistadors, had already traveled to the area and decimated their social structures.

Did democracy exist in pre-Columbian America? The notion seems anachronistic, but the democratic and egalitarian spirit of Indigenous peoples often impressed European philosophers. The fruits of labor (e.g., the bounty from the hunt or harvest) were usually shared, and extremes of power and wealth were narrow in comparison with so-called advanced civilizations, something that impressed some Europeans. The French philosopher Michel de Montaigne painted a portrait of a noble savage, and Rousseau warned that the advance of "civilization" tended to reduce and not enhance the freedom these people enjoyed. These accounts seem hopelessly romanticized, but surviving communities of Indigenous people often fight today to preserve humanitarian values that we "civilized" peoples may have lost in the quest for progress. One such value in the Andean region is that of *buen vivir*, "living well," referring to the idea of living a simpler life, one less focused on material consumption and more conscious of sustainable environmental practices. It is possible that Indigenous cultures also shaped the values associated with democracy in the United States. Charles Mann (2005), reviewing recent and surprising insights from anthropology and archeology, suggests that in North America the "liberal values" exalting individualism were not simply imported from Europe but learned by North American colonists from Algonquin peoples' notions of egalitarianism and freedom from constrictive social hierarchies.

Before Columbus, many civilizations and empires of Indigenous peoples rose and fell (see Table 3.1), but nothing in their earlier history could match the scale of social devastation wrought by the arrival of the Europeans. Their ways of governing themselves and living were often entirely suppressed (as when they were forcibly relocated) or could be practiced in only modified forms dictated by a ruthless and culturally (especially in religion) aggressive imperial system. Many Indigenous peoples had resisted the imperial ambitions of militarily powerful peoples like the Aztec and Inca rulers; the Europeans exploited the ethnic rivalries and resentment of conquered peoples. However, so too did they often rise against European colonialism, demonstrating a persistent desire even to the present day for self-determination, if not democracy.

The Mayan region (mostly modern-day Yucatán and Guatemala) never was fully subordinated to one central colonial rule (Figure 3.1). Other Indigenous peoples lived even closer to nature in highly decentralized communities where political structures were not distinct from religious and family structures. These peoples were less influenced by European culture—though they did not escape the germs and viruses that Europe transmitted to the hemisphere. Authority in Mayan societies tended to flow to men (but not always) from fighting prowess or some other ability, such as hunting.

TABLE 3.1   Chronology: Pre-Columbian Era and Conquest

Formative Era	30,000 BCE*	Hunter/gatherer groups migrate across the Bering Strait; second wave around 10,000 BCE.
	3500 BCE	Formative, pre-classic era begins; ceramic arts and figures appear.
	2000 BCE	By this time village life and agriculture have taken root in many regions.
Classic Era	200 BCE	More sophisticated technical achievements in ceramics, art, and weaving in the middle Andes.
	200 BCE–1000 CE	Cities and more complex social structures appear.
	300–900 CE	Classic Mayan era. Peak of achievements in astrology/astronomy, calendars, mathematics, writing, and architecture. For example, Monte Albán is built in Mexico.
	200 BCE—600 CE	On southern Peruvian coastal desert. Hundreds of huge figures (Nazca lines) drawn in desert without the benefit of perspective from a height. Realistic painting on pottery in northern Peru.
	450–750 CE	Teotihuacán pyramids, near modern Mexico City, center of empire 900 years before Aztecs.
	600–1000 CE	Rise of urban centers and new empires in highlands of Peru and Bolivia.
Post-Classic Era	968 CE	Toltecs, seen by some as ancestors of Aztecs, establish capital at Tula in central (modern Hidalgo) Mexico.
	1000–1476 CE	Chimú Empire in Peru.
Aztec Era	1325 CE	Founding of Aztec capital of Tenochtitlán, site of modern-day Mexico City.
	1345 CE	Aztecs, coalition of three warrior groups, the largest of which was the "Mexica" group, founds an empire based on tribute.
	1440–1487 CE	Aztecs expand under Emperor Moctezuma I; great temple (on site of modern-day cathedral) dedicated in 1487.
	1502 CE	Moctezuma II becomes emperor of Tenochtitlán and rules until 1520, year after arrival of Hernán Cortés.
Inca Era	1200–1532 CE	Incas, beginning with founding of Cuzco, form the Tawantinsuyu Empire based on tribute, outstanding administrative system.
	1438–1471 CE	Inca expansion toward south of Cuzco.
	1471–1493 CE	Tupac Inca conquers further south, into modern Chile, and west to coast.
	1493–1527 CE	Huayna Capac expands north into Ecuador and Colombia, dies in smallpox epidemic, a disease brought by Europeans. Civil war breaks out; two sons battle for succession.
	1532	Atahualpa wins civil war, is leader of Tawantinsuyu, in same year that Francisco Pizarro arrives.
Conquest	1479	Ferdinand II and Isabella I unite Aragon and Castile to form Spanish monarchy.
	1492	Catholic monarchs expel last of Muslims and Jews from Spain, completing the Reconquista, setting a pattern for the "conquest" (e.g., rewarding warriors with grants of control, encomienda, over land and people).

(Continued)

TABLE 3.1   (Continued)

1492	Financed by Spain, the Italian Christopher Columbus accidentally finds a "New World" in the Western Hemisphere. Columbus makes three more voyages (last one in 1502) and takes part in establishing the Atlantic slave trade.
1493	Alarmed by Portuguese and Spanish competition, the pope mediates conflict and divides control along a north-south longitudinal line—the Treaty of Tordesillas, dividing Portuguese- and Spanish-speaking America.
1500	Pedro Álvares Cabral claims eastern extension of Brazil for Portugal.
1511	Treatment of Indians draws criticism from the Church; Atuey leads Indigenous revolt against Spanish in Cuba.
1512–1513	Large-scale enslavement and transport of Africans to the Americas begins.
1513	Ponce de Leon begins eight-year exploration of Florida; Balboa sees Pacific from Panamá.
1519–1522	Cortés conquers Tenochtitlán after death of Moctezuma II (1520); his successor, Cuitláhuac, dies of smallpox after only 80 days; Cuauhtémoc, last Aztec emperor, is captured, tortured, and put to death in 1525 as Cortés extends the conquest south, into Mayan regions and beyond.
1532	Pizarro captures the Inca Atahualpa, puts a puppet ruler in Cuzco.
1534	Conquest is consolidated militarily after the Inca resistance leader, Rumiñahi, is defeated.

*"BCE"—"before the Common Era"—is used here in place of the more common "BC" ("before Christ"), as is "CE" instead of "AD" (*Anno Domini*, "year of our Lord") in recognition of the cultural and religious diversity in the region.

FIGURE 3.1   Map of the Pre-Columbian Empires of the Americas

The Aztec and Inca empires were not "ancient," at least not in 1510 when the conquistadors started arriving. Aztecs were in reality not one but three warrior groups gathered into a coalition by the largest and most powerful group, the Mexica people. In the mid-1400s, they came to dominate the central and northern part of what today is Mexico. They ruled from their capital Tenochtitlán, a city of 150,000–200,000 people and site of present-day Mexico City. In the Andean region, the Inca Empire arose in the early 1400s; its emperor ruled from Cuzco in the Peruvian highlands.

On one hand, the two empires, Aztec and Inca, that confronted the Spanish were highly centralized, with a king and imperial court living off the tribute contributed by other regions. On the other hand, typical of empires based on tribute, local communities retained considerable autonomy and were led by local chiefs, called *caciques*, a word that today refers to a powerful, local political boss. Within the less-centralized Mayan culture of modern-day Central America and southern Mexico, even more political variation existed. A priestly caste ruled larger units, but much local and regional life was organized on a communitarian basis. Land was collectively owned and often worked through a system of mutual aid, a tradition that persists in many Indigenous communities and influences ideas about political and economic life today.

At risk of exaggerating how women fared in pre-Columbian America, we can see in some regions that **patriarchy** was less virulent before the Europeans arrived. In some Mesoamerican (Mexican and Central American) monarchies, women rose to the office of queen. Within Inca society, a kind of "gender parallelism" prevailed. Lines of descent were traced through both male and female ancestry. Irene Silverblatt (1987) has documented how women had a birthright through their mothers to land, livestock, water, and other resources. Women and men performed different tasks by tradition, but relatively equal status was accorded to men's work and women's work. Under the Spanish conquest women lost much of their influence, although the blame cannot be laid entirely on the Iberians. The rise of the militarist, exploitative Inca imperial system had already undermined gender equity (Keen and Haynes 2000: 5–36; Schroeder 2000; Schwartz 2000; Silverblatt 1987).

More than in North America, in South America the European imposition was a "conquest" more than a "settlement." This produced a paradox: a society where for 400 years proving your "whiteness" legally was a prerequisite for holding positions of power, but the relatively small number of Iberian immigrants made intermarriage and miscegenation (sexual relationships between people of different races) essential for population growth. Hence, we can speak of the birth of a "new race," **la raza**, as some Latin Americans call it, that can proudly draw upon three cultures (Iberian, Indigenous, and African); yet we can also speak just as accurately of the "rape of a continent" not only as a figure of speech for the pillaging of its gold, silver, and other natural resources, but also literally in reference to the sexual assault that gave birth to this new people.

"In a way," wrote historian Magnur Mörner (1967), "the Spanish Conquest of the Americas was a conquest of women." By this, he meant that the Spanish—and Portuguese too—used degrees of force to extract sexual and economic labor from native women. Hernán Cortés, conqueror of the Aztecs, had all Indian slaves branded and, by one account, reserved first right to choose which women he would lie with. Sometimes Indigenous *caciques* bestowed women on the Spanish as gifts or were willing to sell them. Many women were forced to enter the conquerors' households as domestic servants and were subjected to sexual domination. Writing back to their homeland, the Iberians praised the extraordinary beauty and sexual prowess of native women. At the same time, women were expected to be nurturers, mothers, healers, restricted to the domestic domain of life. In this way, the sexual stereotypes of *machismo*, hot Latin lovers, and sexually alluring but motherly women (***marianismo***) were implanted during the conquest. Unlike the case in North America, many fewer women than men migrated from Europe to Latin America. It is unlikely that Iberian cultural and political norms could have been so deeply implanted in Latin America without the rape of the continent taking a somewhat literal form. Understanding gender relationships in the colonial era is crucial to understanding how race, class, and gender interact with one another even today in Latin America.

PHOTO 3.1   When Mexico's president in 2019 suggested that Spain apologize for violent acts during colonialism, the very conservative Spanish political party Vox responded, "López Obrador, Mexico and all of America should be grateful to the Spaniards for bringing civilization and putting an end to the reign of terror and barbarism to which they were subjected. Nothing more to say. Spain left New Spain as a rich and prosperous territory." The great Mexican muralist depicted the Spanish role quite differently, as you can see from this image.

Source: Wikimedia Commons.

For Review

What were the most important Indigenous civilizations at the time of Columbus, and where were they located? In terms of the ethnic profile of Latin America today, what difference did it make in shaping culture and society that, unlike in North America, in the Iberian conquest the Europeans came as conquerors, not settlers, and with few women?

The Colonial Era

The Iberians justified their conquest and continued domination (see Table 3.2) of Latin America as a mission entrusted to them by God. In the first few decades after Columbus's so-called discovery, under the **encomienda** system (*encomendar* means to "entrust"), the king entrusted to his conquerors the responsibility to Christianize the native population. The conquistadors in turn received the right to extract tribute from the Indigenous peoples. This usually meant that the Indians were required to work a certain number of days laboring in mines, constructing roads and buildings, doing domestic labor in the home, or working in the fields. Fray Bartolomé de las Casas, a bishop justly famed for entreating the Crown to defend Indigenous people from ruthless exploitation by the conquistadors, once remarked that it would have been better for the Indians to have gone to hell with their heresies than to have been Christianized by the Spanish. Fray de las Casas mused about importing African slaves and Moors to replace the Indigenous people in their labor (Galeano 2001: 45). By referring to the "Moors," las Casas reminds us that the pattern of conquest was influenced by what Spaniards even today call the "Reconquista." The Moors were Muslim people who had lived in Spain for 800 years before being expelled by Ferdinand and Isabella in their "reconquest" of Iberia. Las Casas and other religious protestors managed to persuade the Crown to repeal the *encomienda* system, but the systems that came later never truly freed the natives from the yoke of the landlords.

To an important degree, the Spanish imperial structures replaced the Indigenous tribute systems, which in economic and political (but not religious and cultural) terms resembled one another. However, now the system was adapted to the Crown's voracious appetite for gold and silver, imposed on societies whose internal integrity was crushed by disease and conquest. Within the Inca system, tribute was rendered in the form of labor or production not by individuals but by clans. In successive waves over several centuries, Europeans and their descendants attempted to replace Indigenous customs and economic relationships with systems of individual property and contract. Over centuries, colonialism introduced a system whereby people exchanged labor, goods, or services based on market relationships and not mutual obligations defined by kinship or sanctioned by tradition and religious authority. Independence did

TABLE 3.2   Chronology: Colonial Era and Independence

1524	Council of Indies set up by Spanish Crown to administer empire.
1531	According to much-contested accounts, Juan Diego, an Indian, reports seeing Virgin of Guadalupe near Mexico City, which later becomes a central myth in fusing Hispanic and Indigenous elements into Mexican identity.
1537	Pope decides Indians have souls; hence, they are humans.
1545	Large-scale importation of slaves to plantations in North Brazil begins. Silver boom begins in Bolivia.
1570–1571	Inquisition established in Lima and Mexico City, where Spanish viceroys (stand-ins for king) are based.
1571–1572	Unsuccessful revolt of Tupac Amaru I in Peru.
1588	Spanish Armada defeated by weather and British fleet; beginning of long decline of Spain as world power.
1610	Jesuits establish missions among the Guaraní in Paraguay.
1700	Philip V becomes king of Spain as Bourbon dynasty replaces Hapsburgs, ushering in an era of reform designed to enhance colonial economy for the benefit of the mother country.
1780 and 1781	Revolt of Tupac Amaru II in Peru and Revolt of Comuneros in Colombia demonstrate weakening power of Crown but alarming the *criollo* ruling elite.
1791–1802	Slave revolt in Haiti leads to independence, frightens other slaveholders in hemisphere.
1793–1815	Napoleonic Wars in Europe disturb political order. In 1807, France invades Portugal, and the royal family flees to Brazil. In Spain, Napoleon forces the coronation of his brother, Joseph, in 1807, followed by a French invasion and occupation. Creoles establish ruling councils in several cities, including Caracas; they express loyalty to the Crown but alarm Spanish authorities. The year 1814 sees restoration of the Spanish Crown.
1810–1815	Bloody failed insurrections in Mexico led by Hidalgo and Morelos.
1810–1811	Venezuela and Paraguay declare independence.
1815	Simón Bolívar retreats to Jamaica, after leading war of independence for three years, and writes famous *Carta de Jamaica*, which among other things calls for unity in Latin America.
1817–1821	José de San Martín undertakes military campaigns, marching across Andes from Argentina into Peru, paving way for independence of southern portion of continent.
1821	Mexican independence declared.
1822	King Pedro, living in Brazil after fleeing Napoleonic invasion, declares Brazil independent of Portugal.
1823	Monroe Doctrine, by which the United States warns Europe not to try to establish colonies in the America, is issued.
1824	Victory by Bolívar's forces, led by José Antonio Sucre, in Battle of Ayacucho assures independence of South America.
1830	Gran Colombia, created by Bolívar, splits into separate countries of Venezuela, Colombia (including Panama, at the time), Ecuador, Peru, and Bolivia.
1838	Central American republics (Guatemala, Honduras, Nicaragua, El Salvador, Costa Rica) established after breakup of regional federation.

not reverse this shift; in fact, it became more broadly and deeply embedded after 1850, when a period of top-down efforts to modernize took place.

A good example of the legacy of *encomienda* would be the *huasipongo* system in Ecuador. In the late colonial period, landowners extracted labor from Indigenous peoples and poor peasants through a draft system, called *mita* or *quinta*, which required them to provide a certain number of days of labor per year to municipal authorities, who in turn were controlled by landlords. Around 1850 this system was replaced by one called *concertaje*, whereby poor peasants would exchange labor for loans and for the right to live on and work a small plot of land, called a *huasipongo*. Superficially, this system introduced a more liberal economic relationship between owners and workers, an improvement over the *mita*, because workers were not legally forced by law to work for landlords; now they simply "agreed" to work by entering into a contract. But peasants had little choice of whether to work. Usually, the landowner paid in advance or made loans to his "employee." Peasants desperately needed access to land and were not in a position to bargain. Inevitably, they would fall behind on payments, run deeper into debt, and be forced to keep on working—or give up, perhaps fleeing (leaving women and families behind to cope) and allowing the landlord to repossess his land. We refer to this system as **peonage** and those caught in its web as "peons." It persisted deep into the twentieth century, not only in parts of Ecuador but also throughout much of Latin America.

In general, Indigenous peoples were more sedentary and densely populated in the areas of the Aztec and Inca empires and the Mayan region, and this allowed them to be more readily assimilated into Iberian imperial structures. Many Caribbean and Amazonian peoples were completely wiped out by European guns, economic exploitation, and germs (more on this shortly). In Chile and Argentina, the wars between Indigenous peoples and settlers stretched into the modern era and more closely resembled the similar conflicts in North America. Even today, mining and oil companies often encounter sometimes violent resistance to their expansion into ever more remote parts of the world. Their motivation—exploitation of mineral wealth—resembles that of the Iberians. Like earlier conquistadors, they have religious allies who seek converts, but today, they are more often evangelical Protestants, a development that alarms the Catholic hierarchy.

For Review

How did the Spanish conquistadors see the Indigenous peoples, and how did they go about putting them to work? Can you describe the difference among systems like *encomienda* and *huasipongo,* of slavery, and of peonage?

Why Did the Conquistadors Succeed? Why Does It Matter Today?

Why did the conquest succeed? After all, only a few hundred Spanish, in the cases of Cortés in Mexico and Pizarro in Peru, managed to defeat Indigenous empires that were highly organized, experienced in war, and densely populated. Experts dispute the size of the pre-Columbian population of the Americas, both in the north and in the south. Recent research suggests a population of 57.3 million people, divided roughly equally in thirds among central Mexico, the Peruvian region, and other regions combined. One plausible estimate sees a total population of 90–112 million (Keen and Haynes 2000: 9–10). Were the Europeans responsible for the decimation of the Indian population to anywhere from a fifth to a tenth of its pre-Columbian size (and for the extinction of some peoples, especially in the Caribbean)?

These questions are laden with political ramifications. For those who see history as a playing out of the Darwinian forces of natural selection (survival of the fittest), the conquest could be seen as proof of the superiority of European civilization. Some Latin Americans (such as Arturo Sosa Pietri, the Venezuelan oilman we encountered in chapter 2) prefer to emphasize the heritage of Iberia; they celebrated the 500th anniversary of the Columbus "discovery" in 1992. In the 1800s, British historians tended to emphasize the cruelty of the conquistadors and the generations of colonial masters who followed them. This "Black Legend" theory tended to disparage all things Iberian and justify the deep involvement of British interests in Latin America in the 1800s. This version of history became commonly accepted in the United States as justification for the war of 1898, when the United States expelled Spain from Cuba and its remaining colonies in the Caribbean and elsewhere.

In a best-selling book, Jared Diamond (1997) explained the Iberian conquest of the Americas in terms of "guns, germs, and steel." He argued that a few hundred Spaniards could conquer the great Inca and Aztec empires because the Europeans possessed superior military firepower (guns), technology (steel, though navigation also counted for much), and immunity from diseases (germs) that devastated the Indian populations on contact with the Europeans. Diamond calls these factors the "proximate" (i.e., immediate) causes for the Iberian success.

Diamond traces these proximate causes to long-range, "ultimate" causes that can be traced to the luck of the historical draw. Those parts of the world where geographical conditions encouraged cultural and technological exchange, early domestication of a variety of plants and animals, and large settled and diversified societies had a large advantage, he argues, over regions where there were obstacles to these processes. However, the Indigenous cultures of the Americas had remarkable cultural and technological achievements. Where Diamond may be right is that climate and geography limited how much cultural and technological exchange went on among these cultures. Also, they had fewer domesticated species of animals than did the Europeans, who as a result of centuries of interaction with these animals and each other had more immunity to the diseases they carried to the New World. Native Americans might have suffered fewer devastating plagues in their history, but this made them more vulnerable to the diseases carried by Iberians. Indeed, these were factors. For example, smallpox and other diseases may have taken the lives of up to 95 percent of the Indigenous population in the early 1500s. They had calendars, remarkable architecture, and medical technology (such as brain surgery, in the case of the Incas). Their scientific accomplishments rivaled those of the Europeans but were of limited use in resisting the particular advantages held by the invaders.

Diamond's stress on long-run historical factors as the explanation for the enormous gap between poor and rich countries is controversial. If the conquest of Latin America was merely the result of biological and geographical tendencies dating back millennia, then perhaps the cries for justice for descendants of those conquered seem less compelling. After all,

if the luck of the historical draw accounts for poverty and vulnerability to foreign domination in Latin America and other parts of the Third World, then there is little use in arguing
about moral responsibility in rectifying global inequality. In fact, it could be argued that
survival of Indigenous peoples would have benefited the conquerors, who were in need of
labor to work their mines, plantations, and *haciendas*.

Mann (2005) agrees with Diamond that geographic factors limited cultural and biological exchange in the Americas, but he takes issue with Diamond's conclusion that European
military technology was a deciding factor. Recent evidence suggests that Indigenous peoples
did have adequate technologies to defeat the tiny coteries of invaders led by adventurers such
as Cortés and Pizarro. For example, their arrows flew farther and struck targets with more
force and more accuracy than did European bullets shot from primitive firearms.

We are also learning that pre-Columbian civilizations had technological and scientific
knowledge long before the Eurasian cultures came to dominate globally. For example, the
Olmec people of central Mexico had zero in their mathematics at least 550 years before it
first appeared in Mesopotamia (modern Iraq), almost 1,200 years before Europeans managed
to figure it out. Mann points out that corn, perhaps the most important crop in the world,
seems not to have been developed from nature, as is the case for other grains; we cannot find a
primitive, wild ancestor that yielded something edible and comparable with what we know as
corn. Indigenous people accidentally or purposefully were genetic engineers. Spanish soldiers
in Mexico quickly discarded their wool clothing for lighter cotton garments obtained from
Indigenous peoples. Sometimes, our romantic stereotype of Indigenous peoples living har-
moniously and lightly with nature obscures how they shaped the environment, leaving, perhaps unintentionally, with the notion that they were primitive technologically for their times.

Alfred Crosby Jr. (1991), a historian who did much to bring the impact of disease on
Indigenous people to our attention, points out that the introduction of European plants and
animals undermined the stability of the environment in the New World, reduced the genetic
pool, and "caused such vast erosion that it amounts to a crime against posterity." Columbus
and the first Europeans who followed him were interested mainly in gold and silver. As the
mines gave out, Europeans found natural conditions in different regions of the hemisphere
suitable for production of coffee, cacao (for chocolate), sugar, and other crops and minerals
in demand overseas. Even small Caribbean islands, mere microstates today, yielded enormous wealth when their fertile soils were tilled by slave labor. For example, in 1773, the value
of sugar exports from the small Caribbean island of Grenada, a British colony, exceeded the
total value of exports of all Britain's New England colonies, New York, and Pennsylvania
combined (Williams 1970: 151).

Diamond's book is an extended response to a question posed to him by Yali, a local
politician from the Pacific tropical island of New Guinea, who asked, "Why is it that you
white people developed so much cargo and brought it to New Guinea, but we black people
had little cargo of our own?" Are we to believe that the answer is merely, "Well, you had
the bad luck to be born in the wrong part of the world"? Would all cultures have been as
aggressive and ruthless as were the Europeans? Do long-term technological and biological
factors adequately explain why the Europeans visited the holocaust of the transatlantic
slave trade on Africans and imposed devastating forced labor and land expropriation on
Indigenous peoples?

Accidents and nature played a role in the European conquest of the Americas, but
colonialism was neither natural nor accidental. As Mann proposes, we might do well to

concentrate less on moral culpability in history and more on our own responsibility to address inequalities and prejudices inherited from the past.

In colonial times, the Spanish and Portuguese crowns regarded the natives as little more than children to be civilized through conversion to Christianity. As such, church authorities, often backed by the Crown, defended Indigenous people from some of the harshest forms of exploitation on the part of those "entrusted" with responsibility for this task. This pater-nalistic attitude was not always welcomed by the **criollo** elite—that is, those members of the predominately European elite who made up the colonial ruling class in the Americas. (The word in English is usually translated as "Creole." We will use this term interchangeably with "*criollo*," but keep in mind that in the U.S., "Creole" refers more to mixed-race people, and not necessarily those of the upper class.) They had little use as well for Indigenous culture and knowledge.

After independence, the *criollos* faced a new question: What made them nations with a right to claim sovereignty—that is, the right to claim independence? Over time, the *cri-ollos*, few of whom could trace their ancestry solely to Iberia, began to include Indigenous culture as part of their identity as Colombians, Mexicans, Venezuelans, and so on, without necessarily respecting Indigenous people as equals. For example, in Mexico after expulsion of a French occupation in 1867, Indigenous culture was elevated in a way useful to defining a sense of national identity. Mexicans discovered a past that preceded and perhaps even exceeded what it had inherited from Spain. However, this was expressed more in museums, artistic movements, folklore, cuisine, and tourism and not in respect for the rights of Indig-enous people to govern themselves or regain control of their land. As Benedict Anderson (1983), a student of nationalism, would put it, they were "imagining" themselves as a nation.

One of the places where this happened was in the kitchen, where Mexican women continued to prepare corn-based meals despite the attempts of *criollos* to "Europeanize" the country and replace the traditional Indigenous cuisine with wheat (Pilcher 1998). Women not only cooked but also collected and printed recipes. In this way, women helped to keep alive a heritage thousands of years old, keeping it available to be incorporated into Mexican culture when the governments after the country's 1910 revolution promoted **mestizaje** as the "real Mexico." But the notion that the real Latin America is **mestizo** is something that Indig-enous peoples have come to challenge recently.

For Review

Why were the Indigenous people of the Americas vulnerable to European diseases? What other factors made them vulnerable to conquest by the Iberians? Why do these questions have any relevance to politics today?

Slavery

Not long after Columbus's first voyage, the first "illegal immigrant" took part in organ-izing the system whereby Africans were forcibly transported to the New World as slaves and thrown into the racial stew. In a few cases, such as in the southern Brazilian state of

Minas Gerais, they were put to work in mines. While today Afro-descendant people are found everywhere in the Americas, they continue to populate in greater numbers those areas where the climate and soil were most suitable for plantation agriculture and where the Indigenous population was scarce and especially resistant to exploitation through *encomienda* or its successor schemes. Women once again played an unwilling role in the story. In Brazil, Portuguese planters exercised despotic power over black female slaves. Sexual unions among white, Indigenous, and black people shaped the genetic makeup of the Brazilian population. In 1775, colonial authorities legitimated white–Indian marriages and made their offspring eligible for offices previously limited (at least officially) to whites. However, children from unions involving blacks and whites were not similarly favored (Keen and Haynes 2000: 130).

Hard labor was identified with slavery, so whites often resisted work that in their minds only befitted the slave. If their skin was not too dark, **mulatos** (or in English, mulattos), people of partial African ancestry, might be admitted into higher socioeconomic positions. The uneasy relationship between class and race was further complicated by the way some slaves could acquire an education and even become artisans (skilled workers and craftspeople—e.g., furniture makers and blacksmiths) with their own small businesses in the towns. In Cuba, a house slave named Juan Manzano acquired an education and became a writer of some note. He wrote mostly about the conditions afflicting himself and his family. He left us the only direct testimony we have from this period and region of the psychological burden of being an enslaved man with a free mind. He wrote in a letter, "A slave is a dead soul" (Manzano 1996: 21). One of his poems well describes the evil nature of the slave trade itself:

> The Cuban merchant prosecutes his trade
> Without a qualm, or a reproach being made;
> Sits at his desk, and with composure sends
> A formal order to his gold-coast friends
> For some five hundred "bultos" of effects,
> And bids them ship "the goods" as he directs.
> That human cargo, to its full amount,
> Is duly bought and shipped on his account;
> Stowed to the best advantage in the hold,
> And limb to limb in chains, as you behold;
> On every breast, the well-known brand, J. G.

Slavery was a political powder keg, and the periodic revolts worked both for and against prolongation of colonialism. Slave revolts were more numerous in Latin America than in the northern continent, but there is little agreement among historians about why. You can find a summary of the academic controversy in Holloway (n.d.). He lists 64 significant slave revolts between 1512, when 40 people enslaved by Christopher Columbus revolted (all were captured or killed within months), and 1825, when hundreds of enslaved Afro-Cubans revolted. On the one hand, these revolts frightened the *criollos*. Fear of slave revolts made them reluctant to separate from the imperial state and its armies. On the other hand, revolts constituted one more form of resistance that were precursors to the final break. Enslaved Africans often sought freedom in the vast interior, where they established self-governing communities, *cumbes*.

In 1804, slaves led by Toussaint L'Ouverture revolted against their French colonial masters in Haiti and achieved independence—arguably the first true national liberation movement in the history of anticolonialism. The new Haitian regime carried out a bloody expulsion of white planters (especially after L'Ouverture's assassination), which frightened slave owners throughout the hemisphere, including the southern region of the United States. Colonial elites in several neighboring Caribbean colonies (Cuba, Dominican Republic, and Puerto Rico) resisted the continent's movement into independence for another 70 years. Many looked hopefully toward the United States to replace faltering Spain as guarantor of their dominance, even after abolition. Fear of emancipation also contributed to the willingness of the Brazilian colonial elite to remain loyal to a Portuguese monarch who fled Napoleon's troops in 1807 and set up shop in Brazil.

As we discussed earlier concerning *mestizaje*, the interaction among race, class, and gender was a complex one, and in Latin America the practice of miscegenation and rape quickly gave rise to a large population that was racially and culturally mixed. Those of partial African descent came to be called *mulatos*, *pardos*, or some similar name. More so in Latin America than in the United States, there was room for some economic advancement and social mobility for enslaved people. Certainly enslaved people yearned for freedom, but it did not always mean a better life materially. In the towns, where those freed from plantation life gathered, there developed a large, poverty-stricken class of "free" homeless people, beggars, prostitutes, and others. Their status in colonial society was higher than that of blacks, but their economic condition could be even worse.

For Review

In what regions of Latin America do we find people of African descent? What were the main reasons that Europeans decided to enslave Africans and bring them to the New World? How did the exploitation and subjugation of Indigenous peoples and enslaved Africans affect the calculation of European descendants about the desirability of independence?

PUNTO DE VISTA: DOES BRAZIL NEED AFFIRMATIVE ACTION?

Affirmative action refers to governmental policies that attempt to redress the historical legacy of slavery and discrimination on the basis of race, ethnicity, or gender by favoring individuals who are members of historical exploitation and discrimination. Courts in the United States have placed obstacles in the way of affirmative action by finding most such policies discriminatory against others, most notably whites and males. But in Brazil, recent governments have implemented the most controversial of such measures—quotas.

On October 12, 2012, President Dilma Rousseff approved a new Law of Quotas, which required the country's 59 universities to reach the goal of having half of their students come from public schools, whose own students come mostly from poor neighborhoods. The universities must also ensure that half of the admitted students are representative of the local population's racial mix, a measure that heavily favors those of African descent. Universities were assigned quotas that they had to achieve. The law capped off 20 years of gradual implementation of various affirmative action measures. In April 2013, Brazil's Supreme Court approved the constitutionality of the law. The program was funded and functioned for five years but was targeted for drastic reduction if not elimination when right-wing politician Jair Bolsonaro became president on January 1, 2019. Bolsonaro made clear in his campaign that he regarded affirmative action as divisive and unnecessary. However, at least in his first year, he had not moved forward, and more universities joined the program. However, affirmative action was approved with the proviso that it would run out in 2024. Rather than stir up Brazil's strong Afro-descendent movement, he would wait it out.

Early signs indicated that despite fears of diluted education, students admitted under the quota were doing fine. That may in part reflect the low percentage of Brazilians who make it to college overall—only 19 percent, compared to 45 percent of U.S. residents and 69 percent in South Korea. University education is free, but students must pass qualifying exams to enter. Supporters sometimes point out that the program has had a different kind of benefit, prompting Afro-descendant Brazilians who regard themselves as *pardo* ("Brown") rather than *negro* ("Black") to feel more free to express their identity as they actually feel it.

A slight majority of Brazil's 200 million people identify as Afro-descendent, at least partially. For 300 years in the colonial era, Brazil's export economy depended on enslaved Africans whose labor produced gold, silver, sugar, and other products that enriched an upper class. Brazil imported seven times as many slaves as did the United States, and it was the last country, in 1888, to make slavery illegal. As in Cuba and other regions with a plantation economy, African descendants—including most of the mulatto population—have not relinquished their sense of connection to mother Africa, which is reflected in religion and culture.

Until recently, Brazil shared the myth of racial democracy with the rest of Latin America. However, during a gradual move from democracy to dictatorship in the 1980s, that began to change. Landless workers, people in the *favelas* without legally verified ownership of their homes, women in poor communities, and many others formed social movements. They eventually came to back the political rise of a *pardo* union leader, Luiz Inácio Lula da Silva (Lula), who became president in 2002, and Benedita Silva, a devout radical religious woman who became the first black (and black woman) elected to the Brazilian Senate.

One important feature of quotas in Brazil is that they are based on social class, not just race. Also, Brazil has very liberal criteria for qualification as black—often described as the "one drop" of blood rule. Given these provisions, it is no surprise that a large part of the population benefits, giving the policy a broad base of support politically. Polls in 2008 showed that 44 percent of the population "strongly agreed" with the quota system, and another 18 percent "agreed." Most of the opposition came from the middle class, and the major media all opposed the idea. Bolsonaro appealed to hard racist sentiments, but there are too many Brazilians now who see value in the program for him to make it a priority.

The president's argument, that historical discrimination no longer exists, should be familiar to most North Americans, though with a difference. In the United States the typical argument made by whites is that the present generation should not be held responsible for the injustices of ancestors. They note that many immigrants and their descendants are not even descended from slave owners or others of the past era. In Brazil, the argument is more along the lines that because of miscegenation (births resulting from sexual intercourse among people of different races), the country already is a racial democracy, a claim that lost steam as the social movements of the 1980s began to ask why so few dark-skinned people could be found in prestigious and well-paying professions.

It is too soon to know what positive or negative effects the quota law will have on Brazilian society. Affirmative action may exist in some form in the United States, but it is difficult in a country with such a strong liberal (see chapter 1) ideology to imagine that a quota system will ever be accepted. Clearly, something about Brazil's history and culture is different, something that, even though many Brazilians still oppose the law—would permit such a system to be found desirable by most citizens and legal by the courts.

Point/Counterpoint

Is affirmative action in Brazil consistent with the democratic principle of equality?

If you answered yes, how would you answer those who say that it penalizes those Brazilians who weren't responsible for the original injustices? Also, are you saying yes because in general you also support affirmative action in the United States and other societies or because Brazil's history with slavery and race is different in some way?

If you answered no, how would you answer those who say the legacy of slavery means that Afro-Brazilians and *pardos* do not have the same opportunities as lighter-skinned Brazilians? Would you do nothing?

For More Information and Perspectives

If you want to consult one source that takes you inside race and affirmative action, I strongly recommend you listen to the National Public Radio podcast "Brazil in Black and White," which can be found at www.npr.org/2019/08/20/752866675/brazil-in-black-and-white-update. Other sources include Julianna Barbassa, "Race to the Top," *New York Times*, May 17, 2013 (http://latitude.blogs.nytimes.com/2013/05/17/brazil-has-aggressive-affirmative-action-programs-for-university); Ibram H. Rogers, "Brazil's Affirmative Action Quotas: Progress?" *Chronicle of Higher Education*, November 5, 2012; Edward Telles, "Brazil in Black and White," Wide Angle (PBS, June 1, 2009, www.pbs.org/wnet/wideangle/lessons/brazil-in-black-and-white/discrimination-and-affirmative-action-in-brazil/4323).

Colonial Attitudes and Identity Politics in Latin America

How do the pre-Columbian and colonial eras assert themselves in present-day politics? In the 1990s, the political influence of Indigenous peoples grew to proportions not seen since the conquest. In other places, Afro-descendent peoples emerged to demand not only respect for their cultures but also programs and even reparations for the harm inflicted by slavery.

Colonial Legacy: Indigenous Politics

Mexico has felt the impact of Indigenous reawakening. In the southern state of Chiapas, the local Indigenous people are the country's poorest. However, Chiapas is blessed with considerable natural resources. Its rivers supply power to most of the country, and central planners in Mexico City have designs for expanding the energy grid south into Central America. The growth of cattle ranching has depleted the Lacandon rainforest, driving many peasants onto more marginal lands. Almost invisibly, in the early 1990s, a guerrilla movement of resistance began to form, and it burst into view suddenly on January 1, 1994, when the rebels seized the state capital. They call their forces the Zapatista Army of National Liberation (Ejército Zapatista de Liberación Nacional—EZLN), taking the name from the great peasant leader of Mexico's 1910 revolution, Emiliano Zapata.

The character of this movement has been stamped deeply by Indigenous values. This is evident in its strategy, which rejects the idea of taking power by taking control of the Mexican state. Zapatistas say that they want to rethink the entire idea of the state and power (see the Punto de Vista in chapter 1), placing less emphasis on national government and more on values of community solidarity, common ownership, and local participatory government. Inspired by their Mayan past, the Zapatistas are prepared to work patiently for decades to accomplish their goals. Their slogan, "Change the world without taking power," has been adopted by many social movements opposed to economic globalization.

The movement cannot simply be labeled "Indigenous." Its leader, known as *"subcomandante"* Marcos, is not a native Indigenous person, but he has been embraced by his followers not because of his genealogy but his way of thinking. Farther north, the people of Atenco successfully resisted an attempt during the early 2000s to build a new airport for nearby Mexico City. Only a few hundred of that town's people speak an Indigenous language, but they justified resistance to expropriation of their communal lands by referring to their native past. This sense of ancestry contributes to a growing number of people awakening and embracing an Indigenous identity or seeking a broader identity beyond national boundaries, such as "Mesoamerican" in Mexico and Central America (Stolle-McAllister 2005: 27).

A similar resurgence has happened in the countries that lie within the historical Inca Empire. For example, in October 2003, descendants of the Aymara people swept down on La Paz, the Bolivian capital, from the sprawling urban slums of El Alto to force President Gonzalo Sánchez de Losada from the presidential palace. They were protesting his plans to place Bolivian natural gas deposits under foreign control. Up to 500,000 Bolivians participated. The organizers and participants alluded to something that had happened in 1781—a failed revolt against colonial authorities—though this time they met with more success. Mass uprisings had forced dictators out of Bolivia before, but in those cases, the protests were led by the middle class and workers affiliated with the unions; Indigenous organizations were secondary actors. This time the uprising was being led by the Indigenous sector (Hylton and Thomson 2004). Many heretofore *"mestizos,"* although most did not speak an Indian language, came to see themselves as primarily Indigenous. They chose, in a sense, like the people of Atenco, to adopt their Indian ancestry as their identity.

Indigenous peoples have a historical narrative, and they too may draw on it selectively. An anthropologist sympathetic to the cause of the residents of El Alto encountered some resistance from students at the university where he taught, even though the professor had lived in and researched the city for several years before the uprising. He contends that before the Spaniards arrived, the Indigenous communities (*ayllus*) might not have been as egalitarian as we suppose and that the system of rotating leadership introduced by the Spanish conquerors might have been more democratic in some ways. The students at the Public University of El Alto, he says, did not want to hear it (Lazar 2008: 10–11). Which position was right is not the point of this story. What it exemplifies is that what we *think or prefer to think* happened in history is just as important as what really happened.

In 1990, Indigenous peoples from 120 different Indigenous societies and movements from every part of the Western Hemisphere, north and south, came to Ecuador and issued their Declaration of Quito. They proclaimed that their struggle for "self-determination" had reached a new level of organization, but not in isolation from struggles for social justice waged by other groups. The declaration speaks of "autonomy," not "sovereignty," and in doing so avoids the notion that the people of Indigenous movements are separatists. A key part of autonomy demands that Indigenous peoples have "the right to control our lands, including the management of natural resources under and above ground, as well as control over our airspace." It includes a "rejection of the capitalist system" and calls for "the elimination of all forms of sociocultural oppression and economic exploitation. Our struggle is geared toward the construction of a new society, pluralistic, democratic and based on popular power."

In Bolivia, Evo Morales, a native Aymara speaker, was elected in December 2005 as the first Indigenous president of a South American country. He rose to prominence in Bolivian politics as leader of the *cocaleros*—cultivators of coca, the base for cocaine. Aymara and Quechua people cultivated and chewed the leaf of the coca plant for centuries, long before the Spanish arrived, but Andeans produce coca today also to take advantage of the international recreational drug market. Morales advocated closing Bolivia's markets to imports of luxury goods and to other products that Bolivians can produce themselves. He advocated that the Bolivian state nationalize the country's mines, railroads, and utilities. He opposed the U.S.-inspired and -financed war on drugs, fought partly in Bolivia. He characterized it as imperialism. This anti-imperialist message and economic agenda broadened his appeal across ethnic boundaries. Morales told *New York Times* correspondent Juan Forero he had little interest in compromise. "For more than 500 years, they have not been tolerant of us; now that we have gotten ahead, they want us to be tolerant with them."

Indigenous demands for autonomy are an attempt to defend their culture from disappearing into a *mestizo* nation. *Mestizo* (sometimes *Ladino*) here means "mixed race," and the term sometimes is expanded to *mestizaje* when it refers to an ideology, a way of thinking. In the 1800s, having shaken off colonial rule, a growing middle class had to come to grips with the various strains of blood running through its veins. Gradually, the notion of *mestizaje*, somewhat akin to the idea of a new race, emerged, changing national identity. Morales gave voice to the demands and grievances of the Indigenous population, and once in office he moved to rewrite the constitution and define Bolivia as a "**plurinational state**." Regional and ethnic autonomy were key principles in the charter and to some degree in subsequent laws.

As president, Morales, despite his declaration to the *New York Times* reporter, found it necessary to compromise as he sought to balance the reality of a national economy tied closely to extractive export industries (oil, gas, mining) against demands from Indigenous groups. Local elites, many of which are European immigrants or recent descendants from Europeans, in the energy-rich southeast of Bolivia pressed for territorial autonomy, with the goal of keeping profits in their own hands, away from the central government headed by the Indigenous leader. When Morales backed a controversial plan to open part of a national park to new mining projects, Indigenous groups nearby protested and were met by violent repression. This was only the most serious breach that opened between Indigenous groups who continued to back Morales along with his MAS (Movement Toward Socialism) party and those who felt he had betrayed them. It would weaken Morales when his more right-wing opponents maneuvered to foment a military coup in November 2019.

PUNTO DE VISTA: CAN "PLURINATIONALISM" WORK IN BOLIVIA?

Bolivia's constitution of 2009 begins by describing how in colonial times the country's natural resources were raped and how "this Sacred Earth" was populated by peoples whose diversity was not recognized because of racism. The new constitution, it says, recognizes this legacy and the "plural composition" of its inhabitants. Committed to the "integral development and free determination of its peoples," the constitution asserts it accepts "the historical challenge of constructing a 'plurinational' nation state."

Drawing on Indigenous culture, it seeks to create a society in which "living well" (*buen vivir*, or *vivir bién*) takes precedence over accumulation of material things. These goals inspired many people beyond Bolivia's borders, especially those alarmed by climate change and concerned that material wealth does not equate to happiness.

Many political scientists argue that pronounced ethnic divisions pose a threat to democratic stability (Rostow 1960), but others (Selverston-Scher 2001) contend that few nation-states in the contemporary world are truly homogeneous anyway. The solution, they argue, is a "plurinational" state. In a **plurinational state**, different ethnic groups find a compromise formula permitting shared **governance** and a richer, more diverse society.

Some Bolivians believe the idea of a plurinational state is both unrealistic and undesirable. In 2009, Bolivian president Evo Morales declared that the Wiphala, a rainbow-colored flag used by Indigenous peoples throughout the Andean region, should always be flown alongside the tricolor Bolivian national flag. This prompted protests from some Bolivians, mostly those not identifying as Indigenous, that the unity and identity of the nation were being undermined, heightening ethnic tensions.

In November 2012, Bolivia conducted its first census since Morales became president. In the census, Bolivians were able to choose among a variety of identities, including 38 different ethnic classifications, including various Indigenous groups and Afro-descendant options. But "*mestizo*" was not among them, though those who chose "other" were so classified. Why does it matter whether a Bolivian can choose "*mestizo*"? "*Mestizo*" suggests a melting-pot culture where everyone shares a common sense of nationhood. People might have different skin complexions, but all share a common identity as Bolivians. That is, all Bolivians share the same "mixture" of European, Indigenous, and other values. To be able to choose among a number of different Indigenous classifications suggests this process has largely been a myth. It creates a basis for people in these classifications to make demands about control over their territories, for example, or what children are taught in school. Geofredo Sandoval, a sociologist involved in administering the census, said that the exclusion of *mestizo* this time was "an attempt to correct a centuries-old subjugation of the Indian majority by the dominant *mestizo* classes" (Catholic News Services 2012).

The plurinational idea raised thorny issues about who controls access to land and resources. In 2011, export from extractive industries (mostly oil, gas, copper, and mining) constituted one-third of Bolivia's gross domestic product and over three-quarters of its total exports. Morales, a native Aymara speaker, strived successfully to direct more of the profits from these industries toward the needs of the poor, including Indigenous peoples. However, when Morales moved to open more of the country to mining and natural gas exploitation, some Indigenous groups withdrew support.

Bolivian law requires that government agencies consult with Indigenous peoples before drilling, mining activity, or road building takes place. In December 2011, the Morales government claimed that 80 percent of tribal groups in one Amazonian region agreed with the government's plans to build a road through one such territory, but a critic in the region complained that consultations organized by the government were not well attended, did not adequately inform participants, and framed discussions with promises to provide a variety of benefits and services if the road were approved (Achtenberg 2012).

Ironically, Morales's shift on extractivism temporarily won him cooperation, if not support, from some of his most extreme opponents in Santa Cruz province, which lies on the plains south and east of the Andes. The *criollos* are descendants of more recent European immigrants, and the region around Santa Cruz sits on top of valuable minerals, including large hydrocarbon deposits. They wanted to use new autonomy laws to keep profits in the province and out of the hands of the central government. The area is also close to the Amazonian lowlands, Morales's political stronghold, where Indigenous and other peasants made a living off production of the coca leaf. This added an additional strain on the uneasy truce between the Santa Cruz oligarchy and Morales.

The truce came crashing down in 2019. Morales had lost a referendum to amend the constitution to run for a fourth term, which he subsequently overcame by obtaining a favorable ruling from the country's Supreme Court, dominated by his appointees. Morales won the election, but his opponents and some important Indigenous groups cried "fraud." The Organization of American States

agreed, although its observer team never really substantiated charges that the count had been manipulated. This is not to say that election was without flaws. The constitution of 2009 had not entirely changed a political culture in which to win national elections candidates had to build coalitions with local *caciques*, who could deliver their clienteles (see Anria 2016).

Morales, like other Pink Tide leaders in Latin America, had raised taxes and royalties to capture more of the profits from raw material exports, and he had channeled them toward the poor in ways that substantially reduced poverty (see chapter 2). But the channels were still often controlled by politicians, including many who opportunistically had joined the MAS. Still, the count by national electoral authorities was probably accurate, giving Morales a bare 10 percentage point majority over his main opponent, enough for a first-round victory (see Bowman 2019).

Widespread protests, some violent and encouraged by the *criollo* elite, were backed by police and the military—even though Morales has courted the latter, which alienated some of his popular base. He offered new elections, and then promised he would not be a candidate. With police support, the protests grew more intense and began to target violently members of the government and MAS party offices.

On November 10, saying he did not want to further endanger his Indigenous and political supporters, Evo Morales went into exile, first to Mexico, then on to Argentina. MAS supporters charged that the United States, which had been involved in encouraging separatism in the Santa Cruz region early in Morales's presidency, was part of a conspiracy to overthrow him. The U.S. interest, Morales's supporters said, is partly in Bolivia's subsoil. The country possesses rare-earth minerals in growing demand for high-tech manufacturing, including cell phones. The United States did not recognize the events as a coup, but the destitution of Morales fits the profile of many recent irregular changes of regime in Latin America. They happen where the military does not act autonomously but in support or concert with political opponents of the regime (see chapters 10 and 14). All the recent "coups" have come from the right.

Following Morales's flight, and with him the vice president and other MAS officials in the government, there followed a short period of anarchy, without an obvious constitutional replacement. Stepping into the breech, by design or not, was Jeanine Añez Chávez, the second vice president of the Senate, a leader of Bolivia's far right that fanned the flames of anti-Indigenous sentiment throughout the violent protests. Añez is married to Luis Fernando Camacho, an ultra-conservative Protestant evangelical and lawyer from Santa Cruz who also has ties to paramilitary forces that were deployed against Andean coca growers and other Indigenous groups in the region around that city. During the coup, Camacho went to the government palace in La Paz and vowed that Pachamama (Andean Mother Earth goddess) would never return. He placed a Bible on the Bolivian flag as Morales opponents burned the Wipala, the symbolic flag of plurinationalism, on the streets. Añez and her supporters were already making clear they intended to turn back the clock on Morales's nationalistic investment promises, cultural and political advances made by Indigenous groups (especially autonomy).

As I prepare this third edition, plans were being made by Añez to hold new elections in May 2020. Añez originally said she would only be a transitional leader, but she later declared herself a candidate. Morales and many key MAS leaders were in exile, but in the face of threats, jailing, and violence, the MAS was preparing to run candidates. Morales himself was living in exile in nearby Argentina and preparing to run for the Senate.

Regardless of the outcome, the future of the country looks tense. Even if Morales and the MAS were to make a comeback, the ultra-Christian *criollos* have shown they do not intend to accept a plurinational Bolivia, while Indigenous groups, including many who were alienated from Morales and protested the 2019 election, were seeing that they had underestimated the breadth and depth of the racial prejudice in the traditional elite.

Point/Counterpoint

It may be too late to save it in any event, but do you think that plurinationalism makes sense for Bolivia? Do you think that this idea has contributed to the threat that the country will ultimately come apart, or do you see it as the only solution to preserve it?

What do you think is more important for a census? Is it to count people by how they identify themselves or by other criteria, such as the language they speak or their ancestry? Is there any kind of compromise that might work for this purpose? Remember, the census has much to do with how political representation is structured, whether a region qualifies for autonomy, and other matters.

For More Information

Several documentaries at Journeyman.tv look at Bolivia's Indigenous politics. *Bolivian Voices* (2008) looks at the rise of Indigenous influence, whereas *Two Bolivias* (2007) features critical reactions to Indigenous demands. The short (less than seven-minute) piece *The Struggle for a New Constitution* (2008) shows how complicated Indigenous politics can be. Katie Kuhn sees the emergence of Indigenous influence as a good thing but questions where plurinationalism is workable in "Identify Versus Unity: Solving Problems in a Country with 36 Nations," *Diplomacy and Foreign Affairs* (n.d., http://diplomacyandforeignaffairs.com/identity-versus-unity-solving-common-problems-in-a-country-with-36-nations).

Colonial Legacy: Afro-Descendent Politics

As with the case of Indigenous peoples, the social questions that arise are not simply ethnic but also touch on social class and regional differences. In Brazil and Cuba, almost everyone is Afro-descendent, meaning there is some connection to enslaved ancestors in their genetic makeup. So when we say that the Brazilian census for the first time in 2010 revealed that a majority consider themselves non-white, this could be because of differential birthrates over time, or it could be because people have changed how they think about their ancestry, their identity. In Cuba, the 1959 revolution did not target Afro-Cubans for special treatment, but programs to improve literacy, education, and rural conditions disproportionately benefited the darker-skinned population, who, we saw in chapter 2, make up much of the poorest people in Latin America. Conversely, as the Cuban state has created more space for markets, private property, and employment, lighter-skinned Cubans, many of whom have relatives in the United States willing to send help with money and gifts, are better able to take advantage. Not only does this connection improve their standard of living, it also provides resources to start small businesses when the rules allow.

Venezuela has a substantial number of ***pardos*** (racially mixed) people in its population, but the greatest African influence is most pronounced on its northeast coast, Barlovento, where cacao plantations were the backbone of the colonial economy. After the victory of Hugo Chávez, a *pardo*, in the 1998 election, darker-skinned Venezuelans began to press for more explicit recognition in the new constitution of their distinct cultural identity and of their needs. Like their Brazilian counterparts, they were protesting against the myth of racial democracy. Indigenous peoples were allocated three seats in the national legislature, and some Afro-descendent people feel they merited similar consideration, some kind of guarantee of representation. But even in the favorable context provided by Chávez's victory, they failed to achieve formal recognition in the new (1999) constitution. Some progress was made in incorporating African influence in history education and culture, and Chávez's programs aimed at alleviating poverty disproportionately held by Afro-descendant people, but Jesús Chucho García, a leading spokesperson for the Afro-Venezuelan movement and a supporter of Chávez, complained,

> We, the African-Venezuelan organizations, made a formal proposal for the constitutional assembly . . . There was someone from the left—racism does not respect ideologies—who said, "the articles for the Indigenous already caused so many problems, are we now going to put something in for the blacks? No, we can't do that." Still, in the original constitutional proposal that Chavez had made there was a reference to those of African descent, but it and our proposal were completely taken out by the left. By the left! Because they did not understand the problem.
>
> (quoted in Wilpert 2004)

He went on to say that afterward, as key new laws were passed, such as those dealing with land reform and education, once again problems specific to Afro-Venezuelans were not addressed.

> And since we don't appear in the organic [semi-constitutional] laws, we don't appear in the programs of government institutions. For example, in the ministry of social development, there is a program to support ethnic diversity. If you look at the program, the only type of ethnic diversity it refers to are the Indigenous peoples, but African ethnicity does not appear. . . . So, as you can see, there is a racial exclusion,

discrimination, from a juridical perspective and in the area of public policy. This is one of the great challenges that this revolution has to deal with. There is no real, profound, sincere revolution without the incorporation of the issue of African descent.

(quoted in Wilpert 2004)

García was not opposing recognition of Indigenous autonomy but claiming that descendants of enslaved peoples deserve recognition of their particular identity and the impact of enslavement and subsequent discrimination.

The issue of racial equality can go to the heart of what it means to be a citizen, as illustrated by the terribly complicated issue of land ownership throughout Latin America. In the colonial era, the Crown and the Church often set aside and defended land rights for Indigenous peoples. Rebellions and financial calamity could result in land changing hands, but with those deposed insisting that they still held legal title. Over centuries, land was often bought and sold in irregular ways; multiple deeds for the same parcel came into existence. This laid the basis for land conflict not only in rural areas, but also in urban areas. As relatively sleepy towns grew into major cities, poor people were often expelled from city centers to the outskirts, where they built their own housing on parcels of land that were never registered as theirs or, even worse, were registered to someone else in the form of a deed in some dusty church or municipal archive, laying the basis later for a real estate speculator. This process was often repeated as the small cities became metropolitan areas with millions of people, with half or more living in homes without verifiable legal documents to back them up.

The link to race here is that those living on such parcels, expelled from the city centers and later from other urban areas that became valuable real estate with economic and population growth, are disproportionately non-white. The Brazilian case is instructive. James Holston (2008) notes that Brazilian definitions of citizenship, unlike in North America, allowed for different kinds of citizens, with differences closely related to race. In the colonial era, the government allowed land to be deeded only to residents with sufficient economic means to work it, virtually excluding not only Afro-Brazilians but many freed blacks and *pardos* ("browns") as well. With a huge landmass and small population, "free" but unequal citizens could usually migrate to vacant land or to land owned but not used; in other words, once such land became valuable for agriculture or commercial development, the settlers could have their right to live there challenged. Whites, generally with more resources and lawyers at their disposal, could win out (though they also battled with one another).

Examination of one land-dispute case involving attempts to displace poor residents of a neighborhood of São Paulo (Holston 2008) found that the conflict had multiple sides, including divisions among those fighting to keep their homes. So too were there divisions within the side seeking to evict residents from their homes. They fought one another to establish a dubious legal ownership over the land. Some hoped to collect rents from residents in disputed buildings; other simply wanted a payoff through a negotiated settlement. The situation was made even more complicated by swindlers who were expert at using courts and records to establish supposed "ownership" over large swaths of the neighborhood. Holston (2008: 205) says,

> I soon discovered that no one could make much sense of the dispute in question without following it back in time. Litigants, lawyers, judges, residents, and swindlers themselves study its genealogies to base their present-day arguments on the authority of history, which dates back to 1580.

São Paulo had grown from a small city of 30,000 around 1870 to a megalopolis of over 11 million. Along the way, poor people, mostly black and *pardo*, were successively expelled from the communities they had built to the periphery, building the *favelas*, as the city's urban slums are known.

The result in this struggle was not, as so often seems to be the case, defeat for the poor, but Holton was more interested in an aspect of the struggle over land. He concluded that the illegality and uncertainty in which people in São Paulo live today ignited a broader demand for full equality and inclusion as citizens. The Brazilian struggle to transition from a military dictatorship to an elected democracy in the 1980s (see chapter 7) was rooted in strong social movements that elevated Afro-Brazilians and *pardos* to political leadership. This included former president Luiz Inácio Lula da Silva (Lula) and Senator Benedita da Silva, both of whom would reach the presidency in the 2000s. In struggles like the one in São Paulo, Brazilians began to practice "insurgent citizenship," challenging their historical exclusion—politically but also socially and economically. This exclusion had been built on the foundations of colonialism, slavery, and a system of law designed to ensure that political equality would not shake the social order—racial and class-based—inherited from the past. That has led Brazilians to be much more open than are North Americans, for example, to affirmative action programs that use quotas to increase the numbers of Afro-Brazilians in universities (see the Punto de Vista in chapter 2, "Does Brazil Need Affirmative Action?").

Before we move away from the topic of race and class, I think it important not to leave you with the impression that there is a strict correlation between race and social class in Latin America. One can find lighter-skinned people in poor urban neighborhoods or eking out a living on small plots of land in northeast Brazil. Similarly, few members of the upper class are without Indigenous or African ancestry. The myths of racial democracy and of *mestizaje* persist in part because there is truth in the idea that Latin Americans are more comfortable with social and biological racial mixing than are most people in the United States. But at the same time, we should be wary when this positive aspect of social relations leads to denial that race matters in Latin America.

For Review

Why might a Latin American person's sense of his or her own ethnic identity change, even if the person's skin color and other biological features have not? What are some ways that people turn to history in arguing about issues today in Latin America?

Colonial Roots of Economic Dependency

Of course, the original impulse for Europeans to conquer the Americas rested in economics. Although religious motives were present as well, the Spanish and Portuguese crowns were seeking wealth to consolidate control over the Iberian Peninsula and to finance wars with other European powers. Clearly, we would be failing to understand the legacy of colonialism if we did not make reference to the way that Europeans sought to put their colonies at the service of the "mother country."

In the United States, most schoolchildren learn that one of the causes of the American Revolution was the colonists' resistance to attempts by the English Crown to restrict trade with other countries and limit which ships could carry goods in and out of North American harbors. These restrictive policies were even more rigid and harshly enforced in colonial Latin America, especially in the case of the Spanish colonies. For example, the Spanish Crown would not even let its colonies produce olive oil, requiring instead that they import it from Spain. Economic and political forces combined to create a system of **monoculture** whereby distinct regions in Latin America specialized in the production of a single particular product—cacao, sugar, hemp, and so on.

Thus, the imperial powers limited the ability of their colonies to produce and trade with one another or to import products from rival European powers. This pattern of monoculture and the export of raw materials (beginning with precious metals, and later plantation crops and minerals) and the import of finished goods from abroad set a pattern of economic **dependency**, which many Latin Americans believe is the most significant cause of underdevelopment. Latin America's economic fortunes remain highly dependent on exports.

The reorganization of Indigenous social systems to extract and export raw materials and agricultural products contributed to the devastation of the population and set a pattern for the centuries that followed. As Elizabeth Dore (1991) once put it,

> Because pre-Columbian societies deified nature and were organized to provide food security, their material and ideological structures generated a profound respect for the environment. Despite their significant differences, Maya, Aztec, Inca, and less numerous native peoples each shared key attributes: ruling classes appropriated surplus labor in the form of food (later distributed in times of scarcity), their cosmology was explicitly linked to the material order, and survival was precarious and highly dependent on preserving the eco-system.

During the colonial era, Latin America was integrated into an emerging world system as an exploited area of what theorists such as Immanuel Wallerstein (1974) call the "**periphery.**" This integration meant that Latin America became one of several regions where for centuries a highly exploited labor force produced primary goods (agricultural goods and minerals) for export, exchanging them in the world trading system for more costly manufactured goods. The roots of Latin America's underdevelopment lay here, say dependency and **world systems** theorists.

The Europeans and the European-oriented ruling class (*criollos*) that succeeded the original Iberian masters viewed the New World as a source of wealth. They viewed nature as a woman to be conquered, another reason some call the conquest the "rape" of a continent. Consider the famous boast of Simón Bolívar, the great liberator of South America, who said in 1812 after an earthquake devastated Caracas, "If nature opposes us, we will struggle against her and make her obey."

Earlier, I cited Mann's observation that sometimes we romanticize Indigenous culture and fail to recognize that the "first nations," as the Canadians call them, did not always live in harmony with nature. There can be little doubt, however, that Indigenous people in the Americas had neither the capacity nor the will to conquer nature, much as Europeans had by 1500. Although environmental consciousness and respect for traditional knowledge has increased in recent years, for many Latin Americans (perhaps for everyone else as well) the bounty of nature still exists mainly to be exploited: If a country wishes to progress, it must open that bounty to investment. If domestic capital and technology is lacking, the goal should be to remove obstacles that prevent foreigners from investing and promoting **modernization**. Now, in the age of globalization, many economists say that those countries that open their economies will prosper; those that close them will come to grief. To some Latin Americans, this sounds too much like a recipe for environmental disaster and continuing dependency.

The colonial era lasted 500 years; the postcolonial era has barely reached two centuries. Still, this is a significant passage of time—enough for Latin America, much like North America, to seek its own path forward, less encumbered by the negative aspects of colonialism, but not completely free of the shackles it has left. Indeed, independence has permitted Latin Americans to escape some of the severe consequences of colonialism in the nineteenth and twentieth centuries, but at the same time few would argue that the legacy of economic dependency has been overcome.

Discussion Questions

1. What does it mean to be a "Latin" American? Do you think it makes any sense to describe as "Latin" people as diverse as an Aymara Indian from Bolivia, a descendant of slaves in Cuba, a white landowner in Chile, and an entrepreneur descended from Asian or Arab immigrants in Venezuela? Are nations nothing more than imagined communities?

2. Find a video (e.g., on YouTube) of the popular singer Shakira, who is partially of Arab descent. Find a biography of her on the web. How would you characterize her place in the racial/class pyramid of Latin America? Do you consider her music to be Latin?

3. Latin American *criollos* came to want independence—that is, territorial sovereignty. What did most of them *not* want to happen with independence?

4. Part of the legacy of colonialism is that Indigenous peoples and Afro-descendent peoples still disproportionately populate the ranks of the poor and indigent. Do you think that the persistence of this state of affairs (hardly unknown in the United States, we should acknowledge) is a sign of democratic failure?

Resources for Further Study

Reading: *The Villagers* (*Huasipungo*), by Jorge Icaza, translated by Bernard Dulsey (Edwardsville: Southern Illinois University Press, 1964), is a novel exploring the life of Indigenous people in Ecuador under the *latifundia* system. *Women in the Crucible of Conquest*, edited by Karen Vieira Powers (University of New Mexico, 2005), tells how some women resisted dominance and made a place for themselves in colonial society. *Colonial Legacies: The Problem of Persistence in Latin American History*, edited by Jeremy Adelman (New York: Routledge, 1999), deals with the impacts and influences of colonial life on Latin America today and its likely future relevance. One way to understand the clash between republican values and Creole fears of social upheaval is through the life of Simón Bolívar. A good recent biography is *American Liberator* by Marie Arana (New York: Simon and Schuster 2013).

Video and Film: *The Mission* (1986), set in colonial Brazil, explores the complex relationship between the Church and exploitation of Indigenous people. One of the most important examples of Indigenous politics is Bolivia's first Indigenous president, Evo Morales. A 2008 Tuttle Films documentary, *Bolivian Voices* (www.journeyman.tv/58726/documentaries/bolivian-voices.html) explores Evo Morales's biography and his rise to the presidency of Bolivia. It also ponders a future under his political guidance and notes mixed feelings of anticipation and hope. The documentary *Cocalero* (2007) looks at the movement that brought him to prominence. *También la lluvia* ("Even the Water," 2010) links Spanish colonialism to a modern-day conflict over control of water supplies in Bolivia. *A Place Called Chiapas* (1985), about the Zapatista uprising, can now be viewed on YouTube. Controversy about the Wiphala, the Indigenous flag, is the subject of this news report from Taiwan TV (TITTV): www.youtube.com/watch?v=c6MGKbzFG38. *Buried Mirror* (1994), from the PBS Americas series, focuses on identity in Latin America.

On the Internet: For women and feminism, along with some broader information on gender in Latin America, a good site is livguides.rutgers.edu/LAfeminisms. Perhaps no region is so rich in Afro-Latin history as Bahia, in northeast Brazil (see http://isc.temple.edu/evanson/brazilhistory/Bahia.htm).

4 Political Without Economic Independence

Focus Questions

▶ Why after political independence did most of the social and economic patterns established by colonialism persist?

▶ Why did Portuguese America—that is, Brazil—not break up into smaller nations the way that Spanish America did? How different is Brazilian politics today as a result?

▶ What were the political, social, and economic consequences of the shift of dependency from Iberian Europe to Northern Europe?

▶ Why did countries in the region struggle to establish stable republics, and why did state-building eventually emerge in the final decades of the nineteenth century?

HOW MUCH DIFFERENCE did political independence from Spain and Portugal make in the lives of most Latin Americans? The social class structure stayed largely intact; the majority of Latin Americans remained mired in poverty; and various cultural institutions, including the Catholic Church, retained their privileges. However, in Spanish America the disappearance of the colonial power left a vacuum of power that in most of the new countries was not filled for many decades. Civil war was not unknown in the colonial era, but the Crown provided a degree of political stability. The aftermath of independence saw the rise of **caudillism**, a tendency that continues to mark Latin American politics today. On the other side of the ledger, independence did result in Latin Americans achieving a sovereign status denied to peoples subject to nineteenth-century European imperialism in Africa, Asia, and the Middle East, and it opened the way for a degree of economic and social development in the later 1800s.

The Path to Independence in Spanish America

The roots of independence were multiple. Part of the story was a growing sense of self-confidence among *criollos*, whose economic interests were diverging in the late 1700s from those of the Iberian homeland (see Table 4.1). World events, such as the American and French revolutions and the decline of Spanish power, pushed them further toward that objective. By the eighteenth century, the upper classes of colonial society were 200 years removed from their

TABLE 4.1 Chronology of the Nineteenth Century

1830s	Rise of *caudillos*, civil wars in most countries.
1823–1855	Santa Anna, a *caudillo*, presides over chronically unstable Mexican Republic. Loses Texas in war (1833) with the breakaway republic, later absorbed into U.S. Defeats French forces occupying Veracruz (1838).
1846–1848	Mexican American War culminates in Treaty of Guadalupe Hidalgo, ceding half of Mexican territory to U.S. Mayan Rebellion ("Caste War") suppressed in Yucatán region.
1855	U.S. adventurer (known as a filibuster) William Walker invades and occupies Nicaragua, rules as president for two years, is undermined by forces backed by Andrew Carnegie, and is executed by Hondurans in 1860.
1858–1861	War between Liberals and Conservatives in Mexico.
1862–1864	French Army invades Mexico and sets the rule of Austrian archduke Maximilian in alliance with the Conservatives.
1867	Liberal armies defeat French, Maximilian executed; Benito Juárez becomes president of restored republic.
1864–1870	Brazil, Argentina, and Uruguay (Triple Alliance), backed by British, defeats Paraguay in bloodiest international war, resulting in (estimated) deaths of 300,000 to 500,000 Paraguayans.
1868–1878	Unsuccessful wars for independence in Cuba and Puerto Rico.
1876	Porfirio Díaz takes power, rules Mexico until 1911.
1879–1884	Chile, backed by British, defeats Peru and Bolivia in War of the Pacific, seizes nitrate-rich northern desert.
1888	Abolition of slavery in Brazil.
1889	Pedro II abdicates, Brazil is declared a republic.
1895	José Martí leads a war for Cuban independence but is killed in this year.
1897	Brutal repression (15,000–30,000 killed) in Bahia, Brazil, of Canudos, where thousands of poor peasants had flocked to join movement led by religious mystic and radical.
1898	Spanish American War, United States controls Puerto Rico, Cuba, Guam, and Philippines.

conquistador ancestors. Within the protective umbrella of Spanish and Portuguese military forces, they had begun to experience a degree of local control over their affairs, especially in *cabildos* (town councils) in Spanish America.

Two rising powers in Northern Europe, France and Britain, knew that control of the Iberian countries brought with it the benefits of its vast American empire. *Criollos* had already seen the French Bourbon dynasty replace the Hapsburgs in 1700, and Spanish forces suffered a humiliating defeat at the hands of the British in the War of the Spanish Succession (1701–1713). The *criollo* ruling class in both Portuguese and Spanish America began to seek more freedom to trade outside the confines of the colonial system. Although gold and silver were still being mined, commodities such as sugar, cacao, coffee, rice, grains, and leather, among others, were increasingly in demand. And when the Industrial Revolution took off, first in Britain (around 1780) and later in other parts of Europe, Latin America's raw materials were in demand.

The Bourbons tried to stanch the decline of the empire by making it easier for colonial exports to enter Spanish ports, but they also cracked down on smuggling and illegal trade, which threatened the *criollos'* access to growing markets in Northern Europe. To improve efficiency and fight corruption, the Bourbons centralized administration in the colonies. Just as *criollos* were seeking new opportunities and markets for their exports, the Crown was reinforcing its monopoly on governance. These policies generated resentment among the colonial elite, who were eager to trade freely and control their own affairs. This resentment smoldered again in 1767, when the Crown expelled the Jesuit order, seizing its property and pocketing profits after selling it. Many *criollos* had been educated in Jesuit institutions.

Criollo enthusiasm for independence was held in check by fears of social rebellion by the lower orders. Indigenous resistance to the conquest had never been entirely extinguished. Slavery, **peonage**, and other forms of exploitation required deployments of armies over vast territories to put down revolts. Mass uprisings punctuated the late colonial period. In 1780, a *mestizo* who took the name Tupac Amaru II, after the last Inca emperor, sparked an uprising that blazed across Peru, putting many *hacendados* (landowners) to death and burning their estates. There followed in 1781 the Revolt of the Comuneros, as the inhabitants of present-day Colombia and Venezuela were known at the time. This rebellion started as a *criollo*-led tax revolt and evolved into a mass revolt of Indigenous peoples. These and other revolts (e.g., see Hidalgo's revolt in Mexico, described later) are often celebrated in Latin America today as precursors of independence, but they inspired fear in Creoles.

The American Revolution in 1776 inspired thoughts of independence and admiration for liberalism among some *criollos*, but the French Revolution of 1789 and its political ramifications in Europe had an even greater impact. By 1800, revolutionary idealism had given way in France to dictatorship and empire. The French ruler and conqueror, Napoleon Bonaparte, threatened to overrun Spain and Portugal altogether and impose liberal ideas by force. In Spain, regional governments proclaimed self-government under *cabildos* (councils) or **juntas**, a word that would later become synonymous with temporary rule after the overthrow of a government. Many Creoles looked to fill the vacuum of legitimacy in Spain. Napoleon's main rival, Great Britain, encouraged them to opt for independence.

In the Viceroyalty of New Granada (modern-day Colombia, Bolivia, Ecuador, Venezuela, and parts of Peru), the leader of the *criollo* revolt was Francisco Miranda, who had participated in both the American and French revolutions. The political earthquake in France gave momentum to the idea that people with a common national identity have a right to sovereignty. Miranda's revolt of 1810 was centered in the Spanish captaincy of Venezuela. It was crushed by the colonial governor, who supplemented Spanish troops with an army he raised by promising freedom and land to slaves and peons. The Spanish quickly forgot these promises to the masses (setting a pattern for the next century) and also exacted brutal retribution on many of the *criollos*.

The defeat of Napoleon's army in 1814 brought to the Spanish throne Ferdinand VII, whose father had been deposed by the French. He moved to restore Spanish colonial authority and deployed troops—now freed from the European conflicts—to South America. But European powers, notably Great Britain, were now actively aiding rebel *criollos* with money and arms. The struggle for independence in Spanish America evolved into a prolonged, violent civil war. Miranda's mantle of leadership was picked up by another *criollo*, Simón Bolívar, a brilliant military tactician who bravely marched his army over the Andes to spread the fight throughout New Granada. In Argentina the fight was led by José de San Martín, whose tactical military genius and promises of freedom for slaves and peons allowed him to raise a formidable army by 1816. San Martín swept northward and met up with Bolívar's forces in 1822 in Guayaquil, Ecuador. The cause of Pan-Americanism (unity after independence), championed by Bolívar, was dealt a blow when the leaders failed to agree on a political formula for governing the newly independent lands. San Martín retired into relative obscurity, whereas Bolívar's forces completed the revolt, scoring the final decisive victory at the Battle of Ayacucho in Peru, in 1824.

In Mexico, a defrocked priest, Miguel Hidalgo, issued his *Grito de Dolores* ("Cry of Sorrows") in 1810 and launched a movement for independence. A huge mass of poor, mostly Indigenous Mexican rebels swept down from the north toward the capital of Mexico City. The popular army burned all in its path and summarily executed the Spanish *peninsulares*, the name given to officials sent by the Crown to govern the colony. Here was the nightmare that the Creoles had feared! Frightened, they turned to Spain to restore order.

A second mass uprising in Mexico followed, led by another priest, José María Morelos. Like Hidalgo, Morelos promised to improve the lot of miners and Indian villagers who were losing common lands to renters favored by village leaders. Morelos fought more in the style of a modern guerrilla leader. After he was captured, tried (like Hidalgo, in a church court), and shot in 1815, the revolt continued, though with less force than before. Then an unexpected group decided to seek independence. Conservative Creoles were angered because the Spanish government, briefly in the hands of liberals, abolished some of their military and religious privileges. The Conservatives then made an offer of peace to the main rebel leader, Vicente Guerrero, which paved the way for Mexican independence. It was not Guerrero but General Agustín de Iturbide, a conservative, who took control, proclaiming himself Emperor Agustín I. Thus, Mexico's first generation of leaders broke from Spain not because they rejected monarchy but in defense of it! Most of Mesoamerica broke from Spain around 1830, with support from independent Mexico.

The Haitian Revolution of 1787 quelled Creole ardor for independence in most of the Caribbean. The islands seethed with slave revolts and social unrest, but Cuba and Puerto Rico remained under Spanish rule. Havana, Cuba, was the most important military and economic outpost of Spain's empire in the Americas, which meant that the empire's military power was most concentrated and effective there. As Spain proved increasingly impotent to maintain order, many elites saw the United States, which maintained slavery in its southern states, as a substitute. The United States' defeat of Spain in the war of 1898 ended Spanish rule, but the occupation of the island thwarted native Cuban hopes for more radical social and economic change (see chapter 8). Cuban rebels had been near victory when the U.S. invasion brought occupation instead of national liberation, cutting off the aspirations for deeper social change advocated by the Cuban independence movement. Puerto Rico never gained sovereign independence.

For Review

What are some ways that events in Europe affected the Americas? What internal and external factors in Latin America ultimately reinforced the emergence of an independence movement and the shift of Creoles in support of it?

▮ Brazil's Divergent Path to Independence

Brazil took a different route to independence, one that was less abrupt and violent and did not result in the breakup of the colonial territory. However, as in Spanish America, political sovereignty for the Portuguese colony did not produce a decisive break with patterns of economic dependence, and the chasm separating the masses from the elite remained. In the colonial era, Brazil's vast territory was populated by a mere four million people; almost all lived not far from the coast, and half of them were slaves. Many enslaved workers fled the mines and plantations to the interior, where they often intermarried with Indigenous people, and slave rebellions were frequent. One of these in Salvador, Bahia, in 1835 was organized by free and enslaved Afro-Brazilians inspired by Muslim thought, which they had brought from their homeland in what is now Nigeria, and by the independence struggle in Haiti. They wore amulets with the image of Haitian president Dessalines, who had declared that country's independence in 1804.

The Portuguese colonial administration operated more on its own authority than did Spain's, but authorities in Brazil had to be constantly on guard against encroachment by the Spanish in the south and by the British, Dutch, and French in the north. The Northern European powers took advantage of Portuguese weakness to establish three colonial enclaves along the north coast of the mainland of South America (British, French, and Dutch Guyana). Europe maintained colonial outposts in most of their Caribbean possessions (Curacao, Haiti, Grenada, Jamaica, Martinique, etc.). Even the smallest of these colonies were lucrative plantation economies, possessed of ideal conditions for growing sugar, which had once been an aristocratic luxury and was fast becoming a mass consumption staple in the cupboards of the expanding working and middle classes. Many of these territories would finally achieve political independence after World War II.

In the late colonial era, Portugal, like Spain, attempted to tighten control over its American colony in the face of the challenge from the Northern European powers. This fueled the desire of some Brazilian elites for independence, but as in other parts of the Americas, there was the matter of slavery and social rebellion to consider. Brazilian elites had their problem solved temporarily and unexpectedly when Napoleon invaded Portugal in 1807 and the Lisbon court fled to Rio de Janeiro. Now the capital of a European empire was located in the Americas! The Portuguese prince regent, João, opened trade, permitted local industries, and founded a national bank. In 1815, he declared Brazil to be equal in status to Portugal. A revolution in Portugal in 1820 paved the way for João to return to the motherland, but he left his son and heir, Dom Pedro, behind to rule Brazil. In 1822, Dom Pedro refused an order from Portugal to return home, and thus the new nation of Brazil was born—like Mexico, as a monarchy.

A superficial examination of Brazilian history suggests the country evolved toward independence without civil war and subsequently with more stability than most Latin American countries. The myth persists that Brazil marched progressively toward democracy: from colony to a constitutional monarchy with an elected parliament sharing power, and then to a full republic in 1889. However, as in Spanish America, Brazil's nineteenth century was punctuated by slave revolts and movements for land by the poor free population. The collapse of the monarchy and establishment of a republic was accompanied by social strife caused by the question of slavery, which was abolished only in 1888, a year before the monarchy came to an end.

From 1889 to 1930, Brazil was formally a republic, with legislatures, civil courts, elected executives, and so on—but not a very democratic one. Of a population of 22 million people, only 360,000 voted in the 1910 presidential election. In 1890, the leaders of the new Brazilian republic established a literacy test as a prerequisite for voting—similar to what whites did in the U.S. South after the Civil War. Even after abolition, land remained concentrated in a few hands. Race became less of a barrier to social acceptance and ascent in Brazil than it was in the United States, but as in the U.S. Afro-Brazilians remain (see chapter 2) disproportionately poor. For most, life expectancy was extremely low, and schooling beyond second grade was almost nonexistent. Staying alive was a day-to-day struggle, and citizenship meant little in that context.

In the Brazilian hinterland, the social structure was semifeudal. An oligarchy made up of former slave owners monopolized the land. For the "right" to work small plots to feed themselves, their tenants had to provide personal or military service to the landowners. They were kept in line by Brazil's version of the *caudillo*, the *coronel*, a warlord with his private army of full soldiers. *Coroneles* often fought one another, sometimes with or against bands of bandits who became popular Robin Hood figures. Quasi-religious movements of the landless poor periodically broke out and were brutally suppressed. Brazil's social structure had a "medieval atmosphere of constant insecurity and social disintegration" (Keen and Haynes 2000: 241).

The best-known episode of resistance and suppression took place in the state of Bahia, an arid region populated by ex-slaves, mulattos, and Indigenous peoples. Bahia's marginal geography, far from populated centers with established government and without economic resources, failed to attract much attention from central authorities in the more prosperous south. Its desperately poor inhabitants often turned toward mystical figures—saviors or messiahs who could lead them to a better life on earth or afterward.

Antônio Vicente Mendes Maciel, also known as "the Counselor," was such a man, presenting himself as a prophet predicting the return of a mythological Portuguese king who would redeem the people of the region. Maciel and some followers founded a town, Canudos, and based on his promises of an imminent better world, thousands flocked to the new settlement. Suddenly, the Church and provincial authorities took notice and began to fear sedition. Their fear increased, and the Counselor's legend grew. Two initial attempts to disband the settlers were met with devastating defeats and massacres suffered by police and troops sent by the Republic (as Brazil's government was known), with the rebel forces shouting praise for monarchy. By this time, Canudos's population exceeded 30,000. Another (third) unsuccessful attempt was made to quash the town, at great loss of life on both sides. In September 1897, the government launched a full-scale military campaign, with well-trained troops, modern arms, and professional planning. On October 2, 1897, after additional fierce fighting, Canudos was destroyed, with only 150 survivors (Levine 1995). Estimates of total casualties range from 15,000 to 30,000.

The revolt of the Comuneros, the Haitian Revolution, the Mexican mass rebellions led by priests, and the uprisings in Canudos, and many others, are today part of Latin American historical memory. How they are memorialized can burst into political controversy. In the 1920s, after an abortive coup in Brazil, young army lieutenants led by Luis Carlos Prestes marched through the countryside, attracting tens of thousands of poor peasants, evoking the hopes and fears that had been crushed at Canudos a quarter century before. More recently, landless peasants have organized themselves into the Landless Workers' Movement

(Movimento dos Trabalhadores Sem Terra, or MST), again evoking memories of past agrarian uprisings. While these latter movements lack the religious overtones of Canudos, they were in the tradition of mass risings of poor rural sectors against social exclusion.

Popular culture often bestows heroic characteristics on figures who were little more than bandits, as was the case in Brazil with the renegades known as "Lampião" (Virgulino Ferreira da Silva) and María Bonita (María Dea). The two "bandits" were killed by Brazilian troops in 1938, after they had spent 19 years terrorizing local power brokers and landowners. There is little evidence that the two robbers and their band were politically motivated, but they were popularized as avengers of the common person against the arbitrary authority and greed of the wealthy. Lampião and María Bonita are kept alive in ballads and puppet plays in the Sertão (desert of the northeast) and the city of Recife. Bands that play the traditional and popular music, *folha*, in the northeast often wear clothing and symbols evocative of the marauders. Many *corridos* of northern Mexico today celebrate the coyotes, traffickers of people, drugs, and contraband. For the most part the songs are popular with people who feel poor and excluded. They reflect not popular approval of crime but admiration for the bravery and risks they take in defying government enforcers and the U.S. advisors who support them.

For Review

In what ways was Brazil's path to independence different and in what ways similar to that of Spanish America? Why did most of the rebellions against the Spanish stop short of achieving deeper social and economic change?

New Nations, Failed States

Enlightened Latin American leaders were aware that a new colossus was rising on the North American continent, but in the 1800s the power that mattered most in making and breaking Latin American governments was Great Britain. The British navy dominated the world's oceans, and it was the first and only country to have industrialized at the time of Latin America's independence. This gave Britain a decided military and economic advantage in world affairs, which it used to build an enormous empire that spanned Africa, the Middle East, India, and parts of Asia. In the Americas, the British were satisfied with a few Caribbean possessions, the westernmost of the three Guyanas (to which they brought thousands of indentured South Asians), and later Belize (then known as "British Honduras"), which they carved out on the Caribbean coast of Central America. Other European states, notably France, Holland, and Prussia (part of what would become Germany), competed with the British and at times financed or armed factions favorable to their interests. When nationalist regimes in Latin America threatened common European interests (for example, by renouncing a debt), the European powers usually united to protect the system. Loans, trade treaties, arms sales, and gunboats were tools by which Latin American economic dependency shifted from Iberia to the new, dynamic economies of Northern Europe after political independence.

Bolívar had called for unity and **Pan-Americanism** (i.e., awareness of a common identity among all peoples in the region), but the Spanish empire in the Americas broke up. The scale of the empire had something to do with this, as it stretched from California (part of Mexico) in North America to the Antarctic Circle. The Spanish Crown by necessity had divided this vast territory into geographic units for governance, but even these were large relative to the state of transportation, especially given formidable geographic obstacles. Local and regional power centers grew up, and some territories that had united briefly after independence dissolved quickly into smaller sovereign units. The Southern Cone rebellions for independence were against a colonial viceroyalty far away and over the Andes in Lima, Peru. They split into the two large countries of Argentina and Chile, with Uruguay and Paraguay emerging as buffer states between Brazil and Argentina. By 1830, the northern region of the continent had broken apart into five countries—Venezuela, Colombia (including the province of Panama), Ecuador, Bolivia, and Peru (see Figure 4.1). Farther north, southern regions of the greater Mexican empire broke away to form the Central American confederation, which itself splintered rapidly into five (six counting Belize, then part of Guatemala) smaller

FIGURE 4.1   Map of European Possessions of South America

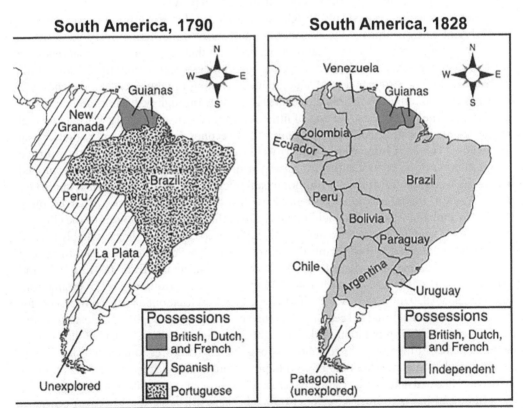

Source: Steven Goldberg and Judith Clark DuPré,
Brief Review in Global History and Geography, Prentice Hall (adapted)

Source: © iStockphoto.com/KURL.

republics—Guatemala, Honduras, El Salvador, Nicaragua, and Costa Rica. Panama would form another Central American republic when it broke away from Colombia in 1903 (with considerable help from the United States, eager to build a canal there with cooperation from a pliant government).

Even these reduced territories were not well integrated territorially and were afflicted by regional revolts against central authority. In most countries, coastal ports were better linked to foreign export markets than to the national capital. Transportation routes were built to connect the hinterlands with these ports, not to enhance economic trade of one region with another or to facilitate effective governance from the political capital. In Argentina, the Spanish had routed all trade to the north and west, over the Andes, to Peru. After independence, tensions between the province of Buenos Aires, with its fine Atlantic port, and the northwestern provinces helped fuel a bitter civil war that ended in dictatorship.

Social and economic conflicts further undermined stability. Landowners often found themselves in conflict with merchant houses in the ports and with banks. Together the merchant houses and the banks controlled two matters vital to the landowners' prosperity: finance and prices for their exported commodities. When overseas demand for exports fell and prices plummeted, landowners faced foreclosure on their property by creditors. Landowners, merchant houses, and banks all turned to the central government for help, leading to grabs for property, bitter political factionalism, and often civil war.

Most Creoles interpreted citizen rights as intended exclusively for themselves and perhaps other literate members of their society, certainly not for the "ignorant" Indians, slaves, and peons. The economic base was land ownership, and their most profitable markets were overseas. Although they were the leading class of an independent nation, they showed little interest in building a strong central state or incorporating the lower classes into political life. Regional economies were linked to overseas markets through ports, but rarely much to one another. The national market was of little importance. The capital city was usually well beyond the horizon, geographically and politically, of economically important regions. Local and regional *caudillos* (*coroneles* in Brazil) were the immediate rulers. Often, they turned on one another or on central authority, raising armies by making promises to the exploited masses. However, central authority was not meaningless. The capital was the most important political link to the international system, giving it military and economic resources, often secured by foreign loans, which could make or break the fortunes of factions of the elite.

Though *caudillos* might seize the capital with their local armies, they inevitably needed support from educated and economically powerful Creoles. Some *caudillos* could not read or write—an example being Rafael Carrera, dictator of Guatemala from 1844 to 1848 and again from 1851 to 1865. Many, such as Juan Manuel de Rosas, strongman of Argentina from approximately 1830 until 1852, were landowners. Others started out as trusted overseers for owners or as vigilantes hired to keep the peace then turned on their employers. Most successful *caudillos* built on their reputation as skilled and fearless fighters to attract large followings of peasants, slaves, or indentured **peons**, hopeful of gaining land or freedom. With this backing, *caudillos* could sometimes fight their way into power, but running a government was another matter, so educated elites in the capital never fully lost influence to military strongmen.

Today, in many countries, regional power brokers still resist the sovereign power of the central government. Brazil is especially notable even today in this respect, a tradition reinforced by federalism. Take the case of Blairo Maggi, first elected in 2002 to be governor of Mato Grosso, Brazil's largest state, located in the heart of the Amazonian basin. He is also known as the "king of soy" because he is the state's biggest landowner and has benefited handsomely from the boom in soybeans, produced in the region for export. As governor, Maggi simply refused to implement the central government's mandates to reduce destruction of the rainforest by curbing logging and clearing for more farms. In 2003, Maggi's first year as governor, the rate of deforestation nearly doubled. The combination of Maggi's economic wealth and Brazil's federalism made Maggi virtually untouchable in his own region, perhaps not a military *coronel*, but virtually sovereign in his own backyard.

In 2009, a Brazilian newspaper columnist (complaining about the use of patronage by President Luiz Inácio da Silva—Lula) described how a traditional *coronel* in the state of Pernambuco once gathered his peasants together on election day and one by one handed out ballots, each conveniently filled out with the *coronel*'s choice of candidates, each placed in a sealed envelope ready to be deposited in the ballot box. "Could the Senhor [Lord] tell me at least for whom we are voting?" asked one of the peasants. "Don't you know that the vote is secret?" the *coronel* responded (Soares 2009).

For Review

How did the phenomena of *caudillos* and *coroneles* arise? How would you explain what enabled such figures to become heads of state in nineteenth-century Latin America? How did they set back the cause of unity and Pan-Americanism that Bolívar wanted? Why did such strong leaders tend to produce weak states?

Rebuilding Nations and States, Modernization

The nineteenth-century Latin American republics were ill-adapted to republican political ideals and, with a few exceptions (e.g., Chile), not very stable politically. Here, by *republic*, we mean states where the authority to govern comes at least theoretically from the people and not directly from god, inheritance, or some other myth. Men and women, like Bolívar, who embraced republicanism were not necessarily representative of Latin America's upper class. Most of the Creoles were repelled by liberal ideals such as separation of church and state, freedom for slaves, mass education, and so on. Of course, the young United States republic failed to implement many of these same ideals, but Latin Americans faced an even more difficult task in constructing a new identity and social order for a diverse people, living in a geographically daunting territory and inheriting a hyperexploitative social structure. Was there one Latin American nation—an ideal expressed by Bolívar as "Pan-Americanism"—or several, as suggested by the proliferation of new republics in the wake of independence?

We are accustomed to thinking of nations as bound together by a common language, culture, race, or ethnicity, but few nation-states of the world have populations in which virtually everyone shares any one of these traits, much less all of them. One unifying factor can be the economic interdependence fostered by a domestic market. Long-distance trade rather than expansion of internal markets gave Europe's monarchies the financial wherewithal to consolidate control over their territory. Their wealth allowed them to create the trappings of and infrastructure for centralized authority—through buildings, the arts, military forces, roads, and so on—over the large territories that would become nations on a map. Spain's Latin American

PUNTO DE VISTA: WHAT CAN WE LEARN FROM PARAGUAY'S UNSUCCESSFUL NINETEENTH-CENTURY BREAK FROM DEPENDENCY?

Latin American history is filled with controversial strongmen who have inspired debate in the present. The debate is not merely confined to academic historians. In popular culture, intellectual salons, and speeches by politicians, these powerful rulers are variously portrayed on the one hand as saints, heroes, or martyrs and on the other hand as devils, cowards, or pathological tyrants.

Perhaps no historical personality has been so shrouded by negatives or positives than José Gaspar Rodríguez de Francia, a leader of Paraguay's struggle for independence (1811) from Spain, who afterward became dictator of that country from 1814 to his death in 1840.

Francia was a complete autocrat who became known as "El Supremo." Most historians describe the dictator as a mentally unbalanced political caricature, but others suspect his idiosyncrasies were exaggerated by his enemies. Francia was austere in dress and customs and determined to make over his country's social and economic structures. He removed Creoles from their positions of power, redistributed land, and stimulated economic development without foreign credits. One hundred years before the Russian Revolution, Francia expropriated large estates, converted them into state property, and rented land cheaply to those willing to till it. He used his power to create an economy in which common people lived better than in most other Latin American countries. He placed emphasis on production of crops consumed at home by Indigenous people and *mestizos*. Almost unique in Latin America, Paraguay became self-sufficient in food.

Francia ruled Paraguay from 1811 until his death in 1840. He was a child of the French Revolution and made an enemy of the Catholic Church. He confiscated its property and abolished tithes paid to the clergy. His government established iron, textile, and livestock industries, employing thousands. Blockaded by Argentina from exporting their production out to the Atlantic, Paraguayans traded overland with other Latin American countries. This trade was carefully regulated through licenses. Neither large-scale foreign investments nor debts were accumulated.

However, the country was far from a political democracy. Francia repressed all dissent; his dungeons were notorious.

Francia's experiment began to take hold to some degree in another region, land disputed by Argentina and Brazil that would become Uruguay. A *caudillo* named José Artigas sought to distribute land formerly belonging to supporters of the Spanish Crown to blacks, Indigenous people, poor whites, and mixed-race peoples. Brazil invaded in 1817 and put an end to the experiment. Brazil occupied the region until 1828, when it was forced by Great Britain, who wanted neither Argentina nor Brazil to control the territory, to give it sovereignty as Uruguay.

Francia's successors kept his experiment going until 1870. Neighboring countries, ruled by traditional elites, looked at Paraguay with alarm, and so did Great Britain, the dominant world power. What if other South American countries tried so boldly to break away from the **free trade** model that Britain sought to maintain? Francia's dictatorial ways, though hardly unusual in the region, were fodder for effective propaganda and revulsion abroad.

Brazil, Argentina, and Uruguay, financed by Great Britain, crushed the experiment in the War of the Triple Alliance (1864–1870), a holocaust that nearly exterminated Paraguay's entire male population, including nearly all adults of the native Guaraní population. The victors occupied Paraguay for five years and completely reversed the system that had generated a higher standard of living and more productive economy than had any of its neighbors.

Countries that embark on revolutionary experiments at odds with the prevailing economic models and interests of wealthy nations can expect to be targets of subversion from domestic opponents allied with foreign powers. Fidel Castro attempted to escape the fate of Francia's successors by allying himself with a great power, the former Soviet Union, which was eager to compete with the world's dominant power, the United States. An economic embargo imposed by the United States, including pressure on other countries to do the same, forced Cuba to develop alternative trading networks and look at alternative, state-controlled economic institutions—although the Cuban economy has yet to demonstrate it can produce economic prosperity.

Although much of the anti-Castro rhetoric in the United States is aimed at Cuba's lack of Western-style democracy, it is arguably Cuba's attempt to experiment with a more autonomous economic development model at odds with most of the region that attracts such hostility from the United States.

Georges Fournial, a twentieth-century Paraguayan intellectual, called Francia "a despicable, bloody tyrant that submitted his people for 26 years to the most ferocious terror, and also isolated his people from the outside world, condemning Paraguay to its miserable fate." But other commentators praised his economic plans. One Scottish observer who lived in the country for four years said that Francia "never would defend an unjust cause; while he was ever ready to take the part of the poor and weak against the rich and the strong" (both views provided in Burns 1996: 76–77).

Point/Counterpoint

How should we view Francia today—as a visionary leader or another brutal autocrat?

If you say "visionary leader," how do you respond to those who say that he was unrealistic, concerning both his own people and the international situation, and thereby led the country to disaster?

If you say "brutal autocrat," how do you respond to the way he tried to rely on his own people to lift the country, rather than foreign interests, as in so many other countries? Given how his powerful neighbors and the British wanted him to fail, could he have afforded to be tolerant in his own country?

Do you think that under some circumstances rule by a strong leader, even a dictator, can be justified?

For More Information

See "Quién era José Gaspar Francia?" (2012), www.ceibal.edu.uy/contenidos/areas_conocimiento/ cs_sociales/090616_donjose/quin_era_jos_gaspar_francia.html. A novel based on this era in Paraguay is *I, the Supreme* (New York: Knopf, 1986) by Augusto Roa Bastos.

empire was governed from several centers of control—Mexico City, Havana, Lima, and Rio de la Plata (in modern Argentina). This was logical given the vastness of the region, but it posed huge obstacles to unification, the goal of Spanish America's independence hero, Simón Bolívar.

Benedict Anderson (1983: 47–66) tells us that the desire to justify independence from Spain led the colonial elite, the Creoles, of South America to confront what their identity would be afterward. A common pattern, especially in larger countries, saw regional export economies develop rather than one national economy. In Venezuela, for example, cacao was grown and exported from the coastal center; both coffee and cacao were produced and exported in the west near Colombia; dried beef and hides were produced in the plains and floated down the Orinoco River in the east. It took days or weeks to travel from any one of these regions to the capital in Caracas, and the contact among peoples in each region with another was limited. Brazil was an even vaster state, with a thriving sugar export economy in the northeast, mining in parts of the south, and later coffee production. Mexico had sisal (a strong white fiber for rope that was vital to sailing ships, rugs, and so forth) plantations in the Yucatán, but mining predominated in the central and northern regions. Each local economy was tied to export markets, with produce flowing from the interior to trading houses in the ports. The interaction among different regions was limited.

Conservatives and Liberals

The century between independence and the **Great Depression** of the 1930s constitutes for Latin America a long, evolutionary period marked by chronic political instability and civil wars, but around 1850 the central state did begin to assert sovereignty over the territory within its boundaries. We should say "more or less asserted" sovereignty, because some Latin American states even today remain vulnerable to foreign intervention or unable to enforce national laws and policies over regional power brokers.

Still, a process of economic and social modernization unfolded as transportation (ports, roads), communications (the telegraph), and other forms of infrastructure were built, usually financed by Europeans, designed to take advantage of growing demands for raw materials on the world market, as well as imports. New schools were built, and universities were expanded. Government bureaucracies grew. Slavery was abolished, to be replaced with new labor systems, though the region's elites remained highly prejudiced against the lower classes, composed mostly of people of Indigenous and African descent. More liberal factions of the elite studied liberal social doctrines emanating from European intellectual circles, but debt peonage and semi-feudal social relationships remained deeply entrenched, especially in the countryside.

Positivism, a form of thinking that science could be applied to solve social programs, was among the philosophies imported. Some of its tenets encouraged progressive ideas, such as the value of public education. However, prominent in positivism was a distortion of the ideas of Charles Darwin about evolution and natural selection. These ideas were popular elsewhere (including the United States) and were known as Social Darwinism. Many Latin American elites argued that the Indigenous and African genes had created an inferior racial stock and that it was necessary to "whiten" the population. A closely related theory attributed "inferiority" to the tropical climate in some countries. Changing the region's racial stock through European immigration was the (racist) formula adopted by many.

The issues that divided Creoles over independence continued to shape politics in the new states of the early independence era. Just about in every country, one faction of the elite came to define itself as the "conservative" party, even when the name of the political club, newspaper, or political party did not always call itself by the term explicitly. Its members tended to support centralized government, resist policies designed to open the economy to more trade, defend the Church and its control over education, and see themselves as bearers of Iberian traditions. Many conservative landowners saw themselves more as aristocrats than as entrepreneurs, though self-interest certainly played a large role in their thinking. In times of depressed prices for exports, they resented attempts by banks and merchant houses to seize their land through bankruptcy, which explains their reluctance to embrace **laissez-faire** and free trade.

Other elite political factions tended to see themselves as modernizers and to view land as a source of profit rather than prestige. They usually, but not always, called themselves "Liberals." They tended to favor policies to allow them to take advantage of new opportunities on the global market—for example, to obtain land to grow coffee for the new markets that opened after 1800, and to build transportation and port facilities to get commodities to ports. In countries with significant Indigenous populations, Liberals sought to break up communal lands collectively owned by villages or the Church. They were likely to favor **federalism** and decentralized government—at least until they took power for themselves. Many also sought to wrest control of education from the Catholic Church.

It is important not to exaggerate the differences between Conservatives and Liberals. Wealthy landowners and elites could be found in both parties, and principle meant little when power and land were at stake. Two of the main characters in the novel *House of the Spirits* by Isabel Allende (a relative of the martyred Chilean president Salvador Allende) are a married couple—the husband a conservative and the wife a liberal. Gabriel García Márquez, the Colombian novelist, once famously sized up the difference as little more than the hour each faction attended church.

Commodity Booms and Busts—New Exports, New Elites

Changing patterns of consumption and production in the wealthy countries (mainly North America, Europe, and Japan) created new opportunities for those controlling land and natural resources in Latin America, generating periodic economic booms—which inevitably turned into busts. In hard times, when **commodity** prices fell on the world markets, elites looked for help from the government against the predatory practices of foreign and domestic competitors eager to seize their lands. Economic crises inevitably caused further misery for the masses. Nitrate miners in Chile, cowboys in Argentina, peons on the cacao plantations of Venezuela and sisal plantations in the Yucatán (Mexico), enslaved workers on sugar estates in Cuba, tin miners in Bolivia, and rubber-tappers in Brazil (just to name a few examples) never lived a secure or prosperous existence. The collapse of markets or the exhaustion of land or mines could cause a precarious existence to become hopeless, especially for women who could less easily migrate and who sacrificed the most to save the family. In such circumstances, economic grievances have always generated popular unrest, alarming established elites and opening political opportunities for new leaders.

Booms (skyrocketing prices) can also be disruptive, as the expansion of coffee production in several countries shows. In many parts of Central America and Mexico, it drastically impacted those Indigenous people who had escaped complete destruction of their way of life in the colonial era. Most of them lived in the highland areas of Mexico, Guatemala, Colombia, and El Salvador—which were ill-suited for plantation agriculture of the coast. If their labor was needed for mining or temporary work, the Indigenous peoples were forced to provide their labor, but they could continue to live in communal relationships to each other and the land. In many parts of Mesoamerica, land was often collectively owned by the local municipality (village) in the form of *ejidos*. Other Indigenous people could preserve communal economic relations on lands owned by the Church. When these lands became attractive to elites eager to take advantage of a developing overseas market for coffee, conflict ensued. Backed by pro-trade liberal governments, Church properties were taken over and peasants, often illiterate in Spanish, induced to "sign" (often with an "X") over their property rights. Some adapted and were able to share in the prosperity, but more were dispossessed.

One of the more famous commodity booms in the 1800s took place in Chile. That country's northern Atacama Desert is the driest in the world and hardly seemed blessed by natural wealth. What it had in vast quantity were bird droppings accumulated over thousands of years. The expansion of agriculture and demand for food made this guano valuable for its high nitrate content, also in demand for manufacture of gunpowder. Chile had seized the Atacama with British help as a prize of war from Bolivia in 1878. An immense flow of wealth flowed to Chilean elites, but all came crashing down during World War I, when the Germans, blocked from access to the Chilean treasure, developed synthetic fertilizer to replace natural nitrates.

A similar story unfolded in the lowland areas of the Yucatán Peninsula of southern Mexico. As late as 1840s, Indigenous peoples continued to live on land collectively owned by municipalities. Their land became more valuable as demand for sisal, an important ingredient for rope and twine, rose in the industrialized world. With the help of new laws and backed by force, a new landowning class converted the land into privately held estates. In the twenty-first century, rope is made largely of synthetic fibers, and tourists today can visit the ruins of what were once palatial estates of hemp plantations, set amid severe, generalized poverty.

Liberals threatened Indigenous communities more than Conservatives did. Their desire to reduce the power of the Church was motivated not just by the secular ideals of the French and American revolutions but also by their desire to get control of the Church's land and the people who lived on it. The coffee boom, from roughly 1840 to 1870, brought out this conflict in Mexico and Central America. In El Salvador, a new oligarchy arose based on the seizure of land to meet the growing consumer demand for the aromatic bean in North America and Europe. Robert Williams (1994: 124) describes it this way:

> When coffee growers came to power in the 1870s and 1880s, they began to solve both their land and labor problems. National legislation in the early 1880s abolished *ejidal* and communal rights to land, reinforcing a process of encroachment that was well under way. Coffee growers acquired private titles to lands traditionally cultivated by peasants, and with funds from a coffee tax, militias were created with the power to evict previous tenants from the land.

The process was more complicated; many Indigenous people and Latinos took advantage of the same laws to become small, commercial growers themselves. The consolidation of an oligarchy came later—in the 1920s. However, the more general point made by Williams is still valid. Booms, not just busts, can cause political change because they generate winners and losers. Coffee booms also enriched newly prosperous elites in Colombia and Venezuela, and they challenged for power in both countries toward the close of the nineteenth century.

Even Chile and Brazil, the two most stable of the new nation-states, saw regional uprisings, rigged elections, strongmen, and irregular transitions of power. But conflicts were less frequent and devastating than civil wars elsewhere. In Venezuela, independence was achieved in 1821 after one-third of the population perished in war. Over the following seven decades—from 1821 to 1888—730 battles and 26 major insurrections occurred. The Federal War of 1858 to 1863 took between 60,000 and 100,000 lives, and the population fell from 1.9 million to 1.6 million people. The survivors faced a ruined economy, and the cattle herds were decimated, falling from 12 million to 1.8 million in only five years (Ugalde 1978: 29).

Mexico: From Failed State to Modernizing Dictatorship

New opportunities in world markets, we see, often changed the life fortunes of people in different parts of the social class structure, sometimes for better, sometimes for worse. External factors played an important role, given that foreign loans paid for the infrastructure (roads, railroad, ports, etc.) needed to link regions to overseas markets. Northern Europeans established trading houses, and they often became important new players in elite politics. The export economy gave both Latin American elites and foreign interests reason to seek stronger states capable of defending property rights, taming unrest, and building needed infrastructure. Rarely were the thin layer of elites effectively taxed, and there was little to extract from the rest of the population. Customs taxes in the ports were the governments' main source of income. But there never seemed to be enough money to pay for loans. Mexico is a prime example of what ensued.

Mexico's internal conflicts not only decimated the population and its economy but also left the country vulnerable to foreign invasion and the seizure of two-thirds of its territory by the United States via the war of 1846–1848. The U.S. victory was greatly facilitated by mistrust among Mexican generals, each a *caudillo* with his own regional base of power. They were mutually suspicious of each other and of the conservative president, General Antonio López de Santa Anna, of Alamo infamy.

Fourteen years later, in 1862, hopeful of restoring order and beating back the challenge of Liberals, Mexican Conservatives welcomed a French invasion of 45,000 troops. Napoleon III (nephew of Bonaparte) managed to briefly install Austrian prince Maximilian as ruler of the country in 1864. In 1867, the Liberals, led by Benito Juárez, defeated the French, executed the unfortunate Maximilian, and then cloaked themselves in the mantle of nationalism to implement "reforms" similar to ones underway in El Salvador. One of the liberal generals, Porfirio Díaz, seized power in 1876 and kept it until 1910. This hero of the struggle against the French would rule Mexico for nearly 35 years. His dictatorship came to be resented and eventually generated a revolution in 1910, but he gave Mexico a measure of stability and economic growth during what today is known as the Porfiriato—his period of rule.

The exact timing varied, but sometime in the second half of the 1800s, the majority of Latin American countries emerged from a period of intense civil violence and entered a period of relative stability and economic modernization. This usually was engineered by one of a series of skillful *caudillos* or by local political chiefs, known as *caciques* (e.g., Díaz in Mexico), who seized power in countries exhausted by decades of brutal civil war. These strongmen borrowed ideas, training, and money from European powers eager to see political stability restored and their own influence enhanced. As "modernizers," they brought in Prussian, French, and other European advisors to train professional militaries. They constructed statues and built myths of national unity around independence leaders, many of whom, as in the case of Bolívar, were too controversial among elites to merit such attention earlier in the century. They built new capitols, plazas, theaters, jails, and other public buildings to show the power of the state and to help their citizens imagine themselves as a nation. They constructed roads and railroads not only to link regions to ports but also to ensure their ability to rapidly deploy their smaller but better trained and armed military forces to defeat uprisings. They often ruled at the head of an alliance of regional *caudillos*, *coroneles*, or *caciques*, permitting lesser figures and local landowners to dominate state and local governments in exchange for loyalty.

In sum, in this era **caudillism** did not disappear, but states began to develop some capacity to exert control over the national population and territory. Besides better transportation, new communications technologies increased the ability of central governments to exert control beyond the capital region. Juan Vicente Gómez, who ruled Venezuela from 1908 until 1935, took care to place well-paid, loyal supporters in telegraph offices throughout the country in order to get early warnings of possible region uprisings. What did not change was the economic and social gap between the masses and the elites, even when dominance was masked by **republican** constitutions. Mexico was the place where these conditions would lead to social revolution in 1910, which we examine in chapter 8, but unrest would appear throughout Latin America as modernization for the few unfolded in the late 1880s and early twentieth century.

For Review

We have seen that Creoles seemed to have a common interest in protecting their wealth and power against the masses. What were, on the other hand, some sources of political division among this group after independence? Explain what García Márquez was saying about Liberals and Conservatives in his famous reference to their churchgoing habits. In economic terms, what did modernizers want to accomplish? How did they attempt to build a stronger state? What obstacles did they have to overcome? In what ways did modernization strengthen the state; in what ways did things remain the same?

Independence or Neocolonialism—Or Both?

Much ink has been spilled over the question of why North America and Latin America followed such different paths after independence. Some argue that the prevalence of liberal values in the north, inherited from England, explains much. Culture indeed might have made a difference, but the way the two regions were integrated differently into the world capitalist system is just as important, if not more so. To understand this better, consider the different ways that the South and North developed in the United States before the Civil War.

Just as North America developed differently than Latin America did, the U.S. North developed differently than did the U.S. South. In the southern part of the United States, slaves were crucial to production of raw materials and crops (tobacco, rice, sugar, and cotton) for export to the world market, just as hyperexploited Indigenous peoples and slaves were in Latin America. In both cases, wealth became concentrated in the hands of a few landowners, and the pattern persisted after independence from colonial rule. Traveling down the Ohio River between the slave state of Kentucky and the free state of Ohio, Alexis de Tocqueville (1835), the famed French thinker, noticed how much more economically prosperous and energetic the north bank of the river was compared with the southern side, where slavery and plantation economies existed. The victory of the North in the Civil War ensured that the United States would remain on the path to become part of the center of the world system. Industrialization and agricultural development complemented one another, and a prosperous export sector complemented a growing domestic economy. Latin America had changed from colonial days, but the region was still dominated by oligarchies tied to exporting raw materials using hyperexploited labor.

These features of its history and economic development give Latin America much in common with most of Africa, the Middle East, and Asia, what came to be known in the 1960s as the Third World—that is, countries that were neither wealthy capitalist nor communist states, most of which were once European colonies. However, Latin America differs from most of the rest of the Third World in the timing of its independence from colonial rule. It was not until the period between 1948 and 1990 that most of Africa and large parts of the Middle East and Asia achieved independence. Leaders in these regions fought not just for independence after World War II but for something called **national liberation**—that is, elimination of **neocolonial** relationships of economic dependence—though it has rarely been achieved.

Simón Rodríguez, Bolívar's teacher, advocated the creation of national education systems that would not only lift the formal education levels of the population but also draw upon the cultural and technological knowledge of the non-European peoples. The failure of Latin American leaders to pursue such a path meant that the region's separation from Spain and Portugal produced independence in the form of territorial sovereignty, but not independence from underdevelopment and neocolonialism. This fact became clear as the nineteenth century unfolded.

We should disabuse ourselves of the notion that all Latin America's problems are inherited from Iberian colonialism. Most of Latin America was sovereign throughout the nineteenth century. It was neither the Spanish nor the Portuguese who introduced banana plantations in Colombia, Ecuador, and Central America, nor were the Portuguese in charge when coffee and rubber production on a large scale was introduced into Brazil. The landed oligarchies that came to dominate Central America's coffee-export economies were native to the region in the 1800s. British loans, not Spanish viceroys, tied Argentina's beef exports to European markets. Northern European nations financed the wars that shifted desert lands rich in nitrates from southern Peru and Bolivia to the sovereign control of Chile, more friendly to their interests at the time. U.S. invaders cost Mexico half its territory in 1848, and

PHOTO 4.1   This image is of a banana train in Guatemala around 1915. The United Fruit Company owned the train. Where are the bananas going? Do you think that United Fruit's activities were helping develop the economy by providing employment and building a railroad?

Source: Library of Congress.

French forces laid the country prostrate later in the century. After 1900, European and U.S. capital developed oil fields in Mexico and Venezuela, as well as massive new tin and copper mines in the Andes. In Cuba, Puerto Rico, and the Dominican Republic, it was the United States that came to control the vital sugar estates and mills.

Hence, Spain and Portugal set the pattern, but it was the rising industrial powers of North America and Northern Europe that came to dominate the commodity-export economies after independence. The Latin American elites whose fortunes were made in association with this trade were not necessarily descended from the conquistadors or from the old Creole class. Many Indigenous peoples who were left relatively undisturbed by Spanish colonial rulers found themselves dispossessed and forced into the ranks of poor workers once their lands were discovered to be useful for new agricultural exports or mines.

By 1900, Latin American society was becoming more complex, more urban. The period of liberal modernization in Latin America gave impetus to the emergence of new social sectors. Ports, railroads, electric utilities, urban streetcars, slaughterhouses, mines, and so on required workers. Schools, universities, government offices, stores, courts, postal and telegraph offices, newspapers, and other institutions required employees too. Professional associations for lawyers, doctors, professors, and so on grew in size and number. Workers, often faced with terrible conditions and low wages, organized themselves either into unions (especially in mining areas) or into benevolent organizations.

With the growth of working and middle classes and the emergence of a more complex economy, Latin American **civil society** was becoming less hospitable to exclusive domination by a narrow land-based oligarchy. Unions advanced demands through strikes. Students organized protests. Associations of street vendors and neighbors began to make demands on municipal authorities. The middle class pressed for political rights monopolized by the oligarchs. Unions, the military, professional associations, and universities were all social spaces where Latin Americans encountered the influence of foreign ideas. Immigrants from Europe brought the ideas of **anarchists**, socialists, and **communists** from their homelands. Their ideas were often embraced by university and high school students, and young people in Latin America have tended to feel a developed sense of belonging to a political generation since this time.

Although history tends to record the importance of the men who led these organizations and movements, it is hard to see how they could have achieved anything without the involvement of women. Sometimes women themselves organized, as was the case among laundry workers who worked in camps near mines and military installations. In other cases, women organized the solidarity networks that helped strikers survive weeks without pay, to buy food, clothing, and other essentials of life. Even within a fiercely patriarchal social structure, women remained protagonists of history, not just victims or accessories.

With the increased social complexity and the influence of European ideologies, new parties began to emerge, and some older ones changed. New ones included parties that characterized themselves as "radical" or "democratic." Especially prominent in Chile, Argentina, and Uruguay, they tended to attract middle-class supporters, especially teachers dissatisfied with the old conservative or liberal options. Sometimes they attracted labor support as well. In some places, older parties, more often the Liberals, broadened their views and deepened their penetration in society beyond elites. Meanwhile, and usually a little later, leftist parties began to appear, usually tied to workers, sometimes attracting students. As in other parts of the world, the Russian Revolution of 1917 provoked increased interest in revolutionary Marxism but also a split in the relatively new socialist movements and parties. Some aligned with more moderate social democratic parties in Western Europe, while others aligned with the world communist movement headquartered in Moscow.

Because of the strong presence of foreign investment and the history of external intervention, the entire Latin American left identified itself as "anti-imperialist." In the twentieth century, to be a leftist, one had to espouse nationalism and decry the role of foreign investors. This rarely convinced the military establishment that leftists were loyal to the nation. There are notable exceptions, which we will review later in this text, but on the whole, entering the twentieth century, the military excluded leftists from those embraced by the concept of *la patria* (described in the next section).

For Review

List two or three important ways that the Latin American society of 1900 was different from that of Latin America around 1800. What political implications did this have?

Stirrings of Change at the Dawn of a New Century

As the twentieth century dawned in Latin America, not only were economies and states changing, but the makeup of the population was also changing as immigrants were arriving from other parts of the world. The Southern Cone experienced significant immigration from Europe. Asians began to impact most countries, with the Guyanas, Peru, and Brazil standing out. Arab and Jewish names began to appear among the economic and social elite. The industrialization of Europe, North America, and (less directly) Japan created new markets and hence incentives for new foreign investment in Latin America's export sector. The sons and daughters of the prosperous Europeans that owned trading houses identified more with their Latin American homeland and place of birth. They began to become prominent in the social registers and seats of government. In some cases, such as Venezuela, few colonial elite families survived the violent 1800s. The commencement of the oil boom in 1922 provided opportunities for many new fortunes to be made.

Political stability served an economic purpose. Investors needed states capable of protecting property, settling contract disputes, and keeping workers in line. However, one person's political "stability" is another person's system of oppression. On the antidemocratic side of the ledger, stronger states generally meant better-trained military officers who, in turn, became political actors themselves. These professional officer corps affected politics in several ways. First, military officers retained many privileges inherited from the colonial era. Besides their own court system, these privileges often included special licenses for their own businesses. Second, the military defended what historian Brian Loveman (1999) calls *la patria*, meaning "country" or "fatherland." But what was *la patria*? Latin America's ruling class defined national identity by its Iberian heritage, including Catholicism and European values. The military interpreted uprisings by Indigenous peoples, slaves, and peons as threats to civil order and to the essence of the nation's Hispanic identity. The new oligarchic families had little incentive to want to change that mentality, but the middle classes, we shall see, were another matter.

The traditional task of providing security from external threat often became linked in the military mind with defense of its own interests as a corporate body; as defenders of the "nation," they saw themselves above politics. However, as Latin American militaries became more professional, conflicts developed within the ranks. Generals-on-horseback, whose rank owed mainly to their family's traditional **oligarchic** status than their proficiency as soldiers, often treated lower-ranking officers and soldiers trained in new military academies as little more than peons. They chafed at being used to build roads and other projects that made the general's family lands more valuable. Officers trained by professional European soldiers in academies, overseas or in country, were blocked from promotions and grew resentful at the abuse by superiors. Gradually, in many of the larger and more complex countries, the military came to identify more with the middle class and less with the traditional oligarchy. The military would come to play an important role in the next century's politics of change, which we examine in the next two chapters.

For Review

What kinds of forces were shaping the social structure and eventually the military between 1850 and 1930? Why did the military become stronger and more influential in the period of modernization?

◼ Independence: Did It Make a Difference?

Most of this chapter argues that political independence did not do much to change the legacy of colonialism, especially the legacy of economic dependence. It is worth noting, however, that Latin America's achievement of political sovereignty did allow it to escape the worst ravages of direct European colonial rule that have played out in disastrous ways in Africa and parts of Asia. The United States played a small role in discouraging a European "scramble for Latin America" when President James Monroe declared in 1823, in the Monroe Doctrine, that the United States would not tolerate any reestablishment of European colonies. In reality, the United States had little military ability to prevent such efforts, but Europeans were put on notice that there might be a diplomatic cost to such ventures.

So, having dwelled mostly on the shortcomings of independence, it is worth summing up the positive side of the ledger. Latin America's problems today pale in some ways compared with the acute poverty and violence afflicting much of postcolonial Africa. The political systems of the Middle East may be more prosperous, but most of that region compares unfavorably in comparison with the Latin American situation, especially in regard to the status of women, religious freedom, and status of ordinary workers. Some Asian countries have recently advanced more rapidly in terms of economic development, but overall conditions of poverty remain dire in large parts of Asia—even China. If nothing else, after a century of rebuilding state institutions in and export-led economic development, the stage was set for new political developments.

In the nineteenth century, democracy was not on the agenda of Latin America's ruling classes. "**Republics**" existed largely on paper. National legislatures, where they functioned with any degree of real power, were largely arenas in which elite interests played themselves out with little popular influence. Democratization of politics in Latin America is largely a development of the twentieth century, which nonetheless too was marked by revolution, populism, and repression. That century saw an important shift as well in foreign intervention, with the rise of the United States to world hegemonic status and by the great ideological battle between capitalism and communism. Around 1990, this Cold War drew to a close, and in the aftermath Latin America began to experiment with a new wave of liberalism, **neoliberalism**.

Discussion Questions

1.   Just before he died, Bolívar bitterly and famously remarked that in trying to make a revolution, he had "plowed the sea." What did he mean? Can you identify two or three important features of Latin America's political, economic, or social landscape today that can be traced back to the colonial era?
2.   Sometimes we use "counterfactuals" to spur discussion. Here are two for you to consider.
     a.   If Bolívar and other liberators had failed to achieve independence, would Latin American history have been different? (You might take the history of Brazil into account in thinking about this question.)
     b.   If Latin America had been colonized by the British instead of by the Iberians, what difference, if any, might that have made?
3.   It is said that "modernization" took place in the period between 1850 and 1920. What did this mean in political, economic, and military terms?

Resources for Further Study

Reading: John Lynch's *Simón Bolívar: A Life* (New Haven: Yale University Press, 2006) is a
biography that sheds light not only on the liberator but also on his times and conflicts
within the Creole ruling class. Of the many surveys of Latin American history, a relatively brief and lively written account is E. Bradford Burns and Julie A. Charlip, *Latin
America: An Interpretive History*, 5th ed. (Upper Saddle River, NJ: Prentice Hall 2007).
Gabriel García Márquez's *One Hundred Years of Solitude*. New York: Harper Perennial
Modern Classics (2006) is perhaps the best-known novel to come out of the region,
and much of the novel explores how the mythical town of Macondo experienced modernization with the arrival of the banana export business.

Video and Film: *The Battle of Canudos* tells the story of a poor family's fate in the bloody
conflict in northeast Brazil. Searching for "Canudos" on YouTube will provide access
to the film in Portuguese. It is not hard to follow even without knowledge of the
language. *Camila* (1984) is the story of star-crossed lovers, a priest and the daughter
of wealthy landowners in post-independence Argentina, the era of the dictator Juan
Manuel de Rosas.

On the Internet: Paul Hall's Internet Modern History Sourcebook provides thousands of
relevant sources, including many on Latin America. His briefing on world systems
theory is extremely useful. Consult the left-hand column at the following URL: www.
fordham.edu/halsall/mod/modsbook.asp. The world systems summary is located at
www.fordham.edu/Halsall/mod/Wallerstein.asp. You can find an 11-minute segment
on Canudos on the BBC Internet site, www.bbc.co.uk/programmes/p0205w53.

5 Populism, Development, and Democracy in the Twentieth Century

Focus Questions

▶ What is populism, and why does it often revolve around charismatic figures, such as Juan Perón in Argentina and Getúlio Vargas in Brazil?

▶ How were populism and the goal of economic development often tied together by policies called "import substitution industrialization"?

▶ How do more recent populist leaders, such as Venezuela's Hugo Chávez, Brazil's Lula, and Peru's Alberto Fujimori, compare to past populists, their base of support, and their policies?

▶ Why did some parts of Latin America begin to industrialize but others did not in the twentieth century?

L
ATIN AMERICA HAS experienced two great waves of populism. Allowing for significant variance in timing from country to country, the first took place largely between 1930 and 1970. The second can be roughly dated from 1999, when Hugo Chávez assumed the presidency of Venezuela, inaugurating the **Pink Tide** era. When and whether the second wave ended is a matter of debate for two reasons. First, although a number of the most prominent left populist leaders of this wave were swept from office by elections or coups (in the case of Chávez, he died in 2013), populist politicians won elections in 2018 and 2019 in Argentina and Mexico. In Brazil and Bolivia, populist politicians were fighting to reclaim the presidency in 2020. The second reason is that some of the defeats suffered by the Pink Tide were engineered not by mainstream politicians but by right populists (Jair Bolsonaro of Brazil is the most important).

This leads us into the key thing to understand populism: It is not an "ism" (ideology) but a style or way of doing politics. Many political scientists call it an "empty vessel" that can be filled with different ideological content, an idea taken from Argentine intellectual Ernesto Laclau (2005). Laclau saw populism and in particular its "**discourse**"—its style of speaking and way of appealing to the masses—as a way to incorporate into politics those who have been ignored or excluded by elites. Populism appeals to the idea of the sovereignty of the people ("el puebo," in Spanish) against elite power. This is not by any means a theory fully accepted by all, but it is an idea that has pertinence to the emergence of democracy beyond just the elite-dominated, pro-forma constitutional republics of the **modernization** era (see chapter 4). However, on the flip side, populist leaders and movements may also threaten checks on abuses of power by leaders and states, leading in the worst cases to pogroms against ethnic or gender minorities.

Populism is not the whole story of the twentieth century. It is also a century of revolution, especially those of Mexico (1910), Cuba (1959), and Nicaragua (1989). It is also the story of democratic breakdown at the end of the first populist era and the 20 following years of harsh military rule over the vast majority of Latin Americans. And it is the story of a transition back to electoral democracy. Our approach here will be to weave together two key interrelated themes: (1) the quest for development, which for most of the century was equated with industrialization, and (2) the entry of the masses into political life, which produced **populism** and ended tragically in military authoritarianism. Today, the emphasis on industrialization has receded, but the clash over what role the state should play in economic development remains highly salient.

What Is Populism?

Carlos Vilas (1987: 31), like Laclau an Argentine sociologist, once remarked that there is

> a populism for every taste—urban populism and agrarian populism, progressive populism and conservative populism, mass populism and elite populism, native populism and Westernized populism, socialist populism and fascist populism, populism "from below"' and populism "from above."

The nineteenth century saw "populist" *caudillos* rally peons and slaves to their cause. The twentieth-century version of populism was more urban-oriented. The rise of mass media, especially radio and movies, allowed strong leaders to make appeals directly to the people; today those appeals are more directly than ever transmitted via social media. The content of this appeal usually involves rhetoric calling upon "the people," a deliberately imprecise term, to confront social groups said to be putting their wealth and privileges ahead of the national interest. In contrast to **Marxism**, populist discourse puts much less emphasis on the "working class" against the "capitalists"; populists want to rally the people against the "elite."

Rodolfo Stavenhagen (1974: 138) argues that one of populism's main features seems to be the mobilization of "the available working masses . . . in order to build a broader base and provide more maneuvering room for unstable coalitions between certain competing factions of ruling classes." In nineteenth-century Latin America, populist *caudillos* tended to arise when one faction of landowners launched rebellions against another faction, often disputing control over the capital city. In the twentieth century, such rivalries involved new political and economic sectors emerging in urban areas. For the populist to build a mass movement, his or her appeals must be rooted in genuine mass grievances.

Often—but not always—populism forms around a charismatic individual, the most famous (or notorious) being Juan Perón in Argentina in the 1940s and 1950s, whose rhetoric was characterized by inflammatory rhetoric speech and exaggerated **nationalism**. Charismatic leaders usually have forceful personalities and are effective at rallying support through rhetoric. However, charisma comes not just from personality or style of the leader, the German sociologist Max Weber (1947: 328–349) pointed out in 1922. Charismatic authority is something that an eager population projects on the leader. Populism is generated as much from below as from above. The populist often presents himself or herself (e.g., Eva Perón) as a political savior or messiah whom the people will follow and obey without question.

Weber pointed out that to consolidate a regime that lasts beyond his career or life, the charismatic leader must somehow institutionalize the changes made. That has often proven more difficult than winning power. Perhaps the most recent case in point is the great uncertainty and crisis that has enveloped Venezuela since the death of Hugo Chávez in 2013. Chávez rolled up big majorities in five presidential elections (including a resounding "no" to an attempt to recall him from office in 2004), but Nicolás Maduro barely held onto the presidency in the election of April 2013. The opposition, sensing weakness, was emboldened to try to force his resignation through protest, both peaceful and violent. In response, Maduro increasingly relied on abuse of the constitution and repression to hold onto power for the party founded by Chávez, the United Socialist Party of Venezuela (PSUV). As 2020 dawned, Maduro retained power, but post-Chávez Venezuela remained politically volatile.

The leftist **"Pink Tide"** leaders of the post-2000 period opposed free trade and neoliberal economic policies. Their critics argued that the attempt by the left "neopopulists" ("new" populists) to return to state-led development would only deepen underdevelopment and put democracy at risk. But not all neopopulists had this as an objective. Right-wing populists, such as President Brazil's Bolsonaro (2019–), Peru's Alberto Fujimori (1990–2000), and Argentina's Carlos Menem (1989–1999), all implemented economic policies in line with **neoliberalism**. One cannot pin a singular ideology on populism.

Donald Trump's political rise in the United States also shows that populism is not just for leftists. Populism can be understood only in the context of the time and place in which it occurs. Populism does not belong to any particular place on the left–right spectrum of politics. In fact, populist leaders sometimes are difficult to place on this scale, as in the cases of Argentina's Perón and Brazil's Getúlio Varga in an earlier era.

For Review

If you were told that some politician—regardless of what country we consider—was a "populist," what would that mean in terms of (1) style and (2) the kind of appeal he or she would make?

The Mid-Twentieth Century: Latin America's Masses Enter Politics

A recurring feature of populism is that its practitioners appeal across social classes and use anti-elitist rhetoric that identifies an oligarchy as the enemy of a vaguely defined sector called the "people." The United States experienced it late in the 1800s when farmers and workers, mostly in the South and West, organized themselves into local groups and then into a mass. The Populist Party opposed the bankers, railroad companies, and industrial magnates of the East, whom they blamed for their deteriorating economic conditions. During the Great Depression, Louisiana governor Huey Long promised "a chicken in every pot" and to defend the common person against power brokers and businesspeople—even as he made deals with these same "enemies of the people."

Latin American populists are often cut from the same cloth. But despite rhetoric opposing imperialism, populists are rarely entirely hostile to foreign investment and reach out to domestic capitalists. Most preached corporatism—harmony between the interests of capital and labor. Getúlio Vargas of Brazil captured the spirit of populism in a speech given in 1944.

> The possessing classes that genuinely contribute to national grandeur and prosperity, honest merchants, working and fair industrialists, farmers who increase the fertility of the land, have no reason to fear the power of the people. What the law does not protect or tolerate is abuses, unbridled speculation, crime, unfairness, profits by all the castes of favorites, and all sorts of traffickers who feed on the poverty of others, trade in the hunger of their fellow human beings, and sell even their souls to the devil to accumulate wealth off the sweat, the anxiety, and the sacrifice of the majority of the population.
>
> (quoted in Lowy 1987: 34)

In the middle decades of the twentieth century, before manufacturing jobs began to move away from "developed" countries to cheaper labor markets in the Global South, in Latin America economic development and industrialization were regarded as practically the same thing. Populist governments in the larger nations of Latin America pursued industrialization through **import substitution**. This policy included protecting new industries from foreign competition with tariffs and import restrictions, tapping export earnings for state-initiated development projects or subsidies to new factories, and enlarging the domestic market through income redistribution and public spending.

The Political Logic of Import Substitution Industrialization (ISI)

From 1930 to 1964, populist leaders and parties in the larger countries of Latin America appealed to workers, businesspeople, and the middle class to unite behind **import substitution industrialization** (ISI) against conservative forces and foreign investors blocking change. When commodity prices rose with the onset of World War II, governments had funds to make many investments in roads, energy production, and even steel plants. After World War II, Raúl Prebisch and other economists at the United Nations Economic Commission for Latin America and the Caribbean (ECLAC) promoted import substitution through the training of thousands of government bureaucrats. Many countries began to nationalize ownership of the ports, electric and communication utilities, railroads, and other sectors that were vital to national economic development but owned by foreigners. Although considered socialism by some, this mix of private and state capital was more commonly labeled "state capitalism." After 1980, privatization of these assets became a major rallying cry for neoliberals who sought to undo import substitution.

The idea behind import substitution was to promote industrialization in stages, beginning with common items previously imported and with products made from raw materials readily at hand. Why export cacao, for example, only to import chocolate? Why not introduce factories at home to produce confections—and the paper to wrap them in? Could not the same thing be done ultimately with thousands of products, keeping more wealth in the country and generating jobs? Once these early industries were established, Prebisch and his team anticipated, industrialization would deepen and spread, forming a market for a new phase of "deepening" industrialization. New manufacturing would produce durable consumer goods (e.g., refrigerators and automobiles), basic inputs (e.g., petrochemicals and steel), and capital goods (e.g., machinery, mining equipment, and ships).

Under ISI, new industries were protected initially from foreign competition by tariffs, which historically were kept quite high because most of the government's tax revenues came from customs houses. In the chaotic nineteenth century, governments did not have the administrative capability to tax citizens. The early decades of import substitution were years in which factories still tended to produce a single product on assembly lines, drawing on nearby mines for raw materials and other factories for some of the parts. ECLAC economists warned that protection should not last indefinitely, lest it limit competitive incentives to modernize. New technologies, such as transistors and (later) computers, were making industries overseas more productive after World War II, but many industries in Latin America preferred not to adapt. They sought to compete with cheaper labor, protected by tariffs against foreign competition and government subsidies. Eventually those advantages would expire.

ISI did not happen everywhere. The poorer and smaller countries, such as Bolivia, Paraguay, and the nations of Central America and the Caribbean, would not experience nearly the degree of industrialization of larger countries. When manufacturing industries finally began to spring up in the 1960s in the Caribbean Basin, they were usually labor-intensive, low-technology installations, *maquilas*, oriented to export to the United States, a tendency that accelerated after 1980.

ISI was not just an economic strategy. Populists used it to appeal to the masses, expand participation, and incorporate new actors into politics—provided they supported the populists. Many of the entrepreneurs who welcomed state support for new industries were new immigrants from the Middle East (e.g., the Yarur textile group in Chile), Asia, and parts of Europe. In return for subsidies, labor peace, and protection from competition, they provided money and votes (of workers and their families) for populist politicians. Jobs, subsidies, protection from foreign competition, licenses, official recognition of unions, and so forth were all resources for political machines—**clientelism** at work. Populist programs appealed not only to workers but also to the middle class (Johnson 1958), including professional officers in the military. Against these populist forces were conservatives and members of the oligarchies forged in colonial times or in the modernization period of the nineteenth century (see chapter 4).

Nelson Werneck Sodré (1911–1999) was one of many Brazilian intellectuals who saw ISI as the only way forward for the nation. Sodré was a career military officer before becoming a university historian in 1961. He argued that formerly colonized countries such as Brazil inherited an economic structure dominated by foreign interests. Overcoming this legacy was in his eyes a task comparable with the struggle of European countries to overcome feudalism—that is, to take political and economic power away from the old landed aristocracy and put it in the hands of a capitalist **bourgeoisie** that would lead the industrialization. "What for them [Europeans] were feudal relations of development, are for us all that still remain of the colonial past. Nationalism thus presents itself as liberation" (quoted in Burns 1993: 177–179). Those favoring industrialization were also striving for democracy, Sodré argued, because only the people could overcome resistance by foreigners and the local oligarchy to Brazil's desire to become a modern industrialized nation. Take note that populists wanted the state to take the lead in building modern capitalism, not socialism or communism. They did not think that Latin America had a dynamic capitalist class of entrepreneurs, capable of doing it without state help.

Populists were relying, Sodré continued, on a "scheme of coordinating class interests, or reducing them to a minimum common denominator, for the struggle in defense of what is national in us." The national bourgeoisie and working classes, said Sodré, should put aside conflict to show the foreigners—who thought that development could not happen without outside aid and capital—that Brazil could do the job itself. Sodré, like many of his genera-tion, argued that this alliance between social classes would promote growth of a *national* bourgeoisie—that is, capitalists interested not just in profit but also in developing the coun-try. Workers would benefit from more jobs and a higher standard of living. They could be mobilized to support industrialization by an emotional appeal to help build the nation. "New are the people," said Sodré. "Nothing more will occur without their participation."

The policies of ISI were **corporatist** (see chapter 2). The state sought to harmonize relationships between business and labor and dampen social conflict and unite the nation in pursuit of development. Populists did not hesitate in many cases to brand opponents, on the left and the right, as enemies of the nation.

In exchange for providing subsidies, government investments in infrastructure, lucra-tive purchasing contracts, and protective tariffs, populist leaders like Juan Perón and Eva Perón (1946–1955) and Vargas (roughly 1930–1945, 1951–1954) expected in return political support, including cooperation with unions linked to their political parties. Businesspeople did not like unions, but populist politicians disciplined the workers and provided some measure of labor stability in their factories, keeping more radical union movements at bay. Eventually, populists would lose the support from business elites and the middle class when movements of workers, peasants, and poor people radicalized in the 1960s (Nun 1976).

After 1970 ISI lost much of its appeal as economies stagnated and forces for more radical political changed emerged, but its failures were far from obvious in the 1960s. Real per capita income in Latin America nearly doubled between 1950 and 1970. **Developmentalists** on both the left and the right thought that Latin America was poised around 1960 to leap forward. Walt Rostow (1960), an influential development theorist and an advisor to presidents Kennedy and Johnson, took the optimistic view that Mexico and Argentina were already in the initial stages of an economic "takeoff" that would move them from the developing into the developed world (see chapter 6). Few understood that the capacity of ISI to generate the economic growth suffi-cient to meet the rising demands of the population was being reached already.

For Review

What were the essential elements of import substitution? How did import substitution policies strengthen the political power of populists? How could ISI be considered a corporatist approach to development? Why might "corporatist" be a better way to describe the philosophy of ISI dur-ing the populist era?

Case Studies of Populism and ISI

As we review several countries' experiences with populism and ISI, we can see some commonalities. In all these cases, society became more complex as a result of the export-based economic development of the late nineteenth and early twentieth centuries. Working-class and middle-class sectors grew and demanded access to the political system, and the military began to change from an oligarchic to a middle-class institution. These pressures intensified when the Great Depression shook Latin America's economies after 1929. Populist politicians and parties appeared on the scene, promoting ISI and gaining support from workers and the middle class. Populism represented reform and modernization, often cloaked in the rhetoric of "anti-imperialism" but rarely challenging capitalism itself. Most populists supported **state capitalism**—development of a market society with guidance and even ownership of some key industries by the state. With the Cuban Revolution of 1959 as a backdrop, populism took on a more radical dimension in the 1960s. In most cases, the military intervened to defend *la patria* (the "fatherland") and impose an authoritarian "solution" to the crisis.

Although workers and the middle class gained political weight, democracy and economic development were stunted by the incomplete inclusion of peasants and the poor. Elites and the popular sectors who benefited from ISI advocated or tolerated the entrance of workers and professionals into political life, but they were not willing to challenge the political power and fundamental economic interests of landowners, especially in the export sector. There were exceptions. In Mexico, populism grew out of a revolution in 1910, and peasants could not be entirely ignored. In Venezuela, middle-class political leaders organized the countryside as part of an effort to take on the powerful foreign oil companies. Venezuela after 1920 became a petrostate—that is, a country whose economy and society was awash with oil-export dollars that were transforming the country without ISI. When populist democracy and ISI collapsed in a wave of military coups and economic recession (late 1960s–early 1970s), Mexico and Venezuela escaped the wave of authoritarianism that washed over most of Latin America (see chapter 8).

Brazil: Getúlio Vargas and the Estado Nôvo

Brazil is too large and complex a society to have its economy dominated by one export alone. However, the economies of each of the country's highly autonomous regions and states were highly dependent on a particular commodity produced for the world market. Along the northeast coast, the poorest region, sugar and cotton were the most important crops. Rubber ruled in the interior plantations. Further south, gold and diamond mining, coffee, and ranching predominated. The rise and fall of prices for these commodities greatly influenced which region and which elites had the most power. Most states in Brazil (see Figure 5.1) are in territory and population comparable to most countries

FIGURE 5.1   Map of Brazil

Source: © Shutterstock.

in Spanish-speaking Latin America, and they have great autonomy in its federal system of government.

The most important export in Brazil during the Republic (1888–1930) was coffee. Do not mistake "republic" here for democracy. From 1891 until 1930, the central government was controlled largely by oligarchs from two of the most prosperous states, São Paulo and Minas Gerais. State governments in Brazil's federal republic were controlled by *coroneles*, patriarchal heads of ruling families in rural areas (see chapter 4).

Although coffee made some Brazilians very rich, the bountiful production of the crop helped flood the world market from the 1890s onward—something that happened with many agricultural exports introduced throughout Latin America in the period of **liberal modernization** (the late 1800s). The agricultural economy was already in trouble when prices fell by two-thirds between 1893 and 1896. Unable to sell their crop for a profit, but still politically powerful, the coffee growers convinced the government to bail them out by buying much of it. However, now growers could not avoid other groups taking an interest in their affairs.

Everyone was affected because the government financed the coffee subsidies by borrowing abroad and printing money. The growing urban population was taxed to service the debt, and printing additional money led to inflation. To pay the growers, the government devalued the Brazilian currency. In other words, for each dollar or pound sterling (British currency) earned from exports, the government converted it to larger amounts of local money. However, this **devaluation** meant that merchants wanting to import manufactured goods had to charge their customers more *cruzeiros* (Brazil's money at the time) for these products, so that they could pay their suppliers overseas with dollars and sterling. Prices soared, creating widespread political discontent.

The politics of devaluation are complicated. What hurts some groups can reward others. Devaluation, by making imports *more* expensive, was a form of protection for domestic producers; because merchants had to raise prices, goods produced locally became more attractive. For example, as prices of imported shoes went up, customers became more willing to buy shoes made at home, even if they were not of the highest quality or the latest fashion. After the collapse of coffee prices from 22.5 cents per pound in 1929 to 8 cents in 1931, during the Great Depression, the goal of industrialization seemed even more pressing, a way to escape dependency on primary commodities whose prices were so capricious. But with even fewer dollars available to meet demand through imports, Brazilians began to ask why government did not tax some of their profits to help create new industries and jobs. When prices of Brazil's coffee, rubber, beef, and other exports recovered in the 1940s, **import substitution** would get underway in earnest. First, however, the people in the cities had to reduce the power of the landed elites, banks, and merchant houses that dominated the Old Republic. They maintained their control over state governments—which were (and are) much more powerful in Brazil than anywhere else in Latin America—through the power of local *coroneles*. The middle and working classes would have to be mobilized to change the system.

In 1930, two forces united to reduce the power of state governors and *coroneles*. On one side, the oligarchy from states that did not export coffee turned against the coffee magnates from São Paulo, which dominated the old regime. On the other hand, the middle class revolted, led by a movement of army lieutenants, the *tenentes*. This was threatening enough to the oligarchy, but then a key *tenente* leader broadened the revolt. Luis Carlos Prestes, who would join the Brazilian Communist Party in 1934, sought to broaden the revolt to include the masses of rural and urban poor. Most of the Brazilian army was not as revolutionary as

Prestes, but it also was not disposed to defend the old system. Lieutenant Prestes's victory in elections was marred by widespread fraudulent practices all around in 1930. Prestes's main opponent, Getúlio Vargas, a lawyer turned politician, joined a military plot to overthrow and put an end to the First Brazilian Republic (1889–1930). The junta installed Vargas as president.

In a pattern that was common to populism, Vargas astutely took advantage of the crisis and implemented a program that reinforced his own power. In the shadow of Prestes, he promoted reform in order to *prevent*, not to make, revolution. In 1934, he engineered a new constitution and, under pressure from workers' and women's organizations, included in it a minimum wage, support for worker cooperatives, and the right to vote for women. In 1937, the Brazilian president took advantage of conflict between communist and fascist sympathizers (this was the age of Stalin, Mussolini, and Hitler) to declare himself head of Brazil's Estado Nôvo (New State). He was a semi-dictator, and a popular one.

The period between 1937 and 1964 was dominated by Vargas. He centralized economic policy-making, implemented ISI, and in the vacuum left by the collapse of the old Republic built not one but two parties to bolster his support. He did this in corporatist style—top-down. One party, the Brazilian Social Democratic Party (PSDB), was for the middle class. The other, the Brazilian Workers' Party (PTB), incorporated workers through unions controlled by the party with the support of the Ministry of Labor. In 1943, Vargas rammed through his Consolidation of Labor Laws, which directly linked the labor unions to the state. For example, the government collected a "trade union tax" imposed on all workers, whether they belonged to unions or not. The Ministry of Labor then distributed these funds to unions that supported Vargas through the PTB. This clientelism effectively gave workers a stake in the system but also made sure that unions were securely under the thumb of the PTB.

Similar systems linking parties and unions were adopted throughout Latin America. In Chile and Venezuela, the government used money earned from copper and oil exports, respectively, to subsidize unions heavily. The result was the same as in Brazil. Unions and their leaders were co-opted and made dependent on government. Workers lost leverage over their own unions and came to depend on a paternalistic state. However, it must be remembered that before populism, workers were repressed and had little political influence at all. Now at least they gained better wages, some benefits (e.g., retirement and unemployment pay), and protection under labor laws. Employers often complained about unions, but as long as the unions were part of Vargas's political machine, businesses knew there were limits on the kinds of demands they would face. In exchange for working with unions subservient to Vargas and the PTB, business owners received subsidies and favors from government.

Although neither fully embraced the Axis cause in World War II, both Getúlio Vargas and Juan Perón in Argentina admired aspects of fascism in Germany, Spain, and especially Mussolini's Italy. In Brazil, these tendencies made Vargas a target of opposition by democrats and communists. These forces failed to win the election of 1946, but they did deny Vargas victory. Five years later, in 1951, he recaptured the presidency by veering in a more radical, nationalist direction. His presidency was marked by accusations of corruption, which were not entirely unfounded, but also by significant industrial growth. His career ended spectacularly with his suicide in 1954, a year when he was under suspicion for the murder of a prominent opponent. His suicide note was a classic populist statement: He accused foreign interests and the local elite of conducting a campaign of calumny against his government, which he portrayed as a servant of the people and the nation.

During Vargas's first period in power (1930–1945), called the Estado Nôvo, strikes were illegal, but regular wage and benefit increases were granted—a corporatist approach modeled in part on the rule of Antonio Salazar, the dictator in Portugal. In a country where governors have almost always enjoyed great autonomy, he developed patronage networks to undermine governors and to subordinate states to his rule from the capital. Vargas often used a federal "intervener" to take over a state where his programs were being resisted. His programs delivered real benefits to his poor supporters in the cities. His welfare programs earned him the title "Father of the Poor," but his development programs left a huge gap between the industrializing south (Rio de Janeiro and São Paulo) and the impoverished, rural northeast. His import substitution programs were welcomed by businesspeople, but not after he moved toward more radical policies after returning to the presidency (1951–1954). The capitalist class and foreign investors turned on him.

Juscelino Kubitschek was elected president in 1956 and tried to ride the tiger Vargas had created, but it was becoming harder to serve both the rich and the poor simultaneously. Leftist movements, inspired both by Prestes and by the Cuban Revolution of 1959, challenged the Estado Nôvo by mobilizing groups—peasants and the urban poor—left out of the populist system. Kubitschek also urged workers to take radical actions beyond the control of labor leaders tied to the parties created by Vargas. This increase in mass activity occurred just as the economy and the policies of ISI were faltering. In 1960, the system veered further left when João ("Jango") Goulart, who had been elected vice president, assumed the presidency on the resignation of the sitting president. Jango had been a popular minister of labor under Vargas but had been fired for advocating doubling the minimum wage. (Vargas turned around and implemented the raise anyway.) Goulart seemed to be moving in a radical direction, even countenancing the formation of worker militias. This was too much for the military to stomach. As these developments came at the height of the Cold War, and only a few years after the Cuban Revolution of 1959, the United States began to think Brazil might veer toward revolution and communism. In 1964, with U.S. warships offshore, Brazil's armed forces carried out a coup and inaugurated a harsh 24-year dictatorship.

For Review

What were Vargas's political and economic goals, and why did the oligarchy oppose him? How did he manage to gain so much power in a country notorious, even today, for decentralized politics and powerful governors? Why do you think he remains admired by many Brazilians but despised by others even today?

Argentina: Juan and Eva Perón

The quintessential populist in Latin America was Juan Perón. Before Perón, Argentine politics was dominated by competition between the Conservatives, the traditional party of the landed elites, and the Radical Party, which represented the aspirations of the growing middle class (Corradi 1985; Hodges 1976; Page 1983). Neither of the two parties appealed to workers on the railroads and in the ports and slaughterhouses. They were a potential source of power because of the crucial role their labor played in the main export sectors—beef, grain, and leather. Argentina's fertile *llanos* (plains) made it an agricultural powerhouse around the turn of the century. As the Argentine economy grew, immigrants from Italy, Germany, Spain, and other European countries arrived to provide the labor needed to sustain the export sector. They swelled the ranks of the "popular sector"—referring to a bloc of the peasants, workers, urban poor, and sometimes parts of the middle class. They brought with them socialist and anarchist ideas. The Argentine upper class was, on the other hand, thoroughly British in orientation, both culturally and economically. Economically, Argentine elites were cemented to the British by loans and by their

reliance on access to the British market to sell their grain and meat exports. Industrialization would have meant replacing imports from Britain with locally produced products, letting the working class and its unions into the political game, and accepting taxation on exports. The Conservatives had no intention of doing so.

The growth of Argentina's beef- and grain-export economy made the country look incredibly successful in the early twentieth century, with a gross national product (GNP) that rivaled European countries. However, the social gap remained huge, and the prosperity was built on a highly dependent export economy. Things changed when other nations began to compete with Argentina. The economy suffered between 1913 and 1917 during a depression and World War I. The Conservative Party resisted efforts by the Radicals, who had won the presidency in 1916, to incorporate workers into the system. But the Radicals were not really on the workers' side either. When workers—including women, who made up 22 percent of the labor force—revolted against the system in a general strike, the Radical president, Hipólito Yrigoyen, fearing a military coup, crushed the workers with heavy loss of life. As we shall see, the Radicals in Chile followed a different path between 1938 and 1952, ruling in a coalition with the left.

The Radicals held onto power until 1930. They made some reforms under pressure from women's groups and workers, but they failed to address the burgeoning public debt and deteriorating prices of Argentina's exports. The export economy completely collapsed in the aftermath of the Great Depression. In 1930, the military staged a coup, ultimately bringing the Conservative Party back to power. Until 1943, the Conservatives presided over a devastated economy, with soaring unemployment and the largest companies in bankruptcy. Immigrants stopped arriving, and workers now had to be recruited from those fleeing the devastated rural areas. Women were especially important in this migration. The Argentine Association for Women's Suffrage not only pursued the vote (won in 1947) but also demanded welfare, maternity leave, health care, and childcare. One of the migrants, Eva Duarte, emerged from this milieu to become the key ally of her husband, Colonel Juan Domingo Perón.

Perón recognized the political potency of forging an alliance between Argentina's fledgling industrialists (frustrated with the conservative oligarchy) and the popular sectors, including women and the small but militant working class. The colonel was a member of a secretive military lodge that staged a coup against the Conservatives in 1943.

The military officers were nationalistic and angered by the corruption in both major parties. Many, like Perón, saw in Mussolini's fascism an example of how national unity could replace strife and public thievery. But as a group the officers did not share Perón's objectives. The early years of their government saw repression of the women's movement and workers' organizations.

As the minister of labor, Perón, along with his ambitious wife Eva, recognized that ISI was a program that could cement hypernationalism to the aspirations of women and workers. He supported the organization of unions and favored them in collective bargaining. He implemented pension and healthcare systems. Eva built a formidable charitable organization and urged women to organize on their own behalf. Her charitable work and use of glamour played into gender stereotypes, but she was also a shrewd politician. The *descamisados*, the "shirtless ones" who formed the backbone of Perón's movement, adored her. When nervous military officers arrested Juan Perón, still the minister of labor in 1945, the *descamisados*, encouraged by Eva, mobilized to save him (Fraser and Navarro 1980). In 1946, they supplied the votes that carried his new political party to victory and him to the presidency.

Perón was the most personalistic of the populist presidents. His Peronist movement expounded an idiosyncratic ideology called *justicialismo*, combining nationalism and **corporatism**, meant to be a "third way" between communism and capitalism, neither the left nor the right. His party controlled the labor movement completely, and he did not hesitate to repress communists and other leftists, even those who were Peronists. The Peróns saw a threat in any movement to represent worker interests independently of their party. However, their real basis of power was the carrot, not the stick; Juan and Eva Perón delivered real benefits and incorporated the working class into politics.

Other than Eva's charity projects, the couple did little for rural workers. Perón promised to carry out land reform, but he delivered only a few laws favoring peasants renting land from big owners. The land barons hated Perón, but he never decisively moved against them. After all, he needed to tax their exports to finance his industrialization and welfare programs. As in Brazil (and in Chile), the rural sector was left out of the populist equation. This failure to address conditions in the countryside had economic consequences. In the process of industrialization in Europe, Japan, and North America, the rural sector provided affordable food and raw materials for the cities and a market for factories. Land reform was not only a matter of social justice but also crucial to long-term development and modernization of the economy.

Eva's death from cancer in 1952 dealt a political blow to Juan Perón. Industrialists resented worker militancy and union power; they wanted state help but not restrictions. Military officers, always suspicious of their ambitious colleague, grew increasingly restive. In 1955, they overthrew Perón, and Argentina entered a 19-year period of instability. Perón died in 1974 after a brief, unsuccessful return to power in 1971. Without his charismatic personality, right- and left-wing factions in Peronism began to clash, sometimes violently. Communist groups and the left-wing Peronist Youth, inspired by the Cuban Revolution, began to pressure the old guard for revolutionary change. As in Brazil, this surge in militancy happened just as the economy was slowing down as import substitution reached its limits. As street violence intensified, a military government led by General Jorge Rafael Videla inaugurated a vicious "Dirty War" against the left between 1976 and 1978, leaving perhaps 30,000 people murdered or disappeared (see chapter 7).

PUNTO DE VISTA: WHAT KIND OF IDEOLOGY WAS PERÓN'S *JUSTICIALISMO*?

No Latin American leader has personified populism more than Juan Perón, and there are a number of historians who think that Eva Perón, his wife, was even more astute in promoting a close personal identification between Perón and the people. Even if you do not speak Spanish, you may want to go online and watch the many available videos of Juan and Eva addressing masses of Argentines, often in the Plaza del Maya in Buenos Aires, to get a better idea of the emotional connection between these leaders and the people. Following are excerpts from translations of two speeches, one by Juan Perón to the general assembly of his party, the other by Eva Perón to working-class women. Read through both of these before considering the questions that follow.

From Juan Perón's speech "Qué Es el Peronismo?" ("What Is Peronism?"), to the Argentine General Assembly (the national legislature), August 20, 1948:

> A few days ago some legislators of the Congress asked me, "What is Peronism?" Peronism is humanism in action; Peronism is a new conception of politics that does away with the evils of politics of the past. Regarding social questions, it confers a little more equality—more equal opportunities—and assures them that in the future no one in this land will lack the basic necessities of life, even should it be necessary, to benefit those with nothing at all, that those whose hands overflow lose their right to waste [wealth]. In the realm of the economy, it seeks to ensure that everything Argentine should work for Argentina, and it replaces an economic policy that was a permanent and perfect school for capitalist exploitation with a social-

economic model for distribution of the wealth that we take from the land and produce ourselves; one that distributes wealth proportionately among all those who are involved in creating it with their effort. This is Peronism.

And don't say that Peronism is learned; it is something felt, or not felt. Peronism is a question of the heart more than of the head. Fortunately, I am not one of those presidents that isolates himself but one who lives with the people, as I have always lived. I share with working people all their ups and downs, all their successes and failures. I feel intimate satisfaction when I see today a well-dressed worker, or a worker attending the theater with his family. I then feel such satisfaction; I actually feel like a worker. This is Peronism.

Just as I have never conceived of the possibility that in this world there would be groups of men against other groups, nations against nations, even less I can conceive men of different beliefs being enemies. . . . In Argentina there ought not to be more than one class of men alone: men that work for the national good without distinctions. Good Argentines . . . work for the greatness of the Nation; and bad Argentines . . . [are those who] do not every day lift a stone to construct our nation as an edifice of happiness and grandeur.

(Translated from the original Spanish, www.elhistoriador. com.ar/documentos/ascenso_ y_auge_del_peronismo/doctrina_ peronista.php)

In 1949, Eva Perón gave a speech to the Women's Auxiliary of the General Confederation of Labor. After urging women to cooperate with the census and lauding them for their role in defending Perón, in this excerpt, she spoke of Peronist doctrine (translated here from the original Spanish):

> To build a great country it is necessary to do justice by the people; to have a happy country it is necessary to do justice by the people; to speak of peace it is necessary to do justice with the people . . .
>
> For this reason, we have an eminently social doctrine; for this reason, Perón governs with the people and for the people; for this reason every day he delivers blows against the tight circle of traitorous oligarchs.

Already the Argentine people have tired of a small group of so-called "leaders" who constitute a very crude oligarchy and want to govern. The very same ones who are selling out the country to foreigners! The same ones who keep the people down in the worst ignominy and take from them the last thing that a citizen should lose: hope! The same ones who strip the people of their personality! General Perón has restored to each Argentine their feeling of pride, and the greatest thing about Perón is that he stands for men dignifying other men.

I passionately unite with my people, because the more that I interact with them, the more I understand them, the more I love them . . .

Point/Counterpoint

Having read the preceding speeches, and considering the brief history of Peronism, do you think Juan Perón, the populist, was just playing to the masses or was serious about change? What about Eva? Do you think she was sincere in her desire to be one with her *descamisados* (that is, the "shirtless" workers in the slaughterhouses, ports, and railroads)? Why or why not? What alternative motives might she have had?

If you generally answered that the Peróns were serious and well-motivated, how do you account for Juan's later turn to the right and attempts to control the unions?

If you generally see the Peróns as insincere or opportunistic, how do you account for the enthusiasm of the crowds, especially their evident love of Eva?

For More Information

A repository of Peronism can be found at www.pjmoreno.org.ar/documentos/discursoseva3.aspx.

For Review

In what ways was the Peronist era in Argentina similar to that of Vargas in Brazil? What role did Eva Perón play in Argentina's populist experience? Why do you think that the Peróns, even today, inspire either hatred or love in Argentina?

PHOTO 5.1   Why do you think Eva's death prompted such an outpouring of emotion in Argentina?

Source: Wikimedia Commons, Caras y Caretas 2236, Accessed 23 May 2014.

Chile: From the Radical Party to Salvador Allende

Brazil's and Argentina's experiences with populism were stamped by the highly charismatic figures of Vargas and the Peróns. Chile did produce a singular leader, Salvador Allende Gossens, president for three tumultuous years (1970–1973), but not everyone would say Allende was a populist. As a Marxist and socialist, Allende drew upon an ideology that defined the central conflict in society as one between social classes—between the bourgeoisie and the proletariat and not the people and an elite. Rather than see the Communist Party (Partido Comunista in Spanish, or PC) as a competitor, he was eager to work with the PC to achieve this goal. On the other hand, Allende's political coalition called itself the "Popular Unity" and claimed that the middle class and small businesses had nothing to fear from its policies. Thus, Allende resembled a typical populist leader of this period in attempting to build a broad, nationalist political base.

Although he called for revolution, Allende did not intend to replicate the Cuban communist model. He promised to respect the Chilean constitution and the property of the middle class; he claimed local capitalists willing to invest and help the economy grow had nothing to fear from his government. Allende was an experienced politician, a doctor turned professional politician and the product of a competitive party system. He had no substantial base in the military establishment—in contrast to Vargas and Perón, who both first came to power with military support. Allende might be considered more a revolutionary than a populist leader. It is a matter of judgment. Here, we describe how the Chilean populist system worked, leaving the details of Allende's demise to chapter 7.

Chile entered the twentieth century with Latin America's strongest tradition of parliamentary government, but elections were tightly controlled processes. Local governments were responsible for administering restricted laws of suffrage, and it was easy for landowners to dominate the process. One trick was to distribute a shoe to local peasants with the promise that the second half of the pair would be delivered *if* victory went to the landlords' preferred party and candidates. Fraud, repression, and clientelism made it difficult for new parties and social groups to gain a share of power, even for the middle class and its parties. As in Brazil and Argentina, sympathetic military officers, themselves a part of the growing middle class, intervened to open the system to new forces. This happened in Chile in 1924.

Social change was in part fostered by the late-nineteenth-century boom in the export of nitrates mined from guano in the northern desert (see chapter 4). Toward the end of the nitrate era, foreign capital began to pour into Chile to exploit another of its natural resources, copper. Chile had long been an important copper exporter, but a major boom began in 1912 with critical investments by the Guggenheim family.

Landowners benefited from mining exports, but they had little interest in relinquishing their monopoly on political control or dividing up their estates (*latifundia*), where peasants (*inquilinos*) lived like serfs. Landlords had little incentive and peasants had few resources to make investments (irrigation, fertilizers, machinery, new seeds, etc.) needed to modernize agriculture. European and Chilean merchant families, often linked to families that owned the mines and big-landed estates, controlled import-export houses and had little incentive to support state-initiated development plans.

Thus, resistance to political reform went hand in hand with the failure of elites to modernize the economy or to permit other social sectors to pursue this goal. However, the landowners could not profit from mining exports and still expect nothing to change. Teachers, railroad workers, stevedores, lawyers, laundry workers, construction workers, and a host of other new actors joined miners as a new social force. They formed new organizations and movements. Newly formed labor unions demanded recognition, along with better pay and working conditions. Middle-class groups rarely engaged in violent or extreme protest behavior, but they began to infiltrate the ranks of the Conservative and Liberal parties. Then, similar to developments in Argentina in the late 1800s, they created new parties, including the Radical Party, which would rise in the 1930s to become Chile's most important party. (It continues as a small party today.)

Workers and their unions were combative. Some split from the democrats to form socialist and later communist parties. Students often supported the workers. Some politicians in the Liberal Party—the most prominent being Arturo Alessandri, who was called the "Lion of Tarapacá" (part of the northern desert and an area populated by many miners)— saw an opportunity to gain an advantage over their conservative rivals by making populist appeals. Liberals from the northern part of the country and from other mining areas began to appeal to these new actors in politics.

The political pressure cooker heated up when an economic crisis befell Chile after the collapse of the international market for nitrates, a consequence of the German invention of a synthetic substitute during World War I. Alessandri, the Liberal Party *caudillo* from the north, seized on the discontent to win the presidential election of 1920. Many working-class and poor Chileans put more faith in his personal leadership than in their own organizations, whose leaders were skeptical about the Lion's true intentions. Some of Chile's elite and the middle class supported Alessandri because they thought that only his leadership could head off a revolution. But once in office, Alessandri found that both Conservatives and his own Liberal Party refused to support reform legislation in the Chilean parliament (Drake 1978).

The political situation deteriorated as the Chilean parliament and president reached a stalemate. Factions among the civilian elite began to court the military. The army had become more professional and socially complex, not simply an extension of the landed oligarchy. A coup came in 1924. Middle-class officers rammed through social reform legislation. Over the next 15 years, organized workers and the middle class were incorporated into the political system. However, peasants and the urban poor, whose numbers would grow spectacularly, were left out, denied the right to vote. Beginning with the 1934 election, Chile returned to a stability that was the envy of the continent—and much of Europe too. However, peasants and poor people in the cities were left out. Consequently, as in other populist systems, an underlying source of instability remained dormant, but it would eventually come to life, the mass base for Allende's dream of revolution and a "Chilean path to socialism."

Chile in the populist years was not governed by a charismatic strongman. There was no equivalent of Vargas or Perón. True, Alessandri had charisma, but populism in Chile was more about parties than about personalities (something true of Venezuela in these years too, as we shall see in chapter 8). As in these other cases, populist politics was linked to the strategy of industrialization through import substitution.

More so than in Brazil and Argentina, for the next three decades the country enjoyed relatively stable politics and limited social discontent. After a period of turmoil following the collapse of the military government in 1932, a coalition of center and leftist parties, headed by the Radical Party, came to power. Its goal was to diversify the economy and escape the confines of export-based development. The Radicals were joined in the center of the political spectrum by a new party, the Christian Democratic Party (PDC), inspired by Catholic social justice doctrines advocating reforms. The Chilean Corporación de Fomento (Corfo) was created to channel export earnings, generated by taxes and royalties on three large multinational mining companies, into investments in manufacturing to encourage ISI.

Chile's 1932 constitution served as a framework for the Radical Party to lead the process of import substitution. However, Chilean democracy was extremely limited. Literacy tests, property requirements, and poll taxes kept peasants and poor people away from the ballot box. Women got the vote only in 1949 because of a strong suffrage movement but also because Conservatives thought that women would balance leftist tendencies among working-class men. Although the country experienced massive urbanization between 1932 and 1970, representation in Congress was never reapportioned, greatly exaggerating rural areas and thus conservative power. The inability to adapt the 1932 system to social change is a good example of failure of what comparativist Samuel Huntington (1968: 8–31) rightly saw as a crucial feature of healthy institutions—their ability to adapt to new circumstances.

The system remained stagnant while portents of change were becoming more obvious. By 1958, the PDC had eclipsed the Radicals, suggesting the system might survive, but the center began to show signs of strain.

In 1957, reforms to the electoral system eliminated barriers to voting, and between 1958 and 1970, the size of the electorate tripled. The distribution of votes among leftist, centrist, and rightist parties did not much change, but the politicians now had many more voters to please. The economic limits of ISI were being reached at the same time that this rise in political participation occurred. The tensions played out within the parties and in the political system. In the 1960s, young leftist and Catholic youth began to organize peasants and demand land reform. Allende's Socialist Party also felt the tensions within its ranks. Always unruly and prone to splits, the socialists were deeply divided between a revolutionary wing and a more moderate faction that tended to align with the communists during the late populist era and during the Allende years (1970–1973).

When Salvador Allende, with his plan to lead a revolution within constitutional and democratic bounds, won a narrow plurality of the vote in 1970, it was not at all clear at first that the Chilean Congress would ratify him as president (which was its function in the event no one got a majority). Only a bungled kidnapping attempt against Chile's head of the armed forces by right-wing groups (funded by the United States) assured him of the presidency. The centrist Christian Democratic Party, responding to public anger at the murder, decided not to block his ascent. Allende's presidency would not survive even three years into his term. In 1973, he died in a coup encouraged by the United States; General Augusto Pinochet assumed power for 16 years, ending Chile's crisis of populism and replacing it with a brutal military dictatorship.

For Review

During its years of implementing ISI, how did Chile's politics differ from those of Argentina and Brazil in the years of Perón and Vargas? Why do most historians and political scientists think, however, that Chile too went through a populist era?

Mexico: Populism After Revolution

The period of populism and ISI did not end always in military rule. In Venezuela, the oil boom of the 1970s allowed populism to endure much longer than in most other South American countries. In Colombia, the army never fully seized power, although its political influence grew as the country endured 25 years of *La Violencia* (the violence) after the assassination of Jorge Gaitán,

a leftist populist, in 1948. But the most important country to escape military rule was Mexico, a consequence of that country having experienced the first major social revolution of the twentieth century. We will look more closely at the Mexican Revolution and its consequences in chapter 8. Here, we want only to note that as Mexican politics began to settle down after the revolutionary era (1910–1917), the country's ruling party adopted ISI as an economic strategy based on a populist social coalition, if not democracy.

Mexico's liberal modernization had lasted for 30 years under the dictator Porfirio Díaz (see chapter 4). In this time of relative political stability, the export sectors of mining and export agriculture expanded. As elsewhere, the benefits flowed to a small upper class. Small landholdings in the north and the communal-owned lands (*ejidos*) in the south were being taken over by big growers and ranchers eager to export to the growing U.S. market. Miners, railroad workers, and a growing population of urban poor were waiting for some of the new wealth to trickle down to them. The middle class chafed under Díaz's refusal to reform the political system. In 1910, Díaz broke a promise to allow free elections and once again engineered his own victory. Francisco Madero, a liberal opposition candidate, was jailed for protesting the outcome. After his release, he called for towns all over the country to rise up in defense of democracy. Madero got more than he bargained for. He got the Mexican Revolution.

Between 1910 and 1917, Mexico was convulsed by civil war. For 11 more years (1917–1928), the country was racked by sporadic uprisings and assassinations. Nearly all the major leaders of the 1910 revolution were dead by 1928. A formula to end the violence was engineered by Plutarco Calles, who founded a political party that embraced almost all the regional *caudillos* and *caciques* of the country. Calles himself might have become a political patriarch in the style of Díaz, but his chosen successor, Lázaro Cárdenas, elected in 1934, had no intention of serving merely as a puppet for Calles. Cárdenas built his own popular base of support by implementing a program that included land reform (hence, Mexican populism did not entirely exclude the peasantry) and state-supported industrialization—ISI.

The Cárdenas presidency was a vibrant era of union organizing, land reform, cultural innovation, and nationalism, culminating in 1938 with the nationalization of the foreign oil companies, a precedent for the region. Once again, a coalition of the working and middle classes supported reform and ISI, but the rural sector could not be politically ignored. Peasants had been mobilized into the great armies that fought in the revolution. They could not be easily sent back to their villages to live in isolation from each other and as peons for big landowners, who were mostly on the losing side of the revolution. Unlike the **Southern Cone** countries, Mexico underwent land reform in the 1930s. However, the rural beneficiaries were subordinated to the political machine, the Institutionalized Party of the Revolution (PRI). Corporatist structures kept peasants under control of the PRI, which controlled the subsidies vital to their survival.

Cárdenas became a popular, much-revered statesman throughout the hemisphere, but the president opted to moderate his redistributive policies later in his term. This led to divisions within the ruling Party of the Mexican Revolution, which had been founded by Calles as a vehicle to resolve disputes within the revolutionary leadership (and not yet called the PRI). The president's chosen successor, Manuel Avila Camacho, prevailed in the 1940 election, but only with the benefit of considerable fraud, repression, and help from the incumbent government.

After 1940, President Camacho greatly slowed land redistribution and reduced aid for agriculture, even though he maintained policies to promote ISI, and for three decades the Mexican economy grew. But when ISI began to falter in the 1960s, political instability began to grow. Once again, ISI development policies and populism were fatefully linked to one another. The Mexican economic crisis of 1982, when the country defaulted on its international debt, was one of the landmark events that spelled the end of ISI and populism and swung Latin American economic policy toward a more **laissez-faire, neoliberal** model.

Mexico's revolution resulted in some exceptional features in its politics, such as civil control over the military, an independent foreign policy, strong political institutions, and orderly succession of presidents for one six-year term. The PRI held onto power for 18 more years after 1982, but it came to rely much more on fraud and repression than in earlier decades, when people had supported it because it was *the party* forged in the fires of Mexico's great revolution. The military never took power, as in Argentina, Brazil, and Chile, but the political system became decidedly more authoritarian, based less and less on popular consent over time.

For Review

Mexico underwent ISI in much the same way that Argentina, Brazil, and Chile did. Why, then, did Mexico develop a longer-lasting institutionalized political system? Why was the rural sector more incorporated into the populist system than in these other cases?

Assessing Populism and ISI—Lessons for Today

The economic development policies associated with populism included creation of investment funds, nationalization of key economic sectors (sometimes), mediated labor policies, investment in infrastructure (dams, roads, ports, etc.), and taxes on imports and exports to finance ISI. These same development policies provided the patronage (jobs, protection from competition, and subsidies) needed to build parties and networks of support. Populists often sounded leftist, especially when they invoked nationalist and anti-imperialist rhetoric. But they were not communists. Some even saw their task as heading off communism through reform; some (e.g., Perón and Rómulo Betancourt of Venezuela) turned strongly anticommunist during the Cold War (1945–1991).

When the strategy of industrializing through import substitution reached its limits (in the 1960s, in most cases), and the economic pie began to shrink, populist democracy also entered into crisis. We will examine the causes more closely in chapter 7, but here we can summarize some of the problems that contributed to ISI's exhaustion as a strategy for growth in the 1960s. One was the failure of business owners, protected by the state from cheaper imports, to modernize their factories to become competitive with factories abroad. Another weakness in the strategy was its failure to modernize agricultural production for the domestic market, even as the cities were growing. Export taxes generated political resistance from mining and agricultural export sectors, the main source of capital for industrialization. The corporatist networks linking parties and leaders to unions and businesses were riddled with clientelism and corruption, inhibiting the efficient use of resources. Populist leaders (excepting Allende) were willing to go only so far to redistribute wealth and income in a way that would bring more people into the consumer market. Educational systems were not geared to build the capacity to innovate technologically.

Corporatist relationships are based on the notion of political reciprocity. An interest group offers support to the state, a leader, or a political party in return for tangible benefits (jobs, subsidies, contracts, services, etc.) that can be doled out to the group's members (clients). Leaders of groups and of parties can use these benefits to reward other members. In a sense, the populist parties and politicians updated traditional patterns of clientelism. Jobs and bags of cement could be just as effective as **compadrazgo** (see chapter 1); in fact, *compadrazgo* did not entirely disappear in the cities. If rivals cannot be bought off, repression is almost always lurking—the iron fist inside the velvet glove. At an extreme, this dual system of co-optation and coercion resembles fascism, where the state asserts almost complete control over social groups. We saw an example of this kind of power in chapter 2 in the story about Venezuelan workers striking to improve their conditions in a metallurgical plant.

During the populist era, the state became a major economic actor, often owning large industries and expanding its treasury with taxes on export enclaves. The political game revolved around competition among groups and parties seeking to share in these resources, a phenomenon called "rent-seeking." In countries such as Chile, which depended heavily on copper exports, and Venezuela, where oil was king, this behavior was pronounced. Terry Karl (1994), a student of oil-exporting states, argues that the presence of great natural wealth in a country can be something of a disadvantage because it fosters rent-seeking capitalists reluctant to take risks or make investments. Why modernize an old textile plant, for example, if the government will subsidize your purchases of cloth and energy, keep the prices of foreign competitors high, and maybe even subsidize the consumers' purchase of your costly products?

The populist era ended tragically. Populism became synonymous with bad macroeconomic policy and demagoguery. However, it was in this period that the masses entered national politics. Furthermore, economic growth rates were higher, even in the 1960s. From 1950 until 1980, Latin America's economic output increased on average 5.5 percent per year; GDP per capita increased by 2.2 percent. The movements of peasants, workers, and women who either initiated populist movements or took advantage of opportunities opened by political leaders greatly expanded the scope of democracy. Whatever its flaws, ISI, populism's development strategy, was the only sustained effort to develop Latin America's economy by looking mainly inward, not outward, in nearly 500 years of history.

For Review

Clientelism and corporatism were common in Latin America before the populist era. And they did not disappear with populism. Did anything fundamental change about Latin American politics between 1900 and the end of the populist era?

Peasant Politics and the Crisis of Populism

We sometimes think of peasant societies as simple, perhaps varying little from one to another. However, peasant societies are far from homogeneous, which makes it difficult to unite them into broad national movements. Many rural populations are ethnically and culturally diverse. For example, in south and central Mexico, one finds many Indigenous peasants with strong communal traditions. In the northern region, one finds individualist, *mestizo* smallholders. Gender relationships can vary greatly too. Women have different roles and responsibilities, depending on whether their men live at home or must migrate for work on plantations or ranches for months when labor is needed—for example, at harvest time.

Peasants with regular access to land, even small parcels, are generally less responsive to political mobilizations. However, when threatened with being uprooted from their land, they become prime candidates to form political movements. Other rural workers have more in common with workers in the city. Peasants hired to work on plantations generally enjoyed wages and working conditions superior to their rural brethren, or even to poor workers in the cities. For this reason, political activists for unions or parties attempted to organize the export-oriented plantations, strategic enclaves producing sugar, cacao, palm oil, tobacco, bananas, and so on for the world market.

Rural workers in these enclaves were easier to organize into unions and movements than peasants tied to the land through traditional relationships with landlords. They lived closer together, were often less culturally conservative, and had some education. They could be more easily reached with pamphlets and group meetings off company property. Though better paid, they had little rights versus owners and overseers. On fruit plantations in Central America and the Pacific coast of the Andes and in sugar cane fields in the Dominican Republic and Cuba, unions emerged, often spurred by the country's Communist Party, which was finding that its "proletariat," the workers that Marx saw as the base for revolution, was not always in the industrial cities but in the export enclaves.

In this respect, plantation workers, like miners and oil workers elsewhere, had more political leverage than the rest of the lower classes had. Struggles to organize workers in strategic economic sectors often converged with demands for democracy and lent support to nationalists and reformers (Bergquist 1986). However, while there were agrarian leagues (for example, in Mexico), populists did not aim to reform the traditional countryside. Labor laws usually made it much more difficult to organize peasants than urban workers, and the local political power (including repression) that landlords had at their disposal could make organizing dangerous. Land redistribution required interfering with property rights, worrying middle-class and private capitalists, and strengthening the incentives for a coup by conservative military officers. As a result, the countryside neither produced food efficiently for the growing cities nor provided a market for new industries.

To raise money for ISI and other government expenditures, populist governments taxed exports. In some cases, they forced landlords or miners to export through state trading houses that set prices and limited profits. This not only alienated owners of mines, ranches, and plantations, but it also induced them—deliberately for political reasons, or simply because of inadequate profits—to produce and export less. For example, Perón forced ranchers to sell their beef to the state, which set the internal price and attempted to market exported meat at a profit. Not only did this alienate the ranchers; it also angered foreign traders.

The land question did not go away. In the 1960s, agrarian reform would reemerge as an issue in many countries. Rural conflict added pressure to democracies already facing declining economies and increased demands in the cities. In their gestation, the unions and social organizations formed by workers and women's groups had great vitality and democratic promise. Even when they were subordinated to populist parties and leaders, their incorporation made it impossible to ignore their interests. This is one reason populism usually was ended by fiercely repressive military governments.

For Review

Why was land reform not on the agenda of most populists? To what extent was Mexico an exception, and why? Populist governments needed the export sector to promote development. Why?

Did ISI Reduce Dependency?

The compatibility of populism with ISI was based on an expanding economic pie. As long as the economy was growing, the middle and working classes had jobs, and the urban poor had the hope of a better future. Economic growth continued throughout the ISI period in the four countries considered in this chapter and in others all the way through 1979 (Hoogvelt 2001; Daly Hayes 1988/1989), though the Argentine case early suggested troubles were on the horizon. But the growth rates do not tell the entire story. Millions of people were leaving the countryside for the city during the ISI period, attracted by jobs, schools, hospitals, and so on. Strong as growth rates were, they did not approach the 10 percent annual rates that characterized industrialization in the earlier stages of capitalism in the wealthy countries, as they were transformed into mature, market societies. How could all of these urban migrants, much less those left behind in the rural areas, be integrated—that is, find jobs, contribute their labor, and have sufficient income to expand the market for national industries?

So Latin America's economies continued to grow, but the limits to growth by ISI were reached in the 1960s. Industries protected by tariffs, subsidized by governments, and able to draw upon a supply of cheap labor failed to modernize and fell behind competitors overseas. Without income redistribution and land reform, there was not enough demand for many industrial products. Few countries had a large enough class of consumers who could afford cars, refrigerators, and other durable consumer goods. And when export prices fell, so did revenues to subsidize industries and maintain social programs.

Most factories had to import their capital goods (e.g., power looms for textile factories) and other inputs needed to produce final consumer goods. The traditional export sectors remained vital to the economy because the subsidies and patronage that greased the system had to be generated by earnings from abroad. Because the prices of Latin America's primary commodities did not keep pace with manufactured goods in most instances, the export sector could not generate the kind of economic surpluses needed to sustain investments. Although some new industries, such as petrochemicals and steel, produced inputs for factories producing consumer goods (e.g., clothing, paper, processed foods), in general Latin American countries could not "deepen" industrialization by producing capital goods (machinery, technology, etc.) and intermediate goods (automobile transmissions, wire, etc.). Instead of classic dependency being overcome, a new form of economic dependence had emerged.

The middle class wanted access to affordable refrigerators, televisions, washing machines, and so on. Foreign enterprises could meet this demand more cheaply if freed from the constraints of quotas, tariffs, and other measures associated with ISI. Some of the most important new enterprises—for example, automobiles—were the result of investments by foreign companies to build factories inside their key export markets, especially in the larger countries. In this way, they could evade tariff and quota barriers to keep their markets. The purpose of ISI was to jump-start a process of national development and not increase dependency on imports, but import bills were going up, not down. Prebisch and other economists that supported ISI were aware of this and warned that protection was becoming counterproductive, but the political logic built into ISI made it difficult for countries to adjust policies.

The most dynamic capitalists in Latin America were coming to identify progress in their country with attracting foreign investment, not ISI. Fernando Henrique Cardoso, the Brazilian political sociologist who later became president, called this unanticipated result "associated-dependent development." Cardoso and his Chilean colleague Enzo Faletto agreed that foreign capital exploited labor (Cardoso and Faletto 1979, first published in Portuguese in 1971). Indeed, suppressing labor to attract foreign capital was a central function of government in dependent countries. Unlike other **dependency theorists**, however, Cardoso and Faletto rejected the idea that foreign investment *caused* underdevelopment. They argued that foreign capital brought developmental technology and promoted growth of a native capitalist class in the country—one with an internationalist rather than nationalist outlook.

In their view, this new capitalist class was "associated" in a dependent way with foreign capitalists; hence, they coined the term "associated-dependent development." For example, the Brazilian owner of a factory producing industrial paint might have a foreign automobile manufacturer as his principal customer. His economic interest, then, would become linked to the continued presence and prosperity of the foreign manufacturer, who probably has attracted Brazilian partners as co-owners. In a way, Cardoso and Faletto anticipated **globalization** because they saw the development of a different kind of **bourgeoisie**, one that critics of globalization today call a "transnational capitalist class."

Not only was this theory controversial, but also one of its authors, Cardoso, became increasingly controversial himself. He entered politics and became a minister of finance and then president (1995–2003) of Brazil. Cardoso maintained that he was pursuing a pragmatic agenda that neither embraced nor rejected neoliberalism. To many on the left, he had moved from critic to advocate of associated-dependent development.

For Review

From an economic standpoint, what were some of the reasons that ISI faltered? How did ISI on the one hand seem to reinforce economic dependency? What does "associated-dependent development" mean?

Did Populism Advance or Retard Democracy?

Because populism often ended in a coup that inaugurated a long and brutal period of military rule in most of the region, it is easy to forget that populist regimes rarely came to power without the support of the military. Indeed, populists sometimes came from military ranks, as was the case with Perón and Vargas. As president (1951–1954), Jacobo Arbenz, a Guatemalan colonel, attempted to nationalize unused land from the United Fruit Company. Lázaro Cárdenas was a revolutionary general before he became a state governor and then president. A Peruvian general, Juan Velasco Alvarado, came to power in 1968 and embarked on a program of land reform and income distribution. Even today, populist leaders may rise out of military ranks—and later be threatened by their more conservative military colleagues. Hugo Chávez, who came to power in 1998 with a radical leftist agenda for Venezuela, was a colonel in 1992 when he burst upon the scene after leading an unsuccessful coup against an elected but unpopular government. The lesson is that not only is the military involved in politics, but politics also takes place inside the military.

Today, neoliberals see little good about the populist past, but in reality most populists were more interested in promoting capitalism than transforming it. Arbenz sought to nationalize United Fruit's land to promote a social class of small farmers, not collectivize agriculture along the model of the Soviet Union. Arbenz welcomed communist support for his program; the Guatemalan communists were more interested in organizing unions on the fruit plantations than in creating Soviet-style collective farms. However, Perón's anticommunist attitude was more typical of populists in this era. In a speech in 1950 he warned,

> It is beyond doubt that the communist system has its greatest chances of prevailing in the Western World in so far as the capitalist system offers no other doctrine than failed, liberal individualism, while leaving vulnerable its flanks, which are, outside of the United States, people exhausted by poverty and hunger, allied out of desperation with whatever other system is offered them.

Perón promoted his program not as revolutionary socialism but as a third way, an attempt to humanize capitalism and a necessary measure "to battle the communist economic system successfully" (Perón 1950).

Generally, the communists concentrated on organizing workers, both on plantations (e.g., sugar estates in Cuba, fruit plantations in Guatemala) and in the factories and mines (e.g., among copper workers in Chile, among oil workers in Venezuela, and in slaughterhouses in Argentina). But the communists were not nearly as revolutionary as Perón's words or the rhetoric of the U.S. government suggested. They often took the position that Latin America first had to overcome its "feudal" past and experience capitalism before it could move on to communism. Loyal to Moscow's leadership position, they sometimes decried liberal democracy as "bourgeois," but in other times (e.g., when the Soviet Union and U.S. were allied during World War II or during the era of détente between the two countries in 1968–1976), they promoted alliances with reformist parties. Sometimes this resulted in splits between the more pragmatic communists with seats in Congress or with union leadership positions and the more radical party members committed to revolutionary change.

For Review

Why were most populists sometimes in conflict with communists? Why were populists and communists sometimes able to get along, sometimes not?

Populism Yesterday and Today

In the last ten years, a steady stream of books and news analysis, many by political scientists, has painted populism as an inherently antidemocratic force. One of the most influential books in this vein was authored by two political scientists, Steven Levitsky and Daniel Ziblatt (2018), whose main theme is that the "guardrails" are coming off the political systems in the United States and other liberal democracies. The book may be quite timely and relevant about the dangers of the wave of nationalist populism and in locating the cause of its worldwide surge in the economic and social consequences of global inequalities and threats posed to national sovereignty by neoliberal globalization. However, at times the authors assert that populism itself is inherently antidemocratic, which can be questioned.

And given the authors' background as comparativists specializing in Latin America, it is not surprising that no populist, other than Donald Trump, is cited as an example of the dangers of populism more than Hugo Chávez was. Clearly, Venezuela's slide into economic chaos and semi-authoritarian politics in recent years raises serious questions about Chávez's responsibility for the debacle that followed his death, but I want to caution against assuming that Latin America's **Pink Tide** populists fit the rather one-sided, stereotypical image of Chávez, Bolivia's Evo Morales, and other leaders. The history of populist movements in Latin America, like that of populist movements in the United States, is complicated and full of shades of gray.

Discussion Questions

1. What social groups in Latin America gained the most from import substitution policies, and which ones gained the least or lost? How did ISI as a development strategy also help populists build a base of political support? Do you think that overall ISI was a success or a failure?
2. List some of the key factors that brought about the crisis of populism. Do you think the roots of the crisis were predominantly economic or political?
3. Given the experience with populism in Latin America, would you say that calling a politician a "populist" should be a compliment or an insult? Why?

Resources for Further Study

Reading: Separating myth from fact is the object of Nicholas Fraser and Marysa Navarro, *Evita: The Real Life of Evita Perón* (New York: Norton, 1996). Paul Drake's *Socialism and Populism in Chile, 1932–52* (Urbana: University of Illinois Press, 1978) is a good case study of midcentury populism. My own *Venezuela: Tarnished Democracy* (Boulder, CO: Westview Press, 1991) reviews the populist experience in that country.

Video and Film: Three episodes of the Americas (1992) series—on Brazil (*Capital Sins*), Argentina (*Garden of Forking Paths*), and Chile (*In Women's Hands*)—review the twentieth-century rise and fall of populism, military rule, and transitions to democracy. *Hour of the Furnaces* (1968) documents the rise of guerrilla violence and military response in 1968 in Argentina.

On the Internet: You have to be careful with Wikipedia, but the page on Juan Perón is well referenced (see http://en.wikipedia.org/wiki/Juan_Peron).

6

Development and Dependency: Theory and Practice in Latin America

Focus Questions

▶ What are the main debates about the causes and proper way to overcome under-development in Latin America?

▶ What role did colonialism play in laying the basis for economic underdevelopment in Latin America? Why do so many Latin Americans think that colonialism persists today?

▶ How has the role of the state in shaping Latin America's economy evolved in Latin America since World War II? What are the implications of globalization for defining the state's role today?

▶ How well have the major strategies—such as extractivism, import substitution, and neoliberalism—fared in the quest for economic development in Latin America?

▶ What does "economic development" mean? What should it mean?

THE OBJECTIVE OF this chapter is to give you a grounding on the experiences and debates that have brought Latin America to a moment, today, when the quest for economic development remains a key objective of all countries in the region. We mainly focus on theories of underdevelopment and development as they directly relate to the state's role in promoting economic growth, but we also recognize that "growth" is not the same as "development." We put aside for the moment that caveat, as well as the issue of whether growth defined as expansion of the gross domestic product (GDP) is sustainable, especially in environmental terms.

Latin America's search for a strategy to achieve economic development has evolved through at least four different phases.

1. The first post-independence approach took place in the era of **liberal modernization** (approximately 1850 until 1930) (see chapter 4). Outward-oriented national elites sought to foster export growth and create conditions for replicating European social and cultural conditions. In this period, the state had an active role in building infra-structure (railroads, ports, etc.), fostering immigration, and opening natural resources to exploitation by foreign and domestic capitalists.

2. The Great Depression (1927–1945) and World War II ushered in a period in which countries, with the exception of the smallest and poorest, sought to move beyond their high degree of dependence on the export of primary commodities (agriculture, minerals, oil) by adopting **import substitution industrialization** (ISI) (see chapter 5). This strategy was closely associated with **populism** and the entry of the masses into politics.

3. Populism and ISI came to an end around 1970, when highly repressive military governments drove the masses out of public life and implemented pro-business policies that reduced the state's role in promoting development. This strategy resembled the era of liberal modernization in its reliance on technical and economic expertise and faith in the forces of the market, for which reason it became **neoliberalism** ("neo" for "new version"). Around 1980, major technological changes, mainly in communications and computer science, facilitated the rapid acceleration underway among the world's national economy, that is, globalization. Although globalization can take other forms, in this era globalization became inseparably linked with neoliberalism. Neoliberal globalization not only continued after the transitions to democracy; it also took on a character of inevitability.

4. The rise of **Pink Tide** populism has been characterized as a new, "post-neoliberal" period," but that should not be taken to mean that neoliberal globalization ended. In fact, there is little agreement about whether any of the Pink Tide governments, even Hugo Chávez's Venezuela (1999–2013), fundamentally broke from neoliberalism. Much of the Pink Tide has receded somewhat in face of a surge of conservative nationalist populism that seeks to revive the centrality of the nation-state. All we really can say about post-neoliberalism is that the **Washington Consensus**, the widespread belief in the inevitable triumph of an international, liberal capitalist order, has been shaken, leaving the future highly uncertain. The coronavirus pandemic of 2020 added to the uncertainty.

Contending Approaches to Development

The field of "development studies" emerged after World War II. This was a period in which the United States held enormous global power to shape an international economic order predicated on open trade, to be fostered by

1. The World Bank, founded to finance infrastructure projects to facilitate economic development.
2. The International Monetary Fund, given the mission of maintaining a currency stability and avoiding the kind of global financial meltdown that precipitated the Great Depression of the 1930s.
3. The General Agreement on Tariffs and Trade (GATT), which would in 1995 morph into the World Trade Organization (WTO).

A forgotten episode in this post-war proposition, led by Latin American countries at the Havana Conference of 1948, was the attempt to create a fourth agency, the International Trade Organization (ITO). The ITO would have included power to regulate trade in these commodities, the backbone of the economies of the Global South. The countries at the Havana Conference wanted to assign the ITO a mission to stabilize prices and smooth out the destructive cycles of boom and bust (see Hudson 2003). The effort failed when the United States refused to even submit the treaty to the Senate for consideration. In the 1970s, there would be a second attempt by the Global South to regulate the commodities trade, part of a proposed New International Economic Order. It too failed.

We need to keep this international context in mind as we examine development theory, especially as it emerged from social science and history departments of large, prestigious American universities and think tanks, often funded by the United States government. Large grants were made to establish area studies programs, many of them focused on the research relevant to the foreign policy aims of the United States, including "containment" of the rival, the communist bloc in the Cold War. Economic development was seen as key to producing political stability, especially in places where insurgencies or popular leftist governments challenged American hegemony and the international economic regime created after World War II. In this **Cold War** environment, **modernization theory** dominated mainstream academic approaches to development.

Modernization Theory

Modernization has multiple meanings. It can refer simply to efforts by government to update and implement new technologies and the physical infrastructure (roads, utilities, factories, etc.). Good transportation and communication facilities and an education system that prepares prospective employees for the labor forces are also part of modernizations. In the contemporary global economy, countries are virtually compelled to modernize the infrastructure of their economies to compete for investment.

However, the modernization theories of development are usually focused on a different factor, seeing causes of poverty and underdevelopment mainly in "traditional" social values, sometimes referring to the countries of the Global South as "backward" societies. Modernization theorists assumed that Europe's transition from feudalism to capitalism is the model path that societies would follow to development—only more rapidly. Feudal society was mainly rural; its values emphasized the importance of people accepting their place in society, with the aristocracy (lords) naturally ruling over peasants (serfs). The latter owed service to the lords, who in turn provided them protection. The bargain was supposedly blessed by God, and the Catholic Church was itself a major landholder. Serfs were not allowed to leave the estates and work elsewhere; they were not "free" in this sense. However, neither were their overlords "free" to displace them from the land. The land and people on it were regarded as one. A small merchant class existed, but market relations were not very significant to most people's lives; what sustained them was produced and consumed on the manor.

This description is nothing more than a broad sketch of a system that varied a lot from place to place, but it suffices for us to understand how it has influenced modernization theory and its application to Latin America (and other parts of the **Third World**). Modernization theorists generally read the great transition from feudalism to capitalism in Europe between 1300 and 1900 as rooted in cultural change. This transition happened later in Spain and Portugal than it did in Northern Europe, so modernization theorists often held that Latin America inherited cultural features resembling those of feudalism in Europe, while North America benefited from the transfer of the modernization underway in Great Britain.

Modernization theorists drew heavily upon the ideas of the great German sociologist Max Weber. His *In the Protestant Revolution and the Spirit of Capitalism and Other Writings* argued that the advancement of capitalism was driven by cultural changes associated with the values of the Protestant Reformation. The implication was clear: Catholicism was holding back Latin America.

As we saw in chapter 4, Latin America's liberal modernizers believed that economic development required emulating Europe. Some advocated progressive policies in education to prepare their own people for development, but more saw the solution in attracting "modern" immigrants. Many of them believed in the necessity to "whiten" the population.

To some extent, communists and capitalists could agree upon this interpretation of development. They both see interaction between value systems and economic change, and both see development happening in a series of stages that all societies would go through. But Marx put the economic factors at the forefront. The *Communist Manifesto* (Marx and Engels 1848) presented capitalism as a necessary stage of history before socialism or communism. Marxist thought evolved under the influence of the formidable thinking of Vladimir Lenin, leader of the 1917 Bolshevik Revolution in Russia. Marx opposed imperialism, but he thought it would accelerate, not retard, development outside Europe. Lenin emphasized imperialism and colonialism as fundamental causes of underdevelopment.

Perhaps the most influential of modernization theorists was the American social scientist Walt Rostow, who was a student at Yale University and professor at Columbia. His influential treatise *The Stages of Growth* (1960) was confidently subtitled "A Non-Communist Manifesto." His "manifesto," like Marx's, predicted the passing of "feudalistic" social structures into modern capitalist ones, but instead of communism he saw a mature capitalist society, a mass consumer society as the end point of development. The problem, he thought, was that communists were undermining this transition to achieve their goal of an international socialist revolution. He put his theories into action as national security advisor to presidents John F. Kennedy and Lyndon B. Johnson in the 1960s, and he became an architect of the Vietnam War. Rostow recommended providing military aid to fight leftist insurgencies and economic aid to Third World countries, including Latin America, until they were economically developed and politically stable. The Cuban Revolution of 1959 and Fidel Castro's alliance with the Soviet Union provided the "threat" in Latin America.

Modernization theory interprets the Latin culture forged out of Iberian, African, and Indian social values as the major obstacle to development. Tradition is something to be overcome and not utilized. Latin Americans were urged to stop thinking in terms of inherited status, natural inequalities, and the sacredness of old ways of doing things. They needed, the theory suggested, to separate their loyalty to their families and close friends from their responsibility to treat each other as citizens, customers, employers, and so on. Once this occurs, Latin Americans would progress out of the early stages of capitalism, which are always characterized by great inequalities and poverty for workers, and find the path to sustained economic growth and development beneficial to all.

From this perspective, underdevelopment is a condition that has characterized all countries at one time or another and not something imposed by imperialism or colonization. Modernization—and development—theories commonly assumed that Latin America has been left behind and would eventually "catch up" and join the ranks of developed nations. The political challenge facing Latin America after World War II was dealing with an "over-all process of change, which happens to substantial parts of the population in countries which are moving from traditional to modern ways of life," as stated by Karl Deutsch (1961: 394). Governments in Africa, the Middle East, Asia, and Latin America were all dealing with the forces of "social mobilization"—urbanization, industrialization, mass communications, and other changes that undermined the traditional authority typical of the rural village. "These processes," said Deutsch, "tend to go together in certain historical situations and stages of economic development; [they] are identifiable and recurrent, in their essentials from one country to another; and they are relevant for politics" (1961: 493).

Rostow saw the stages beginning with a period of transition in which tradition gives way to modernity. At some point, all the countries that were "developed" were "underdeveloped" until they entered a dynamic period of "takeoff" into high economic growth rates. This "takeoff" was typically a period of economic hypergrowth (about 10 percent per year), for about a 40-year period. Table 6.1 (in the Punto de Vista) shows when Rostow thought this had occurred for some nations that had achieved development at the time (1960) he was writing. By his theory, growth rates level off at "maturity," when growth continues but at a more stable, less dynamic pace. Eventually, then, nations become mass consumer societies, emulating social and economic patterns found in countries that industrialized early. Note that Rostow thought that Argentina and Mexico, then actively pursuing **import substitution industrialization**, were at the takeoff point.

Rostow (as noted previously, an advisor to the Kennedy and Johnson administrations between 1961 and 1968) and others (two influential works were by Lipset 1960 and Huntington 1968) believed that communists were taking advantage of the turmoil in societies transitioning from tradition to modernity. The solution? Most of these intellectuals, often advisors in government, advocated providing military aid to hold off the communists and economic aid to speed the developmental transition. In Latin America, that task took on special urgency in Washington after the Cuban Revolution of 1959.

In *Political Order in Changing Societies* (1968), Huntington took up a theme, mobilization, from Deutsch's work. Huntington defined "social mobilization" as a process associated with the shift (sometimes called the "demographic transition") from the countryside to the city. Here the word "mobilization" has a dual meaning: (1) movement (migration) from the countryside to town and (2) the movement from traditional relationships of inequality and subjection under landowners and religious authority to the world of the city, with its markets, mass communications, schools, employment for pay, and other "modern" experiences. Rural areas are not left untouched. Urbanization puts pressure on the countryside to modernize agricultural production. Eventually, said Huntington, reform-minded groups will mobilize the peasantry in hopes of changing the rural economy, resulting in a "green uprising" that is aimed against "imperial power" and the ruling oligarchy (Huntington 1968: 76–77). In several ways, this interpretation seemed to apply to Latin America in the twentieth century, as cities grew and eventually pressures for change (e.g., agrarian reform) in the countryside threatened the power of traditional oligarchies. Like Rostow, Huntington saw American counterinsurgency wars as necessary for containing communism, complemented by aid programs to support modernization. President John F. Kennedy called the programs for Latin America the "Alliance for Progress."

PUNTO DE VISTA: CAN LATIN AMERICA REPEAT THE STAGES OF GROWTH?

Rostow published *The Stages of Growth* in 1960, when most of the South America was pursuing industrialization using the import substitution policies promoted by ECLAC. In that same year, ECLAC promoted the idea that the 1960s would be the "decade of development." Rostow and most other modernization theorists agreed with this optimism. During the Cold War and rivalry with the Soviet Union, they were worried about how development might destabilize developing countries, leaving them vulnerable to kinds of communist revolutions that had already occurred in China and Cuba. Structuralism, not laissez-faire policies that we associate today with neoliberalism, was the dominant economic ideology of the period. "Globalization" was not in anyone's vocabulary at this time. Only later in the 1960s would any large-scale concern arise about environmental limits on economic growth under consideration; pollution, not global warming, was the main concern about industry.

Table 6.1 is based on a chart from Rostow's book in which he mapped out where 14 countries, including Argentina and Mexico, fit into his scheme. He could have included Brazil and most other South American countries in about the same place as these two nations. We have reproduced his placing of some of the countries, including the two Latin American ones. While one might quibble on exactly when one stage or another happened, by his criteria, his assessment of the countries' "stage" is fairly accurate for the West European, Japanese, and Latin American cases. The most intriguing question is, to what extent did his theory accurately predict the economic future of the Latin American countries?

TABLE 6.1 Rostow's View of Stages of Development, 1960

Country	Take off	Maturity	Mass consumption	Comments
Britain	1780–1810	1855	1938	Generally, fits Rostow; all countries he sees with hindsight.
France	1830–1865	1910	1955	
U.S.A.	1845–1880	1910	1920	
Germany	1855–1890	1910	1955	
Japan	1880–1905	1950	1960	
Russia	1900–1920	1955	Not reached	Rostow staunchly anticommunist, but sees Russia as successful industrializer.
Canada	1905–1925	1950	1925	Maturity after mass consumption?
Australia	1865–1892 and 1940–1960	1940	1940	Interrupted development; agricultural prosperity and late industrialization.
China	1940–	Not reached	Not reached	Real takeoff seems to have come in 1980s.
India	1940–	Not reached	Not reached	
Argentina	1940–	Not reached	Not reached	Seemed to be industrializing, but never "took off."
Mexico	1940–	Not reached	Not reached	

Source: Rostow (1960).

Here is a set of questions that the table raises for us today.

- Western Europe, Japan, and the United States were already mature, mass consumer, developed countries. They had already passed through the period of "preconditions" (social and cultural change) and experienced the "takeoff" phase of sustained growth at approximately 10 percent. Leaving aside the other cases for now, did Rostow get it right in predicting that these had reached a steady state of prosperity sustained by relatively low rates of economic growth? Does "mature consuming" mean the these countries no longer "develop"?
- Curiously, Rostow, a strident anticommunist, saw Russia as having gone through takeoff in the years preceding the Russian Revolution. That certainly would be questioned by much of East European area studies, but what was more generally accepted was that Russia had become a mass consumption society, regardless of how inefficiently its domestic industries operated. Supposedly, once the communist central planning system was dismantled, this should have liberated the Russian economy to finish its journey through the stages of growth. But the decade of the 1990s saw a drastic economic shock treatment—structural adjustment policies and a drastic lowering of Russian standards of living. There has been some recovery, but by both economic and social measurements, Russia is much less economically prosperous than is the capitalist West.

- On the other hand, for China, according to the World Bank, average rates of growth between 1978 and 2011 (33 years) were over 10 percent, and since 2011 they have largely stayed in the 6 to 7 percent range. On a per capita basis, it is even greater, due to policies to limit population growth. For India, the growth rate is less impressive but nonetheless steadily between 5 and 8 percent every year since 1991, well over world averages. In that year, India began to dismantle policies of import substitution. However, both China and India are so large that the equivalent of the entire middle and upper classes of the United States would fit into that of either country, but a large percentage of the population continued to live in conditions characteristic of underdevelopment. It is worth noting as well that both countries "developed" by pursuing an export strategy (not unlike South Korea and Taiwan); these paradigmatic "newly industrialized countries" (NICs) seem to have decisively moved from the ranks of peripheral, underdeveloped countries into the "core" of the world system.
- As for Mexico and Argentina, like Brazil and other countries, as this chapter describes, the 1970s saw steadily falling growth rates and economic (and political) crisis, which was followed in the 1980s by growth without equality in the period from 1990 to 2010.

For Discussion

To what extent have Rostow's theories and predictions panned out? Given the benefit of hindsight, what would you say he failed to consider? Some would say that neither Marxists, modernization theorists (like Rostow), structuralists (like Prebisch and his team at ECLAC), dependency theorists, nor just about everyone else got "development" theory right. Do you agree? Are all of the theories simply obsolete today, or do they still provide some useful insights into the question of why some countries in the world are more prosperous than others are?

If you want more data, you can consult the World Bank's archives at https://data.worldbank.org/country.

For Review

How does Rostow's framework reflect the idea of "stages" of development? Why did he call his most influential book a "Non-Communist Manifesto"? Why does Huntington think that modernization might engender political instability?

Marxism, Dependency Theory, and Latin America's "Structuralists"

In the *Communist Manifesto*, Karl Marx and Friedrich Engels (1848) outline their own theory of historical stages. It asserts that all human societies pass through five stages—from primitive communism (no real social classes, but life is precarious at best); to slave societies (characteristic of the ancient world); to feudalism (Europe in the Middle Ages); to capitalism (developing in Europe around 1800 with industrialization); and finally to communism (a classless, stateless society). Because workers, mostly city dwellers, must sell their labor to capitalists (i.e., find employment; get a job) to survive, the "proletariat" (wage earners) can come into existence only once capitalism emerges. The logic was: without capitalism, no proletariat; without a proletariat, no socialist or communist revolution. Marx and Engels found imperialism to be morally indefensible; imperialism had a historical logic, but its historical role was to accelerate the pace by which countries such as China, Brazil, and India were becoming capitalist. In this sense, like modernization theorists, the classical Marxist view saw foreign investment as developing, not retarding colonial and neocolonial (including Latin American) societies.

This perspective was not just for academic discussion and debate. Communist parties emerged as major actors in several Latin American countries after the Russian Revolution of 1917. Although Moscow's "line" shifted from time to time, for much of the twentieth century communist parties adopted the view that revolution in Latin America had to be postponed until the day that capitalism fully matured. When the Cuban Revolution (1959) occurred, and Fidel Castro later declared the country a "Marxist–Leninist" state, he was endorsing Lenin's ideal about how a revolutionary state should be organized and also the Russian leader's view that imperialism had created "weak links" in the capitalist systems, that is, countries where the bourgeoisie (capitalist class) was weak.

However, Moscow-oriented communist parties still held that capitalism had to develop much further before revolution could take place. A proletariat had yet to fully develop, and because capitalism was an improvement over feudalism, communists sometimes had to make alliances with capitalist, liberal parties. Already, the Chinese Revolution challenged the old theories by mobilizing not the urban workers, but the peasants. At the conclusion of this long, slow process, the cities would eventually fall like ripe fruit. Now the Cuban Revolution challenged both of those interpretations. And insurrection in the cities enabled a rural-based movement of young guerrilla fighters, who started out only three years before with 26 fighters, to topple a regime heavily armed by the United States.

And there was more heresy in the church of communism yet to come. Young leftists all over the hemisphere were ready to embrace the ideas of Castro and his charismatic minister of economic planning, Che Guevara. Guevara believed that the Cuban people could work together in an ethical way to develop the economy. Economic development was not necessary to create a "New Man"; a New Man would create a developed socialist economy. To many Marxists this was heresy, restoring values to a factor in the motors of history. To the young generation in Latin America, it was an inspiration.

Marxism is a broad school of thought, not confined to communist movements. For example, some Catholics, especially those living and working with poor people, have sought to reconcile Marxism with their religious beliefs, questioning the view that Marxists must be atheists. Thinkers such as Enrique Dussel (1980: 117), an Argentine based in Mexico, have called for a new "theory of religion" that "would allow all the people to be impelled with a profound religious consciousness into the liberating process." For some religious Latin Americans, their faith was a motive for revolution.

In the 1960s, Latin American social scientists began to raise doubts about the orthodox Marxist view that Latin America needed to repeat Europe's experience and pass through a stage of capitalism. Brazil's Andre Gunder Frank (1967), perhaps the most influential of these thinkers, pointed out that European feudalism was based on a manorial economy that was largely self-contained, with very little trade. In contrast, Latin America's economies produced raw materials for the world market. In Europe, the Christian religion was shared by lord and peasant, cementing the social structure. In Latin America, Christianity was imposed on native peoples and on slaves brought to work in export-oriented economies. Out of this colonial legacy, Latin American countries should best be called "dependent," not "underdeveloped."

Dependency theory comes in a variety of versions, some very much in the Marxist tradition, others not. The most common version cited was the one formulated by Frank, who argued that underdevelopment is not a condition in which all societies found themselves before progress. Instead, he said, some societies *underdeveloped* others. He wrote,

> Our ignorance of the underdeveloped countries' history leads us to assume that their past and indeed their present resemble earlier stages of the history of the now developed countries. This ignorance and this assumption lead us into serious misconceptions about contemporary underdevelopment and development. Further, most studies of development and underdevelopment fail to take account of the economic and other relations between the metropolis and its economic colonies throughout the history of the worldwide expansion and development of the mercantilist and capitalist system.
>
> (Frank 1967)

By "mercantilist," Frank refers to the way Latin America under colonial rule was integrated into the world economic system as an exporter of primary goods and importer of finished products. There existed, he argued, a systematic inequality that subordinated Latin America to the interest of the wealthier and more powerful nations. This idea was popularized throughout the hemisphere in *The Open Veins of Latin America*, published in 1971 by the Uruguayan journalist Eduardo Galeano (new edition, 1997). "Veins" here had a double meaning: The region's mineral wealth (ore veins) was flowing out and depleting the region's natural capital, and its workers were giving up the blood in their veins to produce materials for the wealthy countries. Other theorists in the Global South, such as the Egyptian Samir Amin (1977), picked up on this dependency thesis.

Modernization theorists see foreign investment and trade as fostering development, not only by providing investment funds, technology, and overseas markets, but also by bringing developed-world social values to "traditional" societies. Frank and the dependency theorists had a more materialist explanation for why Latin America's people were poor. Latin America's commodity exports were undervalued in the world economy. Foreign investment in the region's mines and fertile soil really had the effect of decapitalizing the economy, draining its wealth.

Some political scientists and economists tested Frank's dependency theory using economic data and statistical methods. For example, one study (Kaufman et al. 1975) collected data on foreign investment and correlated it with various measures of economic development. The authors concluded that the higher the levels of foreign investment, the higher the levels of development, contradicting Frank's thesis that foreign investment was a cause of underdevelopment. The poorest countries in Latin America, the ones with the lowest rates of economic growth, usually were the ones that attract the least amount of foreign investment.

Some Latin American social scientists responded that dependency theory should not be reduced to Frank's work alone, nor was it meant to be tested in this way. They argue that dependency should be considered a general approach, one that should include attention to cultural and political—not just economic—dependency. F. H. Cardoso (1977), later president of Brazil, complained that more complex and subtle ideas about dependency had escaped notice in the North. American and European scholars were "consumers" of an intellectual idea fermented in Latin America and not fully understanding of debates about dependency's meaning. Cardoso and his colleague, Enzo Faletto, developed a theory of "associated dependence" that recognized Latin American subordination to developed capitalist countries but also viewed Latin American political and economic processes as having a capitalist dynamic of their own (Cardoso and Faletto 1979).

Most dependency theorists today accept today that the cause of Latin America's "underdevelopment" cannot be reduced to an unfair trading system where primary goods are exported and sold for much less value than goods imported from abroad. Dependency theory today puts more weight on social class structures and class conflicts inside Latin America (Dos Santos 1974; Petras 1980). Some Latin Americans found Frank's theory fatalistic. It implied that Latin Americans themselves could have no control over their futures. Agustín Cueva, an Ecuadorean social scientist (2003: 66–69), argued for dependency theorists to incorporate more Marxist analysis and not let the region's own capitalists off the hook by blaming foreigners. Cueva (2003: 66–67) remarked, "Dependency theory has in fact sought to become a 'neo-Marxism' without Marx."

For Review

What do both Marx and Rostow, despite their differences, seem to have in common regarding the idea of development? Why do some Marxists criticize dependency theory or at least Frank's version of it? Why did the Cuban Revolution challenge some key ideas in Marxism?

Structuralists and Import Substitution Industrialization

Among those who try to relate internal and external causes of underdevelopment to one another is a school of economics called "structuralism." Structuralists were inspired by the work of Raúl Prebisch, an Argentine economist and first secretary general of the United Nations Economic Commission on Latin America and the Caribbean (**ECLAC**; in Spanish, CEPAL), created after World War II, around the time of the Havana Conference. Prebisch's research on historical patterns of trade supported the *dependista* claim that the terms of trade were stacked against Latin America. However, he and other structuralists saw limitations rooted in domestic economic structures. They took aim at "bottlenecks" in the domestic economy. For example, the inefficient countryside could neither provide cheap food for workers in the city nor generate a demand for what urban factories produced. The financial system provided little credit to get start-up industries off the ground.

Prebisch had been head of Argentina's Central Bank during the Depression. Between 1929 and 1932, the prices for food and raw materials dropped about 50 percent (often more), devastating the export-based economies of Latin America. With unemployment afflicting a quarter to half of workers in North America and Europe, the foreign factories that used copper, tin, rubber, and other Latin American exports were closing. With wages plummeting, workers and consumers in the wealthy countries reduced their purchases of beef, sugar, and other commodities. The industrialized countries were raising tariffs (import taxes), making it harder for Latin Americans to access their markets.

As the prices for its exports plummeted, Latin America's capacity to import fell 30 percent between 1930 and 1934 (Furtado 1971: 73). Even people with money found fewer goods to buy on the domestic market. Chile was hit especially hard; in 1932, its copper and nitrates earned only 12 cents for each dollar they had earned in 1929. As a result, the country managed to import only 20 percent of what it had bought before the Depression (Drake 1978: 60–63). In 1920, in Cuba, sugar prices had already fallen from 22.5 cents to 3.625 cents per pound in one year, but they would fall even further, to 1.47 cents in 1929 (Hanson 1951: 107). In El Salvador, the price of coffee fell from US$15.75 per hundred kilograms in 1928 to US$7.50 in 1932 (Armstrong and Shenk 1982). Three-quarters of Cuba's exports consisted of sugar, and 90 percent of Salvadoran export revenues came from coffee. These crops took up nearly all the best land. These countries, though blessed with fertile soil and favorable climate, had little capacity to feed their own people.

World War II (1939–1945) brought a different problem—high prices for exports but not much to buy. Although most Latin American countries capped prices as a contribution to the Allied cause, increased demand for the area's commodities caused a surge in prices, especially for vital goods such as copper, oil, and rubber. The industrial countries were pouring all their industrial resources into the war. Instead of manufacturing clothing, they were producing uniforms; instead of cars, they manufactured tanks. Suddenly, Latin American countries had foreign exchange, but there was a shortage on the world market of the goods they wanted to buy.

Latin Americans thought that the situation would change after the war, but they were disappointed. Some U.S. thinkers were sympathetic to the Havana Conference's proposal to regulate the trade in commodities, but there was little sympathy for it in the U.S. Senate. At Bretton Woods, the diplomats created the World Bank, the IMF, and GATT (the predecessor of today's WTO) to regulate global financial markets and liberalize trade, but the U.S.

vetoed any attempt to stabilize the prices of the agricultural, oil, and mining products that were the core exports of Latin America. The United States implemented a gigantic Marshall Plan for Europe, and Japan also received generous assistance. Even though Latin Americans had held down prices to help the Allies win the war, postwar planning did little to help their economies.

Latin Americans had vivid memories of how a freefall in commodity prices could affect their lives. The situation during the Depression had been desperate and, as might be expected, had led to political instability. Sixty thousand of 70,000 miners were unemployed in Chile. In 1932, the country's military government came crashing down amid calls for social revolution. In El Salvador, a peasant revolt was crushed by the military in "La Matanza," which cost anywhere from 10,000 to 30,000 lives in the tiny country, affectionately called "the flea" by its poets. A revolt by a coalition of civilian reformers and military sergeants in Cuba in 1934 nearly produced a revolution. Instead, it led eventually to the dictatorship of one of the sergeants, Fulgencio Batista, whose despotism was overthrown by Fidel Castro in 1959.

At the same time, Latin America took notice that the Depression experience had altered the attitude of the liberal democracies, even in the United States, about government's proper role in regulating the market. Franklin Roosevelt's "New Deal" began to use the government to stimulate demand and restart the economy. He also introduced reforms, such as social security, major infrastructure projects (e.g., dams and electrification), and progressive legislation to help unions. Latin Americans noticed that, in the rising hegemon of the north, an era of laissez-faire capitalism was giving way to a period of active government involvement.

After World War II, Prebisch assembled a team of economists at the United Nations from Latin America, and in the late 1940s and 1950s they worked on demonstrating the importance of structural problems. ECLAC researchers believed that inequality limited demand, so they advocated measures to redistribute wealth and thus eliminate this bottleneck to industrialization. To address what they saw as a chronic imbalance of trade between Latin America's raw materials and the developed countries' manufactured goods, they urged governments to take measures to develop industries whose production would *substitute* for imports. Thus, ECLAC added intellectual heft to the argument for ISI. Chile, Brazil, Argentina, Mexico, and other governments already had created special financial institutes to fund private and state-owned enterprises, as well as to make low-interest loans to private entrepreneurs.

Import substitution and structuralism stand in contradiction to economic theories based on **laissez-faire** and **comparative advantage**, which are at the heart of neoliberal thought. Modernization theorists were often sympathetic to structuralism. They regarded foreign aid as a way to help industrialize Latin America, providing opportunities for expanding working and middle classes, thereby heading off communists and radicals. In the era of import substitution, many modernization theorists agreed with the structuralists that state leadership could and should pursue developmental objectives, both economic and political. Modernization theorists and structuralists both were called *developmentalists* because they advocated an active state to overcome underdevelopment. Structuralists supported ISI, but they also recognized the need to change the approach over time. Political change would be hard to accomplish once there were entrenched interests behind ISI.

PHOTO 6.1   Look at this photo of a factory built in the era of import substitution in Mexico to produce textile products. Why did Marxists, structuralists, and modernization theorists alike, though they disagree on some things, think that a factory was a sign of development in the country?

Source: Joe Raedle/Staff.

For Review

Why were Prebisch and his team at ECLAC called "structuralists"? Where did they agree, and where did they disagree with *dependistas*? How do structuralists differ from neoliberals?

Institutionalism

During the neoliberal era, structuralism was displaced by a focus on governance. Rather than state-led economic growth, the idea behind governance was that economic development is best promoted by efficient and effective government. A productive capitalist economy needs a legal system ensuring security for property, an impartial system of law, and an efficient bureaucracy impervious to corruption. The theory that getting the politics right is a key to development is known as **institutionalism**. Though institutionalism might have much to offer socialist as well as capitalist economies, institutionalism is usually associated with support for market economies. Institutionalism has attracted additional admirers because of the relative success of Asian economies, which have achieved significant rates of economic growth and development with capitalist economies that benefit from state support for education and infrastructure. Often overlooked is that not just China but capitalist Japan and South Korea have relied upon state planning and support for industries believed most likely to prosper in the global economy.

The World Bank and the Inter-American Development Bank mounted programs to strengthen institutions, such as cleansing courts and the bureaucracy of corruption and helping regulatory agencies operate more efficiently. Development theorists at these and other think-tanks have given impetus to the importance of institutional design, that is, constitutions, laws, and administrative agencies that can facilitate efficient economic growth. They argue that countries with stable institutions are more likely to attract foreign investment and encourage domestic entrepreneurship than those with overbearing, corrupt state institutions. Institutionalism has also been rising as a branch of study in comparative politics. These institutionalists argue that we have for too long focused our attention exclusively on social, cultural, and economic factors to explain Latin American politics.

While fighting corruption and supporting the rule of law seem like goals no one would question, some critics point out ways that institutionalism fails to recognize that corruption and inefficiency may not be ills that once corrected will make capitalism function better, but may be deeply ingrained in capitalist economic systems. We will look more closely at this issue in chapter 14.

For Review

How and why do dependency theorists and structuralists disagree with the laissez-faire approach? How do comparative advantage and ISI differ concerning the role of trade in development? Why might the design of institutions be a factor influencing possibilities for development?

Globalization, Development, and the World System

Although the idea of dependency continues to influence Latin American studies, it is largely understood today with the framework of world systems theory, first elaborated by Immanuel Wallerstein (summarized in Wallerstein 2004). Wallerstein sees the world system as having come into existence around 1500 with the European conquest of the Americas. At this point, there emerged a global capitalist system in which nation-states emerged. At the core of the system are wealthy industrialized states. Also, within the core, one state tends to emerge as the strongest—the hegemon, currently a position occupied by the United States. In the periphery are those that were integrated, usually by force of imperialism, into the world system as producers of raw materials (largely agricultural and mining economies). Latin America's poorest states—for example, Bolivia, Haiti, and Nicaragua—are in the periphery. Some states occupy an intermediate condition in the "semiperiphery." These countries have undergone some industrialization and are better off than the poorest countries in the system, or they have a vital natural resource (e.g., oil) that gives them special weight. In Latin America, this would include Argentina, Brazil, Mexico, and Chile, among others. Venezuela would qualify in part because of its status as an oil-exporting country.

Dependency and world systems theories (in contrast to modernization theory) agree on a diagnosis of underdevelopment as springing from three common elements that Latin America shares with other parts of the Third World, all of which can be traced back to colonialism:

1. As a result of colonialism, *Latin America was integrated into the world economy as a provider of cheap primary goods*—agricultural products (monoculture), minerals, and other raw materials—and an importer of more expensive manufactured goods. While Frank saw this as intrinsic to exchanging raw materials for finished goods, Wallerstein put more emphasis on the way the way capitalists in both worlds built a system that did not work for the global majority. That is, Wallerstein's world systems theory was closer to Cardoso and Faletto's idea of "associated dependent development" than to Frank's unequal trade theory. Industrialization in the Global South was stunted in part because those who controlled the economy and benefited from exports had little incentive to invest in and develop the production of manufactured goods.

2. *Since the colonial period, elites in Latin America have looked outward, not inward*, for models and inspiration. Despite promoting *mestizaje*, the upper classes tended to look abroad for solutions to problems. Because the economy was oriented to production for foreign markets, it is not surprising that the Latin American elite looked abroad for cultural and political inspiration as well. They tended to send their children to Europe for higher education. After independence, they looked to the United States and France for appropriate models for constitutions. They promoted immigration as a way to improve the "racial stock," deemed by many to be "savage" or not inclined to work hard because of the climate. Their ideal of feminine beauty became the light-skinned blonde.

3. The export-oriented economy relied heavily on cheap labor, accentuating the maldistribution of wealth and creating a difficult political climate for liberal and democratic political arrangements to take root. Exploitation began with the **encomienda** (see chapter 3). Although abuses led to the abolition of this system, forms of coerced labor continued in many parts of Latin America throughout the colonial period and well into the independence era. For example, instead of being paid wages, workers often were allowed access to land in exchange for their labor on the big farms and ranches.

Unlike the early *dependistas*, like Frank, Wallerstein saw the possibility of states changing their place in the world pecking order as a result of technological development and interstate rivalries. After all, Spain, once hegemonic, slipped after 1700 into the semi-periphery because it failed to use its colonial wealth to build a competitive economy at home. Since 1970, Spain seems to have rejoined the core as a dynamic economy within the European Union (even allowing for setbacks associated with the global financial crisis of 2008). Some newly industrialized countries in East Asia today, especially China and South Korea, have been migrating from the periphery closer to core. Brazil was not long ago considered a candidate to escape the periphery—the "B" in what journalists still call the "BRICS"—Brazil, Russia, India, China, and South Africa. That prognosis no long looks so promising (see chapter 15).

Dependency theory and world systems theory (compared in Table 6.2) have in common that they challenge the notion, common to modernization theory and to early Marxism,

TABLE 6.2   World Systems Theory, Dependency, and Modernization

	World Systems Theory	*Dependency Theory*	*Modernization*
Relationship between Latin America and wealthy countries	Exploitative. Latin America is part of the periphery, but the poorest countries are the ones most isolated from the global system of markets and investments. Others, e.g., Brazil and Mexico, are part of the "semiperiphery."	Exploitative. Foreign investors benefit from cheap labor and the rape of the region's natural resources, leaving the region poorer than it would be without such investment.	Developmental. Foreign aid and investment from wealthy countries bring needed technologies and capital to underdeveloped countries.
Role of U.S. in the world	Became the dominant, "hegemonic" power of the 20th century and acts not only to maintain its dominance but also to protect the interests of other wealthy nations of the core.	U.S. is a classic imperial power, acting to protect its own capitalists and preventing Latin America from developing stronger ties with competitors (to the U.S.) among core nations.	The U.S. is a model nation whose culture and economy would be emulated by others. Some theorists take a broader view, worrying that the U.S. may be in decline.
Can Latin America develop?	Yes, shifts in global system sometimes allow nations, such as South Korea, China, and Japan, the opportunity to move out of the periphery, while former members of the core have sometimes slipped back to the semiperiphery—e.g., Portugal and Spain after 1700.	Little hope of development as long as capitalism and imperialism exist.	Yes. The road is long and difficult, but the problems and obstacles, such as poverty in cities, are not so different as those once found in the "developed" countries today.

that all countries will pass through similar stages on the path to fully developed capitalist economies. Neoliberals with modernization theorists make the assumption that low wages, poor working conditions, and poverty in Latin America are symptoms of underdevelopment, likely to be left behind as further stages of development are reached.

For Review

What countries are typically part of the "core," the "periphery," and the "semiperiphery," according to world systems theory? What patterns, according to world systems theorists, did colonialism put in place that remained influential in shaping Latin America (a) in its development, (b) in its underdevelopment, and (c) after independence?

State, Market, and Globalization

Dependency theory, structuralism, and modernization were theories of development that emerged in the middle decades of the twentieth century, and all three see the nation-state as the primary unit of analysis. That is, each one views the world largely as divided into approximately 150 nation-states, each with an economy clearly bound from the others. Even today the main news stories, statistics, and analyses focus on national economies or what trends in the global economy mean for the national economy. When it comes to trade, our mindset is not so different from that of the classical economist David Ricardo when he illustrated the idea of **comparative advantage** by showing how England and Portugal could both maximize their economic benefits if Portugal exclusively concentrated on production of wine for export to England, and England exclusively concentrated on production of textiles to Portugal. Each one was wholly producing a good within its territorial boundaries.

Most world systems theorists today recognize that globalization presented a formidable challenge to national sovereignty in the form of **transnational** capital. A common way of understanding this idea is that of the "**global assembly line.**" Henry Ford is famous for having implanted the assembly line to mass produce automobiles, as various components would enter the factory on one side and exit the other as a completed Model T. The various parts would pass in front of workers who would complete one task before the vehicle-to-be would go on to the next. This became a model for all manufacturing. Today, by contrast, an automobile is one "made in America" or "made in Mexico" (etc.) superficially. Finished autos and other products stand at the end of a "**supply chain,**" whereby components are fabricated all over the world, often by contractors who feed into the chain, "adding value" at each step in the process.

Your iPhone is not "made in China." Its accelerometer (which helps protect it when dropped) is manufactured by a German company, Bosch. The battery was made by Samsung, based in China, but its lithium, a rare mineral, may have been produced by a Chinese mine in Bolivia. Qualcomm, a U.S. company, made the camera, some of them in Brazil. Approximately 12 other components come from other parts of the world. The blouse you're wearing? It's a good chance the cotton was grown and put through a cotton gin in El Salvador, perhaps shipped to Honduras to be milled into cloth, but only after having passed through Trinidad to be combined with a synthetic fiber made from oil. The patterns probably were designed by Burlington-Northern or Benneton and sent electronically to a contractor on the northern border of Mexico, where it was stitched into the garment for shipping to a wholesaler in the U.S.

It is possible that import substitution retains some relevance in Latin America. Countries that produce oil might want to build refineries to avoid importing gasoline. Transforming minerals into intermediate products and cookware might be something that Chile and Peru can aspire to. However, given this kind of global economy, the aim of development cannot be to arrive at an industrialized economy that looks like the Japanese, U.S., European, or even the Soviet economy of the twentieth century.

We will come back to this topic in chapter 15, where we look at globalization more closely. In the remainder of this chapter, we will review the political and economic forces that shaped Latin America's place in the global economy today. Of course, there are variations within the region. World systems theory can be helpful in this regard, helping us to understand how more peripheral countries, such as Paraguay, Haiti, and Honduras, face more limited options than semiperipheral Brazil and Chile. And it might also be useful in exploring why no Latin American country has shifted more toward core status than several Asian countries have.

The Crisis of Populism and Import Substitution

Import substitution and structuralism were approaches to economic development closely associated in the twentieth century with populism of the sort we highlighted in chapter 5 (e.g., Peronism in Argentina). The populist era ended in crisis and, in most of Latin America, in harsh military rule. The dismantling of unions, populist parties, and other mass organizations paved the way for a shift away from protectionism and structuralism and toward market-friendly, export-oriented economic policies in most of the hemisphere.

Economic policies swung away from import substitution, which emphasized *desarrollo hacia adentro* (inwardly focused development) and back toward *desarrollo hacia afuera* (outwardly focused development). Although the shift owed something to military rule, broader trends were at work in the international environment that encouraged almost all Latin American governments to implement neoliberalism to some degree. Mexico, Costa Rica, Colombia, and Venezuela—four exceptions that escaped military regimes in this period, the 1980s—also saw a shift away from the ISI policies associated with the populist era. Even Cuba, faced with the loss of support from the Soviet bloc, in the late 1980s introduced some market reforms and policies friendly to foreign investment. Although the domestic politics behind neoliberal measures varied across the region, the new policies everywhere were implemented in the context of crushing national debts that greatly limited the capacity of newly elected governments to pursue any other approach. The pressure was usually applied by the World Bank, the IMF, and the United States, with large global banks allowing them to take the lead.

The exhaustion of ISI as a developmental strategy brought great instability into the lives of the middle class and salaried workers in the form of hyperinflation. Deficit spending, trade deficits, debt, and dwindling confidence in local currencies converged at times into astounding monetary instability. In Bolivia, the inflation rate reached 1,300 percent in 1984 and 11,805 percent in 1985. In 1989, Argentina's rate of inflation reached 3,000 percent. In 1991, Brazil's inflation rate was a ridiculous 2,489 percent over one year. To put this in perspective, the same rate applied to the United States would have meant that US$2,489 would have turned into US$1. In comparison with Argentina and Brazil, Mexico's rate of 110 percent in 1988 seems tame, but someone with a bank account in pesos would have seen their savings halved in a matter of months. In many Latin American countries, people's life savings were effectively wiped out.

Latin Americans sometimes saw prices double or triple before they could spend their paychecks. Only those who were able to convert their savings into dollars before the crash were spared, and this group, of course, was almost exclusively made up of the wealthiest portions of the population. Therefore, the poor, working class, and middle class bore the highest cost of the economic crisis—and women sacrificed and suffered the consequences more than men did. Women tend to be employed in social service sectors (teaching, nursing, etc.) where falling government spending most affected wages and employment. When inflation is high, women face the challenge of providing for families with declining incomes; when inflation is low, they benefit less because so much of their work is unpaid. We should not be surprised to learn that eventually women would play leading roles in challenging military rule.

To maintain political stability but also to carry out fiscal austerity, governments sought to reform welfare programs to bypass politicians and more directly reach poor people—that is, by eliminating clientelism and creating community-based programs. In practice, they were a welfare Band-Aid on open wounds caused by economic shock treatments. In Mexico, President Carlos Salinas de Gortari launched his "Pronasol" program under which a fund was created to match community projects. Total spending was impressive, over $2 billion by 1993, but less than the programs it replaced. Poverty increased significantly in 1994 when the government devalued the peso against the dollar (lowering the value of real wages) and opened up the economy to competition with the United States under the North American Free Trade Agreement (NAFTA). And the Pronasol program failed to eliminate clientelism (Moguel 1994; Gardy 1994).

Sometimes it is assumed that populist economic policies cause hyperinflation. However, a runaway inflation crisis struck most countries *after* the collapse of populist democracy and *after* ISI had been abandoned as the overall development strategy. Some of the worst episodes of inflation occurred under military rule and not populist governments. But politically, it became useful to simply blame left populism and justify harsh austerity.

The Debt Crisis and the "Lost Decade"

The 1980s, often called the "lost decade" (see chapter 6), was nothing less than an economic disaster. A major cause of the economic distress was the **debt crisis**, which afflicted—and continues to afflict—not only Latin America but also the entire Third World. The crisis became visible in the international media in August 1982, when Mexico announced to the world banking community that it could no longer service its debt. "Service," as used here, refers to making scheduled payments. As with a personal loan or mortgage to an individual, the earliest repayments on loans to countries consist of interest and service (administrative) fees, with very little, if any, going toward reduction of the principal on the loan. This is what Latin American governments were struggling to pay—not the loan itself, but interest and service fees.

If we consider export earnings to be the income available to Latin American countries to pay their debt, the crisis was truly alarming. As we have already seen, even in those countries that implemented import substitution, the export sector has been the motor force of the formal economy. Whereas exports typically constitute about 10 percent of the economy of developed countries, in Latin America and the Caribbean they constitute approximately 30 percent (Potter 2000: 80). In 1970, the total debt for Latin America and the Caribbean was US$26 billion; by 1980, it had risen to US$191 billion, with US$69 billion slated to fall due within just a few years (Potter 2000; World Bank 1996; see Table 6.3 and Figure 6.2). The total debt in Latin America was more than twice its total export earnings in 1980; and by 1983, only three years later, it was nearly 300 times that amount. Interest payments alone were nearly 20 percent of total export earnings in 1980, rising to 30 percent by 1983; total service payments rose from nearly 37 times the value of export earnings to nearly 48 times (Franko 1999: 90). To put this another way, in 1983, had Latin American governments met their international loan payments, US$1 out of every US$2 earned from exports (total earnings and not just profits) would have gone to the world's bankers.

If we jump ahead to the years after 2000, you can see from Figures 6.1 and 6.2 that Latin American countries have seen their debt fluctuate, but it has risen in recent years.

TABLE 6.3 Total Debt and Total Debt Service Paid in Latin America and Caribbean, 1980–2000

	1980	1990	2000
Total debt of Latin America and Caribbean, combined	$191 billion	$480 billion	$750 billion
Total debt service paid		$350 billion 1980–1990	$815 billon 1990–2000

Source: Potter (2000).

FIGURE 6.1 Latin American and Caribbean Central Government Public Debt as Percent of GDP

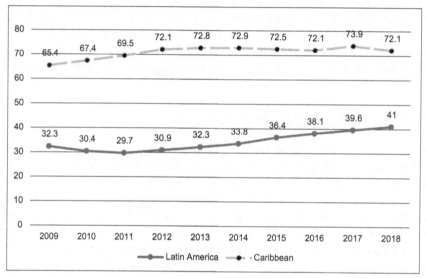

Source: ECLAC (2019).

FIGURE 6.2 Latin America and Caribbean, Total Debt Service as Percent of Gross National Income

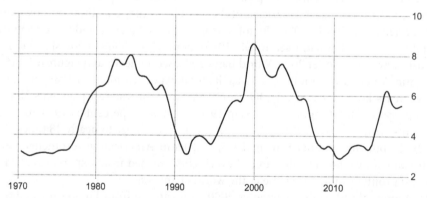

Source: World Bank data, https://tradingeconomics.com/latin-america-and-caribbean/total-debt-service-percent-of-gni-wb-data.html

Figure 6.1 indicates that central government debt as a percentage of GDP rose about 11 points between 2011 and 2018 in Latin America, and that overall, it is more than 70 percent in the Caribbean. Servicing debt (Figure 6.1)—what countries must pay each year—continued to rise as well. In 2019, Brazil's debt had reached 78.7 percent of its yearly GDP; the comparative figure for Argentina was 80.7 percent. The average for Latin America was 43.2 percent (ECLAC 2019a).

What caused the debt crisis? Various factors contributed. In 1973, the Arab oil-exporting countries declared an embargo against the United States and other industrialized countries that supported Israel during the October war of that year, causing shortages and price rises on a vital commodity. The Iranian Revolution and subsequent war between Iran and Iraq caused prices to rise again in 1980–1981. All oil importers suffered economically, but Third World oil importers were hit the hardest. Not only were their economies afflicted by higher energy costs, but demand and prices for their exports also fell because the rise in oil price contributed to a deep economic recession in Europe, Japan, and North America.

The small Central American countries saw their debt escalate with the fall in the price of coffee, bananas, cotton, sugar, and other agricultural exports. El Salvador, Nicaragua, and other Central American countries had modernized and somewhat diversified their agricultural export sectors after World War II, often with the help of development loans and foreign aid. Their sugar, cotton, and beef export sectors were energy-intensive, more so than traditional exports such as coffee and fruit. Pesticides, fertilizers, trucks, and tractors all increased these countries' thirst for oil. To make matters worse, peasants had often been forced off the land to develop the new export plantations. The expansion of plantation agriculture to take advantage of export markets was a major factor behind the revolutions and wars that wracked Central America in the 1980s, especially in Nicaragua, El Salvador, and Guatemala (see chapter 9).

Throughout Latin America, the global economic situation and the local political situation discouraged foreign investors from making the large-scale investments that the generals and politicians hoped to attract. Memories of political unrest and nationalization were fresh in the minds of foreign investors. The prospects for turning a profit with new investments in Latin America's export sector were bleak. Economic recessions in the wealthy countries in the late 1970s and the 1980s meant low demand for raw materials and other goods produced in Latin America. Foreign investors who might put their money into real projects (not just financial instruments—e.g., bonds and investment funds) thought that it was better to wait for renewed growth in the developed countries.

The international banks were much less cautious than direct investors were. Many of them were finding dollars piling up in their accounts in the 1970s. In the years after World War II, the European and Japanese economies had been built with both the real and the symbolic support of dollars, which circulated in great quantity outside the United States. In 1974 alone, the Organization of Petroleum Exporting Countries (OPEC) earned US$74 billion more than the value of their imports. Most put their funds in their Western banks (Wachtel 1977). Most oil purchases were (and are) made with dollars, and OPEC had to dispose of the "petrodollars" flowing into their treasuries during the 1970s oil boom. Why was this a problem? The essence of banking as an industry is to make more money on interest from loans than is paid out in the form of interest on deposits. Banks had to find a way to make new loans, or they would lose money.

With the world industrial economy in recession, where could banks lend the money? One answer was the world's governments. In theory, a government cannot go bankrupt, so the banks paid little attention to the creditworthiness of the borrowing countries or to the degree of corruption in their politics. By the mid-1970s, Bank of America and First National City Bank were so exposed abroad that 108.2 percent and 126.8 percent (respectively) of their overall income was from foreign sources. How can the percentage be over 100 percent? Simple. They were losing money at home and making it overseas. On average, the 12 largest U.S. banks derived 63 percent of their income from foreign sources (Wachtel 1977). The magnitude of the problems did not become clear until Mexico's threat to default on its loan payments in 1982.

The debt burden was made worse in the 1980s by the policies of the U.S. Federal Reserve Bank, the central bank for the United States. The Federal Reserve maintained a high prime interest rate as the administration of Ronald Reagan borrowed heavily to fund deep deficits and increased military spending. Fearing inflation at home and attracted by high interest in the United States, wealthy Latin Americans converted their own nations' money into dollars and sent them abroad. From the point of view of the rich, why invest in the shaky economies of Latin America if attractive profits could be gained from interest on deposits in the United States? This aggravated the problem of capital (money for investment) flight from the region, and it discouraged foreign investors from putting money into Latin America in the 1980s. Economic reactivation became all the more difficult.

We should not attribute the growing debt to external causes alone. Corruption and inefficiencies, the failure to modernize industries, and lack of investment in education and technological development were all contributory factors. Latin Americans found themselves paying exorbitant interest rates for short-term loans, but desperate governments kept borrowing to keep ambitious, large development projects (roads, airports, public buildings, etc.) afloat. This, in turn, kept some workers employed and generated profits for businesses with close ties to the military regimes. Some of these problems in some places can be attributed to populist politics, but the military regimes also borrowed heavily. For example, the military regime that overthrew democracy in Brazil in 1964 and tightened its grip on power in 1968 never entirely abandoned state capitalism. Many projects in the military years were called "pharaonic" because they were often never finished and did little to promote development. Some of the ones that did materialize drove deep into the Amazon rainforest.

After a while, new loans were no longer going into the nations' own economies; instead, Latin American governments were merely refinancing loan payments as they came due. This arrangement was something like loan-sharking: a heavily indebted customer desperate for additional money keeps digging a deeper hole for himself or herself. Without loans to pay back existing debts, Third World countries would find themselves blacklisted from loans needed to sustain government services, finance new investment, or purchase needed imports. It was not a matter of choice. Without finance, it is virtually impossible to do normal business in the world today. Given this context, who is most at fault—the client or the creditor?

Even in the 1990s, when Latin America's economies began to grow again, the debt burden continued to rise. The total debt in Latin America and the Caribbean expanded at the same rate in the 1990s as it did in the "lost decade" of the 1980s. Between 1990 and 2000, countries in the region paid US$815 billion to service the debt, but the amount owed actually increased from US$480 billion to US$750 billion.

If oil prices were high, why did Mexico and Venezuela, two oil-exporting countries, also fall so far into debt? Venezuela borrowed heavily against future oil earnings in an attempt to industrialize overnight (Hellinger 1991; Karl 1994). In the case of Mexico, its oil company (Petróleos de Mexico—PEMEX) had confined itself to producing mainly for the domestic market, partly because the global oil companies tried to isolate it after the nationalization of 1938. In an attempt to break the power of OPEC on the world market, the consuming countries and their banks suddenly became eager to make loans to the government of President José López Portillo (1976–1982), as Mexico was not a member of the OPEC cartel.

What neither Mexico nor Venezuela counted on was the fall of oil prices that began in 1982. Economic recessions in developed countries, conservation efforts, and increases in alternative energy production combined to dampen demand for oil on the world market. Increased production outside OPEC created a glut of supply. Something similar happened to Latin America's other major commodities—copper, coffee, rubber, and so on. Prices recovered only near the end of the century, when India's and China's rapidly expanding economies generated new demand and as OPEC recovered some influence—partly due to Venezuela's leadership in rebuilding the organization. The trend upward lasted until oil prices passed US$147 in 2008, only to tumble with the economic recession that began with the financial crisis in the United States in September 2008.

For Review

Why are the 1980s considered the "lost decade" in Latin America? Why did Latin American governments borrow from the international banks? Why did the banks keep lending, even when it seemed that governments might not be creditworthy?

Sovereignty, Democracy, and Structural Adjustment

Latin American governments, democratic or not, became vulnerable to pressure to conform to economic blueprints, called "**structural adjustment**," promoted mainly by the IMF, the World Bank, and the **United Nations Commission on Trade and Development (UNCTAD)**. Loans made by the IMF to governments are significant in that they signal to other lenders that a country is creditworthy. Often, conditions set by the IMF set the pattern for subsequent deals between debtors and two big consortiums of lenders. The London Club was made up of big private lenders; the Paris Club was for governments of wealthy nations that do the same kind of lending. The IMF and World Bank negotiated terms for their own loans, which set conditions for the clubs afterwards.

Latin American leaders such as Fidel Castro and Alan García (president of Peru from 1985 to 1990) proposed that Latin Americans band together to seek a moratorium on paying the debt or at least to negotiate better terms. Even today, leftist governments in the region are cautious about policies that might isolate them economically. Venezuelan president Hugo Chávez, regarded as a leading critic of neoliberalism, used earnings from the oil bonanza of the post-2000 period to pay down the country's debt rather than save it or spend even more on popular programs. On the other hand, in 2001 Argentina simply declared it would not pay creditors who failed to make concessions. In other words, creditors do not hold all the cards in debt negotiation; if they push too hard, debtors may tip over the game table.

Typically, structural adjustment agreements require governments to implement the following set of policies in exchange for new loans:

- *Free-trade policies.* Governments are expected to reduce protection for domestic enterprises, whether in manufacturing, services, or agriculture.
- *Tax reform designed to increase government revenues.* Because Latin American bureaucracies are notoriously inefficient and because taxes on domestic industries might deter investors, governments frequently imposed value-added taxes, which function something like a sales tax imposed at each stage of production of a consumer goods. Although this tax falls on businesses, it is passed along and embodied in final prices. Generally, it falls more heavily on lower income people.
- *Reduction of the public sector.* Governments are expected to cut the payroll and reduce spending on welfare. The net result is a transfer of funds from programs to pay government employees, pensioners, and others (students, the poor, women with families, the sick) to payments to foreign creditors.
- *Privatization of state-owned enterprises.* The goal here is often to reduce a drain on government resources and to provide an injection of money that can be used to service the debt. The IMF and World Bank urge privatization as a "modernization" policy to increase efficiency and reduce the influence of the government over the economy.
- *Encouragement of growth in the export sector.* More exports mean more foreign currency, especially dollars, entering the economy. More dollars mean greater potential to pay the debt.
- *Conservative monetary policy.* Usually, the demand is that the government devalue the country's money by tight monetary policy (that is, reducing the amount of money in circulation), allowing interest rates to rise, and allowing the exchange rate to fall (for example, more pesos needed to buy each dollar). Devaluation helps exports but makes imports more expensive. Venezuela, for example, was told to devalue in the 1980s and 1990s if it wanted new loans. The problem here is that Venezuela, an oil-exporting country, imports most of what it consumes. Its importers were forced to pay many more *bolivars* for dollars needed to buy goods abroad, increasing the cost of living for the population. The banks also applauded Argentine president Menem's decision to peg his country's peso to the dollar, one peso for one dollar. This was an effective way of boosting investors' confidence and reducing inflation, but when the economy faltered again in 2002, it caused a major crisis. Ecuador went so far as to eliminate its local money and adopt the dollar as its official currency (joining Panama, which has long had the dollar as its official currency). In 2020, the country was early hit hard by the COVID-19 pandemic, devastating the economy. Many other countries loosened their monetary policy to meet the emergency needs for the health sector, but Ecuador could not. It cannot, after all, print dollars.

These measures not only add up to an economic agenda favorable to foreign capital (banks and investors) but also create opportunities for well-connected Latin American elites to take advantage of the weak state. Particularly scandalous was the way privatization of public assets was handled. Wealthy foreigners and domestic elites were able to buy state assets very cheaply, and their purchases were made more profitable by tax relief, mass layoffs of workers, and lax public regulation.

As the "lost decade" drew to a close, Latin America's governments faced restive populations demanding payment of the **social debt**—that is, money obligated to them by law, sometimes (as with pensions) accrued through work and savings (see Potter 2000). Structural adjustment took a toll on Latin America's workers, peasants, and middle class. The gap between the richest and poorest 1 percent of the population increased from 273:1 to 417:1 between 1970 and 1995 (Franko 1999: 228). Between 1985 and 2000, Latin America experienced several urban explosions, including rioting (e.g., in Caracas, Buenos Aires); organized blockades of roads protesting attempts to privatize utilities (Peru, Bolivia); peasant marches on local and national capitals (Ecuador, Mexico, Bolivia); and general strikes (Brazil, Venezuela).

Proponents of structural adjustment often contend that ultimately neoliberal economic policies will strengthen democracy. Their theory is that markets disperse power more evenly in society. They argue that reducing government's role in the economy encourages a more **pluralist**, stronger **civil society** by allowing citizens to assert themselves through independent group activity (Schumpeter 1947; see chapter 1). Despite all the indications of profound discontent with structural adjustment, candidates and parties associated with these plans often had come to power through elections. Notable cases include Carlos Menem (1989–1999) in Argentina, Alberto Fujimori (1990–2000) in Peru, and Carlos Andrés Pérez (for his second term, 1989–1993) in Venezuela. However, as candidates, they usually either espoused a populist position against neoliberalism and then shifted once confronted with hard choices or promised to soften the impact on poorer sectors with aid programs, as with Pronasol in Mexico.

For Review

Neoliberalism refers to an overall economic philosophy, whereas structural adjustment refers to specific policies. How do the policies reflect the philosophy, and how did the debt crisis encourage structural adjustment?

▮ The Decline of Economic Nationalism

The shift from populism and ISI to neoliberalism both reflected and influenced events in the international economy. The fall of the Berlin Wall and the collapse of the Soviet superpower between 1989 and 1990 meant that any country wanting to pursue an alternative to the neoliberal recipe could no longer look to a superpower that might deter efforts by the remaining superpower, the United States, to punish it for challenging the rules of the "new world order."

The period between 1960 and the 1980s had seen the decolonization of Africa, the Middle East, and Asia; the radicalization of the Cuban Revolution; setbacks for the United States in Vietnam; the emergence of Japan and the European Economic Community (today, the European Union) as economic competitors with the United States; and the emergence of OPEC. In this period, Third World nations sought to increase strategic cooperation with one another to regulate supplies of commodities (food and raw materials) in the world marketplace. Now with large majorities in the United Nations General Assembly, the **Third World** began lobbying for a New International Economic Order (NIEO), one that would narrow the gap between the rich nations of the Global North and the poor nations of the Global South, the latter highly dependent on export of primary commodities.

Those who promoted the NIEO often cited the instability of world commodity prices as an obstacle to development. They shared the diagnosis of economists like Prebisch that there existed a chronic gap between the prices of raw materials and those of manufactured goods. In a series of meetings sponsored by the United Nations, nonaligned nations (i.e., a group of mostly Third World countries who asserted independence from the two superpowers engaged in the Cold War) declared that territorial sovereignty had to include the right of governments to control their natural resources. This assertion was made in defense of nationalization of key industries, especially mining and oil companies. The UN Commission on Trade and Development proposed in 1976 the creation of a system of buffer stocks for 22 mineral and agricultural commodities. In times of high commodity prices, UNCTAD would release stocks onto the market; in times of low prices, UNCTAD would buy surplus production.

These measures struck against two fundamental principles underlying a liberal world order and free trade: (1) defense of private property against government expropriation and (2) reliance on the free interplay of market forces to set prices. Through collective action at the international level, national sovereignty would be strengthened versus the power of private capital. Some Latin American nations provided crucial support for this initiative. Cuban diplomats emerged as forceful spokespersons for the initiatives. Venezuela was the initiator of the Organization of Petroleum Exporting Countries; its oil minister, Juan Pablo Pérez Alfonzo (1958–1963), is often called the "father of OPEC." In the late 1960s and 1970s, Chile and Peru, two major copper producers, had populist leaders who initiated nationalization (with compensation) of mining industries and sought to coordinate their policies with other countries. Many thought that the next step in implementing an NIEO would come in the form of an international copper cartel, envisioned to be the first step in implementing the UNCTAD plan.

Some leaders in developed countries embraced the idea. In 1980, a commission headed by former West German chancellor Willy Brandt issued a report (the **Brandt Report**) favorable to the UNCTAD initiative. It called for efforts to narrow the economic gap between North (core) and South (periphery). However, by this time, the NIEO was already in trouble, in part due to changes in Latin America. The leftist governments in Chile and Peru had been replaced by right-wing military regimes that retreated from nationalist economic philosophy. To get the buffer stock system going, UNCTAD was going to need initial financing from the wealthy countries and OPEC. Although Europe and Japan initially signaled support, the United States opposed the scheme from the start. When oil prices collapsed in the 1980s, any possibility of help from OPEC disappeared. OPEC itself failed to maintain prices through regulation of supply.

The final blow to the NIEO came from the debt crisis. To comply with structural adjustment, governments had to privatize state assets. The result was the reversal of many of the sovereign nationalizations of airlines, mines, railroads, and so on, accomplished in the populist era, and the shifting of many other assets created by state investment (roads, steel companies, and communications industries) to private ownership.

If the world had followed the Brandt Commission lead, we might today be talking about a very different kind of globalization, one regulated by international organizations, instead of by relatively unbridled market forces. Instead, globalization took place under a set of liberal economic and political doctrines. President George H. W. Bush in 1991, following the victory of the United States over Iraq in the first Gulf War (after Iraq's invasion of Kuwait), proclaimed the new era a "New World Order" (NWO) in his victory speech. Among other things, the neoliberal NWO elevated security of the property rights of investors over sovereign control of natural resources. New mining and hydrocarbon (gas and oil) legislation followed advice and models provided by the World Bank and guaranteed investors against nationalization or future tax increases. UNCTAD's role shifted to provide technical advice on how nations could best compete for foreign capital by creating a favorable environment for investors. Even the economists at ECLAC embraced some aspects of neoliberalism, but more recently the organization has shifted its focus back to the consequences of inequality and export dependence (for example see ECLAC 2019b).

A series of financial calamities (in Southeast Asia in 1998 and in Argentina in 2001), the resurgence of oil and other commodity prices since 2002, and rapid economic growth in Brazil, Russia, India, and China seem to have shifted power back somewhat toward the Global South. As national leaders began to meet to confront the world financial crisis of 2008, these countries demanded a seat at the table normally occupied by the "G7" group of Western countries and Japan. Luiz Inácio da Silva (Lula), the Brazilian president, was particularly outspoken and successful in this respect. With a quite uncomfortable visiting British prime minister (Gordon Brown) at Lula's side in a 2009 press conference, the Brazilian said, "This crisis was caused by the irrational behavior of white people with blue eyes, who before the crisis appeared to know everything and now demonstrate that they know nothing" (*Financial Times*, March 17, 2009).

For Review

Describe the underlying ideas of the NIEO and how the NWO that actually emerged was different. What role has Latin America played in the shifts of power between the Global North and South?

Adjusting to the Global Market: Three Variations

In this section, we look at three different experiences, not because they are representative but because they illustrate the diversity of experiences and experiments with economic policy in Latin America. In all three cases, countries have had some macroeconomic success, but uncertainty about the future lingers.

The Chilean Neoliberal "Success Story"

Chile is often held up as a success story of adaptation to the NWO. General Augusto Pinochet's government (1973–1989) decreed new laws guaranteeing investors low tax rates that would never be raised. Pinochet did not privatize the state copper company because the military receives (as it still does today) 10 percent of its sales (not profits, *sales*) off the top. However, he offered new concessions (leases to exploit natural resources) to foreign companies at low tax rates and under a new mining law that practically guaranteed the companies would never be nationalized. Mining companies were given leases virtually in perpetuity. Meanwhile, the government starved the state copper company (Codelco) of investment capital to start new mines and modernize old ones.

New mines were started by foreign investors who were guaranteed low taxes and were relieved of any obligation to pay royalties (compensation to the country for using up its mineral wealth). Today, the big private mines produce and export a majority of the country's copper. In some ways, they have a better deal today than they had before nationalization. When copper prices, driven by demand from China, finally began to climb again in 2003, Chile's earnings from copper exports climbed. Codelco was still the largest single copper company in the world, so the government did gain some benefit from the boost. However, the big private companies paid very little to the state despite a bonanza in profits. Suddenly, Chileans began to realize they were nearly giving away their copper for nothing. Under mounting public pressure, enough conservative legislators voted with the Concertación majority to impose a very modest 5 percent levy on export profits of the big mines.

Even these terms were not enough in the 1980s to bring the mining companies back to Chile. Copper prices were low, and foreign investors feared that Pinochet's harsh rule might lead to renewed revolution. These factors deterred large investment until the transition to democracy in 1989. When the centrist and leftist politicians came back, they left the new rules in place, partly because of limits on democracy built into the constitution (see chapter 7) and partly because they were reluctant to disturb an economy in recovery. Rolling back the power of the state, then, was accomplished by dictatorship, but liberal democracy seemed more capable of providing the political security that investors wanted.

Many countries, such as Chile, Peru, and Mexico, became statistically less dependent on export of raw materials, but this does not necessarily mean that they export fewer raw materials. For example, measured by the ton rather than in dollars, Chile actually doubled copper exports in the 1990s, largely because of new large, private mines put in operation. Meanwhile, Chile's percentage of export earnings from copper actually fell from roughly 80 percent to 45 percent between 1970 and 2000. This was not only because Chile diversified its exports in agriculture, forestry, and manufacturing (e.g., armaments) but also because low prices for copper meant that the country was earning less for its mining exports.

A deep recession struck in the aftermath of the 1973 coup, which destroyed much of the economy built up in the populist era. A recovery occurred between 1977 and 1980, but a second deep recession followed in the period between 1981 and 1986, when the economy actually shrank by 0.1 percent. Ten years of growth of between 6 and 9 percent followed, a period that seemed to suggest that Pinochet's neoliberal restructuring, combined with a return to democracy, would pay big dividends. From 1996 until 2000, the rate of growth leveled off at a still healthy 4.1 percent. How was this achieved? The Pinochet regime took advantage of the crisis and fears of the old landlord class to replace the traditional *latifundia* with modern export agriculture. Similarly, it opened the country's rich forests and coastal waters to timber and industrial fishing. Workers who managed to find employment were forced to pay into private pension funds managed by private investors, which provided capital for new investment. The leading growth sectors were fruits, forestry, and new natural resource industries (that is, outside of copper). In other words, Chile relied on diversification of raw material and food exports more than manufacturing, took advantage of repression to lower wages, created new pools of capital for forced savings, and opened the country's bountiful natural resources to exploitation at bargain prices (and with little regard for the environment). Although the terms were somewhat moderated and made more fair by the democratically elected governments after 1990, Chile remains more firmly neoliberal than any other country in the region.

The biggest problem in Chile is inequality. Overall, poverty declined by some measures from 40 to 18 percent between 1998 and 2005, but 15 percent of the population earned less than the minimum wage, about US$204 per month in 2007. Chile's richest citizens earned 55 percent of total national income; its poorest earned only 4 percent. Education became an especially sensitive topic. Graduates of private schools, greatly expanded since the Allende years, tend to make much more money than those from the public system. As a result, although Chile's economic model seems to have produced growth, as the years of democracy wore on, a kind of resignation came over what was once one of the most vibrant of Latin American democracies. It would not last. Since 2013, mass protests led by the youth and Indigenous peoples in the country's southern region have exposed the dark underbelly of the "success story."

Brazil: The Business-Friendly State

Brazil's military government (1964–1985) never fully embraced neoliberalism. In part, this reflects a feature of Brazilian political culture—the nation's sense of *grandeza*, a feeling that so large a country, possessed of so many natural resources, must be destined for economic greatness. During the years of military government, the unions and parties of the populist era were crushed, and the government took measures to open the country to foreign investment. Key policies included government support for developing competitive manufacturing in computers, aviation, small arms, and conventional weapons (for sale to Third World countries) and increased exploitation of the Amazon for timber, soybeans, and ranching.

From 1968 to 1974, Brazil experienced the highest rate of economic growth in the world; its manufacturing exports for the first time surpassed those from mining and agriculture. This experience stands much in contrast to the process of deindustrialization that characterized military rule in Chile and Argentina. Brazil's military rulers sought to "deepen industrialization" by increasing production of steel, petrochemicals, and durable consumer goods (cars, refrigerators, etc.). The oil price hikes of late 1973 put an end to the miracle, even as the military borrowed money feverishly to maintain it. The debt quadrupled between 1970 and 1980, surpassing US$100 billion and giving Brazil the largest foreign debt in the world. Hyperinflation also became a serious problem.

Brazil, the world's sixth largest economy, was facing an economic crisis that threatened to have a hemispheric, if not global, impact. The "Real Plan" (the *real* is Brazil's currency) was adopted in Brazil in 1993 by the finance minister, Fernando Henrique Cardoso, the former socialist intellectual turned politician. In 1994, Cardoso won election as president, promising market-oriented reforms cushioned with an effective safety net. He followed the IMF prescription of privatization, trade liberalization, fiscal restraint, and incentives to foreign investment. Results were mixed. From 2,500 percent in 1993, Brazil's inflation fell to 3 percent by 1998, a remarkable achievement. However, the Asian financial crisis in 1998 threatened Cardoso's plans. Financial speculators and capitalists pulled dollars out of Brazil, forcing the government to borrow dollars heavily to maintain the value of the *real* and economic growth, which was an impressive 4 percent in 2000. Investment started coming back, but a downturn in the United States, an economic collapse next door in Argentina, and the difficulty of continuing to defend the *real* set back Cardoso's plans again. By August 2002, Cardoso's preferred candidate for the presidency in the November elections had lost ground to leftist candidates, leading to the election of Lula as president and contributing to the rising **Pink Tide** in the region.

Lula had been defeated three times earlier in his quest for the presidency. Many businesspeople feared that he and his Workers' Party would enact radical, populist policies that would in turn induce a flight of capital. Lula proved much less radical than his opponents feared. Rather than change fundamental social and economic structures, which his colleague Chávez attempted in Venezuela, Lula attempted to alleviate poverty using the benefits of rapid economic growth. Cardoso had paid a political cost for his macroeconomic policies, but they laid the basis for Lula's popularity; in fact, Lula's popular and successful program to reduce hunger had been pioneered by his predecessor. The leading growth sector has been soybeans, which in turn has raised concerns about the environment and future of the rainforest. Brazil's growth rate during Lula's administration, ending in 2010, hit 5 percent per year, much less than that of China or India, but well ahead of Europe, Japan, and the United States. By some estimates, Brazil could move from the seventh-largest economy in 2005 to the fourth largest (trailing China, India, and the United States) by 2050.

Has economic growth expanded the middle class? One study by a Brazilian sociologist (cited in Osava 2004) indicates that the middle class, defined in terms of a family's ability to own durable consumer goods (television, car, computer, etc.), shrank from 42.5 percent of the population in 1981 to 36 percent by 2000. The ranks of the poor increased from 30.5 percent to 39.5 percent. However, the economic boom after 2002 saw 23 million of Brazil's 150 million people enter the lower middle class. One concern is that much of this mobility is built on debt; the number of credit cards issued in Brazil has almost doubled since 2001 (da Costa 2008). Another reason to temper optimism is the fact that the upturn is being led by agricultural exports, much of it to fast-growing China and India, and some critics anticipated correctly that the economy would be in trouble if Asian growth slackened. A collaborative study (Pérez et al. 2008: 11) of the soybean sector by the Washington Office on Latin America and Tufts University concluded that South American soybean industries are

> undeniably winners from global trade liberalization, but few of the benefits go to rural communities. Based on high-input, industrialized monoculture, farming, employment and wages have both declined despite rising production. Ecological harm from agricultural expansion onto sensitive lands leaves lasting destruction.

The authors believe that government support for smallholder agriculture would yield long-term developmental benefits to rural communities and better supply the domestic demand for food.

Still, Brazil, like many other Latin American countries, has diversified its export markets, sending more of its production to Europe and Asia than in the past. The latest "miracle" is occurring in an era of high oil prices, the variable that burst the last expansion of the early 1970s. In 2007 and 2008, important new reserves of oil were found off the country's coast, raising the prospect of energy self-sufficiency.

For Review

Both Chile and Brazil are regarded by many as economic success stories. Why is Chile, more than Brazil, regarded as a country that has been more fully committed to the neoliberal model of economic development?

Cuba: Escaping the Debt Crisis and Not Escaping Debt or Crisis

Because it is a socialist regime, one might very well question whether Cuba's development model can be compared with that of Chile or Brazil. However, that Cuba has chosen such a different path and that for decades many Latin Americans saw it as an alternative success story makes it intriguing. Today, it is widely assumed that Cuba's economic model is failing. Raúl Castro, since taking over from his brother in 2008, has argued that the basic model is sound but that some pragmatic reforms, including some concessions to the market, can restore the economy's vitality.

In 1986, Cuba's external debt to the noncommunist world stood at US$2.6 billion, a relatively small amount. However, it also carried other obligations to the Soviet Union and Eastern Europe, many in the form of agreements to supply sugar and other agricultural products. These are difficult to quantify in dollars. One study group critical of the Castro regime claimed the external debt was valued at US$9 billion in 1996 (Martínez-Piedra and Pérez 1996: 33–34). However, Russia's own economic woes were Cuba's gain. The *ruble* collapsed in the 1990s, making Cuba's debt technically worth only about US$475 million in 2002 dollars. Cuba's bigger problem was that the Eastern European bloc was no longer available as a trade partner, and the giant U.S. economy 90 miles to Cuba's north was waiting to see the system collapse.

With the collapse of the Eastern bloc in 1989 and the Soviet Union in 1991, the Cubans decided to open their economy further to foreign investment and to compromise on some of the programs of social welfare and equality for which it had earned admiration. The government asked Cubans to accept a harsh deterioration in their standard of living during the "special period in times of peace." The key difference from structural adjustment is that the government made sure that the burden of sacrifice was relatively evenly shared. Still, Cubans who receive dollars from relatives in the United States or who work for foreign investors (e.g., in tourism) live better than those who enjoy neither privilege.

The combination of favorable deals with Venezuela for oil, investments from other parts of the world, and President Barack Obama's opening on tourism and trade lifted the economy in the 2000s, especially after 2008, but life remained hard on the island. The Cuban socialist economy has not proved that it can generate the economic growth needed to make people believe that the relatively good economy of the 1980s will return. President Raúl Castro, after succeeding his brother, implemented measures to expand small private businesses, loosen restrictions on selling private property, and shift employment from the state to the private sector. A visitor to Cuba in 2016 could not help but notice the increase in commerce on the streets but would still hear complaints of people, such as workers in the health sector, whose incomes did not allow them to participate as consumers or entrepreneurs in the economic opening.

With the economic crisis in Venezuela and the tightening of what Cubans call the U.S. economic blockade under President Trump, times on the island are hard again. The revolution's survival of the economic crisis of the early 1990s owed much to the sense of all Cubans that the burdens of adjustment were being equally borne. Although state authorities clamped down quickly on dissent, Cuba's defiance of constant predictions of imminent political collapse owed much to the legitimacy of the revolutionary government. The expansion of markets, competition, and private employment inspired optimism in some parts but worry and discontent in others, even before Trump became president. Cubans, including dissidents on the island, nervously await the outcome of the U.S. election in November 2020.

For Review

How did the fall of communism in Eastern Europe affect Cuba? How did the country adjust? What seems similar to and what is different from the adjustment elsewhere in Latin America?

Democracy in Neoliberal Times

Though in some cases, such as Chile, neoliberal policies were put in place by military governments, they were maintained subsequently by liberal democratic regimes. In some cases, such as Brazil under Cardoso and in Argentina under President Carlos Menem (1989–1999), elected presidents implemented neoliberalism. Given the accentuation of poverty and inequality in this period, some asked, how could we reconcile implementation of market-oriented reforms with democratic politics (see Remmer 1998)? Leslie Armijo and Phillippe Faucher (2000) think that despite increasing inequality in most of the hemisphere, the majority of poor Latin Americans were not much disturbed by the shift away from ISI and toward neoliberalism. Large portions of the population were excluded from the benefits of the inward-oriented ISI policies, so they had little to gain from abandoning them. Hyperinflation at the end of the populist era struck hardest at the poor. More than anything, though, based on an examination of politics in Argentina, Brazil, Chile, and Mexico, Armijo and Faucher say that the taming of inflation accounts for why politicians favoring neoliberalism could win elections.

We need to weigh as well how in the early years after the transitions to democracy there remained a vivid collective memory of the horrors of military rule in the popular mind. As the decades have passed, fewer citizens have lived through those years, and the discontent with neoliberalism has been evident in mass protests, if not at the ballot box. The democratic credentials of **polyarchy** rest on the assumption that fair elections allow the public to communicate their demands and ensure their equal political weight over elected officials. What determines a president's fate in the streets or at the ballot box may simply be a matter of trying to pay international creditors and maintain vital services—water, transportation, cooking oil, etc.—within reach of people living in an increasingly precarious world.

Discussion Questions

1. How and why did countries in Latin America adjust to international pressure to abandon import substitution and adopt market-friendly policies? Why were many of the new policies called "neoliberal"?
2. Does the fact that several leaders who implemented neoliberalism were elected mean that Latin American voters supported neoliberalism? What arguments can be made for and against the proposition that strengthening market forces has strengthened democracy in Latin America?
3. What are the key ways that modernization and dependency theories differ? Why do you think dependency first emerged in Latin America rather than in other parts of the Global South?
4. List ways that you think neoliberal economic policies might strengthen or weaken democracy in Latin America. Overall, what do you think is their impact on the democratic condition in the region?

Resources for Further Study

Reading: David Harvey's *A Brief History of Neoliberalism* (New York: Oxford University Press, 2007) brings a critical perspective to the subject. Pedro-Palo Kuczynski and John Williamson defend market-oriented economic policy in their edited volume *After the Washington Consensus: Restarting Growth and Reform in Latin America* (Washington, DC: Peterson Institute, 2003). Before he became a vice minister and a key shaper of Venezuela's oil policies under Chávez, Bernard Mommer wrote *Global Oil and the Nation State* (New York: Oxford University Press, 2002). Both Rostow's *Stages of Growth* (1960) and Frank's *Latin America: Underdevelopment or Revolution* (1969) are reader-friendly. Frank's "The Development of Underdevelopment" appeared in *Monthly Review* (June 1989). Editor Ronald Chilcote's *Development in Theory and Practice: Latin American Perspectives* (Lanham, MD: Rowman and Littlefield, 2003) provides a good selection of Latin American views on development.

Video and Film: Search "Hernando de Soto" and "economist" on YouTube for various speeches and videos elaborating his pro-market views on urban development. *Capital Sins*, the second program in the PBS Americas (1992) series, focuses on development issues in Brazil.

On the Internet: One good reference on different theories can be found at www.uia.be/sites/uia.be/db/db/x.php?dbcode=pr&go=e&id=11202060, the website for the Australian Union of International Associations.

PART III

Regimes and Transitions in Latin America

Los Presidentes in 1982

Galtieri
Francois Lochon/Contributor.

Pinochet
Eric Brissaud/Gamma-Rapho
via Getty Images.

Figueiredo
Hulton Archive/Staff.

Las Presidentes in 2014

Fernandez
© iStockphoto.

Bachelet
Martin Bernetti/AFP
via Getty Images.

Rousseff
Ernesto Benavides/AFP via Getty Images.

7 Democratic Breakdown and Military Rule

Focus Questions

▶ What economic, international, and social factors contributed to the breakdown of democracy in many countries of Latin America between 1960 and 1985?

▶ What have each of the following factors played in the breakdown of democracy at the end of the populist era: interactions among elites, the international situation, domestic social actors?

▶ What do we mean by the terms "democratic transition," "pacts," and "democratization"? How do political scientists see the relationship between elites and the masses in such transitions?

▶ What kind of economic policies were implemented by the military **juntas** in each country? How did the economic policies of the new democracies change, if at all?

▶ After the transitions to democracy, what human rights issues remained to be dealt with? What were the arguments on each side about an amnesty?

IN THE AFTERMATH of the global financial crisis of 2008 and the Great Recession that followed, a wave of populist **regimes** around the world shook two earlier notions: (1) that globalization is inevitable and (2) that a **third wave** (a term coined by Huntington 1991) of liberal democracy will continue to wash up (though perhaps more gradually than at its inception) on all shores. As the coronavirus pandemic spread to all corners of the world, including Latin America, even more uncertainty prevailed about the future shape of global economic integration and democracy. We will take these issues up again later in the book, especially in chapter 15, but the focus in this chapter is on the notion of regime changes in the late twentieth century—changes associated with the breakdown of democracy at the end of the first populist era (see chapter 5), the nature of the military regimes that followed, and then transitions to liberal democracy (that is, **polyarchy**) that characterized the way the third wave washed over Latin America.

One reason to examine these regime changes is that they inform much of the political science literature that began around 2015 to warn of threats to democracy arising out of populism. Authors of two widely read books (Albright 2018; Levitsky and Ziblatt 2018) warned that a close examination of how fascism and other authoritarian regimes arose shows that populist leaders threatened to hasten democratic demise. The concepts and tools of analysis that political scientists use in such books owe much to comparative politics, in particular to the **pluralist** approach (see chapter 1) that was used to identify why the democracies in Latin America (see chapter 6) were unable to cope with the economic and political crises of the late populist era.

Similar to the books concerned with threats to democracy in 2020, studies of the populist crisis and democratic breakdown in Latin America compared these episodes to democratic collapse in other parts of the world and in other periods of time. The experiences of Brazil and the countries of the **Southern Cone** were compared to the rise of fascism in Europe in the 1920s and 1930s and the brutal military regime that grew from a "colonels' coup" in Greece in 1967 (Sartori and Sani 1983). The most influential of these analyses was a four-volume series edited by Juan Linz and Alfred Stepan, *The Breakdown of Democratic Regimes* (1978). The restoration of democracy in most of Latin America and the larger third wave of democracy brought about a similar kind of approach, a kind of reverse engineering, focused on the reconstruction of social and elite consensus (O'Donnell and Schmitter 1986; O'Donnell et al. 1986a, 1986b, 1986c).

The pluralist approach to understanding the collapse of democracy at the end of the populist era and the transitions from military rule has been criticized for placing too much emphasis on elites and not enough on the resistance and mobilization of popular forces. Given the influence of comparative theories about regime change, examining the breakdown of democracy, the nature of military authoritarianism, and the subsequent transition in Latin America takes on an importance beyond the region itself. **Dependency theorists** and Marxian analysts stress the polarization of social classes and the threat of revolution (e.g., Nun 1976; Zenteño 1977).

My own view is that we need to draw upon both the pluralist/elitist approach and approaches focused on social and economic forces, especially class conflict, operating on both national and international levels. In this chapter, we will look closely at the regime changes (the breakdown of populism, the military regimes, and the transitions back to electoral democracy) in Brazil and the Southern Cone.

The Decay of Populist Democracy

One of the most influential books in comparative politics, *Political Order in Changing Societies* by Samuel Huntington, published in 1968 in the middle of the **Cold War**, viewed communism as a threat because it could take advantage of weak political institutions in the process of modernization (see chapter 6). While cloaked in the anticommunist rhetoric of the Cold War, Huntington's book offered an explanation of the fragility of democracy in regions experiencing development. In Latin America, he argued,

> the wealthiest countries are at the middle levels of modernization. Consequently, it is not surprising that they should be more unstable than the more backward Latin American countries . . . Communist and other radical movements have been strong in Cuba, Argentina, Chile, and Venezuela: four of the five wealthier Latin American countries suffered from insurgency.
>
> (1968: 44)

Huntington's premise was that social mobilization contributed to political crisis and challenged both the economic model and the stability of electoral democracy. His argument was summed up (1968: 55) in three equations:

$$\frac{Social\ mobilization}{Economic\ development} = Social\ frustration$$

$$\frac{Social\ frustration}{Mobility\ opportunity} = Political\ participation$$

$$\frac{Political\ participation}{Political\ institutionalization} = Political\ instability$$

The first two equations refer to the kinds of social tensions that arose in the era that bridge the era of **liberal modernization** (see chapter 4) and the era of populism and import substitution (see chapter 5). It is the third equation that most interests us here.

An institution is "an arrangement for maintaining order, resolving disputes, selecting leaders, and thus promoting community among two or more social forces," says Huntington (1968: 9). Strong institutions are not unchanging; they show capacity to adapt to new situations—such as strains caused by economic change. The relationship is delicate. "In the total absence of social conflict, political institutions are unnecessary; in the total absence of social harmony, they are impossible" (9). In Huntington's Cold War mindset, the disruption of social harmony was a goal of communists; but from the perspective of dependency and Marxist analysis, it can also be seen as a result of imperialism and class struggles.

Political polarization in the late populist era (post-1960) in Latin America partly involved the emergence of strong leftist movements that gained strength within labor unions and began to organize and mobilize the urban poor and peasantry. This organizing was what Washington's Cold Warriors (politicians and officials who tended to see Communist expansion behind every regional crisis) regarded as the "communist threat" in the hemisphere. Most of the region's actual communist parties were much more pragmatic than how they were portrayed in Washington's imagination and propaganda. Communists often founded themselves outflanked on the left by young religious radicals and admirers of the 1959 Cuban Revolution. The revolution was bringing about what Regis Debray, a French philosopher and interpreter of the thought of Che Guevara, called a "revolution in the revolution."

Many leftists questioned the more pragmatic communist theory that a socialist revolution required many years of patient organizing to succeed or that Latin America had to go through capitalism first. The rapid collapse of the Batista regime (see chapter 9) in 1959 suggested that Latin American states throughout the hemisphere rested upon a weak social base and a poorly trained, even if well-armed, military. This proved to be something of an illusion. Cuba's social conditions were quite different from those on the continent and in Mexico. With military aid programs and other forms of support, the capitalist class in Latin America was soon prepared to repel the rising tide of revolution.

Social and Political Polarization

Social class polarization at the end of the populist and ISI era was fueled not just by left activism but also by the middle class's reaction to the threat of revolution. The middle class is a swing sector (see chapters 2 and 11) that might support reform, but it typically fears instability and revolutionary change. When the latter threatens, the middle-class allegiance usually shifts to more conservative sectors and defenders of order (Nun 1976; Zenteño 1977). Typically toward the end of the populist era in Latin America, there took place a social polarization in which the wealthy, the landowners, the businesspeople (the **bourgeoisie**), and the middle class were pulled in one direction, while the working class (the proletariat), the urban poor, and the peasantry were pulled in the other direction, increasingly viewing each other as enemies. Typically, such polarization manifests itself first in street actions and then escalates to illegal and sometimes violent protest. (Nun 1967).

Political polarization is a related process by which politicians, parties, and groups lose the capacity to settle disputes, especially those about constitutional issues. Political polarization can happen even when there is little class polarization. Political factions and parties might simply fight one another over the spoils of government, or ethnic and religious differences may make consensus difficult to achieve. However, class polarization almost always makes political polarization worse. Simply put, when society is torn apart by fundamental issues, the political center cannot hold.

Theotonio Dos Santos, a leading *dependista*, succinctly described the unfolding of this process in Brazil, where a military coup against President João Goulart in 1964 ushered in the long period of military rule throughout most of the region:

> Ideological tendencies polarized. Bourgeois ideology moved further to the right as evidenced by its conciliatory position towards imperialism, in its rejection of reformist slogans, its anti-Communist attitude, and above all its support for political authoritarianism. In contrast, nationalist thought became more anti-imperialist, radical reformist, and pro-socialist. These increasingly radical tendencies led to the awareness of the need . . . [on the left] for armed confrontation.
>
> (Dos Santos 1974: 457)

Business groups, says Dos Santos, began to encourage military intervention and adopt "intensive fascist mobilization . . . culminating in the organization of a massive march for 'God, Liberty and the Family.'" When Goulart, the populist president, settled a revolt by rebellious sailors in a way unacceptable to the high command, the military decided to act (Stepan 1971). Dos Santos sees the 1964 coup as a logical response of capitalists (foreign and domestic alike) to the threat of a democratic revolution made by workers, peasants, and the poor. José Nun (1967), an Argentine political scientist sympathetic to the left, stresses the role of the middle class in abetting the coups by shifting its sympathies from the lower classes in the face of possible revolutionary change. He thus takes issue with the common assumption that growth of the middle class, a product of economic development, is a democratizing force. As mainly middle-class institutions, the armed forces tend to defend that class's interest, argues Nun.

Although Huntington shares little in common politically with Dos Santos and Nun, he takes a similar view of the armed forces. The Latin American military had evolved early in the 1900s from its ragged condition of the nineteenth century. As the military evolved, the professional officers, drawn from the middle sectors, chafed at the limitations imposed by superior officers in high ranks populated by the sons and cronies of oligarchs. They were the "doorkeepers to the expansion of political participation in a praetorian society; their historic role is to open the door to the middle class and to close it to the lower class" (Huntington 1991: 222). Military officers were often at the forefront of opening the closed systems inherited from the era of **liberal modernization** and state-building, abetting the rise of **populism**. But decades later, when populist governments began to radicalize and threaten revolution, the military took on a quite different, reactionary role.

Table 7.1 provides a summary of political transitions that took place in five important Latin American countries, beginning with the establishment of populism, its crisis, and the political changes that ensued. You may find this table to be a useful reference as we discuss timing and consequences of events in these countries in this and the next two chapters.

For Review

What is social polarization? Military officers are mostly members of the middle class. Why might this incline them toward intervening in politics when tensions rise between social classes?

The Final Breakdown of Populist Democracy

In this social context, political leaders became less and less inclined to negotiate a compromised solution to the crisis of populism. In this view, moderate leaders of leftist, populist parties were pressured by leftist extremists to accelerate revolutionary processes, whereas moderates on the right felt pressure from extremists on the right who resisted any reform or compromise with the "communist threat." The moderates on both sides had an interest in saving democracy, but neither side trusted the will or ability of the other to keep the extremist wings in check.

For example, Salvador Allende, the elected socialist president of Chile, and Eduardo Frei, the most important leader of the centrist Christian democrats (then in opposition), were unable to negotiate an exit to Chile's crisis in 1973. In his contribution to a book on democratic breakdowns, Arturo Valenzuela (1978: 109), a Chilean political scientist (who later became a U.S. citizen and assistant secretary of state for hemispheric affairs in the Obama administration), blamed leftists for much of the polarization. Many of them thought Allende was not sufficiently committed to revolution. "By its actions, the revolutionary Left, which had always ridiculed the possibility of a socialist transformation through peaceful means, was engaged in a self-fulfilling prophecy," he wrote.

Alfred Stepan (1971), in his analysis of "breakdowns," also found the cause of decay in the breakdown of elite compromise under the pressure of social polarization. The Brazilian system was simply overloaded by the mobilization of new sectors at a time of "decreasing extractive capability" for the Brazilian state. Put another way, economic and political demands were increasing at a time of slow economic growth. The political party system

TABLE 7.1 A Reference Chart for Understanding Transitions in the Southern Cone, Brazil, Venezuela, and Mexico

	Argentina	Chile	Brazil	Mexico	Venezuela
Populism and its origins	1945–1968 Juan Perón (1945–1955)	1932–1970 Popular Front of parties, 1932–1952	1946–1964 Vargas + successors	1934–1982 Lázaro Cárdenas (1934–1940)	1945–1989 Rómulo Betancourt, Pact of Punto Fijo (1958–1998)
Crisis	1968–1976 Cordobazo (1968)	1970–1973 Allende and Popular Unity	1964–1968 Joao Goulart, coup in 1964, resistance	1968 Massacre of student protestors; 1982 debt crisis	1989 Caracazo revolt; 1992–1993 failed coup and resignation of Carlos Andrés Pérez
Peak of repression	1976–1982 Dirty War	1973–1976 Pinochet's "Caravan of Death"	1968–1973 "Economic Miracle" and silencing of critics	1968–1988 Continual, less visible repression; never military rule	1989 Hundreds die in repression of *caracazo*; never military rule
Crisis leading to transition	1982–1983 Inflation, defeat in Malvinas War, military retreats	1982 Recession; 1986 protests; 1989 Plebiscite leads to transition	1984–1985 End of "Economic Miracle," pressure in streets, gradual transition	1988 Election fraud; 1994 Zapatista revolt in Chiapas	1989–1998 Frustration with failure to reform closed nature of party politics
Civilian neoliberalism	Menem 1991–1999	Concertación 1990 to present	Collor and Cardoso post-1990	Salinas and Zedillo, 1988–2000; NAFTA, 1994	C.A. Pérez, 1989–1993
New parties or electoral movements	New Left Alliance; later left-Peronists	PPD on left, UDI on right	PT	PRD	Causa R, MVR, later PSUV (chavismo)
Post-BA military status	Conflict over amnesty— *Carapintadas* revolt of 1987, Menem reduces size, restores amnesty	Amnesty in 1883; strong influence, Pinochet still heads until 1998; declining influence since	Gradual transition and amnesty for both sides, military still influential but little threat of coup	Civilian control but rising repression after 1968 raised specter of militarized politics, especially in Chiapas	Radical, nationalist sector, led by Chávez grows after repression of *caracazo* 1989; coup attempts in 1992
Status around 2010	Amnesty revoked, some trials under Kirchner	No repeal of amnesty, but criminal prosecutions	Recent signs of prosecution for human rights abuses	Pres. Fox fails to keep promise to open files, but pressure remains	As president, Chávez uses military for civilian projects. Dissident sectors purged after failed coup 2002

Note: BA refers to the bureaucratic authoritarian military regimes in the region; NAFTA, North American Free Trade Agreement; MVR, Fifth Republic Movement; PRD, Democratic Revolutionary Party; UDI, Unión Demócrata Independiente; PPD, Partido Para Democrácia; PSUV, United Socialist Party of Venezuela; PT, Workers Party in Brazil; Causa R, Radical Cause Party in Venezuela.

fragmented under the load, but collapse was not inevitable. Stepan thinks that President Goulart might have staved off a military coup had populist politicians and leaders of movements (e.g., the peasant leagues) not pulled politicians away from a negotiated solution to the conflict.

In Argentina, the military had already intervened several times after the overthrow of Juan Perón in 1955. So we might argue that Argentina never had a populist, institutionalized democracy to start with. But in these coups, the military was acting out what some call the "moderator" role. In this role, the military typically comes to power announcing its intention to act as a caretaker or to rule in the name of honesty or patriotism (Stepan 1971: 61–66). This was typically the case with military coups in Bolivia, which had averaged about one per year since independence. Brazil's General Castelo Branco seems to have had this goal in mind in 1964, but by 1968 the military had shifted to much more ambitious goals of political and economic engineering. Guillermo O'Donnell (1978) found a similar process at work in Argentina between 1956 and 1966, as several military governments came and went as they unsuccessfully tried to marginalize the Peronists. But by 1966, Peronism itself had split between a more radical, revolutionary wing and a more conservative, **corporatist** wing. Democracy was never in good shape in Argentina in the twentieth century, but its descent into a brutal military dictatorship was hastened by a process of acute social and political polarization that led to a breakdown of consensual politics at both the elite and mass levels.

PHOTO 7.1   The Argentine military this day consider what most Argentines call the "Dirty War" to be the "War Against Subversion." Why do you think they see it this way?

Source: STR/AFP via Getty Images.

The International Context

Like all revolutionaries (including the American patriots who attempted to "free" Canada from England's rule in 1812, the Cubans thought their revolution was part of an international wave that they were duty-bound to help along. Cuba offered moral support, some training, and—at least until 1965—arms to revolutionary movements. At the same time, the United States exaggerated the influence of Cuba and the Soviet Union—at times even inventing it—to justify intervention and repression of leftist political movements, democratic or not (see chapter 16).

The administration of President John F. Kennedy came to power in January 1961 determined to commit Americans to a crusade against communism. "Bear any burden, pay any price," the new president said in his famous inaugural address. Kennedy, advised by academics such as Huntington and Rostow, also called for reform in Latin America, especially agrarian reform (land distribution, unionization of rural workers, etc.), to quiet the restive peasantry. This program was called the "Alliance for Progress." Concretely, this meant foreign aid packages and advisors (including volunteers in the new Peace Corps) to help centrist parties, such as Chile's Christian Democrats, Venezuela's Democratic Action party, and Brazil's social democrats. At the same time, however, Kennedy and his successor, Lyndon Johnson, actively deployed strategies that encouraged reactionary forces in the region.

The CIA is estimated to have spent US$40 million (US$20 million in each case) to influence the outcome of state and congressional elections in Brazil in 1962 and Chile in 1964 (Cockroft 1996: 541, 639). These funds greatly exceeded what parties and candidates could themselves muster in these countries. When such tactics failed to quell the threat of revolution, the United States turned to measures, overt and covert, to destabilize the political system and encourage military intervention. Kennedy opened the spigot of military aid; he upgraded the firepower and training of Latin American militaries, which were schooled, like their contemporaries in Vietnam, in counterinsurgency tactics and anticommunist doctrines.

Much as Rostow (see chapter 6) and Huntington advised, Kennedy strengthened Latin American militaries to fight the "communists" while promoting reforms. The latter included breaking up large landed estates, supporting health and education programs, and promoting "nonpolitical" unions to replace those closely linked to parties. Aid was targeted at centrist parties in an attempt to strengthen them against leftist challenges, but right-wing groups saw the American reforms as playing into the hands of the communists. The military accepted aid but not the "strings" attached, such as land reform and respect for human rights. Latin American generals correctly calculated that for the United States, defeating the left (elected or not) was a higher priority than reform or rights.

The post–World War II model for destabilization was set by the CIA's successful operation to overthrow the elected government of Jacobo Arbenz in Guatemala in 1954. That operation too had a precedent in operations elsewhere in Europe (Greece and Italy) and the Middle East (Iran in 1953). In Central America and the Caribbean, American military intervention played a direct role in bringing despotic governments to power, keeping them there, or bringing down regimes deemed too radical for comfort. A U.S. military invasion ousted a democratically elected government in the Dominican Republic in 1965. An invasion of the tiny island of Grenada in 1982 made sure that no new revolution would emerge from the ashes of a collapsed revolutionary regime. The Nixon administration (1968–1975) employed the CIA to engage in economic sabotage, kidnapping, psychological propaganda, and other tactics designed to bring down elected governments that were unacceptable to U.S. interests in the Third World, including in Latin America and the Caribbean.

For Review

How did the Cuban Revolution affect politics in other countries in Latin America? What was the response of the United States to the emergence of the radical left in Brazil and the Southern Cone?

Case Studies of Democratic Breakdown

The study of the breakdowns of democracy and (later) transitions back to electoral democracy in Brazil and the **Southern Cone** were influenced by similar experiences of countries elsewhere in the world, especially the Mediterranean. The way that both Spain and Portugal underwent transitions from regimes that openly identified with **fascism** (Franco in Spain, Salazar in Portugal) drew attention from Latin American area specialists not only because the Iberian countries had colonized Latin America but because in the mid-twentieth century their social structures and levels of development were relatively comparable to those in the southern part of South America.

Breakdown in Brazil: Setting the Trend

After World War II, Brazilian presidents attempted to maintain the same **import substitution** policies championed first under Getúlio Vargas, who committed suicide in 1954. After Vargas, Brazil seemed to be jumping forward under President Juscelino Kubitschek, who in three years built a new, gleaming capital, Brasilia, in the Amazon interior. Brazilian elites had always believed the future lay there. But by 1960, the economy was beginning to slow. When Jânio Quadros became president after winning election in 1960, he vacillated between a more conservative, corporatist version of Vargas's **Estado Nôvo** and the more radical, leftist brand of populism represented by his vice president, João Goulart. Goulart assumed the presidency in 1961 after Quadros had resigned under pressure from the military and conservatives opposed to his friendliness toward the new regime in Cuba. They were also suspicious of his pro-labor policies and his attempts to tax the wealthy, including landowners, to keep import substitution going. But Goulart proved even more radical than Quadros.

Goulart faced a hostile parliament that stripped away some of the presidential powers built by Vargas. In 1963, Goulart won back much of his authority in a **plebiscite**. He then moved to carry out nationalization of several industries, land reform, large concessions to labor unions, and so on. Goulart hoped to keep the support of Brazil's businesspeople, who had benefited from years of state support under import substitution. However, Goulart's turn to the left alarmed the capitalist class in general. They feared the growing radicalism in the labor movement, and this outweighed the subsidies and other incentives Goulart offered to get the economy moving forward again. It is important to remember that fresh in the minds of both the left and the capitalists was the 1959 Cuban Revolution.

Inflation was an especially thorny issue, and attempts to control prices and wages made no one happy. Small farmers and the poorest urban workers were seeing their living conditions deteriorate. Skilled and organized workers defended their pay more successfully, but this further antagonized business. The highly unequal distribution of income in Brazil limited the possibility of renewed growth through ISI, but internal redistribution of wealth and income was blocked politically. The option of new industrialization through exports to markets abroad would require major adjustments in the economic model to make factories more competitive with manufacturing in other countries. The growing strength of popular movements not only posed a political obstacle to such a change but also deterred foreign investment.

As the Brazilian military—already deeply drawn into the complex web of negotiation among Brazil's political parties—mobilized for a coup in 1964, the United States signaled the go-ahead. President Lyndon Johnson's instructions to his foreign policy advisors in a telephone call were captured by tape recorder (National Security Archives, www.gwu.edu/~nsarchiv, accessed August 8, 2007). Johnson is heard to instruct Undersecretary of State George Ball that revolution in Brazil would be unacceptable. "We just can't take this one," he says. "I'd get right on top of it and stick my neck out a little."

The catalyst for the coup that ended Brazil's first experiment with democracy was concessions that Goulart made to rebellious naval officers, which the high command saw as intrusion on their domain. Politicians welcomed the coup, believing it would, like so many other Latin American coups of the past, simply break the political impasse and open the way for a new election. In his inaugural address of April 15, 1964, General Humberto Castelo Branco promised to "observe and maintain the laws of the country" and said he would call upon the participation of "all the citizens" in his endeavor to continue "striving for progress and advancement." He promised, "My behavior will be that of a head of state who will permit no delay in the process of electing the Brazilian to whom I shall transfer my office on January 31, 1966." The general also promised that his government would work not only to benefit private enterprise but also to extend well-being for "those who toil and suffer in the less-developed regions of the country" (quoted in Sigmund 1970: 132–134).

In 1964, the military junta might very well have had these goals in mind, but it first tried to bring inflation under control at the sole expense of the workers. The political situation grew even more polarized. The violence spilled over into the kidnapping of several foreign diplomats. In 1968, the hardliners in the military consolidated their rule with Institutional Act #5 (see Stepan 1978). The act "legitimized" serious abuses, including torture, disappearances, and limits on political rights. The act's preamble specified, "subversive acts on the part of different political and cultural sectors prove" that the relatively liberal system established in 1964 were "being used as a means to combat and destroy it." It authorized the military president to close down national and state legislatures indefinitely, to rule by decree, to "suspend the political rights of any citizen for a period of ten years," to declare at will states of siege and suspend habeas corpus, and to confiscate the property of anyone it found (without a trial) guilty of corruption (Sigmund 1970: 142–145).

The regime was less brutal in many respects than its counterparts in Chile and Argentina were, but the legacy of repression remains a controversial factor in present-day Brazilian politics. Hundreds were killed, and many thousands more tortured or imprisoned. The military would retain power until 1985. The events in Brazil, the largest and most influential country in the region, proved a harbinger of what would follow in almost every other country in Latin America.

For Review

What factors led the military to carry out first the coup of 1964, and then the coup of 1968? In what ways did the populism of the Vargas era become much more radicalized in the Goulart era?

Breakdown in Argentina: The Dirty War

The 1964 coup in Brazil was only the first act in a series of setbacks for democratic rule. In Argentina, the final turn toward tyranny came in 1976. Twenty years before, in 1955, Juan Perón had been overthrown by the military. Perón was anticommunist, but like other populists, he angered foreign investors and local capitalists alike with pro-labor policies and nationalization of some foreign assets, most importantly the oil company, ports, and railroads. The United States welcomed his overthrow. At the time (1955), the Argentine military intended not to govern but only to "restore order" and then hold elections to be contested between two other parties, the Conservatives and Radicals, without the Peronists.

The problem for the military was that the political party built by Perón was the best organized and most popular one in the country, and the old parties had no solution to Argentina's severe economic problems, which were growing worse (O'Donnell 1978: 149–155). Inflation soared to 113 percent in 1959 and ranged between 20 and 32 percent for most of the next decade. In the late 1960s, workers' wages fell to levels below where they had been (in real terms) in 1947. Negative growth rates of –3.7, –5.5, and –2.2 percent were recorded for 1962, 1963, and 1966, respectively. ISI had reached its limit, and Argentine meat and grain exports were incapable of sustaining the new urban economy.

As in Brazil, the economic crisis contributed to a radicalization of populism. The Peronist Party was deeply divided between a revolutionary leftist wing and a conservative wing. The Peronist Youth were aligned with the left. Like young leftists throughout Latin America, they were inspired by Cuban events (Che Guevara was an Argentine) and by the emergence of a Marxist-influenced movement (**liberation theology**) for social justice in the Catholic Church, and they grew more discontented with the party's labor oligarchy. What kept the dysfunctional Peronist Party together was the desire to win elections, defense of the labor movement (the leadership's main electoral base) from military repression, and the personality cult around the deceased Eva and the exiled Juan.

The military would not find it easy to expunge Peronism from Argentine politics. Some politicians in the middle-class Radical Party, notably president Arturo Frondizi (1958–1962), tried to strike a deal with the Peronists, but the military moved to block prospects of Perón returning to power. Meanwhile, the intractable economic situation undermined the chances of compromise. A cycle developed: Elections were held, but the winners found they could not govern. Strikes and student demonstrations then would escalate until the military would intervene again to prevent the resurgence of Peronism. Coups occurred in 1962, 1966, and 1976. The military would tire of dealing with economic problems and unrest and call elections in which the Peronists would show their power. Then the cycle would start again.

Meanwhile, conservative Peronists became alarmed as worker groups began to move beyond traditional demands for better wages and benefits to challenge ownership and management for control. Inspired by the Cuban Revolution, but also frustrated by repression at the hands of Peronist Party leaders, some on the left concluded that only armed struggle could bring change, so they formed a guerrilla movement. The most important were the Montoneros, who adopted the theory that in the cities, where most Argentines lived, the people could serve as a refuge for guerrillas, substituting for the mountains, where guerrillas elsewhere typically install themselves. A key moment came in 1969 in the city of Córdoba. Workers and students seized control of the automobile factory and other factories in the city and called for a revolution. The Cordobazo uprising was brutally repressed, but it was evident that populist forces were growing more radical and stronger.

The military now began to think of how to interrupt the cycle of elections and coups, and some thought working with the Peronists might be a solution. General Alejandro Lanusse became president in 1971 and decided to lift the five-year-old ban on political parties, hoping to head off the radicalization process by strengthening moderate and right-wing Peronists. In 1972, he allowed Juan Perón himself to return from exile. After his victory in the July 1973 presidential election, Perón launched a "purification" campaign against the leftists in his ranks. A year later, he died at the age of 78 years. His third wife, Isabel, who had run with her husband for the vice presidency, was no Eva. She took office and continued the purge, with support from the military.

Isabel Perón veered wildly in policy, crushing strikes and rejecting large wage increases, only to reinstate them in the face of huge, militant protests and new strikes. Inflation reached 335 percent in 1975. Meanwhile, the combination of falling prices for Argentina's staple export products (beef and wheat) and skyrocketing oil prices (following the Middle East war of October 1973) devastated the economy. Perón accepted stringent restrictions on government spending and wage increases to get a desperately needed loan from the International Monetary Fund (IMF). Right-wing death squads appeared, and the Montoneros escalated their actions, including kidnappings and bombs that took civilian lives. Their targets included rival unionists within the Peronist Party. In 1974, the guerrillas obtained US$14 million in exchange for a captive executive of Exxon Corporation, heightening Washington's support for a coup.

As the situation deteriorated toward civil war, the economy was jolted when the price of imported oil tripled in 1973–1974. The popularity of the government plunged. In March 1976, a military junta seized power. The coup had substantial support from the middle class, which saw the government as inept and recoiled at the prospect of a leftist revolution (Nun 1976). Many Argentines thought that the coup was just one more coup in the cycle. This time, however, the generals had other intentions. General Jorge Rafael Videla launched what the military to this day calls the "War Against Subversion"; more generally it is known as the "Dirty War."

Already, Brazil's generals had decided to stay in power and ratcheted up repression in 1968; violent military regimes had seized power in Uruguay and Chile in 1973. From 1976 to 1982, the military killed or "disappeared" as many as 30,000 people (Andersen 1993). The military saw its "War Against Subversion" as part of an international struggle against communism. There were guerrillas, the Montoneros, operating in the cities, but the military acted with a free hand to crack down as well on the Peronist leftists in the unions and youth movement. There were only a few thousand guerrillas, but the military targeted anyone (clergy, students, professors, union leaders—anyone) they viewed as possibly connected to "subversion." Merely having your name in the address book of someone detained was enough to find yourself arrested, tortured, disappeared, or murdered.

The military operation went far beyond what might be justified by Montonero violence (see Andersen 1993). In a campaign of terror, the junta disappeared as many as 30,000 people. With the encouragement of Argentina's wealthy oligarchy, support initially from a fearful middle class, and tolerance from Washington, one of the most murderous military regimes ever to rule a Latin American country won its war to the death with the Montoneros—by eliminating anyone remotely connected to them. The military officers banned unions and took control over social institutions, even soccer clubs. Simply having your name in the address book of some thought to be a Montonero was enough to lose your job or your place in the university, to be jailed, tortured, or even worse. The middle class found that it had traded one form of insecurity, anarchic violence, for another: state terrorism, unleashed with little moral or political restraint.

For Review

The military was never very content with Peronism. Why? Describe the divisions within Peronism and how they contributed to polarization in Argentina and ultimately to the Dirty War.

Breakdown in Chile: The Allende Tragedy and Pinochet

September 11 (9/11) is one of those days that "live in infamy," but it has a different meaning for Chileans than for most other people in the world. On September 11, 1973, the Chilean Air Force bombed La Moneda, the presidential palace, putting an end to four decades of electoral democracy in Chile. Salvador Allende, Chile's elected socialist president, died in the bombing. It was only the most dramatic of the coups that brought military rule to most of Latin America.

Chile's history includes episodes of military rule and civil war, but more than in most other Latin American countries Chile's elite has governed the country through parliamentary institutions—which is not the same as saying it was democratic. When Salvador Allende, a Marxist, was elected president in 1970, Chile was being governed under a constitution written in 1932, which had admitted the middle class and parts of the working class into the political game, but still left others excluded. Until 1949, the right to vote was limited by property and literacy requirements that kept most peasants and much of the urban population entirely outside the system. In the countryside, control over registration and the voting process was in the hands of local authorities holding to big landowners. Women finally won the vote in 1949, partly through a suffrage movement but also because conservatives thought their votes would offset the influence of the newly enfranchised males. And there was another barrier to political equality: Despite **hyperurbanization**, seats in Congress were never reapportioned after 1932, leaving representation grossly skewed toward the rural areas dominated by the political right.

Political conflict intensified when Allende achieved the highest vote total (but not a majority) among three major candidates in the 1970 presidential election. Besides entrenched opposition in Congress, Allende would inherit judges and a bureaucracy that were heavily biased against his goals and able to obstruct his programs, such as land reform. These same institutions had obstructed the much less radical reforms that Allende's predecessor, Christian democratic president Eduardo Frei, had attempted (Kaufman 1972).

Populism in Chile from 1932 to 1973 revolved much more around political parties than a single charismatic leader, as in Brazil and Argentina. For much of the era (1938 to 1958), the country was governed by a coalition of urban-based parties, led by the Radicals. The coalition, called the Popular Front, included the Socialist Party and, until 1945, the communists. It implemented a program of ISI (Drake 1978), providing cheap loans and subsidies through a special government development agency funded by taxes on the exports of the foreign copper companies—Kennecott and Anaconda.

Just as the parties founded by Perón and Vargas provided labor stability for new industries, the parties in the Popular Front did the same—in exchange, of course, for political support. Union contracts improved conditions for the growing working class, but unions were subordinate in **corporatist** style to the parties. The Popular Front never attempted to redistribute Chile's wealth or redistribute land. It never challenged the right's control over the rural areas, largely in the hands of Liberal and Conservative parties founded in the era of liberal modernization.

The coalition began to falter after World War II. First, President González Videla of the Radical Party outlawed the Communist Party in 1948, after the outbreak of the Cold War. The Socialist Party split into a moderate faction that favored an electoral strategy for change and a faction that favored revolutionary action. The Radicals were a middle-class party of reform whose days were passing. A new political party, the Christian Democrats, formed in the center and by 1958 had displaced the Radicals, who would never recover their old role as the country's largest party. In the 1952 election, a retired general won the presidency, an indication that the old party system was in trouble. In the 1958 election, a Liberal Party candidate, supported also by the Conservative Party, barely defeated Allende and the candidate of the Christian democrats. A small splinter vote for a radical, defrocked priest was all that prevented the socialists from achieving the highest vote. A year later, the Cuban Revolution intensified the right's fear of an Allende victory in 1964. The United States now entered the picture, secretly providing heavy financial backing for the Christian democratic candidate, Eduardo Frei, who won the 1964 election with 56 percent of the votes, in part because the right-wing parties, under pressure from the United States, chose not to run a candidate.

Six years (1964–1970) of mild reforms under Frei satisfied nobody. Landlords hated his agrarian reform program, but peasants were resentful because Frei delivered land to only one-fifth of the families who had been promised a parcel. Land was also an issue in the cities, where poor workers pressed the government to give them titles to unused land they had occupied. The Christian democrats divided over these issues, with a conservative, business-oriented wing providing the financial muscle and a youthful reform-oriented wing providing a political ground army more committed to more radical change. Radical Christians and Marxists (many dissatisfied with the Communist Party's go-slow approach) organized and exhorted disaffected workers, the urban poor, and restive peasants. Electoral reforms allowed the electorate to triple between 1958 and 1970, and peasant unionization surged. Both developments threatened the landed oligarchy's power, based on congressional representation weighted heavily toward rural areas.

The Kennedy administration (1961–1963) made Chile a major target for foreign aid, but with ISI faltering, this was not enough to keep the economy growing. Frei hoped to increase ownership of the country's copper mines. His government bought a majority of shares in the two big foreign mining companies—just before copper prices began to fall, a disaster for an economy that depended on copper exports for 80 percent of its foreign exchange earnings. Businesspeople faced declining profits; wages fell; and the middle class faced mounting inflation.

Under the Alliance for Progress, the Kennedy and Johnson administrations promoted and provided aid for a moderate land reform. President Frei welcomed the help, but the Chilean right was outraged. Despite their fear of Allende's revolutionary plans, in 1971 they would vote for Allende's nationalization of the two large American copper companies. They reasoned that there was no reason to protect the property rights of Americans eager to support land reform.

The stage was set for a dramatic election in 1970. Could Chile's institutions stand the strain? Despite the polarization and underlying tension, there was some reason for optimism. Chile's political party system seemed adaptable. The Christian Democrats had replaced the Radicals in the center, and parties on the left and right had shown an ability to form coalitions and compromise. Chile had strong labor unions, but the parties exercised considerable restraint over them. And overall, the percentage distribution of the vote for the left, right, and center candidates in 1970 was similar to that of 1958, when the politicians worked through the crisis. Compared with most of Latin America, and in fact compared with most of Europe, Chile's military had largely refrained from intervening in politics since 1932.

The center virtually collapsed. In the 1970 election campaign, the Christian democratic candidate, Radomiro Tomic, in some ways sounded a more populist and radical note than did Allende. What was left of the Radicals had mostly shifted left into Allende's Popular Unity (Unidad Popular—UP) coalition. The process of polarization would accelerate over the next three years, but already it was acute enough in 1970 to put into doubt whether the Chilean Congress, which was constitutionally charged with choosing the president in the event no candidate achieved a majority (50 percent, plus one) of votes, would follow well-established tradition in the event of a victory by Allende.

Allende won 36 percent of the vote, more (barely) than any other candidate, but not a majority. Congress convened to choose a president. The United States pressured it to elect someone other than Allende but also sought to short-circuit the process and provoke a military coup by staging the kidnapping of the commander of the armed forces and blaming the left. The plot was exposed after the general involved died resisting the kidnappers. Now the Christian democrats agreed to vote for Allende in Congress in exchange for his promise to leave the public administration, judiciary, and armed forces independent. Allende controlled the presidency, but Congress, the judiciary, the bureaucracy, and the military were beyond his control.

Allende's plan was to nationalize key sectors of the economy, beginning with the vital copper industry. Revenues from copper were intended to accelerate land reform (compensate owners and help peasants become more productive) and to improve living conditions in the *barrios*. He hoped that populist programs (health, education, welfare, price controls, and so forth) would win broad support for an overhaul of Chile's constitution. He never intended to do away with elections, opposition parties, rights, and so on. His goal was to make it easier for a majority to pass laws socializing a larger portion of the economy. In keeping with the nature of populism in this period, Allende hoped to keep the allegiance of the middle class and sectors of business by targeting his reforms only at landowners, foreign capital, and the largest private capitalists, especially those resisting his revolution. The UP called this plan "the Chilean path to socialism."

It did not work. Chile's nationalization of copper mines, one of the few things that passed Congress with support from all parties, came just as world copper prices were falling. Also, the large mines, after decades of exploitation, were in need of new investments to maintain production, something the country did not have. The economy suffered. At the grassroots level, workers and peasants, impatient for real change and improvement in their lives, began to take over factories and form neighborhood organizations. Some began to arm themselves, to the consternation of the police and military. Most of the popular organizing was profoundly democratic, as anthropologist Peter Winn (1989) showed in his path-breaking study of a textile factory taken over by workers. But land and factory takeovers forced the hand of the government, which had to choose between tolerating these actions or enforcing laws protecting the property rights of owners, which would require using the police and military to evict the workers and peasants. Allende was pursuing a relatively moderate strategy, but Carlos Altamirano, the leader of his own Socialist Party, was pushing for a more radical approach.

Polarization now took on a dynamic of its own. Each side tended to take on the attitude "If you're not with us, you're against us." Rhetoric escalated; and neighbors chose sides. Politics became intensely personal. At the grassroots, local leaders ("cadres" or "militants") of leftist parties often discriminated against people who did not support revolution. When local organizers denied milk or other benefits of redistributive programs to eligible people because of their politics, the effect was to drive them further into opposition. Meanwhile, on the right, with the aid and support of the United States, an extraconstitutional, disloyal opposition emerged, engaging in sabotage and provocative activities, including propaganda that alarmed Chile's devout Catholic population by raising the specter of atheistic communism. President Richard Nixon and Henry Kissinger, Nixon's national security advisor, ordered the CIA to "make the economy scream" and bring down Allende via a military coup (Kornbluth 2013).

The Popular Unity coalition divided into factions. One was a "consolidation" faction, headed by Allende himself and including moderate socialists and the Communist Party. Other parts of the Popular Unity coalition wanted an "advance without compromise faction." This was favored by more radical socialists, a majority of the president's own party. The mass media, the Church, and the Christian Democratic Party moved deeper into opposition and began to raise the specter of a military coup. As the economy worsened in 1971, more women were drawn into the struggle. In December 1971, wealthy and middle-class women staged the "march of the empty pots," a protest tactic that came to be known as the *cacerolazo*. The tactic drew attention to shortages and led to considerable street violence. Greater numbers of poor and working-class women participated than the government would have hoped. Meanwhile, in 1972, the United States doubled military aid, a clear sign of Washington's preferred outcome, and it ratcheted up destabilization (Roxborough et al. 1977).

Allende was losing his grip. Leftists called on him to arm the workers, which probably would have brought an immediate coup. Strikes became more common, but the economic situation did not allow the government to offer workers a better deal. In March 1973, congressional elections were held; Allende's coalition increased its share of the vote but was far from the majority needed to enact sweeping changes. The opposition fell far short of the majority needed to remove Allende from office before the next scheduled election in 1976. In fact, the UP percentage had increased to 43 percent from 36 percent in 1970, increasing the opposition's unease. Allende brought generals into his cabinet to try to assuage the opposition, but this was taken as a sign of weakness by the right. A coup was barely averted in June 1973. In August, several naval officers tried to warn the president of an impending coup; they were arrested by their superiors and tortured into implicating some leftist leaders in alleged plans for an uprising. Allende apparently could not even defend his supporters in the armed forces.

On September 11, 1973, American and Chilean naval maneuvers were underway off Chile's coast. Tanks rolled through the streets. Allende rushed to La Moneda, the presidential palace, after hearing news that a coup was underway. He armed himself and broadcast a final message (Allende 1973) to the Chilean people.

> My words are not spoken in bitterness, but in disappointment. There will be a moral judgment on those who have betrayed the oath they took as soldiers of Chile. . . . They have the might and they can enslave us, but they cannot halt the world's social processes, not with crimes, nor with guns. . . . May you go forward in the knowledge that, sooner rather than later, the great avenues will open once again, along which free citizens will march in order to build a better society. Long live Chile! Long live the people! Long live the workers! These are my last words, and I am sure that this sacrifice will constitute a moral lesson which will punish cowardice, perfidy and treason.

The Chilean Air Force bombed the palace in Santiago. Allende's body was later recovered from the ruins of the palace. Most likely, he committed suicide, feeling he had let down the Chilean people. Either way, he was among only the first of many victims of the military. General Augusto Pinochet emerged soon afterward as the strongman of the new regime. He would rule Chile for 17 years. Officially, 3,129 people were killed, most in the first four years. As in Argentina, the military's goal was to purge the left entirely from political life. Tens of thousands of Chile's 14 million people suffered imprisonment, torture, and exile. Even after Pinochet turned power over to an elected civilian in 1990, he retained considerable power for another decade as a senator-for-life and, most importantly, as commander of the armed forces.

In 2013—40 years after the coup—Chileans were still trying to draw lessons from the breakdown of democracy in 1973, and so were political scientists. Can a revolution, especially a socialist revolution, be accomplished within a pluralist, constitutional framework? Or are revolutions by necessity violent? Was the collapse a failure of elite negotiation, or were deeper social and economic factors responsible? To what degree can the collapse be attributed to the destabilization plan launched by the United States, or would a coup have taken place regardless of U.S. actions?

For Review

What was the Chilean Path to socialism? How was it supposed to work? What were some of the reasons that it failed? What difficult choices did Allende face?

Bureaucratic Authoritarianism

Guillermo O'Donnell (1973), an Argentine political scientist, coined the term "**bureaucratic authoritarianism**" (BA) for the harsh dictatorships that followed the populist crisis. By qualifying the term "authoritarianism," O'Donnell implies, rightly, that not all authoritarian regimes are the same. The leaders of the BA regimes came to power convinced that they could not simply restore the status quo. Influenced by the national security doctrines of U.S. training missions, they came to see their mission as that of defeating the threat of another Cuban-style revolution. The prospect of turning government back over to professional politicians seemed unappealing.

The military juntas did not necessarily seize government with a preconceived plan of what would replace import substitution as an economic development strategy, but they did understand that the threat of revolution required more profound change than a "moderating" role would imply. The coup makers were convinced that they had to radically restructure the economy, even if that meant bulldozing not only anything associated with left populism and **ISI** but also the resistance of the inefficient landlords and businesspeople who simply wanted them to oust Allende.

Each of the BAs brutalized the population not only to crush insurrections but also to destroy the power of unions, peasant movements, and leftist parties. Then they turned to economists and other experts to construct a new economic policy. This marked the entrance of the so-called technocrats into power, completing the bureaucratic–authoritarian alliance. The advice of these technocrats could vary. Chile perhaps represents the case where the threat of revolution was most pronounced and the swing toward neoliberalism was most decisive. Brazil, on the other hand, opted to retain some state control over the economy.

By destroying the institutions of populist democracy and putting an end to ISI, the military in the Southern Cone and Brazil prepared the way for the rise of pro-business policies (see chapter 6). Chile was where **neoliberalism** struck its deepest roots. The "nonpolitical" experts recruited by Pinochet were known as the "**Chicago Boys**," because many of them were taught by free-market, antigovernment professors from the University of Chicago. They were schooled in the laissez-faire doctrines of Milton Friedman and Friedrich Hayek. These doctrines emphasized minimizing the role of the state in all economic affairs. This included allowing businesses dependent on subsidies and protective tariffs to go bankrupt and forcing native producers to compete with imports and foreign investors. On the other hand, business would be favored by reducing taxes and regulations. The regime destroyed unions and permitted unemployment to soar, driving down labor costs. Almost all industries nationalized by Allende were privatized again. The Pinochet regime did not privatize the state copper company, Codelco, but it opened the country's rich copper ore veins on very lucrative terms to new investors.

The fate of land reform perhaps best illustrates how the Pinochet regime went far beyond the expectations of those who supported a coup in 1973. Agrarian reform was indeed reversed, but the land was not simply returned to former owners. The land reform and peasant organizing of the Frei and Allende years had fundamentally altered the relationship between peasant and landlord. The social and cultural structures of the past could not simply be restored. Therefore, many landowners tended to accept compensation offered by the government instead of the return of their land. The government then turned around and sold the properties to more efficient, large-scale capitalist farmers who started producing fruit, wine, and other products for export. Some peasants were allowed to keep land gained under the Frei and Allende reforms, though in the form of small individual plots, not under collective ownership. An economic collapse in the first two years of military rule further changed agrarian Chile, as large-scale capitalist landowners were able to buy smaller or inefficient properties cheaply through bankruptcy and foreclosure.

Like landowners who could not simply go back to their old ways, the businesspeople (and a few women) who benefited from import substitution faced the choice of adaptation or ruination. Tight money supplies and cuts in spending (except for the military) tamed inflation but threw the economy into deep recessions in 1974–1976 and the early 1980s. Many businesses would not survive the elimination of protection for industry and the regime's commitment to free trade, spurring a process of deindustrialization. Closed factories meant unemployment and plunging wages for workers, which provided a ready pool of cheap labor for new and surviving businesses. A new social security law forced workers to put some of their earnings in accounts that were then used to finance new projects launched by capitalists. U.S. president George W. Bush (2001–2008) proposed using Chile as a model to privatize the American social security system, but one of the main issues in massive protests demanding a new constitution in 2019 was the failure of the neoliberal pension system to meet obligations to retirees.

Codelco, the state copper company, was squeezed for higher profits. The regime reduced miners' pay and safety to increase production. Chile is to copper exports what Saudi Arabia is to oil; increased production helped to create a glut of the red ore on the world market and made the price fall even further. Facing low global demand and fearful that the unrest of the Allende years might return, big transnational companies hesitated to return; most waited until the return to civilian rule (1989). In the 1990s, some big, profitable mines paid no taxes or royalties at all to the new government, thanks to the generous system put in place under Pinochet. Other natural resources were treated similarly. For example, the bountiful virgin forests in south Chile were opened for clear-cutting timber operations.

Brazil's generals took a somewhat different approach. Their solution to the problem of a stalled import substitution model was more nationalist and **corporatist**. If Brazil was not producing enough steel, then it was up to the government to make a partnership with Brazilian capitalists to create a steel industry. If Brazil was to escape technological dependence, the generals decided it would have to create its own computer industry. If other Third World militaries wanted to buy arms on the international market, why should Brazil not become an exporter of such goods? In other words, although Brazil's technocrats shared a desire with Chile's economists to diversify exports and attract foreign capital, the Brazilians did not abandon the idea that the state should play a key role in the economy. Argentina occupied a somewhat middle ground between these two orientations. All three countries, however, shared a strong pro-business and anti-worker posture.

As for political engineering, all these military regimes undertook a "tutelary" role concerning democracy. Having purged the left and limited the voice of centrist and even conservative politicians, the regimes aimed to prepare a transition to democracy in which the parties would basically accept the new economic model. Brazil went the furthest in this regard. In 1964, the military created a party entirely controlled by the military, the National Renovation Alliance (ARENA), and an official opposition party, the Brazilian Democratic movement (MDB)—what one critic called the "Yes" party and the "Yes, sir" party. This failed experiment sought to artificially produce a two-party system similar to that in the United States. In fact, by abolishing Brazil's old populist system in which unions were subordinate to the parties, this strategy helped clear the way in the 1980s for a new type of labor party, the Workers' Party (PT), which became a major player in the system after the return to democracy.

In Chile and Argentina, the military plan was somewhat different from that in Brazil. In these cases, the generals sought to purge the old left from the system and gradually allow the remaining parties to reassume their role in the system—but under terms similar to those spelled out by Pinochet, quoted previously. The mainline leftist parties survived, but as we will see in the next chapter, their left wings had been sharply clipped.

The political strategy of the BAs was only partly successful; their economic strategies were even less so, at least in the short run. The political violence and disruptions to the economies in Argentina and Chile discouraged investment by foreign capital. The Southern Cone and Brazil suffered an additional shock from the sudden rise in international oil prices—by a factor of four in 1974 and by a factor of ten over the entire decade. The rise struck an especially harsh blow to Brazil, which had little oil of its own and which had greatly increased consumption of energy in modernizing industry and agriculture. In addition, almost all export commodities important to these countries (copper, coffee, beef, wheat, rubber, etc.) saw dramatic drops in prices. Countries needed more dollars to buy oil and other crucial imports but were earning less from exports. The "solution" was to borrow, which ultimately led to the debt crisis of the 1980s. Even Brazil, whose economy boomed from 1968 to 1974 in what was called a "miracle," entered a new period of crisis. Brazil and Argentina saw rampant inflation. Suddenly in the 1980s, the BA seemed no more capable of promoting economic development than did its populist predecessor.

For Review

What were the main political and economic goals of the bureaucratic authoritarian military governments that took power in South America after populism? How was Chile's economy transformed into the most neoliberal model in the hemisphere, if not the world?

Regime Change and the "Third Wave"

The 1960s and 1970s were decades of the "breakdown of democracy" in Brazil and the Southern Cone, and the following period saw transitions to democracy—more specifically, **polyarchy**—as part of a **third wave** of democratization around the world (see chapter 1,

Figure 1.2). In most cases, the transitions were facilitated by pacts—that is, agreements among key actors about rules of the game and policies to be followed in the new democratic era. These pacts facilitated the return of control of government to civilians and restored elections, but at a cost to democracy. The new rules of the game limited the ability of the new democracies to hold bureaucratic authoritarian rulers accountable for human rights violations and to make significant changes to the economic model. Chile in particular was left with a constitution that left its people with little possibility of modifying the neoliberal model.

A political transition is a kind of "**regime change.**" A "regime" refers mainly to the relationship between society and the state and to the rules of the political game, some formally embodied in the constitution and others not, that determine who governs. A regime in a liberal democracy includes, among other things, rules determining what parties are competitive, what groups have the most influence, and what elites are most powerful. It includes an overall philosophy regarding the degree and kind of political control the state exercises over the economy. Polyarchies, for example, can have a capitalist system that is highly weighted toward the free market (a liberal regime) or toward a regulated economy with a welfare state and a highly planned economy (a social democratic regime).

Revolutions might be regarded as the most extreme of regime changes because they involve not only changes in the political game but also the state's role in the economy and a radical redistribution of wealth and power among social classes. While many regimes in Latin America refer to themselves as revolutionary, the description really applies to only a handful, such as those in Mexico (1910) and Cuba (1959). We examine revolutionary change in chapter 9.

The most influential studies in comparative politics see the transition from authoritarianism to democracy as the result of a pact in which political elites representing different interests compromise in the midst of uncertainty about the future. Guillermo O'Donnell and Philippe Schmitter (1986: 65) wrote that popular pressure "may be an efficacious instrument for bringing down a dictatorship but may make subsequent democratic consolidation difficult, and under some circumstances may provide an important motive for regression to an even more brutal form of authoritarian rule." This danger exists, they say, because the negotiating process is not orderly but "tumultuous" and "impulsive." As they put it, main players in the transition to the democracy game are elites negotiating with one another while outside are

> people challenging the rules on every move, pushing and shoving to get to the board, shouting out advice and threats from the sidelines, trying to cheat whenever they can—but, nevertheless, becoming progressively mesmerized by the drama they are participating in or watching, and gradually becoming committed to playing more decorously and loyal to the rules they themselves have elaborated.
>
> (O'Donnell et al. 1986a: 66)

What is all the tumult about? In Brazil and the Southern Cone, the military wanted amnesty for alleged human rights crimes; victims and their families wanted to hold them accountable. Businesspeople and foreign capitalists wanted to guarantee respect for their property rights, even if the property was attained through questionable or corrupt processes. They also wanted a guarantee that labor and other leftist movements would not break from the neoliberal economic model. They wanted built-in limits on the popular majority's ability to raise taxes, increase regulation, or do anything to jeopardize profits. Labor unions looked to recapture the power lost during the era of repression. On the other side, leaders of people in the streets were calling for accountability of those responsible for torture, investigations into disappearances, as well as social justice and redistribution in favor of the poor. The Catholic hierarchy (cardinals, bishops, etc.) typically supported human rights demands but sought to keep its role in education and limit changes in family laws, such as those on abortion and divorce. Women's movements wanted not only economic equality but to broaden reproductive freedom for women. Having participated in movements to restore democracy, women grew more audacious in challenging male privilege, both in the public arena and in the home. High-level religious clergy, usually male, resisted such change.

The image of elites tensely negotiating while the unruly people press them on the sidelines presents us with a rather conservative theory of the process. The people, the demos, are more the chorus than the protagonists in the drama. O'Donnell, Schmitter, and other contributors to a series of books on transitions (O'Donnell and Schmitter 1986; O'Donnell et al. 1986a, 1986b, and 1986c) seem to be saying that transition is and ought to be a spectator sport. The people are portrayed as an unruly mass whose behavior must be tamed—or at best as the chorus in a Greek tragedy—commenting while gods and heroes struggled with fate. More recently, specialists on democratization, including some from the pluralist school, have tended to give more positive recognition to the role of popular pressure (see Welzel 2009), but the studies focused on elite pact-making remain the better-known and more influential approach to studying democratization.

For Review

How does a transition involving regime change differ from one that simply changes control of government through an election? How is it different from a revolution?

Cases of Transition in the Southern Cone and Brazil

Adam Przeworski's (1986: 47–63) contribution to the four-volume series on *Transitions to Democracy* lays out the nature of the "game" of transition played by elite actors. The concept of politics as a game, borrowing from the study of economics, is known as "rational choice theory." In the case of transitions, we are looking not only at the behavior of individuals (mainly elites) but also at the behavior of groups (labor leaders, social movements, the military, etc.).

Transitions begin, Przeworski says, when certain conservative sectors among business elites and politicians begin to protest the dominance of a small clique of military officers and civilian allies in control of government. Business elites are dissatisfied with persistent economic problems, such as inflation, slow economic growth, and the cronyism and corruption that favor some of their number over others. Politicians who once favored military rule begin to leave government and express criticism in the press. Inside the military, there are *duros* (hardliners) who want to keep power, but increasingly officers become uncomfortable with the politicization of their services and their loss of prestige within the general popula-tion. These **blandos** (soft ones) begin to urge a quicker transition to democracy, providing political cover for civilians to express dissent openly. Once conservative sectors pry the lid off dissent, other sectors become bolder, and the fear needed to keep critics in line begins to dissipate. Criticism spreads to other sectors, and the populace becomes emboldened to challenge the regime more openly in the streets.

Przeworski groups players in the transition game into four categories: right hardliners and moderates on the government side and radical opponents and moderates on the opposi-tion side. He argues that the threat of force underlies their search for agreement on new rules of the game. The success of their negotiations depends not only on public pressure for an end to military rule but also on a fear of return to repression. That is, in societies not far removed from the trauma of state terrorism (especially relevant to Argentina and Chile), a significant part of the population might favor democracy but also want to avoid a return to the crisis years at the end of the populist era.

Think of the range of issues to be discussed. Are the military and police to face criminal prosecution for allegations of torture, disappearances, and murder, or are these matters to be put aside in the interest of reconciliation and hastening their willingness to return to the barracks? Will neoliberal economic policies (see chapter 6) be subject to repeal by a legis-lative majority, or will these policies be made irreversible by limiting majority power? Will conservative judges and bureaucrats appointed by the military hold onto their jobs-for-life, or can they be replaced by the elected government?

According to Przeworski, moderates on the government side want to negotiate a transition that prevents a return to populism and preserves what they like about the pro-capitalist policies of the military era. However, they worry that the longer the dictatorship lingers, the greater the threat of revolution, the more impatient the opposition becomes, the more militant the protests become, and the more urgency they feel to achieve a transition. A similar logic motivates moderates in the opposition to conclude a pact with their moderate colleagues in the BA. Opposition moderates worry that their negotiating partners will decide to stick with the devil they know, dictatorship, rather than risk the outcome of a democratic game. Pushed too hard, the military *duros* will crack down and delay a return to democracy for many years, at the cost of many lives.

The centrists in both camps keep a wary eye on the protestors in the streets. Culturally, perhaps even politically, elites at the negotiating table probably have more in common with one another than with the people in the streets or the hardliners in the military. Some of them were colleagues in cabinets or legislatures in the era before military rule.

This game was significantly influenced by international events. Two important Third World revolutions, in Iran (1978) and Nicaragua (1979), heightened the sense that delay could lead to radical outcomes. On the other hand, in the Philippines, a dictator, Ferdinand Marcos, was driven from power in 1986 by a popular movement before the armed forces completely collapsed, leading to a moderate, elected government. Preferring the Philippine outcome, Washington began to back the idea of a "democratic transition" in Latin America. Even the administration of U.S. president Ronald Reagan, which blamed Reagan's predeces-sor (President Jimmy Carter) for allegedly abandoning pro-U.S. regimes in Iran and Nicara-gua, took this view (Robinson 1996).

The collapse of the Berlin Wall in 1989 and then of the Soviet regime itself in 1991 removed communism as an excuse for repression. Cuba remained communist, but it had long ago shifted away from support for insurgencies, seeking normal trade and diplomatic relationships with other Latin American countries. Cuba's economic problems and uncertain future diminished leftist enthusiasm to adopt its system as a model. One prominent Mexican intellectual, Jorge Castañeda (1993), claimed in a widely read book, *Utopia Unarmed*, that the entire notion of revolution through guerrilla warfare had been discredited and abandoned by the left. The ink was barely dry in 1994 when the Zapatista uprising in the southern Mexican state of Chiapas proved him partly wrong. Still, Castañeda identified an important trend within much of the "old left"—a movement away from viewing Cuba as a model and a shift toward contesting power through elections.

For Review

How can a transition from an authoritarian regime to a military regime be considered a game? What can be said on both sides of this question? Who are some of the key actors, and what do they want?

Chile's Controlled Transition

By 1976, three years after the coup that brought General Augusto Pinochet to power, fierce repression had completely erased the prospect of socialism. An official truth commission (Rettig 2000) documented over 2,279 killed for political reasons, over 90 percent by forces linked to the military. Nearly 1,000 were "disappeared," an especially fear-inspiring tactic. Later estimates put the dead at over 3,000. Beyond this, hundreds of thousands of people were exiled, tortured, and imprisoned (some in prison camps in the remote parts of the country). Officially, in 2011 the government recognized over 40,000 people eligible for compensation as a result of acts committed by Pinochet's junta. The vast majority of acts took place in the first three years (1973–1976), which effectively snuffed out all political activity in the aftermath of the intensely polarized atmosphere of the Allende years.

It is doubtful that Pinochet could have "modernized" Chile's economy without the threat of revolution, which induced Chile's elite to give his regime a blank check to "save" capitalism. Nonetheless, as early as 1977 some supporters of the government were questioning the desirability of indefinite military rule. General Pinochet responded by tightening his grip—ruthlessly. In 1980, after several high-profile political murders of opponents, more Chileans began to yearn for more lawful rule. In response, Pinochet proposed a new constitution that opened the possibility that he would leave the presidency eight years later, but only if he lost a plebiscite on his rule. Even then, he would remain the supreme commander of the armed forces. In September 1980, with no public opposition permitted, Pinochet won a referendum ratifying his new constitution, promulgated in 1981 (see Garretón 1986).

The early 1980s were difficult. Pinochet had tamed inflation, reducing it from more than 500 percent to 10 percent, but a recession devastated the business community. Living standards declined, while foreign investment remained reluctant to return. Much of the world believed that the dictator's days were numbered. However, by 1986, the plunge in world oil prices was helping the Chilean economy to recover. In September of that year, a failed assassination attempt on the dictator strengthened his hand and that of the military *duros*.

By the Przeworski model, the game of transition probably had already begun in 1983 when a group of centrist politicians approached the minister of the interior, Sergio Onofre Jarpa, a conservative politician, and asked for the resignation of Pinochet and modifications in the constitution. Minister Jarpa rejected both demands, but he agreed to open a dialogue. Then a prominent Christian Democrat, Patricio Aylwin, who in 1990 would become the first elected president after Pinochet, made a crucial concession on behalf of the opposition politicians: The transition back to civilian rule could take place under the guise of the 1981 constitution. Accoring to the elite bargaining model of transition, we can see this as a way of reducing the risks facing the military and capitalists in returning to electoral democracy. The price was that the decision would severely limit the Chilean people from changing the economic model or the generals responsible for human rights violations.

The concession deeply divided the opposition. Moderate socialists and members of the Christian Democratic Party were eager to strike a deal, but more radical socialists and the communists, who were more connected to rising protests in poor neighborhoods, rejected the deal. An assassination attempt on Pinochet (which raised fears of instability in the mind of the population) and the visit of Pope John Paul II later in 1986 boosted Pinochet's stature. The pope was critical of neoliberal economic policies, but he expressed approval of Chile's conservative laws making divorce and birth control illegal. Still, there remained general fatigue with military rule and street protests.

The socialists who had advocated a go-slow approach or moved toward the center in the Allende years were brought more easily into the moderate alliance, whose largest proponent was the Christian Democratic Party (PDC). In this way, Aylwin's PDC and moderate socialists (divided into two parties) began to forge a relationship that would later became an electoral coalition, known as the Concertación. As the moderates negotiated with conservative politicians interested in engineering a controlled transition, the two sides developed confidence that each would respect the pact in the future. A transition was also encouraged by the United States. Pinochet had friends in American conservative circles, but he was wearing out his welcome with pragmatists in the administration of President Ronald Reagan (1981–1988).

Although the Communist Party of Chile (PCC) was playing an important role in organizing popular resistance to the dictatorship, the center alliance would not bring that party, which represented those seeking more profound regime change, into transition negotiations. The communists had suffered the purge and exile of its moderate leaders; its young and remaining cadre threw themselves into the dangerous work of organizing the poor in shanties. One legacy of this trial by fire is that the PCC of Chile today, though it mobilizes fewer votes than before 1973, continues to play a role as a critic of the system that emerged after 1988.

In the 2006 election, the party's presidential candidate garnered about 5 percent of the national vote, enough to prevent the Concertación candidate, Bachelet, from winning on the first round. In 2013, the highly visible leader of the student protest movement, Camila Vallejo, joined the PCC. Vallejo won election to the country's House of Deputies. Bachelet sought and received Vallejo's endorsement as she ran for a second term as president in 2014. Bachelet was hoping to revitalize the center-left's image in the face of popular fatigue with the

Concertación after 20 years of dominance by the PDC and socialists. She won the election as leader of a "New Majority" coalition, made up mostly of the old Concertación and the Communist Party.

In 2009, the major right-wing parties formed the "Coalition for Change." The name emphasized their sense that Chileans, though favorably inclined toward President Bachelet (who was constitutionally ineligible for reelection), were fatigued and disappointed with the Concertación's 20 years in office. The Coalition's candidate, billionaire tycoon Sebastián Piñera, who had campaigned against Pinochet (that is, he favored ending the dictatorship) in the 1988 plebiscite, ran as a moderate and defeated former President Frei (the younger) in January 2010, ending the Concertación's grip on the presidency. However, the fundamental regime, the rules of the game, had not really changed. Reflecting this status quo, Bachelet returned to the presidency and won a new term in 2014, and Piñera did the same four years later. But both presidents in their second term faced massive protests, indicating that the mechanisms of polyarchy were not sensitive enough to popular demand for change.

In her second term, Bachelet delivered some political reforms and modest new taxes and royalties on the copper companies. She left office in 2018 to accede to the position of High Commissioner of Human Rights, notable in part because her father was a dissident military officer who was killed by Pinochet. She remains popular, but how much she left unfinished became evident in the first year of her successor (Piñera). He faced an explosion of popular anger, once again touched off by student protests squarely focused on poverty and even more so on inequality (see chapter 2). His reputation was tarnished by the ensuing repression by security forces, which by late 2019 had left 29 dead and over 12,700 wounded, including hundreds blind by pellets shot deliberately into their eyes. Piñera was forced to apologize and make concessions that may lead to a new constitution being written in 2020.

For "transitionologists," such as Przeworski, the story of the return to democracy in Chile is the story of how moderates forged an agreement despite the pressure from the extreme left, which organized in the streets. But did the transition succeed despite or because of popular pressure? Another view holds that the transition was really the story of how the mobilization of the *barrios*, and not negotiations among elites, forced the military from power. Lois Hecht Oppenheim (1993: 138) says of the period 1983–1986,

> The popular mobilization of this period was characterized by its grassroots nature. Civil society led the way, with political parties, especially at first, following their lead. The mobilization period demonstrated how civil society could organize itself autonomously from political parties. It also highlighted the divisions between parties (especially party elites) and grassroots groups. What happened in Chile was similar to what took place in many Latin American countries as they threw off the yoke of military rule.

In fact, the politicians' meeting with Jarpa (the interior minister for Pinochet) took place only after the first signs of popular resistance to the dictatorship. The process began on May Day (May 1) in 1983, when the copper miners called for a day of protest and the public responded with several days of street demonstrations. Some of the politicians who met with Jarpa urged the grassroots leaders to ease up, but the communists and others, with women especially prominent, organized more protests.

As we will see again in the other cases, in the grassroots struggles for democracy it has been women who have the most visibly organized protests in public plazas. They sometimes pay a severe price for their political courage. Torture all too often includes sexual humiliation, reflecting the ugliest side of human nature. Rape and sexual torture are ways that men punished women for stepping "out of their roles" and assuming political leadership. They are brutal statements of patriarchy, but at the same time they can have the effect of bringing women into politics, not keeping them out. During the 2019 protests in Chile, this became evident once again as several women were raped by security forces repressing the demonstrations. Las Tesis, a feminist cultural troupe in Valparaíso, performed *Un Violador en Tu Camino* (A Rapist in Your Path). A video of the songs and dance moves went viral as protesters transmitted it via social media around the world.

Within the opposition camp, much of the left felt betrayed by the acceptance of the plebiscite, feeling that it legitimated the very undemocratic constitution of 1981. However, after years of repression, most of the population was ready to join the centrist politicians in a campaign of "No" to Pinochet's desire to rule for another ten years. Pinochet threw the resources of government behind a campaign based on fear, but "No" won 56 percent of the vote behind the slogan *"Vuelve la alegría"*—"happiness is coming back." In 1990, Aylwin was elected president as the candidate of a broad alliance, the Concertación, based on the willingness of the left and center parties to coordinate both their electoral strategy and their platform for government. The alliance was dominated early by the PDC and then after 2000 by the Socialist Party.

Although the opposition celebrated his exit from the presidency, Pinochet remained commander of the armed forces for another decade after his exit in 1990, periodically rattling the sabers when he felt the government threatened to modify the economic model put in place by his regime or to investigate military officers for human rights abuses or corruption. The 1981 constitution inherited by President Aylwin (1990–1994) included a Senate with enough nonelected, lifelong members to block any legislation unacceptable to the general's supporters. If that were not enough, each state elected its two senators by a system that made it almost impossible for the Concertación to win enough seats to counteract these so-called bionic senators. Even after the bionic senators were removed from the Senate, the Concertación could win 60 percent or more of the votes nationally but still win only half the seats in the Senate. Changing the most important laws ("organic laws," see chapter 14) left behind by the dictatorship requires a super majority in both houses of the Chilean Congress. Most of those laws were decreed by the military junta in the Pinochet years.

The ministers of the Concertación governments found themselves in charge of implementing the very same economic policies that they had fiercely criticized during the dictatorship, but they had the good fortune to come to office just as the global economy improved. As a result, the confidence of foreign investors in Chile's political stability and friendly business environment improved. Foreign and domestic capitalists began to take advantage of the extraordinarily generous tax breaks and incentives for foreign and domestic capitalists enacted by the Pinochet regime. The neoliberal economic policies achieved impressive macroeconomic results; the gross domestic product (GDP) per capita grew by an average of 8 percent from 1991 to 1997. The share of the population below the official poverty line was cut in half, but the gap between rich and poor grew larger than ever. Under the pension system, Chilean workers are forced to pay 10 percent of their wages into accounts managed by private banks. These forced savings provided capital for new investment, but around 2005, as workers started reaching the age of retirement, they found that the accounts were under-funded and vulnerable to corruption.

Pinochet had ruled for 18 years. His legacy was defended by local officials, judges, and bureaucrats, who were left in place from the dictatorship and by law could not be replaced. As commander of the armed forces, Pinochet held a big trump card if this wasn't enough. Whenever it seemed that the government might undertake some unacceptable action (such as threatening to prosecute human rights offenses), he could rattle the sabers—usually in the form of noisy military maneuvers in the streets.

The three largest parties in the Concertación and now the New Majority were the PDC and two socialist parties, the Socialist Party (PS) and the smaller Popular Socialist Party (PPS), whose ideological differences are not enough to detain us here. On the PDC side, many politicians had to explain their support for the coup of 1973, but the two socialist parties seemed even more chastised. Rather than demand accountability for the overthrow of an elected government, most of the politicians in the PS and PPS seemed eager to offer apologies for their actions during the Allende years.

Concertación politicians pointed to constitutional limitations as the reason that they did not change course, but they also seem comfortable with the system. For example, in August 2003, Chile's national union confederation launched its first general strike since the dictatorship in protest against the neoliberal model. Rather than recognize and address the grievances, President Ricardo Lagos (2000–March 2006), a socialist, criticized the unions for putting Chile's international credibility and reputation for stability in doubt and threatening its economic future.

The New Majority bloc in Chile remains similar to the Concertación but today faces opposition mainly from two conservative parties. One is the Renovación Nacional (RN; National Renovation), which to some degree groups together the forces that constituted the right before Pinochet. It has a reputation for more pragmatic politics than the other right-wing party has, the Unión Democrata Independiente (UDI). The UDI openly defends the historical legacy of the dictatorship and promotes extremely traditional Catholic views on divorce, birth control, and other "family issues." The UDI, then, is more a party of right populism. Like their center-left rival bloc, the two conservative parties bitterly contest one another but usually come together in the interest of defeating the opposing coalition. In 2006, under the banner of the Alliance, it ran a common candidate, Evelyn Matthei, and Chile became the first Latin American country to feature two women as the main candidates for president.

This milestone was reached even though political pacts more often seem to reduce the political influence of women rather than enhance it. Women found themselves on the outside looking in during the years after the transition, even if there was no explicit pact among the parties to exclude them. They had been prominent in the mobilizations against the dictatorship, but no women were included in the first cabinet. This time, though, women would not remain excluded from government indefinitely. They continued to be politically active and began to win electoral posts. Although they remain far from having achieved equality with men, their progress became apparent when Bachelet won election in 2006.

In the Allende years, women were often treated as though they were little more than the ladies' auxiliary on the left. The Allende government failed to tap full support from women who would most benefit from populist programs to help families. Women in the opposition who helped to topple Allende, such as the middle-class women in the noisy marches (*cacerolazos*; clanging of empty pots), were treated in a similar way by the generals. Some political scientists argue that the transitions to democracy, therefore, were "gendered" (see Friedman 2000). With the return of democracy, women went, or were sent, out of the public space, back into the home—hence, the importance of Bachelet's victory. A socialist woman from a military family, who had been tortured by Pinochet but served under Lagos as minister of defense, would become president. However, Bachelet, though personally popular, failed to stem a general decline in the fortunes of the Concertación, who lost the January 2010 presidential election to Piñera.

Because of coalition politics, Chile, though it has a multiparty system, has politics more like those associated with a two-party system; that is, politicians and candidates move toward the center. The party coalitions, if not the parties themselves, tend to be **catch-all** types (see chapter 12); they are less ideological. Although this may contribute to political stability, many citizens have felt their interests are not represented and are discouraged from participating (Moulian 2002). That seemed to be changing with the protests of 2013 and 2019.

The Chilean transition looks like a classic example of Przeworski's transition game. Moderates in opposition and in the government cooperated to make the 1989 plebiscite possible. The dictatorship's *blandos* had to worry that street protests led by the left might eventually trigger a revolution that would jeopardize the neoliberal model put in place by Pinochet. They also wanted to moderate the arbitrary excesses of the military regime. Center and center-left politicians feared the specter of indefinite military rule and crackdowns. Both sides had reason to help the other control more extreme factions, but both had to wonder whether their negotiating partners across the table could deliver the promised moderation. Defenders of the outcome say Chile has compiled an enviable macroeconomic record and degree of political stability. Many others feel that the limited democracy has made "*Vuelve la alegría*" ring very hollow.

In a book widely read and discussed in his country, sociologist Moulian (2002) argued that Chilean society had experienced not only a widening gap between rich and poor but also an impoverishment of its national soul. Moulian says that Chileans have become market-oriented, individualistic, and consumer-oriented at the cost of social solidarity. Moulian had little nostalgia for the polarized ideological battles of the Allende era, but he lamented the lack of dialogue and debate about how to create the "good society" of the era before the dictatorship. The crisis of Chile now, he wrote, "arises in reality from utopian neoliberalism, which tends to make politics a technical matter, killing off other ideologies" (62). It would seem that neither those who think that Chile was put on the right track by Pinochet nor those, like Moulian, who despaired for its political soul were entirely right.

As 2020 opened, it seemed likely that a new constitution will be written, but a familiar divide has opened again. Many voices from the grassroots protesters have called for their movements to directly choose representatives to write a new charter, which would likely result in a more radical attack on inequality. It represents a strong challenge to the political class, which favors choosing the constitutional assembly through the political parties. How this issue is resolved will probably determine how different the new regime will be from the old one. The onset of the

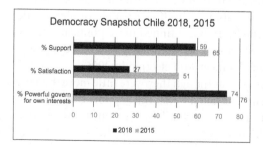

coronavirus epidemic has put brakes on the process and helped the government tamp down protests, leaving the future uncertain.

For Review

Who were the major players in the game of transition in Chile? Why did the more centrist actors "win" the game against those who wanted a more radical transition or wanted to keep Pinochet in power? How did the pact among the centrists affect politics after Pinochet? How have Chilean politics changed since 2009? Are we seeing new regime change in the wake of the 2019 protests?

Argentina's Transition and National Humiliation

The Argentine transition resembles what took place in Chile, but with a major difference: The military's departure from power was hastened by a disastrous defeat in a war launched ostensibly to reassert Argentine sovereignty over the Malvinas Islands, known to the British as the Falklands. After a devastating defeat, the generals decided to retreat to the barracks. They rapidly threw up as many barriers as possible to avoid being held accountable for massive human rights abuses of the Dirty War. In part, the officers were successful because many Argentines feared a relapse into violence (a factor in Chile, too) and because of divisions within the most important party, the Peronists.

Like the Pinochet government next door, the junta favored more laissez-faire policies and privatization of many state-owned companies. Many considered it a victory that inflation had been brought down to 88 percent in 1980. But Argentina's economic problems went deeper. Workers suffered the most, but businesspeople also could not cope with a worldwide recession and lack of access to foreign credit. Although the junta implemented business-friendly policies, many foreign investors preferred to avoid visible collaboration with a pariah state.

The Argentine transition began, one might argue, on April 30, 1977, barely a year after the coup, when a small group of mothers of the disappeared, frustrated at authorities' lack of response to their entreaties about their sons and daughters, decided to go to Plaza de Mayo, in front of the presidential palace. There every week, until the coronavirus pandemic intervened against public gathering, they have silently borne witness to the atrocities of the military regime. The military, accustomed to fighting guerrillas, had little notion of how to cope with a protest by a group of middle-aged and elderly women. After all, what threat could such a group pose to these men? The junta failed to anticipate how much international attention and solidarity the women would engender and the way their ranks would steadily grow. They became a powerful international symbol of resistance to repression—Las Madres de la Plaza de Mayo.

The junta stood firm for five more years, but on April 2, 1982, the largest antigovernment demonstration since 1976 took place. The junta, now led by General Leopoldo Galtieri, needed a distraction. Confident of support from the conservative administration of U.S. president Reagan, the generals launched an invasion of the desolate Malvinas

(Falkland) Islands (population 1,800) in the Atlantic Ocean. It is easy to see why the military thought it would be a good, patriotic rallying cry. Argentines have been contesting British control of the Malvinas for a long, long time—and continue to do so today. The junta hoped that the British colonial government would simply abandon the islands. After all, in London, a bill was pending in Parliament that would have stripped the Falklands residents of their equal status as British citizens. As Galtieri hoped, the Argentine public enthusiastically supported him. However, the government of Prime Minister Margaret Thatcher, fiercely conservative itself, was not prepared to be defeated by a Third World country. After 257 British deaths and 649 deaths on the Argentine side, the British forced the surrender of Argentina's 7,500 troops.

Government propaganda had portrayed Argentina winning handily. Public euphoria in Argentina swiftly changed to anger, made worse when inflation shot up to 200 percent. Galtieri resigned in favor of a retired general, Reynaldo Bignone, who promised an election and return to civilian rule by 1984. In July 1983, the junta decreed an "amnesty" for itself. A demonstration of 50,000 people dissuaded the parties from endorsing the move. Raúl Alfonsín, of the Radical Civic Union, won the election and took office in 1983, partly on his reputation as a defender of human rights and his promise to prosecute those responsible for the Dirty War.

The centrist Radicals won a majority in the Chamber of Deputies. With the military thoroughly discredited, Alfonsín seemed poised to consolidate democracy without a limiting pact. Defying the military's self-pardon, Alfonsín's government indicted nine generals and admirals, five of whom were convicted and sent to jail. The high command—it seemed—would be held accountable. But a barracks revolt in 1987 induced the fearful Congress to grant an amnesty to all officers below the highest rank and to end further prosecutions. The Peronists in the end they were no more willing to punish those responsible for the Dirty War. This became obvious when they came to control the presidency in 1989.

President Alfonsín's hand was limited by several factors. The international economy was stagnant when he took office, so Argentina's export earnings remained dismal. Inflation had not been tamed (soaring to 400 percent in 1983), and—with the military's demolition of import substitution—factories were closing. Unemployment and poverty were on the rise. Overall, per capita income fell by 25 percent in the 1980s, Latin America's "lost decade" (see chapter 5). The Peronist unions, motivated both by politics and by the severe erosion of their members' living standards, resisted wage controls, which fell apart, unleashing inflation again. Food riots broke out in 1989. In that year, the Peronist candidate for president, Carlos Saúl Menem, won a clear-cut victory (47 percent) running under the slogan "*Argentina a vuelve tener peso*." The double meaning was "Argentina will have weight again" in the world after its humiliations in war and debt negotiations, and "Argentina will again have a peso"— that is, a viable currency. Alfonsín surrendered the presidency right after the election, even before his term ran out.

Menem forged an alliance between his wing of the Peronists and the military, mortal enemies of each other since the fall of Juan Perón in 1955. In December 1990, a group of nationalist officers (*carapintados*, or "painted faces") revolted. Menem defeated the revolt but then pardoned the convicted officers. He was now in a position of strength to deal with the military. But his intentions were not to return to the old populism. Against expectations, Menem, the Peronist, proved to be an enthusiastic neoliberal reformer. He privatized major industries (railroads, communications, energy, airlines, etc.), fought the unions at the bargaining tables and in the streets, and replaced all savings accounts with ten-year bonds—essentially confiscating the savings of the middle class for a period of time. However, in return, the middle class got protection from inflation. To halt the freefall of the currency, Menem pegged the new Argentine peso directly to the dollar—one to one.

President Menem tamed Peronism with divide-and-conquer tactics. He favored careerist politicians loyal to him over nationalists and leftists. The labor ministry helped the union leaders willing to endorse his overall policies to obtain relatively favorable labor contracts; those critical of neoliberal policies and deals with the IMF were isolated. Pegging the peso did restore monetary stability for about ten years, which made Menem popular until the tactic began to fail in his last years in office. He rewrote the constitution and won a second four-year term in 1995. But opposition was gathering. In 1994, human rights advocates and disaffected Radicals and Peronists formed a new, leftist alliance, offering voters a third alternative to the Radicals and Menem's Peronists. In the election of October 1999, Fernando de la Rúa, joint candidate of the new coalition and the Radicals, won the election to succeed Menem.

To understand how Argentina's economy fell on hard times in the late 1990s, we have to digress to consider the politics of monetary supply and exchange rates. Menem had tamed inflation by abolishing the old currency and guaranteeing that the new peso would always be exchangeable at one to the dollar. For a while, the strategy worked, but when the economic growth rate began to decline, the guarantee suddenly turned into a huge liability. Holders of the peso fled to the dollar at the guaranteed rate of one to one. These dollars, concentrated in the hands of the wealthy, flowed abroad out of Argentina into foreign banks. Now the government had to find more dollars to meet the guarantee, which meant more borrowing—and also a more drastic devaluation once dollars ran out. The one-to-one peso guarantee became unsustainable—and a political albatross.

Devaluation is a policy whereby a government reduces the value of the national currency against foreign currencies—that is, one dollar, for example, buys more money (e.g., more pesos) than before; conversely, it takes more money (e.g., more pesos) to buy one dollar than before. Even the possibility of devaluation can disturb an economy. Anticipating devaluation, those with savings take their money out of the economy to seek shelter in, for example, dollars safely deposited in overseas bank accounts and investments. Matters are made worse when those with connections to the government know in advance that devaluation is coming. Corrupt public officials and speculators can make a tidy profit simply by buying dollars in advance and then selling them later. As tawdry tales of corruption and speculation filled the headlines, they took a toll on the legitimacy of government and Menem's popularity plunged.

It was the misfortune of Fernando de la Rúa to assume the presidency of Argentina as years of economic stagnation reached crisis levels. Although elected in response to Menem's plunging popularity, de la Rúa did not attempt to overhaul Menem's neoliberal policies. Debt payments bled the economy. In the year 2000, the growth rate was actually negative (−0.8 percent), and things got worse in 2001. De la Rúa's response to the crisis was to try to (1) eliminate the government pension system, (2) reform the tax system to fall more heavily on businesses, (3) privatize some government operations (including parts of the tax collection system), and (4) freeze federal spending. He asked governors of the provinces to do the same. Not surprisingly, labor unions, people dependent on welfare, and small businesses rebelled. The Peronist opposition, despite Menem's role in creating the economic mess, was content to let the president stew in it.

De la Rúa now confronted rising popular anger about the **social debt**. In Argentina and throughout Latin America, the majority of poor people felt that they had seen little or no benefit from the rash of government borrowing that had begun in the 1970s. They felt no obligation to pay these bills, especially when the funds to service the debt would come out of their pensions, wages, and already inadequate government services. Nonetheless, de la Rúa continued to pursue unpopular policies because the IMF, Washington, and private banks insisted on fiscal austerity as a condition ("conditionality," or structural adjustment) for renegotiating overdue foreign debts. Without such an agreement, Argentina could not hope to obtain the injection of new dollars that it so desperately needed to keep the peso stable. We will encounter (see chapter 8) a similar situation—Venezuela in the 1990s—with somewhat similar political results.

In December 2001, violent street protests in Buenos Aires left 27 people dead. De la Rúa resigned, and his vice president declared a state of siege. The real value of the peso would have plummeted were it not pegged, but no one trusted the government to keep it that way. Wealthy people and speculators kept changing the peso into dollars, sending much of this money abroad, forcing the government to borrow more to meet the demand. As capital fled and investment fell, unemployment and poverty increased. In January, the government finally abandoned the one-to-one peg. The exchange rate plunged, and inflation skyrocketed. Savings were wiped out; factories were closed. Provincial governments lacked money to provide basic services (schools, police, sanitation, and health care) and took to issuing promissory notes (bonos) that, of course, had even less value than the peso itself.

Devaluation allows a government to convert the dollars it has in its reserves to much more of its own currency, so it has more money to meet promises in its budget. Devaluation also encourages exports—every dollar or euro earned abroad buys that much more of the local currency at home. However, this also means that everything imported will cost more to businesses and consumers. Devaluation causes the real value of salaries and wages to fall, at least in the short run. At the same time, rising costs for imports raise prices. Not surprisingly, governments are reluctant to risk the unpopularity that comes with devaluation, and they are especially keen to postpone or avoid it in election years.

Things finally bottomed out in late 2002 but not before a political crisis that saw a succession of presidential resignations and changes. Finally, investment began to return to the country, which for all its problems has a relatively educated workforce and rich farm and grazing lands. The peso began to make a comeback in 2003, and overall the economy grew, largely on the strength of exports (beef, grain, and soybeans), much of it to China. A new president, Nestor Kirchner, a leftist Peronist and opponent of Menem within the Peronist Party, defeated the former president's bid for a comeback and took office in May 2003. Kirchner faced on one side pressures from the IMF (the debt remained at US$60 billion) to implement austerity and, on the other side, an aroused populace. He turned toward populism in an international context much more favorable to resistance to neoliberalism than his Peronist predecessors had faced.

Kirchner reached out to other leftist presidents in Chile, Brazil, Venezuela, and Cuba and made clear his dissent from the Washington Consensus. He also won popular approval at home for meeting with the Madres de la Plaza, which resulted in Congress repealing Menem's amnesty for the military. The president replaced the military high command with officials less tainted by the Dirty War. Venezuela's president, Hugo Chávez, flush with petrodollars from a new oil boom, came to his aid with oil shipments and a willingness to buy up some of Argentina's debt, much to the dismay of the United States and the IMF.

One result of the unrest during the depths of the economic crisis was the formation of neighborhood and factory committees all over the country. *Piqueteros*, a movement of poor and unemployed workers, blockaded roads and supported popular actions to create an alternative economy. Neighborhood groups sought to pool resources to survive the economic collapse; the worker committees reopened factories abandoned by their owners and ran them themselves—what some leftists say is the essence of socialism, worker democracy. With economic recovery, the hard work of the former employees was paying off, but the owners in many cases wanted their factories back (Trigona 2006).

This posed a challenge to Kirchner and to the country's judicial system. Should property rights be respected and factories returned to the owners who had abandoned them, or did workers deserve to keep control over enterprises they had rescued through risk, sacrifice, and hard work? In the end, new bankruptcy laws opened the way for 600 factories to remain "recovered" and run by cooperatives of workers under self-management schemes. The recovery of the economy in the 2000s, fueled by agricultural exports (especially soy; see chapter 15) to growing economies in Brazil and Asia, slowed momentum of the *piqueteros*. The movement fragmented over whether to support the Kirchners. However, as a protest movement the *piqueteros* left a legacy. "Pickets" have continued to crop up as a way Argentines protest unpopular governments.

Argentina's politics and economic policies have careened more wildly than Chile's, and once again in 2020 the country was facing a major debt crisis—this time with the coronavirus pandemic looming. At the same time, Argentina's transition to democracy closed off fewer options for the future than did Chile's transition. Both economic and human rights issues have remained contested. As it hastily retreated to the barracks in 1983, the Argentine officer corps had called for a concertación (agreement) under which the major parties (Radicals and Peronists) would agree to continue basic economic and social policies and not prosecute officers. However, the military's prestige and power had been undermined by defeat in warfare. It retained influence, but far less than exercised by the Chilean military in post-transition Chile.

In Argentina, it was not the constitution that restricted democracy in the subsequent period but the realities of power, both economic and political. The Menem government was outspoken in support of U.S. foreign policy, committed to free trade and privatization, and willing to service the international debt at a high cost to Argentina's people. He also benefited from saber rattling by *duros*, reminding the public of the military's power and discouraging dissent. Support from Washington and Menem's acceptance of the military's self-proclaimed amnesty allowed the Peronist to reduce the size of the armed forces. But his popularity lasted only as long as Menem seemed to have restored stability and economic growth. When it faltered, protests returned and the Kirchner faction of the Peronists, resistant to neoliberalism, ascended.

Argentine democracy is "pacted," but less so than Chile's. Until the 2000s, Argentina was the only state to prosecute any officers for political murders during the bureaucratic authoritarian era. Still, the military retained enough power to prevent a full accounting for its crimes. Argentina's most influential political party, the Peronists (Partido Justicialista), survived the repression, but it has become much more of a "catch-all" than a solely labor-based party. Kirchner, who died in 2010, was succeeded in 2008 by his wife, María

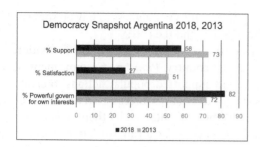

Democracy Snapshot Argentina 2018, 2013

Cristina Fernández de Kirchner, a career politician and senator herself. The Radical Civic Union remained the largest opposition party, but it was Mauricio Macri, an independent candidate who, like Menem, promised to put the economy back in order, who defeated Fernández de Kirchner in 2015. His neoliberal economic policies aroused protests from opposition movements, one reason he lost the 2019 election to Albert Fernández, the Peronist candidate in 2019, who ran with former President Cristina Kirchner as his vice presidential candidate.

Confused? You can be forgiven. The key takeaway is that the power game in Argentina had evolved by 2020 into one that takes place as much within the ranks of Peronism as between Peronism and the opposition. The latter is not clearly organized into a single party or stable coalition, as in Chile. The post-military regime in Argentina shows a more fluid, changeable relationship between state and society, a mixed economic system that has partially but not completely rolled back neoliberalism, and a fluid party system less institutionalized than in the case of Chile.

For Review

How did the Malvinas (Falklands) War hasten transition in Argentina? The military failed to destroy Peronism, but Peronism after military rule was different when it returned, under Menem. How and why? How have the Peronist presidencies of Menem, on one hand, and the Kirchners, on the other, differed from each other?

Brazil's Gradual Transition

As in Chile and Argentina, mass movements in Brazil lent political weight to the entreaties of politicians and moderates inside the regime for a transition back to civilian rule. The military junta had used torture, imprisonment, restrictions of civil liberties, and disappearances. The repression took its toll in lives and constituted state terrorism, but it was more selective than in Argentina and Chile, where victims numbered in the tens of thousands. Brazil experienced 240 killed and 150 disappeared in 21 years of military rule. One Brazilian political scientist suggests that today the country experiences higher rates of violence in the form of

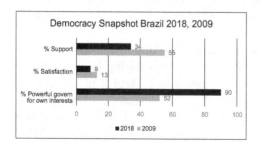

Democracy Snapshot Brazil 2018, 2009

crime, police abuse in urban *favelas*, and violence used by ranchers and landholders against peasants (Avritzer 2002: 112–117). The unflattering thought is that Brazilians are more tolerant of political violence because the society itself is more violent.[

The Brazilian military did not pardon itself. In the late 1970s, human rights organizations, the Church, and exiled or disenfranchised politicians proposed reconciliation as part of a process to resume democratic political life. In 2004, a group called Torture Never Again (GTNM)—formed by relatives of 150 Brazilians killed, tortured, or disappeared—successfully pressured the new president, Lula, to open secret archives dating back to military rule. When a newspaper published photos of a prominent journalist who had died during the dictatorship after undergoing torture, the military insisted that its actions were "a legitimate response to the violence waged by those who refused to engage in dialogue and opted for radicalism and illegal actions" (Osava 2004). When the president and his party protested the army position, the military refused to retract the statement, issuing instead a weak statement of regret for the journalist's death. Human rights issues remain, as in Chile and Argentina, as a residue of the transition process, even if they are less potent in Brazil.

In 1968, the military empowered itself to act without limits by an infamous decree known as Institutional Act #5, issued by a junta that had replaced a more moderate military government. However, it acted with more restraint than the juntas that came to power in Argentina and Chile. The Brazilian junta closed Congress for only a few months and did not seek to prohibit all political activity. Its goal was to channel political participation within narrow limits. The military created two officially recognized political parties, one pro-regime and one opposition, in an attempt to engineer a two-party, centrist system to replace the populist system overthrown in the first coup of 1964. The junta silenced left-wing politicians by exiling them or by taking away their citizenship rights. There were enough disappearances and murders to create an atmosphere of fear, but the political class of the old regime was never totally banned from politics.

As the economic situation worsened in the late 1970s, talk of a transition began. The pro-regime party (called ARENA) began to experience defections, and the official opposition party (the MDB, later PMDB) began to assert more independence. At the same time, the presidents (Generals Ernesto Geisel and João Figueiredo) responded to deteriorating economic conditions, growing social protest, and bolder opposition from the MDB with more international borrowing and with political reforms. Among the latter was an electoral law that permitted new parties to form, a tactical effort to split the opposition that produced unexpected results for the generals. Instead of dividing, the opposition broadened.

In the period of 1968–1974, the Brazilian government adopted many pro-business policies typical of the bureaucratic authoritarian states. It repressed unions and held down wages. It stressed exports rather than production for internal consumption. It used financial policies to stabilize the currency. The military welcomed foreign investments on favorable terms. The military also opened the Amazon to economic penetration, touching off a huge ecological disaster with the burning of thousands of square kilometers of Amazonian rainforest. But government was not fully committed to the neoliberal model.

Rather than abandon all industries to their fate in a competitive world market, as did Pinochet and (after the transition) Menem, Brazil's generals and technocrats favored big infrastructure projects (dams, roads, etc.) and subsidies to heavy industries. The regime fostered partnerships between Brazilian industrialists and foreign corporations. Their hope was that industrialization would move past the import substitution stage and deepen—that is, factories would produce durable consumer goods (refrigerators, cars, etc.), basic industrial goods (e.g., steel and chemicals), and military arms for Brazil's own forces and other Third

World countries. The result was a fourfold increase in exports and an astounding average growth rate of 10 percent per year, the "Brazilian miracle." But the "miracle" only lasted six years. Limited domestic demand, skyrocketing oil prices, and the mounting debt crisis took their toll after 1974.

The military had always planned to engineer a lengthy, guided transition back to civilian rule, but divisions arose in its ranks. The *blandos* favored a faster return; the *duros* thought that it was important to complete the remake of the economy and political system before returning to the barracks. However, the pace of change was ultimately not of the military's own making. Led by the vigorous new democratic labor movement, the Brazilian people would have much to say about the timetable. The Roman Catholic Church, influenced greatly by the doctrines of Vatican II and the philosophy of a "**preferential option for the poor**," provided significant political cover for the opposition. This was true in other cases as well, most notably in Chile, where the Vicariate of Solidarity of the Archdiocese of Santiago was for many years the only voice capable of speaking up against human rights abuses.

By destroying the old unions and breaking their clientelist ties to populist parties and leaders, the military removed some considerable obstacles to new actors in politics. A new union movement started in the metallurgical sector in the belt of heavy industries in the suburbs of São Paulo in the 1970s. Its leader was Luiz Inácio da Silva, "Lula." Lula would be elected president in October 2002 and became leader of a new political party, the PT (Partido do Trabahaldores), launched in 1980.

Organizing itself openly but illegally and hoping to avoid the negative experience of political parties during the populist era, the PT emphasized political participation at the base. It developed a set of democratic norms that attracted new social movements forming among blacks, landless peasants, environmentalists, human rights organizations, neighborhood movements, women's organizations, the Catholic and religious left, and others (Keck 1992). This solidarity proved crucial when the military attempted to control the pace of the transition by arresting Lula in 1981. Massive demonstrations posed the question of whether the military was prepared—17 years after initially seizing power and with the economy uncertain—to direct firepower against the people. The *duros* had to recognize that taking this option would exhaust the regime's remaining prestige at home, invite international condemnation, and risk a more revolutionary upsurge. The military retreated and freed Lula.

Next, the Brazilian opposition sought to accelerate democratization under the banner of "*Diretas Já!*" ("Direct elections now!"). The gradual transition began to accelerate as a new party system was emerging. Lula and the workers' movement had created the PT. The two parties created by the military in 1976 began to act on their own. ARENA morphed into the pro-military, conservative Party of Social Democracy (PDS); the Brazilian Democratic Movement added "party" to its name to become the PMDB. Another left party, calling itself the Party of Democratic Workers, emerged in the important state around Rio de Janeiro. All coalesced to demand direct elections. Failing to achieve this concession, they united in 1984 around one slate for president and vice president and won the indirect elections. The winner, Tancredo Neves of the PMDB, underwent surgery just before his scheduled inauguration in March 1985 and died shortly afterward. His vice president, José Sarney, assumed the presidency.

The new president confronted a grave economic crisis, including spiraling inflation. In February 1986, he implemented a new economic program, the Cruzado Plan. The plan created a new currency (the cruzado), increased the wages of the poorest workers, and froze prices and other wages. Sarney appealed to Brazilian citizens to enforce price restraints by directly confronting retailers who tried to raise prices. Rising consumer demand gave the economy a temporary shot in the arm. The popularity of the president allowed his supporters to win the congressional election of 1986, which had added importance because the Congress was to write a new constitution (of 1988). The Cruzado Plan faltered because consumer demand increased but productivity did not. The economy lapsed into crisis in the late 1980s. Sarney limped to the completion of his term. The new direct elections of 1990 were won by a governor, Fernando Collor de Mello, completing the formal transition from military to elected civilian regime.

Collor defeated Lula, who had entered the election as the favorite to win. The new constitution (still in effect today) provided for a runoff election if no candidate achieved a majority in the first round. Lula emerged from round one with the most votes but not enough to win outright. Lula's formal education was limited, and his presence on TV at that time was much less impressive than Collor's. The business community and big landowners, fearing a union leader as president, lavishly financed the Collor campaign. The country's media barons made sure that coverage was heavily slanted toward their candidate, constantly warning of chaos if Lula were elected. Lula was also swimming against an international tide. The Berlin Wall was falling, and the United States was trumpeting the **Washington Consensus**, which painted pluralist democracy and a free-market economy without alternatives in the New World Order.

Collor won but proved corrupt even by Latin American standards. Brazil's Congress impeached him in 1992. In doing so, the Brazilian legislature showed an unprecedented degree of institutional power in the region. Collor's vice president, Itamar Franco, succeeded him and put Brazil's economic policies in the hands of the political sociologist Fernando Henrique Cardoso. Cardoso, author of an influential neo-Marxist analysis of **dependency theory** (see chapter 6), was appointed minister of finance and implemented the Real Plan, named after the country's new currency. Leftist critics assailed Cardoso for implementing a conservative monetary plan that reduced inflation but did little to compensate workers for two decades of falling real wages. Nor did Cardoso take direct aim at redistributing income and land, a serious problem in Brazil. However, the economy rebounded; Cardoso got much of the credit.

Cardoso and Lula faced off in the 1994 elections. Lula again was the early favorite, but again he lost, as the opposition, media, and international forces coalesced to prevent the "radical" PT candidate from taking office. Brazil's economy continued to grow, and Cardoso, at the peak of his popularity in 1997, resorted to a frequent political tactic in Latin America. He amended the constitution to make himself eligible for another term; he defeated Lula again. However, his second term was less successful, as economic stagnation returned after an international financial crisis, which had originated in far-off Thailand in 1998 and had thrown the world economy into a recession. Economic conditions worsened in Brazil. The center and right had no respected figure of the caliber of Cardoso to contest Lula, who finally won the presidency in 2002.

PHOTO 7.2   Luiz Inácio da Silva (Lula), a union leader with only a second grade education, led the struggle to end military rule in Brazil and eventually, in 2002, was elected president of his country.

Source: Claudinei Petroli/AFP via Getty Images.

In Lula's eight years in office, it was clear that even a president elected directly out of the ranks of Brazil's working class was not going to totally change the direction of Brazil's gradual transition. Many high PT officials were enveloped in corruption scandals, some of which involved bribes to members of other parties whose support was needed to ensure control of the Congress. In short, Brazil's transition had opened the possibility of the establishment of a more radical democracy than normally associated with pluralism, but the prospects of an innovative democratic experiment faded as the PT failed to purge itself of the corrupt practices of the past. According to the Latinobarómetro report of 2018, satisfaction with democracy in Brazil was among the lowest in Latin America, and it still is today (see Figure 0.1, Introduction).

Still, one cannot say that the country simply returned to politics as usual. Lula expanded education and anti-hunger policies, which led many of his opponents to accuse him of communism or (heaven forbid!) vote buying. Lula's origins were themselves an indication of change, given his ***pardo*** complexion and class background. More indicative of change was the rise of the PT's Benedita da Silva (no relation to Lula), who broke down race, class, and gender barriers to enter the Senate in 1994 and headed Lula's successful reelection campaign in 2006. Da Silva emerged out of the *favelas* of Rio de Janeiro through her involvement in an evangelical

Protestant movement (influenced by **liberation theology**) and in several local struggles to improve living conditions in her Rio de Janeiro *favela*. Da Silva not only led on gender issues but on efforts to redress racial discrimination, something long denied in Brazilian culture.

In 2010, Lula was succeeded in the presidency by another PT leader, Dilma Rousseff, a former guerrilla who had been captured and tortured between 1970 and 1972. After the 2013 election in Chile, all three of the countries considered in this chapter had women as presidents. But corruption, deeply rooted in Brazil's political system, had tarnished the PT and left it vulnerable to a right-populist backlash that led to the impeachment of Rousseff, jailing of Lula, and, eventually, to the presidential electoral victory of Jair Bolsonaro in 2019.

For Review

In what way was Brazil's transition gradual compared with the other two we have examined? The only really new party to come out of the transition in these three cases was the PT. What was its original base? What did it stand for? Who is Lula, and what were his main accomplishments and shortcomings?

PHOTO 7.3   A Uruguayan woman carries a photo of a disappeared person at a 2010 protest against amnesty for human rights abuses during the military regime.

Source: Miguel Rojo/AFP via Getty Images.

PUNTO DE VISTA: URUGUAY'S STRUGGLE BETWEEN HUMAN RIGHTS AND AMNESTY

The case of Uruguay shows how difficult it has been for Latin Americans to deal with the issue of accountability for human rights violations committed during the era of military rule. Like Brazil, Chile, and Argentina, Uruguay, a country known for having one of Latin America's most developed welfare systems and strongest middle classes, fell under bureaucratic authoritarian rule between 1973 and 1985. The populist crisis began in 1968, when an elected conservative government signed an agreement with the IMF that rolled back many economic rights won in prior decades by unions. Protests followed, and the government ratcheted up the use of military force to keep order. This spurred an urban guerrilla movement, known as the Tupamaros, comparable to the Montoneros in Argentina.

In early 1973, the military proclaimed that the Tupamaros had been wiped out, but in the face of a severe economic recession, the junta nonetheless closed Congress and undertook to reengineer the economy and political system. Half a million books were burned; universities and cultural institutions were purged of their intellectuals; one in every 50 citizens was detained; and nearly one-fifth of the population was forced into exile. The country became infamous for ingenuous new types of torture, much of it

directed toward women and children in front of men, a blatant attempt to demonstrate total power through humiliation.

Economic failure and popular anger at human rights abuses in the 1980s led to negotiations between the military and the Colorados, the largest political party. However, the transition and exit was initiated by the generals and negotiated "with political elites in a secretive, top-down process, which enabled them [the generals] . . . to maintain a political role after the elections" (Mallinder 2009: 2). The generals, who had always governed behind a civilian façade, permitted elections won by the Colorados in 1986.

One of the first acts of the new government was to proclaim an amnesty for all military personnel. Before the vote, then President Julio Maria Sanguinetti explained why he favored amnesty and was refusing to prosecute gross violators of human rights:

> First . . . there wasn't enough evidence [to prosecute cases]. It was going to disturb society, and there would be a lot of confrontation. Second . . . it was a question of moral equivalency . . . A lot of those involved in left-wing groups had never been to jail at all. To begin the arithmetic of judging levels of responsibility, we would have been faced with complications of such magnitude that we thought it best to amnesty everybody—the left and the military. Third . . . it was necessary to have a climate of stability to consolidate democracy . . . Finally, for historical reasons. Traditionally after all great conflicts in a country there is an amnesty.
>
> (quoted in Mallinder 2009: 41–42)

Outraged citizens responded with a massive petition drive that placed the question of repeal of the amnesty on the ballot for a referendum. More than 600,000 citizens signed the petition, more than one-fourth of all voters. However, in April 1989, the electorate voted by a 58 percent majority to uphold the amnesty. Human rights advocates were demoralized, but some continued to fight for accountability. They took their battle to the Inter-American Commission on Human Rights, which in 1994 said that the military's amnesty law was incompatible with the country's treaty obligations and added that it

> notes with deep concern that the adoption of this law effectively excludes in a number of cases the possibility of investigation into past human rights abuses and thereby prevents the State party from discharging its responsibility to provide effective remedies to the victims of those abuses. Moreover, the Committee is concerned that, in adopting this law, the State party has contributed to an atmosphere of impunity which may undermine the democratic order and give rise to further grave human rights violations.
>
> (quoted in Mallinder 2009: 60)

A moderate leftist president, Tabaré Vázquez, elected in 2005, reopened a number of cases, with focus on the military's transporting of prisoners to Argentina, where the prisoners were killed or disappeared. Popular pressure resulted in the second referendum in 2009. Once again, the vote went against repeal of amnesty, but the issue was not closed. In July 2011 a presidential decree permitted prosecutions of the military for certain types of crimes, and in October 2011, the Uruguayan Congress, pressured to comply with its treaty obligations, finally voted to repeal the law—by only one vote (16 to 15) in the Senate. Then in February 2013, the country's Supreme Court threw out two key provisions of the 2011 decree permitting prosecutions, effectively nullifying it.

These arguments about amnesty and prosecution for perpetrators of gross human rights violations are found in many countries. In sum, those who oppose reopening the cases against the military argue that it risks renewing conflicts and weakening democracy. To this we can add the argument, in the case of Uruguay, that a popular vote was taken on the question. On the other side are the moral arguments of victims and their supporters and the concern

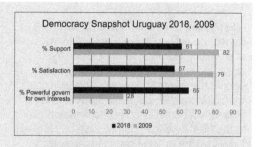

Democracy Snapshot Uruguay 2018, 2009

that impunity for past crimes will someday lead to new ones.

Point/Counterpoint

Should Uruguay's government continue attempts to prosecute former government and former military officials for the human rights atrocities committed in Uruguay?

If you say yes, how do you respond to the arguments that it is wrong to go back on the amnesty, especially because it was submitted to a plebiscite, and that the country needs to move on?

If you say no, what do you say to the hundreds of thousands of relatives of the victims? What about the argument that failure to hold former officials responsible makes it more likely that the past will be repeated?

For More Information

See Francisa Lessa and Leigh Payne, *Amnesty in the Age of Human Rights* (Cambridge University Press, 2012). Long before WikiLeaks, the National Security Archive, a private repository at George Washington University, was legally collecting declassified U.S. documents, including candid descriptions of the military regime's actions in Uruguay. It is online at www2.gwu.edu/~nsarchiv. *State of Siege* (1972) shows events leading to military rule.

Forbidden to Forget

Although the transitions to democracy occurred 20 to 30 years ago, the experience of military government remains as a specter hanging over politics. In Argentina and Uruguay, the issues of human rights remain especially acute. In Chile, in addition to human rights issues, there remain many critics who say that the country's enviable record of economic growth is compromised by inequalities that can be attributed to deals made to secure the transition to democracy.

As Rubén Blades, the salsa star, put it in one of his songs, "Prohibido olvidar"—"It is forbidden to forget." Yet we are now well past 20 years since the military dictatorships, and there are signs that the military is once again restive. Several left, Pink Tide presidents (Rousseff in Brazil; Morales in Bolivia; Manuel Zelaya in Honduras; Fernando Lugo in Paraguay) have been deposed in what their backers call a "coup." In Venezuela, Nicaragua, and Cuba, the militaries were an important base of support for leftist governments. Blades's warning seems more pertinent than ever in 2020.

Discussion Questions

1. Why were the military regimes that took power at the close of the populist era determined to keep power instead of playing a "moderator role"?
2. What seems more important to you, and why, in explaining the democratic breakdowns and the transitions back to democracy in the three countries discussed in this chapter—the role of underlying economic and social forces or the actions of elites?
3. Given the way that negotiated transitions result in pacts limiting human rights prosecutions and changes in economic policies, should current governments respect them? Does a vote approving amnesty, as happened in Uruguay, make amnesty legitimate?
4. What do you think most influenced the transition from dictatorship in the Southern Cone and Brazil? Which do you regard as more important in inducing change—the international context or domestic politics? Would you weight domestic versus international factors differently for each case, or the same?
5. The new rules of the game that followed transitions from military rule in the four countries considered in this chapter were negotiated among elites in the context of popular pressure in the streets. Did the elites on the opposition side give away too much to achieve the transition?
6. Can it be coincidence that all three countries analyzed here have seen women advance to the presidency since the transitions? If not coincidental, what might account for their success?

Resources for Further Study

Reading: The sequel to *The Breakdown of Democratic Regimes* was *Transitions From Authoritarian Rule*, four volumes edited by Guillermo O'Donnell and Laurence Whitehead (Baltimore: Johns Hopkins Press, 1986). Manuel Puig, *Kiss of the Spider Woman* (New York: Vintage, reissued in 1991), deliberately tangles the themes of political and sexual repression. It was adapted to film in 1985.

Video and Film: Search for Rubén Blades and "*olvidar*" (to forget) on YouTube to find the Panamanian's salsa warning. *La Historia Official* (1985) tells the story of a schoolteacher who must come to grips with her story and her country's story when she suspects her adopted children may have been birthed by a victim of the Dirty War. *Johnny 100 Pesos* (1994) is set in Chile right after the transition (1994) and poses a test for the new democracy about how much violence it should use in a hostage situation. *No* (2012) tells the story of a young advertising executive who donates his skills to design TV ads for the winning 1989 campaign to force Pinochet to leave the presidency. *Capital Sins* (1991), in the Americas series, looks at the "Brazilian miracle" and the transition to democracy. *Operation Condor* (2003) details U.S. covert support for state terrorism in the three countries examined in this chapter.

On the Internet: *Inside Pinochet's Prisons* is a Euro TV film with real footage and interviews from within the prisons that gives an interesting look at the cruelty of the government and at the different political views of Chile's people. It can be found at www.journeyman.tv/8946/documentaries/inside-pinochets-prisons.html. The comparative democratization section of the American Political Science Association, which is associated with the U.S. government's National Endowment for Democracy, can be found at www.ned.org/apsa-cd/home.html.

Bolsonaro
Andressa Anholete/Stringer.

Fernandez
Stephane De Sakutin/Contributor.

Pinera
Javier Torres/AFP via Getty Images.

8 Transitions From Party-Dominant Regimes: Mexico and Venezuela

Focus Questions

▶ Why did these two countries avoid the wave of military rule that engulfed so much of Latin America after the populist period?

▶ What was the relationship between the political parties and social and economic associations in these two countries? What was different, and what was the same in the two cases?

▶ What were the main features of the political pact that established the Mexican political system after the revolution? How did President Lázaro Cárdenas consolidate the regime? In what way did the 2000 election signal significant change in the regime created by the pact?

▶ What were the main features of the political pact that established the Venezuelan political system in the transition from military dictatorship to polyarchy in 1958? How did the oil export economy influence relations between the state and social and economic groups? In what way did the election of Hugo Chávez in 1998 signal significant change in the regime created by that pact? What kinds of issues have clouded the future of the Bolivarian regime?

▶ What conclusions might we draw about "regime change" from consideration of the six cases examined in this chapter and the previous one?

MEXICO AND VENEZUELA both avoided military rule, though like almost everywhere else in the region they experienced tensions and problems toward the end of the populist era. Both countries, however, did experience a significant change of regime, mainly concerning the political party system and the relationship of the state to the market and to **civil society**.

In Venezuela, in 1958 and after ten years of military dictatorship, Venezuela's noncommunist political leaders negotiated among themselves a power-sharing agreement that became known as the Pact of Punto Fijo (named for the house in Caracas where it was negotiated). The two-party system seemed extraordinarily stable and came to be regarded by many political scientists as the key to consolidating democracy in Venezuela (e.g., Levine 1978). However, the party system came crashing down in the late 1990s, leading to the election of President Hugo Chávez Frías, a former army colonel cashiered for attempting a coup in 1992. Chávez attempted to engineer a revolutionary type of democracy based on participation by creating "twenty-first-century socialism."

Contributing to the illusion of stability and optimism about the future in both the Punto Fijo era and Chávez's administration were the seemingly inexhaustible resources at the disposal of the state, derived from exports of oil, the bounty of the country's subsoil. Venezuela is often described as a petrostate, but Venezuelan sociologist Fernándo Coronil (1997) called it a "magical state." Oil revenues were so plentiful that populist leaders believed it could conjure up spectacular and rapid development. During the 1970s' OPEC oil boom, Carlos Andrés Pérez (1974–1978) dreamt of using petrodollars to transform Venezuela into the "Ruhr of South America" (Germany's Ruhr was the heartland of its industrialization). In the 2000s, Hugo Chávez tried to create a new kind of socialism based on highly participatory councils networked across the country into communes.

The pact underlying Mexican stability went back further in history, traceable first to the decision in 1928 by Mexican leaders of its great social revolution of 1910 to put aside their violent conflicts with one another. They did this by creating a single party, eventually known as the Institutional Revolutionary Party (PRI). Its consolidation took place in the 1930s, led by their President, Lázaro Cárdenas. During his administration, the PRI formally incorporated the middle class, the working class, and much of the peasantry under its organizational umbrella, delivering significant benefits to members of unions, peasant associations, and professional groups from these sectors.

To some, the seven-decade rule by the PRI was a "perfect dictatorship"—because it monopolized national political power without military rule and without rigged elections. To some political scientists, despite significant defects the PRI regime was for much of its existence a form of democracy appropriate to Mexico's own history (Middlebrook 1986). Today, comparative political scientists might call the PRI rule a "**hybrid**" regime or "**illiberal**" democracy, combining features of authoritarianism and democracy.

As in Brazil and the Southern Cone, **import substitution industrialization** (ISI) was the economic engine for this combination of **populism** and **corporatism**. In Venezuela and Mexico, populism in the twentieth century also saw the incorporation of masses of people into political processes. In Mexico, the exhaustion of ISI contributed, as in those cases, to the erosion of the political regime created by their founding pacts. The Venezuelan case differs, as the collapse of the populist system created in 1958 had more to do with discontent over the mismanagement of the natural bounty of its subsoil. Still, neither country experienced **bureaucratic authoritarianism**. But both entered 2020 facing a serious crisis of social and political violence that threatens the stability of regimes—though more acutely in Venezuela.

Venezuela and Mexico have in common that between 1968 and 1989, citizens increasingly saw the political party systems as unrepresentative and unresponsive to groups and movements demanding change. In both cases, Mexico in 1968 and Venezuela in 1989, the military was called out to quell protest and unrest and acted with an excess of force and loss of life that contributed ultimately to a transition to a new regime. This transition included popular pressures to make democracy more genuine through political decentralization, reform of political parties, and participation of social movements in public life. Large segments of the ruling elite agreed to restructure the economy, to implement policies typical of **neoliberalism**. These reforms tended to impose the greatest sacrifice on the poor, and in both countries, the traditional parties paid a heavy economic price for adopting them. However, the new regimes were quite different from one another. In Mexico, conservative candidates were

PHOTO 8.1   Newly elected populist President of Mexico, Andrés Manuel López Obrador celebrates his victory before throngs of supporters on election night.

Source: Alfredo Estrella/AFP via Getty Images.

declared winners (though with considerable and plausible complaints of fraud) of competitive multiparty elections in 2000 and 2006; in 2012, the PRI candidate won, but two other candidates were competitive. In Venezuela, Hugo Chávez proclaimed himself dedicated to making a "Bolivarian Revolution," but instead, since his death from cancer in 2013, the country has descended into a social and political crisis so devastating that approximately one of every seven Venezuelans left the country. Chávez's chosen successor, Nicolás Maduro, hung on to power in 2019, but rival Juan Guaidó laid claim to be the country's legitimate president.

Mexico From Revolution to the Neoliberal Era

The 70-year dominance of PRI arose directly out of the most radical type of transition—revolution. The Mexican Revolution of 1910 put an end to a 40-year dictatorship but gave birth to a 20-year period of violence, including assassinations that claimed the lives of most of its leaders. It was a pact among the remaining leaders that formally gave rise to a political party that enabled them to compete for power within a framework of political rules. The new regime was consolidated after Latin America's most revered leader, Lázaro Cárdenas, implemented reforms that delivered on at least some of the key social demands of the revolution (land reform, labor rights, educational opportunities, etc.). Cárdenas also put Mexico

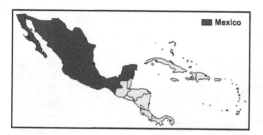

on the path of **import substitution**. Like the countries examined in chapter 7, Mexico experienced exhaustion of ISI and a populist crisis of its own, leading first to a change in the state's relationship to the society and economy and later to a change in the political rules of the power game.

The Mexican Revolution was the first mass revolution of the twentieth century. It began with a cry for political rights, but the subsequent uprising went far beyond this limited objective. In the 1800s, Mexico suffered invasion and defeat by both the United States and France and the loss (to the United States) of almost half its national territory—clear indications of the weakness of its central state. Behind this weakness lay fractious elites and warring *caudillos* who were unable to organize a defense of the country. Mexico was hardly unusual in this regard, but this liability proved especially disastrous because of its proximity to the United States. "Poor Mexico, so far from God and so close to the United States," said Porfirio Díaz, the strongman who finally put an end to the political chaos. However, his policies also sowed the seeds of revolution (see chapter 4).

Roots and Legacy of the Revolution

General Díaz, a liberal *caudillo* and hero of the war to expel French troops, presided over decades of significant economic growth in Mexico after 1876, even as he ruled behind a façade of liberal constitutional government. Díaz opened the country to foreign investment, while allowing conditions for the workers and rural masses, especially Indigenous people, to deteriorate. In Mexico, after years of growth under Díaz, fewer than 200 families owned one-quarter of the land, and much of the best land (perhaps one-fifth of all acres) was foreign-owned. Some rural estates were larger than ten million acres, keeping land beyond the reach of Mexico's rural poor, many of whom were Indigenous people whose common lands had been lost to big landowners during the liberal era. Rural peons earned much less than a dollar a day. Meanwhile, prices for basic goods, such as corn and chili peppers, doubled; the price of beans rose six times. *Mestizo* workers in the newly built railroads, mines, ports, and (few) factories were poorly paid and blocked from organizing unions.

In designing policies, Díaz relied on a group of lawyers, businesspeople, landowners, bankers, and intellectuals called *científicos*, who besides lending their expertise accumulated great fortunes during the dictatorship. The small but growing middle class faced limited opportunities to rise in a social system dominated by Creoles. Rigged elections ensured that only reliable allies of Díaz could win political office. To some degree, these frustrations were kept in check by economic growth, but this slowed in the final decade of the Porfiriato.

In 1910, Francisco Madero, a liberal landowner who had rallied popular support for a transition to constitutional government, was jailed by Díaz and then expelled from the country. From exile, Madero called for Mexican villages to revolt against the old *caudillo's* attempt to perpetrate another electoral fraud and extend his rule. Madero did not know he would ignite a much broader social conflict that would not settle down until after 1928. That was when Plutarco Calles, Cárdenas, and others created a political party, eventually called the PRI (Partido Revolucionario Institucional), to resolve conflicts among revolutionary forces.

Under pressure, Díaz first announced he would not run for an eighth term as president, but then he changed his mind and won reelection by fraud in 1910, prompting Madero to call for "effective suffrage and no reelection"—that is, political democracy (Burns and Charlip 2002: 200–211). Díaz recognized that his days were numbered. He fled to Paris but warned Madero that he would now have to "ride the tiger." Madero indeed found that Mexico's people wanted more than fair elections and freedom of speech. Like many revolutionary leaders, he learned that the hardest part of revolution is not overthrowing the old regime but constructing a new one.

All revolutions are complex, but it is especially difficult to tell the story of the Mexican Revolution because there was no one central leader, movement, or party responsible for leading the insurrection. A generation of regional leaders raised armies by recruiting peasants displaced from land that big owners had seized to produce crops and beef for export—not so different from the forces that unleashed revolution in Central America 60 years later (see chapter 9). Some revolutionary generals were little more than ambitious *caudillos*, but others were remarkable idealists with charismatic appeal. In the north of Mexico, General Pancho Villa raised an army based on peasants who worked their own small plots of land, few with well-documented property rights. During the Díaz dictatorship, many lost their plots to owners of big new mines and ranches. Many were owned by Americans like William Randolph Hearst, the newspaper tycoon. These *haciendas* produced for the growing U.S. market.

In the southern state of Morelos, 1,500 miles away, Emiliano Zapata rallied peasants squeezed off land being converted into large sugar plantations (see Womack 1968: 3–9). Zapata was most emblematic of the democratic and social justice goals of a revolution that would, unfortunately, slide later into more chaotic and internecine violence. Zapata took up arms reluctantly, after extended and widespread consultation with villagers throughout Morelos. His land reform program, the Plan de Ayala of 1911, was proclaimed in support of Madero's call to arms, but Madero was more interested in political reform than redistribution of the wealth. "*Tierra, justicia y ley*" (land, justice, and law) was the rallying cry of the Plan de Ayala, linking social justice to political change.

Madero remains today a historical hero for his courage in challenging Díaz in Mexico, but he showed little interest in or understanding of peasant demands. Villa is famed, among other things, for defying the United States for meddling in Mexican affairs. Zapata remains alive in spirit, especially in the poor southern state of Chiapas, where a "Zapatista" rebellion made in his name broke out in 1994.

For a while, after 1914, the most radical leaders, Zapata and Villa, seemed to have the upper hand, bringing their forces together in Mexico City in December 1914. However, the "bandit" from the ranching north, with its independent small landholders, and leader from the south, with its Indigenous values of communal ownership of land, failed to unite, leaving both vulnerable to defeat by ambitious *caudillos*, notably Venustiano Carranza and Álvaro Obregón. Even Carranza and Obregón, however, recognized the need for land and labor reforms—if nothing else to undercut support for Zapata and Villa.

PHOTO 8.2 Pancho Villa, the charismatic leader of small, individual landholders in the north, and the equally charismatic Emeliano Zapata, the soul of the more communal peoples of the south, meeting at a once elite café in Mexico City. Neither would survive the revolution.

Source: Wikimedia Commons, via DeGolyer Library, Southern Methodist University.

The Revolutionary Civil War

Madero was deposed in February 1913 (and assassinated four days later) by an opportunistic ally of Díaz, General Victoriano Huerta. The U.S. ambassador supported the conspiracy, thereby stoking the flames of Mexican nationalism. Huerta raised an army of Federales to fight the insurgents organized in armies raised by Zapata, Villa, and other revolutionary generals. Among the latter, Calles, Venustiano Carranza, Cárdenas, and Álvaro Obregón all eventually became presidents of Mexico. After defeating and killing Huerta in 1914, the revolutionary armies fell into battling one another. The United States settled on Venustiano Carranza as the most acceptable alternative among the rebels and helped to arm and finance his fight against Zapata and Villa. Carranza offered the best deal to American oil companies, who hoped to get leases and displace the British as Mexico's main producer of the newly valuable resource. Villa was furious and in 1916 staged a retaliatory raid on Columbus, New Mexico, earning a reputation in the United States not unlike that of Osama bin Laden after the attacks of September 11, 2001. President Woodrow Wilson sent General John J. ("Blackjack") Pershing with an expeditionary force to punish Villa, but in rugged northern Mexico, the army had little success. Villa assumed legendary status in his homeland.

As Burns and Charlip (2002: 203–204) put it, "the Revolution swept all before it. The destruction was as total as the chaos. It cost more than a million lives. It ruined much of the agrarian, ranching and mining economy. No major bank or newspaper that predated the Revolution survived." In the pitched battles, Mexico's masses were uprooted from village life to fight with and against other Mexicans from all over the country. In the 1920s, many of these illiterate fighters were—not unlike illiterate commoners of the Middle Ages in Europe—shown what to believe in the great murals and paintings promoted by a new set of rulers. However, the message was not religious piety or the flames of hell; the revolutionary message was social justice wrapped in the mantle of nationalism.

In 1917, various leaders and their followers came together at the town of Aguascalientes and framed a new constitution that embodied Madero's initial demands for democracy but added land reform, labor rights, **secularism** (stripping the Church of its privileges), and sovereign control over natural resources as founding principles of a new Mexico. However, it would be another two decades before the new political order was firmly established. Only when President Cárdenas (1934–1940) delivered on some of these promises did Mexicans successfully reconstitute the state on the foundations of the constitution of 1917.

Zapata and Villa fought separately. Zapata was ambushed and killed in 1919, on the orders of Carranza. Villa was bought off and eventually assassinated. Although the United States provided money and arms to Carranza, the general could not restore order. Obregón, more sympathetic to railroad and rural workers and more nationalistic, resisted Carranza's bid to dominate. Carranza emerged victorious, but he too was assassinated, and in 1920 General Obregón took power. He patronized the generation of great Mexican muralists, including Diego Rivera, José Clemente Orozco, and David Alfaro Siqueiros, whose art glorified a radical new vision of what it meant to be Mexican, drawing upon the country's Indigenous past, glorifying *mestizaje*, and linking this new identity to demands for social justice. Rivera was the husband of the great Mexican artist Frida Kahlo. The Mexican cultural giants were influenced by the Russian Revolution of 1917 and other currents of radical thought. Obregón saw in their work a way to channel the mobilization overflowing from the cauldron of revolution into consolidation of a new, *mestizo* national identity.

Under Obregón, the revolution appeared to be settling down; indeed, its most violent episodes were now in the past. But the shape of the new political regime remained unclear. Obregón survived his term and passed the presidency to one of his cabinet ministers, Plutarco Calles. In 1928, Obregón was elected to a new term, but then he was cut down by an assassin's bullet. Fear of death can be a motivator. Mexico's fractious revolutionary generals, led by Calles, now settled on a pact to compete for power within the structure of a new political party, later called the Institutional Revolutionary Party—the PRI.

The *criollos* were replaced by a new elite that exalted *mestizaje*, in part by promoting the Indigenous past (though not necessarily Indigenous rights) through the fabulous images of Rivera and other artists. The imposing murals were painted in chapels, convents, and churches that had been seized from the Catholic hierarchy. In countless kitchens, national identity was being created in a popular way. Women began to replace European cuisines with tamales and other foods that you have probably tried in Mexican restaurants but that were denigrated in prerevolutionary Mexico because of their association with Indian culture (Pilcher 1998).

As with just about every major revolution since the French explosion, the place of organized religion in the new order posed a vexing problem. The Mexican Church had inherited many political privileges from the colonial past. It controlled much of the education system, resisted changes in women's status, and was itself a major property owner. The leaders of revolutions mistrusted the Church hierarchy, and they held social philosophies that saw religion as a drag on progress. At the grassroots level, many of the clergy were not that conservative, especially priests and nuns working with the poor, but the new constitution reflected the leaders' resentment of the Church's conservative social philosophy and its accumulated wealth.

Tensions between Catholicism and the revolution burst open in the Cristero War of 1926–1929. In Mexico's central heartland, conservative Catholics were preaching a kind of mystical religious ideology that attracted peasants, whose lives had been disrupted by political violence and wild swings of the economy. Their way of life had been turned upside down, but the revolution had delivered neither land nor stability. President Plutarco Calles (1924–1928) moved to limit the number of Catholic priests and took other measures to enforce anticlerical provisions in the 1917 constitution. As priests fled the countryside, baptisms, masses, local feast days of saints, and a variety of other customs and practices central to rural life were suddenly absent (Meyer J. 2006; Murphy 2019). However, we should not reduce this conflict to religious issues. The Vatican had finally begun to respond to socialist and communist appeals to the working class and poor with doctrines calling for social justice. This was unwelcome competition and suspicious to the revolutionaries. The conflict culminated in a three-year, bloody revolt in Jalisco and several other states, with terrorism exercised on both sides.

From Revolution to ISI and Populism

Madero had called for political democracy in the form of competitive, fair elections. Out of revolution came a system in which no one strongman could dominate as Díaz had done. Instead, a single political party amassed power to nearly monopolize Mexican politics for the rest of the twentieth century. Many peasants got access to land in the form of the *ejidos* (municipally owned lands). But after 1940, land reform was virtually halted (briefly revived in the 1970s), and support for those peasants who got land (credits, irrigation, roads, etc.) was reduced. Peasant organizations and unions that formed between 1910 and 1940 came to be dominated by the party, whose very name, the PRI or Institutional Revolutionary Party, seems a contradiction in terms.

Can a revolution be "institutionalized"? Although Calles engineered the pact that put an end to the violence, it was Lázaro Cárdenas who, beginning with the election of 1934, rooted the new political system in the populace. Although he had already virtually won the election, Cárdenas used the campaign to build national support for his own administration. When Calles challenged the president after 1934, the old *caudillo* was packed off into exile in the United States. Cárdenas then implemented a series of policies that became associated in the popular mind with the social questions raised by the Mexican Revolution. Though these promises were never fully achieved, millions of Mexican peasants benefited from land redistribution; millions of workers benefited from unions; millions of children benefited from new schools and educational reform; and millions of Mexicans found new opportunities in working-class and professional jobs. Much of this was made possible by the success of **ISI**.

The land reform in particular was of enormous symbolic—not just economic—importance. Most of the land in the central and southern parts of the country was distributed in the form of municipally owned, communal parcels, called *ejidos*, a form of property linked to the Indigenous past, glorified by the muralists. Enshrined in the constitution, *ejidos* could not be bought and sold. Fifty years later, to create appropriate conditions to implement NAFTA—which allows foreign investment in agriculture and favors the development of large, export-oriented farms relying on high-tech cultivation—the government of President Carlos Salinas de Gortari (1988–1994) amended the constitution to eliminate protection of *ejidos*.

Cárdenas rallied Mexican nationalism through his confrontation with U.S. oil companies. Land and control of natural resources had been a major rallying cry of the revolution. In 1938, Cárdenas nationalized foreign oil companies, a move aided by the refusal of the companies to obey Mexico's labor laws. The U.S. administration of President Franklin Delano Roosevelt (1932–1945) refused to help the companies survive a crisis of their own making. Cárdenas even capitalized on compensation to the companies. He mobilized Mexicans, including children who broke open their piggy banks, to make contributions toward the fund used to pay for nationalization. After 1938, the Mexican state oil company (PEMEX) was not merely another state-owned industry; it enjoyed mythological status as a symbol of national independence (Levy and Székely 1983: 213–242). This is one reason that U.S. negotiators failed to get Mexico to agree under NAFTA to privatize PEMEX or to allow direct exploitation of Mexican oil by U.S. companies (Orme 1996: 139–145).

Cárdenas was not attempting to create a socialist or communist state in Mexico. His land reform benefited 800,000 families but did not reach all Mexicans in need of land. The *ejidos* were communal organizations, but they had to operate as enterprises in the marketplace. PEMEX was state-owned, and its profits were a major source of patronage for the PRI. Cheap energy subsidized both industry and consumers, encouraging import substitution.

More radical sectors of the PRI wanted to build further on the reforms of Cárdenas, but the president slowed the momentum of revolution by agreeing to nominate Manuel Ávila Camacho, a moderate conservative, to succeed him. Camacho won, but the election of 1940 was rife with fraud. In the same election, a pro-Church party, the National Action Party (PAN), emerged. The PAN drew strength in traditionally Catholic regions and also had a regional base in the north, where the spirit of individualism was strong among small farmers and ranchers. Over time, the PAN would become less religious and more business-oriented; it was its candidate, Vicente Fox, who scored the breakthrough against the PRI in the 2000 election (Shirk 2005).

Cárdenas, by stepping aside in 1940, reinforced the most fundamental rule of the game in Mexican politics, a product of the pact engineered by Calles and not found in the country's constitution. From 1928, every sixth year (the length of the presidential term), the outgoing president of the country selected his successor from fellow party officials. Technically, he was only choosing the candidate of the PRI, but no other party could seriously compete in the general election. By tradition, the president then stepped aside, allowing the new leader of the country a free hand to rule without interference. Mexicans called this process the *dedazo* ("fingering"; Langston 2006).

The revolution made Mexican politics distinct from the rest of Latin America in several respects. (For a general history, see Meyer and Beezley 2000; also Handelman 1997: 1–46.) Mexico under the PRI did not suffer a military coup or full military rule, as did almost every other country in the region at some time in the twentieth century. Mexico's foreign policy, although not hostile toward the United States, has been marked (until recently, anyway) by insistence on its independence. For example, Mexico maintained diplomatic relationships with Cuba after the communist revolution of 1959 and offered a degree of sympathy and refuge for revolutionary movements in Central America in the 1980s. *Mestizaje* may not have truly addressed the plight of the Indigenous population, but it did legitimate Indigenous culture and make it difficult to ignore entirely demands from that sector.

Mexico's politics in the PRI era was highly **corporatist**, and in this respect typical of the relationship between parties and social groups in Latin America. The PRI exercised control over unions, professional organizations, peasant groups, and so on through an immense patronage network, symbiotically linked to the import substitution strategy. From 1940 to 1970, Mexican economic growth averaged 6 percent per year. The PRI incorporated peasants politically, but this does not mean that its development strategy adequately addressed the need for rural sector development.

Some (e.g., Padgett 1966) regarded Mexico's political system as a good example of an alternative Third World path to modernization and democracy. Although Mexico lacked a competitive party system, significant debate and conflict over policy and allocation of resources occurred within the ranks of the PRI itself. However, Mario Vargas Llosa, the Peruvian novelist-turned-politician, called it the "perfect dictatorship" in a 1990 debate with Octavio Paz, a Mexican intellectual, and the phrase stuck.

A U.S. Library of Congress study (Merrill and Miró 1996) neatly describes the major features of the system:

> The PRI has been widely described as a coalition of networks of aspiring politicians seeking not only positions of power and prestige but also the concomitant opportunity for personal enrichment. At the highest levels of the political system, the major vehicles for corruption have been illegal landholdings and the manipulation of public-sector enterprises. In the lower reaches of the party and governmental hierarchies, the preferred methods of corruption have been bribery, charging the public for legally free public services, charging members of unions for positions, nepotism, and outright theft of public money. This corruption, although condemned by Mexican and foreign observers alike, historically served an important function in the political system by providing a means of upward mobility within the system and ensuring that those who were forced to retire from politics by the principle of no reelection would have little incentive to seek alternatives outside the PRI structure.

The government dispensed subsidies, jobs, land, welfare, and myriad other benefits. Its structures of clientelism reached deeply into almost every corner of Mexican society, even the most remote villages. Dissenters had a hard time mobilizing opposition against a party that enjoyed stature as a symbol of revolutionary nationalism and used the resources of the state to co-opt challengers. The PRI allowed the PAN and a few small leftist parties to hold some local offices in regional pockets, thus burnishing its democratic image without having to deal with any significant opposition on a national level (Camp 1999).

If we were to look for a comparable political institution in the Third World, we might look at the Congress Party of India, founded by Mahatma Gandhi and Jawaharlal Nehru after India's revolt against British colonial rule after World War II. Both the PRI and the

Congress Party monopolized national power in constitutional systems that were formally, at least, pluralistic. That is, neither Mexico nor India was officially a single-party state, but one political party ruled for a long period after a revolution. Both pursued industrialization through a strategy of import substitution. The power of both parties came from (1) their standing as the embodiment of national independence, (2) their very popular commitment to using the state to foster industrial development in partnership with private capital (i.e., state capitalism), and (3) their use of patronage resources to maintain control. Perhaps it is not surprising that with the passing of generations, the strategy of state-led development has been replaced by a more laissez-faire approach in both countries. Also, India and Mexico have, in the last two decades, seen the emergence of party competition, without the complete collapse of the former ruling parties.

Beginning in 1982, the state's relationship with society and the economy began to change. Neoliberal policies were carried out by a series of technocratic presidents. Many of the socially advanced policies of the Cárdenas era have been rolled back but remain hot-button issues in Mexican politics today (see Collier 1999). As with the military dictatorships elsewhere, popular pressure built against the authoritarian and corrupt practices. A combination of elites seeking to dismantle old corporatist structures and populist movements invoking the original values of the revolution brought about a political transition to a pluralist party system, complementing the shift to neoliberal economic development strategy.

For Review

How did the Mexican Revolution help forge Mexico's modern national identity? Why do Mexicans continue to revere Lázaro Cárdenas? Why was the PRI able to establish a near monopoly of power over Mexican politics for nearly 70 years? In what ways was Mexican populism similar to, in what ways different from, that of Brazil and the Southern Cone countries?

Onset of Populist Crisis in Mexico

In 1968, about the same time that bureaucratic authoritarian governments began to emerge in South America, the violent side of PRI hegemony became visible, and by the 1990s, the party was fully in crisis. It was not hard to imagine Mexico relapsing into the kind of bloody civil war that had marked the period between 1910 and 1917. Instead, in 2000 Mexico marked a watershed in its politics when the PAN's Vicente Fox defeated the candidates of, respectively, the PRI and the leftist Party of the Democratic Revolution (PRD) that had emerged in 1988. An offshoot of the PRD, called MORENA, led by Andrés Manuel López Obrador (commonly referred to as AMLO), would win the presidency in the 2018 election.

By 1988, Mexicans were disillusioned with the corrupt and increasingly repressive PRI regime. Clean elections would reduce the power of precisely those elements in the PRI most opposed to rolling back policies associated with the revolution, which provided the material resources needed for **clientelist** politics. However, the party was already relying less on material incentives and resorting to fraud and more frequently resorting to repression.

Some sectors in the PRI were ready for a change and a closer economic relationship to the United States. To convince the country's northern neighbor that it was ready for integration, the PRI "reformers" had to reduce the power of **populists** in their own party (NACLA 1994). The populists in the PRI stood opposed, for both ideological (nationalism) and practical reasons (the need to protect local jobs, state enterprises, subsidies, and welfare programs, all of which provided patronage). Just as Menem changed the stripes of the Peronist Party in Argentina, Presidents Miguel de la Madrid (1982–1988), Carlos Salinas de Gortari (1988–1994), and Ernesto Zedillo (1994–2000) sought to change the PRI. The last of them, Zedillo, whose 1994 victory came after a particularly violent and bitter internal contest in the PRI, did the most to open up the system to more competition.

Despite the experience of revolution, Mexico's socioeconomic profile does not differ drastically from the other larger countries that underwent import substitution and populism. The country escaped military rule, but after 1968, security forces assumed a more prominent role in curbing protest. Since 1982, Mexico has struggled with a debt crisis and adopted many neoliberal policies that seem contradictory to the ideals of the revolution. Although Mexico had asserted control over its land, oil, and mineral wealth, in the 1990s the PRI began to open the economy and allow important basic sectors to be foreign-owned.

Through this period, Mexico's civilian rulers remained firmly in control of the government, but with increasing reliance on repression. The first crack in PRI hegemony became visible in 1968 when the PRI rulers used the security forces to repress a student movement demanding reforms. The students were generally sympathetic to Cuba, where Fidelismo seemed to be producing more social justice than they saw in Mexico. Their movement was attracting support from other sectors. Despite the promises of the Mexican Revolution and three decades of economic growth, illiteracy and poverty were growing in the countryside, and economic development could not keep up with a swelling urban population (Levy and Székely 1983).

Things came to a head as the 1968 Summer Olympics approached. Students protested expenditures on the games and dramatized the gap between the aspirations of the revolution and the limited accomplishments of the PRI since 1940. The government wanted to use the games to show the world Mexico's strides toward modernity. Its response to the students was a turning point for the country's political future.

On October 2, 1968, paramilitary troops and police, including deadly snipers on rooftops, opened fire on student protestors in the Plaza of Tlatelolco in the capital. Hundreds were slain, and hundreds more were wounded, in front of a shocked national television audience. The government said that demonstrators opened fire first, but the claim was never really convincing. Decades later, after the Fox government permitted some long-closed files to be reopened, we learned that hundreds of Mexicans, including students, poor peasants, labor activists, and others, were brutally murdered or tortured by the military and police in the subsequent period. Mexico, in other words, had its own **Dirty War**, but with civilians running the government instead of military men.

In development policy, Mexico's government remained oriented toward **ISI** at this time. In fact, President Luis Echeverria, the minister who had deployed the security forces against the students, even briefly resuscitated land reform during his presidency (1970–1976). However, the country was beginning to feel economic stagnation (inflation with low economic growth rates) and political strains associated with the end of populism and ISI. Still, Mexico had an asset that might have pulled it through: oil.

The United States, drawing for many decades on its own oil production, had shown little interest in buying oil from Mexico, where a state company monopolized the business. That attitude began to change after Arab countries cut off oil exports to the West for a few months in late 1973, and after OPEC (Mexico was not part of the cartel) began to flex its economic muscle. Now the United States became eager to build up Mexico's productive capacity, so the Mexican government borrowed huge amounts of dollars to finance an expansion of the oil industry—and also to stabilize the peso against inflation and keep the patronage machine humming. Private international banks were eager to lend to governments as the market for loans dried up and dollars began piling up in their vaults. Most Latin American countries borrowed heavily from the willing lenders, but few so freely as Mexico. Under the PRI, the government accumulated US$57 billion in debt by 1981 and US$80 billion by 1982.

By the early 1980s, Mexico's oil industry was ready to enter the world market, but the market was not ready for it anymore (Mommer 2002: 82–83). Deep in recession and wary of dependence on foreign suppliers, the United States, Europe, and Japan were now importing less oil, not more. Prices, sustained for a while by OPEC's cuts in production and the Iranian Revolution of 1978, began to fall. Mexico was out of dollars to make payments on the interest and service of its debt. The debt crisis had arrived in Latin America and the world, showing its face first in Mexico in 1982.

Dissatisfaction would produce a new left party formed out of the populist candidacy of Cuauhtémoc Cárdenas, the son of Lázaro, who bolted from the PRI to seek the presidency in 1988. He put together a coalition of dissident members of the PRI and small leftist parties. Afterward, this coalition would form itself into the Party of the Democratic Revolution (PRD; Partido de la Revolución Democrática), which remains one of the four major parties in Mexico today. Cárdenas appealed to Mexicans unhappy with the PRI's embrace of neoliberalism, which had become obvious with the administration of President Miguel de la Madrid (1982–1988), a **technocrat** trained at Harvard. De la Madrid had been chosen via the *dedazo* of José López Portillo (1976–1982), whose speech leaving office was a tearful apology for having led the country deep into debt and economic crisis. The new president had never won an election—something that would be true of the next two PRI presidents. In effect, Portillo felt it more important to please the **IMF** than the Mexican public, and it hardly surprises that de la Madrid implemented a **structural adjustment** program while in office.

In addition to the economic shock treatment, Mexico experienced another one, literally. At 7:19 a.m. on September 19, 1985, a devastating earthquake struck Mexico City. International observers estimated that 10,000–30,000 people died, and 100,000 homes were destroyed. The government mustered a completely inadequate response to the tragedy. This brought two interrelated consequences. First, it raised more questions about the legitimacy of the government. Second, Mexicans began to organize self-help groups outside the corporatist, **clientelist** structures that linked groups to the PRI (Foweracker and Craig 1990). It spurred a movement of neighborhood associations, women's groups, and human rights organizations. Civic action groups began to press for fair elections, a tendency that would ultimately help guarantee respect for Fox's victory in the 2000 presidential election.

De la Madrid's *dedazo* fell on another U.S.-trained economist, Carlos Salinas de Gortari, his minister for planning the budget. This choice indicated that the neoliberal approach was to be continued, but now the political scene had become more complicated. There were deep rifts in the PRI, fomented by anger at technocrats from two sources within the party. One came from the party's left, which thought the PRI might still embrace the values of Villa and Zapata and saw neoliberal reforms as a betrayal of the revolution. The other came from the PRI's professional politicians, who were loath to give up the patronage and corruption that flowed through the party's arteries and veins. A combination of social movement resistance to **neoliberalism** and PRI defectors laid the basis for the Cárdenas candidacy of 1988 (La Botz 1995).

The election was a three-way race between Salinas, Cárdenas, and a PAN candidate. Between them, the PAN candidate and the coalition behind Cárdenas won nearly half the seats in the lower house of Congress. Cárdenas ran strongly in urban areas, especially in Mexico City where neighborhood movements were strongest. The PRI kept its grip on rural areas where patronage politics and manipulation of the voting process were easiest to carry out. The PAN carried record-high votes in the northern region, its stronghold; it took control of the governorship of Baja California. But the presidency was where the stakes were highest. The presidency was the big prize, and on election evening, Cárdenas was ahead in early returns when suddenly and conveniently a "computer glitch" suspended reports until the next morning. Remarkably, when the count resumed, Salinas de Gortari was pronounced to have captured more than 50 percent of the vote, with Cárdenas garnering about 30 percent. Cárdenas reasonably cried "fraud." No one knows for sure who won.

In Washington, the rise of Cárdenas set off alarms. The hardcore-right advisors to President Ronald Reagan had little love for the PRI, whose rule and penchant for state influence over the economy they saw as communism next door. More moderate Republicans realized—along with Democrats—that a storm was gathering in Mexico, one that could launch a new Mexican revolution. Nearby in Central America, Nicaragua had already had a revolution in 1979, and Guatemala and El Salvador were seething with unrest. Instability threatened a refugee crisis right on the border of the United States. Hence, when Salinas approached George Bush (the elder, president from 1989 to 1993), who had just won the election in 1988 and had the idea of linking Mexico's economy to that of the United States, he was well received. There were economic and political motives on both sides to pursue the initiative that led to NAFTA (Orme 1996).

The PRI technocrats were less interested in preserving the party's monopoly on political power than in making the transition to a more market-oriented democracy. A more pluralist political system might weaken the grip of the old party guard—the "dinosaurs," the party's *caciques* and *caudillos*. The dinosaurs were resisting privatization of state assets vital to the patronage machine. The old guard also was not eager to introduce more transparency (to foster foreign investment) in economic and political affairs. With the populist wing of the PRI restive and a new left party, the PRD, now challenging the PRI, the United States foreign policy establishment and Mexican reformists saw **NAFTA** as the key to prevent any future Mexican president from deviating from the neoliberal model. In 2019, when President Andrés Manuel López Obrador (AMLO), a left populist, was confronted by President Donald Trump with a demand that NAFTA (discussed later) be renegotiated to fulfill his (Trump's) "America First" campaign propaganda, the Mexican leader had little option (short of dealing with major disruption to the country's economy) but to cooperate and broaden and extend the treating as the **USMCA, the United States–Mexico–Canada Agreement**.

The Transition to Multiparty Politics

Salinas, whose family was itself mired in corruption, initially pointed the *dedazo* at a politician—party president Luis Donaldo Coliseo. Coliseo was assassinated under still-unexplained circumstances in March 1994. Salinas turned next to a technocrat, Ernesto Zedillo, who won the 1994 election, which was once again marred by fraud, though there is little doubt this time that the PRI candidate obtained the most votes. The new economic model was now in place, and Zedillo made it his goal to complete the regime transition by completing the transition from a near-PRI political monopoly to a competitive party system—**polyarchy**.

Zedillo first had to deal with a peso crisis. To keep the Mexican economy looking stable during U.S. congressional debates over NAFTA, President Salinas had pegged its currency to the dollar, much as Menem did in Argentina. As in Argentina, the government continued to borrow dollars to keep the exchange rate level. It was easy (as Argentina would later discover) for speculators to make a lot of money by getting their hands on pesos (using other countries' currencies or borrowing) and then trading them for dollars, and repeating the cycle. The "easy money" got even better when it became clear that devaluation was inevitable. Still, the PRI government was not going to take action before the elections that year. In December 1994, a few months after NAFTA and with Zedillo safely elected, the PRI government allowed the peso to rise. It skyrocketed, doubling overnight, effectively cutting savings and wages in half.

Zedillo, in a sense, completed Mexico's transition to democracy by refusing to use the *dedazo*, which resulted in a bruising but more democratic internal fight within the PRI for its nomination. But Zedillo and NAFTA could not restore the living standards of most Mexicans. The aura of invincibility of the PRI had been broken by the Cárdenas challenge. Then, on the day Zedillo was inaugurated in 1994, poor peasants in the poor southern state of Chiapas marched into and occupied the state capital, demonstrating that the leftist guerrilla movements had not been relegated to the dustbin of history.

The PRI's political monopoly at the national level was broken in 2000 with the electoral victory of Vicente Fox. In Fox, the PAN offered a candidate who was well-financed, articulate, and able to extend the party's appeal beyond its original base in the north. In 2006, the PAN rejected the Fox-preferred nominee and nominated Felipe Calderón, more conservative in both social and economic policy. Calderón was declared victorious over the PRD's (future president) López Obrador in another highly disputed election. Although the PRI had declined, it did not disappear, finishing ahead of the PRD and PAN overall in local and congressional elections in 2009. Calderón pursued with Washington's aid a highly unpopular war on the drug cartels.

The PRI's Enrique Peña Nieto prevailed in an election over the PRD candidate, AMLO, and the PAN's Josefina Vásquez became the first woman to run for president as the candidate of a major party. AMLO bitterly charged electoral fraud. The PRI also captured the most congressional seats as well. López Obrador again claimed that the election had been stolen. Although Peña Nieto was a politician, unlike the three PRI president between 1984 and 2000 who preceded him, he did not retreat from the economic or political reforms of the prior 30 years. In fact, he dared to seek privatization of many of PEMEX's operations, taking on a symbol and an institutional bulwark of Mexican nationalism. He also opened bidding, allowing foreign companies access to new fields. AMLO retreated from the plan in the face of nationalist opposition upon taking office, though whether permanently or temporarily was not clear.

Peña Nieto failed to curtail the violence and wars among the cartels, and his modest economic reforms failed to spur economic growth, especially when oil prices dropped drastically in 2014. AMLO would leave the PRD after taking criticism for the loss. He founded a party called MORENA (Movimiento de Renovación Nacional), and both he and the party were victorious in 2018. That López Obrador could win showed that the Pink Tide in Latin America was not entirely at low ebb. However, whether he could carry out a *cuarta transformación* (fourth transformation; earlier ones being independence, liberal reforms of the 1850s, and the Revolution) was highly problematic. In 2019, in the face of threats from President Trump to abandon NAFTA altogether, he moved the renegotiated United States–Mexico–Canada Agreement through the Mexican Congress. Even more humbling, he had to agree to cooperate with Trump's plan to allow people seeking asylum in the U.S. to be housed in camps in Mexico while they awaited processing.

Was the Mexican transition merely the result of a game played by elites—in particular the reformist, modernizing faction of the PRI and the business-oriented PAN? As in Brazil and the Southern Cone, democratizing forces were bubbling at the grassroots level. One important new movement sprang up in reaction to the fraud of 1988, as seven different human rights organizations united in 1993 to form the Alianza Cívica (AC; Civic Alliance) to monitor the 1994 elections. More than 18,000 Mexican citizens monitored the election in more than 10,000 voting stations (Avritzer 2002: 97). The AC went on to champion electoral reforms and undertook to monitor public officials, sponsoring an "adopt an official" program to root out corruption.

In electing Fox and Calderón, the Mexican electorate was not much different from voters in Brazil, Chile, and Argentina in the early elections after a transition. In all these cases, centrist politicians who promised a degree of stability after decades of political repression and turmoil won the first elections after military rule. In fact, it can be argued that the real regime change in Mexico occurred during the three PRI presidencies before Fox. It was in those years that the relationship between the state and the economy shifted significantly from the developmentalist role of government during the era of **ISI** to the **laissez-faire** approach that culminated in NAFTA. NAFTA required substantially reducing the role of the state in the economy—privatization, economic deregulation, elimination of protection, and so on. These neoliberal economic policies looked suspiciously like those implemented by Díaz, with similar results—enriching a handful of wealthy elites and increasing the influence of the United States in all things Mexican (Ruiz 2000).

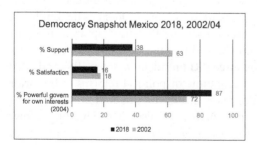

Democracy Snapshot Mexico 2018, 2002/04

Zedillo, in a sense, completed Mexico's transition to democracy by refusing to use the *dedazo*, which resulted in a bruising but more democratic internal fight within the PRI for its nomination. However, Zedillo and NAFTA could not restore the living standards of most Mexicans. The aura of invincibility of the PRI had been broken by the Cárdenas challenge and Zapatista revolt in Chiapas.

For Review

Mexico did not undergo military rule, nor was a new constitution written. Can we speak, then, in any sense of "regime change" or "democratization"? What similarities and differences are there in the way that ISI and the first populist era came to an end in Mexico compared to the cases we examined in chapter 7?

Venezuela's Transition From Pacted Democracy to Radical Populism

In February 1992, Lieutenant Colonel Hugo Chávez led a coup attempt against the elected government of President Carlos Andrés Pérez. The uprising stalled, and Chávez himself was captured. Defeat was turned into political victory, however, as a result of the electrifying moments in which Chávez appealed on national television asking for the revolting troops to surrender. He accepted sole responsibility for the defeat, something that impressed Venezuelans accustomed to politicians dodging responsibility. His claim that the objectives had not been met "for now" (*por ahora*) stirred popular hope that the struggle had only begun. On the streets, civilian supporters, especially younger members of the population, began appearing in red berets similar to those worn by the paratroop commander and his followers.

Why were so many Venezuelans ready to support this military coup? After all, the country had enjoyed 34 years of political stability and regular elections between 1958, when the last dictatorship fell, and the February coup attempt of 1992 (a second failed coup occurred in November). Polls at the time showed no great enthusiasm for military rule, even though the economy had been rocked by nine years of low oil prices. Why then did Chávez's popularity soar after 1992?

The short answer is that Venezuelans' faith in democracy had been shaken because their dream of rapid development into a modern society had evaporated after decades of economic growth generated by oil exports (Hellinger 1991). The widespread perception was that the oil money had been stolen by corrupt politicians associated with the two political parties that dominated the electoral process: Democratic Action, Pérez's party, and the Political Electoral Independent Organizing Committee—a Christian democratic party better known by its Spanish acronym, COPEI (Comité de Organización Política Electoral Independiente).

Venezuelans take pride in the role the country played in South America's independence struggle with Spain, under the leadership of Simón Bolívar, the Liberator. Bolívar's forces liberated not only Venezuela but also modern-day Peru, Bolivia, Colombia, Panama, and Ecuador. After the war, he promoted Pan-Americanism, that is, Latin American unity to prepare for the inevitable expansionism of the newly independent United States toward the south. He also promoted social policies to prepare all Venezuelans for incorporation into republican politics. His *criollo* allies were not enthusiastic, to say the least, so Bolívar attempted to impose his progressive ideas from the top down. He failed. His liberated republic quickly divided into five states (six, counting Panama, which was part of Colombia), slavery remained, and the Indigenous peoples who remained fared little better than enslaved people. Venezuela itself was a poor agrarian society whose main export was hides and cacao, as well as coffee later in the nineteenth century. Blacks and *pardos* escaped to the sparsely inhabited interior plains where they were periodically mobilized into wars that devastated the population and the economy.

After the most brutal of these civil wars, Juan Guzman Blanco, the victorious liberal general, carried out some modernization, including a successful effort to create a cult of Bolívar, with statues in the main plaza of every tiny village in the country. However, the country remained poor, and in 1890 a *caudillo* army swept down from the Andean region to displace the rulers of the day. General Cipriano Castro challenged European powers, who sent gunboats to control the country's ports and collect customs taxes to repay loans made to feuding *caudillo* armies and to fund revolts against Castro. The United States intervened, not so much to back Venezuelans as to show the Europeans that, true to Bolívar's prediction, the colossus of the North was the arbiter of such disputes. In fact, the U.S. was not happy with Castro's nationalistic policies, including his intervention in favor of rivals of the New York–based Bermudez Company, which claimed rights to produce asphalt from what most regarded as a not terribly important substance that oozed from the country's soil—oil.

In 1908, Yankee gunboats stood by as a former ally of Castro, General Juan Vicente Gómez, seized power. He would rule Venezuela until his death in 1935. A tyrant, Gómez was also a state-builder, finishing Castro's efforts to train a professional army that ended the ceaseless wars among regional *caudillos*. He put the country's finances in order. All this was before Venezuela was changed forever when an oil gusher exploded near Lake Maracaibo, in the west. Gómez used the ensuing oil boom to reward his family and friends, but beyond his control the torrent of oil dollars entering the economy virtually destroyed the already indolent rural economy as peasants rushed to the cities and oil camps. A working and middle class quickly emerged, first challenging Gómez in student-led demonstrations in 1928. Among the leaders was young Rómulo Betancourt, who went into exile and returned in 1936 to found an organization that would become Acción Democrática (AD, the Democratic Action party). The Venezuelan Communist Party (PCV) already existed, and the PCV and AD bitterly contested each other for leadership of the unions. AD broadened its organizing effort to peasants and the middle class. A middle-class officers' coup brought AD to power for three years (the *trienio*, 1945–1948). This period also saw the founding of COPEI by middle-class Catholics fearful of the secular tendencies of AD. It was more conservative than AD, but also modernizing.

Already the government that was ousted in the coup of 1945 had passed an oil reform law (1943) that significantly increased Venezuela's share of the profits of the three major foreign companies (Shell, Gulf, and Standard Oil) producing in the country. AD tried to carry out ambitious social reforms in housing, education, health, and so forth, but in 1948 a coup brought to power an ambitious General Marcos Pérez Jiménez. One reason AD was vulnerable was that its opponents resented its use of power and oil money to consolidate its power. The communists resented how the AD regime, led by Betancourt as head of the party, tried to push them out of the unions. As for Venezuelan businesspeople, they had no use for any unions at all at this time. Pérez Jiménez's regime was brutal against opponents, but this was not a **bureaucratic authoritarian** regime. Pérez Jiménez was also a populist, especially regarding housing. Rural Venezuelans continued to flood into the cities, particularly Caracas (Velasco 2015; Tinker-Salas 2009), where they populated the massive housing projects and poor, hillside *barrios* that were bastions of support for Hugo Chávez (see later).

Puntofijismo: Venezuela's Pacted Democracy

Venezuela's "pacted democracy" was founded soon after Pérez Jiménez fled the country in January 1958, leading to the election of Betancourt, founder and leader of AD, in December of that year. Betancourt turned power over to a successor from AD after elections in 1963, but democracy really seemed to be consolidated after Rafael Caldera, founder and leader of COPEI, was elected president in December 1968. Six more presidential elections, every five years, brought either an *adeco* (member of AD) or *copeyano* (member of COPEI) to the presidency. That ended when Caldera broke from COPEI to run and win a new term in 1993. Even so, the two large parties continued after that election to control both houses of Congress. They knew that accepting popular demands for a **constituent assembly** to rewrite or change the 1961 constitution would put that control in jeopardy.

If Mexico's single-party system was a perfect dictatorship hidden in democratic trappings, in many ways Venezuela had an even better disguise for a system in which parties came to smother civil society rather than to represent it (Hellinger 1991; Karl 1986). AD and COPEI competed to control not only government but also unions, professional organizations, peasant leagues, student associations, and neighborhood groups—just about every civic association, but in the face of challenges from other parties they united to repel them.

The Pact of Punto Fijo among the noncommunist parties after the fall of Pérez Jiménez in 1958 was just the most important of several agreements that social and political actors negotiated to lower the risks in the complex game that, according to Przeworski (1986; see chapter 7), laid the foundation for a transition to democracy—that is, to a **polyarchy**. The military, labor unions, professional associations, business associations, and unions were among the most important actors. The military was determined that there would be no retribution directed toward the officer corps as individuals or as a group. The Church sought to ensure that it would continue to have influence, especially in education, which the secular-oriented AD had long wished to modernize by asserting state control over the curriculum. Business groups had become disenchanted with the dictatorship because it had reneged on paying debts. They wanted a government that would continue subsidies and protection, but one that would eschew socialism. Unions were not so easily mollified, but most of the leaders, and especially those affiliated with AD, were drawn into the agreement by the business sectors' acknowledgement of collective bargaining.

The explicit exclusion of the Communist Party from negotiations and the Pact of Punto Fijo was a sign to most of Venezuela's capitalists that the new regime would not be a revolutionary one; that is, it lowered the risk factor. They had reason to fear a more radical regime change because communists and leftist youth in AD had led resistance to the dictatorship. The centrists put aside their differences in the interest of political stability—heading off revolution—and agreed to support an elected government.

Venezuela is either cursed or blessed, depending on your point of view, with oil, which generated one-third of its GDP, 80 to 90 percent of export earnings, and more than half the government's revenues. The taxes and royalties paid by the major foreign companies into state coffers provided the wherewithal for a huge patronage system. Most businesses in Venezuela were (and are) in private hands. What has never been in private hands is oil in the ground. Democracy became linked in the Venezuelan mind with sovereign control of its subsoil wealth and with the fair and effective use of the super-profits to develop the country. This mindset would be one reason why Venezuelans would one day turn against *puntofijismo*.

Betancourt insisted that only a directly elected government could be counted on to "sow the oil," a phrase coined by the novelist Arturo Uslar Pietri (1936), in projects of economic development and improvement of health, education, and other aspects of human welfare. But the emphasis was not necessarily on import substitution industrialization so much as agricultural modernization. Textiles, food processing, and oil refining were typical of where the government wanted to "sow" the oil until quite late in the Punto Fijo era. In fact, it was Pérez Jiménez who undertook the first substantial investment in heavy industry, largely in establishing steel and aluminum production in the underpopulated eastern region. And those industries were envisioned as having export markets as much as domestic ones. With oil revenues available to import goods, import substitution industrialization simply was not as high on the agenda in Venezuela as in governments of the populist era in Mexico, Brazil, and the Southern Cone.

Betancourt won the presidential election of December 1958. His economic agenda was reformist but far short of what the left of AD and the PCV envisioned. A month later, Fidel Castro's forces marched into Havana and began a radical experiment that inspired the left, especially the youth sectors of both parties that felt betrayed by Betancourt and the AD elders. Most of the communist leadership were reluctant to embrace the enthusiasm of their youth, but faced with a rebellion in their ranks, the PCV joined *adeco* leftists and launched a guerrilla war to overthrow the new system. It proved to be a disaster. Whatever shortcomings the new regime had in terms of respecting civil liberties and delivering social justice, it enjoyed the legitimacy bestowed by fair elections. Many peasants and *barrio* dwellers sympathized with the leftist youth, but they were not ready to take up arms themselves, and some of the violent tactics of the FALN (Armed Forces of National Liberation) alienated their popular base. After 1968, most of the guerrillas returned to party politics, many in the mainstream parties. They accepted an amnesty extended by President Caldera, the founder of COPEI, who had evolved from the archenemy of Betancourt to cofounder of the Punto Fijo system.

Punto Fijo as a Model Polyarchy

The Venezuelan political scientist Juan Carlos Rey (1972) described the new system, based on the Pact of Punto Fijo and the constitution of 1961, as a "populist system of reconciliation." What he meant was that the pact allowed Venezuela's elites to compete with one another and reconcile their differences with each other through elections. The prize was access to the country's oil-export earnings. Probably no country in Latin America was so dependent on a single export product, but this product had an unusual ability to generate profits.

Unlike Mexico, Venezuela's regime had competition between incumbent and opposition in elections. But this disguises an important similarity in the way the party system functioned in each case. Although the competition between COPEI and AD was fierce, they would unite with one another in the face of any challenge from a breakaway group. In many ways, the two parties dominated groups in Venezuela in the same way that the PRI did in Mexico: through the promise of economic development, nationalism in defending sovereign control of the country's natural wealth, use of patronage to ward off challenges, and in the end—if necessary—fraud and repression. More colorfully than Rey put it, another political scientist referred to this system of cooperation with limited competition as a "cartel" (Cyr 2013).

Venezuela's populism differed from that of Brazil, Chile, and Argentina in that it revolved more around the vaguely defined idea that "imperialism petrolero" was denying the country a just share of the profits generated by oil exports. Oil nationalism was, we have seen, important in Mexico too, but there it was associated with Cárdenas's nationalization. Until 1973 no major thinker, party, or political leader was interested in nationalizing the oil industry itself. From 1935 onward, Betancourt and his followers said that democratically elected governments would challenge the companies, capture a fair share of the profits, and use them to develop the country. Venezuela's capitalists were more interested in profiting off commercial ventures and finance than becoming industrial barons.

The political elites who dominated the post-1958 era repeatedly associated military rulers of the past with the unpatriotic giveaway of the country's wealth. Actually, some generals had often been as nationalist as civilian rulers were. The reform of 1943 by President (and General) Medina Angarita significantly raised royalties and taxes; just as importantly Medina forced the companies to acknowledge the Venezuelan state's right to set tax rates, a recognition of the country's sovereignty. From 1943 until the nationalization of oil companies in 1976, whenever the economy faltered, the political class could raise taxes and royalties. Royalties are fixed payments that a landlord levies as compensation for the exploitation of a natural, exhaustible resource. In this case, it was something foreign companies had to pay to extract oil from the subsoil.

Venezuela's experience exercising sovereignty over its natural resources had international repercussions. Facing rising competition from Middle Eastern producers and the unwillingness of the United States to agree to import more Venezuelan oil, in 1960 Betancourt sent his oil minister to the Middle East to explore cooperation. As a result, Venezuela, Iran, Saudi Arabia, and three other major oil producers formed the Organization of Petroleum Exporting Countries (OPEC), which began to coordinate efforts to boost export earnings by regulating global production and setting "reference prices" for taxation (Mommer 1988: 119–218).

By the 1970s, in part because of the growing power of OPEC and in part because their 40-year concessions were running out, the companies were ready for change. In 1973, a Middle East war and Arab oil boycott (Venezuela kept producing) sent crude oil prices soaring, and they stayed there. In 1976, the companies actually encouraged nationalization (with compensation). President Carlos Andrés Pérez (1974–1978) proclaimed that Venezuela was now master of its own fate for the first time because "*el petroleo es nuestro*" ("the oil is ours"; see Hellinger 2003). He decided to invest the flood of petrodollars of the 1970s into a crash program to industrialize the country overnight. In fact, he tried to accelerate the program by borrowing heavily against future petrodollars. This was not simply import substitution to meet demand at home. Pérez saw Venezuela using oil profits to produce heavy industry for export to Brazil, Argentina, and other countries. As Fernando Coronil (1997) put it, the petrodollars allowed the "magical state" to conjure up automobile and tractor factories, fertilizer plants, and steel and aluminum industries, not just schools, roads, and food processing and textile industries typical of the early ISI years. And it would do it overnight with the aid of so many petrodollars that Venezuelans began to refer to their country as "Saudi Venezuela" (see Karl 1997).

This strategy proved disastrous; the economy was not able to absorb the enormous flow of petrodollars, and Pérez was nonetheless borrowing against future production. Venezuelans became accustomed to what economists call "rent-seeking"; that is, political competition came to revolve around gaining access to the financial resources of the state. The way to get rich was not to invent something or build an industry but to obtain contracts or subsidies from government. Not surprisingly, corruption, graft, and inefficiency became widespread. For a while, when things went wrong, the government could fix them simply by spending more petrodollars; losses were easily absorbed for most of the decade. The day of reckoning came in 1983, ten years after Pérez had promised to use the great OPEC oil bonanza of those years to turn Venezuela overnight into the "Ruhr" (the industrial heartland of Germany) of Latin America. Until 1976, Venezuelan politicians could always blame oil imperialism for economic failures. Now, after nationalization, facing failure in 1983, they would have to account for themselves.

Collapse of the Punto Fijo System

In the 1980s, the dream of overnight progress through oil exports collapsed. Oil prices fell from well over US$40 in the early 1980s to US$9 in 1986. Corruption became more visible and less tolerable during this period. In May 1988, the military announced it had killed 16 Colombian guerrillas in a firefight along the Apure River on the border. However, two of the so-called guerrillas survived and set the record straight. The military had killed 16 Venezuelan fishermen and tried to cover it up. A subsequent investigation suggested that the military was mixed up in a protection scheme involving extortion of money from ranchers. Human rights scandals, daily headlines about corruption, and even murder plots among quarreling elites began to raise questions about the impunity of politicians and wealthy families in supposedly democratic Venezuela. And in the barracks some Venezuelan officers began to worry about the military's role and how it conflicted with the military's historical self-image as defender of the people, a heritage dating to the struggle of Simón Bolívar (a Venezuelan) in the independence era (Jones 2007).

Like Mexico, Venezuela escaped the wave of military rule that swept Latin America in the 1970s and 1980s, so the fear of military rule was not nearly as strong. In fact, historically Venezuela's military had portrayed itself as the defender of the people against rapacious elites. Military populism became potent as a counterweight to the designs of Venezuelan elites who, during the second presidency of Carlos Andrés Pérez, attempted to implement reforms not unlike the ones championed by Mexico's technocrats (McCoy and Myers 2006).

In December 1988, Pérez had won a new term as president after a populist campaign in which he promised to bring back the good old days of his first presidency, during the 1970s boom. He probably really believed he could do it, but he did not count on how deeply in debt the country had fallen. Instead, he signed a structural adjustment agreement with the IMF that included raising gasoline prices—which were ridiculously low but regarded by most citizens of this petrostate to be a sacred right. The package was harsh economic medicine and clashed with the fundamental connection that Venezuelan politicians had made between democracy and sovereign control over oil: Ownership of oil guaranteed development to be shared by everyone. It did not help that wealthy elites with close ties to politicians continued to live a fast, hyper-consumerist lifestyle in the cities. The contrast was especially vivid in Caracas, where millions of Venezuelans living in shanties perched on mountainsides could observe the social life of those living "à la *adeco*" (like a politico of Acción Democrática) in the glittering valley below.

The popular response to Pérez's economic package began on February 27, 1989, the day transportation fares were due to rise with the price of gasoline, with an astounding, spontaneous revolt—the Caracazo uprising, which engulfed 22 major cities. Caracas was rocked by looting for nearly a week. Pérez sent in the army, but only after the riots had pretty much subsided. Human rights organizations estimated that the death toll was well more than 1,000. U.S. training and the successful counterinsurgency of the 1960s had led academic experts on Venezuela (including me) to assume that the military was firmly linked to the status quo. But the Venezuelan military was not the Chilean or Argentine military. It turned out that Chávez and others had been meeting for many years with former guerrilla leaders from the 1960s. The ex-guerrillas had hopes that they could win the army itself to their cause (Jones 2007).

The 1989 riots were a turning point. The old political class and the political parties associated with the pact of 1958 were in complete disrepute. This disconnect between political elites and the masses is often called a **crisis of representation**, and Venezuela in the late Punto Fijo era is a prime example. An explosion of popular organizing and protest characterized the early 1990s, and it continued, albeit at a lower level of intensity, through the Caldera presidency (1994–1998). Chávez tapped into this surge of participation and protest. Released from prison in 1994 in a gesture of reconciliation, he entered the political stage as a candidate promising to overhaul the system radically, to sweep the old parties from power, and to put the oil money back in the hands of the people. The old parties lay in ruin after his victory of December 1998. The new president convened (after a referendum) a constituent assembly that wrote a new constitution and renamed the country the "Bolivarian Republic of Venezuela." The expressed goal of the new charter was to institute participatory democracy—though whether the objective was to replace or to strengthen representative democracy was less clear. In any case, on paper at least, the reforms promised more direct power for people through social movements and popular organization in governance (see chapter 11 on social movements).

For Review

How was oil linked to democracy in Venezuela after 1930 and in the Punto Fijo era? Venezuela's first populist era differed in some ways from the other countries we have examined thus far. How? Mexican and Venezuelan nationalism were both shaped in part by oil, but how did they differ from one another on the oil question?

The Chávez Era

In the first four years of his term, President Chávez survived several attempts by his opponents to oust him from the presidency prematurely. The most serious was an attempted military coup (April 11, 2002), followed in December by a three-month partially successful general strike and shutdown of oil exports. Behind the plotting for a coup and economic warfare was a coalition of his political enemies—the big private media, executives of the state oil company opposed to his nationalist oil policies, labor bosses associated with the old parties, and much (not all) of the business community. The United States not only welcomed these attempts to oust Chávez, it also it provided money—overtly, in the form of programs ostensibly to promote democracy, and also covertly. It quite possibly actively aided the conspirators in the attempted coup. Having failed to remove Chávez through these methods, the opposition finally decided to try a constitutional route and remove him from office via a recall vote in August 2004. Chávez, already directly elected twice (1998 and 2000) with solid majorities, won the recall with nearly 60 percent of the vote. He won reelection in December 2006 with 63 percent of the vote. He cannot simply be dismissed as an autocrat out of step with "democratic" trends (see Ellner and Hellinger 2003)—although that is how he is largely portrayed today in the burgeoning literature on populism and illiberal democracy (Albright 2018; Levitsky and Ziblatt 2018).

In 2000, Venezuela was one of the top 10 producers of crude oil in the world and the third-largest supplier of petroleum to the United States. In addition, in 2008 major new discoveries brought Venezuela's proven oil reserves to 300 billion barrels, the largest in the world. Not surprising, Venezuela rates high on the diplomatic radar screen in Washington. Depending on the rate of increase of oil consumption globally in the future, the country may become even more important. If technology and economics develop favorably and Venezuela's vast reserves of heavy oil (a tar-like substance, difficult to get out of the ground and transport) become viable to produce, the country could someday return to its former status as the world's leading oil exporter.

Oil revenues powered Chávez's ambitious populist programs to build socialism at home, and it also provided Chávez some diplomatic clout. Any other Latin American leader bold enough to question the conduct of the war in Afghanistan, to visit Saddam Hussein in Iraq, to refuse to cooperate with the U.S. drug war in Colombia, and to question the wisdom of free-market economics probably would have felt the wrath of economic sanctions, or worse, from Washington. Indeed, these finally did materialize in 2017 against his successor, President Nicolás Maduro. Perhaps Chávez's most serious challenge to Washington came in 2005 when he torpedoed U.S. proposals for a **Free Trade Area of the Americas (FTAA)**, which might be described as NAFTA for the hemisphere. Furthermore, he advanced his own alternative for Latin American economic integration independent of the United States. Not surprisingly, the right-wing factions in the United States called Chávez, along with Lula of Brazil, Rafael Correa of Ecuador, Daniel Ortega in Nicaragua, Evo Morales in Bolivia, and the Castro brothers in Cuba, an "axis of evil" in Latin America.

The Punto Fijo regime and ascension of Chávez was not a transition from military authoritarianism but an attempt to build a new populist regime in the wake of the collapse of a political elite that lost connections to the broader society. The elite had failed to use the country's great economic advantage, oil, as leverage to develop the economy. They were perceived, accurately enough, as thoroughly corrupt. A large part of the army's officer corps

PUNTO DE VISTA: WAS CHÁVEZ'S 1992 COUP ATTEMPT IN VENEZUELA FOR OR AGAINST DEMOCRACY?

On February 4, 1992, Lieutenant Colonel Hugo Chávez and his Bolivarian Revolutionary Movement (MBR 200, referring to its founding on the 200th anniversary of Bolívar's birth) attempted a coup against the elected president of Venezuela, Carlos Andrés Pérez. At the time of the coup, more than 80 percent of Venezuelans expressed no confidence at all in the country's political parties. In the aftermath, Venezuelan politicians called on the people to defend democracy, but to their surprise, many Venezuelans came out to demonstrate against the existing system—though not necessarily in support of a coup.

Chávez, who died in March 2013, became president in 1999. Ever since, government supporters have annually commemorated the February 4 date. The opposition instead celebrates January 23, the anniversary of the overthrow of the last military dictatorship in 1958. Chavistas accuse the opposition of being "golpistas" because the opposition tried to oust Chávez in a short-lived 48-hour coup in April 2002. The opposition questions the late president's own democratic credentials because of his leadership of the 1992 coup.

In 2002, two months after the April coup, Chilean journalist Marta Harnecker interviewed Chávez and asked him to explain the motives behind his 1992 uprising.

> Chávez: When the people of Caracas came out into the streets en masse [the "*caracazo*"] on February 27, 1989 to reject the economic package that had been approved by the then-president Carlos Andrés Pérez, and we saw the massacres that took place in response, it made a huge impact on my generation . . . When [Pérez] sent the Armed Forces into the streets to repress that social uprising and there was a massacre, the members of the MBR 200 realized we had passed the point of no return and we had to take up arms. We could not continue to defend a murderous regime . . .
>
> We discussed how to break free from the past, how to move beyond the kind of democracy that only responded to the interests of the oligarchy, how to stop the corruption. We always rejected the idea of a traditional military coup, of a military dictatorship, or a military junta . . . We agreed to issue decrees to convene a constitutional assembly . . . We began to prepare for the rebellion.

Chávez went on to describe the preparation, including planning with leftist groups to encourage civilians to come into the streets in support of the coup, hopes that fell short of expectations that day. "There was no popular mobilization. So it was just us rebelling," Chávez told Harnecker. However, afterward, he claimed, people began to see the military as allies.

> Chávez: The popular protest movement was really unleashed when the people realized that a group of the military was with them . . . . After the February 4 rebellion, the MBR 200 changed substantially, because until then we were a small, clandestine military movement, a group of young officers, a few civilians, a few leftist movements that were incorporated into the MBR 200 . . . [When we got out of prison] we went from being a clandestine military organization to a popular movement; though there was always a military presence, it was a civilian–military movement.
>
> Later in the interview, Chávez said,

I am very much aware of what Bolívar once said: "I am but a light feather dragged along by the revolutionary hurricane." Leaders find themselves in front of an avalanche that drags us forward. It would be very unfortunate, sad, if a revolutionary process of change were to depend on a caudillo.

Point/Counterpoint

Do you think that Chávez persuasively defended his coup attempt of 1992?

If you say yes, how do you respond to the criticism that whatever his policies were, Carlos Andrés Pérez was an elected leader? Can a coup against an elected president ever be justified?

If you say no, how do you respond to the argument that there was a crisis of representation in Venezuela—that elections were not doing the job of keeping government responsive to the people?

For More Information

See Marta Harnecker, *Understanding the Venezuelan Revolution: Hugo Chávez Talks to Marta Harnecker* (New York: Monthly Review Press, 2005). See also Bart Jones, *Hugo!* (Hanover, NH: Steerforth Press, 2007). More critical of Chávez is Cristina Marcano and Alberto Barrera Tryszka, *Hugo Chávez: The Definitive Biography of Venezuela's Controversial President* (Random House, 2007).

identified with popular frustration. Venezuelans seemed to welcome military rebellion but not necessarily military rule.

What we can say is that the period between the *caracazo* of 1989 and what persisted through the Chávez presidency, to his death in March 2013, was not just an explosion of popular anger but a mass mobilization by poor Venezuelans demanding access to the benefits provided by the state. This produced the new Bolivarian constitution in 1999, one that envisioned a participatory democracy with a "protagonistic" role for civil society. That is, political movements and organizations were vested by the charter with the right to participate in making policy and filling important judicial and watchdog offices (to combat corruption and protect human rights). The most controversial and debated part of this plan was advanced in 2007, when Chávez decreed a law (under authority given to him by the National Assembly, elected and controlled by his supporters) to create community councils directly funded by the petrostate. To his Bolivarian grassroots supporters, this was the democratization of the benefits of oil. To the opposition, these councils were little more than an attempt to circumvent representative democracy and construct a new, stronger system of patronage controlled by the executive branch of government. Much of the opposition charge Chávez and his successor, Nicolás Maduro, with attempting to import the Cuban model.

Chávez's successes, both international and domestic, now seem transitory, as a political and social economic crisis began to wrack the country 15 months after his death in 2013. Even if Maduro were to survive the crisis, the Bolivarian regime is unlikely to live up to the innovatory democratic ideals of the 1999 constitution. Venezuela's regime change in the Chávez years is not as secure as the Mexican one, even accounting for the problems facing the latter. What regime change in Venezuela shares with the case of Mexico is the collapse of a developmentalist regime and a party-dominated populist system.

For Review

The "old regime," *puntofijismo,* featured two parties competing in elections, with alternations in power, characteristics associated with polyarchy. What caused an apparently stable polyarchy to weaken?

Venezuela's Polarized Politics

Even before 2007, however, Venezuelan politics and society had begun to polarize. In the first 20 months of his presidency, Chávez had concentrated on dismantling the Punto Fijo regime, which was something that many people who had not voted for him in 1998 supported. But in November 2001, Chávez decreed (as with the later laws about communal councils, under authority granted by the National Assembly) a series of laws promoting land reform and some other property rights.

What really stirred the political pot was the new oil law. In the 1990s, the executives of PDVSA, the state oil company, convinced desperate politicians to lower barriers to foreign investment and increase production of oil, even if it might conflict with obligations to OPEC to manage world supply. The plan was called the *apertura petrolera* (oil opening). They also convinced the politicians to allow foreign companies to own shares of joint projects with PDVSA. The plan did raise production, but in 1998, as the presidential campaign was underway, oil prices fell, and oil glutted the world market. The economic consequences helped Chávez win the election, and he was determined to pursue a nationalist agenda in oil policy. In 2000, he convened what was only the second summit of leaders of OPEC nations in Caracas. And in November 2001, he used powers given him by the National Assembly to decree a new oil reform law.

The reform did not block foreign investment from returning to the oil fields. It raised royalties and taxes. Chávez later insisted that all basic operations in oil be majority-controlled owned by Venezuela. In taking these actions, Chávez took on the most powerful group in the country, the high executive class of PDVSA. The executives became deeply involved in the efforts to overthrow Chávez. They and their allies had failed to appreciate how popular he was among poor Venezuelans. When the coup occurred on April 11, 2002, tens of thousands descended from the poor *barrios* above the Caracas valley. Their intervention, divisions with the coup plotters, and the actions of troops loyal to Chávez enabled him to return triumphantly.

Venezuelans rallied behind Chávez again when his opponent tried to force him out with a shutdown of oil production. After the opposition obtained sufficient signatures on a petition to hold a recall election, the election was held and they voted to keep him in. Chávez's government rewarded the people with social programs, called "missions," that nearly eradicated illiteracy, put high school and college education in reach of most people, and spread health clinics and state-run subsidized markets throughout the country. He was able to do this because oil prices and earnings rose substantially in the decade following 2000. The price rise was partly because of demand in industrializing Asia, but also because Chávez took the lead to reinvigorate OPEC's discipline over production. Because of the oil reform law, the government maximized its share of the profits from exports, even permitting the foreign companies to their profits.

However, the Venezuelan transition was never complete. The Bolivarian constitution of 1999 established many innovative new institutions and ways for people to influence the state, but these institutions were never functioned independently of the leadership of Chávez, who died in March 2013. Chávez established a party, the United Socialist Party of Venezuela (PSUV), in 2006. His opposition, though divided into several parties, united to form a coalition, the Democratic United Roundtable (MUD). The MUD never came close to defeating Chávez in a presidential election, but it saw its vote total rise between 2010 and 2013, and in the April 2013 election to replace the deceased Chávez, it came within a whisker of defeating Maduro, the popular president's anointed successor.

The MUD candidate against Chávez in December and then Maduro in April was a governor, Henrique Capriles. Capriles said he would adhere to the 1999 constitution. Some questioned his sincerity. Even if sincere, Capriles would have faced tremendous pressure from his constituents to end some popular programs. For example, Chávez had negotiated a deal with Cuba that included that country sending 10,000 medical personnel to work in the poor *barrios* and rural areas, as they were still doing in 2020. In exchange, Cuba receives oil. The MUD is to this day committed to ending oil exports to Cuba, but then how would they replace the doctors?

Grassroots Chavistas wanted more resources and power transferred to the communal councils, but professional politicians, including many mayors and governors in the PSUV, are not keen to lose their control over local funding. Chávez held the reins of power closely to his own chest. He had the support of the military, which he now controlled. He had the ability to make final decisions when members of his cabinet quarreled over economic policy. Maduro, by contrast, was a bus driver by trade and leader of the unions. His performance in the April 2013 election to replace Chávez raised many doubts about his political capacity; Maduro defeated Enrique Capriles by less than two percentage points—in comparison to Chávez's victory over Capriles by almost 11 percentage points in October 2012.

Partly what enabled Maduro to survive in 2020 was his opposition. Opposition leaders have said they do not intend to dismantle social programs, but much of the population, including those now alienated from the PSUV, can see that conservative governments elsewhere in the hemisphere have moved back toward neoliberalism. Much of the opposition is still tainted in the public mind with the Punto Fijo past and with the coup of 2002.

In February 2014, rivals to Capriles seized on the emergence of an opposition student movement protesting high rates of violent crime and economic shortages. The movement had some legitimate grievances to protest, but it was quickly politicized when Leopoldo López, a former mayor in the Caracas metropolitan area, put himself at the head of the movement and called for the "exit" (i.e., resignation) of Maduro and his government. By April, some of the demonstrations had turned violent, and dozens of security personnel, demonstrators, and bystanders were killed in confrontations. López himself was upstaged in December 2018 when Juan Guaidó, head of the National Assembly, declared the presidency vacant and with the support of the United States and conservative governments in Latin America proclaimed himself the legitimate president.

Almost all the protests originated in middle-class parts of large cities. The poorer parts of the cities were noticeably quiet by comparison. However, this does not mean that the *barrios* are as enthusiastically behind the Bolivarian government today as they were when they saved Chávez from the 2002 coup. In 2017, protests began to appear in *barrios*, often more focused on economic privations and corruption in government programs that are supposed to ameliorate the impact of the economic crisis on the poor. But Bolivarian police, the National Guard, and armed groups of *"colectivos"* (not all are armed) have reacted by stepping up operations against opponents in poor urban areas, not just against middle-class protesters.

A report by the Office of the UN High Commissioner for Human Rights in 2019 stated that the government has "aimed at neutralizing, repressing and criminalizing political opponents and people critical of the government."

All the blame for Venezuela's faltering democracy should not be laid at the feet of Maduro. On the opposition side, the coup and oil shutdown of 2002 did great damage to the economy. Chávez was vilified in the mainstream press, which openly campaigned for his overthrow. Pro-Chávez demonstrators were routinely described as *"turbas"* in the streets, while middle-class protesters were described as "civil society." Guaidó has openly worked with Washington to encourage the military to oust Maduro via a coup. For his part, although Chávez could be magnanimous, for example, after his return from the coup attempt, he routinely characterized all opposition as *"la oligarchía"* and *"los escuálidos"* (the squalid ones). While he seems to have sincerely wanted to implement participatory democracy through community councils, he centralized control over the funds to implement projects in a social fund and in the oil company. His presence was so commanding over the state that ministers and other officials could not take decisions of any importance without Chávez's approval. Like President Pérez in the 1970s, he put rapid social economic transformation (in this case, various "twenty-first-century socialist programs") ahead of preparing for the inevitable fall in oil prices.

Rather than serving to democratize the distribution of oil rents, in the crucible of political polarization and economic crisis the communal councils and other grassroots organizations evolved into new clientelist networks, controlled by politicians administering programs funded directly by the executive branch and an oil company–controlled fund.

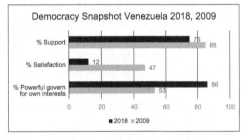

When the old Punto Fijo regime was swept away, most Venezuelans, even those who opposed Chávez in the 1998 election, regained a sense that they have democratic rights to demand influence over government. There has been regime change, but how democratic it will be is still an open question. As of 2020, Maduro seemed to have weathered the demands for his ouster, but the political system envisioned under the 1999 constitution is certainly not institutionalized and, even less so, democratic.

Everybody in Venezuela has "lost." Maduro proved resilient but heavily dependent on the security forces, and he remains vulnerable to new challenges to his power, some of which could come from within the PSUV or the left. Guaidó had clearly lost ground and was more heavily dependent on support from hemispheric allies. The United Nations says that the number of refugees that have fled Venezuela is now at four million, approximately one of every seven of its people. New National Assembly elections were to take place in 2020. There were some indications early in the year that some sectors of the opposition might decide to participate. The most likely (but not certain) outcome elections would be a PSUV (Maduro) victory in a low turnout election, with charges of fraudulent counting and other irregularities, some of them manufactured, some of them factual. In a country where "pacts" are strongly associated in the public mind with elite disregard of the needs and desires of ordinary people and with tremendous mistrust on both sides, it will be difficult to hold a democratic election.

Conclusion: Pacts and Polyarchy

The notion that a pact is the underlying basis for democratic government is deeply rooted in pluralist theory and the conception of democracy as a polyarchy. The idea is that democracy cannot itself ensure consensus and acceptance of fundamental principles. Consensus is what makes democracy possible. It would seem, then, that the foundation of polyarchy is something like Venezuelan political scientist Juan Carlos Rey's populist system of reconciliation— that is, a system whereby elites contest their differences with one another but keep popular participation in check.

As Brazilian social scientist Leonardo points out, Huntington's famous analysis of political stability tends to see political participation as a threat to democracy. Huntington (1968; see chapter 7) proposed that we see institutions as mechanisms to control and channel participation. That is, as participation increases, it eventually can overtake institutionalization and increase instability. This was made quite explicit by Huntington and like-minded colleagues at the dawn of the neoliberal age (see Crozier et al. 1975).

Avritzer points out that the framework of the "transitionologists," especially Przeworski (1986), tends to emphasize the importance of elite pacts. Popular participation and protest are largely seen as part of the environment in which the elites negotiate. The people (*demos* in Greek) are seen not as protagonists constructing democracy but as the unruly mob that makes elites put aside deep-seated animosities and conflicts. The unruly chorus encourages them to negotiate a solution before the protests take on revolutionary dimensions or before the military once again takes over. Avritzer, drawing mostly on the Brazilian and Mexican cases, argues that the people themselves ought to get more credit for what has been achieved in the transitions to democracy.

Although the Latin American transitions treated here differ from one another in several important respects, there are some significant ways that the Southern Cone countries, Brazil, Mexico, and Venezuela resembled each other.

- In all of these cases, the combination of the exhaustion of economic growth strategies and falling prices for key commodity exports contributed to an economic crisis that resulted in slowing rates of growth and eventually a debt crisis.
- At the very time when economic growth slowed, sectors that had only marginally benefited, if at all, were being mobilized by radical sectors.
- Political polarization became more pronounced at both elite levels and social levels.
- The polarization was accentuated by the policies of the United States, which materially supported the opposition, as it has consistently done (see chapter 16) where a left-populist government has engaged in programs deemed in conflict with U.S. interests.
- In all cases, the populist regimes gave way to increased authoritarianism, though the

degree of repression varied, from increased abuses of human rights by security forces still subordinate to civilian authority (Venezuela and Mexico) to the intense violence of "dirty wars."

- Neoliberal economic policies began to be implemented not only as a response to international debt but promoted under the Washington Consensus as the only possible response to the exhaustion of state-led developmentalism under ISI.
- A combination of frustration with the corruption and **clientelism** of the populist era, the disruption of the corporatist relations of that era, and the openings encouraged by the global human rights movement increased the leverage of mass movements for democratic transitions or democratic reforms.

Venezuela's crisis of representation toward the end of the Punto Fijo era, as well as the burst of protests that since 2013 has punctuated the myth of a successful neoliberal economics and democracy in Chile since 2013, revealing how pacts safeguarding elite power can threaten liberal democracy. However, the Venezuelan crisis post-Chávez is so acute that it is hard to see how any reconstruction of the country's economy and political peace can happen without a pact of some kind. It would seem that as a practical matter, pacts are almost indispensable to exit authoritarianism and extreme political polarization, but they have to be renegotiated in a process that involves people, not just elites, in establishing regimes that exceed the democratic possibilities of **polyarchy**.

Discussion Questions

1. Would it be fair to say that neoliberalism undermined democracy in Venezuela but strengthened it in Mexico? Why or why not?
2. Some political scientists credited the Pact of Punto Fijo with preventing Venezuela from experiencing the military rule that swept much of the rest of the continent in the 1970s and 1980s. Would you agree? What lessons should Latin America's relatively new democracies take from the Venezuelan case?
3. Do you think that in either case true "regime change" took place, and if so, when do you think it took place? Both countries went through a crisis of populism. Do you think that the Mexican regime is any more institutionalized than the Venezuela case? Why?

Resources for Further Study

Reading: Bart Jones's *Hugo! The Hugo Chávez Story from Mud Hut to Perpetual Revolution* (Hanover, NH: Steerforth Press, 2007) is a sympathetic biography but very accessible and a good window into many different aspects of Venezuela's transition. Steve Ellner and I edited *Venezuelan Politics in the Chávez Era* (Boulder: Lynn Rienner, 2003). Miguel Tinker Salas's *The Enduring Legacy: Oil, Culture, and Society* (Durham: Duke University Press, 2009) examines the profound influence of U.S. investment and consumer values on Venezuela. Matthew Gutmann's *The Romance of Democracy* (Berkeley: University of California Press, 2002) looks at ordinary people's hopes and disappointments during the Mexican transition. The fifth edition of Roderic Camp's *Politics in Mexico: The Democratic Consolidation* (New York: Oxford University Press, 2007) is an optimistic but critical look at Mexico's political reforms.

Video and Film: *The Revolution Will Not Be Televised* is a remarkable documentary of the attempted 2002 coup against Chávez. *¿Puedo Hablar?* (2007) looks at the 2006 presidential election, crediting Chávez for helping the poor but raising questions about the health of democracy. *A Place Called Chiapas* (1998) is one of the many good documentaries on the Zapatistas.

On the Internet: Venezuela Analysis, www.venezuelanalysis.com, disputes the general U.S. media view of Venezuela but also provides critical analysis and debate. An opposition viewpoint that generally avoids hysterical rhetoric is Caracas Chronicles at www.caracaschronicles.com. You can find good perspectives from different points of view on Mexican politics at www.latinamericanstudies.org/mexico.htm. Spanish language *La Jornada* (The Work Day) is a good center-left newspaper. The great Mexican muralists are explored at http://smarthistory.khanacademy.org/los-tres-grandes.html.

9 Democracy in Times of Revolution

Focus Questions

▶ What were the underlying causes that gave rise to the Cuban Revolution?

▶ What challenges face Cuba as a new political generation enters the political stage?

▶ Cuba is often placed among the bottom three countries in terms of democracy. Is that a fair evaluation?

▶ Why does the U.S. seem to single out Cuba for economic sanctions and efforts at regime change?

▶ To what degree has the settlement of civil conflicts in Central America addressed underlying social tensions in that region?

▶ What is an insurgency, and what ramifications do insurgencies have for building democracy in the post-conflict era?

THE CUBAN REVOLUTION is now over 60 years old. Almost all the young *barbados* (bearded ones) who marched into Havana on January 1, 1959, have either passed away or retired. Fidel died in 2016; Raúl has resigned his government posts, though he still wields influence as head of the Cuban Communist Party. A second generation of party leaders now makes policy, and in 2019 they set out to write a new constitution, though clearly Cuba will remain a single-party state. A certain degree of economic liberalization was implemented during Raúl's eight years at the helm, and it seemed that some political liberalization would likely follow. But as 2020 opened, the Cuban regime found itself under siege once again, both economically and politically. The collapse of Venezuela's economy threatens the flow of oil, vital to the island's economy, and the administration of Donald Trump has mostly reversed the limited opening of the United States. The prospect for expanding commerce and U.S. tourism in Cuba are bleak.

The hope of hardliners in the Trump administration is that strangling the Cuban economy will encourage the Cuban people to rise against the communist government, leading to a regime transition. That was supposed to happen after the collapse of Eastern European communism 30 years ago, but the Cuban system survived. Now even fewer residents on the island were alive during the revolution of 1959; those under 40 were too young or not yet born during the hard years after the fall of the Berlin Wall in 1989. We must take into account the passing of generations to assess how politics might evolve in the 2020s.

The last of the revolutionary generation is retired or elderly. Fidel is in his grave. Although Raúl Castro still heads the Cuban Communist Party, he has transferred governing responsibilities to younger party leaders. This transference indicates that the Cuban **regime** has achieved a degree of institutionalization and is no longer dependent on the **charismatic** authority of the Castro brothers or other first-generation revolutionary leaders. In fact, considering "regime" not in the pejorative sense of "authoritarian rule" but "order of things," we cannot rule out a consolidation of a single-party system, a variant of what the PRI was in Mexico between 1928 and 2000. Some possible alternatives for Cuban politics include transitions (1) to a less personalist, more bureaucratic form of autocracy; (2) to a social democratic political system closer to that found in Costa Rica or Uruguay, the Latin American countries with the strongest social welfare systems; or (3) to a hybrid state with a dominant single party but with more space for opposition and channels of popular influence.

We need to look at Cuba's politics through a lens less clouded by stereotypes, positive or negative—especially those portraying the island as a totalitarian dungeon, ranking barely above the autocracy in North Korea. Later in the chapter, we will consider the legacy of revolutionary insurrections in Central America that ended with pacts settling civil wars but left scars that have yet to heal.

The Nature of Revolutions

The philosopher Hannah Arendt (1963: 27) argued that revolutions have two things in common: (1) They are characterized by a striving for freedom against repression, and (2) they attempt to create a new social order—what we might take the liberty to call "regime change." But not just any kind, she said. The quest for freedom in a revolution is tied to the "social question." The makers of revolution seek freedom but believe that it cannot be fully achieved without radical changes in social and economic conditions (55–61). Latin America's break from colonialism brought about a political revolution accompanied by violence and social upheaval, but it would not qualify as a revolution in the terms defined by Arendt. The Creole social class wanted "freedom" from Spanish rule, but not change in the social order. Bolívar's frustration and bitterness reflected that fact.

Revolutionary *movements* have been relatively common in Latin America, but revolutionary *regimes* are rare. What distinguishes these few "success stories" from the more numerous failures? Once in power, revolutionary movements rarely carry out their political plans as promised. Why? Do they ever achieve freedom and a more just social order, or do they merely culminate in a new system of repression—old wine in new bottles?

Latin America's revolutionary movements have usually linked the "social question" to breaking economic dependence and asserting national sovereignty. Latin America's mythic revolutionary heroes—for example, Venezuela's Simón Bolívar, Cuba's José Martí, Argentina's (and Cuba's) Ernesto Che Guevara, and Nicaragua's José Augusto Cesar Sandino—all saw the United States as a threat to the region's independence and ability to reform its social order. It is no coincidence that the revolutions in Mexico (1910–1917), Cuba (1959), and Nicaragua (1979) took place in three countries that have suffered direct military occupation by U.S. forces in their history. Mexico lost half its territory to the northern colossus in 1846–1848 and endured several subsequent interventions. The United States invaded Cuba in 1898 as it was on the verge of achieving independence from Spain and then occupied it for three years. Nicaragua, thought to be a desirable site for a trans-isthmus canal, attracted frequent intervention by the United States and European nations vying for influence and control of such a project. (Ultimately, the United States built the Panama Canal.)

The Mexican and Cuban revolutions gave birth to a long period of rule by a single party that tried to unite the population behind a program of national economic development and resistance to U.S. pressures. Cuba's rebels consolidated their control after 1959 in a state modeled on Marxist–Leninist principles; the one-party system was formally incorporated into a constitution in 1976. Mexico, we saw in chapter 8, finally moved after 72 years to a multi-party system. In both of these cases, however, the catalysts for revolution included rebellion against dictatorship and a demand for fair and competitive elections. The same can be said for Nicaragua, where the Sandinistas seemed at first after 1979 to be pursuing representative democracy and social justice, and today both democratic and social conditions have seriously deteriorated. In other words, the Latin American experience raises questions about whether revolutionary regimes can really deliver on both the social question and democracy.

The Cuban Revolution

The commitment of Fidel and Raúl Castro and the Cuban Communist Party to preserve Cuba's current political system grew out of a long history of resistance to U.S. domination (see chapter 16). The Castros believed that maintaining a one-party state is crucial to unity against the threat of Cuba becoming once again a virtual colony of the United

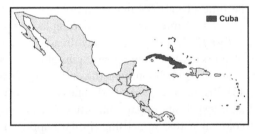

States. Given the sad history of U.S. intervention in Guatemala, Chile, and (in the 1980s) revolutionary Nicaragua, we can question but not dismiss this perspective. Critics, including some who are sympathetic to Cuba's revolution, argue that the party is clinging to a type of political system discredited nearly everywhere in the world today, that the aversion to competitive party elections constitutes an admission that the government dares not put its legitimacy to test in an election.

Origins: Nationalism and Neocolonialism

Cuba was among the very last of Spain's colonial possessions to achieve independence. Havana, the capital, was the departure point for Spain's armada of merchant vessels and warships during the colonial era, a military stronghold of the empire. The colonial economy was based on plantations producing sugar and tobacco for export. Slaves were imported into Cuba as late as the 1870s, which gives the island deep historical and cultural connections with Africa. The *criollo* elite chafed under Spanish rule but feared social rebellion and emancipation, lest they suffer the fate of French slaveholders in nearby Haiti. As in several other Caribbean nations, the elite seriously considered exchanging colonial rule for entry into the United States as a slave state. Several promising movements for independence were thwarted when elites, fearful of social revolution, changed sides (Pérez 1988).

The last of these revolts was led by the extraordinary patriot and intellectual José Martí. Visitors to communist Cuba are often surprised that Martí's busts, statues, and portraits are more prominent than are images of Fidel Castro and Che Guevara. Martí mobilized Cuba's Afro-descendant population (those enslaved on plantations, plus some blacks and *mulatos*) by promising to create a race-blind social order of opportunity for all (De la Fuente 2001). Martí was killed in battle in 1895, but not before warning his countrymen and women about the expansionist ambitions of the United States. Still, in 1898 most Cubans welcomed U.S. intervention, believing it would shorten the bloodshed. Cuban elites hoped that U.S. intervention, by ending the independence struggle quickly, would forestall deeper social revolution.

U.S. troops left in 1903, but only after forcing the Cuban government to accept the Platt Amendment, which gave Washington the "right" to intervene in Cuba to maintain stability. Under Platt, the United States established the naval base at Guantánamo Bay, which it still occupies despite Cuban protests and which it uses as a prison in its "war on terror." The U.S. embassy became a major player in Cuban domestic politics. Whenever any political faction disliked the outcome of an election, it could organize civil unrest and appeal to Washington. In both 1905 and 1917, the United States invoked the Platt Amendment and occupied the island. Platt was repealed in 1934, but not before U.S. interference in Cuban affairs had become a fact of life in Cuban politics—but one resented by most of the population.

The United States also had replaced Spain as the key foreign actor in Cuba's economy. Before 1898, North Americans already owned many of the plantations and sugar mills; Cuban planters became their agents or employees. After the war, North American investments went from US$50 million near the end of the 1800s to US$1.3 billion by the 1920s (Pérez 1988: 13). Britain and the United States set the price of sugar, the island's crucial export, through an international sugar committee. Cubans soon came to link economic distress to this neo-colonial status. Something similar happened throughout Central America and much of the Caribbean, including the Dominican Republic, Haiti, and Puerto Rico. U.S. interests owned the banks, port facilities, railroads, utilities, and so forth. Their investments modernized the infrastructure, but mostly to facilitate an export-based, highly dependent economic system. The dominance of foreign capital and the buying out of the planters meant that in this region the domestic **bourgeoisie** was numerically and politically weak, even by Latin American standards. U.S. companies did provide some employment and opportunities for a middle class to develop, but at the top levels of society, there was an economic and political void.

Martí's promise of racial egalitarianism posed a direct challenge to the U.S. ruling class, especially to the white southerners who maintained racial supremacy in the former Confederate states. Here was a revolution promising racial equality only 90 miles away from Florida. After the war, the U.S. exported Jim Crow to the region. The U.S. armed forces were segregated and would remain so until the end of World War II. Their presence in bases and on shore leave in Cuba reinforced racial segregation, accentuating tensions on the island.

Cuba's politics post-independence became an elite game, full of corruption and fraud. Two parties, Liberals and Conservatives, competed for power behind a façade of democracy. Corrupt politicians and an inefficient bureaucracy were certainly not unique in the region, but in the Cuban case they were associated with frustrated revolution, compromised sovereignty, and a government that depended more on a foreign power than its own people for support. In 1924, the Liberal Party's Gerardo Machado was elected, and then he changed the constitution to grant himself a new six-year term. Then the world economy collapsed, sending Cuban sugar prices plummeting and unemployment soaring. Machado met strikes and protests with harsh repression.

In Latin America, many such crises have spawned a cohort of student activists, many of whom later undertake political careers and assume a generational identity. Some of the key political leaders of the populist era—for example, in Venezuela, Peru, Bolivia, and elsewhere—came out of student movements. In Cuba, a young "Generation of 1930" sprung up to oppose the Machado dictatorship. Fidel Castro was not of the 1930s cohort, but he began his political career at the University of Havana and was influenced by the radical nationalists of 1930. Many would join him in revolutionary struggle after World War II.

Despite President Franklin Roosevelt's (1932–1945) "Good Neighbor" policy, the United States intervened to quell radical changes demand by the Generation of 1930 through the machinations of Ambassador Sumner Welles. Welles worked to replace the dictator Machado, and the dictator was driven from the country by a revolt of army officers. His replacement (Carlos Manuel Céspedes) was too close to Machado to please the opposition. Meanwhile, workers in the sugar cane fields pressed their demands in the midst of a worsening economic crisis. The government moved to freeze military pay, and in response a group of noncommissioned officers, led by sergeant Fulgencio Batista, staged a coup that ultimately brought a reformist university professor, Ramón Grau San Martín, to power.

Grau instituted some reforms, such as nationalization of the electric utilities and expansion of legal rights for unions. His approach was moderate, but it alarmed both the Cuban ruling class and the United States. Welles began to plot Grau's removal. He found an ally in the ambitious Batista. As the U.S. fleet made an ominous appearance in the harbor, ostensibly to protect American lives and property, Batista staged a *golpe* (in Spanish, "blow"; used as a synonym for "coup" throughout Latin America) against Grau. For the next 25 years, Batista ruled Cuba—either in the presidency or as the power behind the throne. Grau managed to win election as president in 1944, but by this time he and his Cuban revolutionary party (called "Auténticos") had been tamed. He failed to deliver any more progress on the social question, even though significant social and economic rights were embodied in a new constitution written in 1940. Grau, his successor (Carlos Prío Socarras), and his Auténtico Party were drawn into the corruption.

Cubans were becoming frustrated with the failure of electoral democracy. The most active opposition came not from the Communist Party, which pragmatically aligned with Batista at times, but from the Cuban People's Party (Orthodoxos). Eduardo Chibas, a member of the Generation of 1930 and a fiery orator, was their leader. The head of the party's youth wing was a law student at the University of Havana, Fidel Castro Ruz.

For Review

How did the U.S. war with Spain over Cuba cut short the revolutionary aspiration of Martí? How might we apply Arendt's ideas of revolution to the movement Martí led? How did the role of the U.S. in Cuba's economy and politics influence Cuban politics between 1898 and 1952?

The Rise of Fidel Castro and the Revolution of 1959

In 1952, Batista canceled elections and moved from behind the scenes into the presidency. Batista—corrupt, brutal, mafia-connected, and U.S.-supported—would be overthrown in 1959 by a few hundred guerrillas under Castro's leadership in the countryside and by tens of thousands of other Cubans in the cities, especially Havana. A signal event occurred when Castro led an attack by students and workers on the Moncada army base in Santiago, in eastern Cuba, on July 26, 1953. The attack failed. Most of the rebels were eventually killed, but Castro survived. The bold move sparked the 26th of July Movement, formed officially in November 1956. Under its umbrella, opponents of Batista united behind a program calling for both political democracy and deep social change.

Fidel Castro drew a connection between these goals in his famous speech made in 1953 at his trial for leading the Moncada attack. In "History Will Absolve Me," Castro laid out the stark injustices afflicting Cuba's laboring masses, the corruption and brutality of the government, and other problems. He argued,

> The problem of land, the problem of industrialization, the problem of housing, the problem of unemployment, the problem of education and the problem of people's health: these are the six problems we would take immediate steps to solve, along with restoration of civil liberties and political democracy.
>
> (quoted in Brenner et al. 1989: 32)

Castro concluded his speech at the trial with an appeal to Martí's words—"a true man does not seek the path where advantage lies, but rather the path where duty lies"—and with a defiant proclamation:

> I know that imprisonment will be harder for me than it has ever been for anyone, filled with cowardly threats and hideous cruelty. But I do not fear prison, as I do not fear the fury of the miserable tyrant who took the lives of 70 of my comrades. Condemn me. It does not matter. History will absolve me.
>
> (quoted in Brenner et al. 1989: 35)

Fidel's speech brought together the two aspects of Hannah Arendt's conception of revolution—the quest for freedom and the social question. "History Will Absolve Me" galvanized them as the banner for a revolutionary movement—just as they were galvanized in Mexico when Francisco Madero's call for clean elections in 1910 was supplemented by the demands for social justice themes enunciated by Pancho Villa and Emiliano Zapata (see chapter 8). Similarly, the Sandinista Front for National Liberation would pair social justice and the fight against dictatorship in the struggle leading to the 1979 revolution in Nicaragua.

Castro served 22 months in prison and then was released after Batista, under popular pressure, declared an amnesty. He left the country for exile in Mexico, where he met the free-thinking Argentine Marxist, Ernesto Che Guevara. As the urban fighters of the 26th of July Movement drew Batista's army into the cities, Fidel, his brother Raúl, Che, and others landed an insurrectionary force in eastern Cuba in November 1956. They were nearly wiped out and fled to the nearby Sierra Maestra mountains. It was there, protected by sympathetic, poor peasants, that the rebels' commitment to revolutionary change and understanding of Cuban society was deepened. It is worth noting that Raúl Castro and Che were already Marxists by this time; neither, however, was a communist.

In 1957, Herbert Matthews, a journalist for the *New York Times*, would report that Castro had "a political mind rather than a military one. He has strong ideas of liberty, democracy, social justice, the need to restore the Constitution, to hold elections. He has strong ideas on economy, too, but an economist would consider them weak." Matthews said Castro expressed no animosity toward the United States, and he quoted him as saying, "Above all we are fighting for a democratic Cuba and an end to the dictatorship" (Matthews 1957).

From their base in the mountains, the rebel band reorganized and grew into an effective fighting force, often taking weapons and gaining new recruits from captured soldiers. At the same time, the 26th of July Movement kept up the pressure in the cities. Batista's heavy-handed response brought death or torture to thousands. Altogether, 20,000 civilians died in the fighting, creating deep popular anger against anyone associated with the regime. Batista's political support crumbled, as did the army with it. This same scenario of an isolated, repressive dictator vulnerable to revolutionary insurrection would repeat itself in 1979 when the Sandinistas overthrew the Somoza regime in Nicaragua.

In January 1959, Batista fled. Castro and his guerrilla forces moved across the country toward Havana, slowly, gathering support and adulation along the way. They entered Havana in February with wild and enthusiastic crowds. Fidel did not make himself part of the new revolutionary government, but no one could rival his political influence. His guerrilla force rapidly transformed itself into the new national army, stepping into the void left by the total collapse of Batista's forces. This makeover of the military meant that the rebels would have the decisive element of power on their side in shaping the new order. Castro had something going for him that Jacobo Árbenz of Guatemala lacked when overthrown in 1954, and Allende too in Chile in 1973—that is, control over the coercive apparatus of government. However, we should not exaggerate this single factor. The Sandinistas would take power in 1979, and they too controlled the armed forces. Yet they lost control of government only 11 years later.

Batista's collapse surprised everyone. Superficially, it seemed as though Cuba's new leaders had defied the notion that revolutions require patient organizing. Perhaps Latin American governments everywhere were weak and doomed to collapse—if only a dedicated band of rebels would dare to take up armed struggle. A new theory, a "revolution in the revolution," as the French writer Regis Debray (1967) put it, took hold in the form of the theory of the "armed *foco*." Rather than concentrate patiently on developing a social base among workers and peasants, the "armed *foco*" theory stressed insurrection. This view failed to take into account adequately the importance of broad opposition to Batista in the cities organized by the 26th of July Movement. It also assumed wrongly that other Latin American states were as weak as that of semi-colonial Cuba, and it failed to recognize that the United States and these states were also analyzing why Batista had fallen, to prevent the same thing from happening elsewhere. But the gospel of revolution spread by Cuba was embraced by a generation of young Latin American leftists. Here at last was a leader, Fidel Castro, ready to make a real social revolution. In the 1960s, Cuba's young rulers saw their revolution as a harbinger of change on a global scale and supported young Fidelistas elsewhere.

Once Washington realized that Fidel Castro was determined to carry out his agenda of social and economic reform, the Eisenhower administration reacted as it had to efforts by Árbenz to make radical change in Guatemala in 1954. The Central Intelligence Agency developed a campaign of propaganda, sabotage, and economic sanctions against the new regime, measures continued by presidents John F. Kennedy (1960–1963) and Lyndon Baines Johnson (1963–1968). Perhaps Castro and his close collaborators would have moved against dissenters in any case, but Washington's external threats and subversion reinforced an inhospitable climate for tolerance of opposition. In this climate, the new government turned to dealing with the popular rage directed toward the dictator and his circle, who had committed gross atrocities, including assassinations and tortures. Batista had left the country on a mobster's plane, but most of his henchmen were left behind. Many were put on trial, and 550 were executed. These actions prevented mobs from exacting their own revenge, but the firing squads alarmed some parts of the anti-Batista coalition and splits began to appear.

They widened as Fidel Castro and his companions were prioritizing their radical agenda of redistribution and social restructuring, and the imperial power with a long history of intervention against such regimes grew restive 90 miles away. The Cuban revolutionaries were well aware that the United States had destabilized and overthrown an elected reformist government in Guatemala only five years before. Washington saw Castro defying U.S. hegemony in an unprecedented way and feared the establishment of a communist regime in the hemisphere. In some ways, the latter proved a self-fulfilling prophecy.

On a visit to the United Nations in New York in 1960, Castro shocked the U.S. State Department and many in his own entourage by refusing to ask for economic aid, a symbolic demonstration of his determination not to subordinate Cuban sovereignty to Washington's influence. Upon his return, Castro consolidated his popular base of support by implementing a far-reaching land reform, expropriating (with compensation in bonds) all parcels of land of more than 1,000 acres. Other measures quickly followed. Big wage increases and price freezes were proclaimed. Mandatory reduction of rents alone redistributed about 15 percent of national income. In 1960, more than US$1 billion in U.S. property was expropriated, as Cuba seized control of its oil refineries, transportation system, and utilities. In that same year, hundreds of thousands of young students went to the countryside on a campaign to eradicate illiteracy. This far-reaching populist program is crucial to understanding how the rebel leadership was able to fend off U.S. intervention and consolidate a regime distinct from the kind of **pluralist** democracy originally promised by the young rebels. Heavily influenced by his brother Raúl, Fidel Castro looked to the Communist Party, the best-organized force on the left (but slow to have joined the revolution), to provide support, and they moved to rapidly transform the guerrillas into a new army. These actions alienated centrist leaders of the 26th of July Movement and even some leaders of the guerrilla army. By moving decisively toward radical change, the Cuban Revolution's young leaders were closing the door to the kind of negotiated pact that might have resulted in **polyarchy**, but they also had a free hand to implement radical economic and social changes. This stood in contrast to what happened when reforms implanted by electoral government failed to fully address the social question.

The United States stepped up its efforts to exploit divisions within the revolutionary forces, raising the specter of a repeat of the Guatemala episode of 1954. Castro forced dissident members of the governing council to resign. Some of them were arrested, charged with collaborating with the enemy, and imprisoned for decades. It is impossible to know how many opponents were jailed for collaborating with CIA subversion versus how many were jailed for merely dissenting from the direction Fidel was taking. Was fear of U.S. intervention driving repression, or was the imperialist threat a convenient excuse to repress?

Many opponents of Castro went into exile in Miami, where they plotted and organized a counterrevolution. At the direction of the Eisenhower administration, the CIA planned and encouraged acts of sabotage and terror, which were implemented during the Kennedy administration. For example, one six-man CIA team blew up a Cuban industrial facility in 1962, killing 400 workers. Among the angriest enemies of the new regime were *mafiosos* who had enjoyed Batista's patronage. They had turned Havana into one of the world's most decadent playgrounds for the rich, and now they had lost their glittery hotels and casinos to a bearded Marxist. We know that some of them eagerly collaborated with the CIA in attempts to assassinate Castro (Hinckle and Turner 1981). In response, the Castro regime cracked down on press freedoms and other civil liberties, hastening the exodus to Miami. Not all those fleeing to exile were collaborators with the old regime. Many were members of the middle class understandably alienated by the loss of their property or status as the revolution leveled the social class system. Others felt the democratic ideals expressed in the Moncada speech were being betrayed, or they rejected the growing influence of the Popular Socialist Party (PSP), Cuba's Communist Party in the pre-revolutionary era.

On April 17, 1961, the Kennedy administration put into action a plan devised under President Eisenhower (1952–1960), modeled on the overthrow of Árbenz. Cuban exiles trained by the CIA in southern Florida and Guatemala invaded Cuba at the Bay of Pigs. Just a few days before the invasion, the exile force had carried out the terrorist bombing of the seven-story El Encanto department store in Havana in an attempt to sow fear. The exile army was routed by Cuban forces at the beach, Playa Girón. Kennedy had temporized by withdrawing promised American air cover for the invasion, but more serious was the miscalculation that the Cuban population would rise against the new government. Castro defeated the invaders. The die was cast. Cuba now moved firmly into the communist bloc of nations. In October 1962, the world would be brought to the brink of Armageddon with the Cuban Missile Crisis. Castro permitted the Soviets to base intermediate-range missiles on the island. Kennedy reacted with a naval blockade that could have led to nuclear war. The Russians, without consulting Castro, agreed to pull their missiles from Cuba in exchange for, among other things, a promise from Kennedy that the United States would not invade Cuba again.

For Review

Why do Cubans celebrate July 26 as the anniversary of their revolution? What promises did Fidel Castro in the Moncada speech make about politics after the revolution? What kinds of social promises did he make? What actually happened? Why?

PUNTO DE VISTA: THE STRUGGLE FOR THE LEGACY OF CUBA'S JOSÉ MARTÍ

Fidel and Raúl Castro, Che Guevara, and the other "bearded ones" created the first and only self-proclaimed Marxist state in the hemisphere. However, the social thought of José Martí resonates more deeply with the Cuban people than Marxism does. Both the government and the exile community in Miami have sought to tie themselves to Martí, the former by linking his thought to socialism, the latter by linking it to liberalism. Both have an argument to make.

Martí never embraced socialism or Marxism, but he also feared that no significant change could come to Cuba unless deep social reform accompanied independence. Martí and his collaborators kept their ultimate plans hidden from view of the colony's elites. He feared that they would trade colonial status with Spain for a neocolonial dependency on the United States to protect their wealth and status. And though he admired much about the United States, where he lived and traveled, organizing Cubans abroad to support the fight for independence, he feared U.S. imperialism would overrun not only Cuba but all of Latin America. In an unfinished letter, written on the day he died, May 18, 1895, Martí told a friend,

Now I can write, now I can tell you how tenderly and gratefully and respectfully I love you and that home which I consider my pride and responsibility. I am in daily danger of giving my life for my country and duty, for I understand that duty and have the courage to carry it out—the duty of preventing the United States from spreading through the Antilles as Cuba gains its independence, and from overpowering with that additional strength our American lands. All I have done thus far, and all I will do, is for this purpose. I have had to work quietly and somewhat

indirectly, because to achieve certain objectives, they must be kept undercover; to say what they are would raise such difficulties that the objectives could not be achieved.
(Martí 1999: 234)

Martí went on to use an analogy drawn from the biblical story of David and Goliath. "I have lived in the monster and I know its entrails; my sling is David's."

Cuban exiles believe that by consolidating his personal power, Fidel Castro has contradicted Martí's spirit, that Martí never would have made Cuba so dependent on the Soviet Union, as it was before 1990. A Texas-based exile found this quotation from Martí to post on her website (xld.com/public/Cuba/marti.htm, accessed on February 13, 2004):

Socialist ideology, like so many others, has two main dangers. One stems from confused and incomplete readings of foreign texts, and the other from the arrogance and hidden rage of those who, in order to climb up in the world, pretend to be frantic defenders of the helpless so as to have shoulders on which to stand.

Another dissident website (Cuban-junky.com, accessed February 13, 2004) in the Netherlands argued,

All of Marti's teachings . . . condemn all despotic regimes and the abridgment of human rights. Furthermore, he goes on to denounce the lack of spirituality and type of arrogance that we find in the current dictatorship. For this reason, the publication of Marti's thoughts, in all its force, is of the greatest importance today. His beliefs, which can guide democracies and if heeded, offer them greater security, speak more eloquently against the Cuban apostasy than all the accusations that others might make.

Fidel sees himself as following in Martí's footsteps. Consider his remarks (Castro Ruz 1991) to a party congress called to deal with the harsh economic conditions threatening the revolution in the wake of the collapse of the Soviet Union in 1991:

> The world is looking at Cuba today with great hope. The world wants us to resist and win because it will be their victory. The world admires this small country. The world admires this island of freedom and dignity that defies all and is capable of defying all. The world admires the Cuba of today and will admire it more and more, to the extent that we are capable of courage, that we are capable of fighting, and that we are capable of winning.

Martí without a doubt saw himself as a liberal republican. After all, Marxism in his lifetime was largely a European intellectual and working-class movement. The Russian Revolution was two decades away. But he also, like Bolívar, believed true independence required deep social and economic change. Cuba had to become a "country for all," he said, cognizant that slavery had left a racial hierarchy that had to be overturned by revolutionary means.

Point/Counterpoint

So who has the better claim to Martí's legacy—the exiles or Havana?

If you say "the exiles," how do you respond to the argument that the more moderate parts of the coalition that fought Batista would have ultimately subordinated the Cuban Revolution to Washington's hegemony and failed to achieve the social gains (health care, education, more equality for Afro-Cubans and women) made by the Fidelistas?

If you say "Havana," how do you respond to the fact that Martí never embraced Marxism and, like Fidel in his Moncada speech, envisioned Cuba as a republic after independence from Spain?

For More Information

See Esther Allen and Roberto Gonzalez Echevarria, *José Martí: Selected Writings* (New York: Penguin Classics, 2002). The PBS program *Latino Americans* has an episode on José Martí at http://video.pbs.org/video/2365053101.

▪ Consolidation of the Cuban Revolution

Havana met the U.S. challenge not only by repressing dissidents but also by mobilizing the population to defend the revolution. Most important were a militia and Committees for the Defense of the Revolution (CDRs). The CDRs, which continue to exist today in a less central role, are composed of neighborhood residents who volunteer to participate in revolutionary activities in their neighborhood. They formed a nationwide grassroots network that exercises surveillance over dissidents, but as neighborhood organizations they also carry out a range of other functions. They intervene against domestic violence and check on the welfare of children. In the 1960s until approximately 2010, they provided a low-technology apparatus for security against the infiltration of Cuban exiles intent on carrying out sabotage. They continue to exist today but have been significantly scaled back. Walking major cities, one sees many CDRs closed or with old men (mostly) in rocking chairs out front. Other mass organizations and local government "popular power" organizations have more responsibility for social programs.

Fidel Castro declared himself a Marxist–Leninist in 1961, but the communist party (that is, the PSP) remained but one element in a revolutionary coalition. The ruling group displaced the old party in 1962 and formally declared itself the Partido Comunista de Cuba (PCC; Cuban Communist Party) in 1965. Still, no party congress was held until 1975. The decisive move toward the economic and political model of the Soviet Union came after a series of economic setbacks, most notably a failure to reach the goal of a 10-million-ton sugar harvest in 1970. The objective had been to capture a larger share of the world sugar market and use the profits for an ambitious program of economic development. The country's entire human and physical infrastructure was thrown into an effort that fell 2.4 million tons short, an economic disaster. Facing crisis, Cuba joined the Eastern bloc and synchronized its economy with these nations. The Cuban leadership abandoned humanist economic ideas implemented by Che Guevara, who thought that Cuba's "new men" (presumably women too?) could voluntarily work in the spirit of socialism, something he offered as an alternative to the model of centralized planning promoted by the Soviets. Another factor was that by 1970 it was clear that revolutions elsewhere in Latin America were unlikely to happen. The Soviets were relieved because in this era they were more interested in détente than confrontation with the United States. Facing U.S. hostility and an economic blockade by Washington, Cuba pursued better relations with Latin American governments.

To this day, the PCC remains the only legal party in Cuba, but its relationship to Cuban civil society has been more complicated than it was in other communist nations in Eastern Europe. Before the PCC became the official party of the revolution, mass organizations (CDRs, women, unions, rural workers, youth, and so forth) linking the society to the state had been created. In addition, the Communist Party in Batista's time was still adhering to the idea that socialism would only come at a later stage, and in some ways they opposed the more radical agenda of the Castros and Che. By 1970, the Fidelistas had displaced many older communist leaders from leadership of the party.

There is no disputing the fact that the PCC is the most powerful institution in Cuba, but the party does not nominate or campaign for candidates. That does not prevent it, however, from stepping in to veto the candidacy of any office-seeker who advocates radical free-market reforms or multiparty politics. The party can exert strong influence over the state bureaucracy and major social institutions. You can rise to significant positions of authority and not be a member of the party, but you cannot rise or keep those positions if the party decides you are unfit.

Was Fidel Castro a closet communist before 1960? Was he sincere about restoring political democracy? Had he immediately called elections after taking power, could he have delivered on the social and economic agenda promised in the Moncada speech? Years later, would Castro warn Salvador Allende in Chile (see chapter 7) that a revolutionary social and economic change is incompatible with liberal democracy? The Cuban leaders might remind us that they had tried electoral democracy, and it had failed—for example, after the 1933 revolt against Machado.

It was Machiavelli (1947: 48) who noted 450 years earlier that for new rulers, "[A]bove all it is impossible not to earn a reputation for cruelty since new states are full of dangers."

The Italian thinker also warned that only "armed prophets" succeed in founding new states; "unarmed prophets" fail. Cuba's new rulers acted accordingly. Fidel Castro and his comrades relied on swift and effective suppression of opposition to consolidate their power; to this day, Cuban leaders operate under a siege mentality, justifying repression of dissent deemed outside the boundaries of the revolution.

Machiavelli also warned against excessive reliance on cruelty and fear, counseling new rulers to commit necessary cruelties early so that they do not alienate the people in the longer run. That lesson also seems to pertain to Cuba. The hardcore Cuban-American opposition in the United States seeks to maintain the image of the Castros as mass murdering dictators. To the extent they deserve that reputation, it is largely based on the public trials of Batista's henchmen in the first two years of the revolution. Today, dissidents are often detained, and prison conditions are harsh for those incarcerated for long terms for political crimes. However, states of siege and death squads are unknown in Cuba. We may judge the Castros harshly for the violations of human rights in Cuba, but they pale in comparison to the crimes of many regimes friendly to the United States since the revolution.

Those who think that force is the only factor holding the regime together are overlooking the significant accomplishments of the Cuban Revolution and the political spaces it opened for significant public participation in shaping policies. In addition to the CDRs, Cubans are integrated into government and politics through "mass organizations" that are formed by artists, women, labor unions, and so on. Even among Cubans who have become disaffected with the regime, many remain proud of Cuba's place on the world stage; they may want change, but there remains a deep commitment to defense of its sovereignty. Cubans tend to view their army positively because of its performance in Africa in the 1970s and 1980s, especially in Angola and Namibia, where it backed new governments against rebels backed by the apartheid regime of South Africa. The army fought impressively against a white South African military force in battle in 1988. The army today no longer has the capability to fight so far abroad, but it has been entrusted with managing much of the tourism sector, the most important generator of foreign exchange today.

In February 2013, Raúl Castro (at age 81) was reelected to a five-year term, but he promised not to seek another one; he did not but remains the head of the PCC. The first leaders not to fight in the 1959 revolution will soon hold the reins of power, and they already have begun governing today. Without the prestige of that struggle to their credit, can a new generation hold the allegiance of Cubans fatigued by decades of sacrifice? Do Cubans still see socialism as the way to develop their economy and keep their independence from the colossus 90 miles away? Did limited reforms whet their appetite for more capitalism? We address these issues in the next section.

For Review

Around 1970, how did Cuba's political system change from what it had been in the first years after the revolution? In what ways is Cuba's political system, as it has evolved, like the old Soviet Union and Eastern bloc communism? How is it different?

Taking Stock of Cuba's Revolution

Cuba's social accomplishments are what have always attracted admiration in Latin America, but they have been put in doubt since the Eastern bloc communist states collapsed between 1989 and 1991. Suddenly, Cuba lost almost 87 percent of its trade, including imports of vital machinery, fertilizer, and energy. Between 1989 and 1993, oil imports were more than halved, leading to planned, rolling blackouts. In these four years, the size of the economy was cut in half. It is difficult to find any comparable case among the world's nations where such contraction occurred; however, the system survived, and after 1994 the economy began to recover.

By 2014, the economic situation had much improved but not yet recovered to pre-1990 standards. It is worth reviewing where Cuba stood before the Soviet demise, because to some extent the survival of the regime can be attributed to its social accomplishments. Also, these statistics represent a standard of living that still represents "normality" for Cubans, even in times like the present, when they are hard to sustain under the pressure of the Trump administration and the threats posed in 2020 by the coronavirus pandemic.

By the early 1980s, Cuba had dramatically reduced infant mortality from 60 per 1,000 to 19 per 1,000 (the U.S. rate was 14 at the time), largely by eliminating gastrointestinal inflammation and respiratory infection. The number of medical practitioners was doubled, despite the fact that most of Cuba's existing doctors had fled the island in the early 1960s. Malaria, diphtheria, and polio were eliminated. Advances against tuberculosis were recorded. In 1959, there were 18 refrigerators per 100 homes; in 1985, there were 63. There were 49 radios per 100 homes in 1959; by 1985, there were 135. There were only six televisions per 100 homes in 1959; in 1985, there were 79. Before the revolution there were 1.3 million housing units, of which only half had access to electricity; by 1982, of 2.4 million housing units, 79 percent had access to electricity. The literacy rate was 32 percent before the revolution; by the 1980s, it was 98 percent. In the days before the Internet, the United Nations said that every country should have 100 newspaper copies, 50 radio receivers, and 20 cinema seats for every 1,000 people. Cuba was the only Third World country to meet all of these criteria.

Although the other economies of Latin America contracted by 8 percent in the 1980s, the "lost decade," Cuba's grew by 33 percent. The real material conditions of Cuban life improved in the 1980s. A good comparison can be made to the second-largest Spanish-speaking Caribbean country, the Dominican Republic. Cubans lived 12 years longer, on average, than Dominicans. Infant mortality was four times higher in Santo Domingo than in Cuba. Illiteracy had been eradicated in Cuba; the literacy rate was only 77 percent in the Dominican Republic. Cuba had twice as many doctors per capita and 8.5 times as many nurses. Unemployment in Cuba was 5 percent; the informal sector and unemployed rate were more than 60 percent in the Dominican Republic. Cuba's most important source of foreign earnings was sugar exports; the Dominican Republic relied more on remittances (money sent home) from emigrants.

Despite recovery after 1994, Cubans were still coping with shortages 20 years later in 2014. By this time, tourism, exports of nickel (used to make steel), and remittances from Cubans living abroad had replaced the sugar industry as the most important source of foreign exchange. In 2002, the government closed down half of the sugar mills. Fortunately for Cubans, political events in Venezuela had brought an ally, President Hugo Chávez, capable of relieving some of the pain. Discounted Venezuelan oil eased energy shortages in that period. A combination of urban gardens and increased production of fruit and vegetables in the countryside had improved diets. In 2008, Raúl Castro, having taken over leadership after the retirement of his brother, began to lift some regulations and open some space for markets. But even before the Trump administration began to twist the tourniquet, which had been somewhat loosened in the Obama years, there were signs of increasing inequality, threatening the moral authority that carried the Cuban system through the terrible 1990s. Minimum nutritional standards were being met, but meat, eggs, and other common goods were in short supply. More ominously, for the first time in 50 years, slums and social exclusion were beginning to reappear in urban areas.

Ironically, Cuba's success in education may be breeding frustration. A highly educated workforce lacks job opportunities in Cuba and can earn much more abroad. Many have looked to immigrate legally or illegally to the United States. Women and Afro-Cubans, who benefited the most from post-revolutionary advances, suffered the most from the economic contraction of the 1990s. Women had to absorb more of the stress that difficult economic conditions placed on the family. Despite enormous progress in reducing racism in Cuban society, Afro-Cubans were still disproportionately in occupations most affected by cuts, and some discriminatory practices reappeared.

The benefits from highly discounted oil provided by Venezuela could disappear entirely should the party (the United Socialist Party of Venezuela—PSUV) of Chávez, who died in March 2013, lose control of government. As it is, the economic collapse of Venezuela has already reduced scarce energy resources on the island. Global oil prices had plummeted to under $30, so that has eased the pain, but at the same time Trump administration sanctions of oil companies doing business with Cuba put strains on supplies.

Washington seeks to prohibit not only its own citizens and companies from doing business in Cuba, but also those of other countries (see chapter 16). Pressure increased after the release of many Cuban political dissidents from jail in the summer of 2010. A majority of the Miami Cuban community favors ending the blockade, but its powerful anti-Castro lobby remains firmly opposed. The Obama administration (2008–2016) lifted many restrictions on travel and on the ability of Miami Cubans to send remittances to relatives. Under "people-to-people" programs made available by travel agencies in the United States, most Americans were able to travel easily to Cuba. Americans could still go legally as of early 2020, but the Trump administration has cut off all flights to and from Cuba other than flights between Miami and Havana. It also has made it much more difficult for Cubans living in the U.S. to send money and other resources to family on the island.

Sugar prices continue to widely fluctuate but have been overall somewhat higher since 2008. However, yields are lower, partly because of a deliberate policy of reducing dependence on sugar exports, but also because of inadequate capital to renovate farms and mills. At the same time, despite repeated experiments, the agricultural economy languishes. The physical infrastructure—communications, roads, railroads, etc.—on the island is in disrepair. And with all Caribbean nations, rising seas and severe hurricanes take a devastating toll. The country is benefiting from a large investment made in a pharmaceutical industry whose patents and exports of medicine are a source of export earnings. But despite still having a health system that is the envy of the Third World, common medicines are in short supply. A black market has appeared for drugs and other basic goods, eroding social solidarity.

Human Rights, One-Party Rule, and Cuba's Uncertain Future

Cuban politics is more complex than the simple image of dictatorship so often portrayed in the U.S. media. How the Cuban political system actually functions, and what exactly the balance is between consent and repression, is hard to answer.

Visitors to Cuba are often struck by the lack of heavily armed police and military, a common sight in other Latin American countries. Assassinations, disappearances, and states of siege, common throughout much of "democratic" Latin America, have not occurred at all in Cuba. However, there are political prisoners, and counts vary. Amnesty International in a 2018 report listed 18 prisoners of conscience, and its reports also list a number of ways that dissidents are kept in line by methods other than jailing, for example, by discrimination in employment. The Human Rights Watch World Report for 2019 estimated that there were 2,000 detentions (i.e., people taken into custody by police and later released) between January and August 2018. Most of these detentions are used to break up public protests. Prison conditions can be harsh, and there are reports of beatings of detainees.

Cuban elections (see Roman 2003) are contested by multiple candidates, open to all, not just party members. Elections are held for local, provincial, and national assemblies. At lower levels, many successful candidates are not PCC members, but PCC members are prevalent at higher levels. Candidates present themselves in meetings at the local level; these meetings in the past were well attended and vibrant, but in recent years they have fallen off in both respects, especially among the young. Incumbents often lose (Roman 2003). Mass organizations can influence the outcome and pressure officials in office. Many economic policies are debated and discussed at grassroots meetings and in these organizations. The year 2018 saw Cuba write a new constitution that mostly incorporated social reforms but few political ones. The process certainly was "guided" by the PCC, but grassroots assemblies across the island involved millions in discussions before the new text was approved by over 90 percent in a secret vote in February 2019. The PCC's monopoly over party politics was off the agenda from the start, but the party does not appear to control leaders of groups or government agencies in the way Eastern European parties did under communism.

Usually, the general direction of policy, especially economic policy, has been set by the PCC, and for many years debate would occur only after Fidel—or now Raúl—had pronounced the matter open for debate. For example, the decision to allow private business to operate was a matter of policy set from above; how large those businesses may be or how they are taxed is subject to discussion and debate.

Clearly, Fidel Castro had played a crucial role in Cuban politics for nearly 50 years. During Fidel's illness in 2006–2007, Raúl took center stage; he formally became president of the Council of State in 2008. Contrary to what Miami and Washington hoped, Cubans seemed to react more with concern than with elation at the prospect of life without Fidel. Raúl made several cautious but significant moves. For the first time, Cubans could own cell phones and personal computers. Farmers were told that they could produce and sell crops grown on up to 100 acres of land, an attempt to rectify a situation in which Cuba imports 80 percent of its food. Raúl opened the media to facilitate criticism of the government, and millions of suggestions for change have been generated from thousands of grassroots meetings.

In August 2010, Raúl Castro announced that as many as 1.3 million state employees would be discharged and expected to find work in the private sectors. To absorb these workers (one-quarter of the workforce), the government has been allowing small private businesses to form. Some observers think Cuba might be headed for the Chinese model—a one-party state that retains control over the most important economic sectors (finance and key industries) but otherwise aims to produce economic growth through capitalism and the market. In January 2013, the government lifted the requirement for Cubans to secure an exit visa to travel abroad.

Raúl Castro articulated this as modernizing socialism, not compromising it. However, greater political space for the market and private property potentially threatens one of the regime's key political resources, the sense of the population that they are all making a common sacrifice and that egalitarianism prevails in distribution of goods and services. These were the political resources that allowed the regime to survive the devastating economic consequences of the collapse of the Soviet Union in 1991. The right to own cell phones and computers and to travel is indeed liberalization—but along with the good (more freedom to communicate and criticize) comes the bad. Only those who can afford consumer goods, tickets abroad, and good Internet service can fully enjoy the new freedom (just as under capitalism, it should be noted). A Cuban who receives US$100 per month from relatives in Florida can live a comfortable life because he or she does not pay for health, education, or housing and can buy basic foodstuffs at subsidized prices. Cubans without relatives abroad continue to struggle. And to start up a small business requires capital—which has to be accumulated or provided by relatives abroad. In either case, that favors some Cubans more than others, and it favors white males more than blacks and women.

In 2019, Miguel Díaz-Canel, 52, a former education minister, became president of Cuba. In addition, the constitutional revision created for the first time the position of prime minister, which was filled by the president in December 2019. All indications are that Díaz-Canel would continue the economic and (more limited) political openings championed by Castro. However, the Castros (and those of their comrades from the Sierra Maestra who are still living) enjoy a prestige that no successor can match because of the heroic mythology surrounding the 1959 revolution. It will be a challenge for the PCC to take on this role institutionally. As in any political system, there are factions within the party and government with different degrees of interest in broader reforms. By 2017, 40 percent of Cubans (including some still formally employed by the state) were working as "*cuenta propistas*" (on their own account), and some were operating small construction companies, restaurants, taxies, repair shops, and so forth. A small middle class, but large enough to provide a consumer market for other producers, had visibly emerged.

A key issue for the PCC but also more broadly for all Cubans is to what extent market forces should be allowed to allocate resources. The evidence for market reform undermining the egalitarian culture comes mostly from studies of prices and incomes, but Cuba's economy is monetized far less than the vast majority of countries in the world. Recently a team of Italian and Cuban researchers took a novel approach by examining the assets of households. Their study of inequality of households looked into changes over the period 2008 to 2014, and they take into account not only wages and income (monetary assets) but also goods and services distributed by the state (such as health care, rationed goods, transport). These include tangible ones, such as appliances, tools, furniture, etc., and less tangible ones, such as skills that enable people to exchange services with one another. They found that by monetary measures Cubans who work in the state sector, still about 70 percent of the work force, cannot cover their basic needs, "no matter how austere," from their pay. There has emerged, they say, a small sector that has "relatively high personal monetary incomes." However, they add,

> [T]the capability on the part of the state to ensure universal access to the so-called "equality spaces" (by means of nonmarket allocation of services, goods and assets) remains far superior to what would be the norm in countries with a similarly low degree of economic development. This structural feature is at the heart of the "Cuban paradox", i.e. the well-known stylized fact that Cuba's degree of human development compares favorably to those of the most advanced developing countries—and also to those of many developing and even (in some domains) developed OECD countries.
>
> (Echeverría et al. 2019: 366)

This relatively optimistic outlook on how market mechanisms may influence Cuban society was based upon a study in years when relations with the United States were improving, and that has been anything but the case since 2016. Additionally it only considers economic inequality but not the way the growth of a private civil society may change the relationship among the state, the PCC, and various groups. Cuban unions are largely populated by state workers, but now many more workers in small offices, restaurants, cafes, and so forth no longer are represented. Owners of small businesses want to expand; restaurants and beauty salons want to be free to buy from private wholesalers, not just the state; workers in state jobs in vital areas like health care are being drawn into working as waiters or drivers in the tourist sector. A family can open a restaurant in a spare room, but only those with a relative abroad may be able to provide the capital to buy an espresso coffee machine.

The PCC and the government try to "update" the Cuban economy without abandoning socialism, but questions about social justice will inevitably arise, and political processes to determine "who gets what, when and how" will have to address them. Besides, allocating resources among employment sectors and labor vs. capital, there is considerable justifiable concern that with the opening of market forces racial and gender divides will also widen. While both women and Afro-descendent Cubans without doubt made gains under the revolution, deep-seated prejudices remain.

My own view, based on several trips to Cuba, is that there are many Cubans who want a "regime transition" in the sense of more room for market mechanisms and political pluralism but without abandonment of three things that are overwhelmingly valued in Cuba. One is personal security; Cuban children play all night, and neighborhoods are secure from crime. Another is the remarkable healthcare system; and the third is free access to high-quality education at all levels. However, personal security without ever-present armed police depends upon a sense of solidarity that can erode if gender, class, and racial gaps widen. The health care and education systems require resources that demand productivity gains, which have thus far been hard to achieve, and skilled professionals in these sectors are not among the minority of Cubans who have formed a small consumer class. Finally, educated young people are leaving Cuban universities with limited opportunities for careers. They may find similar limitations if they emigrate, but living on an island so close to the material attractions to the north is frustrating to many, and alienation among the younger generations is growing.

Many on the outside of the island, especially in the large exile community, expected that the passing of Fidel Castro would usher in regime change. Cuba is changing, but thus far the regime, the "order of things," on the island has not undergone a transition of the kind we have examined in the prior two chapters. That is not to say there are no scenarios where the Cuban regime collapses and undergoes a transition more like that which occurred in Eastern Europe. One can imagine the regime shifts to a gray, bureaucratic party dictatorship, like the ones that prevailed in communist Eastern Europe. Yet another possibility is the emergence of a Cuban version of China's hybrid state, one that mixes one-party rule with a market economy. However, one can also imagine a future in which Washington returns to engagement and eases economic pressures, widening the possibility of liberalization and defending the social gains of the revolution as trumping these alternatives. Although a "transition to democracy" of the sort that happened in Eastern Europe, Brazil, or the Southern Cone might not happen, so too the Cuban people might construct an alternative unforeseen by Washington, the Castros, or the Miami exile community.

Despite the sanctions imposed by Trump after 2016, international pressure has continued to mount on the United States to lift the economic blockade (which the U.S. calls an "embargo") that it imposed on Cuba in 1962. On March 25, 2020, a cohort of Cuban doctors and medical technicians flew to Italy to help treat thousands of patients with COVID-19 in the hard-hit region of Lombardy, Italy. The U.S. State Department issued an absurd warning, via Twitter, against accepting Cuban humanitarian support. "Host countries seeking Cuba's help for #COVID-19 should scrutinize agreements and end labor abuses," the message stated. "#Cuba offers its international medical missions to those afflicted with #COVID-19 only to make up the money it lost when countries stopped participating in the abusive program." The countries referenced were Brazil and Bolivia, where the conservative presidents that had replaced **Pink Tide** governments had ended Cuban medical aid agreements. The U.S. message is even more tone-deaf than it appears. Cuba has a track record of developing antiviral drugs, and its program for rapidly dispensing aid in response to hurricanes is well known outside of the United States.

The interesting question about U.S.-Cuban relations just a few years ago was whether the end of economic sanctions by the United States would boost the regime by giving the economy a lift, or whether the sudden influx of U.S. tourists and consumer culture would ultimately further undermine the egalitarian values, the legacy of Jose Martí's influence over Cuban national identity. The question now is whether the Trump administration has definitively ended the U.S. opening to Cuba. You might note that I refer to the "U.S. opening," not the "Cuban opening." The Cuban government has always sought more trade and tourism with the U.S.

For Review

How did the Cuban regimes survive the economic impact of the collapse of Eastern European communism? What dilemmas and difficulties does opening more space for the market pose for Cubans? To what extent have market reforms and the passing of the revolutionary generation brought about changes in the political regime?

Insurgency, Revolution, and Post-Conflict Central America

We could have a lively debate about whether revolutions can happen without insurgencies—that is, armed revolutionary movements that attempt to overturn an existing regime. Here, we concentrate on the way revolutionary insurgencies may leave a significant mark on politics even without succeeding. In fact, the Zapatista uprising in Chiapas, Mexico, has questioned the very idea that revolutionary movements should even aim to take over the state. Insurgencies by their nature require violence and a paramilitary organization. If successful in taking power or gaining a share of power (as a result of a negotiated end of civil conflict), they bring this experience and culture into the state or politics.

The Central American nations experienced insurgencies in the 1980s. In the case of Nicaragua, an insurgency led by the Sandinista Front for National Liberation succeeded (1979) in taking power through a mass revolution. In two other cases, El Salvador and Guatemala, left-wing insurgencies failed to overthrow existing regimes but did achieve some significant democratic political reforms. The fallout reached Honduras, which was militarized as a base for U.S. intervention in these conflicts. By the end of a decade of acute civil violence, the civil wars were settled by negotiations, but the region as a whole was left with a troubling set of social questions left unresolved by the pacts ending armed conflict.

Revolutionaries seek support by offering answers to deep-rooted problems of poverty and injustice. These issues become more pressing, say some political scientists (Goldstone et al. 1991), when rising expectations are frustrated. This often happens when a period of economic growth feeds expectations in the population that life will get better, at least for their children, but instead things get even worse. If the benefits of growth fail to reach most people, that can also cause resentment. These factors seem to have been at work in the case of Mexico during the Porfiriato era (1876–1910; see chapters 5 and 8), and they were at work in Central America in the post–World War II era. The region saw high rates of economic growth generated by export booms. Just as in the Porfiriato period in Mexico, this boom disrupted rural economic and social life, and economic benefits were concentrated in a few hands.

In the period between 1850 and 1920, traditional life in much of the Central American countryside was uprooted by the force of **liberal modernization**. The process was complex, and peasants were not simply passive victims of the process (see Lauria-Santiago 1999). However, by the early twentieth century a new oligarchy had formed, and many peasants had been driven from the land to make room for export agriculture, mostly coffee and fruit. In El Salvador, the coffee *fincas* (plots of land) were generally owned by an elite so closely knit that it was known as the Fourteen Families. Oligarchies in other countries benefited from fruit plantations that were developed by foreign companies, such as Castle and Cook and the United Fruit Company. Neither economy generated the kind of export wealth that provided capital for industrialization in Mexico and most of South America. A new era of "modernization" began in the region after World War II, and once again peasants were victimized and oligarchs—old and new ones—benefited almost exclusively.

Allowing for some variation, we can say that El Salvador, Nicaragua, Honduras, and Guatemala all evolved into oligarchies—in which a small clique of wealthy elites ran the country with no regard for the broader interests of the people. A family clique came to dominate Nicaragua and ruled it like a private *hacienda*. In El Salvador, a proud, nationalist, landed oligarchy liked to run things themselves with the help of the military. In Guatemala, dominance of the foreign fruit companies suffocated the development of a local bourgeoisie. After the 1954 overthrow of the reformist President Árbenz, the fruit companies sold much of their land to wealthy or politically connected Guatemalans and to retired military officers. These elites had little experience or commitment to democracy, and they were heavily prejudiced against the nation's large Indigenous population.

After World War II, the World Bank encouraged Central American governments to embrace a strategy of development that involved borrowing money for infrastructure (roads, ports, etc.) and to take other measures to encourage investment in new exports. U.S. investors began to see the region as a place for investments in new forms of export agriculture and for light, labor-intensive industry, often working with local associates in the region. Central America recorded great increases in the export of nontraditional products, such as cotton, sugar, and meat, but also labor-intensive manufacturing products, such as blouses, jeans, and pajamas (Barry and Preusch 1986).

The new export model brought several consequences, including the emergence of some new elites and expansion of the middle class and the working class. At the other end of the social pyramid, thousands of peasant families were displaced from the land to make way for new pastures and plantations. They had to live on the margins and seek work from landowners or work in the new export factories. The new manufacturing sectors (making bras and pajamas; assembling transistor radios and TVs for export) could not absorb the displaced poor. In the 1960s the oppressed peasants, workers, and urban poor attracted organizers. This cadre was drawn from leftist students inspired by the Cuban Revolution and from clergy and Catholic lay workers inspired by social justice messages. The Second Vatican Council blew winds of change through Latin America as threatening to the oligarchies as those emanating from Havana.

On the surface, Central America's economic signs looked great between World War II and 1975. The economy was booming and diversifying. Then, the new economic model was slammed by the energy crisis that hit in 1974. The new export agriculture economy depended heavily on oil for crop dusters, transport, fertilizer, irrigation, and other inputs that had been much less important in the labor-intensive, prewar export economy. At the same time, consumers abroad were feeling the pinch of energy prices; demand for the region's exports slackened, and prices fell. By the end of the 1970s, the economies had stopped growing and debt was at record levels. The oligarchy showed little concern for the impact on the masses. Hundreds of thousands of additional landless and unemployed workers were available to answer the call for revolutionary change or to take jobs in the only growing sector, the military. The United States blamed Cuba for the unrest, and the oligarchy saw communism behind every call for reform.

Liberation Theology

Liberation theology emerged out of forces unleashed by the Vatican II council called by Pope John XXIII in 1962. Though less committed to change than John XXIII was, Pope John Paul II ratified the notion that Catholicism would have to address the concerns of the Third World, where a majority of its faithful lives. Latin American bishops at Medellín, Colombia, and at Puebla, Mexico, proclaimed their adherence in 1968 and 1979 to the doctrine of a "preferential option for the poor," a concept that gave momentum for clergy to work on behalf of social reform, even revolution.

Liberation theology grew out of the experience of clergy who came to identify with the needs of the poor as they carried out pastoral work. Their experiences and others shaped the development of the theological movement, not vice versa. Bishops attending the Latin American Episcopal Conference in Medellín endorsed the concept of *concientización*—the responsibility of clergy and delegates to educate the poor to their political rights. Although the earliest developments took place within Catholicism, the movement also gained a foothold within the swelling Protestant missionary movement and spread to Africa and Asia.

One of the central insights that liberation theologians, using Marxism as a tool of analysis, brought to the Church was recognition that, as an institution, it is shaped by social class conflict. More Catholics live in Latin America than anywhere else in the world. Because it is one of the poorest areas (only Africa is poorer) and the one with the widest gap between rich and poor, the shift in the Church inaugurated by Pope John made its greatest impact there. Some priests, nuns, and brothers adopted Marxism as a tool to understand how to put the preferential option into practice. Liberation theologians turned to Marxist analysis because it seemed pertinent to what their brethren were doing in the field, often drawing a violent reaction from oligarchs and generals.

In Central America, hundreds of clergy and lay "delegates of the word" worked to raise the consciousness of the poor and helped them self-organize, a process replicated in many other countries. These grassroots leaders formed "Christian base communities" where people met to discuss both the Bible and their local problems. Although some bishops were sympathetic, after 1980 the Church hierarchy began to assert opposition and roll back the movement somewhat. Catholicism stresses the role of ordained (male) priests as intermediaries between the faith and God. Only priests can say Mass and perform "transubstantiation"—the transformation of bread and wine into the body and blood of Christ, the central ritual of the Catholic Mass. The emergence of base communities led by lay "delegates," basing their understanding of scripture on discussions rather than received wisdom from clerics, threatened the patriarchal authority of the hierarchy.

Radical Christians often participated in developing a broad network of women's organizations, Indigenous groups, human rights organizations, and other groups whose practices informed the development of liberation theology. More and more, they interpreted the Bible as a mandate to struggle for social justice. The inspiration often came from peasants themselves who, having been taught to read by using the Bible as a text, often interpreted its stories quite differently from the standard, middle-class, developed worldview. They looked to stories of Jesus driving moneylenders out of the temple as condemnation of rapacious businesspeople. If it was harder for a rich man to get into heaven than for a camel to pass through the eye of a needle, then quite clearly God has a preference for the poor. In the Old Testament, prophets from God often appeared when his "chosen people" had gone astray from the principles of social justice, such as worshipping a golden calf.

The great example of the "praxis"—that is, the relationship between practice and social theory—advocated by liberation theology can be seen in the evolution of the greatest martyr of this movement, El Salvador's Archbishop Oscar Arnulfo Romero. Romero was assassinated for condemning repression in El Salvador in 1980, telling soldiers in his Sunday homily that they did not have to follow orders to kill in violation of God's law.

Romero assumed his position in 1977. The Salvadoran oligarchy was somewhat relieved that a more radical priest had not been appointed. Weeks later, Romero found himself officiating at the burial of his friend, Father Retulio Grande, who had been killed by landowners. Grande's murder led Romero to learn about and appreciate the courage of those clergy working with the poor to raise their material—not just spiritual—well-being. Father Grande was not organizing a peasant revolt but teaching peasants to read and dig wells, but in doing so, he was helping them reduce their dependence on landowners. The murder of Grande and others set Romero out on the road that led to his martyrdom at the hands of Salvadoran soldiers using U.S.-supplied weapons.

Faith-motivated activists often exerted a humanizing influence over their secular, revolutionary brethren. The Nicaraguan Sandinistas, for example, were as much influenced by changes in the Church as by any explicit Marxist doctrine. Tomás Borge, a communist and atheist and one of the founders of the Sandinista guerrilla movement, kept a crucifix on the wall of his office and wrote a book titled *Christianity and Revolution*. Borge said that his encounter with radical Christians helped him forgive a torturer who had brutally maimed him and raped his wife. The Somoza guardsman had fallen into his hands after the Sandinista triumph. Borge wrote a poem expressing how he would "take revenge" by insisting on the right of his torturer's "children to school and flowers" and would "show you the good in the eyes of my people," who although "always unyielding in combat" are also "most steadfast and generous in victory" (Borge n.d.).

To some clergy, Vatican II's call for the Church to adopt a preferential option for the poor was a call to revolution. To others, it was not just religious insubordination but a heresy to suggest that the Church should profess one social philosophy more holy than another. Revolutionaries in Central America portrayed the opposition of conservative bishops in Nicaragua to the revolutionary Sandinista government of the 1980s as hypocritical, charging that the hierarchy had itself taken sides, aligning with the business community.

As the conflicts in Central America were becoming more intense, more conservative members of the Catholic hierarchy were laying plans to roll back the influence of liberation theology. They were heartened when Bishop Karol Wojtyla, a Pole from communist Eastern Europe, assumed the papacy as John Paul II in 1978. Aided by conservative Cardinal Joseph Ratzinger, who would himself accede to the papacy as Pope Benedict XVI in 2005, the new pope began to discipline leftist theologians and radical bishops. The new pope, though he considered neoliberalism to be "savage capitalism," had experienced the repressive communist regime in his native Poland and had little sympathy for democratizing the Church's hierarchical structure. To hasten the exit of leftist bishops, John Paul instituted mandatory retirement of bishops at the age of 75 years (though he did not follow his own policy in this regard). For example, he forced Bishop Samuel Ruiz's resignation from the Chiapas diocese in 1999 and appointed a less outspoken successor.

Still, the institutional Church is unlikely to return entirely to its traditional position as defender of the privileges of the local oligarchy. Many clergy who do not fully embrace the philosophy of liberation theology have lent the authority and resources of the Church to defense of human rights. Also, Catholicism faces intense competition from Protestantism in Latin America, so it can no longer take the adherence of the poor majority in Latin America for granted. Religion and Catholicism shape Latin American social struggles, but the reverse is also true.

PUNTO DE VISTA: LIBERATION THEOLOGY IN LATIN AMERICA— SHOULD THE CHURCH HAVE A "PREFERENTIAL OPTION FOR THE POOR"?

Pope Francis, since his accession in 2013, has said little directly on liberation theology, but his actions and willingness to meet with some prominent liberation theologians have encouraged many Latin American clergy.

CARTOON 9.1   Nicaraguan cartoonist Roger plays on the biblical saying: "It's easier for a camel to pass through the eye of a needle than for a rich man to enter heaven."

Source: *Cartoons From Nicaragua: The Revolutionary Humor of Roger*, Managua: Committee of U.S. Citizens Living in Nicaragua (1984), p. 31.

A document titled "Peace" issued by Latin American bishops meeting in Medellín, Colombia, in 1968 was a major statement on this movement. Following are excerpts. You can find the whole document at www.shc.edu/theolibrary/resources/medpeace.htm.

As the Christian believes in the productiveness of peace in order to achieve justice, he also believes that justice is a prerequisite for peace. He recognizes that in many instances Latin America finds itself faced with a situation of injustice that can be called institutionalized violence, when, because of a structural deficiency of industry and agriculture, of national and international economy, of cultural and political life, [quoting Pope Paul VI] "whole towns lack necessities, live in such dependence as hinders all initiative and responsibility as well as every possibility for cultural promotion and participation in social and political life," thus violating fundamental rights. This situation demands all-embracing, courageous, urgent and profoundly renovating transformations. We should not be surprised therefore, that the "temptation to violence" is surfacing in Latin America. One should not abuse the patience of a people that for years has borne a situation that would not be acceptable to anyone with any degree of awareness of human rights. . . .

Also responsible for injustice are those who remain passive for fear of the sacrifice and personal risk implied by any courageous and effective action. Justice and therefore peace conquer by means of a dynamic action of awakening (*concientización*) and organization of the popular sectors, which are capable of pressing public officials who are often impotent in their social projects without popular support . . .

We address ourselves finally to those who, in the face of injustice and illegitimate resistance to change, put their hopes in violence. With Paul VI we realize that their attitude "frequently finds its ultimate motivation in noble impulses of justice and solidarity." . . .

If it is true that revolutionary insurrection can be legitimate in the case of evident and prolonged "tyranny that seriously works against the fundamental rights of man and which damages the common good of the country," whether it proceeds from one person or from clearly unjust structures, it is also certain that violence or "armed revolution" generally "generates new injustices, introduces new imbalances and causes new disasters; one cannot combat a real evil at the price of a greater evil." . . .

To us, the Pastors of the Church, belongs the duty to educate the Christian conscience, to inspire, stimulate and help orient all of the initiatives that contribute to the formation of man. It is also up to us to denounce everything which, opposing justice, destroys peace.

In 2009, Pope Benedict (Joseph Ratzinger) sent a letter to a gathering of Brazilian bishops warning them about embracing liberation theology. He reminded them of an earlier pronouncement he had made:

It stressed the danger that is entailed in an a-critical acceptance on the part of certain theologians of theses and methodologies that derive from Marxism. Its more or less visible consequences consisting of rebellion, division, dissent, offence, and anarchy make themselves felt, creating in your diocesan communities great suffering and a serious loss of vitality. I implore all those who in some way have felt attracted, involved and deeply touched by certain deceptive principles of Liberation Theology to consider once again the above-mentioned Instruction, perceiving the kind light with which it is proffered. I remind everyone that "'the supreme rule of her [the Church's] faith' derives from the unity which the Spirit has created between Sacred Tradition, Sacred Scripture and the Magisterium of the Church in a reciprocity which means that none of the three can survive without the others" (John Paul II, Fides et Ratio, n. 55); and that in the context of Church bodies and communities, forgiveness offered and received in the name of and out of love for the Most Blessed Trinity, whom we worship in our hearts, puts an end to the suffering of our beloved Church, a pilgrim in the Lands of the Holy Cross.

Point/Counterpoint

Should the clergy restrict its work to pastoral mission, or should it denounce social injustice? Do you agree that *concientización* should be a responsibility of clergy?

If not, how do you respond to the bishop's argument that they have a moral responsibility to get involved? How would you respond to the argument that the Church has long taken sides on political and social issues, from the conquistadors to the present day?

If you believe that the clergy should take a position on social injustice and raise consciousness among the poor, then how do you respond to those who would argue that democracy requires separation of religion and politics? What answer would you give to a bishop who said that the Church should not discriminate against the rich? How would you respond to the argument that if the clergy takes on this role, the Church might lose some of its ability to mediate on human rights issues? Finally, how would you respond to the argument that without social consciousness, religion would just become the "opiate" of the masses?

For More Information

On liberation theology, a good source is Robert McAfee Brown, *Liberation Theology: An Introductory Guide* (Westminster/Know Press, 1993). Pope Benedict's full letter on liberation theology can be found at www.vatican.va/holy_father/benedict_xvi/speeches/2009/december/documents/hf_ben-xvi_spe_20091205_ad-limina-brasile_en.html.

For Review

Why was access to land a major issue in Central America leading up to the insurrections of the 1980s? How was the economy evolving in the cities? Religion is often viewed as an obstacle to revolutionary change. How did liberation theology bring that into question?

The Nicaraguan Revolution

Nicaragua until 1979 was ruled by the Somoza family, a regime inaugurated in 1934 with the help of the United States. Anastasio Somoza was the U.S.-appointed commander of the country's National Guard. The Guard was a constabulary trained by the Americans to fight the nationalist patriot José Augusto Cesar Sandino. Sandino had worked in Mex-

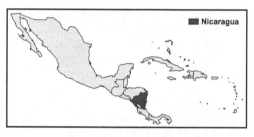

ico and had the support and sympathy of its revolutionary government when he took up arms against the U.S. Marines, who had occupied the country periodically since 1910. Sandino drew his support from Nicaragua's poor peasantry. In what was a forerunner of U.S. policy in Vietnam 35 years later, the United States decided to retreat from Nicaragua because the casualties inflicted by Sandino's forces were increasingly costly in political terms at home. The U.S. idea was to train a professional army that would carry on the fight against Sandino but stay neutral in political battles between liberal and conservative *caudillos*, allowing the country to settle conflicts through elections.

This early experiment in "democratization" imposed from abroad proved disastrous for the Nicaraguan people. Instead of a professional, apolitical military that would allow political disputes to be settled through elections, the U.S.-trained and armed Guard served as an instrument for Somoza, a modestly wealthy liberal landlord and patriarch of a family that used its power to amassed a huge fortune and repress all opponents (Millet 1977).

The elder Somoza was assassinated in 1956. His sons were just as ruthless as Batista in Cuba and even greedier. They used their power to extort other elites and move in on their wealth. After an earthquake devastated Managua in 1972, Anastasio Somoza Debayle used foreign aid to rebuild family businesses while withholding help from competitors. This induced many middle- and upper-class Nicaraguans to take their chances with the Sandinistas. Fearing a repeat of the 1959 episode in Cuba, the Carter administration (1976–1980) exhorted the dictator to leave, but he stubbornly refused to go. After the popular uprising showed how willing Nicaragua's people were to make the ultimate sacrifice for change, the Sandinista National Liberation Front (Frente Sandinista de Liberación Nacional, or FSLN) gained momentum. Somoza clung to power with air assaults and brutal repression. As the FSLN was closing in on Managua, Washington reluctantly abandoned the dictator. He fled on July 19, 1979. The collective leadership (nine *comandantes*) entered Managua to a cheering reception, like the one that greeted Fidel Castro in Havana in 1959.

The FSLN took power with an agenda of radical land redistribution, union organizing, political reform at home, and friendly relationships with Cuba. As in Cuba, there was euphoria and a spirit of national unity in the beginning. The Sandinista leadership and their supporters included an important component of grassroots Catholic clergy. Priests occupied three of the most important ministries in the new government—culture, education, and foreign relations. A significant gap opened between the hierarchy of the Church and many grassroots clergy over the role of religion in revolution.

The Cuban Revolution served as an inspiration for Sandinista programs in Nicaragua in a number of ways. The Sandinistas organized mass literacy brigades, carried out land reform, and implemented many other measures that resembled the mobilization campaigns of the early years of the Cuban Revolution. As in Cuba, mass organizations of peasants, Indigenous people, *barrio*-dwelling workers, and so on came into existence. Although the government kept an official distance from events in nearby El Salvador, sympathetic FSLN commanders and government officials lent support to the guerrillas fighting that country's military regime. Friendly relationships were established with Havana, irritating the United States. The Carter administration kept the door open and induced the Sandinistas to limit support to their Salvadoran brethren, but the election of hardline, anticommunist President Ronald Reagan in 1980 led to a change in policy.

The Reagan administration organized and armed a counterrevolutionary army—the *contras* (a name derived from the Spanish word *contrarrevolución*). This mercenary force touched off a bloody civil war that wracked the country, setting back further progress on social development after 1984. Reagan could do this in part because the Sandinistas had not carried out a bloody purge of Somoza allies, most of whom had escaped the retribution that was experienced by Batista's henchmen. Somoza's Guardsmen had been allowed to flee to Miami; no mass public trials or executions were held. As a result, forces from the old regime in Nicaragua were available to wage a counterrevolution with Washington's support. This raises an interesting question: Should we praise the Sandinistas for a generous and procedurally just policy toward their former enemies, or should we condemn them for naïveté in allowing their enemies to remain a threat?

The FSLN held power ten years before losing the 1990 elections. Besides impressive policies addressing the social question—literacy and health campaigns, land reform, and so on—they experimented with participatory democracy. In their first two years, they governed through a Council of State in which mass organizations (unions, women's groups, entrepreneurs, students, peasants, students, etc.) were directly represented. In 1982, under pressure from European and other governments, the FSLN sought international legitimacy by writing a constitution erecting a more familiar set of institutions, a **polyarchy**. The Council of State was replaced with a national assembly of representatives chosen by vote of the people for candidates nominated by political parties.

In the first elections in 1984 under the new constitution, the Sandinistas did well. They hoped the election would show the world that they were democratic and would put diplomatic pressure on the United States to end the *contra* war. However, intransigent sectors of the opposition, under direction of and with financing from the United States, decided to continue the war. It is difficult to sort out how much of the subsequent suffering in Nicaragua was due directly to the war or could be attributed to the actions of the Sandinistas. The U.S. government is estimated to have spent nearly US$1 billion in a ten-year campaign to oust the Sandinistas through military and political means, including a harsh campaign of terror that included burning down new schools and health clinics, killing teachers and doctors, mining the country's harbors, and causing as much havoc as possible. For the 1990 elections, Washington spent US$30 million (US$20 per voter) to influence the outcome (Robinson 1992: 60–65).

When the FSLN entered Managua, there was a shared collective leadership of nine *comandantes*, not one outstanding personality, like Fidel Castro. Daniel Ortega, one of the nine *comandantes*, was elected president in 1984. Already having emerged as first among equals after the 1979 triumph, Ortega gradually asserted control over the FSLN as it was transformed from an insurgency to a governing political party. Ortega had to respond to a difficult economic situation. The 1980s were Latin America's lost decade, which itself dictated austerity (Prevost and Vanden 1996), but he also faced the burden of fighting the *contras*, proxies for the United States. He had little choice but to bleed the economy to fight the war—exactly what the Reagan administration had hoped would happen. At the same time with the shift to polyarchy in 1984, the FSLN began to act more like a party of politicians eager to preserve power than a revolutionary party carrying out social transformation. No one in the party is more representative of this trend than Daniel Ortega, who returned to the presidency in 2006 and was twice re-elected afterwards.

In a major surprise, Nicaraguan voters voted in 1990 for Violeta Chamorro, whose husband was a crusading newspaper editor assassinated by Somoza's forces but who also opposed the FSLN. The brutal economic and military war waged by the United States helped make her promises of peace and reconciliation appealing, but it is likely that voters also punished the Sandinistas as Ortega and some former guerrillas drifted away from the masses. Voted out, the Sandinistas further tarnished their revolutionary credentials by transferring ownership of many assets taken from the Somoza dictatorship to the party or government officials, a practice known as the *piñata*. The FSLN did not just disappear. The Sandinistas could still rally labor and other social sectors to oppose neoliberal austerity measures, but the party just as often supported these measures in deals to protect themselves from prosecution for the *piñata*—and to protect Daniel Ortega from being prosecuted for alleged sexual abuse of his niece.

Chamorro inherited an impossible economic situation, but neither did she show much leadership in addressing the issues. The period between her leaving office in 1996 and Ortega's return in 2006 was largely a period of unseemly bargaining between the FSLN, now completely controlled by Ortega, and the old Liberal Party, itself deeply divided and corrupt. The Liberal Party (the party of Somoza) seemed to have learned nothing from the fall of the Somoza dynasty; the Sandinistas seemed mostly to have forgotten why they had won the revolution.

Still, the FSLN remained the most coherent single party in Nicaragua, on the right or left. In 2006 Ortega won election once again to the presidency; he was reelected in 2011 and 2016, and has made clear his intentions to run again in 2021. One clear sign of the FSLN's evolution was Ortega's acceptance of a severely restrictive ban on abortion, legislated in November 2012. Women were on the front line of battle during the revolution, and their mass organization after victory was one of the most influential sectors represented in the State Council. Thirty-two years later Nicaragua became one of only a handful of countries that ban abortions without any exceptions. On the other hand, there were ways that Nicaragua under Ortega remained aligned with more radical governments of the **Pink Tide**. The FSLN became staunch allies of Hugo Chávez and joined the Bolivarian Alliance for the Americas (ALBA), an economic integration scheme, promoted by Chávez, that was supposed to empower small-scale, worker-owned businesses and cooperatives. That conception of development was hardly compatible with the alliance that Ortega forged with Nicaragua's national business council, once a bitter enemy of the FSLN.

Ortega's deal making and cautious economic record made clear that the FSLN was no longer the party of revolutionary politics. Ortega cultivated a base of support among the poor and unionized workers, but in a corporatist style that limited their capacity to dissent from the neoliberal, export-led development model that the FSLN had once opposed. A tight circle of friends around Ortega and his wife, Rosario Murillo, including the national business confederation (which supported the *contras* in the 1980s), profited from the unholy alliance between capital and the FSLN.

In 2018 and 2019, Ortega's hold showed some fraying as protests against cuts to pensions were brutally put down by security forces, leaving 30 dead. Students joined in protest activities that led the government to outlaw all demonstrations in September. Mothers of prisoners, who had fled to a church after being attacked in a protest, became symbols of resistance and forced Ortega to release prisoners. In

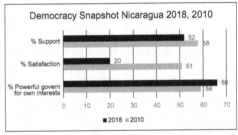

May 2019, five banks in the city of Masaya, a town legendary for its heroic uprising against the Somoza regime in 1979, were looted in mass attacks. The government blamed foreign interference from the U.S. for the violence. Given U.S. attempts to punish the Ortega government for its relations with Cuba and Venezuela, the charge of intervention could not be simply dismissed. However, the protest movements emerging in Nicaragua have their roots in anger with the economic and political dominance of a ruling family, just as it did when the young Sandinista rebels and Nicaragua's people chased the Somoza dynasty out of the country in 1979.

For Review

Who was Sandino and why was he an inspiration for the Nicaraguan Revolution of 1979? Who were the contras, and why were they supported by the United States? What factors led to the Sandinistas to be voted out in 1990? How are Daniel Ortega and the FSLN different today from what they were in the early 1980s?

El Salvador's Near Revolution

In El Salvador, military dictators and right-wing oligarchs, the "Fourteen Families" (see earlier), had dominated politics in partnership with the military since the era of **liberal modernization**. In 1934, they crushed an uprising led by Agustín Farabundo Martí, a communist union organizer whose followers were protesting the canceling of elections they were expected to win that year. The slaughter

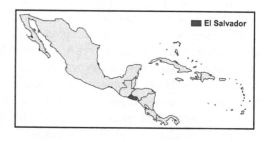

of 10,000–30,000 of the country's Indian population that year is simply known as *La Matanza* (Anderson 1971). In the 1960s, Christian and secular leftists began again to organize El Salvador's poor. As in the liberal modernization era, social and economic changes were shaking lives. New cotton and sugar plantations, as well as large ranches, had displaced many peasants from land that already provided only a meager living. Some fled for the cities, seeking jobs in labor-intensive factories producing pajamas, bras, electronic goods, toys, and so on for export north.

In this environment, religious and social justice activists made progress organizing unions, peasant leagues, and other organizations. They joined professional groups and reformist parties to challenge the Salvadoran oligarchy's monopoly of power. By the late 1970s, they had made significant progress, but they were blocked by the oligarchy and the army. In 1979, in the aftermath of the FSLN victory in Nicaragua, a ray of hope appeared when a military–civilian junta seized power and attempted to implement economic reforms and political reform. It appeared the country might become a democracy, but the right-wing oligarchy struck back, brutally, determined to crush change just as they had in 1934. As in Nicaragua, the insurgency took on the name of the popular hero of the earlier uprising and formed the Farabundo Martí National Liberation Front (FMLN), a coalition of five different guerrilla movements. A revolutionary civil war loomed (Armstrong and Shenk 1982).

The United States feared the oligarchy's resistance to change would lead to revolution, as it had in neighboring Nicaragua. The oligarchy had already instigated a coup against a reform-minded government in 1980. The ranks of the guerrilla forces and their supporters swelled. In response, but much to the consternation of the oligarchy, Washington invested heavily on organizing the election of a Christian Democrat, José Napoleón Duarte, in 1982. The Reagan administration sent civilian advisors to shore up the Christian democrats; at the same time, military aid was sent to keep the fledgling insurgency at bay.

The United States promoted new unions to rival ones that had connections with the left. Washington also promoted a land reform program aimed at creating a small capitalist peasant class, an effort to take the land reform issue away from the insurgents. The oligarchy, on the other hand, was accustomed to responding to "communist" threats in the way it had in 1934. It formed a political party (ARENA) that would eventually defeat the Christian Democrats in the 1989 elections. The founder of ARENA was Roberto D'Aubuisson, a former army death squad leader, notorious torturer (known as "Blow Torch Bob"), and author of the assassination of Monsignor Oscar Arnulfo Romero, the archbishop of San Salvador. Romero had become a spokesperson for the poor and an outspoken critic of the army's human rights atrocities. Romero had pleaded to U.S. president Jimmy Carter, "You say that you are Christian. If you are really Christian, please stop sending military aid to the military here, because they use it only

PHOTOS 9.1 & 9.2   View from the steps of the National Cathedral as Salvadoran troops open fire on mourners at the funeral of slain Archbishop Oscar Arnulfo Romero with weapons supplied the United States. How could this happen in a Catholic country? Does the United States apologize for its role in these events?

Sources: 9.1: Keystone/Getty Images.

9.2: Wikimedia Commons, Grupo Cinteupiltzin CENAR El Salvador.

to kill my people." Carter refused. In an interview two weeks before he was killed, Romero said, "Christians do not fear combat; they know how to fight . . . The Church speaks of the legitimate right of insurrectional violence" (available at www.infed.org, accessed January 29, 2020).

On March 30, 1980, some 250,000 people attended Romero's funeral. Twenty to thirty were killed when military snipers opened fire on people gathered on the cathedral steps. Two days later, the U.S. Congress approved another round of military aid. El Salvador's progressive politicians and social leaders, moderates and radicals alike, coalesced into a Democratic Revolutionary Front, a political group, while the FMLN fought an increasingly aggressive war. The guerrillas tried to touch off a mass insurrection in early 1981. They gained ground but not power. Meanwhile, the Reagan administration was determined to prevent an FMLN victory at any cost. The stage was set for a decade of civil war, which ended only after an internationally brokered agreement among all parties in 1990. An estimated 75,000 people died in the ten-year conflict, the vast majority killed by government forces.

Duarte had become highly unpopular by the time the 1989 election approached. The U.S. needed a candidate to continue pairing counterinsurgency with mild reform. ARENA had always resisted the American project, welcoming military aid but without strings attached. But the business community in El Salvador was feeling the economic consequences of the war. Under pressure from Washington, ARENA put forth as its candidate Alfredo Christiani, a businessman without the baggage of the internationally reviled D'Aubuisson. Christiani won. Under prodding from the new administration of George Bush (senior) and, more importantly, diplomatic pressure from the European Union and a number of Latin American countries, Christiani negotiated with the FMLN to end the Salvadoran civil war, much to the displeasure of his party.

At the end of the bitter war, the FMLN had achieved some of the democratic reforms it sought in 1980, but El Salvador had made little progress toward resolving its social question, which in many ways had been worsened by war. The FMLN became the single largest political party in the country, and in 2009, its candidate Mauricio Funes won the presidential election. Funes said that his election was a mandate to reduce poverty and make good on some of the unrealized promises in the pact that had ended the civil war. However, the FMLN's commitment and ability to bring about social change has been tested by the global recession and the continued presence of the right in the courts and public bureaucracy. Funes acted cautiously, being careful not to offend the military and the United States. He assumed office the same month as Honduras suffered a coup, in part a retaliation against a president who had allied himself too closely, in the view of the military, with Chávez and had challenged the economic model.

El Salvador, then, emerged from brutal civil war with a polyarchy strong enough to survive the election of a candidate from the FMLN. But one year after the election, many of Funes's supporters were wondering what they had truly won. Funes officially apologized for the state violence of the 1980s and opened the country's institutions to ensure more transparency and less corruption. But no trials of those responsible for truly horrible mass atrocities of the 1980s were in the offing. A nearly bankrupt economy limited the president's economic options, but he advanced no long-term plan for addressing the social questions that had sparked revolution.

In 2014, the FMLN candidate Salvador Sánchez Cerén, a former guerrilla, defeated the ARENA candidate. It was a narrow victory, but the leftist victory suggested more reform might be forthcoming. The FMLN benefited from the positive impact that Venezuelan aid programs were having, including on small businesses and farmers. But Cerén failed to make progress on three key issues: curtailing murderous gang warfare, reducing corruption, and raising living standards. ARENA was a spent force, but a new, populist right party formed out of the ranks of the FMLN itself. Nayib Bukele was a popular former mayor of San Salvador, but he had been expelled from the FMLN for physical attacks against a councilwoman. He ran as the candidate of a small party that had split from ARENA, and he defeated both parties to become president.

The FMLN, more than Nicaragua's FSLN, remained more committed to popular programs in health and education, but its economic policies were still based on the neoliberal export model, and its inability to curb gang violence also hurt it. The left party may yet return to power through elections in the future, as Bukele as maintained the economic model and cooperated with the Trump administration on curtailing immigration to the U.S.

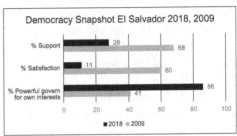

Democracy Snapshot El Salvador 2018, 2009

For Review

What is the FMLN, and how did it evolve from the civil war to the present time? What challenges did it face and does it continue to face in the current era? What were the origins of ARENA and how did it evolve?

Genocide and Revolution in Guatemala

One reason that pluralist democracy is suspect to many revolutionaries is the apparent vulnerability of pluralist systems to outside intervention. Perhaps no experience has reinforced that concern more than the overthrow of Jacobo Árbenz, Guatemala's reformist president, in 1954, a case in which the CIA acted with cold calculation to abet the overthrow of a democracy.

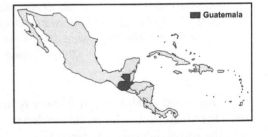

In 1944, a military coup in Guatemala brought a reformist, democratically oriented government to power. After several years of reforms, most supported by the country's small middle class, the outgoing president, Juan Arévalo, handed power to Colonel Árbenz, who was committed to deepening the reforms. Árbenz had won an internal battle in the reform movement against a more conservative candidate. In 1950, he won the election with 65 percent of the vote and the support of Guatemala's small but influential Communist Party (PC). The party was not really a threat to the United States, but it was no phantasm either. Although small in numbers, the communists were the single best-organized party and had a mass base by virtue of unions it had organized in the foreign-owned fruit plantations, the railroad, and the utility companies.

In 1952, Árbenz took the radical step of expropriating unused lands, including those of his own family and of the country's biggest landowner, the United Fruit Company of Boston (UFC). He also expropriated (all with compensation) utilities, roads, and other parts of the country's infrastructure controlled by UFC, which because of its tentacles everywhere in the economy was known as "the Octopus." The PC, rather than urge Árbenz on, warned Árbenz that he had made a powerful enemy. The company's allies in Washington included Secretary of State John Foster Dulles and his brother Allen, director of the CIA. They convinced the Eisenhower administration that Guatemala was being drawn into the orbit of Moscow.

The U.S. Central Intelligence Agency found ready allies when it launched an operation to destabilize and overthrow the Árbenz regime. The agency's disdain for Árbenz was reflected in an internal memorandum that summarized his program as "an intensely nationalistic program of progress colored by the touchy, anti-foreign inferiority complex of the 'Banana Republic'" (Doyle and Kornbluth 1997). Some of the same CIA operatives that helped to organize a coup against a nationalist government in Iran in 1953 went into action in Guatemala, boosted by the US$2.7 million authorized by President Dwight Eisenhower. It was not difficult to alarm anticommunist sectors in the military. Local elites were recruited to form a "liberation army" and invade the country from Honduras. Inept and ill-armed, the counterrevolutionary forces had little chance of succeeding, but conservative army officers showed no restraint in putting down the rebel offensive, which quickly stalled. Meanwhile, the United States launched a diplomatic and propaganda war, openly encouraging the army to overthrow the government.

In 1954, the conservative factions of Guatemala's military overthrew Árbenz, leading to an era of almost three decades of fierce repression by the military, most of it directed against the Mayan Indian population. An American University report summarizes what happened:

> The civil war took a turn for the worse in the early 1980's, when the Guatemalan army, backed by the CIA, began a campaign of genocide against the Maya peoples. Several hundred Indian villages were obliterated and their inhabitants, presumed to be guerrilla sympathizers, were either killed or forced into exile in Mexico.
>
> (https://mandalaprojects.com/ice/ice-cases/peten.htm, accessed September 14, 2020)

Árbenz had said his objective was to redistribute land and use the country's infrastructure to breed capitalists who would develop the country. However, in Cold War Washington, under the grip of right-wing hysteria (McCarthyism), the only thing visible was communism. Che Guevara was an eyewitness to the events in Guatemala. In Mexico, a young Fidel Castro took note of Washington's actions and had to wonder whether democracies could defend themselves adequately against outside intervention. The prospect of revolution reappeared in Guatemala in the 1970s. The military officers who had carried out the coup used power to elbow their way into the ranks of the economic elite (Jonas 1991). For the next 35 years, the country lived a nightmare of repression. Various guerrilla movements struggled with mixed success to resist the army.

By 1977, army repression reached levels that caused the Catholic Church to speak out and the Carter administration to cut off military aid. The Israeli government, which was eager for arms sales and diplomatic support in its conflict with the Palestinians, and Argentina, which was then engaged in its Dirty War, stepped into the breach. In 1981, the Reagan administration restored aid. Backed by military advisors from these countries, the Guatemalan government embarked on a scorched-earth campaign. The Guatemalan president at the time was General Efraín Ríos Montt, a born-again Christian with ties to the right wing of the U.S. Republican Party, including televangelist Pat Robertson and Attorney General Edwin Meese. Ríos Montt unleashed a wave of terror to flush out the guerrillas. Between 1981 and 1983 alone, more than 100,000 Indigenous people were killed and 440 of their villages destroyed. The army engaged in **ethnic cleansing**, forcibly relocated the population into government-controlled towns, and obliged Mayan Indigenous people to join "civil patrols" to hunt down guerrillas. The violence continued until the United Nations fostered successful negotiations to end the war, at least for the time being, in 1992.

Not much changed politically until 2007 when a leftist candidate, Álvaro Colom, won election as president. In 2009, Colom began to open security files on the civil war. He managed to stabilize the economy in a difficult global environment, but he has made little progress addressing the social question. In 2011, former general Otto Pérez Molina defeated a centrist candidate. Unlike the case in El Salvador, the guerrilla movement in Guatemala never approached the levels of support needed to gain concessions in the negotiations that

PHOTO 9.3   Colombia's FARC guerrillas agreed to a peace treaty with the government in 2016 and are trying to compete for power through elections. What do you think the chances are that the war may finally come to an end? We take this up in Chapter 10.

Source: AFP, Agence France-Presse via Getty Images.

ended the civil war. Its supporters were scattered in the highlands, mostly Indigenous peoples, many of whom were forced into refugee camps in neighboring Mexico. An indication of this weakness is the fate of Ríos Montt. In 2013 he was tried and found guilty of genocide against the Ixil Mayas, only to have the country's Supreme Court—heavily lobbied by the Guatemalan business community—annul the verdict against the dictator.

A succession of presidents and parties have occupied the presidency and legislature in Guatemala since 1991. The most significant development was the sudden emergence of a mass movement against corruption in 2015. In December 2006, a conservative government under popular pressure agreed to cooperate with an International Commission Against Impunity in Guatemala (CICIG), supported by the United Nations. After a decade of investigations, the CICIG efforts began to bear fruit in 2012 with exposure of widespread tax fraud and embezzlement schemes that involved almost the entire political establishment. The fallout and subsequent years of new scandals and mass demonstrations touched off massive demonstrations and helped bring a maverick outsider, Jimmy Morales, to the presidency. Morales at first cooperated—until his own family members were ensnarled. He terminated the CICIG mandate in January 2019. Presidential elections were scheduled later that year, and the one candidate in the presidential election who promised to renew the CICIG mandate had a fighting chance to win. She was disqualified on shaky grounds, being herself accused of corruption, although it was never proved. The eventual victor was the current President Alejandro Giammattei, former director of prisons, an unlikely a candidate supported by the old guard. Turnout was only 42 percent in the election.

Clearly, Giammattei has no real plan for regime change. He fits the mold of a right-wing populist, like Brazil's President Jair Bolsonaro. He demonstrated his loyalty to Donald Trump by agreeing to accept undocumented Guatemalans appealing for asylum in the United States. In March 2020, after Guatemala City airport officials expressed concern that some the deportees were infected with COVID-19, the program was suspended for two days, then renewed. In April, another incident forced Giammattei to suspend the program again.

The willingness of Guatemalans to take to the streets in 2015 against corruption must be seen as remarkable considering the 60 years of ferocious repression that preceded it. Like El Salvador, Nicaragua, and Honduras, the coronavirus pandemic adds to the challenges of gang violence, poverty, and dislocations of rural people from the land to make way for new agro-businesses (see chapter 15). Central America may not be as close to revolution as it was in the 1980s, but the underlying situation is such that the social question is likely to arise again.

For Review

What was Jacobo Árbenz's program? Why was the United States intervention in 1954 a turning point for Guatemala? Guatemala's insurrection did not nearly approach the success of the FSLN in Nicaragua or the FMLN in El Salvador. What would you say are the reasons?

■ Violence, Civil Society and Revolution

One problem with revolutionary organizations is that by their nature they require tough internal discipline. The extreme consequences of someone being captured and facing torture to disclose the identity and location of colleagues partly explain this fact, so secrecy and discipline must be maintained. These habits, essential to insurrection, might be unhealthy for democracy. Another factor is the revolu-

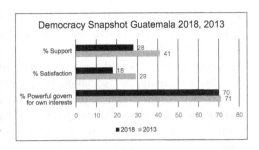

Democracy Snapshot Guatemala 2018, 2013

tionary fighter's understanding of his or her role in organizing a popular insurrection and effecting social change. Those who take up arms or engage in risky nonviolent actions in support of revolution are usually trying to raise the consciousness of ordinary people. This requires an educational process by which those already "enlightened" (in the forefront or vanguard) try to convince others that a new society is possible.

Out of the Russian Revolution of 1917 came a model that has influenced would-be revolutionaries ever since. Vladimir Lenin viewed it as necessary for revolution that a small, committed core of leaders of the new social order form a political party to help the oppressed. Lenin's formula for revolution, points out C. B. MacPherson (see chapter 1), argued for a vanguard to take control of the state and "forcibly transform the basic relations of society in such a way that the people would become undebased and capable of a fully human existence, at which point compulsive government would no longer be needed." That approach has yielded tyranny in many parts of the world, notes the Canadian philosopher.

This pessimistic assessment of revolution has to be balanced against the fact that guerrilla armies must rely on the support of the population to survive. To a certain extent, an armed movement can survive by instilling fear of reprisal for people who refuse to cooperate. Ultimately, however, the willingness of people to provide food, hide the rebels' location from government forces, care for the wounded, and perhaps even to rise up themselves at a key right moment depends on their sense of identity with and sympathy for the revolutionary fighters. This is one reason why revolutionary wars are among the most brutal: both sides are asserting their right to be the state, to exercise legitimate violence against those opposed to their ends. Revolutionary terror, counterrevolutionary terror, and state terror are all used in the battle for hearts and minds. It is hardly an environment friendly to democracy.

All three of Latin America's major social revolutions (Mexico in 1910, Cuba in 1959, and Nicaragua in 1979) resulted in a period of single-party dominance for a period. All three faced counter-revolutionary violence that heavily influenced the course of events afterward and reinforced the other tendencies running against a more pluralist political system. In Mexico, it would be 90 years before a peaceful transfer of power to an opposition party would take place after an election. Cuba remains today a single-party state. In Nicaragua, FSLN dominance was short by comparison. Sandinistas gambled on elections and were rudely displaced from power after implementing polyarchy.

History suggests that revolutionaries are not without grounds for being suspicious of the pluralist brand of democracy. Counterrevolutionaries often claim they want to restore democracy, but they often show less commitment to democracy than the new ruling class. Both in Guatemala (1954) and Chile (1973), the United States, as the hegemonic power in the region, worked diligently and with success to destabilize elected governments it did not like. Washington supported opposition groups that resorted to economic sabotage and terror to achieve their objectives. Although it won the 1984 elections, the Nicaraguan FSLN was punished by a more intensely violent counterrevolution that significantly contributed to defeat at the polls in 1990.

Revolutionaries find it necessary to appeal to democracy to build broad popular support, but addressing the "social question" with deep change conjures up enemies within and abroad. Revolutionaries tend to come to see themselves as saviors and prophets with a special mandate to rule without submitting themselves to democracy. When counterrevolutionaries are financed from abroad, antidemocratic tendencies are reinforced. Would-be democrats seem to put aside their principles when the poor majority uses the processes of democracy to challenge their wealth and privileges. Yet, the idea of "revolution" remains what the Sandinista rebel Omar Cabezas (1985) once called the "fire in the mountains" in Latin America.

Discussion Questions

1. The outbreaks of revolution in Cuba and Mexico took place nearly 50 years apart. Nonetheless, do you see any common factors that led to both? Why do you think both cases veered away from the pluralist model (polyarchy) after defeating the old regime?
2. Why do you think that Cuba came to identify its revolution with communism rather than with some nationalist label?
3. Would Cuba's socialist system crumble if its leaders abandoned the single-party system? What do you think would be the impact on Cuban politics if the United States ended its economic embargo?
4. El Salvador, Guatemala, and Nicaragua are poorer and more violent today than before the insurgencies of the 1980s, but for all their flaws, they now have 25 years of experience with elected democracy. When all is said and done, can we say that the insurgencies in Central America accomplished anything?
6. Based on the Latin American experience, can revolutions succeed in addressing both of the issues cited by Arendt: freedom *and* the social question? If revolutionaries must choose, which should take priority?

Resources for Further Study

Reading: Two excellent biographies capture the essence of revolution in Cuba and Mexico, respectively: Sebastian Balfour's *Castro*, 2nd ed. (New York: Longman, 1995) is an evenhanded look at the Cuban leader, and John Womack's *Zapata and the Mexican Revolution* (New York: Vintage Books, 1968) is an accessible classic. *A Nation for All: Race, Inequality, and Politics in Twentieth-Century Cuba*, edited by Alejandro de la Fuente (Chapel Hall: University of North Carolina Press, 2001) puts the shortcomings and accomplishments of the Cuban Revolution into perspective. See also Walter LaFeber's *Inevitable Revolutions: The United States in Central America*, 2nd ed. (Norton, 1993). Marc Frank's *Cuban Revelations: Behind the Scenes in Havana* (University of Florida Press 2015) is by an American reporter who has lived for decades in Cuba with his family.

Video and Film: *Strawberry and Chocolate* (1995) is remarkable for its commentary on gay life and frustrated idealism, all the more so for having been made in Cuba. *Continent on the Move* (1992) in the Americas series looks at the economic factors behind migration within Mexico and out of Mexico to the United States. *The Uncompromising Revolution* (1992) looks at Fidel's leadership style on the eve of momentous change. *Yo Soy Cuba* (1964) is a Russian-made documentary with a surprisingly objective point of view. *El Norte* (1983) tells the story of a young Guatemalan boy caught in the counterinsurgency. *When the Mountains Tremble* (1983) is about the Guatemalan army's assault on the Mayan people, narrated by Nobel Prize winner Rigoberta Menchú.

On the Internet: The Center for Cuba Studies at www.cubaupdate.org offers a sympathetic view of the revolution. The Cuba Transition site at http://ctp.iccas.miami.edu/main.htm at the University of Miami promotes pluralist democratization of the island.

10 Civilians and Soldiers in Illiberal Times

Focus Questions

▶ What are some signs and conditions indicating that a military coup might soon occur against a civilian government?

▶ What is an "*autogolpe*"? How has the use of the term "coup" changed in some ways since the transitions to democracy of the 1980s?

▶ What are some of the different kinds of military coups? How does a military junta that assumes a moderating role differ from some other kinds of military regimes?

▶ How does the military exercise influence?

ON SUNDAY, FEBRUARY 9, 2020, El Salvador's President Nayib Bukele marched into the National Assembly and demanded its members pass a bill authorizing a $109 million loan to finance a campaign against violent crime, which is rampant in the small country. The money was being blocked by both the leftist Farabundo Martí National Liberation Front (FMLN) party and the right-wing ARENA party. Bukele did not come alone. He was accompanied by a group of uniformed soldiers in battle gear carrying automatic weapons. He told the deputies, "Now I think it is very clear who is in control of the situation. And the decision we are going to make now, we are going to put it in God's hands. Let's say a prayer" (*Washington Post*, February 12, 2020).

Bukele, riding a wave of public approval as an outsider expected to clean up government, also brought with him a large crowd of Salvadorans, weary of corruption and their inability to move about the capital city of San Salvador because of violent crime. Outside the assembly building, Bukele told them that his message to the assembly's deputies were words that God put in his head. Later in the day, the FMLN and ARENA accused him of attempting a coup, and many Salvadorans expressed concern about his alliance with the army, which was responsible for most of the 75,000 deaths and 8,000 disappearances during the civil war of the 1980s (see chapter 9). The FMLN and ARENA accused him of attempting a coup against the assembly. Bukele responded, "If I were a dictator or someone who didn't respect democracy, I would have taken control of everything right away."

We usually think of a coup as an action taken by the military to seize power from an elected civilian government. However, since the era of transitions to democracy of the 1980s and 1990s, the threat to elected governments has often taken shape as an alliance between certain civilian sectors and the military. In several cases, including Bukele's action, the threat of a coup or an actual coup has been initiated by an elected president against an elected legislature tarnished with the stain of corruption. These "*autogolpes*" (self-coups) and other signs of growing military influence have been taking place in an international context unfavorable to liberal democracy. A wave of right-wing, nationalist leaders (and some leftist, as well) have challenged what once seemed an unstoppable momentum of neoliberal globalization.

◼ Democracy in Illiberal Times

The universal acceptance of liberal democracy and capitalism in the 1990s formed part of an ideology of globalization that promoted the idea of the world advancing toward one universal form of state, **polyarchy**, and a single world market, knit together by **multilateral** "free trade" treaties and by similar agreements under the umbrella of the World Trade Organization (WTO). These developments led to optimism that Latin America had finally shed its predilection toward military coups. The region seemed to be swimming with the **third wave** tide.

While acknowledging that militaries still exercised political influence in the region, two political scientists who are experts on military–civilian relations in Latin America expressed optimism in a recent book (Pion-Berlin and Martínez 2017: 1), writing,

> Less it be periodically called upon to lend a hand in crime suppression, disaster relief, or peacekeeping abroad, the military is mostly confined to the barracks and kept off the front pages of newspapers. Governments, no longer anxious about what the armed forces might or might not do, turn their attention to the more pressing matters of the day. Democratic rule in many parts of Latin America seems more settled than it has been in generations.

There were doubters, however. Two prominent political scientists (Dominguez and Lowenthal 1996) early on took note that several new democracies had conceded to the military a strong role in promoting social and economic development, linking this goal to its traditional responsibility, security. Rut Diamint (2002: 15), an Argentine specialist on civilian–military relationships in Latin America, pointed out,

> We have also witnessed new forms of military involvement in guises that preserve the semblance of democracy: military control of vast quantities of economic resources, intelligence services with close links to governments, military putschists following populist policies, paramilitary intervention in political disputes and control of society through militarization of domestic law enforcement.

The reference to "illiberal times" in the title of this chapter refers to several different features of populist challenges to the principles of liberal democracy in the world. When authors allude to "the people vs. democracy" (Mounk 2018), "how democracies die" (Levitsky and Ziblatt 2018), and "fascism" threatening to come by way of the vote rather than by military coup (Albright 2019), they usually find **populism**, whether on the left or the right, to be the main danger to democracy. **Pink Tide** presidents Hugo Chávez (1999–2013, Venezuela), Evo Morales (2006–2019, Bolivia), and Rafael Correa (2007–2017, Ecuador) figure prominently in these books as threats to democracy. Levitsky and Ziblatt (2018: 22–24) say that these and other Latin American populist leaders say they are the "voice of the people [and] wage war on what they depict as a corrupt and conspiratorial elite." They include Chávez, Morales, and Correa among those who rejected or weakened the democratic "rules of the game," denied the legitimacy of their political opponents, tolerated or encouraged violence, and curtailed civil liberties of opponents and the media.

Other area specialists take issue with such a broad generalization about populism in Latin America and tend to put more of the responsibility for weakening democracy on the opposition to the left populists of the Pink Tide. Steven Ellner (2019: 5), editor of an issue of the academic journal *Latin American Perspectives* devoted to Pink Tide populism, sees social polarization and class politics at the root of the deterioration of democracy in the region. Ellner attributes these forces mostly to opposition groups, saying they sought to restore **neo-liberal** economic policies (privatization, cutbacks in social spending, opening of natural resources to foreign capital) and align themselves closely with the United States' attempts to undermine leftist governments. The opposition's main goal, he says, was to restore power to privileged and wealthy groups that had lost ground to social movements supporting leftist parties and leaders.

The brashest populist in this era was Venezuela's Chávez, who first launched his political career in the form of a failed coup (in 1992). When he assumed the presidency via election in 1999, he brought with him into government many of his military colleagues, which prompted one political scientist to characterize his government as "democracy uniform" (Norden 2003). Chávez's program (see chapter 8) was influenced by another experiment in military populism, one led by Peru's General Juan Velasco Alvarado from 1968 to 1975, an experience that Chávez studied while he was barely out of the military academy. At the dawn of the populist era, Getulio Vargas rode to power in 1930 on an alliance of political outsiders and rank and file in the army (see chapter 5), that is, a civilian–military alliance. The same can be said of Argentine Colonel Juan Perón's Grupo de Oficiales Unidos (GOU; Group of United Officers), founded in 1943 to promote national unity, modernization, and order. As minister of labor, Perón developed a mass base of support among the *descomisados* ("shirtless ones"), the poorest workers in the ports, railroads, and slaughterhouses crucial to Argentina's ranching and agricultural export economy.

Ecuador's Colonel Lucio Gutiérrez was a staff officer in the army high command when in 1999 he assembled a group of lower ranking officers to support the Confederation of Indigenous Nations of Ecuador (CONAIE) when in 2000 it rose against President Jamil Mahuad. CONAIE had formed in 1986 to advance Indigenous demands, including land reform, **plurinationalism**, bilingual education, and opposition to neoliberal economic policies. On several occasions, its activists had already occupied and virtually shut down Quito, the capital, to protest budget cuts and intrusions of mining and oil transnational corporations into their territories. In 2000, CONAIE protested because Mahuad, facing an economic crisis, had frozen all bank accounts and decreed a 150 percent rise in gasoline prices.

With Gutiérrez's soldiers clearing the way, CONAIE occupied the capital. Mahuad fled, and Gutiérrez was named to the junta that replaced him. Gutiérrez's audaciousness and his alliance with Indigenous people were not welcomed by the army's high command. They pressured the junta to turn over the government to General Carlos Mendoza. Mendoza had no intention of acceding to the demands of CONAIE, but Gutiérrez put his loyalty to the army above the movement's political objective. He was briefly jailed for his role in the uprising. Released, he would be elected and serve as president from 2003 to 2005.

Gutiérrez incorporated many of his allies from the uprising into his government, but he left the control of key economic policies in the hands of the traditional elite. For two years he dealt with an unstable situation, beset with charges of corruption and under attack from both the right and left. The Ecuadoran Congress deposed him on the rather shaky constitutional grounds that he had abandoned his position as president.

These episodes (and others) should caution us about too readily generalizing about the political role of the military in Latin America. In Latin America, the military has never been as insulated from governing power as in wealthy, stable political democracies. In the nineteenth century, *caudillos* and *coroneles* were rarely trained soldiers; they came to power by putting themselves at the head of peasants and rural cowboys hungry for land or freedom from debts. Many of the *golpes* of the twentieth century were "moderating" coups that sought to separate contending civilian political factions, but usually they were urged to act by civilian opponents. Usually, they had no policy agenda of their own. Between 1955 and 1973, the Argentines acted to suppress Peronism with three coups. In the Cold War era, militaries (urged by the United States) would oust governments in Central America, acting against progressive governments that were a "communist" influence.

The bureaucratic authoritarian governments ousted leftist governments in Brazil and the **Southern Cone**, but the generals relied on technocrats to design neoliberal economic policy. In Central America the military has had a history of close association with oligarchies, often (as in Guatemala) using control or influence over government to gain economic power and enter into the national circle of elites (Brömmelster and Paes 2003). Chapter 7 dealt largely with the ascension of hard-right bureaucratic authoritarian military regimes that gained power in the context of extreme polarization and the specter of another Cuban Revolution.

As the year 2020 opened, no country in Latin America was governed by an active military officer. The president (or in some Caribbean countries, the prime minister) of the country was a civilian. That does not mean, however, that the military has entirely retreated from the political arena. This chapter looks at how the military influence exerts itself over civilian regimes, with a close look at the experiences of Peru and Colombia.

Delivering a *Golpe*: When and How?

The Spanish term for *coup d'état* is *golpe*, literally "a blow." One stereotype we have of these *golpes* is that they are executed by generals or colonels from traditional, landed families or that they frequently install a pathological brute in power. One of the most notorious cases of the latter was General Maximiliano Hernández Martínez, the model for novelist Gabriel García Márquez's *Autumn of the Patriarch*. Martínez once proclaimed, "It is a greater crime to kill an ant than to kill a man." However, as we have already seen in examining Latin American history, military officers have sometimes been agents of modernization, at times even staging coups in alliance with civilians who want to implement democracy.

PUNTO DE VISTA: COSTA RICA—THE EXCEPTION THAT PROVES THE RULE?

There is one often-cited exceptional case in the history of military rule in Latin America, and that would be Costa Rica. In 1948, after a brief civil war touched off by allegations of a fraudulent election, the winning side, led by Pepe Figueres of the Social Democratic Party, actually abolished the military. In the end, the forces of Figueres defeated an unusual coalition of convenience between Conservatives and Communists. The Conservative Party president from 1945 to 1948, Rafael Angel Calderón García, was something of a populist who had conceded to workers an eight-hour day, created a social security system, instituted an income tax, and built a social welfare program. The communists, bitter rivals of the social democrats, were at the time the largest force in the labor unions that were prominent on the fruit plantations, the key export sector.

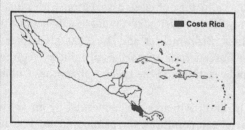

The U.S. government and President Harry Truman supported Figueres's revolt against the conservative candidate, handpicked by Calderón, who had won the 1948 election with support from the communists. Fighting broke out. Washington and its ally, General Anastasio Somoza in neighboring Nicaragua, provided Figueres with aid to defeat the country's armed forces, which had stood by Calderón. Figueres disbanded communist unions and the Communist Party, but the social democrats also took Calderón's reforms even further—expanding labor rights and the welfare system. At the same time, he boldly abolished the army, replacing it with a "Civil Guard," whose mission was to serve as a

national police force. Money saved by disbanding the army helped fund the expansion of social programs.

Since 1986, Costa Rica has celebrated the abolition of its army, now also part of its constitution, on December 1. The absence of an army goes a long way toward explaining why Costa Rica escaped the Cold War wave of military rule and brutal dictatorships in Central America, but this has to be set against the economic reforms that reduced social inequalities and lessened political polarization in the country.

Costa Rica has had continuous democratic rule since 1948, for the most part with power alternating between Figueres's Social Democrats and the Conservatives. But there are reasons to wonder about the future. Costa Rica did not escape the social polarization and economic crisis that enveloped Central America in the 1980s. The United States provided military aid (US$18 million in 1984–1985) to train and modernize Costa Rica's Civil Guard, which began to look more and more like an armed forces establishment. Under weight of debt, the country began to retreat from the welfare programs enacted after 1945 and, as elsewhere, began to open up to market forces and free trade. Inequality, historically low in Costa Rica, increased. In 1980, the Civil Guard opened fire on striking banana workers, and in 1982, the government allowed the United States to train the Guard in "counterinsurgency." Today the Guard has 4,500 members that supplement a police force of 10,000, for a country with only 4.5 million people.

More recently, Costa Rica has found itself dealing with drug trafficking and the infiltration of a Mexican crime organization. It has a dispute with Nicaragua over its river border with that country. In 2011, it created a special border unit to deploy along its borders (Sánchez 2011). It would be an exaggeration to say that Costa Rica now has a military establishment typical of the region, but the increased social class polarization, the continued economic struggles, and the size and mission of the Guard at least raise the question of whether Latin America's great "democratic exception" is immune from democratic breakdown.

In the post–World War II period, Latin American militaries have been deployed more often against internal "threats," real or manufactured and often at a great cost in lives, than against external enemies. On the other hand, even Costa Rica has had to respond with military-like solutions to modern security problems, such as globalized crime syndicates.

The Democracy Snapshot for Costa Rica report shows Costa Rica to have experienced a significant erosion in public satisfaction with democracy since a high point in 2009, falling from 51 to 27 percent. Support has also fallen off. In 2013, it fell to only 53 percent, but as the snapshot shows, it rebounded to 63 percent. Back in 1996, the percentage saying they supported democracy as the best form of government was 80 percent. Seventy-five percent of Costa Ricans think the country has a government run by a few groups for their own interests. In sum, while liberal democracy is still in good shape in Costa Rica compared to most other countries, there certainly has been slippage in public attitudes favorable to democracy.

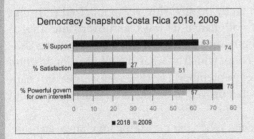

In April 2014, an independent leftist candidate, Luis Guillermo Solis, defeated the candidates of the two main parties in a landslide. Solis had been in fourth place before the first round of voting in February. Corruption, growing poverty, and inequality were the factors behind his ascent. The new president campaigned on a platform of higher taxes on the wealthy. His presidency ran into three serious problems that almost gave the 2018 election to the candidate of an ultra-conservative Christian party.

First, although Solis promised and then partly implemented his campaign promises to redistribute income with higher taxes on the wealthy, the global economic crisis exacerbated the country's economic problems and worsened the fiscal deficit, leading Solis to seek raising the value-added tax (a regressive tax) and cutting spending. Second, he was accused of complicity in a corruption scheme involving cement contracts. The charge was especially explosive because Solis had run as an independent in 2014 after breaking with the National Liberation Party (founded by Pepe Figueres) over corruption scandals. He was ultimately acquitted, but the country's conservative press made the most of the charges to weaken him. Third, the Inter-American Court of Human Rights issued a ruling against anti-gay laws, which produced a surge in support for an ultra-conservative, fundamentalist Christian candidate.

Costa Rica remains a relatively stable social democratic regime, but the main political parties that build the regime have been decimated, the government remains under great pressure to reduce spending on the welfare programs that have contributed to political stability, and right-wing populist parties have grown in strength. Costa Rica may not have a military, but it does have a Civil Guard that looks more like an army that it did before the Central American civil wars of the 1980s.

Point/Counterpoint: Is Costa Rica Really So Different?

If you say yes, how would you answer those who see rising inequality and poverty occurring despite the country's unusual democratic stability and lack of a military? Has the loyalty of Costa Rica's Civil Guard really been tested?

If you say no, then how would you respond to the argument that the lack of a standing military might allow the new president to address some of these problems before they get worse?

Whichever way you answered, based on this chapter's review of military intervention, what should we consider in evaluating whether Costa Rica might move toward democratic breakdown?

For More Information

See Steven Palmer and Iván Molina, eds., *The Costa Rica Reader* (Durham, NC: Duke University Press, 1998); John Booth and Christine Wade, *Understanding Central America* (Boulder CO: West-view Press, 2008); Judith Eve Lipton and David P. Barash, *Strength Through Peace: How Demilitarization Led to Peace and Happiness in Costa Rica, and What the Rest of the World Can Learn From a Tiny, Tropical Nation* (New York: Oxford University Press, 2018).

Shall We Coup? When Does the Military Intervene?

Coups rarely occur when societies, democratic or not, are prospering and calm. Without implying any order of importance, political scientists have identified some combination of kinds of stresses that often precede a coup.

A breakdown of consensus among political elites. Not all the rules of the political game are spelled out in constitutions. The functioning of any regime, but especially democracy, requires leaders of different factions and parties to seek compromises with one another. Opportunism, mistrust, vengeance, deep philosophical differences, and pressure from powerful social and economic groups can erode the willingness of political leaders to "muddle through" and seek an exit from a crisis. Things seem to reach a boiling point when political elites begin to speculate openly about the possibility of a military coup or call upon the military to defend the nation from the "threat" posed by the existing government (Stepan 1971; Sartori and Sani 1983). Usually this opposition tactic begins with well-publicized warnings of the danger of coup should the government not change its ways, and over time it escalates to calls for the military to intervene in the name of defending the constitution. Usually their objective is to induce a moderating coup, which is what the Chilean opposition to Salvador Allende expected from the coup of September 11, 1973. As we saw in chapter 7, once installed the regime of General Pinochet proved to be intent on much deeper and longer-lasting regime change.

Abuse of authority by incumbent governments. When people asking for change encounter violence or fraud, they are more likely to resort to street protests, strikes, seizure of public buildings, or (eventually) violence. Sometimes it is difficult to know whether opponents are protesting because the system is rigged or simply because they are too weak to win. If one player knocks over the chessboard, is it because the other side is cheating or because the other player has achieved a superior position in the game?

Abuse of democratic processes by an immoderate, disloyal opposition. One hallmark of democracy is respect for "loyal opposition," the right of an opposition to use constitutional means to replace the government of the day. However, not all opposition to democratic government is loyal. While a conservative or a centrist elected government can be threatened by disloyal opposition, more often this problem confronts elected leftist governments. Some examples are Guatemala in 1954, the Dominican Republic in 1965, Chile in 1973, Nicaragua in the 1980s, Bolivia in 2019, and Venezuela in the 2000s. All of these cases have in common that the traditional ruling elite, supported by the United States, engaged in an extralegal, sometimes violent, attempt to overthrow a government legitimized by election.

In the Andean countries of Bolivia, Ecuador, and Peru, coups were so chronic for much of the nineteenth century that they almost became ritualized between 1930 and 1970. Protestors, often students, would take to the streets. Tanks would surround the palace. The president would leave, knowing that his time was up. After a period of military government, a transition back to civilian rule, often through elections, would take place, and the cycle would begin again. Bolivia experienced 14 coups between 1899 and 1980. Ecuador experienced four between 1925 and 1972, and Peru seven between 1914 and 1992. We could count several more in each case if we included times that military pressure forced a president to resign and give way to another civilian, short of a general taking outright power.

Economic stress. One famous definition of politics is that it is about "who gets what, when, and how" (Lasswell 1936). Logically, it is harder to divide a shrinking pie, or at least one not growing as fast as before. This is what happened to the economies of Latin America with the exhaustion of import substitution industrialization (ISI) in the 1960s. Slower growth and lower profits at the end of the import substitution era put pressure on wages and reduced jobs in the swelling cities. Social activists—including Marxists and leftist Christians—supported peasants demanding land reform and slum dwellers demanding housing and better conditions (see chapters 5 and 7). **Hyperurbanization** (see Table 2.1 in chapter 2) exceeded the capacity of the cities to absorb migrants, increasing social frustration. Strikes became bitter, and in many cases the labor movement split between leftists and leaders tied to the old system. Leftist calls for revolution, rural land invasions, urban unrest, and inflation all frightened the middle class, whose fears were then exploited by the most conservative groups in society (Nun 1967; Sartori and Sani 1983).

Polarization of social classes. Resistance to and frustration with the pace of change through constitutional procedures can together accelerate the centrifugal social forces in a liberal democracy under strain. Elected leftist governments often find themselves caught between groups seeking to accelerate revolution and an opposition that has enough power to forestall change. Caught between the two sides, either the government must speed up or radicalize its policies and thereby risk alienating the loyal opposition and moderates in its own ranks, or it must use force against workers, peasants, and poor people protesting the slow pace of change. As just mentioned, governments in Chile between 1964 and 1973 attempted to implement an agrarian reform, but landowners used the courts and bureaucracy to slow the process to a crawl. Peasants frustrated by years of delay took matters into their own hands in the form of land occupations.

An unfavorable international context. The populist crisis developed in the decade after the Cuban Revolution (1959), the first successful communist revolution in the hemisphere. The United States, the most powerful nation in the world, was fighting leftist movements and insurgencies in a variety of places, most notably Vietnam. In the 1960s, the Cuban government morally and sometimes materially supported revolutionary movements in Latin America. Cold Warriors in the U.S. saw any form of leftist, nationalist radicalism as a threat and carried out counterinsurgency warfare against revolutionary movements and programs to destabilize leftist regimes, elected or not.

If the large number of countries that democratized between 1974 (when Portugal transitioned from dictatorship to democracy) became known as the "third wave" of democracy (after Samuel Huntington's book title by that name [1991]), the erosion of liberal democratic norms of the last decade has prompted some political scientists to speak of a "third wave of autocratization" since 1994 (Lührmann and Lindberg 2019; Senem Aydin-Düzgit et al. 2019). By their count, since that year there have occurred 75 significant shifts toward greater autocracy, with 37 of them having affected democracies. Much of this recent political science literature recognizes that short of outright military government, what has occurred is "backsliding" from liberal democracy. However, one widely read popular book warns of imminent fascism (Albright 2019), and so do articles in an influential edited volume (Sunstein 2018) entitled "*Can It* [fascism] *Happen Here?*"

The long historical record of intervention by the United States includes very few instances in which Washington has fostered democracy when elections threaten to bring or actually result in leftist regimes unacceptable to the United States (see chapter 16). However, there have been periods in which the United States has encouraged democratic transitions from autocratic regimes because it fears a prolonged dictatorship risks a more revolutionary outcome as a result of popular uprisings against the regime. In the period between the presidencies of Jimmy Carter (1977–1980) and Barack Obama (2009–2016) promoting **polyarchy** (Robinson 1996) was diplomatic principle, though hardly consistently applied.

The election of Donald Trump effectively brought that policy to a halt, however temporarily. For the Latin American right, his embrace of authoritarian regimes, not to speak of his own dismantlement of liberal "guardrails" on U.S. democracy (Levitsky and Ziblatt 2018), has signaled that they need not worry about displeasing Washington for violating **pluralist** political ideals. The administration's ire is reserved only for the regimes under the influence of the populist left.

Triggering Factors for a Coup

Every Latin American country except Mexico has experienced at least one military coup since 1945. Why do coups happen? Huntington's theory of praetorianism (taken from the Roman Praetorian Guard) focuses on the weakness of political institutions; that is, weak civilian institutions encourage the tendency toward military rule (Huntington 1968). The transitions literature focuses more on political polarization and a breakdown of elite consensus. Marxist theory emphasizes the military's role as watchman over the interests of capitalists. These approaches and theories find the causes of coups in the nature of political and economic systems. There is also comparative politics literature focused on politics in the military (see Stepan 1978), an attempt to examine the "proximate" causes of coups, not just the sociological and economic ones described earlier. What induces officers to take the bold and risky step of attempting an armed uprising?

The recurrence of coups might lead us to believe that they are easy to organize. Consider, however, the personal risks involved. Some person or small group must initiate a conspiracy and feel out potential collaborators. If even one participant decides to reveal the plot to superiors, the coup may fail, and its organizers may be punished or purged. Where social discontent is widespread and high-ranking officers are alienated from civilian authorities, the risk may be diminished somewhat. When political uncertainty prevails, even soldiers who oppose a coup may opt for neutrality, lest they find themselves suddenly answering to a new government led by officers they betrayed. Although soldiers take an oath to defend the constitution, the nature of military life makes insubordination, even to orders to take part in a coup, dangerous. Military training and corporate identity work to create networks of personal loyalty within the military organization. In addition, the legacy of military involvement in politics involves a certain degree of tolerance in the ranks for dissenters. Today's rebel may be tomorrow's commander, or even president.

Within the military, the would-be coup maker must be a conspirator willing to risk his career. (No coups have been led by women—yet.) The military itself may be rife with factions. Not infrequently, it is divided into pro-regime, anti-regime, and constitutionalist (neutral) wings. If one faction moves, will the others resist? Will soldiers fire upon one another in that case, or is loyalty to the military caste likely to restrain the potential for violence? Externally, there may be civilians encouraging or even entering into the conspiracy. Are they to be trusted? Will they be dependable allies in a post-coup government?

Then there is the attitude of the rank and file to be considered. Ordinary soldiers are recruited (sometimes forcibly in the countryside) or drafted, and their ethnicity and social class (but much less so, gender) reflect to some degree the composition of the entire society. The recruit is often poorly educated, subjected to harsh living conditions inferior to those of high-ranking officers, and lacking even the most elemental rights within the military hierarchy. He (most often "he," sometimes "she") is put through a harsh physical regimen designed to instill patriotic values and unquestioned obedience to superior officers. More often, the "enemy" against whom the Latin American soldier is deployed is his fellow citizen. Most of the time, soldiers follow the orders of their commanders, even if they are asked to move against their own government. However, discontent deep within the ranks is not unknown. Occasionally, noncommissioned officers (e.g., sergeants) and field officers have led revolts. One of the most famous cases occurred in 1934 in Cuba when a "sergeants' revolt" rose up against superior officers resisting the progressive president of Ramón Grau San Martín. Subsequently the leader of that revolt, Fulgencio Batista, would become a strongman president, eventually to be overthrown by Fidel Castro's revolution in 1959.

We have been examining the *internal* military politics of coup making, but these must be put in the context of the political environment at any particular moment. We have already listed some of the contextual factors that make democracies vulnerable to collapse, which usually leads to military rule in some form. What are the more immediate circumstances that prompt military intervention? Not all of these factors are present in every case, but we can identify some signs of a civilian government in trouble before a coup actually occurs.

- *Civilian politicians and other elites begin to speculate about the possibility of a coup, often in a manner that seems to invite intervention.* Typically, military officers are "reminded" of their duty to put allegiance to the nation or the constitution above their loyalty to the president and commanding officers. For example, in March 1964, the Brazilian newspaper *Diário de Notícias* editorialized that extremists had "co-opted the president [Goulart] himself" and led him to subvert the rule of law. For this reason, it went on, the president had lost "the right to be obeyed . . . because this right emanates from the constitution. The armed forces, by article 177 of the constitution, are obliged to defend the country "and to guarantee the constitutional power, law and order."
- *Civilian groups take up arms, threatening the military's monopoly of force.* The military

has a strong interest in maintaining its status as the sole repository of legalized violence. In 1959, upon seizing power, Cuba's revolutionary government abolished the regular armed forces in favor of a militia, sending shivers down the spines of the hemisphere's military elite. (Today, Cuba has a regular army again, but it also has a well-trained militia.) However, the military rarely views threats from the right with the same alarm as ones from the left. The military has been known to assume a direct leadership role in right-wing death squad activities in Central America (see chapter 9) and in Colombia (see later). Landowners and oil and mining companies make use of retired and sometimes even active members of the armed forces to attack peasant movements or defend themselves against guerrillas. Military rank and file and police, often very poorly paid, can be lured into private security services and paramilitary activities in the countryside and the cities.

- *The military sometimes resents being deployed against the population by the incumbent government.* Although Latin American militaries have a well-earned reputation for repression, they sometimes blame the corruption or inadequacies of politicians for putting them in the position of repressing citizens from the same social strata as the rank and file.

- *Political struggles among civilians spill over into military affairs and become factors in promotions and other matters that the military would reserve for itself.* As the executive branch becomes more concerned with the possibility of a coup, the president seeks to ensure that key positions in the command structure are held by supportive officers, or at least by those opposed to a coup. Sometimes officers with more time in grade or impressive records are passed over for promotion by more junior or less qualified colleagues; this, of course, only exacerbates existing dissension in the ranks. This was a source for discontent of the first generations of military officers graduated from academies in the era of liberal modernization. It is also a factor that can undermine military juntas that govern for a long period.

- *The United States expresses alarm about the policies of the existing government and signals its approval of military intervention.* In some cases, the United States is directly involved in fomenting a coup. In its public diplomacy, Washington usually condemns intervention, but its actions (e.g., Venezuela in the failed coup of 2002; the coup in Honduras in 2009—see chapters 8 and 13) are often inconsistent with its words.

- *Certain political factions gaining power are deemed threats to the nation.* Under the influence of North American "national security doctrines," Latin American militaries were enlisted by Washington in the fight against communism during the Cold War. In this era, almost any leftist political movement was regarded as communist by domestic elites. Since the fall of the Berlin Wall and then the 9/11 attacks on New York and Washington in 2001, terrorism and drug trafficking have replaced communism as the rationale for aid and alliances with the military.

Sometimes the United States has tried to promote political stability by championing the creation and training of a well-equipped, effective fighting force commanded by officers who stand above partisan political fights. The result is often something quite different. Instead of a neutral military, the training produces a more powerful army that becomes the dominant political force in its own right. The classic example for Central America was the creation of the Nicaraguan National Guard in the early 1930s. The United States had equipped and trained the Guard to take over the fight against the patriotic guerrilla forces of José Augusto Sandino. After the United States withdrew its forces, Sandino agreed to negotiate an end to his resistance with the Guard's commander, Anastasio Somoza. Instead, in 1934, Somoza had Sandino assassinated. He used control of the Guard to establish a family dynasty and amassed a huge fortune (Millet 1977), ruling the country until overthrown by the Sandinistas (FSLN) in 1979.

Generally, the corporate identity of the military is associated with repelling threats from external sources. However, for Latin American militaries the security threat to *la patria*, as political scientist Brian Loveman (1999) called it, is defined as internal. General Jorge Rafael Videla, for example, justified the Argentine coup of 1976 as necessary because "the country [was] on the verge of national disintegration." Events associated with the coup represented

> more than the mere overthrow of a government. On the contrary, they signified the final closing of an historic cycle and the opening of a new one whose fundamental characteristics will be manifested by the reorganization of the nation, a task undertaken with a true spirit of service by the armed forces.
>
> (Loveman and Davies 1997: 160)

On its way out of power in 1983, the military argued that the violence of late populist Argentina had justified the "use of classified procedures," a euphemism for what become known as the Dirty War. Even the generals and admirals, however, had to admit, "within this almost apocalyptic framework, errors were committed" (Loveman and Davies 1997: 166).

In 1967, General Castelo Branco was still describing the goals of the 1964 coup in Brazil in terms suggesting a moderator role. The most "urgent task," he said,

> was to contain the extraordinary rise of the general level of prices, to recover the minimum necessary order for the functioning of the national economy, to overcome the crisis of confidence, and to return to entrepreneurs and to the workers the tranquility necessary for productive activities.
>
> (Loveman and Davies 1997: 174)

However, the military found its policy role deepening and its bases of popular support shrinking. Many civilians who had supported the 1964 coup encouraged Castelo Branco's opponents to act against him in 1968. The Brazilian military moved decisively toward the bureaucratic authoritarianism (BA) model in December 1968. A national state of siege was prolonged, which meant among other things that citizens could be stripped of all their rights for ten years. Congress and all other legislatures were closed. On September 4, 1969, the U.S. ambassador was kidnapped and later executed by urban guerrillas. Now Brazil's own version of the Dirty War began in earnest, although the amount of political violence was not as great as in Chile and Argentina.

Even in the case of Chile, the full consequences of the Pinochet coup of 1973 were not immediately visible. The initial proclamation of the coup makers on September 11 claimed that the Allende government had forfeited its legitimacy, and the coup makers proclaimed their intention to "reestablish normal economic and social conditions." However, like his colleagues in other countries, Pinochet had no intention of returning power to the politicians, even the ones who had urged him to act. In 1983, he explained, "Our historical experience confirms that political parties, as they were called under the old constitutional framework, tended to transform themselves into monopolistic sources for the generation of power; they made social conflict more acute." The military intended to make sure that the political parties would assume again "their true role as currents of opinion framed within a juridical [legal] order which will save the country from excesses, as parties whose bases are those consecrated by the people of Chile in their new [1981] constitution" (Loveman and Davies 1997: 183–184).

Politics Inside the Barracks

Perhaps more than in any other bureaucracy in government, promotions in the military are supposed to be based on rational criteria—for example, education, performance, and leadership qualities (Janowitz 1960). Hence, on one hand, the nature of its mission—defense of the nation from external threats—creates an internal ethos and *esprit de corps* that is unique to a military environment. In a classic study, Eric Nordlinger (1976) argued that the military had a penchant for political stability built into its internal codes calling for order, dignity, and hierarchical relationships. On the other hand, as a department of government, the military competes with other departments for a share of state spending. Also, the way the military defines a *threat* is a highly political matter. Finally, the military is an organization with its own corporate political interests and biases, and it is an organization with its own internal politics. Who gets promoted? What branch gets more money for procurement? Who gets an overseas posting? Who gets command over elite units? These questions rarely are decided on purely rational criteria. Hence, not only is the military often involved in politics, but politics also penetrates military life.

Marxists have almost always seen the military as the "night watchman" of capitalism, ready to defend the interests of the capitalist ruling class against the threat of revolution. Other analysts have seen the military as a transformative force, seeking to modernize society, perhaps even to advance the interests of social forces being blocked by conservatives. As the economies grew more complex and urban, Latin America's military officers came from the ranks of the middle class—and not, as in the past, exclusively from the ranks of the landed gentry. Amos Perlmutter (1977: 187–190) calls military governments with an agenda "ruler oriented," distinguishing them from the moderator role (discussed earlier in this chapter) of other military juntas (councils). There is little doubt that the military governments that took power after the crisis of populism were ruler oriented, but not on behalf of justice or democracy.

Military populists, such as Chávez, Perón, Velasco, and others, were not just lone mavericks in uniform. All were part of organized factions within the ranks. Chávez, who came to power through an election in 1998, had organized military officers discontented with the political class long before he launched a coup attempt in 1992. As Perón did with the GOU, in 1982 Chávez founded a brotherhood, the Bolivarian Revolutionary Movement (MBR). The MBR drew in like-minded officers who had become distressed with corruption and the failure of elected politicians to turn Venezuela's oil wealth into a viable project of economic development during the oil boom of the 1970s. By 1992, they were organized enough to try the coup under Chávez's leadership, but not alone. Before they did so, they had developed an alliance with a leftist group that was supposed to foment popular support. The attempt failed, but Chávez emerged as a popular hero.

Chávez had set out from the earliest days to redefine the mission of the armed forces as developmental, conceiving his movement as a "civic–military alliance." Once in power after winning elections in December 1999, the MBR renamed itself slightly get around a law prohibiting a party from using the name "Bolívar," so that its initials became MVR. Once Chávez was in the presidency, he would continue the idea of a civic–military alliance by sending military units to poor parts of the cities and countryside to work with civilians on projects to improve living conditions.

Members of secret organizations in the ranks do not always remain united behind their leader. As happened in the cases of Velasco in Peru and Perón in Argentina, some members of the MVR split from Chávez and joined factions in the armed forces that conspired to overthrow Chávez in 2002. The April 2002 coup seemed at first to have succeeded, but Chávez's allies regained control of the officer corps. Meanwhile, his supporters had taken to the streets demanding his return. Chávez was restored to power after 48 hours of detention by the military. However, retired and cashiered officers continued to articulate fierce opposition to Chávez and his plans for the military, opposing other active and retired military officers who came to occupy key positions of government. Some analysts referred to elected government as "democracy in uniform" (Norden 2003).

Hugo Chávez was elected with resounding majorities five times (1998, 2000, 2004, 2006, and 2012), but retaining military support was a key objective of the former colonel, as it would be for Maduro, whose background was not in the military but in labor union politics.

For Review

From the point of view of a military officer, under what conditions might he (occasionally she) be most likely to join a plot to make a coup? Can you break these conditions down into three categories: (1) inside the military, (2) in the broader political and social system, and (3) internationally? Why might a military officer sometimes be sympathetic to left populism?

Militarized Democracies

After the Cold War, the Latin American military was forced to rethink its mission. The enemy had become far less clear. Economic globalization complicated the question of defining national security in the minds of some military officers. The free movement of foreign capital into strategic sectors of Latin America posed a new kind of threat to the integrity of the homeland, *la patria*, as Loveman (1999) calls it. Nationalist resentment is fueled as well by the fact that the United States, Europe, and Japan—while preaching free trade—protect key sectors of their economies (especially in agriculture—e.g., citrus, fruit, soybeans, and sugar) from Latin American exports. Although vital interests of the wealthy nations are secure, the international debt often leaves *la patria* vulnerable to the imposition of neoliberal, **structural adjustment** policies (see chapter 6) that elicit popular anger and resistance. Militaries in turn are deployed to keep protest in check. Some personnel ask themselves, "Are we no more than guardians of the interests of foreign banks and investors?"

Geopolitics is also cause for concern within Latin America's military. On one hand, U.S. military aid and training missions tie the Latin American military establishment closer to their colleagues to the north. On the other hand, the specter of an unchecked superpower and unilateral use of its power (most Latin American countries opposed, for example, the war in Iraq in 2003) has elicited a nationalistic response from some quarters.

Given the long history of *golpes* in Latin America, the continued influence of the military in a variety of ways short of directly governing is worthy of special attention. The loss of prestige by the military after the particularly brutal episodes following the populist crisis and in the Central American counterinsurgency wars seems to be giving way today to more acceptance of military involvement in government. Much of this can be attributed to the high levels of street homicides and gang warfare. However, even without the rising crime rate, several interventions by security forces show that democratic breakdowns have never entirely disappeared from Latin America after the third wave of democracy washed over the region. Honduras experienced an outright coup against an elected president in 2009. It appears that Ecuador's police may have attempted to oust President Rafael Correa in 2010. In Haiti, President Jean-Bertrand Aristide was ousted via coup in 2004. In this same period we have seen civilian seizures of power that have at least met with the approval, if not the outright participation, of security forces.

In Paraguay, center-left President Fernando Lugo was impeached in a highly irregular manner in 2012 by the country's Congress after proposing a relatively moderate land reform to benefit Indigenous peoples. His other main accomplishments were providing free treatment for the poor in public hospitals and a housing program. In strict legal terms, the impeachment was constitutional; Lugo was charged with the responsibility for the deaths of 17 people in a clash between landless farmers and police. He was given two hours to prepare his defense before Congress voted for his removal. Several Pink Tide presidents at the time termed his ouster a coup.

The military has become a significant economic actor in several countries. As late as 2009, the Chilean military directly received 10 percent of the copper export sales earnings (not only the profits) generated by the state copper company, Codelco, the largest single copper mining company in the world. Recent changes somewhat restrict military control over the funds, but the principle of tying a portion of the natural wealth of the country to the armed forces remains. In Cuba, the military has been entrusted with running the domestic tourism industry. Retired military officers own or control key economic assets in a number of countries, including Brazil.

In Venezuela, former military associates of the late President Hugo Chávez continue to hold important posts in government, with one of them, Diosdado Cabello, president of the National Assembly until early 2018, seen as the second-most powerful person in the country, waiting in the wings to succeed President Nicolás Maduro. Opponents of President

Maduro have sought to provoke the military into ousting him. They accuse Maduro of having executed an *"autogolpe"* when he stripped the opposition-controlled National Assembly of its legislative power in 2017. There is little doubt that Maduro relies heavily on the security forces, especially the National Guard.

Mexico's military has been drawn more deeply into the regime's war on drug lords, and in Colombia, talks between the government and guerrilla leaders have stirred discontent among right-wing civilians with allies in the military. In Peru, Ollanta Humala, a former officer with a questionable record during Fujimori's war on the Shining Path guerrillas (see next section), won Peru's presidential election of 2011. In Honduras, elections took place in 2013, but the impact of the coup of 2009 still is felt. Honduran security forces today act with impunity reminiscent of the worst years of the civil wars in Central America. Banks under control of the military in Guatemala and Honduras are highly influential not only in these countries but in neighboring ones too (Brenes Castro and Zamora 2003; Painter 1987: 46–50, 151).

Peru: Fujimori's Autogolpe

As we observed in the first part of this chapter, the causes of coups cannot be reduced to the ambitions of generals and admirals. Civilians have usually played an important role in inducing the military to act; once in power military men, since the nineteenth-century *caudillos*, have relied on civilian politicians, intellectuals, and technocrats for governing expertise. Military coups were important to ushering in populist parties (such as Democratic Action in Venezuela) and semi-democratic, modernizing regimes (such as Getulio Vargas's Estado Nôvo in Brazil and Juan Perón's *justicialismo* in Argentina; see chapter 5).

In 1992, only a few years after the transitions to democracy on the continent and the ending of Central America's civil wars, came the first of the new civilian–military coups, the *"autogolpe"* in Peru. An elected president, Alberto Fujimori, with the support of the military, shut down Congress, suspended the constitution, and purged the judiciary. Congress and the judiciary were highly unpopular, and public revulsion at the violence of an ultra-extreme guerrilla insurgency helped prepare the grounds for the coup.

Peru was certainly no stranger to coups before the *autogolpe*. Like other Andean countries, nineteenth-century Peru was torn by strife between rival *caudillos* who either emerged from or allied with the Liberal and Conservative parties (see chapter 4). This contributed to the defeat of Peruvian and allied Bolivian forces in the War of the Pacific of 1879–1883 by the Chileans (who occupied Lima in 1818 and enjoyed significant aid from Great Britain). Consequently, Bolivia and Peru lost much of the Atacama Desert and its rich nitrate deposits. In addition, Bolivia lost its outlet to the Pacific Ocean. This military disaster gave impulse to a modernization project, finally producing a centralized state. As elsewhere, this project unleashed new social forces that the two old parties, really contending factions of the landed oligarchy, could not contain.

As in many other Latin American countries, modernization of the military meant the opening of a military academy and foreign trainers—in the Peruvian case, French instructors. The creation of a well-armed and -trained army would spell the end of regional **caudillism**. Even when outnumbered, the better-armed and -organized troops of the central government, aided by improvements in communications and transportation, were able to respond effectively and quickly against regional uprisings. However, caudillism in the form of long and often brutal personalist dictatorships hardly disappeared.

In Peru, modernization was carried out relatively late, in the period between 1890 and 1930 under what was known as the Aristocratic Republic, rule by a tightly knit social elite in Lima, the capital. This elite brooked no challenge from social movements or new parties for a more inclusive political order, but it could not keep the lid on as pressure grew. Arguably, the "republic" ended after a military coup installed Augusto B. Leguía, a member of the Lima elite, in 1919. He ruled until 1931, but that did not mean pressure for reform from the middle and the working class subsided. The year 1924 saw the founding of the American Popular Revolutionary Alliance (APRA), led by Victor Haya de la Torre, who was living in exile in Mexico at the time. Haya was influenced early both by the Mexican Revolution and Marxism, although like other rising middle-class leaders he soon distanced himself from the revolutionary doctrines of class struggle. APRA forged a social coalition between the emerging middle class and workers, especially those in the economically crucial mining sector. Haya expressed cultural respect for Peru's Indigenous population, but his base was largely in the *mestizo* working- and middle-class sectors of the population.

At the same time, a Peruvian Socialist Party was founded and gravitated toward Marxist–Leninist doctrines, later becoming the Peruvian Communist Party (PCP). From its ranks came one of the most original socialist thinkers of the twentieth century, José Carlos Mariátegui, who argued for adaption of Marx's ideas to Peruvian reality. The most important part of that reality, one that neither APRA nor the PCP would fully embrace, was the need to incorporate Peru's Indigenous people into a class-based revolutionary struggle. Mariátegui rejected as unrealistic the idea of forming an Indigenous republic in the Andes, a project that the Moscow-based Communist International entertained (Becker 2006), but he argued stridently that Peru could never truly advance until the Indigenous population was respected and fully incorporated into politics and society. Mariátegui died in 1930, at age 34, and today his writings are widely read and respected by the Latin American left.

Ultimately, the PCP too would concentrate more on organizing *mestizo* workers in crucial nodes of the export-oriented economy. Both parties adopted anti-imperialism, which concretely meant criticizing the influence of European (especially British) mining capital and the country's growing dependence on foreign loans. While Haya was the undisputed leader of APRA, Peruvian populism revolved as much around the party as the personality.

Lima's elite and the military made little distinction between APRA's reformism and the PCP's formal affiliation with communism. Mining unionization and peasant organizing were anathema to the oligarchy. Peru's Indigenous peoples were probably about 40 to 50 percent of the population at the time (and 25 to 30 percent today), lived in almost feudal conditions similar to the *huasipongo* system in neighboring Ecuador. The elite had reason to quell any sign of Indigenous discontent. The colonial era was punctuated by several mass Indigenous uprisings against Spanish and **Creole** elites by a population that never lost memory of the glorious pre-Colombian past. Inca rule was not nearly as benign and loved by its subjects as "remembered" today, but to many Indigenous peoples it stands for a civilization that was displaced by European invaders. Mass uprisings in the colonial era appealed to sentiments for restoration and were sometimes led by quasi-religious, charismatic leaders. These kinds of revolts, found in many different corners of the world, are known as "millenarian" movements. In some ways, the violent Sendero Luminoso movement of the 1980s and 1990s fit that pattern.

The conservative Lima elite and the military were determined to bar from governing not only APRA but also any politicians willing to work with APRA. Electoral fraud and outright military intervention kept Haya and APRA from displacing the elite. Over time, new centrist parties arose to challenge both the conservatives and APRA. Haya finally clearly won a presidential election in 1962, but the military barred him from office. APRA over this period moved more to the right. In 1968, just about everyone was stunned by a coup that brought a left-populist military junta, headed by General Velasco Alvarado, to power—testimony to just how opaque an institution the military can be for study by outsiders.

Velasco Alvarado governed as a left populist. He nationalized the large copper mines and carried out a significant land reform that ended the semi-feudal system on the *latifundias* of the Central Valley. The reform created a large class of small holdings, but like so many populist land reforms in the populist era, it failed to provide the support and conditions to allow peasants to prosper. Velasco Alvarado was overthrown by another general in 1975, but not before an initially small, little-noticed guerrilla organization, Sendero Luminoso, began operating in the countryside. It began to attract more adherents in the 1980s, Latin America's **lost decade**, and it grew into a major insurgency during the presidency of Alan García Pérez, the first and only APRA leader to become president.

For our purposes, the details of this winding and complex history need not be fully explored here. What is most important for us is understanding that the violence that engulfed the Peruvian countryside in the 1990s was the product of decades of failures by Peruvian elites to adapt to the forces unleashed in the modernization era, their excessive reliance on the military to resist reform, and the simmering resentments of a proud but impoverished Indigenous population. These factors help us understand why Peru between 1985 and 1992 would suffer seven years of cataclysmic violence, and how a Japanese-Peruvian immigrant would win election and carry out an *autogolpe*.

The Shining Path (Sendero Luminoso—SL) guerrillas adopted a Maoist strategy of prioritizing a takeover of the countryside over urban organizing. The group had considerable success in the 1980s appealing to Indigenous peasants, especially those in the Ayacucho highlands, long excluded and subject to racist discrimination by the more prosperous populations of Lima and the Pacific Coast. SL also protected lowland coca growers in the Amazonian region from abuse by traffickers and the Peruvian military, which was carrying out drug-eradication operations with aid from the United States. These activities netted the guerrillas support from the peasant cultivators and "taxes" from the traffickers. SL spoke to the peasants' long-standing grievances and hunger for land in the Quechua language of the Indigenous people. SL's founder, Abimael Guzmán, a philosophy professor at a regional university, saw in Maoism, a Chinese adaptation of Marxism that viewed the peasantry, not the urban working class, as the basis for revolution in a country with a vast countryside seething with resentment toward landlords, as a tool to mobilize Peru's Indigenous peoples. Here were the descendants of the Inca Empire, poor and exploited, but with a shared oral history of past glory and resistance to European **hegemony**. Guzmán developed a cult-like following, not just from Indigenous people but also from other sectors of Peru's cities who fled to the countryside to join the insurrection. For this reason, the Peruvian historian Gustavo Gorriti (1999) describes the conflict between SL and the Peruvian army as a "millenarian war," as Guzmán was viewed by his followers almost mystically, as the messiah come to redeem greatness lost.

As the peasant war intensified, in 1990 President Alberto Fujimori of Peru won the presidential election promising to resist neoliberalism and effectively combat the extremely violent Sendero Luminoso uprisings. An immigrant from Japan, his Asian appearance helped him among Indigenous voters. In office, Fujimori completely reversed his stand on economic policy, but he kept his promise on crushing SL. To accomplish this, in 1992 he closed the Congress, which at the time was highly unpopular with voters, and turned to the military for support. In exchange, the military was given a free hand, freeing itself to commit gross violations of human rights in fighting the internal war. At the same time, a top circle of generals, headed by the president's intelligence secretary, Vladimiro Montesinos, made millions of dollars from drug trafficking, arms smuggling, and other questionable businesses. Fujimori's closing of Congress became known as the *autogolpe* and for setting a pattern for the future: an elected president who allies with the military to exert dominance over the other branches of government.

Under Fujimori (1990–2000), the Peruvian military's tactics did not lower but instead intensified the violence as Peruvians found themselves caught between state terror and revolutionary terror. SL ruthlessly carried out massacres in uncooperative villages and assassinations of dissenters. As military forces repressed the rebellion in the country, SL targeted not only the government and the Peruvian right but also human rights workers, leaders of neighborhood organizations, religious base communities, and any other individuals or groups who did not fit its vision of a society cleansed of European colonialism—in the cities, not just in the countryside. Peasants and progressive groups found themselves caught between SL and Peru's well-trained 70,000-man army. The army employed classic counterinsurgency tactics (taught by U.S., Israeli, and Argentine instructors) that included massive relocation of villagers, much like the scorched-earth policy employed by General Ríos Montt in Guatemala (see chapter 9) and American counterinsurgency forces in Vietnam. Police units massacred suspected sympathizers, in one case by the thousands.

Ultimately the military–civilian government of Fujimori subdued Sendero Luminoso, but at a high cost to prospects for democracy in Peru. The capture of SL's leader, university professor Abimael Guzmán, in 1992 severely weakened the organization, as did the arrest of other leaders in 1995. Since 2000, small cells of SL have carried out some spectacular actions, but the movement has also suffered defeats and arrests of other leaders. However, the movement has never been fully extinguished. Nor has any Peruvian government seriously addressed the social conditions that gave rise to it.

As the war wound down, so did Fujimori's popularity and that of the military. Fujimori fled the country in November 2000 rather than face charges for corruption and gross human rights abuses. His intelligence chief, Montesinos, had strong connections to the U.S. Central Intelligence Agency; he fled after incriminating videotapes put him in the center of several criminal conspiracies and enterprises.

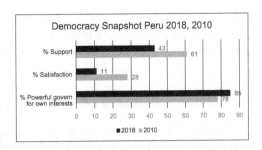

Democracy Snapshot Peru 2018, 2010

Alejandro Toledo was a self-made man with Quechua roots who rose from the ranks of informal workers to achieve advanced degrees in business schools in the United States. He led the political opposition to Fujimori in 2000, and then defeated García in the 2001 election by campaigning on a populist platform that promised policies favoring both the redistribution for the poor and laisse-faire economics. Of course, it proved impossible to reconcile those objectives. Toledo thought he could reconcile his economic policies with his promises to Indigenous peoples by encouraging decentralization, and that Indigenous people could assert themselves at that level. However, his plans to open the country's resources to extractive industries soon mobilized resistance. Mass protests erupted in the streets of the large city of Arequipa touched off by his efforts to privatize the electric utility and to sell rights over the collection and distribution of water to a German firm. These became known around the world as the "Water Wars."

In 2006, Alan García returned to the presidency. He benefited from robust economic recovery due to rising prices on Peru's mining exports, but he was caught up in corruption. The **Panama Papers** revealed his money laundering with funds obtained from Brazil's **Obredecht** construction company. In 2019 García shot himself to death over the scandal. In 2011, Humala Ollanta, a former military officer dogged by accusations of human rights abuses in the war against SL, won election after running on a center-left platform, but he did not introduce any significant reform. He would be indicted in 2012 on charges connected to the Obredecht scandal, referring to revelations of bribery and extortion involving the huge Brazilian construction company. The same fate awaited Pedro Pablo Kuzcynski, who openly embraced neoliberalism but had a reputation as an honest technocrat. He too was swept up in the Obredecht scandal. Since 2000, then, four Peruvian presidents have been indicted on corruption charges.

Vice President Martin Vizcarra took over the presidency following Kuzcynski's resignation. Vizcarra may prove to be an effective leader, but Peru's political party system lies in shambles. The country's economic dependence on extraction will pose problems for him as China's voracious appetite for Peru's minerals has slackened and Indigenous resistance to intrusive transnational mining operations has grown in intensity. Vizcarra initiated a popular anti-corruption campaign and constitutionally dissolved Congress in order to hold new elections in May 2020. Members of the legislature faced loss of their immunity from being charged with crimes should they lose in the elections.

The popularity of Vizcarra and (at least in his first year) his clean record enabled him to defeat the Congress's efforts to manipulate the judiciary into voiding the call of elections, but there was an additional factor in his favor. After members of the right-wing-dominated Congress accused him of carrying out an *autogolpe*, the army, navy, air force, and police announced their support of Vizcarra, ending the standoff between the president and the legislature. On the one hand, Vizcarra may prove to be the first president to actually carry out a campaign against corruption, but at what might prove to be the crucial moment for his ambitions, the deciding factor was not the country's elected representatives but the military.

Colombia: Militarized Democracy

Colombia has experienced guerrilla warfare almost constantly for 50 years. The roots of the conflict can be traced to 1946, when the Conservative Party launched a war against peasants who had supported its Liberal Party rivals. This gave birth to the ten-year period known as La Violencia. The violence intensified as a liberal and leftist firebrand, Jorge Eliécer Gaitán, seemed poised to win the presidency in the 1950 elections. He was assassinated in 1948, touching off rioting all over the country. In Bogotá, the capital, approximately one-third of the city was burned down.

In the next ten years, La Violencia would claim the lives of one of every 40 Colombians (in a population of ten million at this time). Many of the Liberal forces consisted of guerrillas operating in rural areas; the Conservatives, for their part, tended to make use of government forces. As often happens with civil wars (for example, in the United States), the violence became communal; that is, sparked by personal vendettas, banditry, and clashes between small peasants and big landowners. The Colombian military found itself in the middle of a highly partisan, violent conflict. In 1953, the generals finally intervened, with the approval of Liberal and Conservative party leaders, who saw the military government playing a moderator role. General Gustavo Rojas Pinilla, who headed the junta, governed under martial law and reduced, but not entirely eliminated, the violence. Against expectations of the Liberals and Conservatives, Rojas Pinillas also adopted a populist demeanor, much like the Andean dictators General Marcos Pérez Jiménez in Venezuela and Manuel Odría in Peru. All three harshly repressed both the communist parties and the moderate left reformists but also carried out programs, especially urban housing projects, designed to attract popular support. This was enough for liberal and conservative oligarchs. As public protests mounted, the parties negotiated a pact. After a *golpe* against Rojas Pinilla, sometimes called "the coup of public opinion," the parties took back control of the government from military hands.

The era of La Violencia came to a close in 1957 when leaders of the two parties met and agreed to share power in government after elections in 1958 and created a "National Front" that would govern the country until 1974. Another "pacted democracy" was born. As with Venezuela's "Punto Fijo" agreement (see chapter 8), the Colombian pact was accompanied by other accords that protected the interest of other major actors. Even more so than Punto Fijo, the Colombian pact excluded the interests of the lower classes. Colombia was not, after all, a petrostate with a large volume of export-generated revenues to distribute in populist fashion.

The Liberal and Conservative parties continued to dominate the government after 1974 for another two decades, after which a number of new parties formed. Some were left parties founded by allies of former guerrilla movements. However, two of the larger ones were founded by liberal dissidents unhappy with that party's move toward a more progressive stance. One important split came in 2016 when Alvaro Uribe, an ultra-right former liberal president, broke away to form what he called, despite his clearly right-wing sentiments, the Democratic Center Party.

Given La Violencia, the assassination of Gaitán, the monopoly of power exercised by the National Front, and the determination of the oligarchy to continue to resist change, it hardly surprises that guerrilla movements sprung up again in various regions of Colombia after 1957. As in many Latin American countries, left guerrilla movements were encouraged by the success of the Cuban Revolution of 1959. Some fighters in the Colombian movements had been involved in the factional violence of La Violencia; others were frustrated by the machinations of the Liberals and Conservatives to block rival new parties. One guerrilla movement, M-19, arose after claiming (with good reason) that fraud had deprived its candidates of victory in the 1970 elections. Attempts to negotiate a political settlement were futile. In 1985, M-19 seized the Supreme Court building and the justices, demanding that the government publish a report showing the military's violations of a cease-fire agreement. Instead, the military attacked and burned the building to the ground, killing more than 100 people, including the chief justice and 11 of his colleagues. M-19, though divided, eventually did return to civil politics, but it suffered the murder of hundreds of its candidates and of allied leaders of unions, peasant associations, and other civilians. Another smaller guerrilla organization, the Popular Liberation Army (EPL), suffered a similar fate after agreeing to a truce in 1991 (on violence in Colombia, see Tuft 1997).

Two large guerrilla movements in Colombia that remained active are the National Liberation Army (ELN) and Revolutionary Armed Forces of Colombia (FARC). The latter reached a peace agreement in 2016, and many of its fighters have demobilized (see later). The FARC grew out of the Colombian Communist Party, which formed a force in 1965 to protect peasants who were supposed to be resettled in another part of the country. Most were small holders who were evicted from their lands as the government and landowners consolidated properties in a drive to expand agribusiness exports. Colombia's landed oligarchy had long resisted peasant organizing, using its close ties with the state through the two major political parties. The massive rioting that took place after Gaitán's assassination had only made them more determined to repress labor union and peasant organizing. The Communist Party, on the other hand, had a long history of organizing peasants to defend or occupy land and to form peasant leagues. These leagues are counterparts to unions in that they organize rural workers to demand better pay and working conditions for landless rural workers and access to land for those seeking to produce for subsistence or local markets.

In 1968, 16,000 Colombian army troops attacked 48 armed communists protecting the small community of Marquetalia. The armed members and 47 others fled to the countryside and formed the FARC. At its peak, the movement had about 10,000 fighters (FARC-EP, "popular army") and perhaps 200,000 non-combatant supporters (the FARC). By 1982, the FARC had found a bountiful source of financial support by taxing the drug trade, which in Colombia largely involved chemical processing units that prepared coca brought mostly from Peru and Bolivia for transport to lucrative markets in Europe and North America.

The ELN was formed in 1965 by Colombian students who were inspired by the Cuban Revolution. The two groups differed in strategy, at least initially, with the FARC generally following a longer-term strategy of peasant organizing and the ELN more focused on sparking an insurrection to take control of the Colombian state along lines achieved in Cuba. Over time, these differences were less important than their geographic base, with the FARC more rooted in central, lowland regions and the ELN operating in the eastern areas closer to Venezuela. Colombia shares a long ill-defined border (because of shifting rivers) through the *llanos* (plains). ELN forces and the right-wing paramilitary units fighting them frequently cross over into Venezuelan territory.

Besides taxing the drug trade, both guerrilla groups finance their operations through kidnapping, extortion, and taxation of extractive industries (more the ELN), including oil companies that expanded operations in Colombia after 1980. The ELN also extorts protection payments from oil companies operating in its zones of control. Rural Colombians often find themselves caught in the crossfire. The paramilitary groups and death squads, which are well connected to the military and right-wing landlords, adopted the same practices. Both eventually went beyond taxing the drug trade to direct participation in trafficking.

Coca products became for a while the country's most important export, and the traffickers, like all wealthy interest groups, make heavy donations to politicians. Even the U.S. State Department in 1997 labeled Colombia a "narco-democracy." Big transnational companies and ranchers privately funded a paramilitary group, the United Self-Defense Forces of Colombia (AUC), composed of many former and active soldiers. In 1983, 59 members of the armed forces were found to be members of one of the death squad organizations. Like the FARC, a major source of AUC funds came from drug trafficking. Both the FARC and AUC have appeared on the U.S. State Department's list of "terrorist" organizations; the FARC remains so designated today. The AUC, which at its peak had about 20,000 members, was officially dissolved in 2006, but successor groups, such as the notorious Black Eagles, have continued to operate.

In 2001, the United States decided that the Colombian government had made enough "progress" in distancing itself from the drug lords to justify President Bill Clinton's signing a US$1.3 billion package of mostly military aid. Clinton's decision came over the objections of human rights organizations and Colombian civilian organizations caught in the crossfire. Between 2000 and 2016, the United States provided $9.94 billion in aid under Plan Colombia, which mostly went for military equipment and training, both by U.S. military advisors and private contractors (Alpert 2016). The military aid contributed significantly to reducing FARC territorial control and the depletion of fighters in its ranks. The FARC-EP retaliated with attacks on civilians, especially against targets in wealthy areas of Bogotá. The most notorious was the 2003 bombing of a nightclub that killed 36 people. The FARC's turn toward kidnapping and targeting civilians with violence contributed to the erosion of sympathy and tolerance in Colombian civil society, which has been a factor in public apathy, if not opposition, to attempts to implement a peace accord frame in 2016.

Under pressure from the United States to curb right-wing violence, in 2005–2006 Colombian president Álvaro Uribe declared an amnesty for AUC members who turned in their weapons. Human rights organizations condemned the action, which absolved the AUC for thousands of serious human rights atrocities. Declassified cables obtained by the (private) National Security Archive (2018) showed that Colombian sources repeatedly told U.S. embassy officials that Uribe himself was involved in drug trafficking during his political rise. In 1991, a detailed U.S. Defense Intelligence Agency report linked Uribe to the notorious Mexican dealer Juan Pablo Escobar and to the Colombian Medellín Cartel. Uribe, also under suspicion of having led an AUC force (*Colombia Reports*, August 29, 2013), has always insisted that the charges are false (National Security Archive 2004). President Uribe did preside over a vigorous military offensive against drug trafficking. On the other hand, as pointed out in chapter 14, it is not unusual for crime cartels and traffickers to attempt to move from the illicit activities into the realm of the aboveground economy and politics.

As with other attempts to reintegrate guerrilla movements in Colombia into non-violent politics, attempts to reintegrate the FARC have been frustrated by repression organized or tolerated by the military. M-19 claimed that 3,000 of its members were assassinated in 1990, and the EPL said that more than 100 of its members were killed in 1991. In the mid-1980s, the FARC set up a political wing, the Patriotic Union, to test the possibilities of abandoning armed struggle for an electoral strategy. An estimated 2,000–4,000 of the Patriotic Union's members were murdered. In 1987, the minister of the interior listed 137 rightist death squads. In 1987, there were more than 1,500 political assassinations; in that year, dozens of leaders of a banana workers' union were assassinated. In 1988, 40 banana workers were mass-murdered in front of their families.

Despite the violence, in 1991 the M-19 and the Hope, Peace and Liberty Party (formed by former EPL fighters) won more than one-third of the delegates to a **constituent assembly** that wrote a remarkably progressive constitution, promising land reform and social justice. The Colombia Human Rights Network (CHRN) (2001) details the aftermath:

> People assumed that the political landscape would be transformed by the Constitution but, in reality, it had no impact on the level of violence and the search for peace. One reason was that the FARC and ELN, the two largest guerrilla groups, did not participate in the process because, rather than a few representatives in Congress, they wanted social and land reform and restructuring of the army. The M-19 collapsed from political ineptness. The dirty war resumed and violence tripled. The guerrilla movement grew stronger, with activity in two-thirds of the municipalities, but was politically weak and no longer commanded the support of students and the middle class.

All sides in the conflict have committed atrocities. The CHRN stated, "Over 25,000 homicides took place in Colombia during 1995. The paramilitaries are believed responsible for 60 percent of political killings, the guerrillas for 25 percent, and the military for 10 percent." President Uribe, before leaving office in 2010, achieved significant success against the guerrillas, especially the FARC, but the toll on Colombian civil society was high. A 2015 Human Rights Watch documented the killing of thousands of civilians by Colombian security forces between 2002 and 2010, and the report cast some doubt on the army's claims of success. Known as the "false-positive scandal," military personnel dressed up corpses as guerillas in order to boost the FARC body count.

At the same time, the FARC progressively lost much of its appeal to the general population, alienating many Colombians who most wanted to end the long era of violence in their country. Still, applying the label "terrorist" to the ELN and FARC, as the United States has done, oversimplifies their character and masks the deep roots of the unrest. It mainly serves to simplify the ability of the United States to funnel military aid to the Colombian government, as well as establish nine military bases in the country.

Juan Manuel Santos, Uribe's minister of defense, succeeded Uribe to the presidency in August 2010. Against expectations, Santos initiated negotiations with the guerrillas. In

contrast to Uribe, Santos looked to Raúl Castro and Hugo Chávez to urge the FARC to negotiate, and talks began in Havana in 2011 under Cuban mediation. Santos by no means can
be considered part of the Pink Tide; his government remained Washington's closest ally in
the region. Santos's breakthrough was no small feat. Although severely weakened by the
killing or capture of several leaders and by the success of the U.S.-aided counterinsurgency,
the FARC at the time remained a strong presence, with an estimated 8,000 men and women
under arms and present in 25 of 32 provinces. In the negotiations, some progress was made
on issues such as land reform and reintegration of the guerrilla into political life, and in 2016
an agreement was reached. In response, ex-president Uribe broke from Santos and the Liberal Party to found the Democratic Center Party.

Uribe campaigned for rejection of the accord in the plebiscite, which initially was expected
to pass easily. His campaign stressed provisions that would prevent the prosecution of FARC
members for its atrocities, but polls showed a majority of Colombians favored the accord.
Uribe's campaign and voter complacency prevailed. In a low turnout election, the accord was
rejected by 50.2 percent of the voters. Santos and the FARC returned to the table and negotiated
changes that Santos submitted to Congress rather than to the voters, and they passed handily
but with no votes from the Democratic Center Party. Santos was ineligible to run for reelection
in 2018. Instead of a contest between the Conservative and Liberal parties, the election came
down in the second round to a choice between Iván Duque Márquesz, the candidate of Uribe's
Democratic Center Party, and Gustavo Petro, the candidate of a new party, Humane Colombia.
Duque won in an election that attracted only 53 percent of voters to the polls.

There are a few signs of hope for the future.
Claudia López, a member of the LGBTQ+ community, became mayor of Bogotá, the capital, in
2020. She boldly defended a wave of protests
against Duque's economic policies. Protestors
marched in defiance of threats from armed
right paramilitaries. The cities of Cartagena and
Medellín have shed their reputation as violent
centers of drug trafficking. Still, as 2020 opened,

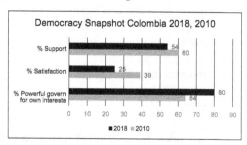

the peace agreement appeared to be on shaky ground. The military continued its attacks of
FARC communities and on members of progressive social movements. Some FARC fighters
that had not yet turned in their weapons threatened to return to warfare. More than 170 FARC
members who had disarmed were murdered in the last few months of 2017 and in 2018.

The state and paramilitary violence vitiated the spirit and letter of the progressive 1991
constitution. In 2020, Colombia's presidency remained controlled by the extreme right "Democratic Center" Party. Its leader, Uribe, has been repeatedly connected to drug trafficking, presided
over severe human rights abuses, and carried out a campaign of sabotaging implementation of
the peace accords. John Dugas, a political scientist specializing on Colombia, lists five fundamental reasons why the promising 1991 constitution will fall short of its promising democratic
aspirations. These apply as well to the other Andean states. Not necessarily in order they are:

1. Weak territorial control and presence of the state authority leaves great geographic
    space available for both guerrillas, traffickers, and paramilitary forces. Not only does
    this mean week public security, especially in rural zones, but also it means inadequate
    access to health care, education, and other services.

2.   Political parties and politicians rely on access to and distribution of state resources to provide jobs, services, and other rewards in exchange for votes. The extensive and direct exchange of resources for votes subverts equality of citizenship and undermines campaigns appealing for votes based on the welfare of all.
3.   Clientelism readily spills over into corruption.
4.   Judiciaries are weak, especially in delivering impartial justice on ordinary political matters.
5.   Most seriously, Colombian democracy continues to be weakened by the direct and indirect participation of the state security forces in human rights abuses.

(Dugas 2016)

According to Manuel Rozental, a surgeon and prominent peace activist in rural Cauca province, nearly 800 leaders of Indigenous and communist groups have been murdered since the peace agreement was signed. Rozental attributes the killing to both dissident members of the FARC that have rearmed or never disarmed and official and paramilitary members of the security forces (*Real News Network*, November 8, 2019).

Colombia, like Venezuela and Mexico, might have escaped the harsh bureaucratic authoritarian dictatorships of the Southern Cone and Brazil, but it might be the most militarized "democracy" in the Western Hemisphere.

Militarized Democracy

Civilian control of the military is a somewhat idealized hallmark of democracy. No democratic institution anywhere is fully insulated from military and police influence, including in the United States. After all, President Dwight Eisenhower, a former general, warned citizens in the United States in his farewell address, "In the councils of government, we must guard against the acquisition of unwarranted influence, whether sought or unsought, by the military-industrial complex. The potential for the disastrous rise of misplaced power exists and will persist."

Max Weber, the German sociologist, differentiated the state from other forms of human organization because, he argued, it is a human community that successfully claims a monopoly on the legitimate use of physical force within a given territory (Weber 2013, original 1916). One can dispute whether that definition applies to all time periods and cultures, but it certainly is one way to describe the modern territorial state. To be a democratic state requires that the institutions that exercise "legitimate" violence not only be subject to control by civilians; it must also be committed to and thoroughly imbued with the democratic spirit.

Discussion Questions

1.   Colombia is often cited as one of the few Latin countries that escaped the wave of military governments of the 1970s and 1980s. Would you agree?
2.   Do you think that a military coup is ever justifiable? If so, under what circumstances? If not, how do you think the military should react if it finds itself called upon by large sectors of a society to defend the constitution against abuse of power by a president?
3.   Why do you think that in the last 20 years we have seen so many instances of irregular takeovers of power but not outright coups? Should we call these incidents "coups"?

Resources for Further Study

Reading: *The Colombia Reader: History, Culture, Politics*, edited by Anne Farnsworth-Alvear, Marco Palacios, and Ana María Gómez López (Durham, NC: Duke University Press, 2017), with many pieces translated from Spanish providing Colombian perspectives. Editors Carlos Iván Degregori, Steve J. Stern, and Nancy Appelbaum provide a human rights perspective on Peru in *How Difficult It Is to Be God: Shining Path's Politics of War in Peru, 1980–1999*.

Video and Film: *Dancing With the Incas* (Intuitive Productions) looks at Peruvian musicians caught between the army and Sendero Luminoso. *The Atlantic* magazine combines an article with a 20-minute film about the difficulties of implementing the agreement between the FARC and Colombian government.

On the Internet: *Colombia Reports* (colombiareports.com) provides highly reliable coverage of Colombian politics, violence, and other matters from the perspective of civil society. English language news from Colombia can be found at the *Peruvian Times* (www.peruviantimes.com).

PART IV

Civil Society, Institutions, Human Rights

Source: Marcelo Benitez/Contributor.

11 Social Class and Social Movements in Latin America

Focus Questions

▶ What are the major features of the social class structures of Latin America?

▶ How do economic inequalities interact with other social cleavages in the region?

▶ How do social movements in Latin America relate to the market on the one hand and the state on the other? How are they shaping civil society?

POLITICS, THE ARENA of our lives where we compete and cooperate to defend our interests but also to build a good society, takes place not only through the formal institutions of the state but also at the level of group life, what is often called "**civil society**." Like so many other key concepts in political science, the meaning of this term is contested. **Pluralists** conceive of civil society as groups, movements, and associations that occupy the social space between the individual and family on one hand and the government and state on the other. From the pluralists' perspective, the marketplace is a part of civil society, the place where people, as Adam Smith (1776) put it in *The Wealth of Nations*, "truck, barter, and exchange" goods and services with one another.

A strong civil society, in the view of pluralists, is a check on tyranny. In fact, the idea of "totalitarianism" is often conceived as a situation in which the state has entirely obliterated the boundary between state and society, including the market. As some critics (e.g., Barber 1969) have noted, this way of thinking about "totalitarianism" is closely wedded to the *liberal* tradition of thinking about freedom as something we enjoy as individuals who freely choose to organize groups and make choices in the marketplace. The tradition of liberal political philosophy, and the **hegemonic** way of thinking in Western capitalist societies, is that markets and societies are constructed by individual human beings. That is, society arises from the "propensity to truck, barter, and exchange." The state and government are in turn created to carry out tasks that are limited by what constitutions, which are contracts between society and the state, authorize them to do—and no more. We give up so freedoms for security and a neutral arbitration of our disputes with one another, including those that arise out of our business in the marketplace. In sum, individuals create markets and groups, the stuff of "civil society." These individuals then created states with constitutions that limit the authority of the state, that preserve our basic rights.

However, what if people are not individuals but naturally social and political creatures, as the ancient Greeks believed? Did society emerge because people were engaged in "truck, barter and exchange," or did "truck, barter and exchange" emerge because we are naturally social beings? There have been markets throughout recorded history, but capitalist societies, where market relations permeate just about every area of social life, are at most a few hundred years old, and less than that in most parts of the world. Indigenous societies of the Americas had markets, but none were "market societies" like those that exist today. Rather than think of government only in terms of a necessary evil that must be kept at bay to protect our freedom, it is also possible to think of government as a desirable force for the general welfare and to enhance our freedom.

In recent decades, grassroots social movements and left-populist (**Pink Tide**) governments in Latin America have taken a view that synthesizes these two different ways of thinking about the state and civil society. **Social movements** are loosely associated individuals or organizations that take action in resistance to common problems, in defense of common interests, or in the quest to force the government or other social actors to respond to widely supported demands. They are wary of attempts at subordination by populist parties and politicians, but they also mistrust the market. Whereas **neoliberals** see the market as enhancing freedom in civil society, many social movements fear that the competitive nature of the market, left unchecked, will corrode the social solidarity needed for a strong civil society and impose the greatest costs of economic change on those least able to bear it. They want a strong, democratic state that works in and with civil society, not standing apart from it. Whether they can achieve this without **clientelism** and **corporatism** is a significant issue.

In this chapter we focus on movements, groups, and social classes, three types of associational life that make up civil society. We already looked at some aspects of social class in Latin America in chapter 2, which focuses on inequality. We return to that subject but flesh it out more by relating it to occupational structures and ownership of the means of production.

The Social Class System

Few social scientists would argue anymore, as some Marxists have, that all other divisions, such as race and gender, would simply disappear if social classes were abolished, but some would argue that not enough attention is given to social class. Two distinguished students of Latin America's class structures have argued that the international organizations that study poverty and inequality generally do not describe the distribution of wealth and income in terms of class "because of its Marxist origin and consequent evocation of notions of conflict, privilege and exploitation. Yet its omission obscures significant aspects of contemporary social dynamics and deprives us of a valuable analytic tool" (Portes and Hoffman 2003: 42).

Portes and Hoffman use Marx's definition as people's relationship to the **means of production**—land, machinery, buildings, and so on, used to produce other goods and services. The conception of class sees this relationship as impacting all other areas of human endeavor, including culture and politics. This means more than just "occupation." In narrowest terms, Marxists define the **bourgeoisie** as owners of the means of production; the **proletariat** are those who must sell their labor (for wages) to gain access to the means of production. However, Marx himself recognized that social class structures are more complex. Also, politically, just as important as how we objectively group people into social classes is how people think about themselves, the "subjective" factor. Class-based social movements emerge when people see themselves as having common interests with each other as a class and begin to act collectively on them (Thompson 1966). Put another way, how people self-classify themselves helps to define the politics of social class in a society.

The most in-depth study of the social class structure in Latin America was published by Portes and Hoffman in 2003. Their results are summarized in Tables 11.1 and 11.2. Keep in mind that social class structures have evolved somewhat since the study was published. Many studies show that Latin America experienced a growth of its middle class and a significant decline in poverty in the 2000s, but after the global financial crisis of 2008, that tendency

TABLE 11.1 Urban Social Class Structure

Social Class	Characteristics	% Labor force
Capitalists	Owners and high-salaried managers of large and medium companies	1.8%
Executives	Managers and administrators of large and medium companies	1.6
Well-off middle class	University-trained salaried professionals in public service, large and medium companies, e.g., engineers, accountants	2.8
Petty bourgeoisie (small capitalists)	Small-scale entrepreneurs who have employees and/or provide a professional/technical service, e.g., doctor, owner of auto-repair shop, computer technician	8.5
White-collar wage workers	Skilled or professionally educated employees typically found in offices, e.g., bank clerks	12.4
Workers, classic proletariat	Manual workers, formally employed for wages, often unionized or protected by labor laws, workers on modern farms	23.4
Marginalized, informal workforce	Day laborers, street vendors, family workers; undercounted because temporary contract workers in large companies are not included	45.9

Source: Portes and Hoffman (2003: 46–49).

TABLE 11.2 Variations in Urban Class Structure in Latin America[5]

	Brazil %	Chile %	Colombia %	Costa Rica %	El Salvador %	Mexico %	Panama %	Venezuela %
Upper class[1]	3.8	2.6	3.0	4.1	2.7	2.9	6.0	3.9
Middle sectors[2]	8.8	16.9	17.0	14.0	14.8	12.2	13.5	21.2
Working class[3]	33.4	45.2	35.0	42.3	33.0	39.1	37.2	36.4
Informal sector[4]	48.1	34.9	44.9	38.9	50.0	45.7	43.0	38.0

[1] Owners of large companies and highly paid executives.
[2] Professionals, small-scale capitalists, skilled or professional employees.
[3] Formally employed wage workers.
[4] Urban poor, marginalized.
[5] Percentages do not add up to 100 because different sources were used to estimate the categories; figures most likely underestimate percentages at bottom of class structure.

Source: Adapted from Portes and Hoffman (2003: 52).

ceased. The net result may be that Latin American social structures had not dramatically changed since 2000. Also, as we saw in chapter 2, much of Latin America's "middle class" lives very precariously. The coronavirus pandemic of 2020 has the potential to impact the way people see their relations to each other and their assessment of how much market forces should determine life chances.

Portes and Hoffman estimated that around the year 2000, between 1 and 2 percent of the economically active population in Latin America owned medium or large companies. If we include managers with high incomes, we can expand the size of the upper class (*bourgeoisie*) to about 5 percent. To this wealthiest sector we can add professional people (engineers, doctors, lawyers, etc.), who make up 5 to 10 percent of the workforce. They have significantly more control over their work lives. They interact personally with counterparts in other parts of the world through conferences, professional associations, trade shows, and leisure travel. They often work for **transnational corporations** or in sectors linked to the global economy; they are "plugged into" the Internet, satellite radio and television, and other information systems. Through such networks, this social class has considerable capacity to meet, plan, and exchange views, nationally and internationally. They form a class of people able to make their own political opportunities and not just take advantage of the ones that present themselves. This social class—the "bourgeoisie"—as Portes and Hoffman define it, constitutes from 5 to 15 percent of those working.

Small capitalists (the *petit bourgeoisie*) in Latin America are middle-class professionals—for example, teachers and technicians—and micro-entrepreneurs (shopkeepers) who employ a handful of workers, often drawn from the ranks of family. They specialize in providing low-cost services for consumers (e.g., shoe repair and plumbing) or for businesses (janitorial services, message services, etc.). This sector grew in the late twentieth century as a result of neoliberal economic policies. Employees of downsized public bureaucracies and closed factories suddenly had to fend for themselves. A teacher now becomes a personal tutor. An architect becomes a cab driver. Perhaps the metalworker in an aluminum fabrication plant hires him- or herself out for construction jobs or roof repair. Under better circumstances, this individual might start a small business that fabricates parts for auto shops. In the worst cases, these individuals fall into the ranks of the informal sector. As we saw in chapter 2, much of the middle class lives a very precarious existence. To express it differently, in a time of relative prosperity, **precarity** affected a little less than half of the population of Argentina and nearly nine out every ten Hondurans. Both figures are high, but the difference should give us pause about too widely generalizing of social classes for the entire region and on matters like how the coronavirus pandemic may impact Latin America.

Brazil, because of the enormous size of both its territory (only slightly smaller than the U.S., including Alaska) and its population (209 million), is worth a closer look, and it illustrates tremendous variance. Figure 11.1 shows how much class structure can vary from region to region in the country. If you look at the last column, the Northeast, where an enslaved population produced the sugar and generated extraordinary export wealth in the colonial era, has the highest concentration of people, mostly *negro* and **pardo**, in the two poorest sectors of the population. Conversely, the southern region has the highest concentrations of upper- and upper-middle-class families. Not surprisingly, this disparity generated a large migration of poor from the north to the south during the import substitution era and the brief Brazilian economic "miracle" of the early 1970s.

FIGURE 11.1   Regional Variation of Social Classes in Brazil

Percent population in social classes based on family assets and monthly income in Brazilian reales in January 2016. 0.252 real = $1 (approximate).

REGION/Class	Class A >12,419	Class B >6,209	Class C >2,484	Class D >1,242	Class E<1,242
Northern	1.5%	13.7%	42.6%	42.1% combined	
Northeast	1.1%	12.3%	39.4%	47.2% combined	
Central-West	3.7%	26%	48.5%	21.8% combined	
Southeast	3.3%	29.7%	51.2%	15.9% combined	
South	3.2%	27.6%	53.5%	15.6% combined	

Source: "Social Classes in Brazil," The Brazil Business, January 26, 2016, based on data from Instituto Brasileiro de Geografia e Estatística. Classes D and E combined in original.

The Brazil Business (2016), a public relations and consulting company, provides on its website (thebrazilbusiness.com) information on the occupations typically found in each class category. As this company provides business and marketing advice to foreign companies, its judgment of what occupations are found in each class provides some further insight on how the relationship to the means of production shapes the class structure. People in Class A tend to be connected to financial businesses, to own large businesses or land, and/or are "people with extraordinary skills" (probably including top-level athletes and entertainment celebrities). Class B tends to consist of people high up in public and private bureaucracies, successful professionals in universities, engineering firms, law offices, and so forth. Class C consists largely of workers who provide services to the first two sectors—teachers, mechanics, appliance installers and preparers, health workers, and so forth. While Class D and E are combined in Figure 11.1, they are occupationally somewhat different. While people in Class C live somewhat precariously themselves, many people in Class D can be found working for these families directly as domestic servants, restaurant and bar personnel, drivers, and other such occupations. They may work in construction or in small stores, possibly in their own small businesses, such as corner bodegas. Those at the bottom of the class pyramid include street cleaners and unemployed people scraping by. People in Class D probably have not finished high school; those in Class E do not have even an elementary education and may be illiterate. The Brazil Business does not list rural occupations, but undoubtedly most peasants and rural workers fall into Class E, or at best Class D.

Hernando de Soto (1989), a Peruvian entrepreneur who founded the neoliberal think tank the Institute for Liberty and Democracy (Instituto Libertad y Democracia), has promoted the idea that many members of the informal class are highly entrepreneurial and could lay the basis for a prosperous capitalist economy—if only the burden of government regulation were lifted. De Soto's critics say that government regulation is less of a threat than the market, where they mostly compete with larger, more efficient businesses and transnational corporations. Everyone who has visited Latin America will probably recall that there is a great variety of low-cost, tasty street food on offer. However, these tiny businesses certainly cannot compete with the large, transnational corporate food chains— McDonald's, KFC, etc.

Many small-scale entrepreneurs are not enamored of laissez-faire capitalism. For example, El Barzón (The Yoke), a movement of small business owners and farmers in Mexico, has criticized neoliberalism and called for reform of campaign financing in Mexican elections. Also affiliated with El Barzón are indebted credit card holders, the National Confederation of Small and Micro Businesses, and the National Union of Agricultural Producers. In 1992, they set up blockades of streets and banks to press their demands for debt forgiveness. They did not achieve that goal, but El Barzón forced the government to grant a moratorium on paying their debts (Senzek 1997).

On the other hand, small-scale entrepreneurs often oppose radical change, especially when they feel that their property is threatened by a leftist government. Such was the case with Patria y Libertad (Homeland and Liberty), a right-wing group that used violence and sabotage to help destabilize the Allende government in Chile between 1970 and 1973 (see chapter 7). Truck and bus drivers, both self-employed and those working for small businesses, participated in strikes with the same goal in mind. Abetted by intervention and funding by the United States (see U.S. Senate 1975), they heightened the polarization that brought about the breakdown of Chilean democracy.

According to Portes and Hoffman (2003), a slightly larger sector is made up of white-collar employees and technicians with vocational training—teachers, accountants, clerks, computer programmers, and so on. Adding this group to the small business sector and adjusting for evidence of growth in the middle class since 2000, we can estimate that the middle class constitutes 30 to 40 percent of the population, perhaps more in some countries, such as Brazil. The quality of their lives, however, remains precarious, as we saw in chapter 2. Inflation and unemployment can strike quickly and devastate this class. For example, in 2005–2007, Argentina, a relatively wealthy country, experienced a wave of education strikes as teachers protested that their salaries had fallen below the poverty line—equivalent to about US$270 per month. An increase brought them to about US$330, but inflation of the peso virtually wiped out their gains in the next year. This precarity makes the Latin American middle class very sensitive to fiscal cuts or other kinds of discipline exercised by governments, whether on the left or right.

The blue-collar working class (the classic proletariat)—that is, manual workers who are paid wages—made up about a quarter of the Latin American workforce at the height of import substitution, but their number has shrunk. These workers, many employed by the state, are the backbone of organized labor. They are formally covered by social security, some form of pension plan, or welfare rights. Though usually far from adequate, these benefits help to get them through illness, unemployment, or old age. They are a varied lot, ranging from relatively well-paid skilled workers in automobile and small arms industries to women working in *maquilas*—labor-intensive factories located in "free-trade zones," often located near ports or (in Mexico) near international borders.

At the bottom of the urban social class pyramid is the informal sector of unpaid family workers, sex workers, street vendors, and day workers who made up almost half (45.9 percent) of the workforce around 2000. As we saw in chapter 2, this sector may have shrunk between 2000 and 2008, but it may be expanding again. Besides "informal," this sector is sometimes called "marginalized" or "excluded" because its members are usually not integrated into the nation's social networks—schools, welfare systems, healthcare systems, and so on. This sector is even larger if we take into account the rural sector, where peasants and small farmers live a precarious existence. The informal sectors' children are least likely to be in school; their neighborhoods suffer the highest crime rates and are scenes of vigilante justice; their jobs are day to day, with few rights versus those who employ them. This is especially true for women, particularly those who work in domestic service and as maids and caretakers of children. It also affects the elderly, whose pensions, if they have them at all, rarely keep pace with inflation and changes in the cost of living.

Overall, most analysts conclude that neoliberal economic policies made inequality worse in Latin America. Portes and Hoffman (77) were prophetic in 2003 when they summarized the political consequences:

> Neoliberalism has proven more successful as a political than as an economic project, as the transformations that it has wrought in society have weakened the basis for organized class struggle and the channels for the effective mobilization of popular discontent. Nevertheless, the dislocations wrought by economic orthodoxy on Latin American societies—rising inequality, rising crime and insecurity, forced entrepreneurship, and emigration—lead to the expectation that the present situation will be unsustainable and that new forms of popular and political organizations will emerge.

For Review

Starting at either end of the social pyramid in Latin America, describe the major social classes. What do we mean by the "informal sectors"? Roughly how large is the middle class in Latin America, and how much does that vary in the region? Portes and Hoffman were writing at a time when in macroeconomic terms Latin America was experiencing growth and democracy seemed to be consolidating itself in most of the region. Why did they think that this situation would prove unsustainable?

Business Interests: Merchants, Banks, Landowners, and Industrialists

At one time, the image of a Latin American businessperson was that of a male descendant of a landowning family, unwilling to take risks and mainly interested in accumulating enough wealth to become a landowner. Latin America's oligarchs were thought to want to keep their fingernails clean. Allowing for significant exceptions, especially among the considerable number of them whose forebearers came as immigrants in the liberal modernization era, they fit a certain stereotype. They were socially conservative and tended to favor corporatism rather than **laissez-faire** capitalism; they were not especially friendly to the idea of a competitive market society. They ran their companies much like landowners ran their estates and the people on them. Employees with proper deference and the right family connections (*compadrazgo*) might receive extra benefits and promotions. Latin American businesspeople showed little interest in paying their workers well and regarded unionization as little more than communist subversion. In the populist era this changed somewhat. Businesspeople favored by **ISI** policies looked to government, using their personal connections to obtain commissions, contracts, subsidies, and protection from competition. Many large businesses in Latin America are still often organized into groups under the dominance of a single family. This limits the ability of competitors to bid for contracts or create business associations because these families prefer to associate only with one another and frequently have privileged ties to the state.

The degree to which these business organizations are coherent and can influence policy varies considerably from country to country. One study (Schneider 2004) found that businesses were better and more effectively able to coordinate their influence in Mexico, Chile, and Colombia than in Argentina and Brazil. In the first three countries, at crucial moments in the import substitution era, governments explicitly granted certain business confederations exclusive access to government. Businesses that refused to join the associations were thereby frozen out of subsidies and protection from foreign competition. In Argentina and Brazil, however, the populist governments dealt individually with enterprises and business interests, reducing the power of big business confederations. Still, in the face of a radical threat, business interests tend to unite regardless of their earlier relationship with the government.

In contrast to the **ISI** era, the largest and most influential businesses in Latin America must think of finding markets globally, working with transnational corporations as their entry into local markets. The path they follow is to find ways to integrate their businesses into global "**value chains**" (see chapter 15). For example, Honduran commercial elites operate labor-intensive factories and grow export crops under contract to European, Asian, and North American companies. More so than in other Central American countries, the most powerful Honduran business elites emerged not out of the old landowning class but out of new businesses in services (travel, shipping, advertising, and so forth), banking, telecommunications, and media. Many are immigrants or their descendants are from the Middle East and Europe. Their business connections abroad have helped them obtain capital for their investments. Their political influence has come to rival or even exceed that of the old landowning class or even the owners of labor-intensive *maquila* factories around San Pedro de Sula, the commercial capital.

Honduran urban entrepreneurs have in recent decades moved economically into the countryside. InSight Crime (2016), a not-for-profit investigative journalism organization, found these elites worked with the military to execute the 2009 coup that ousted the left-populist president Manuel Zelaya, who advocated land reform and participation in Venezuelan-financed grassroots programs associated with **ALBA**. To forestall any negative repercussions for the coup from Washington, the Honduran chapter of the Business Council of Latin America paid its lobbyist in Washington to influence the State Department not to support an **OAS** demand for Zelaya's restoration. The lobbyist was in a good position to help. Lanny Davis is a close friend of Secretary of State Hillary Clinton and served as one of President Bill Clinton's team of lawyers during his impeachment trial.

Transnational Crime and Drug Lords

Latin America's most dynamic "business" sector may be narcotics production and trafficking. Because the drug trade is illegal, it is conducted underground and is often linked to political violence. But like any business, it is increasingly transnational in character; from field to customer there is a "value chain." Drugs must be cultivated, which means clearing land, planting, harvesting, and packaging for shipment to a processing center, for which the proper chemicals and capital inputs are required. Then they must be packaged and shipped— by planes, boats, and/or trucks. There are wholesalers and retailers, and now for some drugs, legal dispensaries. The value (money paid) added by their enterprises must find its way back through the chain, and ultimately those who organize and manage the chain ("organized crime") make the largest profits. The famed Mexican trafficker, Juaquín Guzmán (el Chapo), made the *Forbes* billionaire list in 2009 and 2011. Colombian Pablo Escobar owned fleets of helicopters, ships, planes, and remote-controlled submarines.

As with any commodity, the peasant cultivators (***cocaleros***) who provide the raw material make the least amount; the largest profits come from processing and moving the product itself. *Cocaleros* are often at the mercy of the traffickers, who use paramilitary forces to force them to sell cheap. They are also most vulnerable to U.S. and domestic military operations to eradicate their fields. Guerrilla organizations in Peru and Colombia (see chapter 14) build local support by defending cultivators from military and paramilitary forces who force traffickers to pay higher prices. Guerrilla forces also provide security for cultivators and small-scale processing labs from antidrug units that are sent, trained, and sometimes coordinated by U.S. advisors (see chapter 16).

For a while in Colombia, production of cocaine became perhaps the largest business in the country—whether measured by employment, export income, or profit. Under the neoliberal economic policies of the government in the 1990s, Colombia's average annual growth rate from 1980 to 1997 was 3.2 percent, much lower than the 5.5 percent in the previous 30 years. Unemployment rose from a low of 7.5 percent in 1994 to 20 percent in 2000. In this period, between 1995 and 2000, production of coca increased 22 percent. Coffee, Colombia's main legal export, employed 12.5 percent of the population, whereas the cocaine industry is estimated to employ about 12 percent. As coffee prices fell, small farmers were being ruined (Holmes and Gutiérrez de Piñeres 2006). One need only ponder these data briefly to understand why one sector was shrinking and the other growing.

Like any other commodity boom, the dollars generated by narcotics exports circulate in the market, making it easier to import consumer goods from abroad but hurting local producers. Why buy locally produced clothing when you can afford the latest fashions and chic brands worn in Miami? Dollars from international drug sales can be used to buy land in the country's agricultural heartland. In other words, drug lords gradually may become part of the "legitimate" landowning class, shaping the elite contour of civil society, controlling perhaps 30 percent of the wealth in the country. Inevitably, these new oligarchs impact politics, financing candidates and determining the outcome of internal competition for nominations within each of the two major parties, the Liberals and the Conservatives (see the next chapter).

The key here is to understand that we are not simply dealing with a question of the morality of engaging in the drug trade or accepting bribes or contributions from the "businesspeople" who control this sector. The problem is structural. A global market exists for cocaine and other illegal drugs. Profits from this trade will inevitably find their way through legal and illegal channels into politics—including into the pockets of security forces or insurgencies, as in Peru or Colombia. This may take form in antidemocratic parties, such as Uribe's Democratic Center Party in Colombia (see chapter 10), or in a Pink Tide populist party, as in Bolivia. There, *coca* is regarded as a legitimate crop, and *cocaleros* (cultivators) formed the initial base for Evo Morales and his MAS (Movimiento al Socialismo) party.

The coca leaf is consumed domestically throughout the Andes. It has religious significance because of its use in traditional medicine and in ceremonies conducted by Indigenous shamans. In the Andes, the coca leaf is either chewed or brewed into a tea. A United Nations study in 2008 found that in Bolivia only 4.1 percent of the population between 18 and 65 in Bolivia had used cocaine. In nearby Argentina and Chile, the figures were, respectively, 8.25 percent and 6.4 percent. For Argentina, of those who had used cocaine, 45.2 percent showed signs of addiction (United Nations 2008: 48–49). In other words, drug production and trafficking is mainly a problem in its destination, but the problem is being attacked militarily at its source.

Drug trafficking is just one sector among transnational crime industries. In 2017, Global Financial Integrity, an **NGO**, estimated (May 2017) that the total annual value of these trades was somewhere between $1.6 trillion and $2.2 trillion. Of this amount, drug trafficking accounted for $426 billion to $652 billion, trailing only counterfeiting.

For Review

What makes transnational crime and drug trafficking different from and what makes it similar to other kinds of enterprises?

Labor Unions

Before unions, the first worker groups to form were solidarity organizations. Workers would pool a small portion of their poor wages in funereal societies to make sure that they would have a proper burial. These funds, in the absence of insurance or state welfare, provided some small financial support for families left behind. These organizations were incubators for unions that would later emerge. Leadership for the formation of unions was often provided by European immigrants who brought with them experience from home, where labor movements and political parties are typically tightly and formally linked to one another, and where socialist and anarchist movements were influential in the industrial era. These European precedents have influenced labor union politics in Latin America.

More so than in the United States, labor unions in Latin America have closely associated themselves with political parties and ideological doctrines. Many Latin American parties incorporated workers directly into their ranks through an officially sanctioned "labor bureau." Some parties, such as Brazil's Workers' Party (PT) and Argentina's Peronists, historically grew directly out of labor movements, much like the Labour Party did in Great Britain. Although party affiliation can give workers greater political representation, partisanship also is a source of divisiveness. Recall the conflicts between communist unions and Peronists in the early 1950s (see chapter 7). In Venezuela, since 1976, as the country made huge investments in heavy industrial development in the eastern party of the country, political competition for control of unions has often turned violent.

Unions are often strongest in strategic export sectors, in state-owned industries, and in government bureaucracies. As a result, even though a relatively small percentage of the total workforce is organized, labor strife is often at the center of Latin American political struggles. For 1999–2001, International Labour Office (ILO) data indicate that nearly one in six formally employed Latin Americans worked in the public sector. Proportions ranged from approximately one-fifth of unionized workers in Argentina, Ecuador, Mexico, Uruguay, Venezuela, and Costa Rica to a high of one-third in Panama. Public employment is an important source of patronage for politicians, but workers in this sector and in state-owned companies are not necessarily docile. They are especially prone to make demands and strike when the party associated with their union is in opposition; when their associated parties are in power, their tool is their clout inside the party organizational structure.

Workers in key export enclaves played a crucial role in promoting democracy in the mid-twentieth century (Bergquist 1986). By "export enclaves," we mean those sectors of the economy that were crucial to the overall prosperity of the economy. Slaughterhouse workers in Argentina, copper workers in Chile, oil workers in Venezuela, and plantation workers in Colombia crucially supported movements for democracy with their strikes, protests, and votes. We could add examples from every Latin American country to this list, including copper miners in Peru, tin miners in Bolivia, fruit plantation workers in Central America, sugar plantation workers in Cuba, and oil workers in Mexico. Joined by railroad workers, port workers, and other employees in sectors vital to exports, these workers were usually in the vanguard of union organizing and of broader democratic and nationalist struggles. They had leverage because labor stoppages entailed high costs for government and ruling elites. The oligarchs often used repression to end strikes but invariably had to seek long-term political solutions to the strife.

On the other hand, corruption and **clientelism** often limit the ability of workers and their unions to defend their interests or advance broader ideological goals. For example, for decades leaders of the oil workers' union in Venezuela—affiliated with the Democratic Action (AD) party—had the right to actually hire a quarter of the employees in the oil fields. Their Mexican counterparts had similar power, and virtually all hiring of teachers was controlled by the national educators' union. Union leaders were often rewarded with bonuses and lucrative compensation for their expenses when negotiating contracts. Unions often used funds provided by government or collected from workers with government sanction to fund enterprises—stores, resorts, and even banks. In theory, these enterprises served workers, but in reality, they were sinecures for union officials who began to act more like managers than defenders of labor.

In the populist era, Latin American labor movements often came to be dominated by a stratum of privileged labor bosses beholden to politicians and vice versa. Union leaders tended to dampen labor strife when their party was in power; conversely, they intensified it when it was politically convenient to embarrass the government. Either decision might open a gap between the interests of workers and those of the union's leadership.

How workers and their unions were incorporated into the political system left a lasting impression on subsequent political structures (Berins Collier and Collier 1991). "Incorporated" refers to how workers won legal recognition of labor rights and how they won admission to the political game. This incorporation occurred in the populist era, but it happened somewhat differently from country to country. In some cases, such as Chile, Venezuela, and Mexico, organized labor was just one sector under the broader umbrella of multiclass parties—that is, parties that sought votes from both workers and the middle class. In other cases, such as in Argentina with Peronism and communist parties in Central America, left parties were more narrowly built on a working-class base and battled with others more rooted in the middle class. This pattern changed in the 1990s under the neoliberal administration of President Carlos Menem (1989–1999), who attracted middle-class support—at least he did until the initial success of his **neoliberal** policies later collapsed into economic crisis. During the presidential administrations of the two Kirchners (Nestor and Cristina; see chapter 7), middle-class support shifted back and forth. Peronism today is more catch-all, but the party still depends more on labor than on any other sector of the population.

Although labor has played a key role at crucial junctures in Latin America's quest for democracy, its influence has been limited not only by internal divisions, but also by characteristics of the workforce. Latin America suffers from chronically high rates of unemployment and the insecurity of workers in the informal sector—for example, domestic labor, ambulant street vendors, shoe shiners, and construction day laborers. Labor laws usually limit the rights of workers in small and family-run businesses from organizing, often excluding them from benefits legally mandated for others. Peasants usually have even more limited labor rights. This large supply of labor outside the formal economy gives employers the upper hand in wage negotiations. To this source of pressure we can add economic globalization, which has made capital more mobile and has undercut bargaining strength in many labor-intensive industries (textiles, assembly, electronics, etc.). A high proportion of workers in these sectors are women (*maquiladoras*), and their unorganized situation makes them vulnerable to sexual discrimination, harassment, and too often, rape.

In recent decades, traditional industries have shed jobs (especially in Mexico, Argentina, Venezuela, and Chile), as noncompetitive factories closed their doors or modernized with labor-saving technologies. Privatization reduced public-sector jobs, and new owners often have been keen to implement labor savings. The older populist parties can no longer deliver benefits as they did before. As a result, even leaders of older union organizations, especially the Mexican Workers Confederation (CTM) and the Venezuelan Workers Confederation (CTV), have faced competition from new confederations.

The military dictatorships of the **bureaucratic authoritarian** era struck harsh blows against labor organizations. However, by crushing the populist structures inherited from the **ISI** era, the military also weakened or eliminated obstacles to more democratic and broadly organized unions. Even where the military did not seize power outright (e.g., in Mexico and Venezuela), dissatisfaction with ineffective union leadership and the unwillingness of moderate left parties to resist neoliberal policies opened space either for new union federations or for reformist movements within older ones.

In the cases of Brazil and Argentina, the labor movement took the leading role in the struggle to restore democracy. In both cases, labor unions have been disappointed with the economic policies that have followed. This was especially so in the case of Argentina, where President Carlos Menem (1989–1999) implemented a program of monetary and fiscal stability and privatized many state-owned enterprises. Menem used these policies to his political advantage, using a divide-and-conquer strategy, rewarding union leaders who cooperated with his policies while implementing measures, such as privatization, that resulted in many lost jobs.

In Chile, copper workers' strikes in 1982 and 1983, largely around unsafe working conditions, were the first crack in the iron-fisted policies of the Pinochet dictatorship (see chapters 7 and 8). The neoliberal policies of the Concertación governments after the return of democracy caused labor some disgruntlement, but for a decade the threat of a return of the military or the prospects of electoral victories by right-wing parties tempered popular resistance. Labor leaders were reluctant to undertake strikes or other actions that might weaken the center-left parties. Still, in August 2004, much to the chagrin of the socialist president, Ricardo Lagos, unions organized the first general work stoppage since the dictatorship, a protest against the "economic model." Union leaders were warning the politicians not to take them for granted, though their strikes had limited impact at the time. However, since 2010, workers have added their voice to student protestors whose demonstrations against inequality in education proved to be a catalyst for expression of wider discontent. It is fair to say, however, that the Chilean unions do not enjoy the kind of clout they did in the populist era.

In Venezuela, the collapse of oil prices and higher unemployment caused real wages to fall in the 1980s, and the labor unions, tied closely to the political parties, did little to check the slide. In the heart of new steel and aluminum industries in and around Ciudad Guayana, in the eastern state of Bolívar, workers joined a leftist reform movement called Nuevo Sindicalismo (NS, "New Unionism"), breaking the stranglehold of the Democratic Action party (AD) on unions (Hellinger 1996). In 1989, one of its leaders, Andrés Velásquez, successfully ran for governor of Bolívar, and in December 1993 he narrowly lost the presidency—some think that he was denied victory by fraud. This erosion of AD's base in labor was a significant factor in ushering in the regime transition (see chapter 8) from Punto Fijo to the Hugo Chávez era (1998–2013). The largest labor federation in Venezuela today is the Chavista National Workers' Union (UNT). Nonetheless, the labor movement was a thorn in the side of the Bolivarian government in the Chávez years because workers had learned from the Punto Fijo era the cost of subordination to the interests of a party. Chávez's successor, Nicolás Maduro, was a union organizer of Caracas transport workers, but this fact has not meant that worker movements and unions are any more complacent than they were under Chávez. But at the same time, labor unions have been weakened by conflict among factions competing for influence. The conflict has been highly volatile, sometimes violent, not only between Chavista unions and rivals, but within the Chavista ranks, where factions form around whether to press demands on the government or back it uncritically against the opposition.

In Mexico, the CTM long dominated the labor movement and formed (along with the peasant association and a bloc of professions and entrepreneurs) one of the three pillars of support for the PRI. The PRI shifted to the right after Lázaro Cárdenas left the presidency in 1940 (see chapter 8). This shift would have been difficult without the collaboration of Fidel Velázquez, who became head of the CTM in 1941. Thanks to government support, Velázquez had won a battle with a leftist (Lombardo Toledano) for control over the CTM. He subsequently led the confederation into a formal relationship with the PRI in 1946. He remained its head until his death in 1997. In this period of time, Velásquez worked closely with the PRI to repress independent or alternative labor organizing, and he acquired an international reputation for corruption. An aide to a Mexican president once told reporter Tina Rosenburg (1987), "The first thing you do when you're elected president is go to the shrine of the Virgin of Guadalupe and pray for the health of Fidel Velázquez for the next six years." In 1987, Velázquez sought the expulsion of Cuauhtémoc Cárdenas, who would later found the PRD, for advocating reform of the PRI. In the early 1990s he kept labor resistance muted during the controversies over NAFTA, even though the latter was to contribute to weakening of the political dinosaurs that had led the PRI throughout his tenure. Like Menem in Argentina, President Carlos Salinas de Gortari (1982–1988) rewarded friends and punished enemies in labor unions to achieve objectives such as the privatization of state companies.

Several factors have eroded the hegemony of the traditional CTM leadership of Mexico in recent years. Privatization of key industries (e.g., telecommunications) and pressures to eliminate waste and corruption in the state oil company (PEMEX) eliminated some key patronage resources. The labor side agreement of NAFTA, though it lacked any significant enforcement power, put the spotlight on the undemocratic nature of Mexican unions. North American unions, recognizing that more effective Mexican unions might mitigate the incentives to move jobs from Canada and the United States to the south, began providing support for reform. A new federation, the National Union of Workers, and a movement, the Authentic Labor Front, appeared. These groups have tended to favor the PRD, the leftist party that emerged from the ranks of disgruntled PRI members and leftists after 1988. However, they have resisted any formal alignment that might smack of the old relationship between the CTM and the PRI.

In December 2012, the Mexican Congress passed a labor law reform. To its credit, the law requires greater access for disabled people and women to employment, requires publication of negotiated contracts, and introduces other popular, progressive reforms. However, the price of these democratic advances was the weakening of unemployment compensation, reduced rights to collect owed back pay, and greater ease for companies to subcontract work being done by permanent employees. The new labor "flexibility" allows companies to change jobs into temporary or part-time status, and so on.

The arrest two months later of the powerful teachers' union leader (though her corruption was undeniable) struck a blow against the entire labor union movement, weakening Mexican unions across the board. The changes in labor laws and public confidence in unions broke the resistance of the oil workers' union to privatization of many of PEMEX's operations. Smaller independent unions have been pressuring the government to strengthen protections for workers, especially against employers using subcontracting to break unions, but the CTM has not vigorously supported their efforts (Alexander and La Botz 2014; Cypher 2014). Its position is subordinated to the PRI, within which it is incorporated through the party's Congress of Labor.

Andrés Manuel López Obrador (AMLO), who became president of Mexico in 2019, was a long-time critic of NAFTA, but the trade agreement served its purpose. After 25 years, the Mexican economy was so closely integrated with that of the U.S. (and somewhat to Canada, too) that any move by a populist to break from the neoliberal philosophy embedded by NAFTA was too politically risky, even for a populist like AMLO. In February 2020, AMLO delivered a speech to the CTM, touting his raising of the minimum wage but refraining from the kind of criticism he had leveled for years about its corruption and relations with the PRI.

Perhaps the most powerful new labor movement in Latin America emerged in the region's most influential country, Brazil. The PT (Workers' Party) was founded in São Paulo in 1980 by a coalition of leftist Christians, Marxists, unionists, environmentalists, and others motivated by the desire to encourage workers and the poor to organize themselves. They were searching for an alternative to the way that many previous leftist parties had sought to lead workers by promoting themselves as a "vanguard" (Keck 1992). They were motivated not only by disillusionment with old-style unions but also by social justice movements in the Catholic Church and by the democratic practices of a new labor movement emerging in the industrial suburbs of São Paulo.

Brazil's dictatorship (1964–1981) demolished the old populist parties and unions but was not nearly as repressive as the bureaucratic authoritarian regimes of the Southern Cone. This prepared the way for a new union movement that sought to strengthen the position of workers by seeking support from neighborhoods and from broader emerging movements. Women, environmentalists, and Afro-Brazilians began to coalesce with labor as never before. From the ranks of mulattos came the most important leader, Luiz Inácio da Silva—Lula—a steel worker. When the military regime arrested Lula during a general strike in 1980, the agitated population responded with mass protests that forced the military to choose between bloody repression and concessions. The generals chose concessions (see chapter 7). Forty years after the general strike, with right-wing president Michel Temer having taken power after the impeachment of PT president Dilma Rousseff, Brazilian unions were facing a crisis. The business sector allied with Temer to pass new labor laws that eliminated mandatory union dues, which since 1940 had been collected by employers and passed on to the unions. In one fell swoop, Brazil's unions lost 85 percent of their financing. Although weakened, they remain a key sector of opposition to the current president, that is, to the more extreme right-wing Jair Bolsonaro.

Latin American unions remain more politicized than their North American counterparts do, and today overall they are less beholden to political parties. Certainly, this can be read as a plus for democracy, but on the negative side of the ledger we must enter the erosion of union membership caused by economic and social change, the legacy of corruption that still marks much of the labor movement, and the political divisions that diminish the power of labor in national politics.

In addition to the political challenges facing workers, the dramatic changes in communications technology, robotics, and artificial intelligence have eroded the size of organized sectors in the workforce. Subcontracting, temporary employment, and lower barriers to discharging workers have been a reality in the world of work everywhere for some time now. Now the "gig economy" and replacement of service jobs with electronic transactions has led to what some call the "app" workforce. Outside restaurants of all kinds, dozens of (mostly) young men wait and watch their cell phones for a call for service—delivery of a meal, a ride on the back of a motorcycle, transport of a package, etc. Anywhere from 60 to 80 percent of Latin Americans have cell phones, and the smart phones are now universal in the middle class. Flexible labor allows links in the supply chain to ramp employment up or down to match demand from enterprises further up the chain. Robots with artificial limbs may replace many manual labor jobs now left to informal workers. The profits flow to those who control the chains and the technologies. Work is done by "associates," not workers. These forces are hardly unique to Latin America, but they are reshaping the working class and leaving it weaker in relationship to capital (Dinegro Martinez 2019).

For Review

Historically, when were labor unions and workers incorporated into the political system? How is their relationship to the state and political parties different? How do corporatist and clientelist relationships affect their relationship with parties and the state?

Rural Workers and Peasant Movements

Although most Latin Americans now live in the city, the absolute size of the rural population has remained constant. Peasants and farmers might organize not only around access to land ("usufruct") but also around government support in the form of cheap credit, roads, organized markets, price supports and subsidies, irrigation projects, and so on.

In most of Latin America, peasants were left out of the political alliances that sustained populism in the middle of the twentieth century. However, struggles around land are as old as Latin America itself, so it hardly surprises that peasant movements have been part of the "new social movements" tendency. They have been especially visible in recent years in Brazil, in Central America, in parts of the Andes where Indigenous peoples make up a large percentage of the population, and in Mexico, where many peasants feel the government has abandoned the promises of the 1910 revolution.

The stereotype of Latin Americans presents rural society as a mass sea of illiterate peasants living in a subservient relationship. Like all stereotypes, this one is somewhat rooted in reality, but the traditional *haciendas*, plantations, and ranches of the past have faded away in most of the region. Even where change has not entirely swept away the old system, peasants live in different kinds of social and economic contexts. Some are landless day laborers, and others work for wages on large plantations; some have small plots of their own to subsidize meager earnings, whereas others live on the traditional landed estates in a kind of feudal relationship to the landowner.

Gender and racial divisions also give peasants different outlooks and interests. For example, men from the Maya villages in the Guatemalan highlands regularly migrate during harvest periods to the coastal plantations to supplement incomes, leaving women behind to hold families and communities together. In the Andean nations of Bolivia, Ecuador, and Peru, peasant unrest is most intense among Indigenous peoples who remain acutely aware that their ancestors once ruled these lands. The traditional *hacienda* has given way in most parts of Latin America to farms, ranches, vineyards, and plantations, in which workers are hired and fired ("proletarianized") as they are in the city. This also means ownership and management of land has changed, eroding the base for traditional, conservative politics.

As we saw in chapter 8, the civil wars that wracked El Salvador, Guatemala, and Nicaragua in the 1980s were rooted in land inequality and the displacement of peasants from land taken for production of cattle, cotton, and sugar (Barry and Preusch 1986: 144–161; LaFeber 1993). The unrest in the countryside and the poverty of those who migrated to the towns and cities fuel revolution and civil war, leaving a minimum of 200,000 people dead or disappeared in the region. Negotiated settlements of civil wars in El Salvador and Guatemala were supposed to address peasant demands for land reform, but only modest redistribution took place. The victorious Sandinistas redistributed much land in Nicaragua in the 1980s, but the agrarian reform of those years was undone after their electoral defeat in 1990.

Nowhere has this change been more pronounced than in Chile. There, until 1973, political parties on the Chilean right counted it among their basic functions to defend landlords against agrarian reform and to preserve a traditional, almost feudalistic culture. Chile remains one of the most socially conservative countries on issues such as divorce, religious education, and gender rights in Latin America, a legacy of this period. However, ten years of land reform (1964–1973), followed by Pinochet's determination to make Chilean agriculture more commercially successful, has stripped the countryside of the social basis for traditional conservatism. What is blocking change are constitutional obstacles that in 2019 came under attack by mass protests against economic and social inequality.

Chile has two right-wing parties that form a conservative bloc, and both court the urban middle class and business interests for votes. However, these parties still rely on and exercise additional clout in the political system because they draw votes from the countryside, which is overrepresented in Congress, thanks to Pinochet's 1982 constitution. This is especially true in the Senate, where they need only about one-third of the vote to win one of the two seats allotted each province. However, the Chilean countryside has changed too, with more capitalist-style big farms replacing the old traditional *haciendas*. The decline of traditional conservatism rooted in this old system manifested itself in 2004 when Chile finally made divorce legal (albeit difficult to obtain).

Extreme concentration of private land ownership prevails in all of Latin America, except Cuba. However, the relationship between landowners varies as a result of historical experience and the kind of product produced. Argentina shares with Chile a highly unequal pattern of land distribution, but agriculture and ranching were organized somewhat more along capitalist lines from the start. Possessed of extremely fertile black earth, Argentina's pampas, about the size of the state of Texas, provided the basis for a highly successful export sector based on ranching and agriculture. Two-thirds of Argentina's arable land is concentrated in 2.5 percent of large estates. Today, soybeans are the main export crop, but historically ranches given over to the production of cattle and sheep generated the country's wealth. Production of meat created the fiercely independent cowboys, *gauchos*, on one hand, but processing meat and moving it to market required railroads and slaughterhouses, where a proletariat sprang up. The latter was much easier to organize than ranch hands and herders.

Brazil has a similar maldistribution of land, with half of the productive land concentrated in 1 percent of farms. Peasants living on these estates are poor, often illiterate, and highly dependent on the personal largesse of landowners, especially in the poor, chronically drought-stricken northeast. Where state-subsidized irrigation projects exist, the benefits go mostly to big landowners, leaving the poor as destitute as ever. The region has seen repeated movements of desperate, poor peasants. In the late 1800s, they were sometimes led by religious mystics and never achieved permanent victory. But now with Indigenous groups having organized themselves transnationally and international environmental organizations pressuring for defense of nature, occupants of the rural sectors have become increasingly important.

The Movimento dos Trabalhadores Rurais Sem Terra (MST; Landless Workers' Movement) in Brazil, which emerged on the scene in the 1990s, inspired a new social movement for land redistribution throughout the continent. The MST grew to be the largest single-movement organization in Latin America, perhaps the world, though it may have lost some size and momentum as it has drawn closer to Brazil's largest political party, the PT.

The MST emerged as a coalition of landless peasants and supportive urban organizers toward the end of the 1970s, as popular pressure for a transition from dictatorship to democracy was emerging. The group organized land seizures to pressure the government to follow through on promises of land redistribution. Usually the group targeted land, much of it unused, that was eligible for expropriation and redistribution under Brazilian laws. From its early experiences a model for occupation developed. Peasants are organized in nuclei of ten and then upward. No major action, such as an occupation, occurs without thorough discussion and a vote by the grassroots base. The same goes for the movement's political decisions, which are also decided only after extensive grassroots consultation.

The MST's decision to endorse Lula was vital to his reelection in 2006—even though the movement sharply criticized the Brazilian president for failing to deliver on his promise on land reform in 2002. The MST avoided divisiveness over the issue of supporting a party, but it exposed itself to co-optation. On the one hand, the PT government did deliver on its promise to make more land available for redistribution, but the MST began to function less as a movement and more as an intermediary between peasants demanding land and the state. This put the MST in a position to assume a role as patron to land-hungry peasants, reducing its reliance on the organizing model. That changed function became evident in the reduced number of occupations in the later years of the PT's administration. With the PT out of power and a hostile right-wing president (Bolsonaro), the MST might now shift back to a more independent, militant strategy of occupation.

The MST adopted environmentalism as part of its rationale for agrarian reform. On its English-language website (www.mstbrazil.org, accessed June 26, 2006), besides calling for land redistribution, the MST invited visitors to read "a portion of text below, written by Benedictine monk Marcelo Barros for the Fifth conference on agroecology—Developing a Popular and Sovereign Project for Agriculture," which you will find in the Punto de Vista on the MST. This meeting brought 5,000 agriculturalists together in Cascavel, in the state of Paraná, to "exchange experiences and discuss agroecological production and sustainable development." The MST also advocates redistributing land to dwellers in poor *barrios* who want to return to rural life.

PUNTO DE VISTA: IS THE MST'S CALL FOR SUSTAINABLE AGRICULTURE ECONOMICALLY REALISTIC?

During the presidency of Lula in Brazil, significant reductions in poverty took place, contributing considerably not only to his popularity but also to that of the Workers' Party (PT). Government funding of programs to reduce poverty was based in part on economic growth through expanded production of and high global prices for mining and agribusiness exports, such as soybeans, beef, and tropical fruits. Lula and the PT have been supported by Latin America's largest social movement, the Landless Workers' Movement (MST). However, the MST's vision of land reform clashes with the existing structure of large landholdings, highly technological agriculture, and production for export. The following extract includes two components of what the MST called in a 2009 proclamation a "People's Agrarian Reform." (For the full document, see www.mstbrazil.org/resource/msts-proposal-peoples-agrarian-reform.)

1. Earth

The land and property of nature is above all a heritage of the peoples that inhabit each area, and must serve the development of humanity. Democratize access to land, to the goods of nature and to the means of production in agriculture to all who want it to live and work. The ownership, possession and use of land and goods of nature must be subordinated to the general interests of the Brazilian people, to meet the needs of the entire population.

Key Measures

1.1. Establish a maximum size of the farm, for each farmer, established according to each region . . . and expropriate all farms above this module, regardless of level of production and productivity.

1.2. Ensure access to land for every family that wants to live and work there.

1.3. Expropriate all farms of foreign companies, banks, industries, construction companies and churches, which do not depend on agriculture for their activities.

1.4. Expropriate ALL large estates that do not comply with the social function. That is, they are either below the average productivity of the region, not respecting the environment, have problems of compliance with labor laws with their employees or are involved in smuggling, drug trafficking, slave labor. The amount paid should be equal to that declared for taxes, discounted by all taxes owed, with loans of public banks, and with environmental and social damage. . . .

2. The Organization of Production in Rural Areas

Key Measures

2.1. Agricultural production will be directed with priority to produce healthy food for all the Brazilian people, thus ensuring the principle of food sovereignty.

2.2. Production will be organized based on the development of all forms of agricultural cooperation, such as task forces, traditional forms of community organizations, associations, cooperatives, public companies, companies providing services, etc.

2.3. Agribusinesses should be arranged near the location of agricultural production in the form of cooperatives under the control of farmers and workers in agribusiness. Technical training programs should be conducted for workers in management of agro-industrial cooperatives.

2.4. Promote diversified agriculture, breaking the monoculture, seeking to promote sustainable agriculture based on agro-ecological principles, without pesticides and GMOs, creating a healthy diet. This new production model also manages a new base and new forms of food consumption, balanced and appropriate to local ecosystems and culturally appropriate.

Point/Counterpoint

Given how much Brazil's economy overall depends on modern, export agriculture, is the MST's vision for the land reform realistic and in the best interest of the country?

If you say no, how would you answer those who say that large-scale export agriculture has not helped most rural Brazilians and is environmentally unsustainable?

If you say yes, how do you respond to those who say that the agricultural exports have provided the basis to lift millions of Brazilians overall out of poverty?

For More Information

Friends of the MST is a worldwide solidarity movement with the Brazilian movement, with a web page at www.mstbrazil.org/whatismst. Among many good grassroots documentaries, a series of three videos chronicling a land takeover and confrontation with the government is at www.youtube.com/watch?v=hWjrTKuYsJg.

For Review

What kinds of demands do peasants typically make upon the government? What else besides land do they need to make the land prosper? How does the MST illustrate the complex issues that face movements' relationship with political parties?

Social Movements

As we have seen already, some of the most important forces for change in Latin America have emerged from social movements. It can be difficult to draw a bright line between an interest (or "advocacy") group and a social movement. The former is usually a well-established player that regularly interacts with government to influence policy and to obtain benefits for its members. The social movements we are examining here vary in degree of formal organization but in general do not have institutionalized relationships with parties and the state. A social movement can be simply a popular cultural movement (e.g., a dance or music craze), but here we are talking about social movements that emerge in civil society with an explicitly political purpose. They are composed of people who work together with a common purpose to challenge authority or demand change, which involves regular interaction with elites, authorities, and opponents (Tarrow 1994: 4).

Tarrow's concept of **political opportunity structures** describes how movements arise in civil society and impact politics by taking advantage of changes within the institutional or

PHOTO 11.1   The members of Brazil's Landless Workers' Movement have occupied vacant land and are holding a sign that says, "Enough of violence in the countryside and criminalization of social movements." They would later peacefully leave after confrontation with the police. Do you think their protest is justified?

Source: EVARISTO SA/AFP via Getty Images.

opportunity structures that allow a movement to emerge or gain strength. The existing political situation may encourage or discourage people from using collective action. Any group that wants to demand something from the state must take into account the environment in which it operates. For example, repression might make it physically risky for opponents to speak out or to demonstrate, which might lead a movement eventually to take up arms. On the other hand, an existing party or politician might open itself to a movement in the quest for votes or influence. Social movements form, says Tarrow, "when ordinary citizens, sometimes encouraged by leaders, respond to changes in opportunities that lower the costs of collective action, reveal potential allies, and show where elites and authorities are vulnerable" (1994: 17–18). When sufficiently organized, they can widen or create new openings thereafter.

For example, we have already seen that politicians and parties in Latin America often work to co-opt new leaders challenging them for influence. In the era of populism and import substitution, movements of workers often obtained material benefits and a quota of political influence but usually at the expense of their autonomy and internal democracy. This system could be maintained until import substitution no longer generated sufficient growth to satisfy expanding demands from the **popular sectors**, contributing to a crisis. Movements that tried to radicalize populism emerged. We saw this happen in Chile, Argentina, and Brazil in the period leading to bureaucratic authoritarianism. Eventually, in the latter era, democracy movements emerged to foster a transition from one institutional system to another.

In some circumstances, social movements might evolve to challenge the structures themselves. This process is often a feature of politics in democracies where institutions have decayed—that is, failed to adapt to new circumstances and drifted away from serving the public interest. This happened in Venezuela to the political parties Acción Democrática (AD; Democratic Action) and COPEI in the waning years of the Punto Fijo regime (see chapter 9). Party leaders resisted demands to change the constitutional game because they feared reform would threaten their joint monopoly of power.

Tarrow places emphasis on how outside factors (e.g., a political entrepreneur's ambitions or an external shock, such as a loss in war or natural calamity) shape movements. It is also the case that movements shape their environments. Charles Tilly (1978), somewhat in contrast to Tarrow, sees opportunity structures as only one of many factors shaping movements and political outcomes. Other factors include the degree to which individuals share a common interest, the capacity they have to mobilize (i.e., the ability of members and scattered groups to create a network and communicate with each other), and the resources at the command of the movement.

Consider the following:

- Employed workers have in common that they labor for a wage. It is difficult and painful for workers to go on strike, but when workers persist and stick together, they have considerable power to wield against more wealthy employers.
- Middle-class citizens can write letters to newspapers, perhaps as a group buy an advertisement to express their grievances, maybe withhold taxes, or demonstrate. Their incomes provide a power resource that is easier to use because it is less risky. On the other hand, they do not have enough income to create an electoral or widespread advertising campaign unless they are mobilized into a group or network—something becoming somewhat easier with the advent of the Internet. The Zapatistas were perhaps the first insurgency/movement to take full advantage of the Internet to mobilize international solidarity with their cause.
- Poor people in the informal ("marginalized" or "excluded") sector often have little influence over day-to-day politics. They are harder to organize than workers are and do not have the threat of withholding their labor. Their main power resource versus the state may be disruption—for example, occupations of the street or public buildings. This is a high-risk activity, but once unleashed, it may have a powerful influence on events.

Now that many of the poorest people have access to social media through cell phones, their capacity to organize may have significantly increased, something that first became visible elsewhere in the world, in the Arab Spring (especially in Tunisia and Egypt in late 2013). But states have learned to adapt. A simple expedient is simply curtailing access to the Internet providers. Surveillance techniques now allow tracking. Facial recognition technology is just beginning to become widely available and already is to some security services. Combined with GPS tracking (commonly activated on cell phones), demonstrators can be tracked and identified. Huge troves of data ("Big Data") exist on just about anyone who has ever used Facebook, and 5G technology, just coming online in parts of Latin America, and artificial intelligence offer states new methods of tracking and disrupting demonstrations and even the most spontaneous of protests. China has pioneered state surveillance and anti-protest coordination, but many of these technologies are already being deployed by private companies and security agencies in the United States. That Latin America is lagging in these technologies, and that many people in the informal sectors live on the poor side of the "digital divide" (or have no better access than to 3G networks) probably will limit the utility of some of these programs, but most students and the middle class are already highly active on social media. Some estimates are that 80 percent of Latin Americans now have cell phones—though percentages for smart phones are lower.

Tilly argues that race, gender, ethnicity, and language offer potential bases for movement politics, but Tilly argues that social class is the most profound. In Latin America, the worsening of class inequalities certainly has been a catalyst for many of the most influential social movements. The year 2020 saw huge mass demonstrations by women and Indigenous peoples, but a variety of other types have sprung up in recent years. Some Latin Americanists would challenge the notion that these groups are really new, but there is little doubt that they are leaving a mark on politics in the region today. On the following pages, we profile some of the most important of these movements, but this is not an exhaustive list by any means. For example, environmental organizations, LGBTQ+ (lesbian, gay, bisexual, transgender, queer plus other gender identities) peoples, youth, and community media are just a few of the other movements that are shaping Latin America's future.

Popular Movement Resistance to Neoliberalism in Argentina

As we have seen (chapter 6), one major force for neoliberal globalization has been the pressure applied on Latin American governments by the **International Monetary Fund (IMF)**, the **World Bank** (International Bank for Reconstruction and Development), and private financial institutions to implement **structural adjustment**. Two great hemispheric forces were joined in the Argentine drama when neoliberal globalization came up against Latin America's new social movements.

After a decade of inflation, with a rate that reached 5,000 percent in 1989, in 1991 Peronist Carlos Saúl Menem tried to stabilize the situation by issuing a new currency pegged at an exchange rate of one peso to US$1. No more pesos would be put into circulation than there were dollars in the country's foreign exchange account. Inflation did indeed recede and new foreign investment and loans arrived, but less of the incoming capital was invested in creating new industries than in buying assets being privatized by the state. Corruption was rampant. Rates of poverty and unemployment for the working class showed little improvement, even though the economic growth rate averaged 8 percent for four years after 1991.

As long as overall economic growth was robust, the peso scheme worked. Argentina's economy was faltering by 1995, but the peso kept its value against other currencies because it was pegged to the dollar. Exports were choked off because the high peso meant that clients overseas had to spend much more (perhaps twice as much) of their own currencies to buy anything Argentina wanted to sell. For example, Brazil, Argentina's largest trading partner, nearly stopped buying Argentina's large rice crop, which could find no other outlet. Usually, these economic setbacks would cause the value of a country's currency to fall, but at the time the U.S. economy was doing well, and hence the peso held its value based on the dollar's strength. By October 2001, the financial speculators were swooping down. They bought pesos cheaply with other currencies and then used the pesos to buy dollars at one to one, subsequently sending them out of the country. The only way Argentina could guarantee the value of the peso was to borrow more dollars, but speculators quickly swept up the additional greenbacks (though most of this money was, in fact, electronic rather than paper currency). Pesos began piling up in government accounts; the dollars kept flowing out. To make things worse, pesos were useless in paying the international debt. Soon the state had no money to pay its own employees and keep social programs, schools, and so on going. The economy began to collapse, and so did the government and what was left of the safety net for Argentine workers.

The IMF's solution to the crisis was austerity, including drastic cuts in the budget. The government, headed by President Fernando de la Rua (elected in December 1999 by a coalition of the Radical Party and a smaller party) decided in December 2001 to freeze all bank accounts, though not before well-connected clients had a chance to move their savings safely abroad. Middle-class Argentineans were cut off from their savings and joined the poor in scouring the streets for food. Argentineans began to engage in episodes of rioting and looting, driving de la Rua from office before his term expired. The country had three more presidents within two weeks following de la Rua's resignation. In January 2002, the government abandoned the one-to-one peg and devalued the peso by 30 percent. The IMF insisted that the budget be cut another 10 percent, even in the face of rising anger from public employees who had not been paid in months.

In middle-class and poor neighborhoods, citizens organized popular assemblies and began to experiment with local solutions and to confront national authorities. Some of the assemblies invaded closed factories and resumed production. When owners attempted to take them back, the assemblies defended them. Some of the assemblies organized economic markets where goods and services, from haircuts to airline tickets, could be bartered, creating a parallel market to the realm of the peso. Groups of unemployed people in the provinces, called *piqueteros*, sprung up around 1996. They began to seize highways and buildings, causing serious disruption. Eventually they organized themselves into a national association (Burbach 2002).

In May 2003, a Peronist, Nestor Kirchner, was sworn in as Argentina's new president. Kirchner had done better than most governors in managing the crisis in the small province of Santa Cruz. By the time he came to office, Argentina had defaulted on several payments due on its US$178 billion public debt. Kirchner took advantage of the situation to drive hard bargains with the international financial community. The situation brought to mind John Paul Getty's observation, "If you owe the bank $100 that's your problem. If you owe the bank $100 million, that's the bank's problem." Kirchner offered the country's creditors US$.25 on the dollar, and some began to accept or at least to renegotiate terms. Kirchner was helped when Venezuela agreed to send several oil tankers to eliminate the prospect that Argentineans would have no oil in the approaching winter. The government prevailed, thereby gaining resources to resume spending and kick-start the economy. Kirchner's popularity soared.

By 2005, as the economy recovered, the popular assemblies and the *piquetero* movement had become less visible. The government had negotiated and not renounced its international obligations. With the economy stabilized and prosperity returning to the middle class, it might seem that the social movements lost all influence. However, people had become more conscious of their power. Even hints that the government might turn back in a neoliberal direction can generate protests, reminding international and national elites of the limits of popular tolerance for globalization as it is commonly understood. Similar scenarios were unfolding in 2019 and 2020 in many parts of Latin America. Right-wing movements and parties trying to restore neoliberal policies run into street resistance when gasoline prices, tuition fees, bus fares, cooking oil prices, etc. go up. Left-wing governments also encounter such issues when drops in export revenues, pressure for more rapid change, or demands from unions and other associations exceed their capacity to respond. As noted in several other parts of this text, **precarity** is not just a concern of the poor and the working class but the middle class as well.

The Urban Poor and Neighborhood Movements

The men and women who make up the informal sector often have a harder time than employed workers have in organizing to exercise political influence. The International Labour Organization breaks the informal sector of workers into three parts: "independent workers," "domestic service," and "microfirms." A handful of highly skilled individuals may fall into the first or third category, but most of this sector is very poor. Its members eke out a living by selling smuggled goods (cosmetics, plastic toys, pirated DVDs, etc.) on the sidewalk; finding temporary work in, for example, construction, or working in other people's homes (see chapter 2). This last group, the domestic sector, is mostly composed of women working as maids, nannies, and so on. Almost none are covered by social security. Most live in the poorest neighborhoods where they and their families must pool their meager incomes, including their children who have little time for school. Often, workers in the informal sector are caught up in the illicit economies of prostitution and drugs, vulnerable to both police abuse and social predators. They and landless peasants suffer the most precarity, which partly explains why the Brazilian MST's conception of "landless workers" includes members of the informal sector who want to return to the countryside.

Despite their social exclusion and vulnerability, the urban poor have entered the political arena repeatedly, organizing themselves in their neighborhoods or places of commerce (e.g., sidewalk vendors). When they do so, class tension escalates. In many countries, this sector is disproportionately of Indigenous or African descent. To the middle class and wealthy, the presence of poor people of color in their neighborhoods (other than when they are working) is disconcerting and threatening. They are the *descamisados* (shirtless ones) who followed Perón, the *turbas* (mobs) who turned out in support of Hugo Chávez, the *cholos* (Indigenous people) blocking highways in the Andean countries, or the *piqueteros* occupying streets in Argentina. To many in the middle class, they represent the opposite of civil society; they are the people who need to be modernized and tutored in the ways of democracy. To the "responsible left" favored by intellectuals such as Mexico's Jorge Castañeda, they are an obstacle to democracy; to politicians such as Chávez and Morales, they are *el pueblo*. They are a ready base for populist leaders.

Latin America's cities, with few exceptions, have populations well beyond their capacity to sustain a good quality of life. Community organizations sometimes begin at the very moment a *toma* (land takeover) takes place, as invaders of vacant land or buildings struggle to gain a foothold in the municipality. With the onset of the debt crisis and economic policy changes that fell most heavily on the poor, neighbors had to rely on one another to survive.

In Chile, *barrio* dwellers came together to form *ollas comunas* ("common pot," i.e., a soup kitchen) during the Pinochet dictatorship. These community kitchens sought more than anything else to maintain minimum nutrition for children. As such, they were not founded with political goals in mind. However, in a society where fierce repression immediately targeted any kind of political organizing, these groups were among the first to raise their voices and demonstrate against the Pinochet dictatorship. The general responded with water cannons and military sweeps through neighborhoods, but the organized neighborhoods were not going to be easily dispersed. Formed to cope with hunger, they could not simply retire from meeting, talking, and in the end raising their voices. Given the origins of these kinds of groups, it should not be surprising that women were most frequently in the vanguard of this struggle to restore democracy.

Asociaciones de vecinos (AVs; neighborhood associations) now network with one another in cities throughout Latin America. In doing so, they have become important actors almost everywhere in the region. In Mexico City, people found they had to organize themselves to compensate for an entirely inadequate government response to the earthquake of 1985. In Peru, neighborhoods organized in response to poverty and to the violence unleashed by both President Alberto Fujimori's security forces and the ultra-extreme guerrilla group Sendero Luminoso. In Venezuela, AVs first emerged as actors in the 1970s and became a force for political change after riots (the *caracazo*) greeted President Carlos Andrés Pérez's announcement of an agreement with the IMF for structural adjustment (see chapter 8) in 1989.

Argentina had for a period one of the strongest efforts by nonunionized workers to organize. The *piquetero* movement emerged in the 1990s when desperately poor people began to block highways and rail lines to protest government cuts. Mayors, governors, and other politicians in the provinces tolerated the actions because *piqueteros* put pressure on the central government to provide states and municipalities with resources needed to carry out government tasks. By 2000, the *piqueteros*, discovering their power, formed national networks. Such action is not limited to poor people's protest. Venezuelan president Hugo Chávez found middle-class opponents adopting *piquetero* tactics in 2003 as part of an unsuccessful effort to drive him from office, and they reemerged again in opposition to his successor, Nicolás Maduro.

Organizations based on where people reside often express social class interests, but their common concerns arise out of where they live, not where they work. Most city residents are now three or four generations removed from the arrival of the first migrants, and more of them are accommodating to urban life. Unlike their predecessors, they are not content with the relative improvement that city life offered over life in the countryside. Struggles against dictatorships, personal insecurity, and economic hardships have generated deeply rooted associational life in many *barrios*, making them more able to press demands outside of **clientelist** networks. While violence and acute poverty still plague many *barrios* and *favelas*, others now address their problems though *asembleas* (popular assemblies). These meetings are sites for developing neighborhood solutions to problems but also to coordinate demands on local authorities.

Although they share some objectives, neighborhood organizations in poor *barrios* differ somewhat from those in middle-class neighborhoods. Both organize themselves in part to articulate demands on local government, but the middle class often focuses on defending urban parks and pedestrian zones from encroachment by developers. They also seek to preserve these spaces from being occupied by vendors and other members of the informal sector. Their actions can be motivated by a sincere desire to preserve common urban living space or by baser motives related to racist or class prejudice—or both. Poor residents often first organized themselves in the land takeovers that created new communities, but they also came into existence as an attempt to pool resources in a struggle for economic survival (e.g., the *ollas comunas*—"common pots"—that sprung up in Chilean cities in the Pinochet years).

In Central America, the guerrilla movements that either toppled dictatorships (Nicaragua in 1979) or achieved political concessions (El Salvador and Guatemala) were mostly based in rural areas, but they also depended greatly on civil society in the towns. Guerrilla armies must be fed, armed, and clothed; their dead must be buried, their wounded cared for, their spiritual needs attended to, and their ideas communicated. In other words, actual fighting is only one part of a revolutionary struggle. The civil conflicts did leave as a legacy a variety of women's organizations, peasant groups, human rights organizations, cooperatives, environmental groups, unions, and so on that have become part of the permanent political landscape in the region. In the past, such organizations in Central America were usually stamped out violently by the oligarchy and armed forces (excepting Costa Rica). They continue to face repression, but they survive.

In Brazil, neighborhood associations in poor areas were critical to the growth of the PT and brought Afro-Brazilians, and their issues, into national politics. Outstanding among the leaders to emerge from the *favelas* is Benedita da Silva, who says in *I Was Born a Black Woman*, a documentary film about her life, "I live in a country of 30 million impoverished people, people who can't read or write, people who live in cardboard shacks in the shantytowns, under bridges, on the streets. I know their stories because I have lived it myself."

Sometimes neighborhood organizations have been formed as a result of initiatives from government. In Cuba, the Committees for Defense of the Revolution (CDRs), although less influential than in the era of Fidel Castro, can still be found every few blocks in every corner of the country. Founded originally to defend the young revolution from U.S. efforts to overturn the new regime, they still serve to identify and repress dissidents. However, CDRs also played an active role in organizing communities to deal with scarcity and social problems, such as child abuse and violence against women. More important today are units call Poder Popular (PP; Popular Power). Every Cuban neighborhood is also organized into a PP. These serve as vehicles for people to voice complaints and demand responses from local officials and the bureaucracy. The PPs are the base units of government and are responsible for organizing elections at the municipal level in Cuba.

Cuba's CDRs, PPs, and other large mass organizations, including women's organizations, cultural associations, and unions, are officially sanctioned. At the national level, their leaders are usually members of the Communist Party. They clearly have a **corporatist** character, but within limits they exercise significant influence over government policies and act to transmit demands from people to government and the bureaucracy (Azicri 2000; Roman 2003). Perhaps the unruliest (from the government's view) of these mass organizations is the Union of Writers and Artists of Cuba. Movie directors, novelists, painters, dancers, and musicians have produced devastating critiques of social ills. Although direct criticism of communism and/or advocacy of multiparty democracy is not tolerated, almost anything else for debate appears, though often subtly, in Cuban art and music.

Venezuela's Chávez (1999–2013), lacking a strong political party, relied greatly on his personal **charisma** but also found a source of support in the early 2000s from

"Bolivarian Circles." The circles were not created by Chávez, as often claimed by his critics. They had appeared in the poor *barrios* in the 1990s, organized by Venezuelans who had already lost faith in the last 15 years of the Punto Fijo regime of 1958–1998 (see chapter 8). The opposition's attempted coup against Chávez in April 2002 further mobilized the *barrios*, as residents turned out in massive numbers to demonstrate for his survival. Chávez now accelerated programs to deliver benefits and solidify his support in these poor neighborhoods.

Various kinds of neighborhood organizations formed to collaborate with the armed forces and government agencies, undertaking "missions" to improve health and literacy. Cuban aid workers were invited to help and were deployed around the country in the poorest areas. Later, many of the circles were replaced by "urban land committees," formed to take advantage of a new law that gave *barrio* residents the chance to register legal ownership of their *ranchos* (poor homes)—but only after the committees worked to carry out a census and establish property lines. In August 2004, when he faced a crucial referendum on whether to cut short his term of office, Chávez found that his political party at that time, the Fifth Republic Movement (MVR), was inadequate to the task, so he turned to these **barrio** organizers to mobilize a "No" vote against his recall. Chávez, after his military background, called the local groups working on his behalf "electoral battle units."

In 2006 and 2007, Venezuela's Bolivarian government launched a campaign to organize communal councils throughout the country. These councils were (and are) made up of a minimum of 200 families in urban areas and 20 in rural areas. The councils receive funds directly from the central government and state oil company to deploy in projects determined by their members. Chávez's goal was, on one hand, to organize a more secure basis of power for his government and, on the other hand, to stimulate local initiatives (cooperatives, land redistribution, and civic improvements) to address the country's deteriorating standard of living and to create a "bottom-up" development model, linking it to participatory democracy and **"twenty-first-century socialism."** The members of the *consejos* (councils) would elect persons to take neighborhood concerns up to high levels. Those elected were called *voceros* (spokespersons), not *representantes* (representatives). They are subject to recall by the organized community.

The model for the program did not simply spring from Chávez's head. It originated in the municipality of Carora, population 90,000, in the west-central region of the country. There the local mayor, Julio Chávez (no relationship to the president), turned over the entire capital budget (funds not allocated to daily operations; 50 percent of the city's available revenues) to the local communities to allocate themselves.

This experiment is highly controversial. Critics claim that Chávez merely built a new patronage structure outside the normal structures of municipal and state government. Much of the Venezuelan middle class was convinced that Chávez wanted to import the Cuban model, complete with CDRs, into Venezuela. Admirers of Venezuela in the heady years of *chavista* rule see a bold experiment in participatory democracy. The truth is somewhere in between. More state money, which largely came from booming oil exports, was channeled to those areas where Chavismo (support for President Chávez) and councils were most strongly organized. But where there were some roots in past organizing and followers more dedicated to community improvement, the communal councils struck deeper roots.

Polarization around Chavismo took on a territorial, not just class, dimension. Massive marches by hundreds of thousands of Venezuelans characterized tactics on both the pro- and anti-Chávez forces during his presidency, with middle class demonstrators mounting the marches from the wealthier eastern side of Caracas and the poor and working class from the massive *barrios* in the western part of the capital city. The largest contingents on the Chavista side usually emanated from the western *barrios* of Caracas, whereas opposition demonstrations always departed from the more affluent eastern areas of the metropolitan area. To some extent, the polarization diminished between the defeat of an effort to recall Chávez in a national referendum in 2004 and his death in 2013, but highly polarized politics reemerged after the narrow electoral victory of Maduro in April 2013 (Mallen and García-Guadilla 2017).

At the time of the death of Chávez in March 2013, Venezuela remained intensely polarized about his plan to construct "twenty-first-century socialism." Since that time the dynamic has changed dramatically, though for the worse, not the better. The Maduro government is increasingly repressive but at the same time negotiates deals with the business community and relies less on mass, popular support. The opposition for its part looks abroad, hoping that U.S. sanctions and pressure from European and conservative Latin American regimes will install Juan Guaidó. Guaidó, president of the opposition-controlled National Assembly, declared in January 2019 that Maduro had vacated the presidency and proclaimed himself to be the legitimate, constitutional president. We will look more closely at this conflict in chapter 11.

Within the organized communities, committees that formed to address local issues and carry out neighborhood programs are called *colectivos*. Many are led by women. In many, but far from all, members of *colectivos* put in energy and time, often to the point of exhaustion, working to carry out the Bolivarian Revolution led by their *comandante*, Chávez. However, facing the prospect that the entire project would be reversed by an opposition victory, they put aside these projects, financed by the executive branch with petrodollars, to prioritize work in the electoral battle units. In this way, not entirely under their control, the *colectivos* became defenders of the political regime. Some of them, mostly armed young men who worked in the valley providing delivery services on motorcycles, began to attack the opposition's demonstrations, party headquarters, and news outlets. In the Maduro years (2013–), these armed *colectivos* began also to target and repress dissent in the *barrios* themselves.

Venezuela offers a cautionary tale about how we evaluate the politics of social movements. Hundreds of thousands of middle-class Venezuelans demonstrating to demand a coup are a movement. Thousands of armed young men intimidating political opposition in a regime that was putatively building a more participatory democracy are also a movement. Perhaps some social movements are better thought of as the "uncivil society."

For Review

What are neighborhood associations? What political role have they played in Brazil, Cuba, Chile, and Venezuela?

Human Rights Movements

Although in North America we tend to think of human rights associations primarily as organizations formed to preserve *civil* rights, most Latin American groups are committed to a broader agenda. The human rights movement emerged as a result of the confluence of international events and regional responses to repressive regimes and persistent social injustices.

The administration of U.S. president Jimmy Carter (1977–1981) can be credited with raising worldwide concern for human rights, but Carter often failed to act forcefully and consistently (e.g., sending military aid to the Argentine and Salvadoran military juntas) on rights issues. The administration of President Ronald Reagan (1981–1988) discovered that the promotion of human rights was a useful tool to embarrass communist regimes; however, soon U.S. allies, especially the **bureaucratic authoritarian** regimes in South America, were being criticized as among the world's most repressive regimes. U.S. policy had helped create an "opportunity" for the movement for human rights in Latin America to press its agenda.

Human rights organizations in Latin America in most cases were formed in the womb of dictatorships, by people who took enormous risks, in many cases losing their lives. In some cases, the Catholic Church provided a protective social umbrella for the first groups. For example, Chile's Servicio Paz y Justicia (SERPAJ; Service for Peace and Justice), part of the Archdiocese of Santiago, was established in 1977 at the height of the dictatorship. One of its activities was training people in "control of fear" and in nonviolent protest. The Chilean Corporación de Promoción y Defensa de los Derechos de Pueblo (CODEPU; www.codepu.cl) devotes itself to preserving memory of the repressive Pinochet era. It organizes people to demand investigations and prosecutions in individual cases and pressures the Chilean judiciary to reopen abuse cases.

Some human rights groups focus narrowly on civil rights, but others extend their work into other areas. In Chile Nizkor (Hebrew for "we will remember," an allusion to the Jewish Holocaust) is one of the networks that link these types of groups throughout the hemisphere. SERPAJ, Chile's chapter of Nizkor, has involved itself in Indigenous and environmental issues. Its web page (www.derechos.org/nizkor/espana/doc/endesa, accessed August 2010) included a call to support the Mapuche Indians in their conflict with a Spanish corporation that wanted to build hydroelectric dams on the Bio-Bio River in southern Chile.

In El Salvador, the Centro de Documentación en Derechos Humanos, a prominent human rights organization, was founded by Father Segundo Montes, a Jesuit murdered by the military in 1989. Based in the Jesuit's Central American University in San Salvador, the organization opened campaigns for the direct election of the country's attorney general, a position of importance because it has independent authority to prosecute corruption and human rights abuses. Like SERPAJ, the organization does not limit itself to defense of civil liberties. On its website, the organization defines its mission as not only to create a safer atmosphere for participation by reducing repression, but also to identify the roots of that repression in poverty, marginalization, and exclusion (www.uca.edu.sv/publica/idhuca, accessed August 23, 2014).

Citizen organizations of a similar nature have arisen everywhere, not just in countries that lived through military rule. In Venezuela, PROVEA (Venezuelan Program of Education and Action on Human Rights) is one of several groups that formed as the economy deteriorated in the 1980s, prompting riots and government repression in 1989. PROVEA certainly takes on civil rights cases, but it defines its mission as defense of "economic, cultural and social rights" as well. In 2006, it was one of several organizations that protested the Supreme Court's decision to void major provisions of a women's rights bill. The sections struck down had authorized government agencies in emergency situations to prevent abusive men from entering the homes and workplaces of threatened women. PROVEA has involved itself in investigating and pressuring the Venezuelan government not just on political rights but also on making good on a variety of social rights, most importantly in housing and health.

Related to the human rights movement are groups that emerged to defend the transparency of electoral processes. These have been particularly significant in Mexico and Venezuela, where the probity of elections has been a major battleground. In Venezuela, Ojo Electoral ("Electoral Eye") emerged after the opposition to Chávez claimed fraud in the 2004 recall election. The group generally rejected these claims, but the organization decided that the country needed an independent, civic group to monitor elections. Ojo itself disbanded but has been succeeded by a similar organization, Observatorio Electoral, that has worked to ensure a fair count of ballots and to build popular confidence in electoral mechanisms. Mexico's Alianza Cívica (see chapter 8), founded with goals similar to those of Venezuela's Observatorio, has gone even further, broadening its focus after 2000 to include anticorruption efforts.

Since 2000, there has occurred a proliferation of groups, agencies, and national governments operating under the banner of human rights that have partisan agendas in favor of or against particular regimes—what is known as "weaponizing human rights." We will return to human rights issues in chapter 13 and deal with the broader landscape of regional and global human rights organizations operating in Latin America.

Gender and Women's Movements

As we have seen already, many popular movements overlap one another, sometimes blurring the boundaries between one social sector and another. Perhaps nowhere is this more evident than in the case of women, whose leadership in democratization was highlighted in chapter 7. Often, women in the past participated in battles to overthrow a dictatorship or in revolutions only to be relegated back to the political margins afterward (Friedman 2000). Certainly, this problem has not nearly disappeared, but supported by a global movement for women's rights, there are signs that Latin American women are not accepting this marginalization without a fight in the current era.

Women's movements are pressing for progress on reproductive freedom, family issues, justice in the workplace, environmental defense, and protection from violence. For example, in Tijuana, Mexico, women workers have organized themselves to battle large companies that refuse to provide workers with severance pay after closing their doors and moving to even cheaper labor markets (cheaper than the US$11 per day earned by the Mexicans). The *promotadoras*, as they called themselves, won their struggle, one they documented in a film called *Maquilapolis*. The leaders collaborated with North American filmmakers who provided cameras, so that the women could document their work. New media technologies in this way are helping grassroots movements support one another on a transnational level.

Social movements often arise in a molecular way, almost invisibly until an outside observer from the world of academia or media takes notice. In Ciudad Juárez, poor women founded Casa Amiga not to seek any benefits from government, but (as in Chile during the Pinochet era) simply to coordinate and exchange services and survival skills. Joanna Swanger (2007: 112) argues that cooperative efforts to build community (*convivir*) are subversive in a subtle but lasting way, "planting the seeds of a workable culture that will grow up underneath the faceless structural forces of globalization." A student doing an internship in Casa Amiga wrote Swanger,

> So now I feel like part of a community of women who respect each other, and it makes me feel so content and secure. Isn't that funny? A little thing like sharing lunch can bring women together, empower them individually and as a group, and build real commitment between them . . . This atmosphere is very different from the one I'm used to in the U.S.
>
> (Swanger 2007: 117–118)

Some of the most vibrant and growing movements in the hemisphere are those connected with countering femicide, the targeting of women for violence. Men too may be victims of gender-based violence, but women are overwhelmingly more likely to be targeted. The United Nations **ECLAC** reported that at least 3,529 women were killed in 25 Latin American countries in 2018, with the highest rates recorded in El Salvador, Honduras, and Bolivia (Agencia EFE, Spain, November 24, 2019). It is likely that many more were killed, because many countries do not classify women killed because of their gender as femicide, a subcategory of murders. Frequently, victims of femicide are women who are political activists. One example of this phenomenon can be found in Colombia. A 2011 law mandates that each party's electoral list (nominees for seats in representative bodies) must be women, which has been effective raising the number of women in local government. Many of these officials come out of grassroots community organizations addressing family and neighborhood issues across a range of concerns. Noting the failures of Colombia to implement peace accords between the government and guerrilla groups (see chapter 10), Ana Güezmes García, United Nations Representative for Women in Colombia said, "To consolidate the peace process, we need to invest in women . . . and create a culture of security for them" (*The Guardian*, London, October 1, 2019).

The movement against femicide and gender violence overall received a major boost in visibility when Lastesis, a Chilean cultural troop, staged a protest against violence targeting women in the mass protests against inequality that erupted in 2019. The group performed a choreographed dance and song in response to several cases of women being raped by police during demonstrations. The song's chorus proclaimed, "It was not my fault/neither where I was/nor what I was wearing," goes the chorus of the chant, called "A Rapist in Your Path." A video of the protest went viral and soon similar events were organized by women in Mexico, Colombia, Spain, and France. The song is more than just a protest against rape; another line in the song says, "The rapist is you/It's the cops/The judges/The state/The president" (*The Guardian*, London, December 6, 2019). In Mexico two months later, photos of the body of a brutally murdered young woman triggered a massive response to a call for protest against machismo and gender-based violence, promoted with the hashtag #UNDIASINNOSOTRAS ("A Day Without Us"). Some estimate that a majority of Mexico's female population were committing to "disappearing" for work that day, with support coming across class, ethnic, and partisan boundaries (*New York Times*, February 26, 2020).

Given Latin America's Catholic heritage, it may surprise us to learn that Latin America has a strong LGBTQ+ movement with some significant achievements. In 2010, Argentina became the first country to legalize gay marriage. One report (Brigida 2018) states, "Latin America's LGBTQ+ push demonstrates how vibrant activist networks, effective messaging to citizens, and access to democratic institutions have made the legalization of same-sex marriage possible." At the same time, LGBTQ+ people face similar problems of targeted violence, partly in reaction to the movement's success. Diane Rodríguez, a director of two of Argentina's LGBTQ+ organizations and an elected member of Ecuador's National Assembly, believes a sharp increase in murders of LGBTQ+ people (May 2017) in the country is part of a backlash to a law allowing people to freely change their gender identity and to a court ruling that allowed a lesbian couple to adopt a child (Reuters, January 20, 2020).

In Puerto Rico, the brutal, execution-style killing of a transgender homeless woman after a viral video showed her being interrogated by police for allegedly peeping at another woman in a rest room elicited a wave of revulsion that forced the government to investigate the crime (*New York Times*, February 27, 2020). But progress in recognizing and protecting the rights of transgender people has run up against another social movement that represents what we might call "uncivil society"—the opposition of small but influential conservative Christian congregations.

Indigenous and Ethnic Movements

As noted in chapter 2, Latin American national identity has been forged around the idea of *mestizaje*, which on the one hand recognized the history of Indigenous and African peoples' contribution to the region's culture, but on the other hand created a basis for denying that racism existed or influenced social class patterns. Andeans and Mexicans learned to glorify the Mayan, Incan, or Aztec past, but not necessarily the Indian present.

In the twentieth century, the most important movements for social justice often included Indigenous peoples in their ranks, but they were almost always led by **mestizos**. Examples include leaders like Haya de la Torre, the Peruvian reformist who founded APRA; Lázaro Cárdenas, the Mexican president who made good on some of the promises of the Mexican Revolution; and Victor Paz Estenssoro, leader of the 1952 revolution in Bolivia and founder of that country's main party of the populist era, the Movimiento Nacionalista Revolucionario (MNR).

The Cuban Revolution greatly benefited Afro-Cubans, but here once again the top leaders (Fidel and Raúl Castro, Che Guevara, and others) were in the great majority either *criollo* or white. While Afro-descendent and Indigenous movements have made significant progress in recent years in gaining cultural recognition and challenging the myth of *mestizaje* (see chapters 2 and 3), their aspirations have moved more assertively toward political and economic equality.

In the last 30 years, new social movements throughout the hemisphere have sought to bring the persistence of racism and race-based inequalities into the open by challenging the myth of racial democracy in Latin America (Rodríguez 1996).

Afro-Descendent Movements in Brazil and the Caribbean

In Brazil, an early initiative to remedy racial inequality was taken by Fernando Henrique Cardoso during his presidency (1995–2003). Cardoso had attracted criticism for adopting fiscal and monetary policies that hurt the poorer sectors, who are more likely to be black, but he showed leadership on the issue of race, which was the subject of his Ph.D. dissertation. One study showed that in Brazil only 2 percent of black students entered universities in 2000, compared with 10 percent of whites. More than 50 percent of Brazil's blacks were illiterate, compared with 20 percent of the overall population, and the rate of infant mortality was twice as high for blacks as for whites (Ikawa 2009). Cardoso proposed affirmative action programs to lift the percentage of black enrollments in higher education. He argued that quotes were compatible with Brazilian laws mandating fair competition through admissions tests.

Below the federal level, three Brazilian states passed laws allocating 40 percent of university slots to Afro-Brazilians (see the Punto de Vista in chapter 3.) Afro-Brazilian members of the PT organized a black caucus. Under pressure from movements of people of African descent, the Workers Party administrations of Lula and Rousseff set quotas for Afro-Brazilians in ministries. Quotas would now be established for admission to the country's prestigious diplomatic academy, the gateway to work in the foreign service.

In liberal democracies, the idea of using measures, especially quotas, to help groups that have historically felt discrimination regain equality of opportunities often encounters opposition from those who say such policies discriminate against men and whites. The privileged sectors of Latin America respond in much the same way, arguing that they should not in some sense be "penalized" for injustices committed by ancestors. Added to this argument is the notion that racism is not prevalent in Latin America because of the historical mixture of ethnic groups—the "myth of *mestizaje.*"

Cardoso's initiatives might not have taken root but for an international black consciousness movement, fed in part by the civil rights movement in the southern United States and the antiapartheid movement in South Africa. Brazilians began to reassess the myth of racial democracy in their country. Like some other social movements we have reviewed, Afro-Brazilian organizations did not begin with avowedly political goals. The movement emerged first in the form of cultural groups, such as Caiana dos Crioulos, a black community of descendants of runaway slaves, and Banda Yle Odara, which practices martial arts, music, and dance. Afro-Brazilian religious groups, including practitioners of Candomble and Umbanda, began to defend their spiritual ways as legitimate. Women's organizations often proved open to views critical of Brazil's prevailing myths of racial equality.

Racism remains a difficult fact of life in Brazil. For example, Kathleen Bond, a Maryknoll missionary working for social justice in Brazil, reports (http://www.hartford-hwp.com/archives/42/132.html) that when Margarida Pereira da Silva launched her candidacy for mayor of Pombal in the northeastern state of Paraiba, she was offered a bribe to drop out of the contest. When she refused, her posters were defaced with "negra feia" (ugly negress), and many of her supporters were paid to defame her reputation. She lost the election badly. Nevertheless, it is worth noting that black women have won some races, and some now even have seats in the Brazilian Congress. In the same vein, the electoral successes of Lula in Brazil and Chávez in Venezuela (along with Indigenous politicians, such as Bolivia's Evo Morales, and female presidents, such as Chile's Michelle Bachelet and Argentina's Cristina Fernández Kirchner) literally changed the "face" of leadership in Latin America, at least until the right-populist wave returned whiteness to the presidencies of Bolivia and Brazil.

Racism divides populations in some parts of the Caribbean. For example, Dominicans occupy one-half of the island of Hispaniola; Haiti is on the eastern side. Both share African ancestry. Haiti has been severely wracked by poverty, nature (hurricanes and an earthquake), and political violence, and while the Dominican Republic is hardly among the more prosperous of Latin American countries, many Haitians have migrated to the Dominican (eastern) side of the island. There they suffer mistreatment and often expulsion, not only because Dominicans resent the additional competition for jobs but also because Dominicans choose to describe themselves as "Indian" or *mulato*—implying that it is better to fit into one of these categories than to be considered black (Sagas 1993).

This denial of African ancestry has been reinforced by the influence of the United States in the Caribbean. Before the integration of the U.S. armed forces after World War II, U.S. military bases and local clubs nearby practiced racial discrimination. Before Jackie Robinson broke Major League Baseball's ban on black athletes, skilled baseball players from Cuba and the Dominican Republic could sometimes find jobs with professional clubs, 300 of them (out of 2,600 total players) in the Negro Leagues. If Latin Americans could convince North Americans that they were "Latin," not "black," they could sometimes play in the Major League or high minor leagues.

Indigenous Movements

Most reformist or revolutionary movements in Latin America since independence have been led by *mestizos* who looked to Indigenous people for support but not for leadership. This was the case with Mexico's revolution, and the situation was similar in Bolivia in 1952. The emergence of strong Indigenous movements in the Andes must be regarded as epochal because they are putting Indian peoples in the forefront of change.

In 1952, Bolivia's middle and working classes, in particular the country's miners, rose up to install the Estenssoro's MNR (National Revolutionary Movement) in power. The party had won the 1951 elections but was prevented from taking power by the army (Cusicanqui 2004; Hylton and Thomson 2003). As the economy deteriorated and mass hunger marches were launched against the capital, the army became demoralized and suffered defections. Miners, mostly *mestizos*, began to arm themselves in support of the MNR. The party, led by Victor Paz Estenssoro, took power after the miners and dissident army forces fought the military for three days, costing 600 lives. Estenssoro proved less radical than his followers hoped and failed to follow through on abolishing the *latifundia*. He focused instead on schools, but rural education meant preparing the Indigenous peoples for Western-style modernization, not learning from Indigenous ways. The MNR divided into factions, and the military began to recover its power. Beginning in 1964, a series of repressive military governments took power.

By the late 1990s, the situation had begun to change; civil society began to reassert itself against the military and against neoliberal economic policies that did nothing to alleviate conditions in South America's poorest country. This time, however, the upsurge came directly out of Indigenous communities. President Gonzalo Sánchez de Lozada ("Goni") was attempting to privatize water services in major cities and to dismantle the state energy company. He planned to grant major leases for oil and gas production on very generous terms to foreign companies, many of which already had obtained lucrative contracts after the energy privatization. On top of that, gas production from new fields was to move through a pipeline to a port in northern Chile, a territory that Bolivia had lost in a war in the late 1800s. Goni sent the military out to quell protests, resulting in 67 deaths. In October 2003, 500,000 people, led by Indigenous leader Felipe Quispe, marched on La Paz, the capital, under the Aymara flag (the Wiphala) protesting privatization and other economic policies, forcing Goni to flee the country for Miami. In 2008, the Bolivian government asked the United States to extradite Goni, so that he could be tried for his role in the deaths, but Washington did not respond favorably to the request.

Meanwhile, impoverished farmers had turned in large numbers to cultivation of coca, a traditional crop now in great demand (though illegal) on the world market. Goni's government had cooperated with a huge U.S. effort to eradicate the crop, part of a drug war carried out in the Andean region. The repression, ecological destruction (caused by fumigation), and economic hardship had generated a movement among the *cocaleros*, a peasant union, and a party (MAS) led by Evo Morales, who emerged as the most popular politician in the country. These forces came together in the massive march of 2003. It originated in El Alto, a suburb of 900,000, where 82 percent of the population identified themselves as Indigenous in the 2001 census. Although this reflected a huge migration from countryside to city, it also reflected changes in the way that people in the lower social classes self-identified—less so as *mestizo* and more so as Indigenous.

The process of organizing Indigenous people has itself meant adaptation of traditional ways to the rules of the modern world system. For example, Inca leaders were not known to use flags, so the use of the Wiphala is an adaptation to the rituals and symbols of modern nationalism. Now the Wiphala has been adopted by Indigenous movements throughout the region—one flag uniting a very linguistically and culturally diverse people covered by the notion of "Indigenous."

In December 2005, not only did Evo Morales become the first Indigenous person to win a presidential election in Bolivia, but he also became the first candidate ever to win a majority of votes and avoid having the decision thrown into Congress. Morales pledged to halt the coca eradication program, nationalize the country's copious natural gas reserves, and reject neoliberal economic policies. Morales faced difficult challenges, not the least opposition from the growing Santa Cruz region in the southeast, where the gas fields are located. Like Chávez in Venezuela, he successfully won a referendum to call a constitutional assembly, but his supporters did not gain enough seats in the 2007 election to engineer all the changes sought by the president. On his left, Quispe was demanding that Morales deliver more on promises of land reform, protection for the *cocaleros*, and strict national control over energy. But on the right, there was mounting resistance in Santa Cruz and other states where a majority of people were *mestizo*. The issue was not just who would control the gas deposits and the land, but whether Bolivia's identity would be redefined in the image of Indigenous cultures. To make matters more complicated, the Aymara and Quechua people themselves were not united on what kind of nation-state Bolivia should be. Eventually, Morales won out with his **plurinational** vision articulated in the constitution, but the question of how much control Indigenous people will have in regions granted autonomy under the constitution was not settled. The *golpe* that ousted Morales in November 2019 brought a stridently conservative and repressive civic–military junta, openly hostile to plurinationalism.

Bolivia

Neighboring Ecuador has also seen political change grow out of Indigenous mobilization (see chapter 14). In 2000, CONAIE (Confederation of Indigenous Nationalities of Ecuador) carried out a massive mobilization of Indigenous peoples to march on the capital, Quito, demanding a "government of national salvation" in the face of an extreme economic crisis. Ecuador's politicians had earned a reputation as the most corrupt elite in the entire hemisphere. This corruption made President Jamil Mahuad's austerity measures—which hit the Indigenous populations the hardest—particularly difficult to swallow. The country's middle class and unions also were fed up with corruption and austerity. Parts of the military officer corps, especially lower-ranking officers whose pay and living conditions were worsening, were growing restless. To the astonishment of the political and social elite, some officers, including Colonel Lucio Gutiérrez, cleared the way for CONAIE protestors to take over Congress, an action that eventually forced the resignation of President Mahuad and established a **junta** that included Gutiérrez and CONAIE.

Subsequently, under pressure from the United States, higher-ranking officers prevailed on the junta to allow the country's vice president to replace Mahuad, thereby applying a fig leaf of constitutional legitimacy over what in effect was a coup. CONAIE and Gutiérrez felt betrayed. Gutiérrez put together a coalition, including a mostly Indigenous political movement called Pachakutik (the Plurinational Unity Movement), and won the presidential election of January 2003. The Indigenous movement had representatives in Gutiérrez's cabinet, but when the president accepted a draconian set of economic policies in exchange for IMF loans, the group left his government. In April 2005, Ecuadorian troops violently repressed a huge protest march called against Gutiérrez.

Into the political chaos strode Rafael Correa, an outsider, a *criollo* economist educated in the United States. Correa put together a coalition of Indigenous support with the disaffected urban middle class and poor. As Catherine Conaghan (2011) put it,

> Out on the stump, Correa seemed to channel Ecuador's past and present in his dueling personas. On one hand, he was the fire-breathing, oligarch-denouncing populist of old . . . On the other, he was the unmistakable candidate of modernity: the hip new guy on YouTube and the uber-technocrat with Power Point slides.
>
> (262)

Correa swept to victory in the presidential election of 2006 and was reelected in a landslide in 2013. His Indigenous supporters increasingly distanced themselves, but his success in rewriting the country's constitution and redistributing oil-export revenues toward the poor sectors contributed to his consolidation of power. Not unlike the MST, members of Ecuador's Indigenous movements apparently found Correa's administration a better alternative than an uncertain future.

What unites Indigenous movements in the region is a common history of exploitation and discrimination; in a very broad way, most Indigenous movements also posit

more environmentally sustainable forms of economic development and challenge capitalist ideas about ownership of land and nature. The Ecuadorian, Mexican (Zapatistas),
Guatemalan (Mayan), and Bolivian cases show that demands by the movements are
expressed as matters of identity. Movements there, but also in places like Brazil (the MST,
for example), mount their own distinctive parties, flags, unions, guerrilla organizations,
and so on. However, Indigenous movements are not trying to turn back the clock, nor
do they seem to want to separate from the rest of civil society. From this point onward,
however, they will shape civil society and politics with more power than at any time since
the conquest.

For Review

What qualifies the different types of groups just described as "social movements"? What makes
a social movement different from an interest group? As social movements get involved in political
struggles, what issues arise for them regarding their relationship to parties and the state?

Uncivil and Civil Society

We should not romanticize social movements or think that a majority of the poor have
been incorporated into their ranks. Some of destructive movements include Central
America's gangs, Andean paramilitary forces, and guerrilla movements that employ violence systematically and criminally, not just as a matter of self-defense or as an occasional
abuse. They make up part of Latin America's "uncivil society" and hardly strengthen
democracy.

One of the great paradoxes in Latin America is that the cities have grown more violent
and uncivil in many ways, but at the same time impressive new movements and associations have sprung up. How "new" such movements are is debatable. Perhaps what is different
about these movements is their determination (not always maintained) to avoid co-optation
by parties and the state, their resistance to neoliberalism (or at least globalization, neoliberal
style), and the greater emphasis they place on "inclusion"—overcoming racial, class, and
gender barriers to full inclusion socially and politically.

Urban and rural inequalities feed on one another, and the situation in Central America is perhaps most illustrative of this fact. The region's cities were swollen by refugees from
the wars, and the great majority of these people have never been resettled. Urban areas are
now populated by legions of unemployed youth; firearms are more obtainable than ever. El
Salvador and Honduras (though the latter escaped the worst violence of the 1980s) have seen
spectacular growth in gangs organized by young men who returned from inner cities in the
United States after the end of the wars.

Social movements can be reactionary, but even here we need to understand why
they form. Consider youth gangs. On May 17, 2004, a fire in one Honduran prison killed
103 young inmates, victims of an overcrowded penal system that cannot absorb prisoners,
most of whom were arrested merely for wearing the tattoos of gangs. They were swept up

in a government crackdown encouraged by a fearful population. Analyzing the tragedy, *The Economist* ("Bring It All Back Home," May 20, 2004) said,

> With no jobs, the deportees set up their own gangs. According to government estimates, 36,000 people are said to belong to gangs in Honduras, 14,000 in Guatemala, 10,500 in El Salvador, 1,100 in Nicaragua and 2,600 in Costa Rica. The true figure is almost certainly much higher. The most notorious of hundreds of gangs, or *maras*, is the Mara Salvatrucha, named for its Salvadoran founders who claimed to be as wise as a trout (*truchas*). Its initials appear in graffiti across the region.

It is difficult to imagine democracy taking firm root in "not so civil" societies. To some degree, all Latin American countries face this dilemma. Crime rates in urban areas are soaring, and justice systems—underfunded and often riddled by corruption—cannot bear the load. Frightened citizens are disposed to give government farther-reaching powers to crack down, leading to increased militarization of society.

Popular dissatisfaction with economic hardship, corruption, and other issues, the "politics of the street" continues to be a major feature of Latin American civil society. This kind of politics often alarms **pluralists**. Some of them generally believe that democracy functions best when citizens use the vote to hold politicians accountable but do not obstruct governance with too much participation. For pluralists, movements to create or restore democracy are healthy; but movements that pressure governments to intervene in the market or shake the prevailing social order are threats to democracy (Crozier et al. 1975).

In contrast, many social movements believe that the problem with democracy in Latin America is not too much but *too little* participation. Their leaders seem increasingly unwilling to accept the logic that governments have little choice but to live up to the agreements to pay off the debt, limit tax increases on foreign investors, put national resources (e.g., water and mineral resources) in private hands, and so on. An irony of globalization is that in certain ways it has fostered the growth and influence of social movements. The Internet, cheaper and faster transportation, and the growth of international nongovernmental organizations (NGOs) have enabled movements to communicate and meet to support one another and exchange experiences.

Social movements are neither smitten with the virtues of the "free market" nor rushing to embrace state control over the economy. The shortcomings of import substitution and the collapse of the former Soviet Union and its "command economy" have influenced the search for an alternative model of development and democracy. Only in Cuba has centralized economic planning ever been tried in Latin America, and even there the political leadership never fully embraced the Soviet model. Import substitution policies, called "**state capitalism**" by some, not only produced considerable economic growth but also fostered clientelism and corruption, limiting the autonomy of the groups that made up civil society. Unions, business organizations, and public bureaucracies were all colonized by political parties that delivered benefits to supporters but allowed for little effective initiative and participation by citizens. We saw examples of that tendency in Mexico and Venezuela (see chapter 8). This helps to explain why new social movements became strong not only in countries where they arose to oppose dictatorships but also in other countries where they grew out of dissatisfaction with the rule of traditional political parties.

Latin America's progressive social movements have usually sought, though not always successfully, to guard their autonomy relative to political parties. At the same time, they seek the protection of the state against globalization's most harmful impacts. New social movements do not generally see civil society as encouraged by the market. They seem in general to regard civil society as existing as public space between the globalized market and the state, something that the Global North might consider.

Discussion Questions

1. Can Latin American countries be considered democracies given the large gaps between rich and poor in the social class system?
2. Labor unions have played a historically important role in struggles for democracy, yet some would say that other types of movements of poor people where they live have become an even more important force in Latin American politics. Why might this be? Do you agree?
3. Land redistribution has been a central demand of peasants for centuries, yet we have seen few successful cases of this. Why do you think peasants have faced such difficulties achieving reform? Can movements like the MST change the record?
4. How might the emergence of social movements strengthen democracy, and how might it threaten it?
5. To some degree, social movements are wary of both the market and the state. But do they really have an alternative to working with both?

Resources for Further Study

Reading: Finding a comprehensive description of social class structures in Latin America is difficult. I rely mainly on Alejandro Portes and Kelly Hoffman, "Latin American Class Structures: Their Composition and Change During the Neoliberal Era," *Latin American Research Review* 38, no. 1 (February 2003): 41–77. Rodolfo Stavenhagen is a Mexican sociologist who has extensively studied social classes, urban and rural. His edited *Agrarian Problems and Social Movements in Latin America* (Garden City, NY: Doubleday, 1970) is a good place to start to appreciate the variety of peasant communities and organization. Hernando de Soto's *The Other Path: The Invisible Revolution in the Third World* (New York: HarperCollins, 1989) argues for freeing small-scale capital in cities by reducing the reach of the state. *El Alto, Rebel City: Self and Citizenship in Andean Bolivia*, edited by Sian Lazar (Durham, NC: Duke University Press, 2008) is a good study of how social change, political change, and self-identity are interrelated. Patricia Fernández Kelly and Jon Shefner's *Out of the Shadows: Political Action and the Informal Economy in Latin America* (University Park: Pennsylvania State University Press, 2006) deals with urban protest movements. Editors Arturo Escobar and Sonia E. Alvarez's *The Making of Social Movements in Latin America: Identity Strategy and Democracy* (Boulder: Westview Press, 1992) was among the first publications to recognize the growing importance of movements and still remains relevant.

Video and Film: *Pixote* (1981) is a portrait of a child's life in the *favelas* of Rio. Simon Romero's report on motorcyclists in Caracas *barrios* can be found at the *New York Times* website (www.nytimes.com) and YouTube by searching for "Caracas barrios." *Las Madres de la Plaza de Mayo* (1985) documents the most famous of human rights movements led by women. *Neighboring Sounds* (2012), called the "best Brazilian film since 1976" by John Powers, film critic for National Public Radio, directed and written by Kleber Mendonca Filho, looks at the life of the new middle class in Recife, Brazil.

On the Internet: Hans Rosling's "Gapminder" website (www.gapminder.org) lets you explore inequality across regions and countries. News from the point of view of social movements, in English, can be found at Upside Down World (http://upsidedownworld.org/main). Information on the *maquiladora* movement of Mexican women can be found at www.corpwatch.org/article.php?id=1528. Searching for "MST" on YouTube turns up several documentaries on the Landless Workers' Movement. Particularly good is *MST—Landless Movement in Brazil*, in three parts.

12 Parties, Media, and Left-Right Populism

Focus Questions

▶ What role are parties supposed to play in a **polyarchy**? What are some of the different kinds of political parties in Latin America?

▶ How does a social movement differ from an organized group? What kind of relationships do movements have with political parties?

▶ What roles have the media assumed in the contentious politics of Latin America in the twenty-first century?

▶ How have the meaning of "left" and "right" changed in recent decades?

▶ What was the initial promise of social media and cyber technology for democracy? How has that played out in Latin America?

THE ITALIAN POLITICAL theorist Antonio Gramsci (1971: 16), writing in the early 1930s, described a political party as an organization in civil society that people join for the purpose of promoting an agenda "with a national or international character." Businesspeople might join a chamber of commerce to promote their particular industry; workers might join a union to negotiate better wages. But by supporting or joining a political party, the same individuals join an organization with broader objectives, some of which might require sacrifices on their part. This conception of a party makes sense in many circumstances. People often ban together in movements, groups, or parties to advance the welfare of all, not just themselves. In most cases, parties differ from other organizations in that they "draw their support from a broad base" and "have as their primary goal the conquest of power or a share in its exercise" (Duverger 1972: 1–2).

There might be a few exceptions. Some small leftist parties hardly seem as though they are interested in gaining office and exercising power at all. They concentrate on agitating for revolution by getting involved in social and economic struggles, such as strikes, land occupations, or environmental issues. Winning elections is not their priority. The Zapatistas of Mexico come closest to this kind of party, but they have always defined themselves more in terms of a movement than as a party. The Brazilian Workers Party might come close to the first definition (see chapter 7), but its founders were part of a movement pressing for a transition from dictatorship to democracy, demanding "Direct Elections Now!" As the party gained electorally, it began to place maintaining its share of power within the state ahead of its commitment to social and economic justice.

Robert Michels would probably find that this experience supports his "iron law of oligarchy" (see chapter 1). Others might quote Lord John Dalton-Acton (1907), who said, "Power tends to corrupt and absolute power corrupts absolutely. Great men are almost always bad men, even when they exercise influence and not authority: still more when you add the tendency or the certainty of corruption by authority." Perhaps the fault lies within human nature, but so too do social and political structures that are biased toward wealth and power. These are subject to change, which is why Gramsci's conception of parties remains as important as Duverger's.

In Latin America, **clientelism** often affects the practices of parties, making distribution of benefits more important than ideology or party platforms. Having a party membership card might be a prerequisite for getting or keeping a job, obtaining an export license from a government bureaucrat, or getting pension payments started. This is typical of parties that serve as a vehicle for the ambitions of a regional politician, such as a governor. Like the *caudillos* that assembled masses of peons to fight behind them with promises of land, a local *cacique* or *coronel* may gather votes to take a seat in the national legislature or even to ascend to the presidency, thereby gaining access to power and controlling patronage resources. But these parties too need a program, even if it is little more than a broad populist appeal to place the "people" before "elites."

Parties whose origins were in progressive social struggles may over time evolve into "catch-all" parties, that is, ones that try to attract votes across different economic and social divisions in the electorate. These parties may be less attractive to those seeking rapid social change, but they may be healthy for **polyarchies**. The need to appeal across a range of social interests to win votes should have a moderating effect, strengthening the center against extremes, lessening the likelihood of the type of polarization that characterized the breakdowns of democracy in much of Latin America 50 years ago (see chapter 7).

The theory does not always work out this way. The two catch-all parties that competed in elections in Venezuela between 1958 and 1998 (see chapter 8) failed to respond to mounting discontent with economic privation and corruption, allowing the country to drift into a crisis of representation that brought the system crashing down in 1998. In a crisis of representation, it may seem that all existing political parties do little beyond aiming to hold on to or expand their power in the state. When parties mainly attract members solely motivated by ambition for power in this way, they are not likely to fulfill the function that Gramsci attached to them.

In this chapter, we will characterize parties in part by their ideologies, but we will also pay attention to the way they relate to the social movements, classes, and groups described in the preceding chapter. Though we risk oversimplifying their ideologies and programs in doing so, there is some use in employing the left-right spectrum, especially as we have seen in Latin America a political polarization between the populist left that rose with the **Pink Tide** and the populist right.

Parties once played the role of mainsprings in the institutional clockwork of **polyarchy**, but they have lost the near monopoly they previously had on organizing the linkages between civil society and government. Lain America is not unique in this respect. Media, both "twentieth-century" print and electronic news media and more recent forms of "social media," have increasingly displaced parties from their role in democracy, at least as the **pluralists** imagined it.

Party Systems

A "**party system**" refers to how parties interact with one another and with **civil society**. These interactions are shaped by electoral rules and systems of representation. Most Latin American countries employ two rounds to elect a president, which tends to encourage more parties to compete. In the first round, electors can "vote with their hearts," and in the second "vote with their heads." This is an oversimplification, but it allows for what political scientists call "articulation" of popular demands. More ideas can enter the "marketplace" and compete for votes than in a "first past the post system" one, in which voters are more likely to feel their only option is to vote for the least bad. The second round requires that voters think more about the viability of the different candidates or, where only two survive, which one they might settle for. This is what political scientists call "aggregation," which might be more eas-ily understood as "compromise," where voters might have to weigh which candidate is least distant from their political views, as opposed to closest.

In a region where strong executive power with tendencies toward **caudillism** is the norm, how the president is elected is a crucial regulator of power. Most countries use a runoff system (e.g., Brazil, Chile, Argentina, and Mexico), but some (e.g., Venezuela) simply award the presidency to whomever gets the most votes (a plurality) in one election. We should note here that many small states in the Caribbean region use a parliamentary system; that is, after the election of the legislature (the parliament), the largest party or coalition of parties selects a prime minister. This is largely because European colonialism persisted in these states into the twentieth century, and at the time of independence the parliamentary model was already in place. Latin America's preference for a presidential system reflects its earlier independence and tendency to emulate the U.S. model.

In Latin America, legislative elections tend toward the German model, whereby pro-portional representation (based on the principle that each party gets a number of seats based on the percentage they have gotten in each state) is mixed with "single member district" representation (one representative for each district in a state, as in the U.S.). Brazil is a major exception in this regard, as it uses proportional representation in each state in choosing members of its lower house. Each state gets three senators, and they serve for eight-year terms, an unusually long period. Furthermore, for reasons rooted in the way Brazil became independent and evolved from a monarchy to a republic in the 1800s (see chapter 3), Brazil has one of the most decentralized systems of federalism. That is, states, and especially the governors of states, enjoy much more autonomy from the central government than any other country in Latin America, even those (such as Mexico) that also have constitutions divid-ing the power between central and state governments. The systems are further complicated by different ways of selecting local authorities. A small change sometimes can make a big difference. In 1989 Venezuela replaced a system, once common in Latin America, whereby governors were not elected but were appointed by the president. The switch to election of governors in Venezuela loosened the grip of central control exercised by national party lead-ers, but this turned out to be too little, too late to save the Punto Fijo polyarchy.

We will return to the theme of how constitutions and institutions shape the political arena in chapter 13, but going into detail about the myriad variations on how Latin Amer-ican countries choose presidents and representatives and divide power between national, state, and local jurisdictions would lead us down a rabbit hole describing voting procedures, powers and limits on powers, systems of law, and so forth. Also, not all the key rules of the game are found in written constitutions. For example, the stability of the Mexican system between 1928 and 2000 was based upon the *dedazo*, the pact made by revolutionary generals to allow the incumbent president to choose ("point the finger at") his successor, with the understanding the president would retire from active politics. This was not in the Mexican constitution, but it was a key feature of how the Mexican state was "constituted" in that era.

One-party systems, whether enshrined in the constitution (the Cuban case; see chapter 9) or rooted in the dominance of a single party over other competitors (Mexico until 2000; see chapter 8), are incompatible with the idea of polyarchy, but across countries with this kind of system there are variations in the degree of internal participation and possibilities for opposition; that is, there is a degree of **pluralism** even in single-party systems. Competition within a single party may permit some opposition and debate even in the absence of competitive elections.

It can be argued that at least until the 1960s, the Partido Revolucionario Institucional (PRI) of Mexico was a **corporatist** machine, but one supported freely in elections by a large majority of the population. For decades, beginning with the presidency of Lázaro Cárdenas (1934–1940), its near monopoly was built on popular support and expectations born out of the country's 1910 revolution. Mexico had a relatively free climate for dissent and some space for political opposition. In the north, in the region around Monterrey, the Partido Acción Nacional generally carried elections and was allowed to govern. Left socialist parties were able to win and take over City Hall in several sizable towns in the central region. Still, the PRI's control over the central government and channels of patronage allowed it to contain party competition to these pockets. Steven Levitsky and Lucan Way (2002), though not referring specifically to Mexico, speak of this kind of state as competitive authoritarianism, one where opposition groups can run in elections and sometimes even be allowed to win, but where unfair procedures and repression of civil liberties make democracy something of a façade.

Although Cuba is often portrayed as a **totalitarian** gulag in the United States, the Partido Comunista de Cuba (PCC) has survived (see chapter 9) not just through prohibiting competition and jailing all dissenters but also through the party's relationship with popular assemblies that provide significant input into policy outcome. However, the fundamental constitutional principles that establish socialism as the economic system and the PCC as the sole legal party are not open to debate. Still, pro-government Cubans argue that the party maintains contact with the country's particular form of civil society. Needless to say, dissenters, both on and off the island, disagree.

Decentralization of government is touted as superior, that it brings decision-making closer to the people. However, decentralization is not always good for **governance**. Brazil is a case in which there is so little party discipline that coalitions must be organized bill by bill— and sometimes by unsavory or illegal financial incentives. Although the Workers Party held the largest bloc of seats in the national legislature, the large majority were held by careerists of other parties, many organized by local or state *coroneles*. The political trajectory of these congressional delegates consists of rising step by step from local, to state, and then national levels, accumulating financial benefits along the way in preparation for a comfortable retirement, with consequences we will examine further on in this chapter.

Multiparty systems are found everywhere outside of Cuba today. Some such systems are very fluid and unstable, as has been common in Ecuador, for example. Some have been highly stable, as in the case of Chile, where parties on each side of the left and right of the spectrum tend to come together in coalitions that make the system function much like the third general kind of party system, the two-party system. A two-party or two-bloc system allows competition but frequently generates the complaint that the parties converge toward the center (as catch-all parties tend to do) and offer voters very limited choice—a criticism often heard in the United States but also echoed in many Latin American countries.

In chapter 8, we reviewed how Venezuela's two-party system dominated civil society through clientelism and corruption, and toward the end of the Punto Fijo era (1958–1998) through manipulation of elections. Despite a troubled six years of coping with economic crisis and political corruption, most political scientists thought the country's competitive party system would be a vehicle of reform. The outbreak of devastating rebellions simultaneously in 22 cities (the *caracazo*, after the violence in Caracas) in February 1989 caught most political scientists by surprise. It exposed a crisis of representation that eventually paved the way for Hugo Chávez to win the 1998 presidential election. In Chile, the outburst of mass protest and violent repression by security forces in 2019 caught many by surprise. The Washington-based Inter-American Dialogue convened a session to discuss the question: "Chile, long regarded as one of Latin America's most stable countries, is experiencing its worst unrest in decades . . . What provoked the recent upheaval that surprised both officials and analysts?"

In Chile, the five largest parties (two on the moderate left, one in the center, and two on the right), routinely have coalesced into two blocs—center-left and center-right—to contest elections. This is partly because the system for choosing a president and especially the Senate makes it difficult for smaller parties to have influence. In assuming the presidency for a second time in 2014, President Michelle Bachelet promised to move decisively to change this system, but she could not attract enough votes from conservative parties to achieve the full overhaul she promised. This experience accounts for why, as 2020 dawned, protests continued despite President Piñera's calling for a constituent assembly to rewrite the constitution. Protestors were not just marching but also meeting daily in street-level assemblies where, with young people in the vanguard, many citizens were demanding direct election of delegates to a constitutional assembly, rather than allowing the existing parties to mediate the process. The coronavirus pandemic interrupted the assembly movement, leaving the issue unsettled as fall and winter approached.

To be sure, political science is unlikely ever to prove itself capable of predicting the imminent onset of social explosions like the *carazo* or the eruptions in Chile. However, there are at least some clues suggesting that these kinds of protests in the neoliberal era are related to **precarity**. The spark that has touched off social explosions in Argentina, Chile, Ecuador, Bolivia, Venezuela, and other countries has been the same—threats to the basic necessities of life: access to water, health, transportation, food, and so forth. The growing precarity of life in the neoliberal era has now been magnified by the coronavirus, with consequences that can only partly be discerned from studying public opinion.

Rather than embark on an endless description of the formal rules of the game in each Latin American country, I prefer that you consider the following idea (which you certainly can debate) as the takeaway: We cannot simply attribute scandals, vote-buying, corruption, clientelism, failure of parties to deliver on promises, and other sources of popular discontent with political parties to the bad faith, greed, vanity, or personal corruption of politicians. The case of Brazil and the Workers Party, among the cases we examine in detail, will show that institutions likewise shape the limits and possibilities of parties that seek, much as Gramsci described it, to advance agendas for the social good.

For Review

How does a party system differ from a party? What are some of the functions that parties serve in a political system, especially in polyarchies? Why can they be considered the "mainsprings" of such systems? What is a crisis of representation, and how might it threaten the health of a poly-archy? Why might some single-party systems still be somewhat pluralist in how they function?

Right and Left in Latin America

The terms "right" and "left" are very subjective and relative everywhere, and Latin America is no exception. Parties such as Acción Democrática in Venezuela and the PRI in Mexico were for decades in the last century generally seen as leftist. Today, most new social movements and the political parties that draw strength from them (whether or not these movements consciously lend support) now regard these parties as part of the "right."

The concept of "left-right" comes from the way that representatives to the French National Assembly have been seated since the French Revolution, with those wanting rapid and deep change seated on the left, facing toward the front of the chamber, and those defending tradition and monarchy seated on the right.

The Right

For many years, students of Latin America tended to ignore conservative parties. Until very recently, these parties were associated mainly with the landed oligarchy. Many industries, economic empires, and businesses were nurtured by the state in the import substitution era, so few entrepreneurs were apostles of laissez-faire policies. Business interests were often incorporated under the wing of populist parties, the dinosaurs. Few conservative parties promoting free-market capitalism could be found.

An exception is Mexico's Partido Acción Nacional (PAN), which was founded in 1939 as a vehicle to serve the interests of powerful industrialists (concentrated in the city of Monterrey) and small landholders who felt threatened by land reform. The PAN also attracted support from religious voters resentful about the Mexican Revolution's strident policies to strip the Catholic Church of its privileges, which sometimes spilled over into attacks on religion itself. Over time, professionals from the middle class began to enter the party, seeing it as a vehicle for protesting the corruption and fraud practiced by the PRI. In 2000, some members of the PRD also supported the PAN candidate, Vicente Fox, for president as the candidate best positioned to break the PRI's monopoly of power. Another PAN candidate, Felipe Calderón, won a six-year term in 2006. The party lost the presidential elections of 2012 and 2018, but it has retained a sizable bloc of deputies and senators in the Congress.

Chile is another of the few Latin American countries where one finds business-oriented parties with a mass base that has lasted over several decades. Two conservative parties vie with each other to promote somewhat different visions of capitalism. One, the National Renovation (RN), is a descendant of the National Party (a product of the merger of the old Liberal and Conservative parties), which opposed the Christian Democrats and Allende's

Popular Unity coalition in 1970 (see chapter 7). The RN's elite base is domestic mining barons and the older businesses that survived the Pinochet era, and its mass appeal is to more moderate sectors of the right. The newer Independent Democrat Union (UDI) was founded by young, ardent admirers of General Pinochet, whose regime swung Chile's economy radically in the direction of a more laissez-faire capitalism. The UDI tends to attract more of its elite support from neoliberal intellectuals and business interests that sprung up in the free-market environment. Both of these parties compete for the votes of social conservatives, especially on issues like education and abortion. Like the leftist parties, they vigorously compete, but like the left they tend to unite around a common candidate in presidential elections.

Chile's electoral politics, then, emerged from the transition to democracy with more centrist electoral politics than in the populist era, with two broad alliances in competition with each other, an alliance between RN and UDI on the right, and the other, now called Nueva Majoridad (originally, the Concertación) on the center-left. This tendency was interrupted in 2005 when Joaquin Lavin of UDI, who seemed to have won the right-wing nomination, was challenged in the general election by the RN's Sebastian Piñera. In effect, the first round of the presidential election functioned like a primary. Piñera finished second and won the right to contest the second round against the Concertación candidate, Bachelet. She won the runoff in January 2006.

This set off an alternation unusual in Latin American electoral policies. Piñera came back as the candidate of a more united right coalition to win the January 2010 elections, and then Bachelet returned to win a new term in 2014. Piñera would return in 2018. This rotation in office of establishment candidates proved frustrating to many Chileans, especially to young people, many of whom are two generations removed from the Pinochet era. This generation has formed the vanguard of massive protests against the country's inequality in late 2019, at least in the capital. Their rising was also connected to environmental concerns in which the country's Mapuche Indigenous people, approximately 10 percent of the population, have played the leading role. Their lands in the southern, Patagonian region have borne the ecological costs of the opening of their forests, lakes, rivers, and estuaries to logging, mining, and fishing industries, which started in the Pinochet era and was continued by the Concertación governments.

Along with the frustration of young generations with the failure of polyarchy to deliver on the promise of democracy, we should also take into account how the harsh dictatorships and widespread human rights abuses (e.g., Chile, El Salvador) of dictatorship have impacted voters, that is, how traumatic violence may motivate those who lived those days to opt for more centrist candidates and parties. Although we are 30 years removed from the bureaucratic authoritarian era and the civil wars in Central America, these conflicts left deep scars on civil society. Voters can be forgiven if they think not only about which party or candidate best represents their interests, but also about which is less likely to make their worst fears of a return to that era a reality.

If today's left in Latin America has a more rosy than red hue, so too has the right evolved from the populist era. Although social issues are the most powerful engines of mass support for the right, being part of the "right" in Latin America today is associated with supporting **neoliberalism**—that is, favoring the economic policies associated with the **Washington Consensus**. So today, to take but one example, Teodoro Petkoff, a guerrilla leader in Venezuela in the 1960s, is seen by *chavistas* as part of the right because he served as minister of planning from 1994 to 1998 and backed many of the structural adjustment policies that

President Rafael Caldera embraced in that era. Few Latin American presidents campaigned openly as neoliberals. When they did, they usually claimed that their administrations would soften the blow on the poor by bringing more efficiency and cleaning up corruption. Examples include Carlos Salinas de Gortari in Mexico (1988), Carlos Andrés Pérez in Venezuela (1988), Carlos Menem in Argentina, and Alijandro Toledo in Peru (2001). Since 2010, the right has surged back against the Pink Tide, often with campaigns featuring not only promises of renewed economic growth and jobs, but also anti-corruption messages, divisive racial appeals, promises to crack down on violent crime, and opposition to reproductive rights and LGBTQ+ rights. If this formula sounds familiar to the campaign themes of the populist right in places as diverse as the Philippines, Hungary, Turkey, and the United States, your instincts are correct. It is not coincidental (we explore this further later).

Throughout Latin America, parties and candidates have run populist campaigns promising relief from economic policies, but once in power, they often leave economic policy-making to policy intellectuals trained in the United States or in "think tanks" heavily influenced by neoliberal ideas. Jorge Domínguez (1997) calls these intellectual politicians "technopols." Unlike technocrats who remain aloof from politics, **technopols** see it as their mission not only to design economic policy but also to build political movements and interest groups dedicated to promote neoliberal ideas.

Typical is Argentina's former finance minister, Domingo Felipe Cavallo, who founded a think tank (Fundación Mediterránea) to promote market-oriented policies. Cavallo moved into the Peronist Party in 1991 at the invitation of President Menem. Chile's Alejandro Foxley, in contrast to Cavallo, had a reputation as an academic leftist before moving in the Concertación cabinet as the first post-dictatorship finance minister under President Patricio Aylwin, a Christian Democrat. Foxley had been severely critical of the economists ("Chicago Boys"; see chapters 6 and 7) who designed the neoliberal policies implemented under Pinochet. However, as finance minister he made few changes—partly because of restrictions imposed by the constitution of 1982 and partly because market-oriented policies seemed to be the *only* possible ones in the era of globalization. Foxley explained what happened in an interview (PBS 2001):

> Interviewer: Is it fair to say that you came to have a greater faith in the role that the market can play in an economy?
> Alejandro Foxley: We have all learned during these years that it's only a very strong person who, when he sees that the world is changing very fast, doesn't adjust his own views to the changes that he's seeing in the world. Today we appreciate the strength and the power of the market much more as a force that will allow an economy to grow fast.

Domínguez says that technopols have a "passion" for a set of ideas and feel a shared responsibility to seek to implement them. He describes them as effectively merging their scholarly experience with political engagement, so they and their teams become "partisans" in pursuit of their ideas. This means they "behave as 'teachers to the nation,' that is, bearers of a more impersonal loyalty to a democratic regime, committed to educate the public about facts that may be inconvenient for their party opinions" (Domínguez 1997: 11). Latin American think tanks have trained hundreds of like-minded technopols who can be imported into key ministries, displacing the politicians from state institutions that have been critical to party cohesion in the past. Out of office, technopols often assume positions as board members of prestigious North American universities, think tanks, and financial corporations, and in similar institutions in their own countries.

One can find technopols in presidential administrations led by politicians that seem totally at odds with their cosmopolitan international social circles. Brazil's conservative populist President Jair Bolsonaro is known for having made "nutty" (*The Guardian*, London, January 2, 2020) appointments to cultural, foreign policy, and educational posts in his government, but his minister for the economy, Paulo Geddes, came to office with a Ph.D. from the University of Chicago where he studied with Milton Friedman. Besides have a lifelong career in finance, including founding a bank, Geddes founded a libertarian think tank and publicly advocated for Bolsonaro, praising him for his anti-corruption stance. Geddes himself, however, has been investigated for fraud.

The Left: Old and New

Latin America's old left, reflecting similar divisions around the world, has long been divided between communist and social democratic tendencies. Although they continue to wage ideological warfare with one another today, both of them represent the "old left." You undoubtedly have seen or heard leftists called "Reds," a term that dates back to the color used by social democrats in the late nineteenth century and then used as a description of communists after the 1917 revolution. As we have discussed in several chapters, the resurgence of the left in elections throughout Latin America has been called the Pink Tide to signify a group of leaders that share a commitment to change, and hence are leftist, but present themselves as alternatives to the old social democratic and communist left.

There are several reasons that Latin American leftists have attempted in recent decades to redefine themselves. Some have to do with internal developments in the region, including the emergence of new social movements (see chapter 11), the search for alternatives to neoliberalism and twentieth-century communism, and frustration with corruption and clientelism. But another reason has to do with the erosion of confidence in the economic sustainability and democratic shortcomings of the Cuban revolutionary model. So, we need to review briefly the Cuban experience to understand why Latin America has turned "pink," not "red," in searching for an alternative to neoliberal capitalism.

Cuba is the only country in the hemisphere and one of the few in the world that enshrines one-party rule in its constitution. The Partido Comunista Cubano (PCC) operates by internal structures patterned on the model called "democratic centralism." This idea was first developed and implemented by Vladimir Lenin. In theory, party members debate policy and by majority vote pass decisions up to higher levels, where debate and voting recur. Once a decision is made at the highest level, all members of the party are supposed to implement it without question. These parties have central organs that have the power to discipline members who fail to do so. On paper, the system should ensure internal democracy, with higher organs merely making sure everyone carried out decisions made, supposedly, by a democratic majority in the party. However, the powers of discipline and control everywhere seem to override democracy. This tendency is understandable when a party is confronted by persecution, often times deadly in nature, but the communism in power has tended to operate with similar discipline. In communist countries, the party is usually the only legal party. In general, party organs must approve appointments to major positions not only in government but also in civil society.

The PCC debated and rejected a proposal to introduce multiparty politics in 1992, and it has not revisited that decision since then. However, the PCC will certainly face the question again. Some small NGOs and autonomous think tanks gained permission to operate independently of the party and state in the 1990s, but most were subsequently shut down or subjected to discipline in later years. Still, Cuban cultural and intellectual life has never been smothered to the degree common in Eastern Europe during the Cold War. Cuba's mass organizations to a degree act like mass movements in other societies, often resisting central directives from the state and the party. Furthermore, though economic reform has stalled in the face of the hostility of the Trump administration, many more Cubans now work fully or partly outside the state sector. This new middle and working class, and the businesses that employ them, have interests that do not neatly fit into the channels of influence and control embodied in the mass organizations. In the post-Fidel era (since 2008), Cuba might experience some of the same kind of tensions between movements and the PCC that other leftist parties in Latin America must resolve.

In his lifetime, Fidel Castro exercised personal authority not just through the PCC but also through direct communication with people and through these mass organizations. With his retirement from the leadership of the government in 2008 (and death in 2016), the mantle of leadership fell on Raúl. He retired from his government position in 2018, though he still heads the PCC. For the first time since 1959, Cuba's government is headed by someone (Miguel Díaz-Canel) who was not part of the generation that toppled Batista in 1958.

As long as the island remains under duress from Washington, it is likely that the direction of Cuban politics in the post-Castro era will remain unclear. At some point, it is likely that a number of key questions will reemerge. What should be the PCC's relationship with the mass organization and new sectors that do not fit well into the old framework? How can Cuba prevent clientelism and corruption, already seen as problems, from eroding democratic tendencies and commitments to social justice? To what extent should the regime compromise its socialist ideology to adjust to external pressures and internal demands for a less statist economy, with a larger sphere of operation for the market? Although no Cuban leader will yet say so publicly, when if ever should there be a transition to a multiparty regime? A veteran foreign observer, a journalist with a Cuban family and decades of experience covering the island east to west, says that this issue will inevitably emerge. "Look at the neighborhood," he says.

Populism on the Left—Chávez and the Pink Tide

The roots of the Pink Tide are in the reaction of Latin American social movements to the experiences of populist and military rule. Indeed, although Latin Americans were no longer looking to Cuba for a political model, they were hardly enthralled with the performance of the old left in Chile or Venezuela, to name only two examples. The breakthrough for hemispheric change seemed to come in Venezuela with the ascent of Hugo Chávez.

Hugo Chávez appealed to Venezuelans as a champion of those disillusioned with the dominance of the two main parties, Acción Democrática and COPEI, over **civil society** (see chapter 8). When he decided to run for the presidency in 1998, Chávez founded what he called an "electoral movement" instead of a party, changing the name of the MBR coalition of military and civilian followers to the MVR (Fifth Republic Movement). The idea was to appeal to widespread antiparty sentiment in the country, but the MVR was not to be dissolved after Chávez took office in January 1999. He needed a vehicle to move his legislative agenda and to contest elections, so in all but name only, the MVR became a party. The party became an instrument to gather votes for the referendums and elections that followed. It was able to discipline Chavista members of the National Assembly created by the new constitution of 1999, but it was much less successful as a vehicle of mobilization for the kind of revolutionary changes Chávez hoped to bring about. Furthermore, it became increasingly obvious that the party had weak roots in the leader's main social base, in the poor *barrios*. The MVR played almost no role in mobilizing the population that descended from the *barrios* to rescue Chávez from the coup that temporarily deposed him in April 2002. It did not dissuade enough citizens from signing petitions to force a recall election in August of 2004. When the MVR faltered in the early stages of the recall campaign, Chávez reorganized his grassroots supporters into an ad hoc system of "electoral battle units" (UBEs). He won handily, but Chávez had to rethink his strategy (Hellinger 2005).

Chávez himself was partly to blame for the weak performance of the MVR. He was a larger-than-life presence who dominated political discourse, and his military background came to the fore as he welcomed his supporters' view of him as, like Fidel in Cuba, *el comandante*. Like Fidel, Chávez was a masterful social communicator, using television and radio on a weekly basis to communicate directly for hours with the people in a different location every week. The program was called *Aló Presidente*. In these programs, Chávez dispensed state resources to solve individual problems, rebutted the often vitriolic criticism of the opposition-controlled media, reviewed history (especially history that seemed to provide lessons favorable to his project), and offered opinions about world economic and political trends. He did this in words and symbols (his "discourse") that resonated with the poor majority, most of whom held him with deep affection. This was the basis of his charismatic appeal.

Charismatic appeal is a great asset for a president, but unless it is used to build institutions, it does not necessarily reinforce democracy. The philosophy of the Bolivarian constitution of 1999 was for institutions not to limit or channel participation but to facilitate bottom-up democracy, to endow the people with a "protagonistic" capacity to legislate and shape the future. The MVR, on the other hand, functioned in some ways like the very parties that Chávez had displaced, that is, as a vehicle to distribute patronage, based on the enormous revenues generated by oil exports, and to discipline members of the governing coalition. In early 2007, Chávez tried to relaunch and reconcile the participatory ideals of Bolivarianism and electoral politics. He founded the PSUV (Partido Socialista Unido de Venezuela), charged with maximizing participatory democracy through grassroots activists working in the communities.

However, soon the PSUV began to show the same shortcomings as the MVR. Even with Chávez alive and in office, the goal of establishing a political party dedicated to fomenting participatory democracy and democratic control over use of the country's oil-export earnings would be difficult. Chávez's death in March 2013 and succession by Vice President Nicolás Maduro makes the enterprise even more problematic.

At least the Venezuelan experiment was an outgrowth of nearly two decades of movements for constituent assembly to create a new regime. In Peru the effort was top-down from the start. A party similar to the MVR, the Partido Nacionalista Peruano, was formed in Peru by Humala Ollanta, who emerged as a serious presidential candidate (endorsed by Chávez) in 2006. Ollanta, a former military officer accused of involvement in human rights atrocities (which he denied) during the war against Sendero Luminoso, emerged (as Chávez had) as the leader of a military faction disgruntled with corruption and neoliberal economic policies. Although Ollanta lost in the second round against Alan García of the Alianza Popular Revolucionaria Americana (APRA), he established his movement as the largest single party in Peruvian politics. García's victory was due in part to ballots from voters who had favored a neoliberal candidate in the first round. They evidently preferred an old pol to the leftist *caudillo*. A torrent of anti-Chávez propaganda in the media helped the *aprista* candidate. Opponents warned that he would make Peru "a colony of Venezuela."

However, the final chapter in the story had not been written in this election, as Ollanta won the presidential election of 2011. The Peruvian stock marketed plummeted, and Ollanta moderated his stance, bringing moderates and technopols into his cabinet. García had bet on economic growth from expansion of mining, logging, and oil and gas extraction, and as long as Asian demand was rising, the overall economy prospered. But the environmental costs and failures to address inequality adequately were not what Ollanta's followers, especially Indigenous Peruvians, expected. The collapse in commodity prices was the final blow, as Ollanta limped to the end of his presidency. Peru's political parties sank even lower in the eyes of the public.

In Ecuador, President Rafael Correa, first elected in late 2006, does not fit the profile of a populist *caudillo*, having attained advanced economic degrees overseas, including a Ph.D. from the University of Illinois. He speaks Aymara, the most important Indigenous language, but he dresses like a *criollo*. Correa was the beneficiary of the frustration of the Ecuadorian people with neoliberalism and the ineffectiveness of their Congress. Like Evo Morales and Chávez, Correa rallied this sentiment not only to win the presidency but also to call a **constituent assembly** to rewrite the constitution. His election shows that the left populism of the Pink Tide after 2000 cannot be reduced to ethnic appeal alone. Like Chávez, Morales, and Ollanta, Correa's success was built on appealing to the overall regional dissatisfaction with neoliberalism. Like MVR in Venezuela, the party he founded, the Alianza PAIS (Proud and Sovereign Fatherland Alliance—*país* means "country" in Spanish), was born as an "antiparty party," cobbled together by its leaders as his vehicle for election.

In Bolivia, the main vehicle for Morales's successful campaign for president in 2005 was the Movimiento al Socialismo (MAS). The MAS emerged out of Indigenous movements, the most important of which was the *cocaleros* (peasant growers of coca, a traditional crop and the basis for the raw material of cocaine). Morales's party is less a personal vehicle than is the PSUV, but it shares many characteristics with its Andean counterparts on the left, especially regarding natural resource nationalism and opposition to neoliberalism. However, the MAS, more so than the PSUV or PAIS, seems to have sprung from a movement rather than a candidacy. For this reason, when the Bolivian right mounted a coup that expelled Morales from the country, the MAS was able, despite whatever some Indigenous groups felt about Morales's own expansion of mining and oil ventures into their lands, to mount a challenge in elections schedule for some time in 2020.

Much of Latin America's old left joined with liberal sentiments in the United States to divide the populist left in Latin America into two categories, something best represented in an article by Mexico's Jorge Castañeda (2006) in the influential journal, *Foreign Affairs*. For Castañeda, Bachelet is representative of a responsible left, and Chávez of an irresponsible "populist left." The first, he said, is modern, open-minded, reformist, and international-ist, and it springs, paradoxically, from the hard-core left of the past. The other, born in the great tradition of Latin American populism of Perón and Vargas, is nationalist, strident, and closed-minded. The first is well aware of its past mistakes, as well as those of its supposed role models, Cuba and the Soviet Union. The second, if Castañeda is to be believed, unfortunately has not learned from populism of the past. For him the unpopular neoliberal economic measures taken by the responsible left presidents are positive and necessary correctives to populist mistakes—adapted to each country's problems and history. To Castañeda, "respon-sible" means abjuring the populist approaches of the past in favor of polyarchy; to critics of his thinking (e.g., Quandt 2007), "responsible" means being faithful to promises to imple-ment an alternative to neoliberal economic policy and respecting the autonomy of social movements. The left-populist experiences at the height of the Pink Tide had some similari-ties to the earlier era, but not all were negative. If the earlier wave of populism was a period of incorporation of the masses into politics, the second one, political scientist Kenneth Roberts says, represented a reincorporation of those masses after decades of social and economic exclusion (Roberts 2018).

For Review

Despite the emergence of new social movements and the Pink Tide, how do caudillism and per-sonalism continue to manifest themselves in elections in Latin America? How did the charisma of Hugo Chávez both enhance and limit his ability to achieve broader goals as president? Why did some populist presidents shift away from their campaign promises once in office?

A Typology of Latin American Political Parties

If we take into account the rise and fall of different political parties in this and other chapters of the text, it should be evident that there are different ways we might classify parties in Latin America. One useful way that relies not just on ideology (left vs. right) is to group them into one of three types: (1) traditional parties, sometimes called the "dinosaurs," that were born out of competition among the *criollo* elite in the 1800s or in the populist era and have survived into the present century; (2) personalist parties, often formed originally as electoral move-ments supporting charismatic personalities or strongmen; and (3) newer populist parties that claim to share the goals of the "new social movements" or are vehicles for the right-wing nationalist movements. The boundaries between each type and others are not brightly drawn; some parties that were founded by *caudillos*, such as the Peronist Party in Argentina, are very dinosaur-like today. Some parties were born out of ideological or social movements that orig-inally had strong leaders, such as the APRA of Haya de la Torre in Peru or the Democratic Action party of Rómulo Betancourt of Venezuela, and became more institutionalized.

Think in terms how party politics works—and often fails to work—in the region. Keep in mind that the parties we describe later are all facing the challenges just discussed: wan-ing confidence of people in government and politicians; new media technologies that allow political elites to directly address voters; dealing with balancing pragmatic policies on economic matters against promises to redistribute wealth, protect the environment, and respect Indigenous autonomy; and keeping promises in the face of making voters even less reliant on parties than in the past. Our goal is to not develop an encyclopedic knowledge of the names, leaders, and histories of parties in Latin America but to better understand the roles that different kinds of parties are playing in democracies constituted as polyarchies.

Dinosaurs: Traditional and First-Generation Populist Parties

The epithet "dinosaur" has been used in Mexico to refer to the PRI, especially to the older generation of politicians who dominated the organization during its long reign as Mexico's only viable national party. These politicians were challenged internally by technocrats (see chapter 8) whose base was in the bureaucracy and not electoral politics. Externally, they were challenged by the rise of the leftist Partido de la Revolución Democrática (PRD), created by a coalition of smaller leftist parties with *pristas* (most prominently, Cuauhtémoc Cárdenas; see chapter 8) and by the surge of an older party, the conservative Partido Acción Nacional, which won the 2000 presidential election. The "dinosaur" proved not to be extinct, however, since its candidate, Enrique Peña Nieto, won (at least officially) the 2012 election. The 2018 election was won by the left-populist Andrés Mieguel López Obrador, known as "AMLO," who broke away to form his own party, MORENA (Movimiento de Renovación Nacional).

In many ways, the determination and ability of Mexico's dinosaurs (PRI and PAN) to remain relevant in national politics typifies the challenge faced by other Latin American parties that first emerged either as factions of the oligarchy in the nineteenth century or during the populist era. Latin America's first important parties emerged in the 1800s when intellectuals and other elites organized themselves into political clubs to compete for control of national legislatures and regional governments. Two main currents formed, usually (but not always under the formal party names), Liberals and Conservatives, with Liberals tending to favor more openness to the world market, greater separation of church and state, federalism, and overall modernization (see chapter 4). Conservatives defended the privileges of the Catholic Church and the traditional *criollo* elite. In fact, neither Liberals nor Conservatives struck very deep roots in mass society, except when *caudillos* mobilized peasant armies to fight under one banner or against one another in civil wars. Most of these parties eventually disappeared, but if they recognized early enough that they needed to appeal to new groups and classes, they survived.

The growth of the middle and working classes in the late 1800s challenged these first parties and laid the basis for new ones, such as the Radicals, who were especially significant in the Southern Cone. This kind of centrist party survives as the Blancos (also known as the Partido Conservador) and Colorados in both Uruguay and Paraguay. Today they tend to draw votes from the middle class, having lost their working-class appeal to socialist-oriented and other leftist parties. A more left party, the Frente Amplio (Broad Front), emerged after the harsh military dictatorship, bringing together a variety of movements dissatisfied with the lack of human rights accountability and economic policies of the earliest post transition governments.

The late nineteenth and early twentieth century saw the emergence of socialist parties, which came in several varieties. The biggest and often bitter divide is between socialists who admired the Russian Revolution of 1917 and formed what we know today as communist parties and those socialists who followed the more moderate and reform-minded path of "social democracy." These social democratic parties (which sometimes use that name, sometimes not) no longer seek to overthrow capitalism but to make it more humane. Unionized workers have been their most secure base of support, but over time most have become catch-all parties that attract middle-class, not just working-class, support. Venezuela's Acción Democrática (AD), Costa Rica's Partido Social Democratico (PSD), and two Chilean socialist parties, the Partido Por la Democrácia (PPD) and Partido Socialista (PS), are good examples of these kinds of political parties.

Communist parties still claim to seek the replacement of capitalism by communism, but by now you should realize that most of the parties that hark back to the 1917 revolution have often made compromises. Nonetheless, there exists a legacy of bitterness between the two major factions of socialism, born out of not only ideology but also their intense competition for the votes of the working class or control over unions. Cuba's PCC is in some respects not representative of other communist parties, as the old communist party (the PSP) that existed until 1961 was merged with the leadership of the 1959 revolution. Although its internal structure is similar to the Eastern European communist parties of the Cold War, its origins are in the Revolution of 1959, which was more in the mold of national liberation movements that emerged in the **Third World** out of the struggles for decolonization.

A variety of other radical leftist parties have some impact on politics in Latin America. These include Maoists, anarchists, and a radical branch of socialism founded by Leon Trotsky—who was murdered by Joseph Stalin's agents in Mexico in 1940 after leaving Russia in 1928. These parties run candidates, but winning elections is not their main goal. Trotskyite parties have been especially prominent through their leadership in strikes, factory and farm takeovers, and protests, pressuring leftist governments inclined toward moderation.

Another type of centrist party, the **Christian Democratic Parties**, arose in many Latin American countries from the changes in the role of the Catholic Church. Under challenge from Marxist parties in Europe, Pope Leo XIII in 1891 issued an encyclical, *Rerum Novarum*, that addressed the need for social justice by asserting, in corporatist fashion, that both labor and capital had rights that must be respected. The pope rejected socialism and defended private property but also said, "Whenever the general interest or any particular class suffers, or is threatened with harm, which can in no other way be met or prevented, the public authority must step in to deal with it" (see Pecci 1981). The programs of Christian democratic parties in many ways resemble those of the moderate social democrats. Nowhere has this been more evident than in Chile, where two moderate socialist parties created an alliance with the Partido Democrática Cristiana (PDC), originally called Concertación, to contest every election since the transition from military rule and the plebiscite of 1989. Both social democrats and Christian Democrats look to European counterparts, especially in Germany, for material support (foundations, think tanks, publishing houses) to aid their political activities at home.

Outside of Chile, Christian Democratic parties are struggling to remain politically relevant. Venezuela's COPEI (Comité de Organización Política Electoral Independiente) nearly disappeared in the Chávez landslide of 1998. In some ways, the region's communist parties have followed a similar trajectory. By the 1940s, most had abandoned ambitions to lead a Russian-style revolution, though their enemies (including in the United States) always painted them as subversive. During World War II (1939–1945), when the Soviet Union was allied with the United States, communist parties often used their influence over workers to limit strikes and political agitation. After the Cuban Revolution of 1959, revolutionary and leftist youth challenged these more pragmatic politicians, and other leftist parties eclipsed them in most of Latin America. Chile is somewhat of exception; the Partido Comunista de Chile (PCC), after having been excluded from the Concertación for 25 years, in 2013 joined agreed the coalition, called Nueva Mayoría (New Majority), that elected Bachelet to her second term in 2014. The party still has limited electoral appeal, but it has been highly visible in the surge of protests led by youth and the Mapuches.

Both communist and socialist parties have faced competition from smaller leftist parties, though more so regarding influence in civil society than in elections. For example, in Argentina, the Communist Party's (PC) Institute for the Mobilization of Cooperative Funds has provided funding for community economic projects set up by the independent Movimiento Territorial de Liberación (MTL). The MTL preferred to work with the PC rather than risk co-optation by the Peronists, who have a well-earned reputation for clientelism. Asked by a researcher whether MTL members would vote PC in a coming election, a leader of the party responded, "Of course not; they vote Peronist" (Alcoñiz and Scheier 2007: 169).

Personalist Parties

Caudillos sometimes seek to rule "above politics," but most find it necessary or useful to create some form of political organization to support their aspirations. If they hope to legitimate their rule through elections, they must have some organizational vehicle for rounding up votes—even if the main strategy is to mobilize voters through distributing patronage.

Many of the parties that emerged in the populist era typically had strong leaders but never relied solely on their charisma. Examples include several parties that emerged in the populist era in the Andean region, including Alianza Popular Revolucionaria Americana in Peru, led by the dynamic Haya de la Torre; Acción Democrática in Venezuela, led by Rómulo Betancourt; and the Movimiento Nacional Revolucionario in Bolivia, led by Victor Paz Estenssoro. University students and intellectuals were in the vanguard of these parties, which throughout the middle decades of the twentieth century maintained close ties with each other. Like Juan Perón in Argentina and Getúlio Vargas in Brazil, the leaders of these parties sought to unite the middle class, the working class, and some capitalists in a coalition behind import substitution (see chapter 5). They often issued fiery denunciations of imperialism, but the rhetoric often hid a less revolutionary agenda. In the past few decades, several of these parties edged themselves into extinction by promoting unpopular neoliberal policies of the post-1980 period and failing to adapt their political practices to the demands made by new social movements.

In Brazil, parties formed late relative to some other countries (Mainwaring 1995). Vargas founded the Partido Trabalhista Brasileiro (PTB, Brazilian Workers' Party; not to be confused with the PT, the Workers Party founded by Lula and others in 1980) in 1945 to mobilize and control workers. He simultaneously created a party for the middle class, named (despite its class orientation) the Partido Social Democrática (PSD). Vargas created these parties to provide electoral support as he transformed his regime, founded via a *golpe* in 1930, into an electoral democracy after World War II. The PTB and PSD virtually disappeared beneath the steamroller of dictatorship in 1964, but parties with similar names reemerged in the country's gradual transition to democracy. Perón founded the Partido Justicialista (Justice

Party), which, like its Brazilian counterparts, sought to mobilize supporters behind his political ambitions. In some ways, the Partido Socialista Unido de Venezuela (PSUV), founded by Hugo Chávez, is the latest manifestation of this phenomenon, though Chávez unambiguously identified with revolutionary socialism. After Chávez's death in 2013, the PSUV continued to hold power in Venezuela, now with President Nicolás Maduro as its leader. It is questionable whether ultimately it will survive the deep political and economic crisis in Venezuela. If it survives, it could very well evolve into something like Peronism is in Argentina today.

Argentine Peronist president Carlos Saúl Menem (1989–1999) angered much of the Peronist base in the organized working class, but as long as the economy seemed to be recovering, the party easily defeated its rivals. In these years, the Peronists made incursions into the middle class, impressed with government's success in taming inflation. The economic crisis that struck Argentina in 1998 put an end to Menem's political career, and a new generation of left-populist leaders rose to fill the void. Peronism has become a kind of catch-all party within which various factions compete. Argentina uses a runoff system to choose a president, and the first round has become virtually a primary to decide which Peronist candidate will go on, almost certain to win the second round. In 2003, a center-leftist governor, Nestor Kirchner, won, and his wife Cristina, herself a prominent politician, kept the presidency in the family in 2007. Nestor died in 2010. Cristina Kirchner's administration saw the erosion of Peronism's middle-class support. Kirchner lost her bid for a new term to a neoliberal candidate, Mauricio Macri, in 2015. His unpopular economic policies enabled the Peronist candidate, Alberto Fernández, to take the presidency back in 2019, with Christina as his vice president.

Contemporary Populist Parties

Populism in Latin America in the mid-nineteenth century was an era of democratic expansion because it ushered in the incorporation of masses of people previously excluded from political influence and economic rights. Very broadly then, in this book I have considered populism the political practice of appealing for mass support by championing the cause of ordinary people against powerful elites.

Very often the rhetoric employed by populists is highly incendiary and delivered in a way that reinforces the leader's charismatic authority, much in the way that Juan and Eva Perón did so effectively in Argentina in the 1940s and 1950s when they rallied the *descamisados* (shirtless ones) against *la oligarchía*. The latter are often portrayed as captive of foreign interests, of the imperialists. In the case of fascism, the most virulent form of nationalist populism, this sense of an anti-nationalist "other," is made by exploiting deep racial and ethnic prejudices and often gender prejudices as well, since more inclusive and tolerant attitudes toward the place of women and LGBTQ+ people is seen as subversion. I have chosen to classify parties as "populist" that are created or made into vehicles for a leader or a movement to make the populist appeal that poses the interests of "*el pueblo*," the people, against those of the elite, often characterized as the "oligarchy." Although many political scientists see this kind of appeal as inherently "antidemocratic," I agree more with the influential Argentine thinker, Ernest Laclau, who sees populism as an "empty signifier." In plainer English, this means it is more a style or way of doing politics that is not tied to any one ideology and should not be regarded as inherently democratic or antidemocratic. From this it follows that while we can consider both Jair Bolsonaro's Aliança Pelo Brasil and Evo Morales's Movimiento al Socialismo to be populist parties, it is useful to recognize that the two have very different ideological goals and may not equally pose a threat to democracy.

Left-Populist Parties

Left-populist parties are largely those that arose as part of the Pink Tide. Latin America's new social movements (see chapter 11) envision a more participatory civil society that goes beyond the role for citizens envisioned in a typical polyarchy. They also reject the laissez-faire philosophy of neoliberalism and demand a more activist economic role for the state, but they are alienated from the old populist style of co-optation and clientelism. Both left- and right-populist parties often present themselves as "electoral movements" rather than as parties with a well-developed platform and disciplined internal structure, a reflection of general frustration and discontent with party politics in the electorate.

Important new left parties in Latin America have arisen as outgrowths of social movements or as parties organized by maverick politicians or outsiders who build their mass base from followers of social movements. Among these parties are Causa R (Radical Cause) in Venezuela, the Partido dos Trabalhadores in Brazil, the Movimiento al Socialismo in Bolivia, and the Partido de la Revolución Democrática in Mexico. Some of these parties are little more than very loosely formed coalitions—for example, the Frente Amplio in Uruguay, Pachakutik (Plurinational Unity Movement) in Ecuador, and Frente Grande in Argentina.

If we were to summarize the appeal of left-populist parties, our starting point must be their appeal to the "popular social classes" against the elites. By "starting point," I do not mean to reduce their appeal to the dimension of social class. Economic cleavages intersect with racial and ethnic cleavages in Latin America (see chapter 2). This added considerably to the appeal of three of the politicians most visibly identified with the **Pink Tide**—Hugo Chávez of Venezuela, Luiz Inácio Lula da Silva (Lula) of Brazil, and Evo Morales of Bolivia. Their very faces, their adept use of the popular vernacular, and their social origins all added to their popular appeal among sectors in society who felt the sting simultaneously of class and ethnic prejudice. I hasten to add, however, that contemporary right populism certainly has an ethnic dimension in its racially charged appeal to the anti-immigration sentiment of the middle class. Middle-class opposition demonstrations against Chávez were routinely described as marches by "*sociedad civil*" (civil society), while pro-Chávez demonstrations were mounted by "*turbas*" (mobs) (Gottberg 2011).

To a degree that varies from case the case, the language of inclusion is typically accompanied by hypercharged language of exclusion of "others," an oligarchy or elite who are by implication not part of "*el pueblo*." The rhetoric of Peronism, which we examined in a Punto de Vista in chapter 5, is typical in this respect. Left populists veer into demagoguery when they depict all opponents as oligarchs and traitors against the nation. Hugo Chávez was at times magnanimous in his treatment of opponents, but he also accelerated the polarization of politics with his characterization of them as "*escualidos/as*" (squalid ones). He punctuated many of his speeches with "*Horror a la oligarchía*," a battle cry of a general who became mythologized as a popular hero in the bloodiest civil war of Venezuela's tumultuous nineteenth century. At the same time, Chávez was the victim of similarly vit-riolic language from the country's mainstream media and newspapers. Cartoonists depicted the Afro-descendent president as a monkey, and TV pundits pointedly characterized him as psychologically deranged.

Populist parties are sometimes founded not by politicians but by "outsiders," such as economic barons, military figures, and rising personalities (for example, celebrities) who appeal to the discontent of social movements with existing parties by founding "antiparty parties." Examples on the left include parties founded to support the candidacies of Ollanta Humana in Peru, Rafael Correa in Ecuador, and Hugo Chávez in Venezuela. They pre-sented their electoral organizations as electoral movements that attracted support as "anti-party" forces, but they certainly quickly developed into more formally organized parties themselves.

The relationship between the PRD of Mexico and social movements is typical of the uneasy relationship between leftist reform parties and social movements. The PRD origi-nated in a coalition of small leftist parties and dissenters from the Mexican PRI—organizations that backed the candidacy of Cuauhtémoc Cárdenas (see chapter 8). From the start, then, the PRD has had to grapple with differences of style and substance among politicians who were, respectively, former members of the PRI, leaders of small Marxist parties with regional strength, and leaders of social movements. The PRD has had a rocky relationship since 1994 with the Zapatistas, endorsing many of their ideas but unwilling to endorse armed rebellion. The Zapatistas, for their part, are suspicious of the motives and constancy of PRD politicians, so much so that they withheld endorsement from López Obrador, the party's candidate for president in 2006. With their philosophy of making revolution "without taking power," the Zapatistas espoused a strategy of challenging the entire modern concept of the state (dis-cussed later).

Like many other **Pink Tide** parties, the PRD increasingly found itself drawn into the "old game" of politics—not entirely surprising given that one wing of the party is made up of refugees from the PRI. *Caudillo* politics reared its head in the PRD as López Obrador battled other aspirants for leadership within the party in 2006 and especially in 2012. Although the Zapatistas were harshly critical of him, in the 2012 election AMLO attracted support from social movements. While sharing doubts expressed by the Zapatistas, the movements are more pragmatic than are the more ideologically idealistic rebels. AMLO's followers charged fraud after both elections, and they resonated with movements demanding more transpar-ency in Mexican politics. Massive marches against fraud took place after the 2012 election, though these were probably motivated more by demands for clean elections than support for AMLO himself.

The PRD attracted only approximately 18 percent of the vote in Mexico's election for the National Assembly, but AMLO by the official count received 31.6 percent of the presi-dential vote. This result suggested that the *caudillo*'s personal appeal threatened a significant accomplishment by the PRD, its rise to status as one of three major parties in the Mexican Congress. From 1997 until 2015, the party controlled the mayoralty of Mexico City, the larg-est metropolitan urban conglomerate in the world. AMLO's break with the PRD and suc-cessful campaign for president in 2019 somewhat eclipsed the PRD. The party had aligned with the conservative PAN in the presidential election, adding incentives for voters to defect to López Obrador's MORENA. This put the future of the left side of the party spectrum in Mexico in doubt.

PHOTO 12.1   Mexico's "Yo Soy 132" ("I am 132") movement emerged after the PRI claimed that a video showing 131 students protesting the influence of money and the media in the 2012 presidential campaign was staged by the party's opponents. The video went viral and spurred a movement demanding election reform.

Source: Alfredo Estrella/AFP via Getty Images.

As parties rooted in social movements move from the politics of opposition to the politics of government, they usually find themselves facing new and different challenges as a result of success. The parties that draw support from social movements often have difficulty in constructing internal governance structures that simultaneously achieve two objectives: (1) encouraging democratic control from below and (2) providing enough internal organization and discipline to permit the party to act with unity and purpose in national politics. In the media age, electoral campaigns can be an expensive proposition, and there is a temptation to stress image over substance. Even the best-organized grassroots campaign may fail in the face of a coordinated and well-financed media-based campaign mounted by economic elites.

A good example here is the Partido dos Trabalhadores (PT), Brazil's broadest national mass-based party. The PT began as a labor union–based party, but rapidly it incorporated Afro-Brazilians, Indigenous peoples, women, and other identity-based movements. The PT pioneered the use of "participatory budgeting," by which citizens were able to directly influence spending priorities in municipalities through a series of local meetings. The PT's leader, José Ignacio da Silva, more widely known as "Lula," lost runs for the presidency in 1989, 1994, and 1998. Each time he was ahead in early polls and ultimately lost to a well-financed opponent aided by opposition from the largest media groups in the country. After three defeats, Lula and the PT turned to public-relations tactics, and his party leaders turned to established traditions of political bribery to achieve their objectives. Once Lula finally achieved the presidency in November 2002, his supporters expected him to fulfill his promise to abandon neoliberalism and find an alternative economic development strategy. He had promised to make rapid progress toward ending hunger, to reverse the degradation of the Amazonian rainforest, to resettle landless peasants, and to reduce poverty—a daunting agenda.

Although Lula made impressive progress toward eliminating hunger, land redistribution, and schooling, he fell far short of the expectations of the some of the largest social movements. Those expecting a shift from neoliberalism were dismayed that he maintained the conservative fiscal and monetary policies of his predecessor. The Movimento dos Trabalhadores Rurais Sem Terra (MST; Landless Workers' Movement; see chapter 11) was bitterly disappointed that he did not deliver nearly the amount of land reform promised in his campaign. In part, Lula's shift reflected his reluctance to upset the growing agribusiness sector, an export sector that generated through export taxes funds needed for the social programs. It was also the basis for generating much of the high economic growth rates of the 2000s, the new Brazilian "miracle," that was lifting the middle class. Lula was also cautious about any policy that might reintroduce high rates of inflation. Furthermore, the PT, having gained national power, did not attempt to adapt its innovative participatory experiments in the cities to national level politics—something that would have been difficult to impose from above. Even more disheartening to its electoral base, some of its leading politicians proved equally as susceptible to the old-fashioned patronage and corrupt practices associated with the past.

Lula won reelection in a runoff in 2006, but his path was made more difficult by the eruption in 2005 of a scandal known as *mensalão*. *Mensalão* refers to the thousands of dollars distributed to PT legislators and members of opposition parties in return for their support for government programs. The practice is an old and common form of corruption in Brazil. It can be traced to the weakness of national parties and the realities of local politics in a federal system in which states have considerable autonomy and their governors have considerable power (discussed in detail in the next chapter, on institutions). Most legislators, both at the national level and at the state level, have short careers. While in elected office, they are expected to deliver goods and services to constituents in return for a comfortable retirement once their terms are finished. Because party leaders have little leverage to discipline their legislators, they often resort to regular payments, bribes, paid on a monthly basis—the *mensalão*.

One of Lula's closest political advisors, José Dirceu, once famed for his radical opposition to the military regime, emerged as the mastermind of the *mensalão*. Dirceu was an advocate of Lula's reconciliation with the policies associated with Cardoso, including accommodation of the **IMF**, the target of harsh criticism by Lula when he was in opposition. The political party that had promised an alternative to neoliberalism and seemed a paragon of honesty appeared to have sunk into a dunghill of corruption and patronage. Lula and the PT survived, but some of the party's left wing split away. And Brazil's many influential social movements had reason to question whether the political party that had once promised a cleaner, more responsive democracy had become just like the dinosaurs of the populist era.

Right-Populist Parties

Several Latin American countries have been caught up in a conservative populist counter-wave since 2010. Some of the leaders and their movements fit broadly into a pattern associated with the global surge of right-populist parties since 2010. Like left populists, right populists typically inveigh against an elite which they depict as corrupt and out of touch with ordinary people. A touchstone for many is resistance to conservative social values, especially those of conservative Catholics and the growing ranks of evangelical Protestants resistant to pressure from women's movements for reproductive rights and protection from male violence, and pressure from LGBTQ+ groups for lifting restrictions on non-heterosexual marriage, adoption rights, and protection from hate crimes (see chapter 14). (Left-populist movements too often resist or fail to deliver on these issues, we should note, especially on the national level.)

In some cases, the populist right has adopted highly nativist rhetoric, expressed in fear of immigration, something rare (but not unheard of) in Latin America. Noting some of the similarities to the strategies and policies associated with right populism in the U.S., one observer referred to conservative populism in the region as the "Trumpification" of the Latin American right (Encarnación 2018). At the same time, the populist right in Latin America differs from its counterparts in Europe and North America on neoliberal economic policies, especially attitudes about free trade. For example, much of the Latin American right reacted to the U.S. Congress's rejection of a Trans-Pacific Partnership (TPP), which would have created a common trade zone among 12 different North American, Asian, and Latin American countries, by going it alone and increasing bilateral trade and investment agreements with China (see chapter 15).

Conservative business leaders and politicians that embraced **neoliberalism** in the 1990s have learned that appeals to traditional religious moral values, prejudices against Indigenous and Afro-descendant peoples, and resentment at the failures of Pink Tide governments to combat corruption and violent crime have much greater electoral appeal than embrace of free-market ideology.

The "right-wing populist" parties that have emerged since 2010 share characteristics with parties that would also fit into the "personalist" category in our classification scheme.

- President Jair Bolsonaro of Brazil was elected under the banner of the small Social Liberal Party in 2018 and then drew other small parties into a new party, Alliance for Brazil. The Alliance serves as an umbrella organization for opponents of affirmative action (see chapter 2), same-sex marriage and homosexuality (for "family values"), liberalization of drug laws, and Indigenous territorial rights, among other issues.
- Bolivia's Jeanine Añez emerged as de facto leader of Bolivia after the coup that ousted Evo Morales in November 2018. Her Democrat Social Movement too was a small regional party from the Santa Cruz region in the southwest part of the country. Her decision to run, reneging on a previous promise, for the president in the planned elections of May 2020 thrust her party into national prominence as a vehicle to defend the coup. Añez softened her tone on Indigenous matters as she began her campaign, but she and her supporters had already earned notoriety for racially charged rhetoric about the Indigenous peoples and rejection of **plurinationalism**.

- El Salvador's President Nayib Bukele, originally a member of the leftist Farabundo Martí National Liberation Front (FMLN), ran as the candidate of the Gana Party, which had split off from the conservative ARENA party. His campaign largely focused on anti-crime measures and corruption. Once in office he created his own Nueva Ideas (New Ideas) party. In February 2020, he vetoed a law intended to allow the prosecution of crimes committed during the country's bloody civil war, which would have mainly withdrawn impunity from the military, the author of several massacres of unarmed civilians.

- Guatemala's Jimmy Morales entered politics as the ultimate outsider, a TV comedian who launched a quixotic campaign for mayor of Guatemala City in 2011 as the candidate of the small right wing, Action for National Development Party. He finished a surprisingly strong third and ran for president successfully in 2015 as the candidate of another small conservative party under the slogan, "Neither corrupt, nor a thief." He sounded much like a left populist promising to raise levels of nutrition and health, in addition to fighting corruption. His outsider credentials appealed to a surge of anti-corruption protests, and his path in the election was cleared by the indictment of two formidable opponents. He won the second round of the election with more than 67 percent of the vote. Once in office, not only did Morales not deliver on social promises, but he and his family were caught up in several corruption scandals and put an end to a United Nations commission that had been established to investigate corruption in the country.

Conservative parties have won elections over Pink Tide incumbents in several other Latin America countries; however, not all of them fit the characteristics of right populism. President Piñera of Chile is certainly religiously conservative, but his party, Renovación Nacional, has roots in mainstream parties from the era before the Pinochet coup against Salvador Allende in 1973. Piñera in October 2019 proclaimed, "We are ready to do everything not to fall into populism" (*Financial Times*, London, October 17). President Mauricio Macri of Argentina made a similar proclamation to a group of businesspeople at the libertarian-leaning Fundación Libertad the year before. Both Henrique Capriles and Leopoldo López of Venezuela were young mayors from wealthy families who built a social base against Hugo Chávez and Nicolás Maduro largely on promises to more efficiently manage the economy and better administer social programs. These conservative politicians and their parties, some established, some founded to support their ambitions, originally emerged from the two large parties that competed electorally in the Punto Fijo era.

For Review

What are the three major categories of parties used in this section to classify parties? The classifications suggested here are necessarily ambiguous. What are the characteristics of what we here have called "dinosaur parties"? What are the characteristics of "personalist parties"? What are the characteristics of populist parties? How might we contrast right populism with the left populism of the Pink Tide?

▋ Why Do Movement Parties Often Disappoint Movements?

The scandals that tarnished Brazil's Workers' Party raise the question of whether reform-minded parties and politicians have the capacity to surmount the powerful forces that draw them into "politics as usual." Even Venezuela's Hugo Chávez, whose administration drew fierce opposition from the middle class and business community, came under criticism by his own grassroots supporters for continuing the flow of patronage from his government to business and commercial elites with personal ties to his regime. His critics, inside and outside his Bolivarian movement, called the beneficiaries derogatorily the "Bolibourgoisie."

The Sandinista Revolution in Nicaragua revolution gave promise of bold innovations in democracy in its early years, between 1979 and 1984 (Prevost and Vanden 1997: 46–52). The Frente Sandinista de Liberación Nacional (FSLN) had overthrown the 45-year dynasty of the Somoza family (see chapter 9). Afterward, the FSLN experimented with a system where mass organizations (peasant groups, members of unions, women's organizations, and others) would directly elect representatives to a Council of State. Participatory politics were embedded in campaigns to mobilized Nicaragua's population in mass programs to lift literacy and health standards, as well as land reforms. But there were countervailing efforts for the Sandinistas to move immediately toward liberal democracy. In 1984, partly to gain international legitimacy, the FSLN implemented a new constitution establishing a pluralist political system—that is, a polyarchy.

As we saw in chapter 9, the FSLN lost control of government only 11 years after taking power. Undoubtedly, the war and economic pressure, as well as heavy U.S. subsidies to the opposition parties, contributed to the Sandinista defeat. However, the nature of the FSLN campaign in 1990 indicated that the FSLN itself had undergone an evolution from the organic relationship to the masses that rose with it to defeat Somoza. President Daniel Ortega, running for reelection, conducted a campaign in 1990 that relied on image advertising, sexy female campaign workers at rallies (a sharp contrast to the early Sandinista efforts to raise the dignity and living conditions of women), and patronage (Harris 1993). Upon exiting power, party leaders allocated much property confiscated from the Somoza family to themselves (the *piñata*). This included Ortega.

The FSLN survived as a party, but it began to take on characteristics of a personalist vehicle for the ambitions of Ortega. He returned to the presidency after winning the 2006 election and was welcomed to the Pink Tide by Venezuelan president Chávez. In the 16 years since losing the 1990 election, Ortega has proven himself an adept dealmaker with various opposition forces, including sectors linked to Somoza's old party, the Liberals. Just before the election, to earn support from religious conservatives, Ortega's faction of the Sandinistas endorsed a law outlawing abortion, angering the FSLN's women's movement. He was reelected in 2011, partly because of the fracturing of the Liberals and the inability of dissident Sandinistas to organize an effective challenge.

In El Salvador, the FMLN and its noncombatant allies became a political party in 1992 under terms of a treaty that ended the 12-year civil war in the country. The party began to grow in influence, becoming the largest party in the national legislature in 2003. In 2009, its candidate, Mauricio Funes (an independent journalist), won the presidency. And it won the 2014 presidential election with its own candidate, Salvador Sánchez Cerén. The party has remained more consistently anti-neoliberal in ideology than has the Nicaraguan FSLN. No one current politician or personality dominates the FMLN. Although it has suffered divisions, the FMLN tolerates considerable disagreement and debate within its ranks. This not only threatens its unity but also prevents it from being dominated by the force of a single personality, as is the FSLN in Nicaragua by Ortega.

Rubén Zamora, a revolutionary leader who would leave the FMLN after 1990 for center-left alternatives, explained (1997: 176) how FMLN changed as it transitioned from armed struggle to electoral competition. "A history of exile and clandestine operations had transformed the party into a sect. To correct this, we made a conscious decision to de-professionalize the party." That shift helped the FMLN avoid being transformed into a personalist vehicle for particular politicians, like Ortega in Nicaragua. But the party, though it held the presidency, did not have a majority in the country's National Assembly. It had to compromise, but pragmatism morphed into unseemly deal making. The Salvador Sánchez Céren government proved a disappointment and was never fully committed to fighting corruption. The FMLN faced daunting problems that were hard to address without full control of government. Salvadorans live in a country with one of the world's highest rates of violent crime, deeply scarred by the violence of civil war, and whose economy remains heavily dependent on exporting labor-intensive manufactured goods and agricultural commodities to the United States. Disappointment with Cérez's incapability to make progress on these problems and the growth of socially conservative evangelical Protestant churches (aided by congregations in the United States) facilitated the political ascent of Bukele.

Some left parties have turned to primary elections in an attempt to reconnect to their popular base, presuming that voting by party members or all citizens would accomplish this goal better than the highly centralized, indirect methods of candidate selection controlled by national party leaders. However, primaries pose a different set of problems for democracy because they place a greater premium on advertising and other tactics that cost money. This problem is exemplified by the case of Brazil's PT, which was the first political party in that country to choose its candidates through a primary. The cost of campaigning for the nomination added significantly to the need for money to contest for office and helped to create the environment that engrossed party leaders in the *mensalão*.

In Venezuela, Hugo Chávez tried to prohibit expenditures on advertising in the PSUV's primary to choose candidates for the National Assembly election in 2010. The idea was to ensure that candidates had real grassroots support. The professional politicians and wealthier supporters of Chávez dutifully avoided broadcast advertising, but they used donations and patronage to print posters and flyers (and to hire people to hand them out), effectively campaigning under the radar and violating the spirit of the party rules—and with success. The PSUV's main opposition, the Democratic United Roundtable, held primary elections for its presidential candidate for the 2012 election. The strategy helped it maintain unity and gave a significant boost to its candidate, Henrique Capriles, who ran a credible campaign but lost to Chávez and who nearly defeated the late Venezuelan leader's designated successor, Nicolás Maduro, in April 2013.

Media Politics

Social movements in Latin America are mindful of the powerful influence of the media in their societies. Grassroots community radio and television stations have sprung up, and computer technology makes community production more economically feasible than ever. The Internet allows community activists to communicate with one another and share experiences. This development seems promising, but it will be difficult for these groups to wean populations away from Hollywood movies, soap operas, beauty pageants, lowbrow comedy and variety shows, pro-business newscasts, Miami-produced recordings, and so on.

There is little doubt that globally political parties have lost ground to media as the main linkages between civil society and government. Each stage of technological advancement has increasingly permitted politicians to communicate to masses of people "unmediated" by parties, as well as to mobilize them. The advent of motion pictures and radio accompanied the birth of mass advertising and political propaganda 100 years ago. Television broadcasting extended that process and increased the importance of gaining access to financial resources to make media buys and to tailor messages to audiences. In the 1980s, cable and satellite transmission created possibilities for "narrow casting," that is, fragmenting the audience in ways that allowed influence shapers to target specific segments of citizens.

We are now in the middle of yet another communications revolution, the rise of the social media linked to cyber technologies. These technologies have not yet been deployed in full power, and they are more prevalent in the Global North, but there are already indications of how they will affect politics in Latin America. On the horizon are artificial intelligence (AI), Big Data, cyber-analytics, facial recognition, and digital surveillance, all still unfolding and raising serious questions about whether they will be used to enhance democracy or simply to enhance the capacity of a global elite to induce us to self-discipline ourselves.

In the first part of the next section, we will examine the way that twentieth-century media technologies have simultaneously competed with and complemented parties in polyarchies in Latin America. In the second part, we turn to social media and the way that new cyber and communications technologies have begun to be deployed and raise questions about the future of democracy in Latin America. These technologies have important consequences for the world of work as well as politics. We leave this discussion largely to the chapter (15) on globalization. Here I will merely note that in the political world and in the spheres of culture and the economy, these technologies are being pioneered in the wealthier countries of the Global North. As with earlier communications innovations, Latin America is more in a reactive stage in which social movements, elites, parties, and governments are having to adapt to rather than innovate technology affecting their lives.

Electronic and Print Media

Print media in Latin American politics were influential from the earliest years of independence. The emergence of film, television, and radio in the twentieth century changed the political game, as newspapers lost their monopoly of influence to these new media. To some degree, social media and the Internet have changed the game again. They have not yet in Latin America eclipsed the role of older media in influence. One difference, however, is that the technologies of communication of the print and electronic eras were transferrable to private media companies and owners in Latin America itself. Telecommunications remains a sector in which local ownership and control is within the grasp of

Latin American elites. The newer media technologies are more transnationally controlled in this respect. Large transnational corporations (mostly North American, some Asian) own and control major media platforms (such as Twitter, YouTube, Facebook, Instagram, and WhatsApp).

Print and electronic media have not lost as much ground to social media in Latin American politics as in the Global North. Although leftist candidates have often proven adept at using media, the ability to communicate directly using the technique of public relations is of even greater importance to **technopols**. As the Argentine analyst Oscar Landi (1995: 210) puts it, "When I am in a situation of hyperinflation, I am going to turn on the television to guide me in my daily action. I'm not going to visit the local headquarters of a party." Landi overlooks the fact that for many Latin Americans, radio remains the principal source for news. Today, in any case, more than half of Latin Americans probably rely more on social media.

Production of television commercials, focus groups, polls, and advertising cost significant amounts of money. A typical poll in Latin America costs US$12,000–US$15,000 (Rial 1995: 503). These resources can be crucial in blunting challenges from leftist movements, at least temporarily. In Brazil, for example, the PT seemed poised to win the presidency behind Lula in 1989, but international and national business sectors rallied behind Fernando Collor de Mello, a relatively inexperienced politician. Collor owned a television station in a rural state and was supported by the country's most important national TV network. With money, media savvy, and the backing of Brazil's worried business community, Collor put together an effective campaign despite the lack of an established, organized party. News organizations in both Brazil and Mexico, closely linked to monopoly business interests and heavily dependent on a friendly state, have magnified poor performances by replaying heavily biased clips of debates and slanted news coverage.

In Venezuela, after the collapse of AD and COPEI, the owners of the country's major television networks and newspapers moved into the void. The media not only abandoned any pretense of objectivity, but it also coordinated major street protests and civic strikes with opposition leaders. In April 2002, Venezuela's media moguls were among those who collaborated in orchestrating (i.e., more than merely "backed") the military coup that removed the president from power for two days. Chávez responded by revoking the broadcast license of the oldest and largest national television network, RCTV, an action that brought protests not only from his opposition but from many of his supporters in the *barrios*. Not only were the news broadcasts of RCTV banished to much less accessible satellite channels, but so too were the station's massively popular telenovelas (soap operas), evening programs that were literally "can't miss" appointments for most Venezuelans, of all stripes.

Among the most ready sources of money to finance the staggering costs of media-centered campaigns are the lords of the region's most dynamic export commodity, narcotics. Colombia's porous party system is especially vulnerable. Here, "porous" refers to legal provisions that allow several slates of legislative candidates from the same party to run in each state and district. Hence, the parties have a difficult time controlling nominations. The candidate who raises the most money has a huge advantage in pursuing a party's nomination.

Private media are usually owned by families or groups with vested economic interests throughout the country. In Mexico, privatization of communications—TV, telecommunications, and so on—in the 1980s and 1990s laid the basis for the global media empire of Carlos Slim, ranked by *Forbes* magazine as the world's richest man in 2010. Cárdenas and AMLO, the PRD's candidates, have had to battle in an extremely hostile media environment. These media empires are associated in a powerful transnational media organization, the hemispheric InterAmerican Press Association (IAPA), based in Miami, Florida. The term "press" is somewhat misleading in that the association is composed not of journalists but of vast media conglomerates that see any attempt to regulate content as interference with free speech.

Most countries have state broadcasting outlets, usually governed by laws requiring political neutrality or balance in news. In times of political polarization, this requirement is ignored by the incumbent. For example, Venezuela's President Hugo Chávez used a weekly radio and television program, *Aló Presidente*, broadcast on the government networks, to rally popular support against his enemies, including the large private media outlets in the country. Chávez used oil revenues to create a new hemispheric network, Telesur, launched in 2005, in an attempt to provide an alternative news and cultural voice. His Ministry of Telecommunications also provided subsidies and licenses to hundreds of "microbroadcasters," mostly radio and Internet and mostly set up by his grassroots supporters.

In early 2008, Chávez refused to renew the license of RCTV. He relied upon a media responsibility law, which had been revised in earlier years by the National Assembly, under control of his supporters. Critics pointed out that the provisions for non-renewal were not properly followed. Given RCTV's involvement in the 2002 coup, he probably could have acted immediately that year, before the license was up for renewal. We ask whether any government in the world would permit a television or radio station that had participated in a coup attempt to continue operating. There were popular protests not only by the opposition, which drew most of its support from the middle class, as might be expected, but also by many of Chávez's fervent supporters in the *barrios*. Some of that probably reflected concerns about media freedoms, but there was another factor. RCTV carried the country's most popular telenovelas (soap operas), programs that could bring a halt to any other social activity throughout the country and across all social classes. This was a source of no little dismay in the *barrios*.

Financial pressure drove another opposition station, Globovisión, to sell out in 2013 to new owners whose political orientation is not entirely clear. The other two of the four private networks, whose audience dwarf the state television channel, got the message to tone down the often vitriolic criticism leveled at the government. These stations, satellite networks, and the main newspapers continued to run critical coverage of the government, including after Maduro assumed office. Maduro reached a truce with Gustavo Cisneros, the country's most important media baron and scion of the family owners of the country's large agribusiness corporation, much to the consternation of the opposition forces attempting to induce a military coup against Maduro (see chapter 8).

Coverage is more professional and has a less confrontational style in recent years, but that does not mean the press freedoms are well respected either. The Committee to Protect Journalists reports on incidents in early 2020 have called attention to threats and assaults on working reporters by groups of armed *colectivos* (mostly young men on motorcycles) and raids on media outlets by security forces, most of which seem intended to suppress coverage. Some journalists have been arrested for reporting on the worsening of health conditions as the COVID-19 disease began to deal its lethal effects. Two journalists have been murdered and three have died covering "dangerous situations" in the country between 2002 and 2019. Between 1992 and 2020, 22 died in Colombia in the same period.

Generally, discussion of press freedoms and media rights reflects the frameworks in liberal capitalist societies and focuses on negative freedom—the right of the press and citizens to express their political views freely without censorship. This reflects a theory of democracy that presumes that civil society in this way achieves a "marketplace of ideas" in which the best ones win out in competition, much like elections supposedly function in a **polyarchy**. What if some of the best ideas are those of groups of people who cannot afford to promote them through privately owned mass media? Suppose the wealthiest people, or the owners of the media themselves, are interested only in promoting their own interests? In all of the world's polyarchies, even the ones that provide guaranteed access to media or public funding of campaigns, the ability to amass money is crucial to effective communication. Is the freedom to speak sufficient, or is there some positive sense of a freedom to be heard?

In the post-2000 period, several other Latin American presidents were virtually at war with media establishments. Ecuador's Rafael Correa took over two private TV networks owned by corrupt bankers. Then he filed and won a $40 million libel suit against a newspaper columnist, and threatened via a proposal in Congress to prohibit media from taking partisan positions for or against candidates in elections. The private media in Ecuador engaged in an all-out effort to defeat the leftist populist's programs and rising popularity. They failed, as Correa achieved easy reelection and 70 percent popularity in 2013. But the situation changed when Correa was succeeded by his vice president, President Lenín Moreno, who campaigned as a left populist 2017, shifted to the right once in office, and was targeted with mass protests that drove him out of the capital (Quito) to the coastal city of Guayaquil for a while in October 2019. However, by this time Moreno had effectively dismantled the new media regulations put in place by Correa.

In Argentina, the two Kirchners (Cristina and the deceased Nestor) had running battles with the influential conservative newspaper *Clarín* and the vast media empire associated with it. President Cristina Kirchner engaged in bitter battle with Grupo Clarín, a giant media company that owns the most important newspaper, broadcast, and cable outlets. Clarín, founded by a fascist sympathizer during War II, secured its dominant place in the Argentine media during the military dictatorship (1976–1983). Tax agents of Kirchner's government raided the Grupo's home offices, and the government introduced a bill into Congress to strip the conglomerate of its lucrative cable outlets.

■ Ecuador

The actions of these left-populist presidents and the extreme hostility of the media empires under fire raise difficult questions. On one side, many human rights observers abroad condemned the actions as ones that would suffocate free speech in a country where the president had already gathered significant personal power. On the other side, one could ask whether leaving control of media in the hands of the wealthiest elites is really in the interest of democracy.

PUNTO DE VISTA: WAS ECUADOR'S CONTROVERSIAL MEDIA LAW A TOOL FOR CENSORSHIP OR RESPONSIBLE AND TRUTHFUL NEWS?

Freedom of the press has been widely interpreted to apply to broadcast media in addition to print media. In recent years, the more radical governments in Latin America have been accused by some major human rights organizations of attempting to muzzle critics with constitutional provisions and media laws that limit ownership of media by large economic groups, limit the number of media outlets any one owner can control, guarantee the public the right to "truthful reporting" or reporting in context, and support the creation of more state-owned media and also community-based media.

In reality, no **polyarchy** leaves media content unregulated. Freedom of the press is enshrined in the U.S. Constitution as the First Amendment, part of the Bill of Rights. Yet often the right of the press to disseminate information to the public is still questioned, especially when the information is harmful to the reputation of the government (e.g., WikiLeaks, Edward Snowden). Would you argue for some additional regulation of journalism in the United States?

Wendy Pérez has been a working journalist and editor in several Latin American countries, a rapporteur and fellow at Gabriel García Márquez's New Iberoamerican Journalism Foundation (FNPI), and a fellow at the University of Michigan. In March 2013, Pérez summarized the controversy over Ecuador's proposed new media law (see http://latam.portada-online.com/2013/03/28/the-most-controversial-points-of-ecuadors-media-law/#ixzz2Q0k3o520):

One the one side, the IAPA sees the law as an attempt to implement a "gag rule." It objects by the law's provision allocating one-third of radio broadcasting frequencies to community media, one-third to public (state and non-profit) ones, and one-third to for-profit businesses. This is a shift from a situation where about 13 percent of frequencies were allocated to the public sector and

less than 2 percent to community stations. The country's Superintendency of Telecommunications says that 71 percent of television frequencies are licensed to private carriers, 29 percent to public.

As in Argentina and Venezuela, Ecuador's media law says that mass communication is a public service that should be held accountable and of high quality, though it is not clear exactly how this is defined. Community media are those owned and controlled by local units of government and society (districts, communes), nationalities (largely referring to various Indigenous peoples and other ethnic sectors) and nongovernmental groups and collectives, and non-profit organizations. It calls for government funding and training to prepare these groups to offer quality broadcasting on a par with the other sectors, in order to promote "plurality, diversity, interculturality and plurinationality."

To implement these provisions, including allocation of frequencies, the law created a Superintendency of Information and Communication (Supercom) with members from governments—including the president's office, universities, media organizations, and human rights groups. Critics believe the law concentrates power in reality in the hands of the government. The IAPA claims the law violates international agreements signed by Ecuador, including obligations under 1991 Charter of American States, created at the pinnacle of neoliberal influence after the Cold War.

Perhaps the most controversial provision gives the Council power to financially penalize media outlets for refusing to correct what it deems to be false information. The Council is also empowered to limit or prohibit violent, discriminatory, or sexually explicit content.

The law provides requirements that radio stations devote half of music programing to national content; half of television content must be nationally produced. Many countries, including Canada, have national content requirements, but they have long been resisted, arguing that they interfere not only with freedom of expression but also with audience choice. However, in Canada there is strong public resistance to doing away with national content quotas.

A provision in the law requires that published information be verified and imposes an obligation to rectify false or inaccurate information. Any individual can ask for corrections for information that is judged to be an affront to their honor or reputation. Another calls for all journalists to be certified professionally, with exceptions for those writing opinion pieces or reports in Indigenous languages.

In December 2018, Correa's successor, President Lenín Moreno, got the Congress to vote to close down Supercom, doing away with mechanisms of enforcement of rules regarding truthfulness and professionalism of information. Other parts, most notably the distribution of frequencies, remain in place. We should take note, however, that almost all major broadcasting networks in Latin America now have cable, Internet, and satellite capabilities that are not affected if broadcast licenses are revoked.

Point/Counterpoint

Is the government justified in the creation of this new media responsibility legislation? Why or why not?

If you say yes, how would you answer those who say that media control by government is worse than control by private owners? Why not allocate some frequencies to communities?

If you say no, how do you respond to the criticism that media has become very concentrated and has in several cases participated in attempts to overthrow elected governments in Latin America by deliberately distorting news?

Are there some parts of the law that you feel are more justified than others?

For More Information

The Committee to Protect Journalists focuses on intimidation of journalists and has some critical reports on conditions in Ecuador at its website. Its critique of the law can be found at https://cpj.org/reports/2018/07/U-turn-moreno-steers-ecuador-away-correa-media-communication-law.php. The Irish documentary *The Revolution Will Not Be Televised* (2002) illustrates the power of media in Venezuela and its participation in a short-lived coup against President Chávez.

For Review

What has been the relationship between privately owned media and leftist governments in Latin America over the past few decades? What issues are raised by efforts by leftist governments to regulate media content? What would you say is the argument in favor? What is the argument against?

Social Media: Control or Democratization of Communications?

Around 2010, when millions of people in North Africa and parts of the Middle East rose in protests against authoritarian regimes, the world took note of the way that cell phones, computers, and social media facilitated the uprising. In the Arab Spring, access to the Internet seemed likely to hasten the pace of **third wave** democratization, facilitating bottom-up coordination of protests and organizing beyond the capacity of states to repress popular demands for democracy. Unmediated discussions and ideas would flow across national boundaries, reinforcing the liberal democratic ideal of an unrestricted marketplace of ideas where both producers and consumers of information would interact freely.

This optimism had given way a decade later to concerns about how the same technologies, reinforced by remarkable advances in cyber technologies, are being used to create a surveillance society in which individuals themselves willingly provide the wherewithal for manipulation of preferences, if not ideas. This concern permeates much discussion about media in the Global North, where much of the technology is generated and owned. In the Global South, the concern is magnified by the reality that countries have much less capacity, in terms of capital and technological capability, to determine how these technologies will be deployed.

In both the economic and political realm, those who have access to the huge troves of information (Big Data), who have capacity to process that information (artificial intelligence and analytics), and who have the wealth to deploy this information and capacity have a new dimension of power at their disposal. And with fifth generation (5G) technology on the horizon, featuring radically enhanced capacity of networks to interconnect and control machines, objects, and devices, this capacity is likely to significantly increase.

This new capacity is unlikely to mean the disappearance of political parties, but it may further undermine their ability to function as communication channels between citizens and the state. Social media, aided by other cyber technologies, also further undermines the function of parties as organizations that mobilize votes. This also makes parties more vulnerable to capture by ambitious populists who have personal wealth or are otherwise able to access these communication and cyber technologies. The most obvious example of the former is Donald Trump, who was able to parlay his celebrity status and wealth into a virtual takeover of the Republican Party, achieved through what we might call "cyber populism."

An account (Rogers 2020) of how Trump and his inner circle utilize cyber technologies demonstrates how new communications technology makes possible the mobilization of supporters in a way that Juan and Evita Perón would envy. While this may be a digression for our focus on Latin America, it provides an example of how social media, analytics, AI, and Big Data will likely become more influential in Latin America. To some extent, they have played a role already in Brazil and Argentina.

To attend a Trump rally, which combines elements of a religious crusade with a mega-sporting or entertainment event, one must register. At a February 2020 rally in New Jersey, a state that is a Democratic stronghold, nearly 100,000 people registered by clicking on a link at the Trump campaign site and filling out an online form with name, email address, and phone number; in return each person got two tickets. Campaign events are advertised through Facebook and other social media sites, where advertising is bought or messages placed, carefully targeting groups of people selected via analytics, much of which is provided by companies like Cambridge Analytica. According to the Trump campaign, the New Jersey rally had over 160,000 requests for tickets, and surveys of those who requested yield data on their voter history and other data points that can be cross-referenced with information from the party. This data is used to make sure that supporters vote and to tailor messages to people who had not voted in earlier elections or had voted Democratic.

A key aspect of this ability to gather data for analysis is that much of it is supplied unknowingly or voluntarily by users of social media and smart phone apps. Consider what information we provide when we allow a cell phone to provide location data to a weather app, "like" an opinion posted on Facebook, buy a product on Amazon or Alibaba, "Google" information about a celebrity, retweet a piece of news (fake?) on Twitter, post a vacation photo on Flickr or Instagram, join a forum on WhatsApp or TikTok, click on a YouTube video, watch a program on streaming media, and travel with our GPS on. We give Microsoft or Amazon permission to gather data "to better serve us," but also to serve the platform's customers. Every one of these activities that we do several times per day, every day, generates data—enormous amounts of it. It is stored on "the cloud," that is, computer servers. It is so much data, "Big Data," and this is where AI and analytics come in—providing there is adequate computing power and fast enough transmission of information.

Trump's campaign, like all major U.S. political campaigns, solicits contributions and, perhaps more importantly, sells campaign paraphernalia through SMS texts, as well as face-to-face marketing at rallies. In 2016 most liberals and Democrats laughed at what most Latin American politicians have long known: A coffee mug or t-shirt with a simple message can be more effective than millions of dollars of television and radio advertising.

At Trump's New Jersey rally, attendees making purchases with credit cards were asked for their driver's license, which was scanned to the campaign database for contributions—another source of information for Big Data. A similar operation is carried out by a contractor responsible for retailing campaign gear, which like sports gear and clothing is frequently redesigned and often carries the latest rumor or message on conservative social media. A Trump rally itself is carefully choreographed, with the crowd stoked by speakers and media presentations that play to common grievances about the mainstream media, the "sacrifices" being made by Trump and his family, and hot button issues such as unisex bathrooms and the "fake news media."

These technologies are not all beyond the reach of grassroots organizations. The campaign of Senator Bernie Sanders, a socialist who caucuses with Democrats but has never actually joined the party, ran an impactful campaign for the Democratic nomination for president in the United States in 2016 and 2020 that was enabled (including financing) by the ability to use social media and some of the techniques just mentioned. A Latina insurgent candidate, Alexandria Ocasio-Cortez, was able to defeat a Democratic incumbent and go on to take a seat in the U.S. House of Representatives in 2018 using primarily social media. These victories, however one wants to welcome or reject their influence on U.S. politics, also suggest how new media and communication technologies are changing party politics.

So how much of this twenty-first-century populism entered the Latin American political environment? The kind of cyber operations just described requires an infrastructure rapidly developing in Latin America but still not on a par with those of the Global North, and there are considerable variations throughout the region. For example, data from 2017 show that only 73 percent of mobile connections in Brazil, the country with the most developed infrastructure, were on smartphones, and only 35 percent of these were 4G connections. In Bolivia, ranked tenth, in the middle of the pact among Latin American countries, only 33 percent of connections were on smartphones, only 21 percent on 4G. In 2018, half of Latin American mobile users had smartphones with access to the Internet, but this was up from only 32 percent and expected to continue expanding (Lustig 2018).

In 2017, it was estimated that 4G coverage is broad enough to serve approximately 70 percent of the region's population. GSMA Intelligence, an industry newsletter, optimistically concluded in 2018 that Latin America could now provide "a large, scalable platform for entrepreneurism. Venture capital and private equity funding have been especially strong in 2017, with more transactions in the first half of 2017 than in all of 2016" (O'Hara 2018).

In sum, there is enough cell phone coverage in Latin America for the bottom-up type of "spontaneous" demonstrations, such as those that originated in the Arab Spring, Spanish *indignados* (the indignant ones) protests, pro-democracy actions in Hong Kong, and Chilean mass protests in 2019. Social media has also played a role in mobilizing mass actions both for and against the Chavista government in Venezuela and in anti-corruption mass actions in Central America. Protesters have learned to use apps like WhatsApp to encrypt messages, enabling them to convoke demonstrations, coordinate activities by the minute, and evade government surveillance.

The power of social media that revealed itself by the Arab Spring did not go unnoticed by states and by conservative elites. In the Middle East and China, governments have simply shut down cellular networks to disturb mobilization and coordination of protests. States have recognized that the transnational character of social media offers new tools to intervene in the internal affairs of other states. This became evident in investigations into the Russian operations to influence the 2016 election in the United States and the British Brexit referendum of the same year. Sectors in Moscow and allied groups in other countries used Internet bots, software applications that not only can generate messages to target audiences online but can also create fake users to create or augment "trending" topics. Just as important, investigations uncovered the complicity of Facebook and other private corporations in collecting and selling information from users.

A Netflix documentary, *The Great Hack*, revealed the political operations, most them already exposed by investigative journalists in several different countries, of the British tech company Cambridge Analytica (CA), which was operated through subsidiaries in India, Eastern Europe, and Africa—and in Argentina (when it was called Strategic Communication Laboratories—SCL) during the 2015 presidential election in Argentina. In February 2014, CA bought a trove of data on 87 million Facebook users with information gleaned from their news feed, timeline, and messages, enabling the company to tailor political messages. The founders of CA had linkages to military contractors, intelligence organizations, and wealthy entrepreneurs, that is, sectors with interests in shaping the outcome of electoral processes in various parts of the world. Britain's Channel 4 News documented that CA crowed that they had the capability to entrap politicians in liaisons with Ukrainian prostitutes and bribers (Elbaum 2019; Rodríguez 2019).

Cyber political warfare is not the sole province of the political right. Given that Russian capabilities have been well documented, it is quite possible, even likely, that diplomatically it has aided left governments in Cuba, Venezuela, Ecuador, and Bolivia at least defensively, and quite possibly through methods it has used in attempting to influence elections in the United States and the Brexit referendum in Britain. Almost certainly, these technologies have been deployed by Pink Tide governments, parties, and allied groups. However, in Latin American elections, social media and new cyber technologies seem more prevalent on the right.

Cyber technology has created opportunities for the populist right to identify and mobilize two sectors, mainly (1) middle-class Latin Americans who can be a swing sector because of the precariousness of their economic situation, but also can be alarmed by hyperbolic, if not entirely fabricated, "news" warning of Venezuelan and Cuban plots to impose communism on their country; and (2) socially conservative Catholic and evangelical Christian communities. The former group is most likely those who can be reached by cyber populism, but the evangelical communities can be reached through messaging to the clergy.

To reach poor parts of the Latin American public, WhatsApp is preferred not only because it is encrypted but also because it can be used on many flip phones, including those made available by the Chinese company, Alibaba. An analysis by *The Guardian* (London, October 30, 2019) of false information circulated on WhatsApp via its instant messaging platform during Brazil's 2018 campaign showed that the vast majority favored Jair Bolsonaro's candidacy. (To get around encryption, the analysts use a sample of messages from WhatsApp monitor, a database of viral political content on the group forums.) Of these messages, the app is used by 120 million of Brazil's 210 million people. The study sampled 11,957 viral messages in group chats, and fact checkers found that approximately 42 percent of right-wing messages were false, compared to fewer than 3 percent of left-wing messages. *The Guardian* found that 48 percent of right-wing messages promoted a fictional plot, often amplified by Bolsonaro, that there existed a plot to manipulate the electronic voting system. Another group of messages blamed his political opponents, without evidence, for a stabbing attack on Bolsonaro. Another set of messages accused the mainstream media of corruption, and a fourth set, 14 percent of the total, advanced "homophobic tropes and anti-feminist views."

In the case of Argentina, it is not clear how much Cambridge Analytica, now defunct, might have influenced the victory of neoliberal businessman Mauricio Macri over incumbent president Cristina Kirchner in 2015. Alexander Nix, chief executive officer of CA and its predecessor (SCL), testified to a British parliamentary committee and affirmed the authenticity of a message from a company employee referring to "Anti-kirchnerista campaign present to decision maker; awaiting outcome" and the likelihood that it referred to meetings between the company and "either a party of the opposition or a private person." A later investigation by a journalistic consortium put Nix on the record confirming that the model for CA operations had the company aiming to instigate fear and hatred among those segments of society perceived to be susceptible to manipulation (cnbc.com, March 27, 2018). For this, Facebook profiles were cross-referenced where possible with other data from insurance firms, bank transactions, media consultations, and personal communications. In many ways, Macri's campaign followed an anti-Kirchner script much like CA's model, but there is no conclusive evidence regarding with whom the company was meeting or if the strategy proposed was ever actually implemented.

What we do have is an indication from both the Bolsonaro and Macri campaigns of how the cybercommunications revolution can influence the role of parties and media and the mobilization of civil society, the direction this may take in Latin America, and the ways that powerful transnational forces are now infusing themselves into national electoral politics. Artificial intelligence coordinates both the gathering and analysis of accumulated profiles (Big Data), largely through algorithms. In both areas, the technological capabilities and ownership of data are concentrated in the wealthier countries of the capitalist Global North, Russia, and China. Already visible on the horizon are more powerful AI tools to mine and engorge even more massive stores of Big Data, to cross-reference data with one another, and to exploit and communicate it rapidly—providing the political candidate, party, or group has the financial wherewithal (or hackers at their disposal) to deploy these tools.

One company, Clearview AI, now claims the ability, using its facial recognition software, to identify any individual by matching a picture of that person to billions of photos that the company has scraped from social media sites (including Facebook and Instagram, without their permission) and the web. A division of Clearview, Insight Camera, is working with a variety of governmental and private security organizations, as well as other clients (schools, labor unions, corporations) to deploy security cameras, which potentially can yield an exponentially larger database. Other companies, including Chinese enterprises, have compiled powerful Big Databases of location data gathered from smartphones as people move about. The implications became more visible after someone in the industry leaked parts of a dataset to the *New York Times* to alert the public of the implications of this form of surveillance. Two journalists (Thompson and Warzel 2019) reported:

> We followed military officials with security clearances as they drove home at night. We tracked law enforcement officers as they took their kids to school. We watched high-powered lawyers (and their guests) as they traveled from private jets to vacation properties.

Deploying the full power of artificial intelligence, huge stores of data, and fast transmission capabilities requires the capability of 5G networks, which are just now being rolled out.

There are many political economic implications for this rapidly expanding technology, some of which we will explore further in chapter 15, on globalization. The likelihood that new media and cyber technologies will impact democracy grows as our sense of precariousness grows. The coronavirus outbreak of 2019–2020, the masses of people on the move from the threat of war, criminal violence, pogroms against minorities, and consequences of climate change have already created fears and concerns that probably make almost all of us crave security. Big Data, the raw material for artificial intelligence, is stored in the cloud—which in reality consists of huge storage capacity located exclusively in several countries in the Global North and Asia. Ecuadorian journalist Edward Tamayo (2012: 18) summarized the implications for Latin America of developing surveillance technology:

> The new vigilance has for its objective to observe, classify and control not only individual but also social movements and processes. The First World transmits the equipment and technologies of control and vigilance to the Third World for us in many cases to trace the activities of dissidents, human rights activists, journalists, student leaders, minorities, union leaders and political opponents.

The coronavirus pandemic has exposed other ways that surveillance technologies may be deployed for antidemocratic purposes. GPS technology has been suggested as a way to quickly track all personal contacts of some diagnosed with the virus. Hungary's prime minister has already used emergency powers to track people ordered into quarantine. It would not be a large leap to apply this to political dissidents.

As bleak as the outlook might seem for privacy and for Latin Americans to defend their individual rights and defend the sovereignty of their states, the actual situation has not quite reached Orwellian dimensions of dystopia. If indeed Macri won the 2015 election, even with the possibility of even my cyber power behind him, he lost the election of 2019 to a Peronist ticket with Cristina Kirchner as the vice presidential candidate. Although new surveillance technologies have continued to advance, mass protests against government have continued to erupt, including in Chile where citizens have demanded not only a new constitution but an active role for civil society in writing it. In China, activists have learned to make use of networks they have constructed on the Dark Web, outside Beijing's impressive, massive system of Internet surveillance. The dangers to democracy, whether liberal or participatory, are present, but a vibrant community network of cyber-activists throughout the region has formed using the very same technologies they often criticize.

Parties, Media, and Civil Society

Although parties emerged in Europe and North America in the nineteenth century, democratic theorists have seen them as keys to democratic governance. Pluralists have seen them as the crucial intermediaries between civil society and the state. Nationalists have seen them as instruments to forge unity in divided societies facing the challenges of development and foreign intervention. Marxist revolutionaries have seen them as the organizations that can lead exploited classes to power and transform capitalism into socialism. Parties, as organizations dedicated to contesting for control of the state, remain the most important vehicles in contesting for power in a democracy, but the media has increasingly stepped into this role, especially in systems where wealthy and powerful media owners have seen the collapse of parties that defend the status quo. Populist *caudillos* and revolutionary leaders can now address the masses through the media, but they still today find it necessary to organize a party to carry out organizational tasks, especially to win votes.

Parties may be under suspicion throughout the hemisphere, but no other social or political institution has yet shown a capacity to serve as effectively as an instrument of governance and contestation for power. Even though parties that emerge out of social movements may often disappoint their followers, they may leave a mark on politics by changing the rules of the game or bringing new policy ideas into the political arena.

This, of course, could change if the power of social media can be placed at the service of democracy. This was the great hope, after mass protests erupted across the Middle East around 2010—the "Arab Spring." It seemed that social media could be harnessed to reverse information flows from media organizations to passive receivers. However, like the electronic and print media that dominated most of the twentieth century, social media infrastructures soon became controlled by two entities: states and transnational corporations. Their interests are in maintaining control and surveillance or generating big data banks and analytics that treat people less as citizens, more as consumers. Neither seems much interested in promoting more egalitarian and participatory democracy or servicing the groups and social movements that remain suspicious of parties and representative democracy.

Discussion Questions

1. Why are Latin Americans in general so skeptical about parties? Do you think it would be possible for democracy to function in Latin America without parties? Could social media fill the void?
2. Do social movements need political parties to achieve their goals? One could argue that in every case, once in power—or close to power—these parties seem to fall back into

the practices of the older parties. Why? Do you think that this pitfall (at least from the point of view of the movements) can be avoided?

3.   Overall, would you say that social media can be a powerful tool for citizens to reshape democracy, or are they just technologies for elite control and manipulation?

Resources for Further Study

Reading: Julia Buxton analyzes the collapse of the Punto Fijo system in *The Failure of Political Reform in Venezuela* (Aldershot, UK: Ashgate, 2001). Nancy R. Powers looks at the political choices made by poor Argentine voters in *Grassroots Expectations of Democracy and Economy: Argentina in Comparative Perspective* (University of Pittsburg Press, 2001). As for politicians' choices, see Barry Ames, *Political Survival: Politicians and Public Policy in Latin America* (Berkeley: University of California Press, 1987).

Video and Film: Oliver Stone's *South of the Border* (2010) takes a sympathetic view of the rise of leftist politicians and parties in recent years. *Our Brand Is Crisis* (2005) looks at culture clash and democratic values as U.S. campaign advisors try to work with Bolivian elites while Indigenous people demonstrate in the streets. The Netflix documentary *The Great Hack* provides a good look at how new communication technologies are impacting liberal democratic systems.

On the Internet: Latin Pulse (www.linktv.org/latinpulse) carries regular reports on elections and parties in Latin America. The Americas Society/Council of the Americas (www.as-coa.org) is another go-to place for information on electoral politics.

13 Institutions, Constitutions, and Constituent Power

Focus Questions

▶ What role do institutions play today in a region where they have often been ignored or abused?

▶ By what criteria should the quality of "governance" be judged? To what extent are Latin American democracies capable of providing this public benefit?

▶ With some exceptions, constitutions have not had long life spans in Latin America. Why? What is behind the recent tendency for new charters to be written through constitutional assemblies?

SINCE 2015, THE mood about democracy's prospects has darkened, returning us in some respects to the 1970s' preoccupation with democratic breakdowns. In the 1990s, attention shifted toward transition to democracy. Most political scientists expressed cautious optimism about "consolidation" and "deepening" of democracy. Von Mettenheim and Malloy (1998: 178–179) argued that transitions had

> empowered citizens and civil society along new lines of gender, race, ethnicity, and identity, and overcame seemingly intractable problems such as high foreign debt, hyperinflation, and economic adjustment. Although not blind to policy failures and facile appeals to authoritarianism, the series of policy successes through open, pluralistic governance by new civilian leaders in Latin America . . . suggests that deepening democracy is possible.

This optimistic perspective encouraged some Latin Americanists to apply analysis drawn from a school of thought called the **new institutionalism**. The time was right, said some political scientists, to call for more attention "on the process whereby elected leaders, working through the institutions of democracy, make decisions" (Munck 2004: 437). Today's stress on why democracy seems once again endangered has overshadowed the optimism, but at the same time we see for **constituent assemblies** to reform or rewrite constitutions, suggesting that many Latin Americans perceive institutions to be important for a healthy democracy. They want to exercise **constituent power** to reshape **regimes**.

Institutions are political arrangements, rules, or organizations that are valued for themselves as ways to process demands, resolve conflicts, or promote the general welfare of the population. Constitutions define the role of branches of government, the powers of but also the checks upon popular majorities, and major responsibilities of public entities. Latin American constitutions, besides defining ordinary legislative powers, also provide for passage of semi-constitutional **organic laws**, which have a special status as foundational laws with a semi-constitution status. Organic laws are conceived as a direct outgrowth of the constitution and can be created or modified only by an extraordinary majority (typically three-fifths or two-thirds). Typically, organic laws govern taxation, union and collective bargaining affairs, property rights, rules for foreign investment in natural resources, or electoral processes. While such laws may protect human rights and provide some stability in economic life, they can also block legal paths to redistribution of wealth and create impunity for crimes committed by security forces. Embedded organic laws have been a major obstacle to modifying **neoliberal** economic policies in Chile.

One positive sign of an institutionalized process or organization is that those who disagree with its decisions or outcomes continue to respect, or at least accept, the outcomes. For example, if citizens think that the rules and political organizations responsible for conducting elections carry them out fairly and impartially, they are likely to accept the outcomes as legitimate even if their preferred candidate or party loses. That is a sign that electoral processes are institutionalized. There are reasons to believe that since the global financial crisis of 2008, the institutions of **polyarchy** have suffered declining confidence, as our Democracy Snapshots and the figures in the Introduction on support and satisfaction show.

Impeachment of the Street

Twenty years ago, Guillermo O'Donnell (1994), the distinguished Argentine comparativist, warned in an often-cited essay that old patterns of presidentialism and personalism have asserted themselves within the new "democratic" framework. Rather than participatory democracy or pluralist democracy with institutional checks and balances, O'Donnell sees a much weaker "**delegative democracy**," in which legislatures concede enormous powers to presidents whose rule is legitimated by elections that are little more than plebiscites.

Rather than empowering citizens, plebiscitary elections can allow powerful executives to acquire near dictatorial powers beyond the control of legislatures, states, and bureaucracies. However, Latin Americans have shown themselves ready to use mass protests to exercise constituent power to counter the powers of a president or, more broadly, a political regime. In a way, the concept bears similarity to what in the U.S. presidential system is known as "impeachment," a procedure found in Latin American constitutions, one that has played a controversial role in recent cases of removal of a president by the legislature. Since 1990, several elected Latin American presidents have been forced out of office in what might be called "impeachment of the street." In the same period, several Latin American presidents have attempted (with mixed results) to use their popularity to remove limits on reelection by influencing court decisions, pushing legislative changes, or amending constitutions. These include, among others, Alberto Fujimori in Peru in 2000, Hugo Chávez in Venezuela in 2007, F. H. Cardoso in Brazil in 1998, Carlos Menem in Argentina in 1994, Rafael Correa in Ecuador in 2017, and Evo Morales in Bolivia in 2018. What you might notice from this list is that presidents from across the entire political spectrum have sought to extend their eligibility for a new term beyond the constitutional limit.

The recent history of Latin America also continues to be punctuated by irregular resignations or removal of presidents across the ideological spectrum. Fujimori shut down the country's Congress in 1992 but fled the country in disgrace in 2000 (see chapter 10). Venezuela's Chávez initially sought power through a failed *coup d'état* in 1992 against President Carlos Andrés Pérez; subsequent pressure from the military and street protests forced Pérez to resign in 1993. After achieving office through elections in 1998, Chávez himself was temporarily ousted by a coup in 2002, only to be restored 48 hours later, in large measure because of mass protests against the junta that had seized power. Popular anger forced out Presidents Jamil Mahuad and Lucio Gutiérrez of Ecuador in 2000 and 2004 (respectively), Fernando de la Rúa in Argentina in 2001, and Gonzalo Sánchez de Lozada in Bolivia in 2003. Conservative opposition drove out Jean Bertrand Aristide in Haiti in 2004. In Paraguay, a Congress dominated by conservatives impeached and ousted President Fernando Lugo from office in a matter of 24 hours in 2012. Based on dubious claims of electoral fraud, a rightwing military forced Evo Morales to flee Bolivia and go into exile in 2019. In some of these cases, constitutional formalities were observed, but what all have in common is that power politics and social unrest were influential factors and the institutionalized procedures were of questionable validity.

What is more important to democracy—respect for the constitution or the will of the majority? **Polyarchies** are constitutionally designed to limit majority power, and we can readily grasp that protection of minority rights from the tyranny of the majority is a good reason for limiting that power. However, what if, as in Honduras, the restrictions go to the point of making it absolutely impossible to change the rules of the game? What about the other side of the question? In at least several of the cases of presidents who failed to complete terms cited previously, the executives were attempting to carry out policies that were widely and deeply unpopular. Are removals of presidents within constitutional rules but under enormous popular pressure—"impeachments of the street"—signs of democratic health or decay?

"Impeachments of the street," whereby masses of people in the streets call for an elected president's resignation or to induce the legislature to remove him or her from office, might make countries less governable, but at least in some cases, they also are linked to demands for more popular accountability—that is, demands for *more* democracy. The protests that ousted Venezuela's Pérez, Ecuador's Mahuad and Gutiérrez, Bolivia's Sánchez de Lozada ("Goni"), and Argentina's de la Rúa were all generated by their attempts to implement unpopular neoliberal policies. Sánchez de Lozada and two of his successors in Bolivia were forced to resign under popular pressure between 2003 and 2005 for pursuing widely unpopular policies, including cooperating with the U.S.-sponsored drug war and opening new territory to foreign oil and mining companies. His biggest misstep was planning to develop national gas fields that not only generated protests from Indigenous groups but also stirred controversy because he intended to sign an agreement with Chile for a pipeline through territory that Bolivia lost in the War of the Pacific and has always vowed to reclaim.

In Ecuador, Gutiérrez, who as a colonel had played a key role in the ouster of Mahuad, was ousted himself by a military coup provoked by street demonstrations in April 2004. His political rise had been closely linked to his role, while still a military officer, in supporting Indigenous protests, but he failed to follow through on promises and faced mass protests similar to the ones he had once supported. In 2019, popular protests again rocked Quito and threatened the presidency of Lenín Moreno, who had served as President Rafael Correa's vice president and had won election in 2017 on promises to continue with Correa's popular, leftist agenda. Instead, Moreno veered to right and signed an agreement with the **IMF** that resulted in cuts to popular programs initiated by Correa. Two weeks of demonstrations demanding his resignation broke out in late November 2019, with recurrences in early 2020. The coronavirus pandemic reached Ecuador with devastating consequences, providing Moreno with some relief from the protests, but images of hundreds of bodies piling up in the streets of Guayaquil, the commercial capital on the Pacific coast, threatened to eventually claim Moreno's presidency as well.

Corruption (see chapter 14) usually is a contributing factor to spurring popular pressures. Some presidents have survived scandals that, temporarily at least, threatened their ability to finish their terms and often have subsequently hurt their parties. Brazil's Lula, who took office with high opinion ratings and a reputation for probity, came under fire in 2005 as a result of several bribery scandals touching close aides. In 2017, Lula was convicted and jailed after a controversial conviction based on a corruption scandal called *Lava Jato* (Operation Car Wash; see later). The judge in his trial was later found to have cooperated with the prosecution to get a conviction of the ex-president. Lula gained his freedom at least temporarily as a result, but the air of scandal around his party, the PT (Workers Party), contributed to its defeat in the 2018 elections.

Other **Pink Tide** presidents in addition to Morales have suffered premature removals from office. President Fernando Lugo, a former Catholic bishop elected in 2008, was forced from office by the Paraguayan Congress in a hastily implemented impeachment proceeding after a clash between security forces and peasants who were encouraged by Lugo's plans for land reform. José Manuel Zelaya's removal was even more controversial because the military seized him in the middle of night and flew him out of the country in June 2009. The Honduran military said it acted because Zelaya had ordered them to cooperate in holding an unconstitutional referendum. Both incidents attracted criticism from most other Latin American nations, while the conservative opposition to both presidents argued that the removals were constitutional, not coups. The argument and causes are laid out in the "Punto de Vistas" on Honduras and on Lugo in Paraguay in this chapter. After the leader is ousted, the new regime calls elections that "legitimize a successor" but effectively block the predecessor's efforts at social change (Maher 2012). This scenario seemed to be repeating itself in 2020 in Bolivia with elections in May scheduled to replace Morales.

PUNTO DE VISTA: DID A COUP OR AN IMPEACHMENT TAKE PLACE IN PARAGUAY IN 2012?

In June 2012, President Fernando Lugo of Paraguay, one of the poorest countries in Latin America, was impeached and removed from office. An estimated 60% of Paraguayans were living in poverty, and Lugo was known as the "bishop of the poor" before he left the priesthood and entered politics. In 2008 he won Paraguay's presidential election, promising to end corruption and to carry out an agrarian reform, angering the tiny percentage of citizens who owned 80% of the country's land. Lugo promised to deliver land to 87,000 landless families and refused to take a salary as president.

On June 22, 2012, a clash between police and peasants over disputed property left seven police officers and ten peasants dead, and Lugo's opponents blamed him for the violence. He was impeached by a 76 to 1 vote in the lower house and then convicted and ousted the very next day by a 39–4 vote in the Senate, both controlled by two Liberal parties and the Colorado Party. The Colorados had controlled Paraguay's presidency for 61 years, including the dictatorship of Alfredo Stroessner from 1954 to 1989. Lugo was replaced by his vice president, Federico Franco, a member of the Liberal Party. The impeachment motion blamed the violence on Lugo's supposedly poor performance.

There were other reasons for the Paraguayan right's discontent with Lugo. Lugo was working to bring Venezuela and its leftist leader, Hugo Chávez, into the Mercosur trade bloc. The only thing standing in the way was the Paraguayan Congress, as other members (Brazil, Argentina, and Uruguay) had already approved Venezuelan ascension. The impeachment may have backfired, as the other countries condemned the hasty removal of Lugo as a coup and suspended Paraguay's membership long enough to admit Venezuela.

In a March cable (WikiLeaks 2009), the U.S. embassy said Lugo's opponents were maneuvering to impeach Lugo in order to "regain their own political relevance" and would do so "even on spurious grounds." Lugo protested that he had no opportunity to prepare a defense before the Senate vote and called his removal a "legislative coup d'état against the people's will." He said the new government had no legitimacy and had "altered the Republic's institutionalism."

The new president, Federico Franco, a liberal, rejected Lugo's claim. According to *Al Jazeera English*, he said, "I ratify and reaffirm that there was no coup here, there is no institutional breakdown. This was carried out in accordance with the constitution and the laws. It is a legal situation that the constitution and the laws of my country permit us to do in order to carry out changes when the situation calls for it. What was carried out was a political trial in accordance with the constitution and the laws."

A senator whose party favored impeachment, Miguel Carrizosa Galiano, seemed untroubled by the haste with which Lugo was evicted. His party was willing to wait four days to give Lugo time to defend himself against the charge. However, he said, "We lost. That is democracy."

Al Jazeera English quotes Adrienne Pine, an anthropologist, for a different view. "It is clear that this was modeled after the Honduran coup in 2009; the same kind of rhetoric is being used and the same kind of powerful oligarchic figures are behind it . . . It's a very shady justification and one that shows that allowing the Honduran coup to stand has paved the way for other similar procedural coups."

Point/Counterpoint

Was what happened in Paraguay a constitutional process consistent with the rule of law, or was it some kind of a coup?

a. If you say it was constitutional and consistent with the rule of law, how do you respond to those who say the hurried proceedings were unfair and that Lugo was removed from office simply because he sought to make changes unpopular with the elite?
b. If you say it was a coup, how do you respond to Carrizosa Galiano and others who point out that no laws or provisions of the constitution were violated?

For More Information

The June 26, 2008, *Al Jazeera English* report on the constitutional legality of Lugo's ouster can be found here: www.youtube.com/watch?v=7P44ga6PPlc. The U.S. embassy cable can be found at https://wikileaks.org/cable/2009/03/09ASUNCION189.html. *Upside Down World* carried several background pieces on the "coup." See http://upsidedownworld.org/category/archives/paraguay/.

What these cases tell us is that institutions may be designed to function in a neutral fashion on paper, but everywhere they are embedded in social and economic systems that affect how well they operate. If institutions did not matter at all, power would be exercised nakedly. Institutions allow social and political life to function with some stability. However, institutions are rarely neutral, yet at the same time it is difficult to imagine how any kind of democracy— direct, representative, participatory, or other—could function without them. Polyarchies require institutions that limit constituent power, but any other kind of democracy that might replace them would also require rules on how decisions are to be made, political competition regulated, and discourse conducted. Institutions are critical to the function of **governance**.

For Review

What is "impeachment of the street"? What is a "constituent assembly" and why is it seen by some observers as different from the way constitutions have been framed in liberal democracies? Why might some see the role of institutions as needing to control participation? How does an "organic law" differ from an ordinary law?

Fair Elections and Democratic Legitimacy

Whatever we might think about pluralism's strengths and weaknesses as a form of democracy, there is little doubt that, in the post–Cold War world, the holding of fair elections is the minimum standard by which democracy is judged. In a democracy, citizens must have the opportunity to turn out incumbents and elect a new government. Elections may not be a *sufficient* condition for democracy in the absence of equality and human rights, but they are a *necessary* condition. Hence, the health of the institution charged with conducting elections is critical to the overall health of democracy.

During the 1980s, Edward S. Herman and Frank Brodhead, dismayed by what they called "demonstration elections" staged by the United States in the Dominican Republic, Vietnam, and El Salvador, suggested six "criteria of election integrity" (1984: 11–15). "Demonstration elections" are staged by governments supported by Washington to bolster U.S. citizen support for counterinsurgency wars waged in those countries. El Salvador at the time was the site of just such a war, a "low-intensity conflict," against the guerrillas of the Farabundo Martí National Liberation Front. The U.S. insisted over objections of the country's oligarchy that elections be held to legitimize the government of Washington's preferred candidate, José Napoleón Duarte, a Christian democrat. The election served as a case study to illustrate the six criteria suggested by Herman and Brodhead, which can usefully be applied even today to other cases.

1. *Freedom of speech.* Citizens should be able to raise questions and criticize leaders. In El Salvador, in the early 1980s, a state of siege and rampant violence violated this provision. In 1982 alone, 1,500 citizens died at the hands of security forces.
2. *Freedom of the media.* This means a variety of media organs not under centralized control. In El Salvador, independent stations and newspapers had been subject to shutdowns, violence, and censorship in the years leading up to the 1983 elections.

3. *Freedom of organization of intermediate groups.* In effect, this is the freedom to associate and organize for change. In El Salvador, social movements and organizations had been decimated by military and paramilitary violence.
4. *The absence of highly developed and pervasive instruments of state-sponsored terror.* This refers to the use of secret police, the military, and death squads linked to the incumbent regime to intimidate and silence opponents, a well-documented practice in the Salvadoran case.
5. *Freedom of party organization and ability to field candidates.* Organizations and parties must be able to support candidates and make alternatives known to citizens. In El Salvador, leftist and moderate leftist parties and candidates were assassinated and driven underground.
6. *Absence of coercion and fear on the part of the general population.* People need to be confident that their ballots will be secret and not subject them to harm. Salvadoran authorities used clear ballot boxes guarded by military personnel (an attempt in part to reduce fraud, but intimidating nonetheless) and required voting by law. Voters were required to dip their thumbs in ink to show they voted and to prevent them from voting more than once. However, this meant that voters who might choose to abstain were readily identifiable to security forces and death squads.

Note that Herman and Brodhead concentrate less on the issue of fraudulent balloting on the day of the election and more on conditions in the period before the campaign. International observers often fly into a country to observe conditions on an election day, or perhaps the last few days before. Fewer are present to observe the atmosphere and conditions of the campaign itself and, therefore, to judge the six criteria we have just reviewed. That does not mean that observation serves no purpose. Obviously, ballots must be counted fairly on an election day. Too often, that is in question in Latin America—though in the United States we should be somewhat cautious, given growing irregularities in our own election system. In 2016, Donald Trump claimed, though with virtually no evidence, that Democrats deprived him of a national majority by tampering with electronic balloting and by busing voters, many of them undocumented immigrants, to the polls.

The Mexican presidential elections of 2006 and 2012 were extremely controversial. In 2006, the Federal Election Institute (FEI) declared the PAN's Felipe Calderón the winner by only half of 1 percent of the total vote (243,000 of 41 million votes). Andrés Manuel López Obrador (known as AMLO; see chapter 8), the PRD candidate, charged that there were irregularities at 50,000 of Mexico's 130,500 voting places. Some voting places reported turnouts of more than 100 percent. More than 1.6 million ballots were disallowed in areas where AMLO ran strongly. AMLO demanded a vote-by-vote recount, but the FEI only agreed to review the tallies from the voting places. In the end, Calderón was sworn in amid street demonstrations and turmoil. The 2012 election, won by the PRI candidate Peña Nieto, was similarly controversial, generating huge protest marches by a nonpartisan movement, Yo Soy 132. The name, "I am 132," emerged after the PRI claimed that 131 protest videos uploaded to Facebook and YouTube by students had really been planted by Pena's political rivals. The demonstrators took to the streets supporting the students with signs saying they were each "132."

Despite the dissatisfaction with democracy registered in surveys, overall the turnout rate in elections is impressive (see Figure 13.1). The only Latin American country with a poorer turnout rate (percent of the voting age population) than the dismal 47.2 percent

FIGURE 13.1   Turnout: Percent Voting

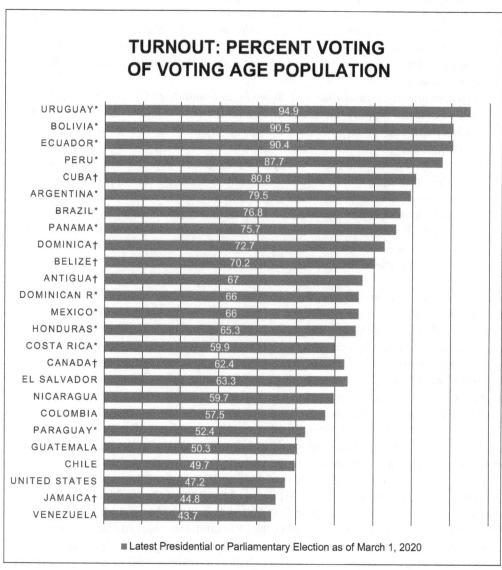

TURNOUT: PERCENT VOTING OF VOTING AGE POPULATION

URUGUAY*	94.9
BOLIVIA*	90.5
ECUADOR*	90.4
PERU*	87.7
CUBA†	80.8
ARGENTINA*	79.5
BRAZIL*	76.8
PANAMA*	75.7
DOMINICA†	72.7
BELIZE†	70.2
ANTIGUA†	67
DOMINICAN R*	66
MEXICO*	66
HONDURAS*	65.3
COSTA RICA*	59.9
CANADA†	62.4
EL SALVADOR	63.3
NICARAGUA	59.7
COLOMBIA	57.5
PARAGUAY*	52.4
GUATEMALA	50.3
CHILE	49.7
UNITED STATES	47.2
JAMAICA†	44.8
VENEZUELA	43.7

■ Latest Presidential or Parliamentary Election as of March 1, 2020

†Parliamentary system; *Compulsory voting

Source: International Institute for Democracy and Electoral Assistance (www.idea.int/vt).

turnout in the United States was Venezuela, where only 43.7 percent turned out for the July 2018 election. In the closely contested election of 2013, 79.6 percent of Venezuelans turned out. The steep decline was undoubtedly due in large measure to a boycott by the opposition over maneuvers by President Maduro, suffering from dismal approval rating in polls, to hold onto power. The National Electoral Commission, with a pro-government majority, had obstructed opposition efforts to force via petition a recall referendum, as provided in the constitution. Maduro had stripped the country's National Assembly of most of its legislative powers after the opposition won control in December 2015.

Chile is another country where turnout rates have fallen off steeply. In 2010, 87 percent of voting age citizens went to the polls; in January 2013, only 42 percent did. The rate somewhat rebounded in 2017, but it remained far below levels achieved in the period between the first elections after the transition from military rule until the 2013 election. One other figure we might note is the relatively high rate (80.8 percent) of voting in Cuba, even more impressive because among the eight countries with the highest turnout, voting is not compulsory in Cuba. In fact, the rate for Cuba's 2018 parliamentary election is significant in that it was a new low and a continuation of falling voter participation since the 1990s, when percentage rates were typically in the upper 90s. It is likely that the decline is most pronounced among youth, who are well educated but disenchanted with limited economic opportunities.

The practice of making voting compulsory is not unique to Latin America; several European countries also regard voting not merely as a right but as a duty. Failure to produce proof of voting (usually on a citizen ID) can result in a fine and loss of privileges, such as the right to obtain a passport or to open a bank account. Turnout tends to be lower where voting is not compulsory. Chile's right-wing parties negotiated the repeal of compulsory voting as a condition for accepting some changes to the Pinochet-era constitution of 1982, the most significant of which was changing the way that Senate seats were awarded by a method that magnified the number held by the right well beyond the percentage of the vote achieved by conservative parties. Higher turnouts generally favor left parties, so a deal was struck that reduced the bias toward the right but still made it difficult for the left to gain enough of a majority to change organic laws.

Electoral laws and procedures are only as good as the institutions charged with implementing them. The emergence of international and national electoral observation as a fairly routine practice has helped in many cases to increase confidence in the fairness of elections in politically polarized societies. Mexico's elections of 2000, when the PAN's Vicente Fox broke the 70-year hold of the PRI over the presidency, were significantly enhanced not only by international observer teams but also by the formation of Alianza Cívica, the mass movement of thousands of Mexican citizens who were deployed around the country to help ensure that fraud would not occur. But a good election requires more than respecting the letter of the law; it requires a commitment to fairness to the spirit. In highly polarized countries, such as Venezuela in the **Bolivarian** era (1998 to present; see chapter 8), that can be in short supply.

Although foreign observers can reinforce electoral fairness, sometimes they arrive with their own political agenda. Such was the case with a U.S. State Department team that observed the 1984 elections in Nicaragua. In that year the Sandinistas, only five years after seizing power through a popular insurrection against the Somoza dictatorship, decided to hold their first direct popular elections. The country had never before had an honest, contested election. In addition to the State Department, delegations came from a wide variety of organizations and countries, including the Carter Center, Canada, the European Community, the Organization of American States (OAS), and the U.S.-based Latin American Studies Association (LASA).

Turnout in the election was 91 percent. Juan Tamayo, reporter for the *Miami Herald*, quoted a 67-year-old carpenter on the difference between this election and the ones he remembered. "Under Somoza you voted once, and someone else voted two more times in your name. These elections have a different air." Not surprisingly, the U.S. State Department observation team was the only one that denounced the elections, won convincingly by the Sandinistas, as unfair. The report of an observer team from the Latin American Studies Association called the elections the "cleanest held in Nicaragua since 1928, when U.S. marines were organizing and supervising the balloting" (LASA 1984: 26). There was a climate of fear in 1984, but the LASA delegation allocated the blame mostly to the U.S.-backed *contras* (see chapters 9 and 16) and to the United States, which sent supersonic jets to create daily sonic booms over the country the week before the election. Despite the generally positive assessment of the 1984 election, many political scientists who are not area specialists date Nicaragua's "return to democracy" from the 1990 election of an opposition candidate, Violeta Chamorro, rather than to the actions of the Sandinistas of that era.

In contrast to Washington's rejection of the 1984 Nicaraguan elections, the United States praised the Salvadoran elections of 1982. In contrast to conditions in Nicaragua, in El Salvador the two main opposition newspapers had been shut down the previous year. Salvadoran military forces and paramilitary groups had killed between 20,000 and 30,000 people in the 30 preceding months. Targets included union and peasant organizers, centrist and leftist politicians, and 200 clergy. Victims' bodies were typically found on roadsides, showing evidence of torture with their thumbs tied together. Not surprisingly, the elections were marked by poor organization, with few polling places in many poor areas and with citizens having to drop ballots into clear boxes guarded by an army guilty of many abhorrent human rights atrocities. Voters had their thumbs dipped in ink to prevent fraud, but this also meant that those not voting would be easily identified and marked as "traitors" by the military and death squads organized by the notorious right-wing leader, Roberto D'Aubuisson. The election, won by Washington's preferred candidate, Duarte, was certified "free and fair" by the State Department (Herman and Brodhead 1984: 93–152).

Elections in Venezuela have been conducted in a highly polarized political environment (see chapter 8), and almost always with some credible objections to aspects of their conduct, but also, until recently, with few doubts about the actual validity of announced results. Still, prior to 2006, the opposition to President Hugo Chávez generally insisted that his victories and those of his party were fraudulent. However, the opposition candidate in the 2006 election acknowledged the reality of his landslide loss to Chávez. The opposition complaint that the National Electoral Council (CNE) manipulated results lost some credibility when voters rejected two Chávez-backed packages of constitutional reforms by narrow margins. The CNE uses computerized voting machines that in addition to tallying ballots checks voters' thumbprints against a national registry to prevent duplicate voting and provides each voter with a paper receipt. In October 2012, former U.S. president Jimmy Carter said, "As a matter of fact, of the 92 elections that we've monitored, I would say the election process in Venezuela is the best in the world."

In April 2013, Henrique Capriles, the opposition candidate, charged manipulation of the tabulations and called for a recount. The CNE was required by law only to audit a sample, but in an attempt to quell suspicion, it completed a complete audit of tabulations and confirmed the results. So does this mean that the 2013 election was "free and fair"? If we apply Herman and Brodhead's criteria, we can say that the opposition had some grounds to contest the fairness of the broader process, but it was not prevented from getting out its message and contesting the election. The strongest case can be made on the charge of *ventajismo*—the illegal use of state resources to promote Maduro's candidacy. This included state vehicles to transport supporters to rallies and to the polls, favoritism on the state-owned television network, and not-so-thinly-veiled messages to public employees that they had to vote for Maduro to keep their jobs. In addition, there were well-founded charges that the government used a list of those who signed a petition to recall Chávez in 2004 to discriminate against opponents.

On the other side of the ledger, despite concerns about suspending some candidates' eligibility for office based on charges of corruption, there were few restraints on the opposition's ability to campaign, and private media overwhelmingly supported the opposition. There is little doubt that Venezuelan voters were well aware of their options at the ballot box. The CNE had taken measures to ensure the anonymity of the vote. Venezuela has a high rate of criminal violence, and there were reports of intimidation by the government. And the opposition also went well beyond virtually unenforceable limits on campaign spending. While the state broadcasting stations virtually ignored their mandate to stay neutral in campaign coverage, the private media, with much larger audiences, waged a ceaseless campaign on behalf of the opposition.

In short, there were legitimate concerns to be raised regarding Venezuela's electoral institutions' capacity to enforce rules of the campaign game and limit *ventajismo* in 2013. However, every election in Venezuela, from local parish councils to the presidency and national legislature, has been fought as a plebiscite on Chávez and the Bolivarian Revolution. In December 2015, the opposition won a large majority of seats in the National Assembly, giving it the ability to threaten the foundations of chavismo by changing organic laws. In the election, the opposition benefited from election rules that previously had magnified the assembly majority enjoyed by the pro-government PSUV (United Socialist Party of Venezuela). Using claims that some elected opposition deputies had bribed voters (charges never tried in the courts), and backed by courts with pro-government judges, President Maduro maneuvered to strip the assembly of its legislative powers—just short of actually closing it. These were some of the factors that led a large part of the opposition to boycott the July 2018 election, which Maduro won against a candidate backed by the faction of the opposition who favored participation. These events prepared the scene for Juan Guaidó, president of the National Assembly, to declare himself interim president of the country in December 2919 (see Punto de Vista, "Doña Venezuela and Her Two Presidents" in chapter 14).

For Review

If you were a member of an electoral observer team, what kinds of homework would you want to do before traveling to monitor the actual balloting on Election Day? What kinds of questions would be on your mind as you prepared to go?

Democratic Governance

While the World Bank, IMF, and conservative think tanks have provided theory and guidance for neoliberal economic policies, the Bank and other NGOs have recognized that for markets to function as they should requires more transparency and efficiency in providing public services. While the neoliberal track record for delivering on promises to limit negative impacts on the poor is not very impressive, international governmental organizations, including the Bank and the United Nations Conference on Trade and Development, have developed model laws and procedures for what they call "good governance." So too have a range of nongovernmental organizations, such as Transparency International (an anti-corruption NGO; see chapter 14) and the National Endowment for Democracy (NED). The NED was created by the administration of Ronald Reagan to promote democracy. It receives funding from U.S. taxpayers, authorized by Congress. For this reason, a better term for it is not "nongovernmental" but "quasi-governmental," what the British call a "quango."

Larry Diamond is a comparative political scientist who serves as a consultant to the NED, although "consultant" understates his importance as the most eminent scholar guiding the organization. The *Journal of Democracy*, edited by Diamond and published by the NED, is a key intellectual forum for this purpose today. Diamond (2005: 14) sees a "triple crisis of governance" in the world, including Latin America. The elements of this crisis, in his view, are (1) lack of accountability and rule of law as evidenced by criminal activity, human rights abuses, corruption, and so on; (2) "inability to manage regional and ethnic divisions peacefully and inclusively"; and (3) economic challenges resulting from failure to carry out neoliberal economic reforms fully. The first two tasks are important elements of the good governance agenda.

The theme of good governance emerged around the time of peak influence of the **Washington Consensus**, which promoted reduction of the influence of the state over the market as needed to produce prosperity that would trickle down to everyone. Good government in this framework generally promotes honesty and transparency to reduce corruption and favoritism—something that neoliberal thought sees embedded in the state-led strategies of import substitution. For the **World Bank**, good governance requires enforcement of contracts and effective enforcement of rules, but also minimum regulatory restrictions on business. Good governance, it said in 1999, means "a well established system of market institutions—clear and transparent rules, fully functioning checks and balances (including strong enforcement mechanisms), and a robust competitive environment—[that] reduces opportunities for rent-seeking and hence incentives for corruption" (Broadman and Recanatini 1999: 2).

"**Rent-seeking**" here refers to a tendency for private actors to seek wealth through their connections to government rather than through hard work and investments that involve risk taking. World Bank economists, critical of **import substitution** (see chapter 5), contended that too much government ownership and regulation of economic goods and services leads citizens to such rent-seeking. However, in the middle of 2008, that "consensus" came crashing down when deregulated banks and financial corporations faced bankruptcy as a consequence of financial speculation linked to the real estate market. In October of that year, the U.S. government moved to "bail out" these corporations by injecting US$700 billion into the credit market and buying equity (ownership shares) of several of them.

Many Latin American leaders reflected sardonically on how poorly governance seemed to function in the Global North, even as it pressed the concept on them. Latin Americans took note of how readily Washington seemed prepared to abandon deregulation of the market and state subsidies when faced with its own economic crisis in 2008. "There was plenty of advice from supposed specialists, to poor, developing countries," said Lula. "What was lacking was advice for rich countries, about the signs of financial mayhem that had been accumulating over time." Reflecting on his own personal history and referring to the G-20, a broad association of key economic ministers from 20 wealthy countries, with Central Bank presidents most prominent among them, the Brazilian president went on to say,

> My whole life when I was a metal worker, for me to buy a TV I had to work another 40–60 hours per month, nearly killing myself. Today someone can become a billionaire without producing a single piece of paper, a single job, without producing a single salary. For this we need serious regulation coming from the G-20.
>
> (Astor 2008)

A broader conception of governance, one less tied to a particular set of economic policies, has been developed by the British Council, which considers governance as the "interaction between the formal institutions and those in civil society. Governance refers to a process whereby elements in society wield power, authority and influence and enact policies and decisions concerning public life and social upliftment" (Global Development Research Center n.d.). In contrast to the neoliberal conception of governance advanced by the NED, this approach recognizes that governance involves the ability of democracy to produce substantive, positive improvement in people's lives. In this respect, it goes beyond the idea that governance (and by implication, democratic governance) is to be judged in terms of efficient procedures.

Good governance and democracy are not the same. For example, an honest and efficient administration made up of aristocrats may produce less social upheaval than a corrupt, populist administration. This argument is made by some Asian political scientists and political leaders. Pan Wei, an American-educated political scientist at Beijing University, argues that the **rule of law** is more important to good governance than is democracy (Wei 2006). Critics of Wei think that only democracy ultimately guarantees rule by law. Without the discipline provided by periodic elections and freedom of the press, it is too easy for ruling sectors to hide their culpability and escape punishment. But Wei responds that many other forms of state have relied on rule of law to provide fairness and wisdom. Indeed, corruption is rife in many electoral democracies—something borne out by the Latin American experience. It seems easier to hold an election than to create fair and honest bureaucracies and judicial systems.

On the other hand, why should Latin Americans, or any people in a democracy for that matter, not expect both good governance and policies aimed at social uplift? Some institutionalists, such as Brian Crisp (2000), advocate that constitutions be designed not only to represent diverse parts of society but also to facilitate decision-making by those elected. Electoral systems and relationships among branches of government need to fulfill two goals that are somewhat at odds with one another: They should ensure deliberation and prevent passionate majorities from dominating minority rights and interests, but they should not throw the legislative and policy-making process into gridlock. This is closer to what Diamond and most of the transition theorists have in mind.

Effective rule of law requires working and respected judicial institutions. Several NGOs, as well as the World Bank and U.S. Agency for International Development, have put resources since 1980 toward expanding the number of judges, training prosecutors, and expanding budgets. Still, research (see Hammergren 2008) suggests that citizens have little confidence overall in these institutions. Criminal justice systems (see chapter 14) have come in for harsh criticism, and the perception of widespread impunity for corrupt officials persists.

Democratic governance can be imagined to be something like Rousseau's concept of the social contract: one in which citizens are politically informed participants not just oriented toward their interests but also concerned about the general will—about what is best for society as a whole. This is closer to good governance as expressed by the British Council and to the approach advocated by the Brazilian political scientist Leonardo Avritzer (2002). Crisp (2000) argues that good institutions encourage good governance by ensuring that participation is channeled and influences elite decision-making, whereas Avritzer sees good institutions as those that foster decision-making through popular participation.

For Review

What is "rule of law"? How does it differ from democracy? What can be said in favor of and against the idea that democracy is necessary to have rule of law? Why do some good governance advocates want better regulation but less of it? Why is this relevant to Latin America?

New Institutionalism and Constitutional Design

The "new institutionalism" departs from the uncontroversial premise that constitutional designs affect the decisions that politicians and citizens make, and in doing so, they may enhance or inhibit effective governance. A few go beyond this assumption to argue that institutions be designed to reflect the assumption that institutions are most wisely structured when they assume that all humans, regardless of culture, act to maximize benefits and minimize costs—that is, they exercise rational choice (Morgenstern and Nacif 2002). This assumes, as the writers of the U.S. constitution did, that when it comes to politicians, they are motivated mainly by ambition. Many area studies specialists, including Latin Americanists, believe that such an approach fails to take cultural and social class differences into account adequately. Still, virtually all of the region's constitutions attempt to incorporate the U.S. tradition of checks and balances, especially concerning relations between the executive branch and the legislative branch. But in their constitutions, Latin American countries differ from the United States and among themselves about how the president is elected, the system of representation used in legislative elections, the rules for passing legislation, and the powers assigned to each branch.

New Institutionalism and Constitutional Design

Institutionalists argue that constitutional design affects, among many things, the ability of leaders to forge coalitions in legislatures, the ability of courts or legislatures to check the programs of presidents, and the ability of people to hold elected officials accountable. When it comes to immediate matters of public policy—for example, the ability of presidents to privatize the banking system, nationalize copper mines, push a treaty through a congress, and so on—the institutions and the rules of the game defined by constitutions can determine success or failure, at least at the moment of decision-making. Of course, social and economic sources of power can be brought to bear upon the institution and its members.

Latin American constitutions have tended to emulate the U.S. system in providing for election of the president and separation of powers, rather than the parliamentary model, more common elsewhere in the world. In a parliamentary model, a prime minister and/or cabinet is chosen by an elected, representative assembly that can also remove the chief executive by a vote of no confidence. This pattern is found often in the small Caribbean republics that were once colonies of Britain, France, and the Netherlands. Few institutionalists advocate substitution of the parliamentary model for the U.S.-style system. Instead, they tend to emphasize strengthening the capacity of the legislative and judicial branches to check the power of presidents to act in excess of the spirit or letter of the constitution (Mainwaring and Shugart 1997).

In general, Latin American constitutions give significant decree powers to presidents. Usually, these powers are limited to "emergencies," but this condition is interpreted loosely, to say the least, by many presidents. Legislatures sometimes grant decree powers to a president to escape responsibility for unpopular policies, thereby allowing the president to assume credit or blame. This was a factor in Argentina when President Carlos Menem, the Peronist who governed for two terms from 1989 to 1999, issued 166 "decrees of necessity and urgency" in his first eight years. In the prior 140 years, presidents had used this power, bestowed by the constitution of 1853, only 35 times. Most of these decrees were anything but necessary or urgent, and the Argentine courts could have acted to curb the president's abuse of authority. However, Menem had packed the country's Supreme Court with supporters to ensure that the decrees would not be overturned (data cited by Mustapic 2002: 30).

Research on the ability of presidents to move proposals through legislatures rather than around them suggests that, in general, legislatures in Latin America do not have the institutional power characteristic of the U.S. Congress, where bills originate before they become law. In one case, Chile, the executive branch has the right to have its own representatives participate in the deliberations of legislative committees, quite a departure from the principle of separation of powers (Crisp 2000; Morgenstern and Nacif 2002). Many of the key measures enacted by President Chávez in Venezuela in 2001 and 2007 were done through decree-making powers granted by the National Assembly, where the government party enjoyed a strong majority. This may have been constitutional, but it precluded widespread discussion of major legislation and direct input into its passage by movements and groups—one of the main principles in the 1999 constitution, written in Chávez's first year by an assembly that conducted widespread consultation with Venezuelans. One of the central ideas throughout the charter is the idea that the people should be a "protagonist" of political change and not just delegate that task to representatives or a president.

The success of presidents in advancing agendas varies in some predictable ways. Obviously, it helps when the president's party has a majority or at least a large plurality in the legislature. This tends to be the case when legislative elections occur at the same time or shortly after the presidential election, so constitutional design can matter here. A second variable that matters is the degree of discipline that party leaders exercise over their delegations in legislatures. This can be an advantage when the president has a majority but a disadvantage (making it harder to pry opposition votes away) when he or she faces a Congress controlled by opposition parties. This situation confronted both Evo Morales and Lula in Brazil (but not

Chávez). To move any of their programs through the legislature required making alliances with legislators more interested in personal enrichment or patronage to secure their political power back home. This context partly explains how the PT became enmeshed in the *mensalão* scandal (see chapter 12).

Cuba would seem to represent one more case of highly centralized power, although it is not clear whether the decisive actor in votes of National Assembly members is the Cuban Communist Party (PCC) or the personal power of the country's president. In the era of Fidel, there is little doubt that his personal authority transcended that of the party, and after 2006 Raúl enjoyed similar prestige as a revolutionary leader in his own right. In October 2019, the baton was passed for the first time to a non-member of the revolutionary generation, Miguel Díaz-Canal. Díaz-Canal seemed secure in that position in 2020. The hostility of the Trump administration probably reinforces unity among major institutional actors—the party, the government, and the military. What may develop if U.S. policy shifts back to the softer approach of the Obama administration is more uncertain, as there are differences within the party and government over the pace and breadth that should be given to economic reforms.

Although the Cuban legislature often reaches decisions on major legislation by unanimous vote, there often takes place beforehand a long period of discussion and consultation with people in local meetings before a consensus among party and government officials is reached (Roman 2003). Unlike the former communist states of Eastern Europe and those of contemporary Asia, the PCC does not seem to act strictly as a shadow government behind Cuba's political institutions. However, the PCC is constitutionally defined as the country's only legal party, and Cuba certainly falls into the category of countries with powerful executives and highly disciplined party politics. Until Raúl retires entirely from politics, he could intervene if he is unhappy with the direction of certain policies. New social forces arising from openings to the market and the passing, finally, of the generation that led Cuba's 1959 revolution may eventually put the durability of Cuba's institutions to the test and generate pressures for political liberalization.

Parties, Legislatures, Executives, and Reform

Party systems, election systems, and the rules by which legislatures operate all interact with one another in ways that vary from country to country. Many Latin American parties exercise a high degree of discipline over legislators, meaning that the representatives tend to vote as party leaders dictate and defy them only at risk to their careers. Sometimes this can be an advantage for governance because it makes it easier to fashion majorities to pass legislation, but discipline can also be used to block compromise. At an extreme, highly disciplined parties that allow for little independent judgment by members of a congress or assembly may result in a "crisis of representation." That is, citizens may feel they have no real representation because politicians are completely at the mercy of their party authorities.

Perhaps the best example of such a crisis was the utter collapse of Venezuela's party system in 1998. As we reviewed in chapter 8, the two main parties that dominated the Punto Fijo era (1958–1998), AD (Democratic Action) and COPEI (Christian Democrats), suffered ignominious falls due to pent-up civic anger at their resistance to democratic reform and inability to respond to economic woes. Throughout most of the Punto Fijo era, Venezuela appeared to be a model **polyarchy** because of its two-party system and accumulated experience with peaceful presidential transitions through elections, standing in contrast to the stark military rule elsewhere in the region. A crisis of representation developed as the party system proved impervious to popular discontent.

The political careers of legislators in both AD and COPEI depended entirely on the will of national party leaders. These leaders could award or deny aspiring politicians a place on the party's ballot anywhere in the country, regardless of the politician's standing at the local level. Disciplinary committees could and did expel politicians who might break ranks on important legislative votes or speak out independently on important issues. This discipline was exerted beyond legislators in Caracas to state and local politicians. The constitutional provisions for federalism and some autonomy for state governments were rendered virtually meaningless. Party leaders could punish maverick party members by denying them resources from the budget, a factor reinforced by the control of the central government over oil-export earnings (see Buxton 2001; Coppedge 1994; Crisp 2000).

AD was the dominant party in the political condominium, but COPEI held the presidency from 1968 to 1973 and 1978 to 1983. Its founder Rafael Caldera also was president, though after breaking from the party, from 1993 until 1998. COPEI presidents had to govern in the face of disciplined opposition from AD, but even *adeco* presidents found they could get little done unless they cooperated with the powerful party leadership in the Congress. This made negotiation necessary to break stalemates. This took place among party leaders outside the halls of Congress, more often a matter of dividing the spoils (oil rents) than negotiations of the content of legislative bills (Coppedge 1994; Crisp 2000). To break legislative logjams, the president often looked outside the legislative process, asking commissions composed of representatives of labor unions, business, and government to reach an accord. There was little drama in legislative votes themselves as the word of party leaders was law within each congressional delegation. Congressional votes could be recorded simply by noting a nod of the head from the leader of the largest party or coalition of parties. Centralization was so complete that central party authorities often imposed nominees from one part of the country on another. Venezuelans called these politicos *paracaídos* (parachutists), because they dropped in out of nowhere, anointed by *caciques* far away in Caracas to "represent" local communities where they did not live.

After the Caracazo rebellion of 1989 (see chapter 8), Venezuela's two main parties finally initiated some reforms, but partial reform in some ways made their problems worse. For example, by allowing governors to be elected by direct popular vote for the first time in 1989, the parties allowed the emergence of political leaders with an independent base of support—the direct support of voters in their home state. They had created a new class of politicians not subjected to their discipline. Meanwhile, the national leaders continued to absorb the blame for squandering the country's oil wealth. Then came political Armageddon when Chávez was swept into office in 1998 and called a constituent assembly to write a new constitution.

Chávez used his overwhelming popularity, including considerable support from the middle class (which later turned against him), to change the rules of the political game in Venezuela. He had most of the constituent assembly elected by the uninominal method—that is, one representative per district—which greatly favored the alliance of parties that backed him in his comfortable presidential victory. He also enjoyed power that emanated from his charisma; Chávez mattered more than the organizational strength of the old parties.

The new constitution of 1999 created a mixed system to elect deputies to a unicameral National Assembly, incorporating both **proportional** and **uninominal representation**, but overall the system had a strong tendency toward magnifying the number of seats won by the largest party—in this case, the one linked to Chávez. It didn't matter so much in 2000; the grip AD and COPEI held had already been broken. COPEI almost disappeared off the political map entirely; AD survived as a moderate-size opposition party, one part of a coalition of parties opposed to Chávez. Chávez also ran as a coalition candidate, but his party (the MVR until 2006, the PSUV afterwards) dominated an alliance of left parties. As previously discussed, in December 2015 the opposition won the election for the National Assembly. This time the bias toward inflating the number of seats allocated to the largest party magnified opposition victory, accelerating the country's descent into political and social crisis.

The new "Bolivarian" constitution, not surprisingly, was written with the maladies of the old system in mind. It requires internal primaries (only sometimes respected in practice) to weaken the grip of party secretaries (leaders), and it mandates quotas for representation of women. In keeping with the spirit of fostering participatory government, civil groups are supposed to be consulted about appointments of judges and three key government posts—the attorney general, human rights ombudsman (someone who acts on behalf of the citizenry), and comptroller (auditor). These are significant changes, but early on the idea of protagonistic, participatory democracy was eclipsed by the personalist, charismatic leadership of Chávez.

Chávez hoped that the PSUV would serve as a vehicle for social movements and grassroots activists to participate actively in making policies. In many *barrios*, dedicated grassroots cadres enthusiastically worked to make this goal a reality in their communities, but the practices of the past soon asserted themselves, magnified by the nature of economic reality in a petrostate. Even among grassroots leaders who were deeply committed to participatory democracy and to bettering their communities, the priority of defending the Bolivarian Revolution in the local, state, and national elections, including referendums, and the political imperative of winning votes took precedence over the internal party democracy and respect for those unenthusiastic about community programs. As oil income, typically 20 percent of GDP and 80 percent of government revenues, is passed from the executive branch to local communal councils, there are myriad opportunities for patronage and graft.

As long as Chávez was alive, there was little question about who had the final word on party nominations or how the party would vote in the assembly. With his death in March 2013, the party rallied behind his designated successor, Nicolás Maduro. Maduro won the April election to replace Chávez but by such a narrow margin (less than two points) that it left the Bolivarian movement stunned, as though Maduro had lost. The national charter lays out impressive mechanisms both to check centralized power and to empower citizens to be protagonists of legislation. However, these principles run up against the reality that the financial resources gained from tapping the profits of extractive industries are accumulated by the state, which manages how the valuable resource below its soil is exploited. In the Chávez era, every election was fought as a plebiscite on his leadership. In the Maduro era, there was little confidence of voters on either side. For *barrio* dwellers, the choice was whether to abandon the fate of popular programs to an opposition likely to dismantle them or a political leadership increasingly viewed as corrupt and incapable.

Mexico's political institutions (pre-2000) arguably responded with more agility to that country's crisis of representation, which was increasingly visible between 1968 and 2000. The 1918 Mexican constitution was written in part to prevent another president from accumulating the power achieved by Porfirio Díaz before the 1910 revolution. However, the dominance of the highly disciplined Institutional Revolutionary Party (PRI) and centralized control over spending defeated this goal. The formation of a disciplined revolutionary party between 1924 and 1940 assured that the new system *would not* be characterized by a weak presidency. In fact, the president's command over the party made the Mexican Congress little more than a rubber stamp. Because the PRI held an overwhelming majority of seats, virtually no institutional check over the president's legislative power existed.

The new legislative majority in 1997, composed of the conservative PAN and leftist PRD, cooperated enough to deny the PRI and the Mexican president, Ernesto Zedillo, a majority in Congress. After Vicente Fox of the PAN won the 2000 election, he faced a similar situation, now with the PRI and the PRD in the majority. Mexico evolved into a three-party system, with little love lost among any of the three for one another. The result was gridlock. President Fox (2001–2006) of the PAN, a fiscal conservative, found it almost impossible to move his budget through a Congress in which his party was a distinct minority. (In Chile, by contrast, the president introduces the budget, and it becomes law in 60 days even if Congress fails to approve it or a substitute.) The populist PRI and the leftist PRD not only had different budget priorities than the business-oriented Fox but also had a political motive to embarrass the president and his party. Fox's successor, Felipe Calderón (2007–2012), who took office after an election tainted by credible charges of fraud, was even less successful in gaining legislative support for his agenda.

Mexican President Ernesto Zedillo (1994–2000) was the victim of his own good intentions. Having refused to cooperate with his party's (PRI) attempts to hold onto a congressional majority by electoral fraud, he now had to negotiate with the two opposition parties to pass his budgets. Though they were ideologically opposed, the PAN and PRD cooperated in the new environment to seize a share of some of the patronage previously monopolized by the PRI.

Does this mean Mexican presidents have lost the ability to move legislation as their predecessors did in the era before the neoliberal economic and political reforms of the 1990s? President Enrique Peña Nieto, who recaptured the presidency for the PRI in 2012, was able to forge a pact among the three parties for some important measures, including opening the oil sector to private investment, creating a new regulatory commission, restricting the power of some of the most corrupt unions, and reducing the monopoly power of the media networks privatized in the 1990s. To some observers, these were needed reforms (*Christian Science Monitor*, editorial, March 24, 2013); to others (e.g., La Botz 2012), they were setbacks for Mexican workers. Either way, they show some recovery of an institutional capacity lacking in the first 12 years after the defeat of the PRI by Fox in 2000.

Most party systems in Latin America impose more discipline on legislators than does the U.S. system. Probably the least disciplined parties are found in Brazil and Colombia, where legislators have incentives to think first of their own interest in getting elected, not loyalty to their parties. They get relatively little help from national parties in elections. In Colombia, primaries within the dominant Liberal and Conservative parties make for intense intraparty competition. This made Colombian parties porous—quite unlike the Chilean and Venezuelan cases, and more like the Brazilian case.

In Brazil, most representatives serve one term in the Chamber of Deputies or the Senate and then return to their states or cities to continue their careers in elective office or the bureaucracy. Their main objective, then, is to deliver enough benefits to their home areas that local political bosses will provide a job or support their political ambitions on their return home. "No one who follows Brazilian politics doubts that pork-barrel programs and control over appointive jobs are the mother's milk of legislative majorities," writes Barry Ames (2002:

196). The large number of Brazilian parties—six major ones alone—further complicates the situation. A Brazilian president must use great skill and all the patronage resources he or she can muster to move legislation through Congress. Fernando Collor de Mello (1990–1992) tried to do this with decrees and outright corruption, and he ended up being impeached and removed from office. Fernando Henrique Cardoso (1995–2002) used a different tactic, giving small parties positions in the cabinet. To some degree, then, Brazil's presidential system functions somewhat like parliamentary systems, where minority premiers must cobble together majority coalitions in the same way (Ames 2002; Neto 2002). The result is coalition politics built around patronage, not an agenda for government. This fact of political life in Brazil partly explains the *mensalão* and the later ***Lava Jato*** (see later) scandals that engulfed Lula and the Workers' Party.

Federalism does not always result in decentralized politics, but in the right circumstances, governors and even mayors (e.g., of capital cities such as Caracas, Mexico City, and Santiago de Chile) can play a key role in determining the ability of a president to carry out a program. In Brazil governors control security forces and have used them to thwart environmental protection of the rainforest and efforts to prosecute landlords who have used violence, including murder, to repress the environmental and the landless peasants' movement in several states. Under the right-wing presidency of Jair Bolsonaro (2017–), this violence has only increased and become more institutionalized.

Electoral Competition Between and Within Parties

The foregoing discussion demonstrates the way that (1) party politics, (2) relationships between the executive and legislative branches, and (3) the degree to which political power is centralized are all interrelated. Despite strong traditions of federalism in Venezuela and Mexico, tightly disciplined parties foster a high degree of centralization. Colombia's parties are extremely porous—that is, less tightly disciplined, looser in their organization. Parties in Argentina, Brazil, and Chile fall somewhere in between the extremes of Venezuela and Mexico on one side and Colombia on the other.

Argentina: Between Populism and Neoliberalism

President Carlos Menem of Argentina (1989–1999) faced considerable opposition to his neoliberal economic program within his own Peronist Party. Although Menem used and abused decree powers to circumvent problems with Peronists in Congress, he sought legislative approval on some matters (e.g., broad tax reform) to make it more difficult to reverse his program in the future. Menem was able to use patronage to exert enough control over the Partido Justicialista (PJ, as the Peronist organization is officially named) to place allies in key positions in Congress.

Four factors facilitated the president's task. First, although unionized workers were the key sector organized by Juan Perón in building his party in the 1940s, the internal structures of the PJ did not give the unions a formal voting power; that is, Perón never *institutionalized* labor's influence in his party, so Menem could ignore the unions in formal party votes. Second, the Peronists returned to power in 1983 after a harsh dictatorship had violently repressed labor, leaving unions significantly weaker than they were before the military government. Peronist politicians now relied less on labor support than on the distribution of patronage in general. They began to think of the party less as a labor-based party and more as a catch-all party seeking broad support to win political office in different provinces. Third, the closing of many factories and the shift to service industries had reduced the weight of organized labor in the workforce. Fourth, the growth of right-wing civilian influence offered Menem some allies to help him prevail over opponents in his own party (Levitsky 2000).

What we see here is an example of how social changes (the shift in workforce patterns, changing attitudes in the electorate) reshaped one of the key institutions in Argentine politics. Menem ruled over and through the Peronist Party, but by the time he left office, the party had become much more of a catch-all party and less of a working-class party. When economic crisis arrived and Menem fell from grace with the public, the party proved incapable of pulling together the needed leadership to emerge from the crisis—until another strong figure, Nestor Kirchner, emerged. Kirchner (2003–2007), with considerable assistance (oil and financing) from Venezuela's President Chávez, was able to resist an IMF structural adjustment plan, and Argentina experienced significant economic growth during his presidency. Like Menem at the height of his popularity, Kirchner ruled over and through the party, but it was not long before events showed how porous Peronism had become.

Kirchner's successor, Maria Cristina Fernández de Kirchner, his wife but also a successful politician in her own right, came to the presidency in 2007. She assumed office in fortuitous circumstances. Argentina's agricultural exports, especially soybeans, were experiencing a boom. Fernández de Kirchner attempted to impose what amounts to a windfall-profits tax on farmers, but they responded with mass protests, including blockades of highways linking the cities to food supplies in the countryside. President Kirchner thought that she would lessen her association with the unpopular measure if she had Congress vote on the tax rather than use executive power to impose it. The lower house approved it by a scant 128–122 margin. Then, to her surprise, she lost the vote in the Senate when her own vice president, a fellow Peronist, broke a tie and defeated the proposal.

By 2009, the Kirchner faction of Peronism had lost the dominance it once enjoyed, faring badly in local elections (though it recovered along with the economy afterward). There may have been an element of gender bias at work as well—a desire to put a female president "in her place." For whatever reason, we see that presidentialism does not always win out in power struggles. Kirchner managed to get reelected in 2011, but she never fully recovered her political power to make changes like the one for agricultural policy. In 2015, the Peronist candidate to succeed her was defeated by a coalition of three sizable parties and some dissident Peronists. Their successful candidate, Mauricio Macri, attempted to steer the country in a more neoliberal direction, reminiscent of Menem. He too confronted a difficult economic situation, inherited from his predecessor. His attempt to implement neoliberal fiscal reforms met broad popular resistance. He lost his campaign for reelection to a Peronist slate headed by Alberto Fernández, with Cristina Kirchner as his vice president.

Chile: The Struggle to Undo Pinochet's Constitutional Roadblocks

Post-dictatorial Chile is where constitutional design has probably left the strongest imprint on presidential powers. Here, the parties are more defined and disciplined than in Argentina, but the constitutional framework greatly limits legislative powers in key areas dealing with human rights and economic policy.

Before 1973 three blocs of parties—left, center, and right—contested one another for power, but the experience of dictatorship and the retreat of the socialists from revolutionary politics brought about a reconfiguration. The Christian Democratic Party (PDC) joined with two socialist parties to form the Concertación coalition in support of the 1989 plebiscite that forced Pinochet from the presidency. The Concertación had incentives to stay together for the subsequent elections. One is success; Concertación candidates won four presidential elections in succession after 1990. Christian Democrats Ricardo Aylwin and Eduardo Frei Jr. were the successful coalition candidates in the first two elections. They were followed by two socialists, Ricardo Lagos in 2000 and Michelle Bachelet in 2006. In January 2010, Sebastian Piñera, candidate of the conservative bloc opposing the Concertación, broke through to win.

Presidents in Chile need party support to move legislation, but they have some leverage. Chilean legislators, unlike most of their counterparts in Latin America, seem oriented toward political careers, not short stays in the Senate or the Chamber of Deputies. Members need to balance pleasing their party (to get on the ballot) with pleasing their constituents because, with some limited exceptions, voters cast a ballot for parties, each of which decides on who will appear on a list of two candidates for each district (or each province for Senate elections). But there is a countervailing influence. Legislators who hope to be reelected also need to deliver benefits at home, and to do this, they must avoid alienating the president, who enjoys very strong control over the budget (Cary 2002).

This system is a legacy of the Pinochet era. The price of ending his dictatorship (1973–1989) was acceptance of his 1981 constitution (see chapter 7), which contained various mechanisms that make it difficult for any profound change in the economic and political model to be put in place. The biggest obstacle has been the Senate. The constitution allowed Pinochet to appoint nine senators, while he himself was a senator for life. Although this advantage would diminish over time until it was finally abolished in 2005, it made the Senate a major obstacle to any attempt to change economic policies or move on issues such as human rights.

Also, it took a three-fifths majority to reform the constitution, and the system of election continued to load the chamber in favor of the conservative parties. In each province or district, two senators or deputies (respectively) were elected simultaneously, with each voter casting only one ballot. One seat went to the party with the most votes; the second went to majority party only if it doubled the total obtained by the party finishing second. In the December 2006 elections, the Concertación won 52 percent of the Senate vote nationally, with 40 percent for the right-wing coalition (the rest going to smaller parties), but it controlled only 20 of 38 seats, far short of what it would need to change organic laws.

The massive 2005–2006 demonstrations, initially led by students demanding educational reforms, allowed President Michelle Bachelet to replace the system for electing the Senate with a fairer, more proportional one. The pressure in the street made possible what had been impossible to do: to overcome the constitutional obstacle posed by requiring a two-thirds majority to change any **organic law**. However, the two-thirds majority still makes it highly difficult to carry out the kinds of changes that Bachelet promised in response to the protests, that is, to attack the acute economic inequality that has angered so many Chileans.

Perhaps there is no better example of how institutions can limit as well as enhance democracy. Many Chileans thought that Pinochet's departure would bring the military to account for killings, torture, or disappearances under the dictatorship. Many thought that the neoliberal economic model, which had been criticized by many Concertación public figures in the Pinochet years, would be modified to narrow the gap between rich and poor. Once in control of the executive, the Concertación did increase social spending in some areas, and toward the end of the 1990s it finally pressed human rights investigations and indictments for some crimes committed under Pinochet. However, the new government largely honored its commitment—arguably made under duress—to accept the 1981 constitution, which severely limited its ability to change basic laws or prosecute perpetrators of gross human rights violations. Defenders of the limits on majority rule point to the relative degree of macroeconomic success enjoyed by Chile under this system, which they attribute at least in part to the political stability the constitution seemed to have brought. In 2009, in her first term, President Bachelet managed to pass a new law that automatically registers all citizens, making them eligible to vote. However, part of the compromise needed to gain enough votes from the opposition was elimination of the law establishing compulsory voting.

It is difficult to assess the degree to which Concertación leaders used the constitution to avoid making significant changes in an economic model they fiercely criticized in the Pinochet era. Were the institutions driving the policy, or was a conservative impulse not to disturb the economic model the motive for a less aggressive attempt to make the institutions more democratic?

PHOTO 13.1   Supporters listening to Michelle Bachelet give a speech on election night after winning a new term. She promised to narrow the gap between rich and poor, but she could not get economic reforms through the congress. Are Latin Americans expecting too much from their presidents?

Source: Marcelo Benitez/latincontent/Getty Images.

As elections approached in 2014, the Concertación decided to expand the left-center coalition to take in the Chilean Communist Party, which had gained in prestige for its support of the protests against inequality. Neither the new coalition, New Majority, on the left nor the Alliance coalition on the right generated enthusiasm from voters. Bachelet (eligible again) ultimately secured the nomination to launch a bid for a new presidential term, promising to seek an overhaul of the system by calling a constituent assembly to rewrite the constitution. She won the presidential election in a runoff, but legislative elections did not provide a large enough majority to call an assembly without some votes from the right. By 2019, with Piñera back in the Moneda, the presidential palace, the mass protests reappeared and were brutally repressed. However, they did have the effect of forcing Piñera to concede to a constituent assembly to rewrite the constitution. That has not settled the unrest; many demonstrators fear that the rules for electing the assembly favor the existing political parties, which they see as hopelessly compromised with the economic elite.

Brazil: Dysfunctional Federalism

Brazil's highly fractured party system, long ridden by clientelism and corruption, raises a question: To what extent is corruption a product of bad people versus bad institutions? The election of Lula in 2003 was greeted as a landmark event. He was one of the 13 children born to Euridice Ferreira de Mello, whose husband left home to work on the docks, carrying coffee sacks onto freighters in the port of Santos. Lula went to work at the age of 12 years and eventually found a good job in São Paulo's metallurgical industry, where he became a union leader. In 1980, he cofounded the Workers' Party (PT) and led it through the strikes and protests that sent the military back to the barracks. Workers with dark skin had little prospects of political success before the PT emerged, but on his fourth try, in November 2002, Lula won the Brazilian presidency with 61 percent of the vote in the runoff.

Lula's own background, the way that the PT had emerged as the bottom-up movement of social movements, and the general swing to the left in Latin American politics around this time suggested that Brazil would become a political and economic laboratory for confronting poverty. Lula did implement an anti-hunger program and a plan (the *Bolsa Familiar*) that considerably improved conditions for the poor. By tying aid to school attendance, he not only had success in reducing hunger but also substantially increased school attendance. It should be noted, however, that Fernando Henrique Cardoso, his predecessor, had initiated the policy.

In international affairs, Lula challenged the United States on several issues, but his economic policies did not radically depart from those of Cardoso. In fact, one of the first laws passed during his term was a social security reform that reduced pension rights. Land reform fell well behind promised goals, prompting the Landless Workers' Movement (MST; see chapter 11) to begin seizing properties it deemed eligible for redistribution, resulting in violent confrontations with local authorities and landowners. To gain the confidence of international banks, but much to the dismay of his supporters, Lula appointed a member of the conservative opposition to be president of the Central Bank. He appointed a member of the PT as finance minister, but one who as mayor had privatized a municipal phone company. The "worker president" began to hear criticism from the ranks of the PT; in response, he expelled the party's left wing, which formed a new party, the Party of Socialism and Liberty.

Despite these policies, not all conservatives were mollified. Some remained eager to corral the president, even to topple him, if necessary. In 2005, they were presented with an opportunity when several serious scandals erupted. Two major corruption scandals involving payoffs to the construction and insurance industries were the first blows, but the hardest came in the form of charges in Congress that the votes of opposition deputies were being bought with payoffs of US$12,000 per month—the *mensalão*. Most seriously, Lula's chief of staff, Minister José Dirceu, was among those indicted for corruption. The scandals severely reduced the president's influence in Congress and left him vulnerable to losing his reelection campaign in 2006.

Lula faced a choice in 2006. One option was to turn left and attempt to mobilize Brazil's poor with a more vigorous popular program, but this would jeopardize the stability of the capitalist economy. The other was to govern within the parameters set by Washington and Brazilian capitalists in the hope that Brazilians would prefer a president symbolically from the ranks of the workers, if he had to abandon making substantial changes to the economic model. The second strategy proved successful. Lula lost the election in the heartland of the PT, the industrial states of the south, but he picked up votes from the middle class and from voters in the impoverished northeast to prevail. His second term did not produce major advances on promises made in 2002, but Lula was more assertive in his diplomacy, challenging Washington on Honduras, Cuba, Iran, economic integration, and a host of other issues.

Legislative elections had already occurred in October, one month before the final presidential runoff in 2003, so Lula's initial victory did little to help his party in Congress. As Lula entered office, the PT held only 14 seats in the 81-seat Senate. Only one-third of the Senate was to be replaced in October 2006, so the party had little prospect of increasing its representation. In the Chamber of Deputies, the PT held only 81 of 513 seats. The entire chamber was scheduled to be renewed in the presidential election year of 2006, but Lula was now damaged goods, mired in scandal, his party divided and demoralized. The party suffered a stinging defeat, falling to just 11 seats in the Senate and gaining only two seats in the lower chamber. Lula would have to build coalitions, as in his first term, to govern.

Brazil's Congress is highly fragmented. No fewer than 11 parties had 12 or more seats in the lower chamber after the 2002 elections. Brazilian politicians are notorious for changing party identifications, especially if they can enhance career prospects near the end of their terms (few run for reelection). Brazil's voters choose elected representatives by the proportional method that ordinarily strengthens party leaders. However, until the advent of the PT, none of Brazil's parties had deployed an effective organized presence throughout all regions of the country. Parties have tended to form in states and regions around powerful personalities, the *coroneles*. Remember, Brazil is a huge country, a landmass corresponding to the entire Portuguese empire in America, which did not break up after independence. Much power remains on the local and state levels. In the age of populist president Getúlio Vargas (see chapter 7), two large national parties formed around his leadership, but these political organizations were often fractured into suborganizations supporting local leaders. Not unlike the United States, a large landmass and strong tradition of federalism have combined to dampen the coherence of national parties—something the PT itself has experienced.

The PT, like other left parties, found it hard to shift from being the opposition to becoming the party of government. The party rose to power in part as a result of public disgust with clientelism and corruption, and it had organically grown out of social movements. Here again the structures and institutions have to be considered, not just the personal morality of Lula and other PT leaders. Just like his predecessors, Lula found himself offering cabinet positions, policy concessions, and patronage to members of other parties to pass laws. The resources at his disposal were considerable—as many as 20,000 government jobs. Leaders linked to social movements became politicians, and experience in government changed the perspective of many. The party has become divided between grassroots members who remain linked to social movements and see the PT as a political tool to make profound social change and more pragmatic members who seek to broaden the party's support in the interest of keeping government power.

Brazil's social movements found themselves in a dilemma. In a "Letter to the Brazilian People" (circulated by e-mail on June 23, 2005), the Coordinator of Social Movements (CMS), which unites the largest popular organizations in the country, attributed the **mensalão** scandal to elites who "with the 2006 election in mind initiated a campaign to demoralize the government and President Lula, seeking to weaken him, to overthrow him, or to oblige him to deepen current economic policy and neoliberal reforms, obedient to the interests of international capital." The CMS called for full investigation of corruption accusations and charged that President Cardoso had employed the same tactics to privatize state enterprises and secure a constitutional amendment allowing his reelection.

The CMS also asked Lula to change economic course, "to prioritize the needs of the people and construct a new model of development," but it also called for political reforms—an indication that the social movements recognized that institutions, not just international economic pressures and personal failings, were behind the president's problems. Specifically, the CMS called for rules limiting the ability of elected officials to change parties, instituting public financing of campaigns and outlawing of private contributions, eliminating minimum percentages needed for small parties to achieve representation (which might increase fragmentation but enhance the influence of social movements), and opening heretofore-closed candidate lists ("closed" in the sense that voters choose parties but do not choose among candidates on a party's list). The CMS demanded that half of the slots on the ballot be reserved for women and ethnic groups (Indigenous and Afro-descendent). The CMS also called for creation of referendums and plebiscites. Some of these measures were achieved in 2007, but they did not seriously alter the "normal" mode of doing politics in Brazil.

Lula's chosen successor, Dilma Rousseff, won the election to succeed him in 2010, and with Brazil doing relatively well despite the global economic crisis, Rousseff won reelection in 2014. But Rousseff too had her popularity dented by revelations of corruption during the Lula years. Lula himself had to face judicial investigation for corruption in 2013, though he was not indicted. The PT ran strongly in the 2012 local elections, but Rousseff and PT leaders seemed just as happy that some of its larger rival parties ran well. Having fewer smaller parties would make the task of forming legislative coalitions easier. This seemed to signal that the PT had fully evolved from a movement party to a party of the status quo.

Rousseff and most of the Brazilian political class hoped that 2014 and 2016 would be years through which they would trumpet to the world the country's economic success and social modernization, with the country set to host soccer's World Cup in 2014 and the Summer Olympic Games in 2016. But 2014 began with protests against extravagant spending on stadiums and infrastructure, wholesale militarization of *favelas* in the name of security for tourists, and scandals arising from shoddy workmanship and graft from lucrative construction projects. Rousseff responded to protests with new populist programs, including one that pays Cuba to deploy 13,000 doctors to work in the poor *favelas*. But these measures bought the government little respite from internal protests and scandals.

The *mensalão* scandal (see chapter 12) wounded the PT; ***Lava Jato*** was devastating. Even though it touched the entire political spectrum, the main focus was on Lula. *Lava Jato* was a carwash that was used to launder funds embezzled from Petrobras, the giant state oil company. It opened the door to broader scandal that involved not only Petrobras but Obredecht, a huge Brazilian construction company. The full extent is still not known, but Obredecht used funds to bribe officials in at least 11 other Latin American countries. As much as $43 billion may have been involved. The reach of the scandal inside and outside suggested that corruption was deeply institutionalized. That is, corruption is not an aberration but a normal, accepted way of doing business. As mentioned earlier, irregularities in the prosecution of Lula exposed how the right effectively "weaponized corruption," singling out the PT official. That the impeachment of President Dilma Rousseff could succeed, even though her alleged crime was a minor and routine shuffling of the budget without congressional authorization, can be understood in this context.

For Review

Why do institutions sometimes make political reform difficult? What are some of the ways they do this? Why did two-party competition in Venezuela not lead sooner to political reform in the Punto Fijo era? How did the Pinochet constitution of 1982 obstruct economic and political reforms in Chile? Why did the PT find itself limited by Brazil's political institutions?

Institutions and Democratic Innovation

Samuel Huntington's (1968) influential *Political Order in Changing Societies* viewed institutions as necessary to channel participation, to control it. However, rather than viewing institutions and participation as separate spheres of politics, we can also think of institutions as guaranteeing and encouraging participation, often in innovative ways. Latin America has become an interesting laboratory in recent years for attempts to institutionalize not just representative but also participatory democracy.

In some large Brazilian cities, citizens gather in local assemblies to set priorities for spending large portions of the municipal budget, a process called "participatory budgeting." Indigenous traditions of collective decision-making (e.g., over use of land and water) remain strong in many areas populated by Indigenous peoples. In Nicaragua, the Sandinista government, between 1979 and 1984, experimented with incorporating representatives of mass organizations directly into the main legislative body, the Council of State. All these experiences differ from the traditional way that representative democracy works in the United States, where citizen participation in and knowledge of local and state government is notoriously low. (Quick, can you name three members of your city council?)

Cuba's government engages citizens in participatory decisions over many activities (police services, education, maintenance of streets, etc.) that immediately touch people's lives. A system of councils (*Poder Popular*, or "People's Power") at the neighborhood, municipal, provincial, and national levels requires representatives to periodically "render accounts" to assemblies of voters at the local level. This system probably helped the regime survive the devastating impact of the collapse of its main economic trade partners in Eastern Europe between 1989 and 1991. For example, in December 1993 the Ministry of Finance put forth a proposal greatly reducing subsidies and increasing prices of many state-provided goods and services. Instead of passing the measure, the assembly sent the proposal for discussion to more than 80,000 local meetings, attended by more than three million workers. Some austerity measures were eventually accepted, but others rejected, whereas taxes were increased on rum and cigarettes to help make up the shortfall. Instead of a tax on wages, a general income tax was implemented (Saney 2004: 51–54).

Venezuela's Bolivarian constitution embodies several bold initiatives in an attempt to institutionalize participatory democracy, to make the people "protagonists" in policy-making. Probably no country has gone so far to make possible the recall of elected officials. In 2004, the opposition successfully gathered enough signatures to force a recall election of President Chávez. They lost, but at least for another ten years, the recall put to rest the question of whether Chávez was legitimate. But Venezuelans remain deeply divided over an institution initiated by Chávez, whereby authority over spending the country's petrodollar earnings has moved from local and state governments to grassroots organizations called "communal councils," and plans exist to eventually give even more authority of spending to these new organizations. Since 2007, the government has encouraged the formation of thousands of communal councils, composed of 200 to 400 families in urban areas, smaller elsewhere. They are supposed to set priorities for local projects financed by the national government and state oil company. Residents are supposed to participate in carrying out these projects, not just decide what government will do. Chávez planned to draw the local councils together into larger geographic networks called communes.

Chávez's successor, Maduro, called a constituent assembly in 2017, charged with the task of rewriting the constitution to create communal democracy. In contrast to 1999, when Chávez put the calling of an assembly to rewrite the 1971 constitution to a national vote, Maduro used a highly questionable interpretation of the constitution to call the new assembly and to set the rules of electing it. As of early 2020, there had been little progress on that project; instead, the constituent assembly took on for itself the legislative authority of the opposition-controlled National Assembly. In another twist, in early 2020, Maduro negotiated a deal with a faction of the opposition to regain control over the assembly.

With Venezuela mired in political and economic crisis, the likelihood of reviving the Bolivarian goal of establishing participatory democracy and decentralized administration of the oil wealth in communes and communal councils seems remote. Could it have worked? Or were the petrodollars flowing through Venezuela during the oil boom of 2002 to 2014 likely to have undermined participatory democracy in any case? Perhaps the direct financing by the state and oil company inevitably created a new network of centrally controlled clientelism. That conclusion is not necessarily the last word. Researchers (e.g., McCarthy 2012) have found it almost impossible to generalize about how successfully the communal councils operated in the Chávez years. In some cases, communal councils displaced older organizations with a history of effectively expressing community demands. In many cases, they have served to empower local leaders, especially women. As mentioned previously, after the death of Chávez, political polarization around the future of the country's institutions and control over the oil revenues intensified, leaving the future of Bolivarianism more in doubt than it has been since the short-lived coup against Chávez in 2002.

Peter Roman (2003), who studied Cuba's electoral and representative system for more than 12 years (1986–1998, mostly on the municipal level), provides extensive empirical evidence that elections, at least in that era, were very participatory, characterized by lively debates among ordinary citizens in local assemblies. Roman claims that Cuban representatives act more like "instructed delegates," faithful to their constituents, and less like trustees expected to vote their own sense of what is best for the country. Delegates are required to keep office hours and respond to constituent complaints, and the local councils have considerable discretion over the budget.

However, Roman admits that the system is still much too top-down. Haroldo Dilla Alfonso (2006), a Cuban social scientist who lost his position in 1995 at the prestigious Center for the Study of the Americas in Havana and was expelled from the PCC in 1999, thinks the Cuban system needs to be more open and to have government operate more autonomously. However, Dilla acknowledges that the participatory institutions of Cuba keep leaders more in touch with the country's people and helped the regime survive the extraordinary hardships that came with the collapse of communism in Eastern Europe. The system produced some important reforms, including expansion of religious tolerance, administrative decentralization, and direct election of the national and provincial assemblies. However, there are signs that Cubans, especially the younger generation, are less politically engaged today.

Social movements throughout the region, and especially in Ecuador and Bolivia, are pressing an agenda to require greater direct popular input into the legislative process, including the right to initiate legislation by petition (another provision of the new Venezuelan constitution). They have also called for laws that require the media, which is dominated everywhere by large corporations and wealthy owners, to be more socially responsible. Some of these measures, such as plebiscites, recall elections, initiatives, and referendums, have worked in other areas of the world, including some states in the United States. Others are controversial. For example, can social responsibility laws for media be enforced without state censorship? How would the boards responsible for oversight be formed? As for the right to be consulted or represented directly in making or enforcing laws, how are authorities to verify which organizations most represent relevant sectors of the population? Who decides, for example, which human rights organizations authentically represent groups of citizens and which are merely fronts for wealthy or politically powerful interests, or for the state itself?

Leonardo Avritzer (2002) has argued that Latin American democracies should be credited with creating more open, egalitarian public spaces than typically found in liberal democracies. He thinks that participatory experiments are extending democracy beyond the formal institutions (elections, party systems, etc.) and engaging more citizens in new ways politically. To be successful, he argues, Latin American governments need to cultivate capacity for **deliberative democracy**, which should include greater civil involvement in organizing and protecting the integrity of elections, better civic education, and more widespread and effective use of new information technology. Avritzer sees these new democratic institutions as an extension of the struggles to restore democracy at the end of military rule, but others (see Cameron et al. 2012) would add that these demands are linked to a more general crisis of representation. Social movements not only want better-quality government under polyarchy; they also want better-quality democracy that goes beyond the limits of polyarchy.

PUNTO DE VISTA: DID THE HONDURAN MILITARY EXECUTE A COUP OR DEFEND THE COUNTRY'S CONSTITUTION IN 2009?

The most contentious case of the removal of an elected president from office occurred in Honduras in June 2009 when the Honduran military ousted President Manuel Zelaya from office and spirited him out of the country. The Honduran case raises an interesting issue: Can a constitution's restrictions on the ability of presidents to amend the rules of the game go too far?

The Honduran elites and the military who removed Zelaya from office alleged that his attempt to hold a nonbinding referendum on allowing presidential reelection violated a constitutional provision that not only limited presidents to one term but also made it unconstitutional to amend the constitution for this purpose! The strange rule was written in 1982, when the country was still ruled by a military junta and while Honduras was the main base for U.S. training and support for counterinsurgency in El Salvador and Guatemala and for the *contras* in Nicaragua. (Honduras borders on all three countries.) In this classic "banana republic," the fruit represented two-thirds of the country's exports, and foreign companies owned over one million acres of the small republic's best land. By the 1950s, though, peasant movements and cooperatives began to fight back, and as in neighboring countries, some labor-intensive manufacturing and a modest middle class began to complicate politics—but not enough to break the stranglehold of the Liberal Party and the slightly more conservative National Party over the country's civilian politics. The military was key to keeping the emerging political tensions in check.

Honduran elites, encouraged by Washington to stabilize politics in the geopolitically strategic country, sought to break a pattern of coups and irregular changes in government. In January 1982, the legislature proclaimed a new constitution that included a provision to prevent presidents from trying to extend their terms in office. Article 373 explicitly rules out the possibility of amending the document to change the presidential term or permit reelection of the president. However, the constitution also explicitly states in Article 2, "The sovereignty of the People may also [be] exercised directly, through the plebiscite and the Referendum." Zelaya saw in this clause a way to get around Article 373.

Zelaya, who took office in January 2006, was viewed as just another liberal oligarch, but he unexpectedly turned toward the left after his election, angering traditional elites and much of the middle class, but striking a responsive chord with poor Hondurans, whose living conditions had deteriorated. Figure 13.4 shows that approximately three of every five Hondurans live in poverty, two of four in extreme poverty. Figures 13.2 and 13.3 demonstrate that inequality and poverty were growing worse leading up to Zelaya's presidency, but some modest gains in addressing these trends were made in his shortened term. His programs included a free education program for children, an 80 percent increase in the minimum wage, subsidies for small farmers, extension of social security coverage to domestic employees (mostly women), free electricity, and other aid for the poorest Hondurans.

Probably what was most alarming to the military and Honduran elites was Zelaya's intention to have Honduras join the Bolivarian Alliance for the Americas (ALBA), Hugo Chávez's brainchild for economic integration, developed explicitly as an alternative to the neoliberal Central American Free Trade Association (CAFTA), to which Honduras belonged. The switch was especially alarming to the newer Honduran business class whose manufacturing profits are based largely on

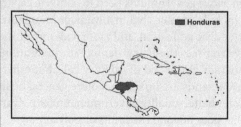

FIGURE 13.2 Honduras: Gini Coefficient

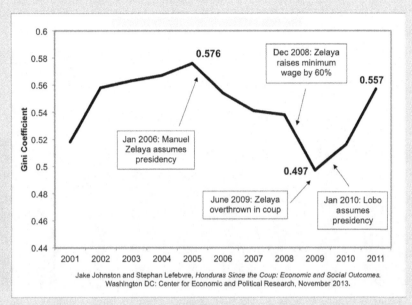

Jake Johnston and Stephan Lefebvre, *Honduras Since the Coup: Economic and Social Outcomes.*
Washington DC: Center for Economic and Political Research, November 2013.

Source: Reprinted with permission of the Center for Economic and Political Research (CEPR).

FIGURE 13.3 Honduras's Average Annual per Capita Income Growth, by Decile

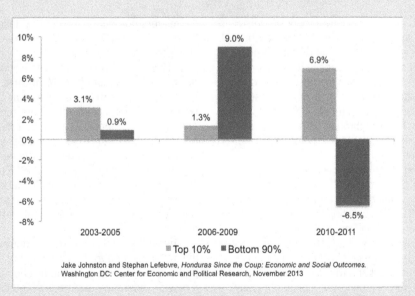

Jake Johnston and Stephan Lefebvre, *Honduras Since the Coup: Economic and Social Outcomes.*
Washington DC: Center for Economic and Political Research, November 2013

Source: Reprinted with permission of the Center for Economic and Political Research (CEPR).

FIGURE 13.4   Honduras: Poverty and Extreme Poverty Rates

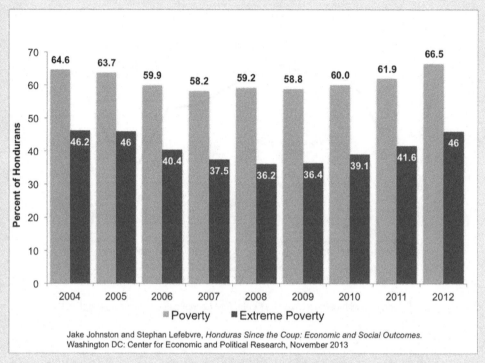

Jake Johnston and Stephan Lefebvre, *Honduras Since the Coup: Economic and Social Outcomes.*
Washington DC: Center for Economic and Political Research, November 2013

Source: Reprinted with permission of the Center for Economic and Political Research (CEPR).

exports of labor-intensive products (electronic goods, clothing, etc.) to the North American market, and the military wanted no part of anything connected with Hugo Chávez. The military's top legal affairs officer made this clear when he told the Salvadoran newspaper *El Faro* (July 2, 2009) that if Chávez followed through on his plans to visit Honduras, he should fear being assassinated by sniper.

The political crisis became acute when Zelaya decided to hold an advisory referendum on amending the constitution to permit reelection. The balloting would have taken place on Election Day, and Zelaya would not have been a candidate, in accord with existing prohibition on reelection. The country's Supreme Court and the Congress both ruled the referendum unconstitutional, but Zelaya ordered the military to deliver the ballots for

the referendum around the country. Instead, the military seized Zelaya and flew him out of the country, to Costa Rica.

Zelaya was allowed to return to Honduras, but not to run for office. Meanwhile, the country has earned a reputation as the poorest and most violent in the hemisphere. The mass movement stimulated by Zelaya's reforms has grown, less so around Zelaya's political ambitions (though the movement supports him and his new party, LIBRE) than around demands for the country to address the issues that he addressed—whether motivated by a sense of justice, political ambition, or both.

The United States initially condemned the action as a coup, but Washington broke ranks in endorsing the election of a new president in November 2009. Latin American countries eventually decided

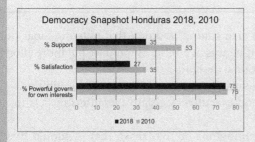

Democracy Snapshot Honduras 2018, 2010

to accept the *fait accompli*. In December 2013, the nominees of the two traditional parties qualified for the January runoff, won by the liberal, Juan Orlando Hernández. LIBRE protested fraud and questioned the viability of elections contested in the context of a highly repressive environment. (See Human Rights Watch, www.hrw.org/americas/honduras.)

Point/Counterpoint

Was there a coup in Honduras?

If you say yes, how do you answer the claim that Zelaya was seeking to change a part of the constitution that is not subject to amendment? Whatever his motives for introducing social and economic reforms, why could he not have simply organized a party to promote a new pro-reform candidate?

If you say no, how do you answer the claim that the referendum was clearly advisory and that it should have been permitted under Article 2? In any event, were not the real motives for the action actually rooted in Zelaya's policies, not legalities?

For More Information

You can find an English translation of the Honduran constitution of 1982 and subsequent amendments at www.constituteproject.org/constitution/Honduras_2013.pdf?lang=en/. For good background on Honduras's history up to the 1980s, see Tom Barry and Deb Preusch, *The Central America Fact Book* (New York: Grove Press: 1986). WikiLeaks documents give many details about the removal of Zelaya and include cables showing that the U.S. embassy regarded the action as a coup. See www.wikileaks.org/plusd/cables/09TEGUCIGALPA645_a.html. The graphs in this section are adapted from articles from the Washington-based Center for Economic and Political Research (CEPR), which has several follow-up articles on Honduras since the "coup" at www.cepr.net.

◼ Institutions Matter

In the end, even the best-designed institutions cannot save a system characterized by deep social and political polarization around basic issues. Those with power and privilege in a society will not give them up just because a majority has demanded change through democratic institutions. The failed Chilean road to socialism of 1973 was but one demonstration of this political fact. However, institutions matter because they establish the rules of the political game, which need to be in place for people to accept the legitimacy of decisions made by the government. Political institutions, many of which are established in constitutions, are the sites where important social conflicts are played out. Even revolutions eventually require institutions to consolidate change.

In contrast to political scientists who think Latin America needs stronger institutions to tame participation, Latin American social movements are asking for participatory democracies. They will need institutions to make them work. They also need laws that provide real protection from violence and arbitrary treatment, whether the protection originates from the state or from private sources. We turn to those laws in the next chapter.

Discussion Questions

1. Most of this book is consistent with the area studies tradition that puts the focus on historical, socioeconomic, and cultural influences in politics. Should we put more effort into examining institutions and constitutional design?
2. To what extent can and should political scientists be involved in designing constitutions—for example, systems of representation and executive–legislative relationships? Is that our job?
3. Is your view of institutions closer to Huntington's or Avritzer's? That is, should they channel participation, or should they become more participatory themselves? Why?

Resources for Further Study

Reading: A good example of the institutionalist approach, enriched by its drawing upon social and economic factors, is Joe Foweraker, Tod Landman, and Neil Harvey, *Governing Latin America* (Cambridge, UK: Polity Press, 2003). Leonardo Avritzer, *Democracy and the Public Space in Latin America* (Princeton, NJ: Princeton University Press, 2002), examines participatory democracy experiments approvingly. Gianpaolo Baiocchi, *Radicals in Power: The Workers' Party (PT) and Experiments in Urban Democracy*, looks at how attaining power affects parties linked to social movements. Álvaro Vargas Llosa examines 500 years of oppression and sees reforming institutions and their underlying culture as the only way to reverse this history in *Liberty for Latin America* (New York: Farrar, Straus & Giroux, 2005). Gabriel L. Negretto, "Replacing and Amending Constitutions: The Logic of Constitutional Change in Latin America," *Law & Society Review* 46, no. 4 (December 2012), reviews recent changes in Latin American constitutions and the causes.

Video and Film: *Beyond Elections* (2009) looks at participatory budgeting and other experiments in deliberative democracy. It can also be found on YouTube. *¿Puedo Hablar?* (2007) documents the Venezuelan electoral campaign and election of 2006, won by Hugo Chávez. *Lula's Brazil* examines the first two years of the presidency of Luiz Inácio da Silva, examining Lula's personal life and critically evaluating his political decisions.

On the Internet: As just mentioned, the documentary *Beyond Elections* can be found on YouTube with a search. LANIC at the University of Texas has a page devoted to government affairs (http://lanic.utexas.edu/subject/government). The World Bank's views on good governance can be found at the "governance and anticorruption" section of www.worldbank.org. The website of the International Institute for Democracy and Electoral Assistance (IDEA, at www.idea.int/index.cfm) provides a wealth of information on voting and election procedures from around the world.

14 Human Rights, Corruption, and the Rule of Law

Focus Questions

▶ How do human rights conditions vary in the region?

▶ How have problems with crime and corruption impacted the quality of and confidence in democracy in the region?

▶ How well do judicial systems and criminal justice systems function in Latin America?

▶ What is "lawfare" and how does it undermine rule of law and human rights enforcement?

IT COULD BE argued that democracy—majority rule through elections—is possible without the rule of law. We have plenty of examples of governments that qualify as democracies but are characterized by rampant corruption. Still, the quality of democracy would certainly seem to depend on whether citizens are protected from arbitrary authority and can hold officials accountable for their actions—and whether they think their fellow citizens obey the law. As Figure 14.1 indicates, in 2011, the most recent year that Latinobarómetro asked that question, not even one in three Latin Americans were confident that this was the case—and this was at a time when overall support and confidence in democracy was higher than it is today.

Certainly, it is hard to believe that democracy can be stable and effective as long as crime, human rights violations, and corruption go unpunished. If citizens sense that some people—wealthier, politically connected, beyond the control of police—are not subject to law ("impunity"), whereas others seem particularly vulnerable to repression and violence by the very authorities charged with protecting them, what faith would they have in democracy as a system of government?

"Rule of Law?" and Democracy

"**Rule of law**" refers to two interrelated but somewhat distinct ideas: the idea that all citizens should be treated the same under the law and the idea that they can rely on the state to guarantee justice and security for persons and property, especially personal property. The implications for democracy go beyond fairness and equal treatment. Personal security—that is, freedom from violence or fear of violence—is vital to democracy. On the most basic level,

FIGURE 14.1   Citizens Obey the Law

TOTAL LATIN AMERICA 1996 – 2011 - TOTALS BY COUNTRY 2011

Q. Would you say that (nationality) obey the law? Here only 'A lot' and 'Some'.

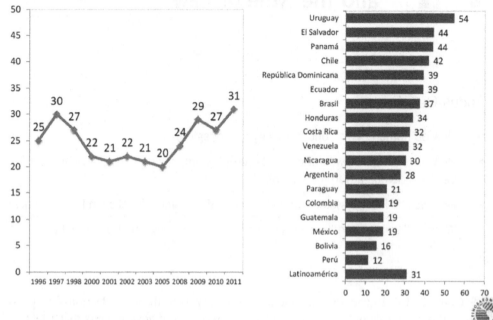

Source: Latinobarómetro 1996–2011.

citizens cannot vote on Election Day or go to a neighborhood meeting if leaving the house puts them at risk of rape, robbery, or murder. Fear of violent crime also makes people more inclined to accept repression and grant arbitrary powers to the state.

The rule of law can be broken into several components.

- *Concern with human rights and impunity.* "Impunity" exists when security forces violate human rights through torture, disappearances, extrajudicial executions, and so on without fear of sanction. Effective courts and a humane criminal justice system are also crucial to what is called the rule of law.
- *Concern about violent crime.* Although there are widespread concerns about police abuses, citizens consider personal security a basic right as well. Violent crime has become a major issue in the region, undermining satisfaction with democracy.
- *Concerns about corruption.* The growing perception of widespread corruption is another factor raising the belief that elites benefit from impunity, eroding public confidence in the fairness of institutions and independence of the judiciary, adding to the sense that elites govern in their own interest.
- *Concerns about respect for constitutional processes* (a major focus of chapter 13). Efforts by presidents to extend their terms in office and doubts about electoral integrity contribute to doubts about the efficacy, if not the actual existence, of democracy.

- *Concerns about international treaties* (a focus in chapter 15). Environmental accords, human rights treaties, and "free trade" agreements all raise issues about sovereignty and, whether desirable or not, are often perceived to weaken the authority of local courts and administrative bodies, placing final judgments about disputes in international tribunals. We will leave this concern to the next chapter, where we look at the impact of globalization on Latin America.

A United Nations–sponsored study of anticorruption (UNDP 2012) sees the incapacity of Latin American democracies to improve the quality of **governance** (see chapter 13) as a major cause of their vulnerability to corruption. This is another way that institutions matter in Latin America. But the study also finds that the growing inequality in wealth and income is another factor inhibiting anticorruption efforts. In fact, the Latinobarómetro survey in 2013 (last year asked) found that the rich are the group Latin Americans most often identify as most likely to break the law—though they are followed closely by politicians (see Figure 14.2).

Wealthy citizens are more capable of insisting on lawful treatment and respect for rights than are the poor. One important example of this inequality in Latin America is visible in the area of land reform. Land reform laws, even in revolutionary situations, such as once

FIGURE 14.2 Rich Seen as Most Likely to Break Laws

TOTAL LATIN AMERICA 2011 - TOTALS BY COUNTRIES 2011

*Q. Which of the following groups do you think complies less the law? *Multiple choice question, totals are higher than 100% **Here only answers with more than 3%*

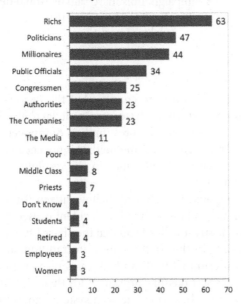
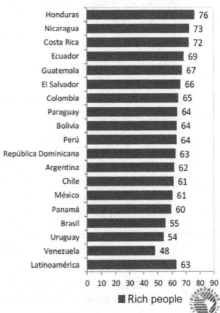

Source: Latinobarómetro 2011.

prevailed in Chile (1970–1973) and Nicaragua (1979–1990), usually have provisions defining the size and type of holdings that can be redistributed. Whether a parcel of land can be expropriated depends by law on the size of the parcel, whether the land is cultivated or idle, what kinds of improvements (irrigation, fertilization, etc.) have been made, and so on. Peasants with little income or formal education, and lacking experience in dealing with courts or a bureaucracy, have to organize and petition in a formal way to press a claim against landowners. Landowners use every procedural method available to drag out the process in the bureaucracy and courts (see Kaufman 1972 on the Chilean case), using their political connections to influence an often corrupt judicial system. Frustrated peasants invade estates to speed up the process. This in turn brings about cries of abuse from landowners and arouses sympathy from other sectors (e.g., the middle class) that fear radical change. Judges and civil servants (bureaucrats) are often holdovers from past governments and do not share enthusiasm for reform.

Sometimes, national and international groups (environmentalists, unions, and human rights groups) help the poor and less powerful to be heard, but more often peasants, workers, and the urban poor feel abandoned by the state, which is often incapable of delivering basic security and protecting them from hired thugs or gunmen. Such is the case in northeast Brazil, where members of the MST (Landless Workers' Movement), inspired by **liberation theology** (see Miller 2003), began seizing land and defending themselves from the small private armies created by ranchers (see chapter 11). The movement claims that around 1,600 peasants had been killed in conflicts, mostly by landowners and state and local security forces, by the mid-2000s (CIP 2006). On April 17, 1996, 19 MST members were killed and 69 wounded by military police in the Eldorado de Carajá massacre in the Amazonas state of Pará. More than 150 police were brought to trial, but only two were ever convicted and sentenced, and in 2001 it remained unclear whether they were ever jailed (Issa 2007: 124–125). Since Brazilian President Jair Bolsonaro took office, violence has ramped up again. In his 2018 campaign, Bolsonaro said he would designate the MST as a terrorist organization (*The Guardian*, London, October 22, 2018).

▌ Crime and Justice

Legal procedures differ in Latin America from country to country, but the region's judiciaries tend to reflect the French legal tradition, which are based on "code law," also known as "Napoleonic law." The Anglo legal tradition includes the presumption of innocence until proven guilty, whereas most Latin American systems presume neither innocence nor guilt. As in continental Europe, precedent has much less importance in the resolution of legal issues than in the United States or Great Britain.

In civil cases, the idea of seeking compensation against a fellow citizen through litigation is unusual in the region. Latin Americans injured in a bus accident caused by faulty brakes or from falling into a gaping hole in the street will tell you that they have little recourse. Trial procedures differ from those of the U.S. In the Anglo-American tradition, an adversarial process decides guilt or innocence in criminal trials and allocates responsibility and damages in civil suits. All involved make the best possible argument for their side, trusting that the truth will emerge from the competition. In Latin American systems, an indictment often means that the accused loses certain rights, and prosecutors are supposed to seek out the truth and not simply pursue conviction.

There is, however, a route for Latin Americans to demand their rights in the legal system. In much of Latin America, this means seeking an *amparo*, a court decision stating that a citizen is "covered" or "protected" by some constitutional right from a government action or from failure of government to act—for example, to rectify unlawful a dismissal from a job, prosecution for an alleged crime, relocation to make room for a highway or economic project, or a prohibition to publish or speak.

If the Latin American and Anglo systems of law differ, one similarity is the difficulty in ensuring that citizens of different economic means have equal access and treatment under the law. Although long incarceration before trial is common in North America, the problem is magnified in Latin America (see Table 14.1). In many countries, more than half of the prison population consists of inmates who have yet to be convicted or sentenced. Panama, Guatemala, Venezuela, Argentina, Bolivia, Uruguay, Peru, Honduras, and the Dominican

TABLE 14.1 Prison Population and Trends, Highest to Lowest Rate of Incarceration

	Year, Total Prison Population	Rate per 100,000	Trend in Rate	Prisoners, in Remand or pretrial	% in Remand or Pretrial, Trend
U.S.A.	2016 2,121,600	655	Down from 683 in 2000	21.1% (2014)	24.6% (2000)
El Salvador	2018 37,714	604	Up from 132 in 2000	32.0% (2016)	54.3% (2001)
Cuba	2012 57,337	510	Up from 487* in 1999	Not available	Not available
Panama	2018 16,183	390	Up from 283 in 2000	62.6% (2014)	63.2% (2000)
Puerto Rico	2017 10,475	313	Down from 383 in 2000	15.3% (2014)	17.0% (2011)
Brazil	2018 690,722	335	Up from 132 in 2000	36.3% (2014)	43.7% (2000)
Uruguay	2017 11,078	291	Up from 135 in 2000	69.4% (2015)	77.2% (1999)
Colombia	2018 118,708	249	Up from 128 in 2000	32.0% (2016)	39.4% (2000)
Chile	2018 42,683	240	Up from 215 in 2000	33.7% (2016)	48.5% (2000)
Peru	2018 87,995	239	Up from 107 in 2000	47.8% (2016)	57.3% (2001)
Dominican R	2018 26,286	238	Up from 173 in 2000	60.2% (2016)	82.2% (2000)
Costa Rica	2017 19,226	374	Up from 193 in 2000	17.2% (2014)	24.0% (2002)
Mexico	2018 204,422	205	Up from 156 in 2000	39.6% (2016)	41.2% (2000)
Paraguay	2017 13,607	191	Up from 60 in 2000	62.6% (2015)	92.7% (1999)
Honduras	2017 18,950	216	Similar to 184 in 2000	54.0%* (2016)	88.0% (1999)
Nicaragua	2017 17,196	176	Up from 128 in 2000	12.3% (2012)	30.8% (1999)
Argentina	2016 81,975	186	Up from 105 in 1999	50.9% (2014)	58.9% (2002)
Ecuador	2018 37,497	162	Up from 64 in 2000	48.8% (2014)	70.4% (2001)
Venezuela	2017 57,096	159	Up from 58 in 2000	63.4% (2015)	44.6% (2000)
Guatemala	2018 24,386	141	Up from 62 in 2000	48.6% (2015)	58.7% (2001)
Bolivia	2018 17,946	123	Up from 95 in 2000	69.0% (2016)	66.4% (2000)
Canada	2016 41,145	117	Similar to 115 in 2000	34.9% (2015)	28.0% (2000)
Haiti	2017 10,512	96	Up from 49 in 2000	70.9% (2015)	83.5% (1999)

*Estimates.

Source: World Prison Population List, *World Prison Brief* (12th edition, November 2018).

Republic all fall into this category, a list that includes countries that have some of the best (Uruguay) and the worst (Honduras) overall human rights conditions (data from World Prison Brief 2017, 2018). The overall rate of incarceration (per 100,000 population) in the Americas excluding the United States has more than doubled (121 percent) since 2000. Those with a more than 100 percent increase include El Salvador, Guatemala, Brazil, Ecuador, Paraguay, Peru, Colombia, and Venezuela. However, large jumps occurred also in Costa Rica and Uruguay, countries often seen as bulwarks of liberal democracy.

Conditions in prisons are degrading, and in recent years inmates have undertaken desperate mass escape attempts and revolts. The problem is especially acute in Central America, where crime rates and problems with youth gangs soared in the aftermath of the civil wars of the 1980s and the deepening economic crises, but prison revolts have also happened in Venezuela, Brazil, and elsewhere. This may seem surprising because the rate of incarceration is quite low, but the underlying factor here may be governance. That is, except for Panama and Costa Rica, Central American political instability and the ineffectiveness of government agencies to deliver basic services extends to an inability to provide security. The low rate of incarceration reflects the inability and unwillingness to invest in prisons.

Mark Kruger (2007), director of the criminal justice program at St. Louis University, attributes the very low crime rate in Cuba to the sense of community and mutual responsibility encouraged by Cuban mass organizations that "provide the glue that attaches individual community members to the larger community." Residents of closely knit neighborhoods are the "eyes of the community" and watch for criminal and anti-social behavior. But this same system can, and sometimes does, get used to identify political dissidents and to monitor plans they may have to conduct visible protests. This enables security forces to round up and temporarily detain organizers or to discourage people from joining them. This tactic of detaining and releasing protestors without formal charges or on charges quickly dismissed is something, we should note, common in the United States as well; it was widely used against protests of police killings of black people in 2015–2020 and now almost routinely in cities during major party conventions and political rallies.

Cuba's rate of incarceration is high (see Table 14.1), though considerably lower than in the U.S. By contrast, its rate of violent crime is low (as indicated by the homicide rate in Figure 14.3). To some degree, detentions for political reasons partly account for this, but there are other likely reasons. One is that criminal sentences for what we would call "white collar crime" are especially lengthy in Cuba. Also, many prisoners convicted of "anti-social" crimes, such as prostitution, petty theft, addictions, and abuse of spouses or children, are detained in low security prisons with few armed guards and programs to prepare for reentry to society. Some detained Cubans are "*balseros*," people who are attempting to migrate to Florida by sea on rafts and other less than seaworthy craft.

Getting a full picture of the Cuban prison regime is not easy. The government had opened its low security prisons to foreign delegations, often allowing visits to jails without warning. For example, a delegation led by a prison reform group from New York State returned in 2016 from a trip to examine Cuban prisons with high praise for the system's enlightened approaches to rehabilitation and the social conditions of those incarcerated. Rather than isolate offenders from society, many of those incarcerated are allowed long furloughs from prison life (Bass 2016). So far, Cuba seems to have avoided the kinds of prison conditions that have spurred major riots with loss of life in Brazil, Honduras, Mexico, the United States, and other countries. However, Cuba does not open its prisons to major human rights organizations. Many dissidents imprisoned in high security facilities depict inhuman conditions in high security facilities and complain of beatings and isolation.

Venezuela, Haiti, Mexico, Paraguay, and Brazil all have seen major deaths as a result of fires and rioting in recent years. Brazil has twice as many prisoners as it has holding capacity. In May 2019, at least 55 prisoners were killed in two days of rioting in several jails in the Amazonian region, and in July more than 50 died in the northern city of Altamira. Twenty-one people died in a breakout from a prison in Belem. In early 2017, around 100 prisoners died in a month—most brutally killed, many decapitated, sometimes even disemboweled (AFP, Agence France-Presse 24, July 29, 2019). In March 2019, apparently spurred by the panic in reaction to the coronavirus in Brazil, as many as 1,300 prisoners may have broken out of four Brazilian facilities (Al Jazeera, Qatar press agency, March 17, 2020).

The Brazilian prison gang, First Capital Command, which formed in 2015, by 2020 was operating in 24 of the country's 26 states (Quirós 2020). The gang has extended operations into Paraguay, where there are strong suspicions that it collaborates with some government officials. There are indications that it has also established networks in Argentina, Uruguay, Bolivia, Venezuela, and Colombia. As a consequence, criminal violence is likely to become more transnational; it likely will prompt a more militarized approach to policing, with little attention to the underlying deterioration of criminal justice facilities.

Violent Crime

As economic conditions improved after 2008, concerns about crime began to show a marked increase, according to the 2013 Latinobarómetro report. Crime surpassed concerns about poverty and economic progress in Brazil, Chile, and Venezuela, among other places. And with this concern has come an increasingly lawless environment where it can be difficult to say what is more threatening, especially for the poor—the criminals or the police. Meagerly paid municipal police are often untrained and treat poor areas as a no-man's-land, where "shoot to kill" is standard operating procedure. In some poor *barrios*, the police no longer provide any security. This usually leads to vigilante justice, including hangings, beatings, and "necklacing," the practice of burning the accused alive by placing a tire around his neck and lighting it. Given this grim picture, some experts on Latin America's judiciary have concluded that "equality of law is a meaningless abstraction since the powerful need not obey the law which is designed primarily to control the behavior of the lower classes" (Schor 2003). In many Latin American countries, the police are widely seen as corrupt and as perpetrators of crime. In 2008, in every Latin American country no fewer than 20 percent of those surveyed in a Vanderbilt University study said they believed that police were involved in crime. In Venezuela and Guatemala, this view was held by more than 60 percent of those surveyed (Cruz 2010).

Particularly distressing in the Latin American case is the number of major cities where police and gangs dispute territory in poor *barrios*. In May 2006, in São Paulo, Brazil, the First Capital Command gang staged what might best be described as a military offensive against the police, carrying out more than 70 attacks over a two-day period, killing at least 70 police and many civilians. The attacks were coordinated with dozens of prison uprisings and the torching of banks and buses. The immediate catalyst for the offensive was apparently the government's decision to transfer 600 prisoners, including First Capital members, to other jails as an attempt to break the hold of the inmates over prison society. The police responded over the next few days with a systematic campaign of revenge against presumed gang members in the city's poor *favelas*, killing 93 "suspects" in one day (Phillips 2006).

Among the 50 cities in the world with at least 300,000 inhabitants and the highest murder rates, cities in Mexico and Brazil were 15 and 14 (respectively; the U.S. stood at 5). The rate in Caracas, Venezuela was 100. That country's rising murder rate between 2000 and 2014 (when a deep economic crisis began to set in) defies the conventional logic that poverty causes crime. Venezuela recorded the region's best record of poverty reduction in that period. Some attribute the rise to a culture of impunity that the Chávez government failed to address; others point to rising drug consumption brought about by the trafficking originating in the nearby Andean countries. Personal security was the number one issue mentioned by Venezuelans responding to poll questions asking them to name the most important issue in the country.

Visitors to Latin America are often struck by the sight of sharp pieces of glass protruding from the top of walls and windowsills. In most cities, private guards armed with automatic weapons patrol wealthy neighborhoods and are stationed outside banks and other public buildings. Guards with automatic weapons are commonly found at shopping centers, banks, and public buildings throughout Latin America; in Central American cities they are also prevalent at chain hamburger joints and at ice cream shops. However, murder rates, fueled by poverty, alcohol, and drugs, are highest in poor areas. Santiago, Chile, Buenos Aires, and Havana are very safe cities with rates of violent crime comparable to U.S. cities. And like U.S. cities, crime tends to be concentrated in the poorest areas. Of course, the large majority of people living in the *barrios* work hard just to live day to day; they are not violent or criminals. They often have well-knit, vibrant community organizations, customs, and celebrations. In some *barrios* or *favelas*, local community leaders take it upon themselves to negotiate truces among warring gangs and with the police. They may prefer living with and regulating conflict over drug trafficking and black markets to factional violence and police abuse.

Some cities have made significant progress curbing crime and violence. For example, Medellín, Colombia, was regarded as a chronically violent city, wracked by violence inflicted by gangs linked to notorious drug wars and clashes between leftist guerrillas and right-wing death squads (often the squads and gangs are indistinguishable). In 1991, the murder rate per 100,000 was well over 350; by 2005, it had fallen to 37, lower than many major U.S. cities. Why? Three factors were involved, says the Center for International Policy (CIP 2006). First, right-wing paramilitary forces, which had gained control over criminal activities, were offered amnesty in exchange for good behavior; second, police and military forces began to reestablish a presence in the poorest sectors of the city; and third, the city government decided to invest money in the poorest areas, offering hope to the poor and an opportunity for demobilized fighters involved in the country's civil war (see chapter 9) to reintegrate into society.

Although increased deployment of police and military seemed to have played a positive role in Medellín, just the opposite result was being obtained in Mexico. President Felipe Calderón (2006–2012) inherited spiraling drug trade–related violence from his predecessor after winning the disputed election of July 2006. Oddly, some of his problems may be the result of the liberal democratization process of the 1990s. The mayors and governors of the PRI might have held power through clientelism, corruption, and electoral fraud, but violence was moderated by a corrupt but effective working relationship between PRI politicians and the drug lords. In many cases, especially in the north, local drug lords—whose business prospered with the increase in traffic across the U.S. border after NAFTA—sought to step into the power void left by the well-intentioned reforms of the Zedillo administration in 1994–2000. However, with the PRI political monopoly broken up, political turf wars erupted.

In early 2007, finding that not only local but also federal police authorities had been thoroughly corrupted, Calderón decided to use the military to deal with his security problem; in the late 2000s, the news was filled daily with stories of violent clashes among local police, the Mexican military, and drug lords, with a rising civilian toll. Unfortunately, the drug lords beat the Mexican government to the punch in terms of preparing for war (Bremer 2007). The most notorious and violent of the gangs targeted by Calderón were the Zetas, who formed a heavily armed, elite network of well-trained former soldiers. The militarization seemed to produce results at first in Mexico City and Tijuana, but the relative peace was short-lived. By mid-2007, violence was escalating and spreading to cities in the south. Dozens of civilians were killed in one firefight alone in a small mining town. Severed heads of rival gang members were rolled out on to dance floors in one incident in Veracruz. Although Mexican citizens initially seemed supportive of using the army to crack down on the traffickers, the rising scale of violence, including grenade attacks that caused indiscriminate casualties among civilians, undermined confidence in a political system already burdened by a disputed election outcome and economic woes. (We should also note that the easy availability of firearms in the United States is a major contributory factor to the violence.)

The escalating violence contributed to the decision of voters to turn back to the PRI in the 2012 election that brought Enrique Peña Nieto to the presidency. Peña Nieto moved to restrict U.S. involvement in the war and, out of concern for the impact on the country's tourism industry, sought to scale down prominence of the war in the media. The government scored some noticeable successes in capturing some of the "big fish" narco-traffickers, but it found itself embroiled in a new problem when citizens despairing of the government's ability to protect them from both gangs and corrupt officials began to take matters into their own hands. In the state of Michoacán, villagers organized to take back land and homes seized by a particularly vicious gang, the Knights-Templar. Rather than disband the vigilante groups, in 2014 the government tried to bring them under control through integrating them into "civil patrols," but it was not clear how successful the effort would be.

Criminal violence spills over into election campaigns in many countries. In the 2007 Guatemalan elections, authorities registered 61 violent attacks on candidates and campaigners, resulting in 26 deaths, including those of seven members of Congress. The legacy of 36 years of civil war (see chapter 9) could be cited as the cause, but the upsurge of violence in 2007 was also caused by "narcotics traffickers and their allies' intent on infiltrating Guatemala's political system" (Lacey 2007). U.S. drug enforcement officials say Guatemala's "dire poverty and lawlessness" create an environment where the traffickers can influence politicians and local government. Police themselves have been implicated in several murders. In this context, citizens showed little sympathy for investigating the deaths of seven inmates killed after being captured when police suppressed a prison revolt.

The degree of coordination among gangs in Brazil and Mexico is particularly disturbing, presenting the possibility of significant social space becoming permanently beyond the reach of state authority. Should this condition become widespread and permanent, it can only lead to further deterioration of the quality of life for poor urban residents. In middle-class neighborhoods there grows an atmosphere of insecurity and fear of a racially distinct, class-distinct "other" mass of citizens.

The inability of Latin American states to provide security from crime for citizens is pervasive and deeply rooted. With the exception of Havana (where the political and social context may be changing), there is probably no Latin American city where citizens can feel safe from violence walking in the evening in all neighborhoods. The *barrios* and *favelas* of Latin America, by contrast, have a reputation as no-man's-land, areas where upper-class and especially white people fear to tread. The poor in these areas, especially when they mobilize to demand social and political inclusion in the broader national community, may be depicted in the mainstream media as *turbas*, mobs, and the antithesis of "civil society." In this way, racial and class divides widen and deepen, reinforcing exclusion of the poor from participation in the mainstream of the social, economic, and political life of the city.

The homicide rate in the Americas (including the U.S.) in 2017 was 17.2 persons per 100,000 residents, according to the United Nations (UNODC 2019); the rate was 3.0 in Europe and 2.3 in Asia. After having been flat from 1950 to 1980, the trend has been steadily upward, approximately doubling since 1980, the beginning of the "lost decade" for the region's economies (see chapter 6). Concerning countries, El Salvador, Honduras, and Guatemala were among those with the highest murder rates (see Figure 14.3), part of what

FIGURE 14.3   Homicides per 100,000 People

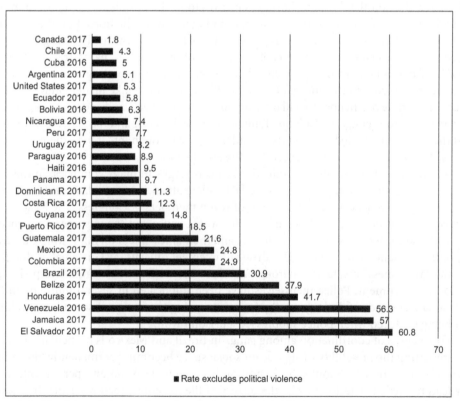

Source: IndexMundi (www.indexmundi.com/facts/indicators/VC.IHR.PSRC.P5/rankings), based on data from UN Office on Drugs and Crime's International Homicide Statistics database.

is driving migration toward the United States. But Venezuela, Colombia, Brazil, and Mexico, much more populous countries, all were in the bottom third of the list. The rate for poor and middle-class youth reached nearly 90 per 100,000. Young men are by far the main perpetrators. Women are equally as likely to be victimized, but that statistic fails to capture a dimension that has finally attracted attention from human rights groups: attacks on women and **LGBTQ+** people motivated partly or wholly by their gender.

It is easy to develop paranoia when reading statistics or hearing anecdotes about crime. In fact, one can visit Latin American countries at very low personal risk, lower than in many U.S. cities. Latin American cities have vibrant cultures, and the countryside can be spectacular. Be street smart, but do not forgo the pleasure of visiting Latin America out of fear.

For Review

Why is rule of law regard by many to be essential to democracy? What factors may impact whether citizens feel they are or are not actually living under rule of law? How does this apply to evaluating democracy in Latin America? What has happened to the rate of violent crime since the transitions from military government and the neoliberal era?

▌ Gender-Related Rights and Violence

It is something of a paradox that women's movements have become a significant force in a variety of way in Latin America, but that only limited progress has been made in expanding gender-related rights (e.g., equality of pay), reproductive rights, and protection from gender-related violence. **LGBTQ+** people face similar problems, though there is evidence in a modest shift in some countries toward recognition of gay rights. In both cases, the limited progress made is jeopardized by the low rates of public approval for gender-related rights, which has been stoked by right-populist parties, politicians, and conservative Catholic and evangelical Protestant religious movements.

Rights and Concerns of Women's Groups

In the case of women, a murder motivated by gender is called "femicide." The Gender Equality Observatory (2012) of the United Nations Economic Commission for Latin America and the Caribbean (ECLAC) estimated that in 2018 at least 3,529 women were victims of femicide. These counts almost surely underestimate "intimate violence," or violence against women by their sexual partners. This is difficult to measure because the rate may rise or fall according to victims' willingness to report such crime and police sensitivity to the issue. The ECLAC Observatory found that the highest rates of femicide were (in order) in El Salvador, Honduras, Bolivia, Guatemala, and the Dominican Republic. The first two of these countries had by far the highest rates, 6.8 and 5.1 per 100,000 people. Both of these countries (and Guatemala) are among those that are suffering highest problems with youth gangs, many of which originated in the United States. It is notable that these three countries are also ones that have generated mass migration northward toward the United States. Despite the horrible conditions, the Trump administration has expelled immigrants living and working illegally in the United States, and also asylum seekers awaiting judicial processing of their appeals, to these countries.

The problem of gender-related violence cannot be separated from the role of female labor in the supply chains of the globalized economy, that is, the "global assembly line" (see chapter 15). Like other border cities, Tijuana, Mexico, with 138 murders per 100,000 inhabitants, is a center of femicide. In Ciudad Juarez, a Mexican city along the border with Texas, Amnesty International reported that almost 400 women and girls had been murdered in the period between 1993 and 2005, most of them employees in the *maquiladora* industries, without charges being brought against anyone. Suspicions fall on powerful local *caudillos* and gangs who have links to or are part of the government in the region. The Mexican attorney general found that 177 officials of Chihuahua were guilty of negligence or omission in investigating, but none were brought to justice on grounds that the statute of limitations (the maximum time period during which one can be prosecuted after committing a crime) had run out (see Amnesty International 2006).

The years 2019–2020 saw a spike in visible mass protest by women around the world, with women's and LGBTQ+ movements in Latin America taking a leading role in making the rights issues and gender-related violence more visible (see chapter 13). But at the same time, this assertiveness has spawned reactions, and sometimes violence, against activists.

Among femicide victims are women who have emerged as movement leaders or entered into electoral politics. Bertha Cáceres was a prominent Indigenous leader who led a successful struggle against a mega-dam project in rural Honduras. She was assassinated in her home by gunmen that have been linked to Honduran elites and ex-soldiers who had been trained by U.S. Special Forces (Mackey and Eisner 2019). In the Cauca region of Colombia, an area long plagued by armed clashes between groups quarreling over control of drug trafficking, mayoral candidate Karina García was found shot to death in her burned-out car in 2019. In Putumayo, a state with a similar history, several women planning to register as candidates were murdered. While assassinations such as these might not be entirely motivated by gender, it is almost certainly a factor. Carolina Mospuera, a feminist organizer, says, "Male candidates are being attacked, but not for gendered reasons—not because they are men." Irina Cuesta, a peace activist, adds, "There is a political message behind these aggressions against women leaders and candidates, particularly in territories where stereotypes and tolerance to gender-based violence are useful tools of illegal armed actors." Laura Montoya, a Colombian journalist and activist who once nearly died after being attacked by a paramilitary group, said, "I work alongside men who are involved in the same activism and they haven't received the threats that I have" (quotes from *The Guardian*, London, October 1, 2019).

Overall, reproductive rights for women continue to be resisted throughout Latin America, the only exception being Cuba. Elsewhere, even women leaders associated with the Pink Tide have hesitated to take up the banner of reproductive freedom. While in office, Brazil's President Dilma Rousseff and Argentina's President Cristina Fernández de Kirchner declared themselves to be anti-abortion and promised to maintain existing restrictions on reproductive rights. Some countries have gone so far as to imprison women on charges of having an abortion. In 2015 in El Salvador, 17 women were serving jail sentences for this offense, some of them claiming to have had miscarriages or pregnancy complications. Some had been released by 2018, but the total number imprisoned had grown to 45. The law used

PHOTO 14.1   This woman is carrying a fake coffin in a demonstration against femicide. Do you think this kind of protest can bring action from the government there?

Source: Orlando Sierra/AFP via Getty Images.

to jail these women was passed in 1997 and labeled the "law against infanticide." The law is increasingly under attack by international human rights groups, but it also has powerful allies, such as the U.S.-based Witherspoon Institute (2020), which is generously funded by several big conservative foundations. Witherspoon claims that many of the aborted fetuses were actually babies born alive, and it accuses groups supporting repeal of advocating "impunity for infanticide." The Pew Research Center reported in 2014 that now more Protestants than Catholics oppose abortion in Latin America. Groups like Witherspoon help promote what U.S. conservatives call "traditional family values" to these evangelical or fundamentalist congregations.

LGBTQ+ Rights and Concerns

The rate of violence directed against LGBTQ+ people also seems to have spiked as the movement has become more outspoken. An August 2019 study by a regional network of LGBTQ+ organizations estimated that 1,300 of the members of this community in nine Latin American countries were murdered in the previous five years. As with femicide, the highest rates are in countries with serious problems of gang violence—Colombia, Mexico, and Honduras accounted for 90 percent of the victims. Young gay men, mostly killed in their homes, and transgender women, mostly killed in the streets, suffered the highest rates of murder (Reuters, August 8, 2019). Marcela Sánchez, a Colombian activist, told a Reuters reporter, "At the bottom of these violent deaths of LGBT people is exclusion, and sometimes total exclusion." She added, "Many of these deaths do not matter to anyone, not even to their own families" (Reuters, August 8, 2019).

A study by the Spanish newspaper *El País* (Madrid, June 22, 2019), using survey data gathered in 2016–2017 in 27 Latin American and Caribbean countries, showed that more of the public accepted than rejected same-sex marriage only in only five—Argentina, Brazil, Chile, Mexico, and Uruguay. In Mexico and Ecuador, court judgments have come down in favor of same-sex marriage, but there is no guaranteeing legislation to enforce judgments. In all of these, an outright majority accepted LGBTQ+ rights only in Uruguay (69 percent). The study found especially dismal the situation in the Caribbean and most of Central America. Only in Costa Rica (25 percent) did the level of approval climb over 20 percent; only 3 percent of Haitians approved.

The *El País* analysis found that some of the harshest anti-LGBTQ+ legislation exists in former British colonies, in part because of the historically deep influence of British anti-sodomy laws that were transmitted to the area before many of them became independent. These are reinforced, as noted earlier, by the influence of religiously conservative Catholics and of conservative evangelical or fundamentalist Protestants. Relations by two people of the same sex remains punishable by death in Guyana and by life in prison in Jamaica. (Elsewhere in the hemisphere, it is legal.) However, "conversion therapy," a pseudo-scientific psychological intervention to "cure" LGBTQ+ people and make them heterosexual, is outlawed only in Argentina, Uruguay, Ecuador, and Brazil.

Pink Tide governments are often rhetorically supportive of LGBTQ+ but rarely make them a priority or vigorously enforce them. Even where modest gains have been achieved, as in Brazil under the PT, they have been rolled back or threatened by the subsequent right-populist governments. In Venezuela, large Gay Pride parades and celebrations are now permitted, but homophobia frequently manifests itself in politics. In 2013, rumors that the opposition candidate Henrique Capriles was gay freely circulated on the pro-Chávez media. On the other side, the opposition media has taunted military officers with gay slurs, suggesting they should have the "*cajones*" to stage a coup. In one incident, dozens of members of the high command were sent women's panties to question their manhood.

For Review

In what ways should we take gender into account in understanding violence and rights in Latin America? How is femicide different from homicide? What political and cultural difficulties confront LGBTQ+ people from achieving their rights in Latin America?

Corruption

Almost anyone who has dealt with Latin American bureaucracies is aware of corruption. The Mexican *mordita*, the "little bite" taken by Mexico City's traffic police officers, is perhaps the best-known example, but the problem is widespread and deeper. Poorly paid civil servants, who often hold their jobs because they have a connection with a local politician or party, make citizens return day after day to secure a passport renewal, to replace a lost *cédula* (identity card), or to obtain a permit to open a business. To initiate home services, such as landline telephones or electricity, from state agencies, residents might need to offer an appropriate "gift" to the dispatcher and crew—though in the age of cellular phones, this nuisance is in decline. These day-to-day irregularities not only are annoying but also sap confidence in government institutions. They feed the perception that having the right connections or being affluent enough to pay a bribe counts more than meeting criteria defined by laws and regulations. In this way, corruption undermines the rule of law and respect for institutions. Citizens are less likely where corruption prevails to believe they have a civic duty to honestly report and pay taxes. Tax evasion by businesses and individuals is endemic throughout the region, even in countries like Costa Rica, generally seen as having more effective governance. Costa Rica's vaunted welfare system is endangered by a rising public debt that would be quite manageable if tax evasion were reduced (ICEFI 2019).

The line between **clientelism** and corruption is not always a bright one. Everywhere in the world, successful politicians reward followers with paid positions in public administration. The problem becomes more serious when appointees not only secure positions through connections but also are unqualified or incompetent. In some cases, this may produce risks to public health and safety—for example, failures to enforce codes for high-rise buildings in earthquake zones, lax inspection of food, and poor maintenance of highways. The problem is that even the most ardent reformer often finds when assuming office that there can be a tradeoff between accomplishing worthy political goals and securing support from allied parties and politicians who expect to be rewarded with patronage resources that they control and distribute.

Transparency International (TI 2005) is an NGO that rates the degree of corruption in national governments. TI's press release accompanying its 2005 report highlighted the costs of bribery in large-scale construction projects, such as the Yacyretá hydropower project.

> The Yacyretá hydropower project on the border of Argentina and Paraguay, built with World Bank support, is flooding the Ibera Marshes [one of the biggest wildlife wetlands in the world]. Due to cost overruns, the power generated by Yacyretá is not economic and needs to be subsidised by the government. According to the head of Paraguay's General Accounting Office, US$1.87 billion in expenditures for the project "lack the legal and administrative support documentation to justify the expenditures."

TI's annual reports are based on compilations of perceptions of what it regards as experts and of businesspeople on conditions in 146 countries. The perception data is gathered by at least three of 12 different organizations that do their own research using expert and business views. These then are compiled into one index by TI. Ultimately, then, it is not based on data about corruption itself. While experts in academia, think tanks, and journalism are consulted, the ranking relies heavily on experts associated with business and banking organizations. This does not invalidate the rankings, but it cannot be regarded as representative of all sectors in the global community. One critical study (Thompson and Shah 2005) of TI pointed out that corruption is better studied by treating different areas of corruption—judicial, taxation, procurement, customs—separately than aggregating them all.

My judgment is that TI's ratings are far from precise, but like most research of this sort, they are the best we have. If nothing else, they provide indications on how global elites see the degree of corruption in different countries. And to TI's credit, its reports and overall conclusions now rely on qualitative assessments drawn from news reports and criminal investigations.

In the TI index, each country is ranked from 100 (very clean) to 0 (highly corrupt). Figure 14.4 shows the rankings and scores for 2019. No country in the hemisphere is among the ten countries that achieved a "very clean ranking," a designation the TI gave only to

FIGURE 14.4 Rank and Score on Transparency International Corruption Index

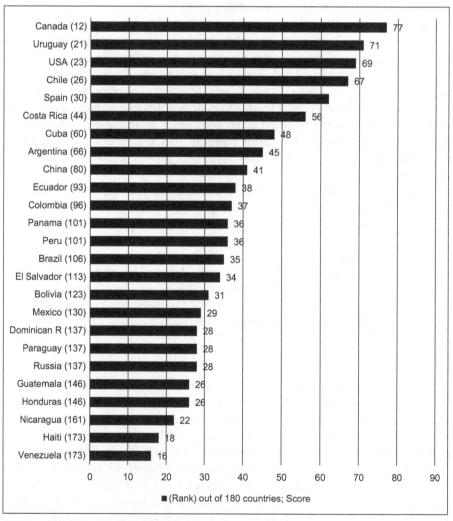

Source: Transparency International, 2019.

Singapore and nine West European countries. In the Western Hemisphere, Canada was by far ranked cleanest, followed by Uruguay, whose ranking was a little above that of the United States. Perhaps some might be surprised that Cuba ranked relatively well, fourth highest among Latin American countries at number 48 (though still only 60th overall). Eleven Latin American countries failed to rank within the top hundred.

TI's report highlighted continuing "evident misuse of state funds at various levels" and criticized the weakness of the judiciary in Bolivia "where parliamentary immunity and a compliant congressional commission responsible for investigating high-profile corruption cases allowed five-year-old allegations of corruption" against a former defense minister to stall. The Brazilian government's anticorruption efforts "continued to be characterized by knee-jerk reactions to scandals rather than a concerted effort to tackle the problem branch and root." Peru, said TI, had failed to put control measures into place in its efforts to decentralize the government, with the result that eight of 25 regional presidents were under investigation for corruption. In October 2008, the entire Peruvian cabinet submitted its resignation to President Alan García as a result of corruption scandals. García himself committed suicide in 2019 as police arrived at his home to serve a warrant for his arrest in connection with the **Obredecht** scandal.

The perception of corruption may be worse than the actual practice. Latinobarómetro (2006) turned up data that suggest that reputation and actual experience are not necessarily consistent. In 2005, (unfortunately, Latinobarómetro has not followed up since), only one in five Latin Americans reported direct knowledge of someone receiving favorable treatment because they were connected with a public official (i.e., clientelism), and likewise only 20 percent of respondents reported that they or a member of their family had direct knowledge of an act of corruption. Corruption is a serious problem, but it may be somewhat exaggerated in popular imagination, at least for some countries.

When civic skepticism becomes civic cynicism, people lose faith in democracy. Military officers often think that they can clean out the stables. Ambitious politicians may close down elected congresses with little protest from citizens, as happened in 1992 when President Alberto Fujimori dissolved Peru's Congress and inaugurated a period of harsh repression. Rather than cleanse the country, Fujimori merely shifted corruption down to other corridors of power. As we noted in chapter 10, even reformist politicians who led the democracy movements, such as Brazil's Lula, seem to have engaged in illegal practices at times. As politicians invoke congressional immunity, manipulate courts, and trade accusations of corruption and mendacity with one another, citizens become even more cynical.

Because of the corruption associated with the first populist era (see chapter 5) and the inefficiency of government, one might think that reducing the size of government by outsourcing public services to private corporations would be popular. However, as the **Panama Papers** and **Obredecht** scandals demonstrate, corruption has been deeply inscribed in neoliberalism as well. A delegation from the Mennonite Church returned from a fact-finding trip to Nicaragua pessimistic about the capacity of Latin American political institutions to cope with privatization. In their judgment,

> Nicaragua is a great example of this. The electric company was privatized five years ago and in its contract agreed to raise the costs for the public [only] once in the next five-year period. In that time the electric prices have been raised at least four times, and the government is unable to control them . . . All the companies that have

> bought out the government utilities (at very cheap prices) are all foreign transnation-
> als, and . . . the government here does not have the power to contend with them.
>
> (Miller 2005)

Wealth and social status draw special treatment from bureaucracies. Although this rule probably holds true in all political systems, the poor feel the discrimination more acutely in Latin America, where inequality is more glaring. Guillermo O'Donnell (1998) writes,

> Perhaps nothing underlines better the deprivation of rights of the poor and the
> socially weak than when they interact with the bureaucracies from which they must
> obtain work, or a working permit, or apply for retirement benefits, or simply (but
> often tragically) when they have to go to a hospital or a police station . . . [For] those
> who cannot avoid this ugly face of the state, it is not only the immense difficulty they
> confront for obtaining, if at all, what nominally is their right; it is also the indifferent if
> not disdainful way in which they are treated, and the obvious inequality entailed by
> the privileged skipping these hardships.

The solution may lie in more democracy, not more police or military action. Robert Putnam's research (1993) on corruption and good government in Italian cities has empha-sized the importance of communities organizing and participating in politics, not just leav-ing decisions to public officials. Of course, this raises the question of how to develop such a culture of civic virtue and active involvement. As we saw in the previous chapter, social movements seem on the upsurge throughout Latin America—a reason for some optimism.

Anticorruption civic organizations have sprung up in several countries. Massive civic protest forced governments to roll back plans to sell public assets in several cases, most nota-bly in 2000 in the Bolivian city of Cochabamba, where citizens mobilized to prevent pri-vatization of water. Anti-corruption protests have broken out in several Central American countries. Sadly, anti-corruption commissions that were established by these states were dis-mantled in 2019, even though they had aid from the United Nations and some NGOs. The question now seems to be, can Latin American nations develop institutions that will make the government responsive and the elected officials accountable to more systematic and peaceful citizen action?

Public attitudes toward corruption are more mixed than the news headlines about indictments, scandals, and protests indicate. As Figure 14.5 indicates, overall 40 percent of respondents to the 2018 Latinobarómetro survey agreed that a certain amount of corruption could be tolerated if the government solves the country's problems. At least one quarter of respondents agreed or strongly agreed with this statement throughout the hemisphere, in a few cases more than half agreed.

In 2018, two-thirds of Latin American respondents to Latinobarómetro believed that corruption had "much increased" (see Figure 14.6); more than half think it has increased. Whether it had actually increased is more difficult to ascertain for two reasons. The recent release of the **Panama Papers** and news of the **Obredecht** scandal may have simply increased public awareness of a corruption already long entrenched. Second, as discussed earlier, pol-iticians have learned how to use corruption to advantage—"lawfare" (see also chapter 13). Either way, the impact can be corrosive to confidence in the institution of the judiciary and by extension to the rule of law. Nearly half the respondents (in Figure 14.6) agreed it was better to keep quiet if one has knowledge about corruption.

FIGURE 14.5   Percent Agreeing a Certain Amount of Corruption Worth the Price as Long as the Country's Problems Are Solved

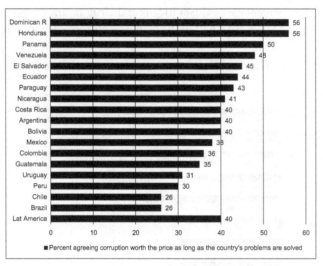

Source: Latinobarómetro 2018.

FIGURE 14.6   Attitudes About Corruption

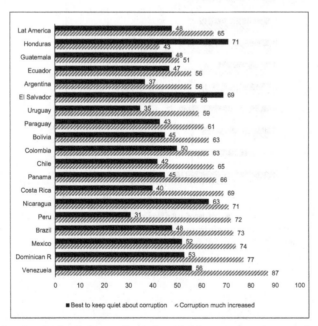

Top bar: In your opinion, has the level of corruption in [country] increased much, somewhat, stayed about the same, or decreased? Here, Much + Somewhat.

Bottom Bar: Please tell me, in your opinion, if you agree or disagree with one of the following: When you know something corrupt is going on, it is better to stay quiet. Agree or disagree? Here: Agree.

Source: Latinobarómetro 2018, p. 63.

In Latin America overall, only 35 percent of respondents to Latinobarómetro expressed confidence in the police, but the judiciary falls well below that mark (see Figure 14.7). Fewer than a quarter of respondents expressed confidence in the judiciary. It should not surprise, by now, that a higher percentage of Costa Ricans and Uruguayans expresses confidence, but even in these countries fewer than half of the respondents looked favorably on the judiciary.

FIGURE 14.7   Percent Expressing "Much" or "Some" Confidence in Judiciary and Police

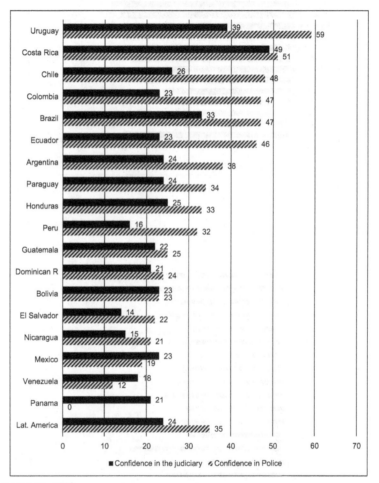

Source: Latinobarómetro 2018.

For Review

What is impunity? What are some of the ways that corruption can weaken support for democracy? Why does O'Donnell think that it is especially corrosive of support for democracy among the poor?

Human Rights and State Violence

More publicized and controversial violations of human rights are those in which governments are accused of carrying out, abetting, or tolerating repression of citizens attempting to exercise these rights. Although human rights reports continue to identify serious abuses, most of the region as a whole showed improvement in the civil rights areas of human rights after the collapse of the dictatorships of the Southern Cone and the end of Central America's civil wars. However, the reality is that no country has a perfect human rights record, and we have already seen in earlier chapters plenty of evidence that in some areas state violence continues to be a serious issue.

The Legacy of Military Rule

To appreciate the scale of state violence during military rule, consider that between 1976 and 1982 Argentina's military junta killed or "disappeared" (referring to citizens swept up by security forces, never to reappear) at least 10,000 people. In Chile, which has two-fifths the population of Argentina, 3,129 people died in the first three years after General Augusto Pinochet seized power in 1973. In Brazil, "only" 400 citizens were killed or disappeared by military forces after 1964.

In these and other cases, the numbers do not reflect the multitude of citizens detained, tortured, stripped of the right to speak or act publicly, or deprived of their places of employment or university study. An estimated 40,000 people in Chile were directly victimized in some way. In addition to deaths and torturing, others were affected in ways from which they still have not recovered. Thousands of students were denied higher education because of their political views, and for the same reason tens of thousands lost their jobs.

In Central America, the human rights toll was even grimmer, especially given the size of these republics. The cases of El Salvador and Guatemala are especially indicative of the causes and consequences of mass human rights abuses. El Salvador was governed for most of the twentieth century by a ferocious and rapacious oligarchy, the so-called Fourteen Families that owned 80 percent of the country's arable land, having forced small producers, including Indigenous people, off the land and having proceeded to create export-oriented estates (Lauria-Santiago 1999).

Accumulated grievances against the oligarchy led to successful peasant organizing in the 1920s by the Communist Party, led by the nationalist patriot Farabundo Martí. After the annulment of the party's victory in the municipal elections of 1931, the oligarchy found a savior in General Maximiliano Hernández Martínez, who unleashed a massacre, variously estimated to have taken the lives of 10,000–50,000 peasants, with Indigenous peoples especially targeted. Forty years later, the tragedy repeated itself. Between 1979 and 1981— while some civilians and a handful of sympathetic military officers supported land reform and other measures demanded by labor—35,000 people, including labor leaders, nuns and priests, and peasant leaders, of a total population of five million people, were killed, often in the most brutal and public fashion. By the end of civil war, 75,000 people were dead in the tiny country, sometimes known as the "flea."

The United States still prefers to be in denial about how its policies in support of repressive regimes have had a lasting impact. The U.S. State Department's evaluation (no longer available online) of the human rights situation in 2004 in El Salvador is typical of the way it uses soft gloves in assessing the human rights policies of its allies in Latin America. It said,

> The Government generally respected the human rights of its citizens; however, there were significant problems in some areas. Some alleged politically motivated killings were under investigation at year's end. There were no reports of politically motivated disappearances. Some police officers used excessive force and mistreated detainees; at times police arbitrarily arrested and detained persons without adequate cause. Prison conditions remained poor, and overcrowding was a continuing problem. Lengthy pretrial detention remained a problem . . . Violence and discrimination against women remained a serious problem. Discrimination against disabled persons also remained a problem. Abuse of children, child labor, and forced child prostitution were also problems. The Government did not adequately protect workers' rights to organize and bargain collectively. Trafficking in women and children was a problem.
>
> (U.S. Department of State 2004)

In contrast, consider Amnesty International's 2002 report of the same government:

> January marked the 10th anniversary of the Peace Accords which brought an end to the armed conflict in El Salvador. Despite improvements in the human rights situation during this period, those responsible for the massive human rights violations committed during the country's 11-year conflict had not yet been brought to justice, an issue central to the peace process. However, local organizations renewed their efforts to ensure accountability for the violations. Economic conditions in some areas of the country deteriorated dramatically as a result of bad weather or low prices for agricultural products in the international market, leading to high levels of child malnutrition, in some cases resulting in deaths.
>
> (Amnesty International 2002)

On September 30, 2013, employees of Tutela Legal, a legal aid organization affiliated with a human rights office founded by Archbishop Oscar Romero (see chapter 9), found themselves locked out of the office in the National Cathedral by the Archbishop José Luis Escobar Alas, who said its work was no longer relevant. Critics said the move was made to separate the Church from a controversial investigation into one the most notorious massacres (*El Mozote*) carried out by the army (*Los Angeles Times*, October 4, 2013).

These are some of many historical injustices, including slavery and ethnic purging (if not genocide, in some cases) that have left their mark on Latin America. This has led to a call for restorative justice to members of groups that have been directly affected or who have inherited harm as a result of these mass-scale injustices. Most recently, the idea has been incorporated into the plan to reincorporate guerrilla fighters and anti-insurgency forces into civic life in Colombia. The concept originally comes from ideas about alternatives to incarceration of criminals, the idea being that the victor and perpetrator of a crime, and the affected community, are brought together to develop methods of compensating for the harm done. It may seem an idealistic solution, but it has been tried with some success at the local level in different places in the world, and one could argue that Brazil's affirmative action for education program (see chapter 2) is to some extent based on restoration.

For Review

How have the civil wars in Central America and Colombia and the legacy of the military governments raised awareness of human rights issues, even though the wars may have ended?

Drug Wars and the "War on Terrorism"

Intervention in Central America was the last major hemispheric conflict of the Cold War. The mission entrusted to U.S. forces in the postwar period is broader today than that of any previous era. Latin America falls under the aegis of Southcom (U.S. Southern Command), one of the five U.S. commands whose areas of responsibility divide up the globe. Southcom has 1,400 staff, making it larger than all other U.S. government agencies in the region (e.g., the embassy and consulate staff) put together. It has an annual budget of US$800 million, and it administers a large military aid program. In 2005, its commander, General Brantz Craddock, told the U.S. Congress that his theater of command was brimming with threats to U.S. national security, listing them as "transnational terrorism, narcoterrorism, illicit trafficking, forgery and money laundering, kidnapping, urban gangs, radical movements, natural disasters, and mass migrations." Craddock attributed the problems to "anti-U.S., anti-globalization, and anti-free trade demagogues" (quoted in Barry 2005). In this way, a U.S. general made transparent what is often the key goal pursued by military aid programs and the rationale given for U.S. aid and intervention in the Americas: U.S. security objectives are hopelessly tangled with broader security and economic goals. We take this up again in the next two chapters, but for this chapter we need to examine how it impacts the problem of criminality and violence in Latin America.

Craddock outlined seven objectives in response to these "challenges." At the top of the list is to make sure that "regional energy supplies will flow freely" to markets and "not be targets of aggression." To achieve this, training will help "partner" nations protect "critical infrastructure"—defined as the second objective. Protecting infrastructure in turn leads to objective number three—training the military of the Andean nations (the "Andean Ridge," in the new jargon of the day) in joint operations to "establish dominion over ungoverned spaces," a clear reference to areas under guerrilla control or in sparsely populated (mostly Indigenous) areas. Most of these "spaces" are in the Amazonian region, where mining and oil companies are operating and want to expand. Training would require deployment of more troops on the ground on the continent. Two other objectives are to support stable democracies and to prevent "rogue nations" from supporting terrorism. Cuba was already on the "rogue" state list, and U.S. conservatives pressed to add Chávez's Venezuela. Two other objectives on Craddock's list remained classified.

The U.S. military presence in South America has been expanded mainly under the guise of the drug war, and counterterrorism, in the wake of the attacks on New York and Washington on September 11, 2001 (coincidentally the anniversary date of Pinochet's 1973 coup in Chile), is sometimes cited as an objective, but usually in the context of the drug war. But, is Washington unambiguously on the side of controlling criminality, or only criminality where it interferes with global economic objectives?

International trade in narcotics has been a major feature of the global economic system since the Opium Wars. It is worth remembering that in these wars, China was resisting drug trafficking being carried out by Americans and Europeans, not the other way around. And in Latin America in recent decades, the United States has sometimes either backed or tolerated traffickers. In numerous conflicts, including the Vietnam War and the Islamic Mujahideen's war against the Soviet occupation of Afghanistan in the 1980s, the United States allied itself with opium producers and traffickers. These alliances often have involved covert operations orchestrated by the CIA. In the 1980s, the U.S. Congress, alarmed at human rights violations by the *contras*, prohibited the use of taxpayer dollars to support the insurgency. One way to keep the proxy army funded was to ignore—if not to actively facilitate—their role in trafficking drugs. Central American operatives aligned with the CIA were implicated in the marketing of crack cocaine in the dawning era of the crack epidemic (Webb 1999).

The illegal global trade in narcotics sustains an enormous slush fund that can be utilized by both states and guerrilla movements. Usually, the armed forces of the group offer protection to growers, processors, or traffickers in exchange for a cut ("tax") of the profits. This is the principal relationship among armed groups, the military, and law enforcement officials in the Andean region. Colombians could be forgiven if they were confused about U.S. intentions. In 2000, the State Department found that two Colombian battalions that had lost U.S. aid because of human rights violations and connections to paramilitary groups were still operating, with new battalion designations created simply to qualify for aid. In 2005, President Uribe's decision to pardon notorious right-wing death squad leaders further shook the U.S. Congress's support for the war. On the other hand, a delegation of conservative U.S. members of Congress in 2000, including future speaker of the House of Representatives Dennis Hastert, encouraged Colombian military commanders to ignore human rights restrictions.

The assassination of a prominent Colombian presidential candidate by a drug lord of the notorious Medellín cartel in 1989 was the occasion for U.S. president George H. W. Bush to announce a significant increase in funds for the drug war in Colombia and for a deployment of U.S. military forces to help in training. These actions were publicly justified as interdiction of the drug trade, the only argument that the U.S. Congress would accept. National security directives and diplomatic correspondence show, however, that fighting guerrillas was just as important (National Security Archive 2009). Under scrutiny from Congress and public interest groups in North and South America, U.S. officials continue to claim that American aid and training are to professionalize the military, and they stress respect for human rights.

Estimating the size of the illegal drug trade is difficult. Some experts think that 90 percent of the street value of drugs in the United States stays in the north. The trade is big enough that exports, especially of coca, exceed the value of any legally exported commodity from the Andean Ridge south of Venezuela (Kawell 2002). The profits are concentrated more in processing and trafficking than in the production of the raw material. In recent years, Washington has targeted Venezuela as a key point of transit for trafficking and used it as a justification for unilaterally imposing economic sanctions on the country, designating it a "narcostate." However, the Washington Office on Latin America, a church-funded think tank that is highly critical of the Maduro government in Venezuela, even to the point of justifying some sanctions, used the U.S. government's own data to show that Venezuela was not a primary transit country. Six times as much cocaine passed through Guatemala, a close ally. Increases in Venezuela trafficking largely corresponded with increased production in its neighbor, Colombia, another U.S. ally. When Colombian production decreased, so did trafficking through Venezuela between 2015 and 2017. The Washington Office on Latin America (WOLA) concluded that U.S. policy would be better served by promoting a peaceful, negotiated solution to Venezuela's crisis than by trying to bring down Maduro (WOLA 2020).

Antidrug efforts measure "success" in terms of reducing supply and land under cultivation, but it is not clear that this does much more than raise prices and open opportunities for new entrepreneurs to fill the gap when older traffickers are detained. But it is the cultivators, mostly poor peasants, who are at the greatest risk. They are the easiest to find, and their lower share of profits deprives them of political influence—something that has begun to change as growers' unions have emerged in the Andes, most notably in Bolivia. Human rights issues almost inevitably arise not only because those at the bottom of the supply chain are poor peasants who suffer "collateral damage" from military operations, including fumigation of their lands and abuse by troops, but also because as an organized movement they challenge the governments that collaborate with U.S. antidrug and antiterrorism operations.

Presidents Bush I, Clinton, and Bush II always justified military aid to Andean nations as part of the antidrug war, but counterinsurgency has always been a handmaiden of this policy (see the official U.S. policy documents in the electronic National Security Archive, www.gwu.edu/~nsarchiv). Coca cultivation in Peru's Huallaga Valley was helping to sustain the Sendero Luminoso guerrilla movement. The Drug Enforcement Agency (DEA), a police bureau, found itself conducting military operations, leading some Bush administration officials in 1989 to recommend turning the task over to regular U.S. forces. Twenty members of the U.S. Army Special Forces were deployed to help train Peruvian units.

Nowhere are human rights concerns more in conflict with U.S.-supported antidrug operations than in Colombia. Colombia's two major insurgencies, the ELN and FARC, both of which are officially considered "terrorist" organizations by Washington, financed themselves in part through protection of growers and traffickers, if not through direct involvement in trafficking. These insurgencies have their roots in political disputes going back to the immediate post–World War II era (see chapter 10), long before the drug trade emerged as a significant part of the country's economy.

Agreements between the United States and Latin American countries have raised an important rule-of-law issue: extraterritoriality. These agreements generally give U.S. troops legal immunity (COHA 2005b) from criminal prosecution in the host country. In 2009, the Uribe government in Colombia signed an agreement to allow the United States to locate seven bases (euphemistically called "forward operating areas" to avoid these de facto treaties from facing scrutiny in the U.S. Senate). Uribe's successor, Santos, accepted the ruling by the Colombian Supreme Court that the agreement is unconstitutional. In 2002, the United States sought to convince Costa Rica, with Latin America's longest continuous democratic constitution, to be the host of an international law enforcement academy, successor to the School of the Americas. However, Washington would not agree to San José's conditions: (1) that only police and not military personnel would be trained there and (2) that the academy's U.S. personnel would not enjoy diplomatic immunity from prosecution for crimes under Costa Rican law. (The United States has sought immunity agreements to shield its soldiers and politicians from the International Criminal Court, which the United States rejects, despite having originally championed its creation.) In 2005, over the objection of human rights advocates, El Salvador agreed to host the academy. El Salvador's reputation could not be any more opposite that of Costa Rica. A United Nation's truth commission documented in 1993 that 90 percent of the violence in El Salvador's civil war of 1980–1992 was perpetrated by government forces (COHA 2005a).

It can be difficult to assess any one country's human rights record. Does one examine the record in absolute or relative terms? One or a few political murders are serious enough, especially when perpetrated by the state, but few would say that the human rights record of Mexico or Venezuela in recent decades is as horrible as that of Colombia or El Salvador in the 1980s. Violations approached the level of genocide in Guatemala. An estimated 200,000 people, the majority of them Mayans, were killed in the civil strife of the 1980s in that country, the vast majority at the hands of security forces. We should look at human rights both in absolute terms, so as not to trivialize any abuse that costs even one life, and in relative terms, to keep some perspective on how countries differ from one another.

Leaders of Venezuela and leftist government have often complained that the commission is biased by norms and institutions influenced by the United States. Venezuela claimed that the Inter-American Commission on Human Rights (IACHR) was particularly tepid in reacting to the short-lived coup against Chávez in 2002, a claim the commission denies (see Emersberger 2010; IACHR 2010). In September 2012, Venezuela formally withdrew from the Convention on Human Rights, which it had ratified in 1977; a year later this meant that it could deny the IACHR jurisdiction. The IACHR claims Venezuela remains obligated to the convention because of the country's membership in the Organization of American States (OAS), with which the IACHR is affiliated. The IACHR has not made the same claim about the United States, which has never ratified the convention or the protocols but provides the lion's share of funding for the commission's operation (see the following Punto de Vista).

PUNTO DE VISTA: DOÑA VENEZUELA AND HER TWO PRESIDENTS. WHICH SHOULD SHE CHOOSE?

(With apologies to Jorge Amado's novel, Doña Flor and Her Two Husbands.)

In 2019, Venezuela suddenly found itself with two presidents engaged in a high-stakes game to control the country's future. The country also had two "national assemblies" and many questions about how the constitution should be applied. So, how did it find itself in this position?

President Nicolás Maduro claimed to be Venezuela's constitutional president because he won the presidential election in July 2018. On January 23, 2019, Juan Guaidó, one month after becoming president of Venezuela's National Assembly, disputed Maduro's legitimacy and declared the presidency vacant. He then took an oath to serve as the interim president of Venezuela.

Although involved in politics since 2009, Guaidó was until recently little known outside political circles. A member of the Voluntad Popular ("Popular Will") party, he was an understudy to Leopoldo López, the party's leader who was then imprisoned for allegedly encouraging violent protests seeking the ousting of Maduro.

The 1999 Bolivarian Constitution, written in the first year of former president Hugo Chávez's presidency, fulfilled a promise Chávez made in his successful 1998 presidential campaign to replace the constitution of 1991. Most Venezuelans had come to see the earlier constitution as a democratic façade, serving the interests of a corrupt, wealthy ruling elite that controlled the only two parties with any chance of winning power through elections.

Maduro was Chávez's vice president and the clear choice to succeed Chávez after his death in March 2013, only five months after winning an election for a third term. Chávez had won five presidential elections (including an attempt to recall him in 2004) easily due to strong support among the country's poor majority, who benefited from social programs funded by the country's oil bounty—which, before Chávez, had mostly gone to the wealthy and middle class.

The Maduro era has seen more questions arise about the fairness of campaigns, but also about official results. Despite Chávez's blessing, Maduro barely won the special election to replace the deceased leader, winning only 50.6% of the vote. Maduro's political standing plunged further in mid-2014 when the price of oil, which can vary from 20% to 40% of GDP in any given year, collapsed, falling from US$130 to US$30 per barrel in late 2015.

In December 2015, Maduro's United Socialist Party of Venezuela (PSUV) suffered a severe defeat in the National Assembly elections. The opposition won a super majority of seats, enough to undo the programs of the Chávez era. Much of the opposition had participated in a failed coup in 2002 and never accepted the 1999 constitution—but all now embraced it as a tool to try to remove Maduro.

The opposition consisted of a coalition of parties, the Democratic Unity Roundtable, the MUD. They gathered enough signatures to force a recall election upon Maduro, but the PSUV used delaying tactics to ensure that an opposition win would result in the vice president taking over. The recall effort faded away.

Stymied on that front, the opposition-controlled National Assembly began to act to slow or end Chávez's programs and to limit Maduro's power. The country's Supreme Court, filled with PSUV appointees, used a dispute over the election of three assembly deputies to rule that the body was unconstitutionally abusing its power. The Court threatened to close the unicameral Congress down.

Maduro instead decided to convene a National Constituent Assembly (NCA) to rewrite the 1999 constitution and create what Chávez had called the "communal state." This state would theoretically shift much power over policies and state spending (generated almost entirely by oil exports) to local and regional citizens' councils. To do this, Maduro used a vague phrase in Article 348 of the constitution that says, "The initiative for calling a National Constituent Assembly (NCA) may emanate from the President of the Republic sitting with the Cabinet of Ministers."

The opposition refused to participate in the election (turnout was 41%) of delegates to the NCA—as a result it is almost entirely composed of Maduro supporters. On August 8, 2017, the NCA took legislative powers for itself, away from the National Assembly, under Article 349 of the existing constitution, which is intended to avoid obstruction of a constitutional assembly's work.

Venezuela's electoral authorities then scheduled the May 2018 presidential election half a year early. Though constitutional, the timing made it difficult for the deeply divided opposition to choose its candidate. A large faction boycotted the vote; another backed a candidate, the governor of an important state. Maduro won with 67.8%. The turnout was 46.7%, low by Venezuelan standards.

Maduro claims this election makes him the legitimate president and accuses the opposition, the United States, and other foreign governments of fomenting a coup. In fact, Guaidó had just assumed the presidency for one year under an agreement that the position would rotate among members of the MUD. It was Voluntad Popular's turn. Guaidó's move seemed to catch the rest of the opposition off guard.

Guaidó claims to be the constitutional interim president after the National Assembly declared the presidency to be "vacant" under Article 233 of the constitution, which allows for an interim president to replace a sitting president "upon abandonment of his position, duly declared by the National Assembly." He defends his action as a constitutional route out of the country's economic and political crises—and his move has been endorsed by much of the mainstream news media in liberal democracies.

Maduro has highlighted that he won an election—and Guaidó has not. Guaidó promised he would call elections once he has actual control of government. Guaidó openly embraces his support of the United States and its sanctions against Venezuela. Maduro cites this as evidence that Guaidó's claim to the presidency is yet another stratagem made in Washington to bring down the Bolivarian Revolution. In May 2019, Guaidó supporters wrote the U.S. Southern [military] Command,

asking for a meeting and stating they would "welcome strategic and operational planning so that we may fulfill our constitutional obligation to the Venezuelan people in order to alleviate their suffering and restore our democracy."

Why did both presidents try so hard to justify their status as "constitutional" when almost everyone agrees the military holds the keys to power? For one thing, many in the military feel it's their job to uphold the constitution. Both claimants want to appeal to international public opinion. Both presidents want the support of Venezuelans in the poor urban neighborhoods and countryside, who see the 1999 constitution as guaranteeing their right, won under Chávez, to be politically included in determining the country's future.

For Discussion

Who do you think has the better claim to be the legitimate president of Venezuela?
What do you think would be in the best interest of the Venezuelan people to resolve the conflict?

For More Information

This Punto is an expanded and updated version of my article, "Venezuela Crisis Explained: A Tale of Two Presidents," *The Conversation*, February 6, 2019. The original can be found at https://theconversation.com/venezuela-crisis-explained-a-tale-of-two-presidents-111198. For an update two years after Guaidó's self-declaration, see chapter 8.

For Review

What are the stated objectives of the U.S. "war on drugs"? How do the objectives of this "war" and other U.S. policies conflict sometimes with support for human rights and the rule of law?

Lawfare

Politicians are skilled at bending the laws and using the courts to tarnish the reputation of opponents or even to prevent them from running for office. This practice is known as "lawfare," the misuse of the legal system and of charges of human rights abuses to tarnish the image of an opponent, or even to jail them on bogus or trumped up charges. It can consist of selective prosecution. For example, after the Venezuelan opposition to President Nicolás Maduro won a super majority (enough to change **organic laws**) in the National Assembly in 2015, the government whittled the majority down to a lower level by indicting three law-makers for vote buying, a charge by which just about every member of the assembly might have been disqualified.

Lawfare can also consist of using a relatively mild offense and making it a cause for disqualification or impeachment. The impeachment of Dilma Rousseff in 2005 was on grounds that she acted illegally in contracting loans to fill deficits in the budget. Carlos Andrés Pérez of Venezuela was impeached and removed from office in 1992 for sending foreign aid to the government of Nicaraguan President Violeta Chamorro. The motive in Rousseff's case was a way to replace the PT in the presidency with the more conservative Vice President Michel Temer. In Pérez's case, his own party joined to oust him on the rather flimsy pretext because his tight fiscal policies and widespread unpopularity for his use of the military to put down the Caracazo revolt of 1989 made him an albatross around the necks of the entire political class.

In Brazil, corruption has felled at least temporarily the political careers of two presidents (Rousseff and Lula) of a political party that rose out of the ashes of military dictatorship by mobilizing most of the populace for a democratic transition. Certainly, there was plenty of reason to be suspicious of both. While Lula was never implicated in bribery in the **mensalão** scandal, his closest advisor indisputably funneled money to regional congressional deputies. It was under his watch and Rousseff's that the *Lava Jato* operation took place. At the heart of that scandal were bribes involving Petrobras, the state oil company, and Rousseff was minister of energy at the time. But no direct evidence implicated Rousseff, and the loans to fill budget deficits were unrelated and a common practice by presidents before her. In Lula's case, the judge coordinated the trial with the investigators, who are supposed to act independently and present findings to the judge. The judge in the case was appointed to a cabinet position in the new government. Several major scandals surrounding President Bolsonaro, one involving a murder investigation, have brought about no charges.

In 2005, Andrés Miguel López Obrador (elected president in 2018), when he was mayor of Mexico City (elected president of Mexico in 2019), was accused of violating a court order against the municipal construction of a road leading from a poor community to a hospital. The Mexican Congress, where his party held only a minority of seats, stripped the mayor of immunity from prosecution enjoyed by elected officials, and he was subsequently indicted. By Mexican law (as in most of the rest of Latin America), citizens under indictment cannot run for office; López Obrador protested that the charges against him were trumped up. He pointedly referred to many contemporary and former Mexican officials investigated for far more serious allegations but never indicted. On April 24, 2005, an estimated one million marchers in Mexico City protested the imminent indictment of the presidential candidate. The mayor, known for his populist campaign style, planned to campaign from prison as a martyr, but two members of Congress from the ruling party of President Vicente Fox thwarted the plan by paying his bail. By May, the government had dropped the charges.

Venezuela's highly polarized politics has also generated "lawfare." The highest profile case involves Leopoldo López, a former Caracas area mayor and founder of the Voluntad Popular (VP; Popular Will), a hardline opposition party in Venezuela. In 2008, the government barred him from seeking election as mayor of a Caracas-area municipality, but on charges unrelated to the coup. He was one of 80 politicians (including many from Chávez's own party) banned from running because they were under an administrative (that is, not judicial) investigation for corruption. He appealed in Venezuelan courts but lost; he then took his case to the Inter-American Commission on Human Rights, part of the Organization of American States, which supported his contention that because he had not been tried and convicted on the charges, the ban violated his right to run for office under the hemisphere's human rights charter. The administrative ban remained in place until 2014, when his term as mayor ended.

In spring 2013 and 2014, López was jailed again, this time on charges that he had incited violent antigovernment protests. The first case was a demonstration protesting alleged voter fraud and the second was a student uprising against a range of government economic policies and alleged human rights violations. While the majority of protesters were peacefully exercising their rights, more extreme agitators attacked a number of clinics and government installations, and there were a number of deaths and injuries to members of the security forces, bystanders, and people aligned with the government. However, credible human rights observers inside and outside the country held the government security forces responsible for the great majority of those killed and injured, which in 2014 numbered 43 dead, over 5,000 injured, and over 3,000 detentions.

Most opposition leaders supported the protests but in 2014 sought to suspend them as the violence was worsening. López chose to urge protesters, many of them young, back into the streets. Choosing his words carefully, the former mayor avoided any call for violent protest; however, in the context of the violent clashes, the government held him responsible for the continuing violence as students went back out to build barricades in the streets, most in thoroughfares in middle-class neighborhoods. National Guard troops dressed in riot gear clashed again with protesters. Residents were divided between those who admired the young people standing their ground and others, although opposed to Maduro, who wanted no part of the violence in their neighborhoods.

The government claimed that López and some other opposition leaders were trying to draw the military into a coup. That was not a far-fetched claim, given that a similar scenario had played itself out in the failed 2002 coup against Chávez. Besides the incident at the Cuban embassy, López had the government's interior minister arrested during the coup. However, a month after López's his conviction in 2015, several government investigators defected and denounced the entire proceedings, saying that evidence was fabricated or simply nonexistent. The judge could not quote anything incriminating from López's speech. The government charged that his call for violence was "subliminal."

After 20 years of government under Chávez and Maduro, the Venezuelan judiciary was now dominated by Chavistas. His supporters' complaints have been supported by the United Nations High Commissioner for Human Rights. López served three years under detention in prison or in his home and was released in April 2019. Earlier that year, a protégé of López, Juan Guaidó, serving as president of the National Assembly, declared the Venezuelan presidency "vacant" and proclaimed himself the legitimate president of Venezuela. Venezuela had two presidents, dividing the country and member states of the international system. (See the Punto de Vista in this chapter.)

It is no easy task to reform a judicial system or carry out an anti-corruption campaign. For one thing, attacking judicial corruption often requires sweeping out large numbers of judges all at once, and replacing them gives the incumbent government a chance to load the judiciary with their own allies. Some constitutional reforms in the regions have strengthened judicial review, the system by which courts in the United States can declare certain laws and policies unconstitutional, make courts more politically relevant, and, as a result, more likely to be politically targeted (Pérez-Liñán and Castagnola 2019).

Few observers of Latin America believe that much progress has been made toward overcoming corruption, reducing crime, or establishing impartial judicial systems. On the other hand, it does seem that significant progress has been made in establishing respect for human rights as a principle of government—although there remain serious issues here too, of course, and significant variations across countries. Most scholars see democracy and rule of law as mutually reinforcing one another. For some, one cannot exist without the other. It is hard to believe that an effective democracy can be stabilized without more progress in all these areas, but there is a viewpoint, we have seen, that argues first for establishment of the rule of law and then democracy only later.

Is It Governance or Capitalism That Is Failing?

We need to question just how much corruption is the enemy of good governance versus how much governance is corrupted by legal and quasi-legal means. Governments and large business direct ad money to media friendly to their interests; corporations and wealthy individuals have privileged access to office holders everywhere; political campaigns raise much money from the private sector; contractors cultivate cozy relations with those who hold the public purse strings; and specialized accounts and lawyers facilitate the transference of wealth to safe havens, as the Panama Papers showed. On the one hand, capitalists in competition with one another want transparency and fair procedures in dealing with the state; on the other hand, there are myriad ways that capitalism as an economic system is institutionally woven into the fabric of the state.

Consider how the United Nations Conference on Trade and Development annual report (UNCTAD 2019) characterized the state of the world's financial system ten years after unregulated speculation in the housing and mortgage sector of the U.S. economy sent the international economic system to its knees in 2008–2009. The language of the report sounded more like a report about organized crime. Unregulated financial markets have led to short-term economic decision-making, "rent-seeking behavior" (profiteering off loopholes in the system) "often in a highly extractive and predatory guise." About a third of the global financial system consists of "shadow banking," made up of "vast networks of financial dealers and intermediary institutions with undisclosed balance sheets." This allows "banks and their shadow arms to package and repackage assets of varying qualities in a process known as securitization," which in turn "creates heightened opaqueness and regulatory evasion." Even the sharpest accountant, economist, or anthropologist cannot ultimately trace who owns what. And the phenomenon is not entirely new, as a similar system created "mercurial flows of hot money" that precipitated the Great Depression of the 1930s (27).

Viewed in this way, one-third of the most vital part of the global capitalist system is placed beyond the reach of the rule of law, which partly explains why so few speculators went to jail after the 2009–2010 financial shock. "Too big to fail" is their ticket to impunity, and impunity means the entire system remains fragile, vulnerable, and, arguably, corrupted.

Discussion Questions

1.   Looking at Latin America, do you think that rule of law and democracy are inseparable from one another, or do you think it is possible to have one without the other? In particular, can one have the rule of law without democracy?
2.   In judging human rights conditions in Latin America, besides civil rights such as freedom of speech, should we also include consideration of substantive rights, such as the right to an education?
3.   Why do you think that prison conditions are so bad (even by U.S. standards) in Latin America? Do you think it is possible for democratic governments to bring (a) crime and (b) corruption under control in the region, or might this be something only nondemocratic governments can accomplish?

Resources for Further Study

Reading: A leading study is Lynn Hammergren's *Envisioning Reform: Improving Judicial Performance in Latin America* (College Park: Pennsylvania State University, 2007). Hammergren examines the difficulties in implementing legal reform in "Latin American Experience With Rule of Law Reform and Its Applicability to Nation-Building," *Case Western Reserve Journal of International Law* 38, no. 1 (2006): 63–93. Robert Samet's *Deadline: Populism and the Press in Venezuela* (Chicago: University of Chicago Press, 2018) is a short and exceptionally well-written study of police and crime in Venezuela. On human rights, see Lars Schoultz's *Human Rights and United States Policy Toward Latin America* (Princeton, NJ: Princeton University Press, 1981), which is particularly good on the Carter years. Martin Edwin Andersen's *Dossier Secreto* is a critical look at the Argentine Dirty War from both a human rights and a security point of view. The September/October 2011 issue of *NACLA Report on the Americas* includes several articles claiming that the human rights issue has been used politically and selectively by the right in an attempt to undermine the international reputation of leftist regimes.

Video and Film: *Cocalero* (2007) depicts human rights issues raised by the drug war in Bolivia. Journeyman Pictures offers several good films on the impact of the drug war in the Andes. See its website at www.journeyman.tv. *Landless* (2007), produced by Sonofed and available on YouTube, documents a land takeover, including the movement's interaction with law and the courts. *Dictator in the Dock* looks at the trial of former Guatemalan dictator General Efraín Ríos Montt, who was accused of crimes against humanity and genocide against the Maya Ixil people. Crime, drugs, and the lower class are all subjects of *City of God (Cidade de Deus*; 2002), a drama directed by Kátia Lund and Fernando Meirelles. This movie, based on a true story, tells of a dangerously violent neighborhood just outside of Rio de Janeiro, Brazil. Here, two boys grow up, one to become a photographer and one to become a drug dealer.

On the Internet: See the websites for Human Rights Watch (www.hrw.org), Amnesty International (www.amnesty.org), and the Inter-American Commission on Human Rights (www.cidh.org). The U.S. State Department posts its annual human rights review by country on the web; the 2012 report can be found at www.state.gov/j/drl/rls/hrrpt/

humanrightsreport/#wrapper. The human rights page at the University of Texas is a useful portal to the sites of human rights organizations throughout the hemisphere. See http://lanic.utexas.edu/la/region/hrights/. A valuable resource for data on prisons is World Prison Brief, Institute for Crime & Justice Policy Research, 2020, www. prisonstudies.org. Information on struggles by the LGBTQ+ community in Latin America can be found at https://outrightinternational.org/region/latin-america. The El País study can be found at https://elpais.com/internacional/2019/06/21/america/ 1561126403_693676.html.

PART V

Latin America in the World

PHOTOS 15.1 & 15.2   Officials in Brazil thought they were prepared for 1,000,000 visitors hitting their streets for Carnival in late February 2020. Ten days later the first coronavirus cases were identified. Two months later, the country officially had counted 50,512 cases and 3,365 deaths, widely believed to be a low estimate. Rio de Janeiro's streets, once teaming with revelers, were on lockdown. Brazil's official tally of deaths from Covid-19 exceed 130,000 by September.

Sources: 15.1: Alexandre Schneider/Getty Images.
        15.2: Fabio Teixeira/Anadolu Agency via Getty Images.

15 Democracy in Times of Globalization

Focus Questions

▶ Is globalization enhancing the prospects for democracy in Latin America?

▶ What challenges does globalization pose to the sovereignty of states in Latin America?

▶ What are some of the key issues in the debates about what kind of hemispheric economic integration is best suited for Latin America?

JAIRO ARTEGAGA PARKS cars under a license from Ecuador's capital, Quito; his clients pay 40 cents per hour; 20 cents goes to Jairo, and 20 cents goes to city. As the coronavirus began to creep across the city, the mayor ordered all municipal employees to work from home, which obviously would not work for him. To make matters worse, the city had just announced restrictions on vehicular and pedestrian traffic. This will also be disastrous for Galo Raul, a shoe polisher on one of the capital's busiest streets. Things are even worse for Elder Flores, a recent migrant from Venezuela, one of an estimated 470,000 who took refuge in Ecuador, fleeing dire conditions and political crisis at home. He tries to feed his family with earnings from selling tequeños (cheese-filled fried dumplings) on the street. Like Elder, Mercedes Almache, a Quito native, sells sweets outside a government building. Neither she nor Elder have sanitary protections to protect them and their clients from the highly contagious virus (EFE, Spanish press agency, March 17, 2020).

It would not be difficult to find similar stories in any of the world's major cities, but that only magnifies the way that globalization has linked the lives of people all over the world. Epidemics are democratic in the sense that all of us are biologically precarious beings, but a contagion like the COVID-19 strain demonstrates the vast differences in vulnerability between rich and poor. That gap has widened as globalization has progressed, but the nature of the challenge posed and other global issues (climate change, migration, illegal trafficking) all require global responses. That is the globalization paradox that faces us today.

A central theme of this chapter has to do with the ways in which the process of neoliberal globalization has impacted Latin America. In some ways one can see positive developments, such as the lessening of Latin America's dependence on the United States for trade and investment, some of it fostered by the U.S. neglect of Latin America in its foreign policy. On the other hand, it can be argued that **transnational** capitalism continues to deepen Latin American dependence as we approach the imminent deployment of new cyber technologies, such as artificial intelligence, facial recognition, global positioning system (GPS), and fifth generation (5G) data transmission.

TABLE 15.1 Top Four Agrifood Companies Ranking Among the Top 100 Non-Financial Transnational Corporations

Firm	Top 100 Rank	Home Country	Total Assets	Assets Abroad	Total Sales $million	Sales Abroad $million	Total Employees	Employees Abroad	Transnat'l Index, Average %
British American Tobacco	5	United Kingdom	190,643	189,214	26,116	25,844	91,402	78,843	94.8
Anheuser Busch InBev NV	29	Belgium	205,173	165,176	47,052	38,429	200,000	156,544	80.2
Nestle SA	7	Switzerland	133,627	106,790	91,186	89,905	323,000	312,867	91.8
Coca-Cola Company	19	United States	87,896	81,191	35,410	24,773	61,800	57,805	84.9

Source: ECLAC (2019: 144).

As we will frequently be referring to "transnational corporations" in this chapter, I will take a moment here to describe the characteristics of these entities, which some believe are more powerful today than nation-states. The United Nations Economic Commission for Latin America and the Caribbean (ECLAC 2019) has developed a "transnationalization index" composed by averaging three percentages: percentage of their assets located in countries outside of where they are headquartered; (2) percentage of their sales outside the home country; and (3) percentage of their employees located outside of the home country. Table 15.1 provides an example for agricultural and food companies that are highly active in Latin America.

At least as important to capture the nature of corporate transnationalism is the extent to which a company's board of directors and high-tier management are drawn from different countries. Corporations draw upon each other's top and highly paid executives for memberships on boards. With today's transportation and communication technologies, these networks are tightly integrated. Both boards and social relationships are interlocking, especially in the Western world and Japan. The result is the formation of elite networks, the infamous "1 percent," whose lifestyle and economic functions transcend national boundaries, and increasingly national identities as well. It is these networks that allow Honduran textile *maquilas*, Mexican telecommunications magnates, Chilean mining barons, Venezuela media barons, and others to network politically with each other and with corporate elites in other parts of the globe. All are likely to invest in and pursue business in lands and cultures far away from their homelands. For this reason, many students of international political economy speak of them as a "transnational capitalist class" (see Robinson 2004).

There are wide differences among those who study the international political economy about the relationships between powerful transnational corporations and elites and nation-states. There is little consensus, for example, about whether the United States, the most powerful economic and military nation, is using its power to promote a neoliberal world order friendly to transnationalism or is primarily pursuing its own "national interest." There was not much question about that issue until Donald Trump used a virulent right-wing populist campaign to reach the presidency. His "America First" economic policies seem aimed more at Europe and Asia than at Latin America.

Challenges to Sovereignty

In March 2012, Brazilian judge Daniela Pereira Madeira ruled in favor of Cristália, a Brazil-ian pharmaceutical company, and annulled the patent held by Abbott Laboratories for Kale-tra, a drug for treating AIDS/HIV. Cristália planned to begin producing a generic version of Kaletra. The decision was not the last in a legal battle that began in July 2005 when Brazil's health minister, José Saraiva Felipe, attempted to renegotiate access to Kaletra and other drugs that he wanted to make more freely available to all Brazilians who need it. Kaletra alone was absorbing a third of the health ministry's budget for antiviral medicines.

Felipe's objective was not only to get a break on the price but also to obtain rights to manufacture a generic version of the drug upon expiration of Abbott's patent in 2015. He won a price reduction from Abbott, but the issue over the patent remained. The judge ruled that allowing foreign patents to be extended beyond their initial term—a "pipeline" process, as it is known in Brazil—is not in accord with her country's constitution (New 2012). Brazil desired to develop its own pharmaceutical industry, for which reason the government was resisting attempts by the United States and the European Union to tighten and enforce intellectual property rights in global talks to expand the **World Trade Organization (WTO)**. Several other transnational drug companies were interested spectators (Benson 2005: B13). In 2019, a Brazilian appellate court ruled that Abbott's extension of its patent was valid, but at least the overall cost to Brazil's health ministry had been cut nearly in half.

At one time Brazil's national sovereignty would have given it a stronger hand in the negotiations. National sovereignty originated in the Treaty of Westphalia in the seventeenth century; it obligated states not to intervene in the internal affairs of other territorial states. The principle was never fully respected (with good reason, in some cases), but it served as the main principle of world order until World War II. Demand of The demand for sovereignty was the basis for the anti-colonial struggles of the **Cold War** era. It is still invoked today by Latin American and other states of the **Global South** to demand control over their natural resources—though with diminishing effectiveness as globalization as advanced.

Transnationalization of corporations was already on the increase because of trade agreements that lowered protectionist barriers of sovereign states (Strange 1996). Begin-ning around 1980, cyber and communication innovations imparted new momentum for extraordinarily rapid changes in the production of goods and services in the global economy. Until 2008–2009, when the global financial crisis struck, the advance of globalization seemed ineluctable. Despite the dimensions of the crisis and the wave of protest (for example, the Occupy Movement in the U.S.; the "indignados" in Spain), by 2014 globalization seemed to be moving forward again. Then in 2020, as the coronavirus pandemic struck, the world was reminded that nature too can be a powerful counterforce against globalization in its capital-ist, neoliberal form.

We define **globalization** as a broad tendency toward greater interaction of peo-ple across national boundaries of all types—economic, cultural, natural, and so on. These interactions pose challenges to states and citizens alike, in different ways. Information flows across borders, especially on the Internet, making censorship more difficult to enforce. Social media, camcorders (portable video cameras), and smartphones all seem to allow citizens, leaders, movements, and groups to communicate in an "unmediated" way. However, infor-mation still flows through an infrastructure, and much of it is owned by large corporations.

Surveillance technologies can scrape cybercommunications and use them for commercial or political purposes. Encryption can mask messages, but only to a certain degree.

Challenges to territorial sovereignty continue to arise out of globalization. Migration of undocumented workers and refugees conflicts with the capacity of states to control movements over their borders. Climate change has unleashed natural forces that require international and not national solutions. Drug eradication policies in Colombia poison rivers not only within its borders but in neighboring Ecuador. Melting glaciers in the Andes are forcing hundreds of thousands of farmers to migrate across borders. Clearing of rainforests in tropical areas is contributing to global warming. Biogenetic and other technologies can move on their own; Brazilian and Mexican farmers find unwanted, genetically engineered crops on their land. Tourism facilitates the transmission of epidemics, such as the HIV virus in the Caribbean and COVID-19. Island and coastal nations are threatened by increasingly powerful hurricanes.

Humans have joined nature in posing new challenges to territorial sovereignty. Terrorism and illicit trafficking have proven resilient against the power of national militaries. Human rights movements press the case that certain crimes require more than national systems of justice, laying the basis for supranational judiciaries, like the International Criminal Court and Inter-American Court for Human Rights. The rules of global trade have moved disputes between nation-states and foreign investors out of the courts of host countries and into international "dispute resolution" forums in London, Toronto, and Geneva.

Pundits like *New York Times* columnist Thomas Friedman (2000b, 2005) and *Newsweek*'s Fareed Zakaria take the position that globalization reduces the risk of war and is key to a more prosperous global economy for all. On the other hand, a worldwide anti-globalism movement, including Latin America's largest social movements (see chapter 11), is loath to see national governments, where they have some influence, losing effective sovereignty to distant international organizations like the WTO and International Monetary Fund (**IMF**).

For Review

Define globalization as a broad tendency. How does it come into conflict with the idea of territorial sovereignty? How was this illustrated in the Brazilian clash with Abbott? The coronavirus was not the first global pandemic. How did it reach down into the lives of Latin Americans in the urban informal sectors?

◼ Latin Americans on the Global Assembly Line

We begin to examine economic globalization out of the conviction that it is the most powerful of global tendencies, underlying many of the others to a great extent. In his books *The Lexus and the Olive Tree* and *The World Is Flat* (2000b, 2005), Friedman, a widely read *Times* columnist, described globalization as driven by technology and increasing interconnectedness. Friedman painted globalization as inevitable, beneficial to most people, and supportive of democracy. Countries that resist globalization, rich and poor, will lose out, he insists, if they resist free trade agreements. Friedman has ridiculed anti-globalization movements, saying their real name ought to be "the Coalition to Keep the World's Poor People Poor" (Friedman 2000a).

The majority of the world's poor people live in the Global South, many in Latin America. Many of them, especially those mobilized in the region's left social movements, seem to think that the kind of globalization embodied in free trade treaties seem designed "to keep the world's rich people rich." Fatoumata Jawara and Aileen Kwa, two researchers affiliated with the London-based NGO Oxfam International, believe that the system of trade does this "by increasing limitations on the ability of governments to enact policies in the interests of their own populations ... effectively [giving] precedence to trade and international commercial interests over people and international commitments and agreements directed at their benefit" (Jawara and Kwa 2002: 5).

Their conclusion is based on research and observation they did behind the scenes at the Doha Ministerial Conference of the WTO in November 2001. "Ministerials" are the most important venues for setting new economic, global rules of the game. Jawara and Kwa conclude, "WTO decisions are taken in a way favoring the interests of the few over the many, and commercial interests over ordinary people's livelihoods." Larger countries may bring more than 50 delegates to these meetings, a delegation size only the largest Third World countries (Brazil being one of them) can come close to matching. Large delegations are needed because negotiations, held in English or French, go on in hundreds of formal and informal meetings. Translations are rarely provided for small or informal meetings. Advanced "mini-ministerial" meetings are difficult for smaller and poorer countries to attend.

"Free trade" is usually associated with the elimination of tariffs, quotas, and regulations that limit exchanges of goods and services between nations. However, trade agreements involve much more. They define the rules for protecting technologies and cultural products (e.g., patents and copyrights, as in the Brazilian case with Kaletra). They often prohibit a nation from treating foreign investors differently from domestic ones, which effectively prohibits policies (such as **import substitution**) that Latin American governments have used to promote national industries. The agreements and their implementation by organizations, such as the WTO, have weakened laws that reserve ownership of national resources to that country's own citizens.

In addition to lowering barriers to movement of goods and services, free-"trade" agreements also make it easier for investments to flow over national boundaries. It is much easier today than it was 30 years ago for money to slip in and out of national economies, encouraging opaque "shadow banking" (see chapter 14). By liberating transnational capital to move with fewer restrictions, free trade agreements provide the international legal framework for what in business and management circles are known as "supply chains" and "value chains." Value chains refer to the sequence by which the components and labor are added in different locations and enterprise to produce a final good sold to a consumer. A value chain refers to how along each link in the supply chain a certain amount of "economic value" is added, until that value is incorporated into the price paid by the consumer. These chains are embedded in the production of just about anything we consume (for example, the book you are reading). A more colloquial term for the two chains combined is "the global assembly line," taken from the title of a documentary about the labor practices as the chains were emerging. *The Global Assembly Line* (Gray 1985) also was among the first to take note that much of the "value added" is the product of the meagerly compensated workers in the Global South, many of them women laboring in poor conditions.

Economic globalization involves two different ways of reorganizing the world economy. One has to do with *the production and exchange of whole goods*, what most people have considered "trade" through the ages. To take a simple example, if Salvadorans produce coffee and Canadians produce ladders, and then they trade them with one another, this division of labor is what most of us think of as trade. This is mainly what the English economist David Ricardo had in mind when he put forth his theory of **comparative advantage**. Ricardo argued by way of example that Portugal and England would both benefit if the first country concentrated on production of wine, the second focused on clothing, and then the two exchanged these products with one another. This is true, he argued, even if Portugal could produce clothing cheaper than England could. The efficiency of specialization produced this counterintuitive result. This remains the underlying argument that supporters of free trade make for the liberalization of sovereign control over international trade.

A second division of labor has to do with *how goods and services themselves are produced*—the *division of labor in production* itself. Adam Smith first recognized that the "wealth of nations" actually resided in the productivity of labor, which in turn depended on both technology and the way in which the labor in a society is organized. Smith's famous example involved the making of a pin. Note how elaborate the process already was nearly 250 years ago. Making a pin, he says,

> is divided into a number of branches, of which the greater part are likewise peculiar trades. One man draws out the wire, another straights it, a third cuts it, a fourth points it, a fifth grinds it at the top for receiving the head; to make the head requires two or three distinct operations; to put it on, is a peculiar business, to whiten the pins is another; it is even a trade by itself to put them into the paper; and the important business of making a pin is, in this manner, divided into about eighteen distinct operations, which, in some manufactories, are all performed by distinct hands, though in others the same man will sometimes perform two or three of them.
>
> (Smith 1766, book 1, chapter 1, paragraph 3)

As a result, Smith says, thousands more pins can be manufactured with the same amount of labor time than could be done if each person were to make the whole pin individually.

In Smith's day, factories for manufacturing items such as pins were just emerging. By the 1930s, Henry Ford had taken the idea of the division of labor in production to a new level with the assembly line, where workers performed different, specialized tasks, adding parts to a chassis along the factory floor. Rather than a pin, the product was infinitely more complex—an automobile. On the global assembly line, a product (be it a pin or an airliner) is passed not just from worker to worker but also from nation to nation, with value added along the way. The process is repeated, often 10 or 15 times, to manufacture, for example, a simple garment. To take an example, consider a "Canadian wood ladder." It may start out in a Canadian forest in British Columbia, now owned by the U.S. giant, Weyerhaeuser. After being cut into component parts it can be shipped on a Panamanian registered freighter from Vancouver to Mexico for assembly, using glue manufactured by a French-owned company in Senegal. Then it can be shipped by truck or rail to a Walmart warehouse in Texas—with the entire process controlled by a computer system maintained in New Delhi, India.

In sum, almost anything of any complexity produced today is not produced in a single factory or country but is passed along from country to country, stage by stage, along the global assembly line. If any link in the chain is disrupted, shortages result. One way the coronavirus threatened to plunge the global economy into crisis was by interrupting multiple links, including in agriculture, medicines, and health supplies. We will return to this problem further on in this chapter.

For Review

Why is it that "free trade" treaties are about more than trade? What is a supply chain, also known as "the global assembly line"?

Manufacturing, *Maquilas*, and Supply Chains

When Henry Ford "invented" the assembly line to produce Model T automobiles, his intentions were to gain control over the quality of components used in making his cars and to reduce production costs by facilitating the specialization of labor. He could then still make a profit on each car but sell more cars at a lower price. To do this, Ford concentrated his production in large factories. Raw or processed materials arrived at one end of his factory, and cars were driven off at the other. Although other manufacturers supplied some parts, an astounding number of components were made fully in-house, brought together in one location, in one country. Much of the raw material, such as iron for steel and coal or oil for energy, was produced in the United States as well. Other industries emulated Ford's approach, and the underlying philosophy, which included the idea that salaried workers could become a mass market for manufactured goods, came to be called "Fordism."

The global assembly line involves the first part of Ford's formula for success with a major difference. Instead of a product moving through a single factory along one conveyor belt, with workers doing specialized tasks along the way, what we now see is a process whereby the "stations" in the production process are scattered around the globe. Technological transformations in communications and transportation have enhanced the ability of corporate managers to move components from one country to another, but also to control production levels at each stage of the supply chain. This "just-in-time production," pioneered by Japanese companies, is carefully monitored to ensure that there are no bottlenecks (shortages) or a large excess of parts that need to be stored. In fact, unlike in the case of Fordism, it is not even necessary to own the process. Production can be divided up in different parts of the world through subcontracting.

Latin America was historically integrated into the world economy as a supplier of raw materials and agricultural products. Industrialization in North America, Europe, and Japan reinforced this pattern in the modernization period, but by World War II, the process of **import substitution industrialization** (ISI) was well underway in larger Latin American countries. Latin America's factories were modeled on Ford's way of organizing production, but the factory owners found it cheaper to import machines with older technology than to invest in research and development. Also, few Latin American universities could come close to matching the scientific knowledge and practical technology developed in the north.

As we have seen (in chapter 6), ISI faltered in the 1960s and gave way to the debt-ridden "lost decade" of the 1980s. "Conditionality" for debt relief required Latin America to move away from state-led development and toward a **neoliberal** strategy. Latin America thus entered the era of rapid capitalist globalization with an economic infrastructure and a scientific and educational sector inadequate to permit its industries to compete internationally. To be successful in the global economy, Latin America must find niches for its exports in global supply chains that are controlled by a few large transnational corporations.

In the small and poor Central American republics, little industrialization had taken place at all. Their economies continued to depend heavily on agricultural exports, such as fruit, coffee, and then after World War II, sugar, cotton, and beef. In this same period, some light manufacturing—pajamas, bras, and so on—appeared for the first time, geared toward export markets, not meeting the needs of the local population. This trend was reinforced in 1983, when the Reagan administration promoted the Caribbean Basin Initiative, under which Central American and Caribbean countries, other than Cuba, were offered duty-free access to the U.S. market for their exports. The initiative was intended to spur development and thereby alleviate the economic factors behind the revolutionary movements in the region.

The tendency accelerated in 2005 with the Central American Free Trade Agreement (CAFTA), modeled on **NAFTA**. This policy laid the basis for expansion of the *maquila* sector—factories where workers do the final assembly of consumer goods with imported components. This kind of manufacturing may not even qualify as "industrialization" since it requires little investment in equipment and technology and relies on abundant unskilled labor. Although some *maquilas* may assemble something as sophisticated and complicated as an automobile, many do little more than stitch the cover on a baseball, cut and sew cloth to make garments, or assemble electronic circuits for computers or Game Boys. Each *maquila* factory is a cog in a broader assembly line of manufacturing of clothing, electronic consumer goods, toys, and so on. Often the *maquila* is the last stop in the process. You may find a "Made in country X" label, perhaps from a Central American or Caribbean nation, on the shirt or blouse you are wearing as you read this book.

Another major step toward a global assembly line was taken in Mexico in 1965 with the establishment of the Border Industrialization Program. Mexico revised its laws to exempt American companies from customs taxes on equipment, machines, and materials brought into Mexico to produce exports back to the United States. The United States in turn reduced tariffs on exports from Mexico. Until 1994, there were limits on how much of the production under this program could escape import taxes in the United States. Unions and companies with factories in the United States did not wish to compete with cheaper Mexican production, but this changed in 1994 with NAFTA (the North American Free Trade Agreement), described later in more detail.

NAFTA contributed to some expansion of the Mexican middle class, but much of the working class has slid into the ranks of the poor. Workers' wages lost 76 percent of their buying power between 1982, when reforms that paved the way for NAFTA were first introduced, and 2012 (Esquival 2011). The numbers of the employed in the new *maquila* factories absorbed some of the dislocations, but not entirely. *Maquila* employment in Mexico rose from approximately 550,000 to 1.3 million between 1994 and 2001, but then it fell by more than 200,000 jobs in 2002 (Papademetrious et al. 2003). The reason for the fall is that other countries have adopted a similar strategy in what critics of neoliberal globalization call the "race to the bottom." Employment figures have continued to fluctuate, rising in the rest of the decade and then falling again with the global recession set off by the financial crisis of 2008.

In 2013, workers in the manufacturing sector in Mexico were typically paid on average US$10 per hour, twice the Mexican minimum wage. A typical *maquila* worker made only about $7.50 per hour. These wages compare to a little over US$19 for a manufacturing job in the United States, and few *maquila* workers have any significant benefits, such as health insurance or social security. Chinese workers in comparable industries earn about $5 per hour, and wages are even lower in poor Asian countries, like Vietnam. In 2018, Mexico agreed to amend NAFTA (now called the United States–Mexico–Canada Agreement). The amended agreement imposes more restrictions on the ability of other countries, mostly Asian, to locate *maquilas* along the border in order to take advantage of NAFTA, and this will probably have a negative impact on Mexican *maquila* workers.

PUNTO DE VISTA: DO YOU KNOW WHERE YOUR T-SHIRT CAME FROM?

A simple cotton t-shirt is a very simple commodity, but there are many steps in the value and supply chain, which together we will call "the global assembly line." The supply chain not only spans the hemisphere; it is global. And if we want to add embroidering, patches, patterns, color, etc., the line will be even more complex. Probably, you would "outsource" this project to a major textile/clothing company; and in fact, the NFL has a division, NFL Consumer Products, that coordinates apparel sales for all the teams.

The first step is the production of cotton, the raw material. If we examine it more closely, we realize that our "primary" stage relies on a lot of other inputs—water, seeds, fertilizer, hoes, tractors, etc. But there is an important sense in which we can still call this "primary": It involves extraction from nature. If our t-shirt is going to be a blend of polyester, a common synthetic fabric, and cotton, then the journey of our t-shirt in fact begins with extraction of oil from nature, because oil is the raw material from which polyester is made. Also, we are going to need energy for transportation and any non-human power employed in production. That would need to be factored into our supply chain as well.

One farm in Mississippi grows enough cotton for 9,000,000 t-shirts in one year.

That's impressive, but how many t-shirts do you own? Multiply that by about 300 million to estimate how much cotton is needed to meet demand in the U.S. In the United States, cotton is generally grown with genetically modified hybrid seeds, and harvesting is automated. For other countries like El Salvador, a producer and exporter of cotton, they need to adopt similar technologies—or make up for it with naturally more productive lands and a higher rate of exploitation of labor. When Salvadoran cotton exports first became an important part of the economy, in the 1960s, large amounts of seasonally employed peasants did the work. Today, immense automated harvesters, consuming huge quantities of oil and gasoline, are employed.

El Salvador increased exports of raw cotton from $60,000 to $1.2 million between 2016 and 2017. A spokesperson for a producer association said that further expansion would require "becoming attractive in segments of the chain which we do not currently have, suppliers of raw materials and high-level clothing," inecessary in order to "go abroad and show investors that El Salvador has clear rules." She added that the country had improved on timely delivery, integrated better with the "synthetic cluster," and increased its share of clothing exports from 2 to 3 percent of U.S. imports. By synthetic cluster, she was referring to processors that specialize in producing synthetic cloth.

Like American large-scale producers, bigger farms in El Salvador need crop insurance, protection against falling prices, and direct subsidies, difficult enough for big Salvadoran producers to obtain and virtually impossible for small producers. Just like the creation of a coffee-export economy in the 1800s, expansion of commercial agriculture means evicting peasants from lands through a judicial process controlled by the country's elite and enforced by its security forces. Injections of foreign aid help build dams and roads, including a project that would create a major north-south highway, connecting with other Central America countries and Mexico. This would facilitate the supply chain, but it would also bring new pressures on land, water, and other features of communities where small-scale peasant farming has survived.

After harvesting, the next stage of the journey is sending the cotton to a gin; seeds are removed, and the product is pressed into bales for export—to where? A likely place would be neighboring Honduras, which has many mills like those that once dotted the landscape of the U.S. South until companies started relocating or contracting out operations to cheaper labor markets. But now everywhere bales go to a modern and productive textile mill, one that is highly automated and operated 24/7. (It is also not at all unlikely that some of it will end up in mills in China or Indonesia to prepare it for production for the voracious Asian market.) After combing and twisting machines have done their work, we now have cotton yarn.

Next, in another location, perhaps in Honduras, the yarn is knitted into cloth—six miles of yarn for one t-shirt. Then the cloth is washed and dried. It is then sent on to its next destination—a good bet would be Colombia or Mexico, where sewing is still done by hand. The garment is then ready for printing the logo of, for example, the Palo Alto Conquistadors. There's a good chance that this was done in New York. But at each of these stages, the work is likely to be done in a country with a free trade agreement with the United States.

The journey is not quite done. The t-shirt needs to be sold and delivered. This is where Amazon, Walmart, and a few other massive retailers come in, with warehousing and either their own delivery systems or access to others—such as FedEx, UPS, USPS, and others. As this is a t-shirt, it might be the

FIGURE 15.1   Simplified Supply Chain for a T-Shirt

| Cultivate cotton | Harvest | Card, spin & weave | Manufacture | Dye, wash & rinse |

| Recycle or discard | Consume | Retail | Package & market | Transport |

Hanes Corporation that organizes the chain. The shirts will move through their carefully coordinated air and ground systems that guarantee "next day delivery."

As the t-shirt is moved about, consider how that is done. If you spend any time near railroad tracks, take a look at the lettering on the side of the cars. It is very likely that you will see a lot of Asian lettering. This is likely to be on a container sitting on top of a platform car, placed there by an automated system that moved it from a barge of an ocean-going freighter. That's how those bales of cotton can get to Indonesia instead of Honduras from El Salvador. Why is that important?

Let's say the Palo Alto Conquistadors finished last in the league the year before and were given no chance of winning the championship, but it's had a Cinderella season. For the season, NFL Apparel ordered 150,000 team logo t-shirts, but as the season comes close to climaxing, it's in the hunt. Now it is anticipated that it could sell 500,000 t-shirts.

To ramp up production you need to coordinate every link in the supply chain. That will not be easy. For one thing, ever since the Japanese innovated with "just-in-time" supply systems to cut down the expense of transporting and warehousing materials, production is carefully calibrated to meet demand in a timely way at each stage. Second, the stages of production are much more complicated than the simple one I have outlined here.

The cost of producing our t-shirt is approximately $13, building in profit along the way. The return to agribusinesses in El Salvador is about 60 cents. The seasonal minimum wage for workers on cotton plantations is $202.82 per month. A conservative estimate assumes the work to take about 200 hours per month, which makes their hourly wage a little more than one dollar per day. By the way, the Dallas Cowboys made $835 million dollars in overall revenue, and after expenses they had $364 million in operating revenue. No data for the Palo Alto Conquistadors was reported.

For Discussion

What kinds of global changes, if any, are needed to address the consequences of the global assembly line for the countries and people who get the lowest percentage of value? Are there any consequences if we do nothing at all?

For Further Study

Much of this quasi-hypothetical analysis of supply chains is based upon:

"Supply Chain 101, Journey of a T-Shirt," www.slideshare.net/TimAumann/supply-chain-101-journey-of-a-tshirt, accessed March 20, 2020.
National Public Radio, "Adding Up the Cost of Planet Money T-Shirt," www.npr.org/tags/190719989/planet-money-t-shirt
On El Salvador, CentralAmericaData.com, "El Salvador Wants to Sell More Raw Materials for Textiles," March 20, 2020.
Sajjadul Karim Bhuiyam, "Story of a Cotton T-Shirt," www.slideshare.net/sajjadbd92/story-of-a-cotton-tshirt

The complexity of the global assembly line varies from product to product. The Punto De Vista about the manufacture of t-shirts demonstrates how transnational and complex, yet controlled, is the assembly line for such a simple product. Figure 15.1 indicates some of the links in the chain. An industry consultant for organizing supply chains has produced a chart that, as I count them, shows 46 "process stages" in the manufacturing of cotton slacks (see http://doctorjane.org, accessed April 9, 2020). Consider an infinitely more complex tech product, the iPhone. A typical iPhone moves through 25 to 30 different countries. Apple hardly has a role in many key components. Samsung makes chips. Texas Instruments makes the chips that makes the phone sensitive to touch. Vishay Intertechnology makes capacitors and resistors, and so forth. Each part has a supply chain comparable to the t-shirt. Apple has 200 suppliers, and a reasonable estimate of the layers behind these companies quickly brings us to 5,000 suppliers and sub-suppliers. One crucial breakdown in the chain can disrupt the rest of it, unless a substitution can be quickly found. This is precisely the problem that erupted on a massive scale when the coronavirus forced much of the world's population into isolation from one another in 2020.

The "race to the bottom" involves more than low wages. Lax environmental and labor protection, poor salaries, and harsh living conditions are fostered by the need of low-income countries to attract foreign investment with the only **comparative advantages** they have—cheap labor and (sometimes) raw materials (oil, wood, mineral ores, etc.). Poor conditions were characteristic of the early process of industrialization in wealthy capitalist countries, answer the globalists. However, during the early ages of industrialization, much of the surplus was reinvested at home, and what we call the supply chain had many more local and national links. Like people in many other regions of the world, many Latin Americans have been impressed with the success of the newly industrializing countries (NICs) of Asia, which

PHOTO 15.1   The Panama Canal, in process of enlargement, as shown here, helps explain why Panama became in 2018 the first country to sign onto China's "Belt and Road" Initiative.

Source: Gerardo Pesantez/World Bank.

have industrialized largely by orienting production toward a world market. At least that seems to be the lesson of South Korea, China, Taiwan, Malaysia, and Thailand. Other development experts argue that the "Asian Tigers" did not simply open their markets and remove government from the economy to succeed. They also stressed education, have sought to limit inequality, and carried out significant land reform—all in contrast to most of Latin America (see various points of view in Dietz and Street 1987).

The companies involved in production all rely on financing to some degree. That creates debt, and this debt is often turned into another kind of security that is bought and sold. Algorithms quickly sense changes in the global economy; buy or sell orders are now automatically placed. So, as much value as the machines and labor just described add in real products used by consumers, the ratio of finance capital to real production has skyrocketed. A downturn in real production caused by a disruption like the coronavirus pandemic ripples through this financial house of cards, hitting hardest those countries, such as Brazil and Argentina, with the highest debts (see Figures 15.2 and 15.3). Companies can go bankrupt; technically, at least, countries cannot on what is called "sovereign debt." Vulture capitalists swoop down to buy securities at much less than face value and then use courts in wealthier capitalist countries to insist on payments on sovereign debt.

Argentina's President Mauricio Macri (2015–2019) attempted to tame the country's debt by curtailing spending and accepting other harsh terms in order to get the biggest loan

FIGURE 15.2   Central Government Debt as Percent of GDP

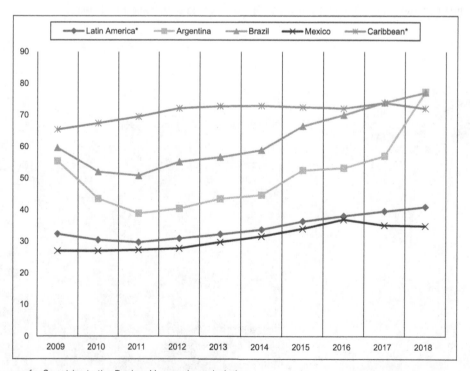

*Average for Countries in the Region; Venezuela excluded.

Source: ECLAC, *Preliminary Overview of the Economies of Latin America and the Caribbean* (2019).

FIGURE 15.3   Interest Payment of Public Debt as Percent Total Expenditure

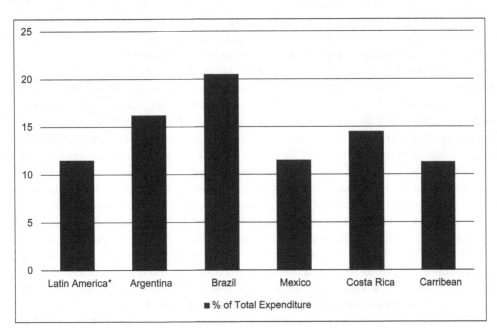

*Average for Countries in the Region; Venezuela and Bolivia excluded.

Source: ECLAC, *Preliminary Overview of the Economies of Latin America and the Caribbean* (2019).

ever provided by the IMF to prevent a full default. Part of his (and the IMF's) problem is that his predecessor, President Cristina Kirchner, put spending to pay down the social debt to struggling Argentine citizens ahead of paying off foreign bond holders. The holders sold off their bonds to vulture capitalists for a fraction of their face value. Backed by a ruling from U.S. federal court, they refused to accept partial compensation and insisted on being paid in full, meaning profits at 300 percent or more than what they paid from the initial holders. Macri attempted to comply, fearing the consequences if Argentina were to be completely cut off from the global financial system. He promised that his policies would soon lift the Argentine economy, but instead the freefall in demand made it crater. This contributed to his defeat in the 2019 elections, and the new president took office facing the daunting task of satisfying voters, somehow renegotiating the debt, and dealing with the onset of the coronavirus.

Fertile Profits: Agribusiness

Supply chains are not unique to industries; they are increasingly evident in agriculture. In fact, rather than separate the agricultural and industrial sectors from each other, economists and business analysts speak of the "agrifood chain," which includes fishing and forestry products in addition to those from farms, ranches, and plantations ECLAC (2019). Here, Latin America has become an increasingly important producer for the world market. The figures are modest; only 11.5 percent of world agro-industrial production came from

Latin America and the Caribbean. However, agribusiness exports were 26 percent of South America's exports in 2017 and had been growing at an annual rate of 8 percent since 2000. Expansion has been especially robust in the **Southern Cone**, east of the Andes, which offers ideal soil (*mollisol*) for cultivation of soy. Rising demand in Asia and Europe has attracted foreign capital and increased trade, with China especially prominent.

ECLAC matter-of-factly states (2019: 131), "In the modern agrifood chain, value creation is concentrated mainly in non-primary production segments where processing operations and services are added to agricultural products." This means that in contrast to cooperatives and small farmers who manage to find niche markets for their products, trans-national agribusiness producers in Latin America must rely on high-tech inputs (genetically modified seeds, fertilizers, livestock feeds), along with financial credit, insurance, and so forth. Big and small farmers must reach markets abroad through intermediaries. For agri-business that means farm and ranching production must be processed. This is an important link in chains within agro-industrial enterprises. It includes preparing frozen dinners and converting grain to breakfast cereal, for example. Enterprises that produce biofuels, textiles (as we just reviewed), and other non-edible products often rely on agribusiness inputs. Even smaller co-ops must link up in most cases with agribusiness for processes. Co-ops produc-ing palm oil in Honduras must find mills to convert the harvest into usable oil, something that requires as many as eight stages of refining. This is a point of vulnerability that can be exploited by land grabbers seeking to move into a growing export sector.

Although some foreign investment goes into the acquisition of land, the bulk of it goes to these forward and backward linkages, and most of that in turn comes from the giant trans-nationals that operate in these areas. From 2012 to 2016, over 90 percent of direct foreign investment in the agrifood chain went into the agro-industrial parts; less than 10 percent went into primary commodities, like soybeans. Almost 70 percent of the total investment in agribusiness in Latin America is in the agri-industrial sector.

Agribusiness and its allies argue that new technologies and their ability to move capital across national boundaries permit farmers to increase yields and feed a growing world popu-lation. In addition to environmental issues, the global expansion of agribusiness has opened issues about "food sovereignty," the willingness and ability of countries with fertile land to regulate land use to ensure the adequate nutrition of their own people. Agribusiness expan-sion has displaced many peasants and small farmers whose production is oriented to local markets and whose relationship to the land is quite different from that of wealthy foreign and domestic owners who live in the cities.

GM seeds are engineered genetically to survive the herbicides and pesticides that kill weeds and pests in the fields. The herbicides can be sprayed by drones flying over fields using GPS coordinates. Harvesters now can be programmed by the same technology that allows cars to self-park and self-drive. The installation of G5 Internet connectivity could enable the entire process to be automated and controlled remotely thousands of miles away, one reason why China is eager to have Huawei, its main cybercommunications company, speed installment of 5G in Latin America. Already the expansion of agribusiness into previously infertile land is destroying the ecosystem of the *chaco* (mostly in rural Paraguay and Bolivia), a region that was once scrub "wasteland" but also home to fast-disappearing tropical birds, armadillos, anteaters, and powerful jaguars.

As of 2005, GM crops were still illegal in Brazil, but their use in the country's fast-growing export sector was expanding. During his term (2003–2011), President Luiz Inácio da Silva

(Lula), whose PT (Workers' Party) includes a strong environmental movement in its ranks, faced a difficult choice. He had made promises to his environmental and Indigenous supporters to limit soy production and ban GM seeds, but he was reluctant to stunt the most dynamic growth sector in the economy—soybean exports. Brazil found itself locked in an international legal battle over the demand of the Monsanto Corporation that Brazil's farmers pay royalties for the use of GM seeds. In 2005, one state government even went so far as to negotiate an accord on royalties with Monsanto, a response to the smuggling of GM seeds into Brazil from Argentina. The federal government found itself being challenged in international courts for failing to enforce payment of royalties for the use of the new technology.

An innovation is poised to move past GM seeds. Nanoscience and nanotechnology will allow humans to see and to control individual atoms and molecules that are 1,000 times smaller than a plant cell. They are designed to get into the cells to introduce nutrients, speed germination, and in other ways influence cultivation. These kinds of technologies are owned and produced largely outside of Latin America and other parts of the Global South. Neither landowners nor farmers have any real say in whether they are introduced, because it is the control centers of the supply chains (see Figure 15.4) that decide what technologies are used and how much is produced in a given period of time. As we just saw with GM technology, even sympathetic leftist governments find it difficult to influence how land is used and for whom food is produced.

The soy boom has encouraged monoculture—that is, the devotion of a large proportion of fertile land in a region to a single crop. Between 1996 and 2008, the amount of land harvested for soy increased from six million to 16.7 million hectares (one hectare—10,000 square meters—equals approximately 2.5 acres). In 2017, ECLAC (2019) estimates 47 million hectares were devoted to soy production, largely stimulated by Chinese demand. However, in Europe as well, soy is consumed indirectly as it is processed into feed for cattle, chickens, pet food, and other uses. Soy imports in Britain come mostly from Argentina and require foreign cultivation of an area the size of Yorkshire—remember, "cultivation" does

FIGURE 15.4 Agrifood Supply Chain

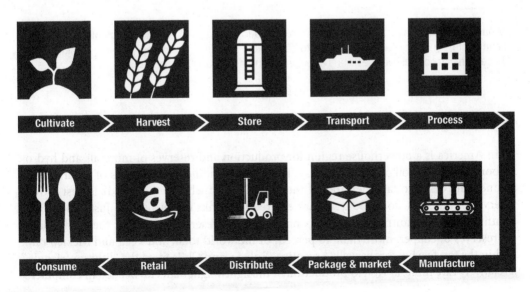

not require ownership. The British newspaper *The Independent* reported (blog, June 2, 3013), "The soya industry is highly concentrated down to a handful of multinational firms who dominate the entire market; from the very first seed through to sowing, spraying, harvesting, post-processing, all the way to the party. This is agribusiness at its most ruthlessly efficient."

Latin America, once stereotyped as a land of traditional *haciendas* with peasants eking out a subsistence living on the land, is passing. However, unjust as these systems were, they were human systems. Agri-"culture" included human culture, with social customs, productions for local and regional markets, and traditional practices of cultivation. As in China, North America, and Europe, rural areas are being drained of people; throughout Latin America today, less than 20 percent of the population lives in rural areas. Those who lived on the land are contributing to a surge of transnational migration. What labor is needed on agribusiness farms is often provided by migrants; in the case of Argentina, many come from nearby Paraguay and Bolivia. Just as in the United States, anti-immigrant sentiment has become more pronounced.

The Argentine government has reacted somewhat inconsistently to the soy boom. President Cristina Fernández Kirchner failed in her bid to raise taxes on soy exports from 35 percent to 44 percent in 2008. Argentine landowners may not control much of the supply chain for soy and other large Argentine agricultural exports (meat and grains), but they were a strategic political ally for transnational capital. They mobilized blockades of highways and put tractors into the streets of the capital to protest any tax hike. However, even at the lower rate, taxation on exports helped fill government coffers—as long as soy prices stayed high. They fluctuated around $15 per bushel in the early 2010s. Two years later they had fallen by one-third. High prices had helped Kirchner expand spending on programs that help the poor (and her voting base) and stimulated the economy; lower prices contributed to her defeat in 2015. A similar political fate hit many Latin American leftist governments, in particular those dependent on another natural resource—minerals, in the form of ores and hydrocarbons.

For Review

What is a supply chain? How does it work in regard to linking Latin American agricultural and manufacturing companies and workers to consumers in wealthy countries? Why are owners not necessarily in control over decisions about what and how much they produce?

Mining, Oil, and Extractivism

Latin America is a powerhouse region for production and reserves of minerals and hydrocarbons (especially oil and natural gas). Though the Middle East reserves of oil are purer, thinner, and easier to tap, they are not the largest. Venezuela has the world's largest proven reserves of oil. Next door, Guayana has entered the ranks of petrostates. Just about every South American country, plus Mexico, has significant reserves. Chile has the world's largest reserves of copper, more than 40 percent of the world total; and Peru and Mexico rank within the top five holders as well. Argentina, Bolivia, and Chile form the "lithium triangle," a relatively rare mineral vital to production of the lightweight batteries needed in computers, cell phones, and just about any "smart" car, weapon of war, or space vessel. This region alone has 54 percent of world reserves. Cobalt, zinc, gold, silver, tin, and just about anything else of value can be found beneath the surface in South and Central America—and even in the Caribbean. Jamaica has long been a repository of bauxite (for aluminum), and Cuba has significant reserves of nickel, important for the production of steel.

From the earliest days of Iberian conquest, Latin America has been prized by foreign investors for its vast mineral wealth. In the colonial era, Indigenous and African labor mined precious metals for export. Industrialization overseas brought increased demand for copper, iron ore, bauxite, and (later) oil. The Iberian Crown insisted on a share not of the profit, but of the value of what was produced—what we know today as "**royalty**," the share of production that belongs to the owner of the land. In the era of **liberal modernization** (beginning in the mid-1880s; see chapter 4), Latin American governments sought to attract investment to extraction by keeping royalties and taxes low as part of the bargain.

In the populist era, governments began to drive harder bargains for access to their "natural wealth." The 1960s and 1970s saw nationalization of mines and oil fields in Chile, Venezuela, Peru, Argentina, and many other countries (Mexico had already nationalized its oil industry in 1938). The **neoliberal** era (since 1980) saw a shift in philosophy—a return to the theory that state ownership, royalties, high taxes (even on super-profits), and regulation were counterproductive. New technologies made possible extraction of lower grades of ore, heavier oil buried deeper below ground, and gas locked in rock formations. Thus, as with agriculture, the capital and know-how to extract natural resources for export to a global market requires dealing with transnational corporations and investors. Neoliberals added a moral argument. They claim that taxing export profits only adds more incentives for corruption due to "rent-seeking"—that is, elites living off wealth generated by export taxes rather than pursuing wealth through entrepreneurship (World Bank 1996).

In the 1980s, the "lost decade" of debt and economic stagnation, Latin American governments felt pressure from the **World Bank**, the **IMF**, and private banks to privatize assets and create incentives for foreign investment. In mining and hydrocarbons, the World Bank laid out a blueprint (1996). It stressed guaranteeing the security of the property rights against nationalization of mining companies, replacing the jurisdiction of national courts with international arbitration, and replacing royalty (compensation for extracting exhaustible resources) with a sliding tax scale. Chile adopted these ideas most fully, and production did rise. However, without royalties and subject to creative bookkeeping by companies (for example, inflating costs of production or manipulating financing), several of the country's largest mines paid nothing to the Chilean treasury in the 1990s. These were years that they were doubling and tripling production of copper for export.

The World Bank–promoted reforms sought to remove any possibility of nationalization, even with compensation, something that was common following the decolonization of Africa, Asia, and the Middle East. An especially strong attack on territorial sovereignty was the Bank's push for "international dispute resolution," which today removes what once was a common feature in contracts, requiring that all disputes over terms be settled in the host nation's courts. Trade agreements, both bilateral (between two countries) and multilateral (more than two), typically include this requirement now. Disputes are currently arbitrated in special international legal forums, one of which is provided by the World Bank.

Another typical feature of free trade agreements calls for "clarity and transparency" in relations between states and transnationals. While theoretically aimed at curbing corruption, the provision also disallows countries from giving advantages to its own investors seeking mineral concessions, thereby limiting the country's ability to grow its own oil and mining industries. This was a common feature of Latin American foreign investment policies in the populist era. Furthermore, the World Bank model called for more access to mineral resources, including transferring those already held back for exploitation by state-owned companies, thereby making them available to exploitation by foreign investors.

The World Bank model would prohibit countries from raising taxes or royalties to increase the nation's share of profits during commodity booms. Countries would no longer be able to restrict production to defend against falling prices in periods of oversupply. This would eliminate for mining and energy a key tool that members of the Organization of Petroleum Exporting Countries (OPEC) have used to defend the price of oil. Global South exporters of copper, coffee, sugar, and other commodities once (in the 1960s and 1970s) saw OPEC's success as a model for defending their own primary commodity exports from the wild swings in prices on global markets. By gaining control over pricing, they could seek to gain equity in their trade relations, ensuring more equity in the trade of their primary commodities for imports from the Global North.

From the Bank's perspective, minerals, hydrocarbons, and nutrients in the soil are all a "free gift of nature" and part of the global commons. The **neoliberal** perspective sees the freedom to discover ("prospecting," "exploration") and then to take them out of "the commons" as the right of the investor. From this viewpoint, the capital investment and labor expended to find and exploit minerals and hydrocarbons (oil, coal, and gas) is what gives them economic value. Together, discovery and exploitation are what we mean by "extraction."

Objections to extraction in Latin America come mainly from two sources. One source is from movements of environmental, Indigenous, and community activists who see extraction as an unsustainable activity that generates harm and caters ultimately to a global consumer mentality. The other source is a relatively new school of thought by political economists who argue that the programs that make Pink Tide governments successful in reducing poverty were dependent on taxing extractive industries during boom times, only to see these programs wither when **commodity** prices fell. With this withering, so too did the political fortunes of the Pink Tide.

On the other side of the debate takes the form of **neo-extractivism** position. It argues that tapping into the profits of extractive industries remains for now at least the only way to generate capital for economic development and addressing pressing needs to address poverty. It is "neo" (new) because it still, as in the past, promotes extraction of natural resources for export and the generation of economic development, but it also demands that mining and agricultural exports pay higher royalties and taxes. Neo-extractivists point out that better stewardship of the earth's ecosystems requires a global effort that should not put the burden of adjustment solely on those people who live in the Global South.

Many countries outside the region have a significant stake in Latin America's policies about extraction. No nation in the Global North has within its territory enough of everything needed to satisfy mass consumption. With Asian countries, especially China, now combing the earth for minerals and hydrocarbons, demand has risen rapidly. The *LatAm Investor*, a British quarterly newsletter for investors, proclaimed in its July 8, 2019, edition that it was a "great time to invest in Latin American mining" because demand was expected to continue unabated. "Latin America isn't just rich in metals—its rich in the right metals," it proclaimed.

Undoubtedly, the coronavirus pandemic in 2020 seriously dimmed this optimism, leaving the future of demand, and perhaps transnational capitalism itself, in doubt.

The voracious appetite for land and what is beneath the surface has expanded transnational investment into the remotest parts of Latin America. This frequently brings them up against Indigenous groups who see themselves as stewards of nature. They are advocates, in harmony with environmentalists, of a less materialist style of life—*el buen vivir*, as Indigenous people in mineral-rich Andean states put it. Many view their land as a sacred resource not to be abused in order to feed mass consumption and transnational profits. Their movements share other objections with environmental movements.

At the same time, we should not romanticize the relationship between Indigenous people and nature. A large but undetermined percentage of this population now live in cities and towns. Furthermore, Indigenous peoples, such as the Pemón in Venezuela, have long participated in small-scale extraction of minerals, certainly more environmentally sensitive than transnational corporations, but still reliant on their operations for community survival. They are engaged in "Indigenous capitalism" (Angosto-Ferrández 2015).

As in agriculture, large-scale production of minerals and hydrocarbons relies on technologies that threaten the environment. Thick oil far below the surface is emulsified (thinned) with chemicals and water. (Sometimes oil and water do mix!) Today, small traces, much less than 1 percent, of copper ore are "leached" from massive quantities of crushed rock by chemical processes. Both leave water pollution and mountains or pools of hazardous waste material. Gold is among the dirtiest minerals to extract. The biggest threat is usually to residents of local communities, but even large property owners, such as owners of tourist resorts, may resist intrusion by mining and oil companies.

There were some signs of a shift away from neoliberal mining and oil policies in the 2000s. Venezuela's late president Hugo Chávez took the lead in the 2000s in reinvigorating OPEC. He raised taxes and royalties and sent advisers to other countries to learn how to strike a better deal with foreign investors. On May 1, 2006, Bolivia's President Evo Morales sent troops into Bolivia's gas and oil fields to (re)nationalize them and demand that operating companies renegotiate terms. Even neoliberal Chile began to rethink policies. In 2005, the Chilean Congress imposed a 5 percent royalty on foreign copper companies, which export two-thirds of Chile's copper but were paying virtually no significant royalties or income taxes—this in a country often called the "Saudi Arabia of copper."

Free trade agreements requiring international arbitration limit this tactic—even when the home country of the investor is not a signatory to the agreement. For example, Exxon-Mobil and ConocoPhillips took Venezuela to the International Court for Settlements of International Disputes over a conflict regarding how much compensation was due to them for nationalization in several large oil fields. Both are U.S. companies, and the United States has no free-trade treaty with Venezuela. The Netherlands does, however, so the companies simply established subsidiaries in that country to serve as conduits for their investments in Venezuela, giving them status to take Venezuela to court (Boué 2013). In fact, statistics on the country-origin of foreign direct investment have become more unreliable because of this kind of practice. The tiny Netherlands is listed as one of the largest sources of foreign direct investment in Latin America today because of its bilateral "trade" agreements in the region.

The kinds of rules promoted by the World Bank model, which in many ways harkens back to the era of liberal modernization when *caudillos*, like Díaz and his *científicos* in Mexico, offered low taxes laws, royalty rates, and incentive to attract foreign investors. Some critics go even further, believing that even booms leave little real progress behind. Latin American history is littered with economic crises that followed when booms became busts. Chile, for example, was thriving off the export of nitrates extracted from immense caches along northern coastal deserts, courtesy of bird droppings accumulated over hundreds of thousands of years that were converted into gunpowder and fertilizer in the nitrates global market. Then, in World War I, German scientists figured out a way to create synthetic nitrates, and the economy went into deep recession.

For Review

What is "extractivism"? How does the economic relationship between transnational mining companies and host countries create conflicts over sovereignty? How does nationalism conflict with extractivism? What about Indigenous movements and environmental movements? How do some trade agreements strengthen the hand of mining and oil companies in disputes?

Tourism

Large-scale tourism has displaced commodity exports as the main source of income for many Caribbean countries. Much of the infrastructure for tourism is owned by foreign companies who export a high percentage of profits out of the host country. The United Nations Environmental Program estimates that of US$100 spent by a tourist in a Third World nation, only US$5 stays in the country. The rest goes mostly to tourist corporations (e.g., international hotel chains, airlines, tourist agencies, and cruise lines) based elsewhere. Mega-developments swallow beaches, mangroves, and other natural features important to the local environment. Tourists demand air conditioning, daily fresh linens, and a variety of comforts that must be imported and are not commonly available to the local inhabitants. The locals often find their beaches and facilities off-limits. If you take your spring break in Mexico or the Caribbean, what kind of accommodations would *you* expect?

The initial economic surge from tourism can hide long-term problems that emerge as the infrastructure begins to decay. The cruise ship industry is especially problematic for the small countries of the Caribbean and Central America. People living on cruise ships do little to spur local employment in hotels or restaurants. Cruise companies operate on the high seas beyond the reach of the state's sovereign power. Tourists tend to come from wealthier, northern nations and expect more and not fewer comforts during their limited vacation time. As Cynthia Enloe (2000) has shown, advertising tends to promote destinations as subservient to First World tourists, using feminine stereotypes. Some governments cast a blind eye toward local escort services or marriage brokers that use the Internet to advertise the availability of young women.

Some countries promote ecotourism as a solution to these problems. Supposedly more environmentally conscious and mindful of local development needs, ecotourism has been touted as an alternative to the exploitative type of tourism. However, a European coalition of religious clergy recently commented to the UN Commission on Sustainable Development,

> Although much promise initially surrounded the ecotourism concept, most ecotourism today is merely a market brand, with the same damaging characteristics. In fact,

ecotourism impacts can be even more acute, due to the ecologically and culturally sensitive areas targeted. As a result, most ecotourism destinations face ruin within fifteen years. Consumers, meanwhile, become desensitized to what constitutes a viable ecosystem or community.

(ECEN 2005)

Cuba has come to rely heavily on tourism, in part because of the crisis in its former key export sector, sugar (Silberman et al. 2004). The country has fared better than most in the region by regulating tourism and keeping tourist dollars in the economy. Hotel workers get typically low salaries but have health care, access to education, and other job protections. To limit the outward flow of tourism earnings, state tourism agencies operate in partnership with foreign investors. In recent years, much of the sector has been turned over to the military; hiring is done through the state labor ministry, opening possibilities for graft and favoritism. Cuba's national women's association attempts to discourage prostitution, which almost inevitably seems to follow the tourist dollar. It does not help that Cuba lures tourists with advertising campaigns designed to create nostalgia for the nightclub atmosphere and tropical stereotypes that made pre-1959 Havana the world's prime destination for a sinful vacation.

Mega-tourism projects have become more common. Any visitor who cares to listen will hear environmentalists talk about the difficulties they have in limiting the impact of these projects on the local ecosystem. Until recently, the state control over tourism was justified because profits were used to subsidize Cuba's free education, health care, and other benefits. However, there has always been something of a compromise here since Cubans working in the tourist trade have had more access to foreigners and their currency (e.g., tips to hotel and restaurant workers). Now, with the gradual economic liberalization launched by Raúl Castro, workers in the tourist sector are better placed, with expertise and access to foreign currency, than their countrymen and -women to launch small businesses.

However, anyone who has visited Acapulco (Mexico) will find a much more unjust system of tourism than anything seen in Cuba. Acapulco's famous hotels nearly surround a bay whose splendid beaches are off-limits to most of the millions of people living in the *barrios* on the adjacent mountainsides. Well-armed police patrol the coastal road to maintain a separation between the hotels and the city neighborhoods. In the evening, the mountainsides are dotted with blazing fires—trash burning in neighborhoods lacking sanitation services. If you visit a Mexican resort for spring break, talk to some of the people who work in the markets and hotels. Ask them where they live, how far they must commute to work, what their life is like. Make your own assessment of who is benefiting from the tourist trade.

For Review

What are some of the benefits from tourism to countries in the Caribbean and Central America? What are some of the dangers? What positives and negatives can be taken from the Cuban experience?

▪ Trade Agreements and Regional Economic Blocs

The U.S. view is that free trade agreements not only bring economic benefits to underdeveloped countries but also strengthen democracy. In 2005, the Office of the United States Trade Representative (USTR) made the following claim in a briefing for a new agreement, CAFTA.

> In the 1980s Central America was characterized by civil war, chaos, dictators, and Communist [sic] insurgencies. Today, Central America is a region of fragile democracies that need US support. Elected leaders in the region are embracing freedom and economic reform, fighting corruption, strengthening the rule of law and battling crime, and supporting America in the war on terrorism. But anti-reform forces in the region have not gone away. CAFTA is a way for America to support freedom, democracy and economic reform in our own neighborhood.
>
> (USTR 2005)

This statement is notable for its characterization of the rebellions of the 1980s as "communist" and its portrayal of a general situation of anarchy. CAFTA eventually was approved, and a sixth country, the Dominican Republic, was added. It is now officially CAFTA-DR.

Similar claims about democracy were made for the North American Free Trade Agreement (NAFTA) and on behalf of a U.S.-proposed Free Trade Area of the Americas (FTAA), which would embrace the entire hemisphere and require that states be democratic. The FTAA ran into trouble at the November 2005 Summit of the Americas, where Venezuela's Chávez led an all-out assault on the idea. He was backed by social movements and other **Pink Tide** politicians. The FTAA ran into trouble domestically in the United States as well. Nonetheless, the idea, if not the multilateral treaty, moved ahead in the form of a series of bilateral agreements (between the United States and individual countries, such as Chile, Peru, and Colombia) and other multilateral agreements.

The argument for integrating Latin America's economies more closely to the United States often invokes the success of the European Common Market (now the European Union, EU; see USTR 2004). The EU contributed to the region's economic recovery after World War II and made Western Europe a force to be reckoned with in global economic diplomacy. However, there are major differences between the EU and the proposed FTAA. The European nations were at comparable levels of economic development, which meant less overall displacement and relative equity among the partners in negotiation and implementation of the accord. Europeans already had achieved progressive and effective protection of workers and weaker portions of the population in the form of welfare, labor rights, and environmental protection. Unlike NAFTA, the Common Market not only committed members to mutually lowering trade barriers but also created institutions whereby the community could represent itself as an entity in global economic talks. Assessing CAFTA, the Washington-based Council on Hemispheric Affairs (Birns and Schaffer 2005) argued that CAFTA's marriage of a US$12 trillion economy, with its "intrinsic advantages," to six economies that in combination amount to only US$12 billion, "is like matching a major league baseball team on steroids against little leaguers and heatedly insisting that, because umpires use the same rulebook, somehow it is a fair match." The rules apply the same to all economies, rich and poor, regardless if they can compete effectively with one another.

Bilateral agreements were once the main instrument for linking economies to one another, but today, they are largely used to incorporate new partners into larger associations. A U.S. bilateral treaty with Chile on January 1, 2005, grants Chile access to the U.S. market on the same terms offered to Canada and Mexico under the NAFTA of 1994. Chile's new pipeline to the U.S. market was sold in the country as a way to diversity its exports. World Bank data do show that Chilean exports in mining fell from 88 percent in 1970 (mostly copper) to 43 percent in 1999. However, the greatest increases were in other extractive commodities and in agri-industries, such as timber, vegetables, fruits, seafood, wine, and dairy products. The ledger also looked more balanced because copper prices were falling.

In reality, Chile exported nine times more copper ore in 1999 than it did in 1970. The basis was laid, at a high human cost, by the Pinochet dictatorship (1973–1988; see chapter 7). In an environment of military repression and economic difficulty, the new seafood and agro-industries found workers in an army of women and peasants displaced from the traditional *latifundia*. By the time electoral democracy was restored, these new sectors were well established. Institutional limits on democracy made it nearly impossible for elected governments to change the generous tax policies and leases of public lands to private interests. The benefits have been sharply skewed in favor of a few, with high public dissatisfaction evident in the maldistribution of income and wealth by the post-1989 elected government. Six-day, 48-hour workweeks are common (see Schurman 2003). The minimum wage in 2003 was only US$150 a month; official unemployment hovered between 9 and 10 percent. Ten percent of the population received 50 percent of national income.

Like other industries, Chile's agro-industry demands (and gets) "labor flexibility," which translates into greater freedom to lay off workers and relief from regulation. In August 2003, Chile's unions organized the country's first one-day general strike, demanding a change in the economic model. President Ricardo Lagos reacted in anger to the action, saying that it harmed Chile's image of stability and friendliness toward investment just as a major hemispheric economic summit was about to take place. Since that time, Latin America's "economic success story" has experience several episodes of mass protests, with the most recent ones of 2019–2020 demanding constitutional changes.

North American Free Trade Agreement (NAFTA)

NAFTA was not the first multilateral trade agreement in the region, but it was a path-breaker that set the model for what the United States hoped would develop into a hemispheric-wide pact. That was not to be, but through a series of other agreements, some of the objectives encompassed by NAFTA have advanced.

NAFTA, signed by the United States, Canada, and Mexico, went into effect on January 1, 1994. It eliminated many national regulations on foreign investment flows and prohibits governments from "discriminating" against those foreign investments by favoring its own companies through subsidies, tariffs, and regulations. NAFTA prevents or strongly limits governments from requiring local purchases of inputs (parts, services, raw materials, machines, etc.). It lifts regulations requiring that a percentage of profits by a foreign company can be repatriated abroad. It bans governments from subsidizing national producers so that they can compete more effectively with foreign firms, and it prohibits favoring national buyers in privatization of state assets. All of these were policy tools aimed at stimulating development in the import substitution era. Hence, "trade" now covers investment, even in areas such as banking. To take one example, Mexico cannot decide that it will reserve at auction 10 percent of land for Mexican mining or oil companies, in order to stimulate their productive capacity. The agreement includes protection of intellectual property rights and allows greater migration among professional and skilled employees, but not ordinary workers.

To gain benefits, corporations must make sure that a certain percentage of the "value added" (to the "value chain") in production of traded goods originates in one of the member countries. That did not prevent Asian companies from taking advantage of NAFTA by locating factories in Mexico. *Labor Alerts*, a U.S.-based newsletter reflecting views of unions, highlighted (June 8, 1997) the plight of workers in Hyundai Corporation's factory in Tijuana, Mexico, during a 1997 strike by workers:

> While the workers assemble and weld at least 26 chassis daily, and the chassis sell for $1800 each, they make 280–360 pesos ($33–$46) weekly . . . The Han Young *maquiladora*, like most *maquiladoras* in Tijuana, pays a government-connected "union" known as the *Confederacion Regional de Obreros Mexicanos* (CROM). Workers do not participate in any meetings of the "union" and have never seen a copy of its contract with the company. It is a standard practice by the *maquiladora* industry to pay for "protection contracts" against independent organizing by workers.

After two years of strife, including a hunger strike by workers, Hyundai simply closed the plant and moved production to a different facility in the same town (Bacon 2004). The amended NAFTA of 2020 would increase value-added requirements, but it largely affects the automobile industry, leaving opportunities intact for other industries.

The original NAFTA included an adjudication mechanism whereby a corporation or citizen could directly bring a case before an international tribunal for violation of value-added limits or abuse of copyrights. However, the treaty provided no similar recourse for violations of environmental, human rights, or labor accords, which are covered only in the side agreements. A study of seven labor cases by five researchers at the UCLA Center for Labor Research and Education (Delp et al. 2004) found that the labor accord had helped expose serious violations that threaten the health and safety of Mexican workers and immigrant workers in the United States, but the authors also found that the accord "failed to protect workers' rights and is in danger of fading into oblivion." The labor side agreement "created a lengthy, bureaucratic process with no ability to protect workers from reprisal" (Delp et al. 2004: 7). The amended agreement negotiated in 2019 is slightly stronger but does not approach levels of enforcement available to corporations for infringement of copyrights or patents.

The story on the environmental side is similar. Stephen Mumme of the Interhemispheric Resource Center credits the Commission for Environmental Cooperation (CEC), created by a side agreement, with having shed light on many serious pollution problems through its investigations and reports. However, Mumme argues that companies have used the antidiscrimination provisions in NAFTA to fight tougher environmental laws in particular countries. Of 20 citizen complaints submitted to the CEC for investigation after 1994, only two had even been recommended as worthy of factual investigation five years later. The CEC can only spur governments to take action; it cannot directly make policies and decisions on issues raised (Mumme 1999).

Mexico has experienced a serious agricultural crisis over the last 25 years (Barkin 2006). Many peasants have been forced off the land by a combination of foreign competition and withdrawal of subsidies and guaranteed land rights (*ejidos*) that were repealed by the Mexican government in anticipation of NAFTA. Rural families became more dependent on money from family members working in the United States. The United States' appetite for ethanol increased demand for corn, provoking the "tortilla wars," a conflict between consumers, Mexican farmers, and the government. To keep prices lower and avert a consumer revolt, the Mexican government opened its market to exports from the United States. This in turn hurt small Mexican farmers who, unlike big growers, are not linked to export markets through transactions that link farms to the U.S. market.

To win approval of NAFTA, the Mexican government overvalued the peso in the run-up to 1994. This was done to prevent a surge in the U.S. trade deficit with Mexico just before the U.S. Congress was to vote and in anticipation of elections in that year. To achieve this, the government borrowed dollars heavily from abroad. After NAFTA went into effect, the government withdrew support for the peso. The subsequent "peso crisis" resulted in a drastic fall in the real wages of Mexican workers. Hence, any recovery in the Mexican economy, especially regarding unemployment and wages, measured from 1994 is suspicious and difficult to attribute to NAFTA. The minimum wage in Mexico in 2016 was less than $4 per day, far below the minimum to escape poverty. The Carnegie Endowment for International Peace, an organization generally supportive of expanded trade, issued a report (Papademetriou et al. 2003) concluding that after ten years, NAFTA had "produced a disappointingly small net gain in jobs" in Mexico. Another study in 2012 found little improvement in workers wages (Johnson 2012). Largely, agricultural imports had reduced employment in the rural sector, while job creation in other sectors had barely kept pace. Things did go much better for workers in the United States. It was not so much levels of employment as wages that were affected. By integrating a low wage nation into two higher wage nations (Canada and the U.S.) NAFTA encouraged employers to plead that they had to compete with factories based in Mexico. This gave them leverage to wrest significant concessions on wages and benefits from American workers, lest they move operations south of the border (Scott 2003). Reviews of NAFTA in 2014, the 20th anniversary, showed increased economic trade among the three countries involved, but also found that things had changed little for workers in the United States, Canada, or Mexico (Aguilar 2012).

CAFTA (or CAFTA-DR, once the Dominican Republic joined the agreement), approved by the U.S. Congress in 2005, is even weaker on environmental and labor protection. Signers are committed only to make "strides" toward enforcement of existing codes, which are weaker than those in Mexico. As with NAFTA, CAFTA was negotiated behind closed doors and drew opposition from many social movements in the region. Demonstrators against the agreement in Guatemala, demanding a popular referendum, were met in March 2004 with violent repression. U.S. and Central American Catholic bishops announced opposition to the treaty. Strikes forced the Costa Rican government to withdraw temporarily from treaty negotiations in 2003. The Nobel Prizewinning former president Oscar Arias, who had been expected to easily win a new term in 2006, barely survived a challenger opposed to the agreement. Arias faced a tough fight but won approval from Costa Rica's Congress. When the Honduran legislature met to ratify the agreement on March 3, 2006, demonstrators surrounded the Congress and blocked all the streets, causing the representatives to flee the building after voting their approval.

NAFTA offered Washington the opportunity to lock in place a model of development predicated on faith in a free market. It poses huge obstacles to any return to more populist economic policies and a state-centered approach to development. Although Mexico's PRD advocates renegotiating, not abandoning, NAFTA, the longer the present treaty remains in place, the more difficult it will be to change. In fact, after left populist President Andrés Manuel López Obrador assumed office, he not only accepted NAFTA but agreed to U.S. President Donald Trump's demand to renegotiate the terms and extend it.

A wave of global protests has slowed down momentum for multilateral trade agreements. At one time, a proposal for a new free trade agreement, the Trans-Pacific Partnership (TPP), seemed almost sure to be enacted. It would have linked together the United States, Canada, Mexico, Peru, Chile, Australia, New Zealand, Singapore, Brunei, Malaysia, Vietnam, and Japan, with provisions for other nations to join later. Together these countries account for one-third of global production. Noticeably absent from the list was China, and not by accident. The United States initiated the TPP proposal in part to respond to the challenge of rising Chinese investment in the Americas and growing Chinese geopolitical influence in Asia. A big stumbling block for both the TPP and expansion of the WTO was intellectual property—that is, the U.S. determination to gain stronger protection over patents and copyrights. Brazil was leery of a proposed Transatlantic Trade and Investment Partnership (TTIP). Latin America also balked at the transatlantic treaty because of the European Union's desire to maintain privileged trade and investment relations with its former colonies, most of which are in Africa and Asia, whose agricultural exports compete with those of Latin America and the Caribbean.

Political opposition in both the United States and Latin America short-circuited the proposal for a hemispheric Free Trade Association of the Americas, modeled on NAFTA. The FTAA collapsed further under the pressure of opposition from the **Pink Tide** in the 2000s. What followed was not a more inward-looking development model, as critics of NAFTA and FTAA agreement hoped, but the entry, for better or for worse, of a new player into the Latin American economy, Asia, especially China.

China, Asia, and Latin America

Judging by the evolving patterns of investment and trade, there is little doubt that the pattern of Latin America's economic relations with the rest of the world has been changing. The period since 1990 was marked by a surge of foreign investment in Latin America, but not all of it from the traditional centers of the world economy. Some of it came from the "developing and transitional" economies (mostly Eastern Europe and the **BRICS**). Investment from these countries increased in the 2000s but fell off after the 2008 global financial crisis. The percentage of foreign direct investment (FDI) coming from the United States and Canada dropped in the second half of the 2000s from 37.8 to 28.2 percent, with a particularly startling drop for Brazil (from 22.2 to 14.4 percent). Undoubtedly, the decline in part was a consequence of the recession in the U.S. economy, but it is also a reflection of shifting markets and the growing influence of the Asian economy, especially China, in the global economy. Still, according to figures from the Organization for Economically Developed Countries (OECD), the U.S. in 2018 remained the most important source of FDI is the region, with more than $1 trillion of accumulated investment.

Tables 15.2 and 15.3 give a good idea of how quickly Chinese economic relations in the region have expanded. In terms of financing, China's loans between 2005 and 2018 went mostly to countries from which it imports food, mainly soy from Brazil and Argentina (see earlier discussion of agribusiness), and minerals, especially oil in the cases of Venezuela and Ecuador. China's earliest investments in Venezuela were just before Chávez assumed the presidency, and it took advantage of the favorable investment climate of the neoliberal "oil opening" in that country (see chapter 8). Like other investors, Chinese oil companies found themselves paying higher royalties and taxes and adjusting to other changes introduced by oil reforms of the 1990s. Still, access in the long term kept Chinese companies and the state interested in expanding in Venezuela, and Beijing has had huge reserves of U.S. dollars to invest.

TABLE 15.2 Chinese Financing in Latin America, 2005–2018

Country	Amount (U.S. billions)
Venezuela	$67.2
Brazil	$28.9
Ecuador	$18.4
Argentina	$16.9
Trinidad and Tobago	$2.6
Bolivia	$2.5
Jamaica	$2.1
Mexico	$1.0
Other Countries	$1.3
Total	$141.3

Source: Gallagher, Kevin P. and Margaret Myers, "China-Latin America Finance Data-Base," Inter-American Dialogue, 2019.

TABLE 15.3 Latin American Exports and Imports, Selected Countries and Years

Trade, billions current dollars	Exports to 2017	Imports from 2017	Exports to 2016	Imports from 2016	Exports to 2007	Imports from 2007
U.S.A.	420.1	293.1	369.5	273.0	325.8	216.8
(Mexico/U.S.A. trade)	(327.3)	(74.1)	(302.9)	(179.9)	(223.4)	(139.9)
Lat. Am. & U.S. trade minus Mexico trade*	92.8	219.0	66.6	93.1	102.4	76.9
China	96.7	170.6	78.4	156.1	35.4	70.2
Brazil	25.3	42.3	23.5	23.5	24.0	38.1
Japan	20.4	30.1	17.2	28.9	17.8	30.4
Netherlands*	19.6	5.7	19.5	6.7	20.4	7.4
South Korea	14.0	27.9	13.1	26.3	9.0	23.7

* Mexico subtracted from Latin American trade only for the U.S.; it is included in trade volumes in the other cases. Netherlands is included because its bilateral reciprocal trade treaties inflate volumes, especially exports.

Source: United Nations Comtrade. Database (https://comtrade.un.org/, accessed September 14, 2020).

Chávez contracted several long-term loans with Beijing to finance his ambitious social programs and keep the state oil company, PDVSA, operating. These are to be paid off in barrels of oil, rather than cash. But then, oil prices went into freefall, from around $130 in mid-2014 (with Nicolás Maduro having succeeded the deceased Chávez) to $35 by the end of that year. This was followed by the further decline in prices into the $25 range when the coronavirus epidemic struck the world economy. They fell also because of a price war between two large, low-cost producers, Saudi Arabia and Russia. For every dollar in the drop in global oil prices, Venezuela owes an even larger quantity of oil still in its subsoil—a prospect made worse by the fact that PDVSA has only one-half the productive capacity that it had in 1999.

Table 15.3 shows that if one subtracts the trade of Mexico with the U.S. from its overall trade with Latin America, Latin America's exports to China now exceed those going to the United States. Latin America still imports more from the United States overall. South Korea and Japan now have substantial trade with Latin America as well, but the biggest increases since 2007 have been with China (see Figure 15.5). In the area of investment, the number of combined Asian and European acquisitions exceeded those of the U.S. in 2017–2018. Only 28 mergers and acquisitions were initiated by Latin America, many fewer than the 172 initiated from other parts of the world (see Figure 15.6), indicating a deepening of dependency. This points to a process of diversification of the region's economic relationship, but it suggests that the Latin American bourgeoisie still looks abroad more than inward for economic integration.

China's increased presence in Latin America is largely economically motivated, but of course it has political implications as well. China's investments are part of its "Belt and Road" strategy. Belt and Road is conceived as another step in restoring China's role centuries ago as

FIGURE 15.5 Growth of Asian Trade With Latin America, $ Billion

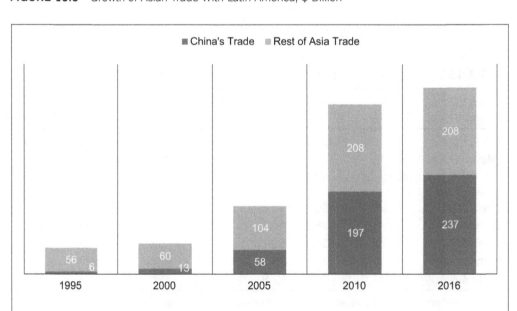

Source: ECLAC (2019).

FIGURE 15.6   Number of Mergers and Acquisitions in 2017–2018, by Origin of the Acquiring Firm

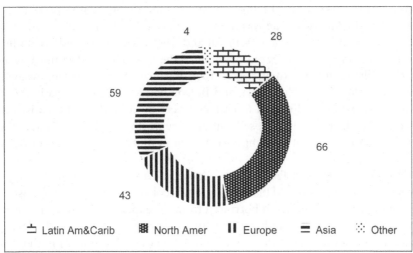

Source: ECLAC (2019: 42).

a great power by building a network of trade evocative of the famous Silk Road that linked Africa, China, and Europe to one another in the days of Marco Polo. Diplomatically, China has used its influence to induce most Latin American countries to withdraw recognition of Taiwan, which China considers to be a province of the mainland. China's policy of non-intervention contrasts with the United States' long history of intervention in the internal affairs of Latin America (see chapter 16).

On the one hand, China's move into Latin America has reduced the region's economic dependency by giving it an alternative economic source of investment and trade. Chinese loans and grants for infrastructure offer better terms than those of Western banks. When the 2008 financial crisis hit, the blow was softened for a few years by Chinese demand for commodity exports. When the Trump administration threatened Latin American countries with sanctions for negotiating with the Chinese tech-giant Huawei to build a 5G network in the region, it backed off after several countries, including Brazil, determined to move ahead.

Other aspects of Latin America's evolving relationship with China share the familiar hallmarks of dependency. Most of its exports to China are primary materials—with oil, soy, and mining products leading the way. China's loans for infrastructure reflects these priorities. Two mega projects on the planning board are a new Panama Canal and a trans-Andean railroad that would run from the Atlantic Coast of southern Brazil to the Pacific Coast of Peru. The latter is further advanced, but both would cut through sensitive ecological zones and have stirred opposition from local communities. Finally, even before the coronavirus pandemic struck, China had significantly scaled back its 2019 investments, perhaps in half according to preliminary data. On balance, China and the rest of Asia are probably involved in Latin America to stay, but with the impact of the coronavirus pandemic still unclear, its role in the region may not be expanding anytime soon at the rate that it did after 2000.

■ Alternative Hemispheric Economic Integration Schemes

In the period between 2000 and 2014, three different economic agendas were competing with one another in Latin America. One was the U.S. proposal for the FTAA, based on NAFTA as a model. The second one was led by Brazil and was closer to the underlying principles in Mercosur, demanding a more rapid opening of the U.S. market. The third agenda was the Bolivarian Alliance for the Americas (**ALBA**), advanced by Venezuelan president Hugo Chávez. By May 2007, Cuba, Nicaragua, and Bolivia had joined Venezuela in ALBA, with Ecuadorian membership pending and several observers. By 2020, these alternative economic integration schemes had largely collapsed, but they are worthy of a brief review, as they were arguably the boldest attempt at building Pan-American unity since the days of Bolívar (see Gardini 2009).

ALBA differed from NAFTA and the proposed FTAA in advocating social as well as economic integration, and it would institute regional economic planning, as opposed to relying purely on market mechanisms. It borrowed from the experience of the European Union by creating a "Compensatory Fund for Structural Convergence" to provide developmental assistance to the poorest countries (e.g., Haiti, Bolivia, and Nicaragua) in the Bolivarian trade federation. ALBA also promoted a Venezuelan socialist program called "endogenous development," including cooperatives and use of Indigenous technologies.

Venezuela's President Chávez used petrodiplomacy to advance ALBA and several other regional programs of cooperation. Preferential payment terms for oil were given to Central America and the Caribbean. Chávez even proposed to create a hemispheric oil company formed through an association of state enterprises, linked by a gas pipeline that would stretch from Venezuela to Argentina. In addition, Venezuela founded Telesur, a semiprivate continental television network independent of the large, transnational media corporations. In 2009, six other South American countries joined a Venezuelan initiative to create the Banco del Sur (Bank of the South), a fledgling effort to provide an alternative to the IMF in times of financial crisis. Venezuela backed with petrodollars the creation of the SUCRE, a "virtual currency" (no actual printed money) that member countries of ALBA would use instead of the dollar for international transactions with one another.

These initiatives lost whatever momentum they had when the Pink Tide receded. Chávez had died in 2013, and Venezuela's own economy began to decline. While Venezuela took the initiative, the backing of Brazil was crucial. Though Lula was supportive, Brazil had other interests to pursue as well. ALBA was predicated on its grand vision of a more autochthonous Latin American economy geared toward the poor, Indigenous peoples, other people of color, women, and so on. However, Venezuela's own developmental policies and international relationships did not always coincide with the agenda of these movements. Brazilian corporations, including the notorious **Obredecht** construction firm (see chapter 14), were major partners in several investment projects in Venezuela that were opposed by Indigenous and environmental groups.

We tend to analyze political trends while holding the present state of the international economy as a constant. However, we have already observed how historical changes in the global economy and political systems reverberate in Latin America. For example, the long-term deterioration of Spain's economy and the political crisis in Madrid set off by the Napoleonic Wars contributed greatly to the cause of independence. The Great Depression and World War II helped bring about import substitution and populism. The coronavirus pandemic will probably prove yet another major shock to the global and hemispheric trade systems, so much of what is to come in the next few years is hard to predict. ALBA is unlikely to survive, but the concepts of increased solidarity and grassroots-oriented development may return as alternative ways to reconstruct after what could be a devastating new episode of economic crisis.

■ Transnational Issues and Global Citizenship

We have concentrated on trade and the global assembly line, but certainly the challenges of globalization cannot be reduced to economics. Some would say that we are seeing the emergence of a "global civil society" to take the place of a world where the most important political decisions are reserved for sovereign nation-states. "Transnational" (or global) issues call forth global citizenship. On the other hand, the 2010s have seen just the opposite in some important respects, a retreat into nationalism and fear or hatred of "others." It is difficult to know just how the corona pandemic will influence the 2020s. Will it induce countries to turn inward and try to make their economies more autochthonous, or will it induce greater cooperation in developing effective medical and social responses?

Major new technological advances in robotics continue to reshape production by replacing human labor with artificial intelligence and robotics. These technologies may significantly reduce Latin America's comparative advantage in cheap labor. Robots rely on sensors, motors, and energy supplies to do "work," especially repetitive work, the kind done in *maquila* factories. Artificial intelligence combines analytics (powerful computer applications) for mining and studying Big Data. There are data sets so large that typical apps and computer operating systems cannot handle them rapidly. Analytics allow the rapid processing that can tell managers where to send robots out to pave potholes or what driverless trucks need to detour to alternate routes. Robots can be do the kinds of work done by the people we met in the first part of this chapter.

The data can be supplied from the constant influx of "likes" and "thumbs down" on social media, the hits made on "click bait" ads, the purchases made on Amazon or Alibaba, the pinprick signals that track GPS positions on smartphones, the photos posted on social media, the choices we make on streaming video, and a variety of other places. China has already begun to use Big Data and GPS technology to track gatherings of demonstrators in Hong Kong, which has not escaped the notice of other governments, including those in Latin America.

Much of this data is collected from cell phones and smartphones, and is much more reliant on the latter. Estimates of the percentage of Latin Americans who own smartphones vary widely, and the countries vary among themselves. One middle-range estimate (Newzoo 2019) indicates that almost half of the population of Latin America are "active smartphone users." But most of most Latin American infrastructure is only at a 3G level of connectivity for smartphones, for better or worse; this limits the potential to fully implement cyber technologies requiring 5G capability. This in turn has ramifications for foreign investment in the region, as more sophisticated analytics allow transnational companies to tighten control over the links in the supply chain.

As pointed out in chapter 12, analytics has begun to play a role in Latin American electoral politics. The United States has committed itself to developing cyber defenses to prevent attacks on U.S. infrastructure and to shield the U.S. public from Russian disinformation campaigns. The same techniques can, and probably have been, deployed into Latin America (with Venezuela and Cuba the most obvious targets) to influence public opinion, hack into databases, and influence public opinion. Facial recognition programs are in demand from security forces, ostensibly to fight crime. However, these programs have been shown to be especially error-prone when it comes to tracking darker-skinned people. Whether we are speaking of Cuba and Venezuela, with leftist governments, or Colombia and Brazil, with right-wing regimes, all have an interest in using these technologies to rapidly track and repress demonstrations, identify protest organizers, and collect photos and messages for storage in Big Data files. The U.S. government has been reluctant to share 5G technology with Latin American forces, not so much on human rights grounds but out of a desire to maintain its global military and commercial advantages.

The Defense Innovation Board, a Federal Advisory Committee to the U.S. Defense Department, rather bluntly made these objectives clear in a report (2019) to the Pentagon:

> Historical shifts between wireless generations suggest that the first-mover country stands to gain billions in revenue accompanied by substantial job creation and leadership in technology innovation. First movers also set standards and practices that were then adopted by subsequent entrants. Conversely, countries that fell behind in previous wireless generation shifts were obligated to adopt the standards, technologies, and architectures of the leading country and missed out on a generation of wireless capabilities and market potential.
>
> (Defense Advisory Board, 2019)

Latin American countries stand to be among those falling behind and therefore to remain technologically dependent. As the United States has chosen to move slowly with little technology transfer, several have looked to China. Mexico, Brazil, and Argentina all had plans to allow Huawei to introduce 5G networks in 2020. This makes sense for China's investment in soy agribusiness. A 5G network makes it possible from afar to sense and process data on wind, temperature, rainfall, quality of the soil, plant growth, pest infestation, and applications of pesticides and herbicides. That is, Chinese transnational agribusiness, not Brazilians, will control the soil, something that U.S.-based transnationals would prefer for themselves.

Climate Change

Although the United States has refused to recognize the gravity of the situation, climate change is affecting the Americas in ways that demand—and are evoking—transnational solutions. Global warming is plunging Antarctic ice into the seas and causing the retreat of Latin America's glaciers in the Andes and parts of Mexico. In such tropical regions, glaciers are found only in regions three miles above sea level. Four of six glaciers in Venezuela's Andes in 1972 had disappeared by the end of the century.

Peruvian experts said in 1999 that 12 billion cubic meters of ice had melted over 27 years from glaciers in that country's Andean mountains (Lama 1999). Should this source of water disappear, deserts will advance on Peru's western slopes, and the ecosystem of the

Amazon will be affected. Some of the loss can be attributed to unusual movements of the warm El Niño current, but this too may be related to global warming. The human consequences will be felt most acutely in terms of scarcer drinking water, less hydroelectric power, and more costly irrigation. In Peru, the loss of water for irrigation can be calculated as a cost of US$1 billion. People will migrate from the most affected areas, risking new kinds of international and political conflicts. Flooding and mudslides are other "natural" catastrophes that could result. Melting of glaciers and the polar ice caps threatens small Caribbean nations and low-lying coastal regions with the prospect that rising seas could claim the homes of hundreds of millions of people in the next few decades.

Water resources are a growing issue between the United States and Mexico. A water use treaty between the two countries regulates exploitation of the Rio Grande (Rio Bravo to Mexicans), but an increasing amount of water is taken upstream on both sides of the border, causing large parts of the river to dry up. In some years, the river does not reach its mouth on the Gulf of Mexico. Farmers near Brownsville, Texas, face ruin, but things are even worse in nearby Matamoros, Mexico. Matamoros now has no water at all for parts of each summer. Further upstream, the river basin is heavily contaminated by industrial pollutants and increased use by Mexican residents who have migrated north within the country, seeking jobs in *maquilas* close to the U.S. border.

One likely cause of global warming is depletion of the tropical rainforests, including the Amazonian region in Brazil and Mexico's Lacondon forest in Chiapas. Called the "lungs of the world," the vegetation in the rainforest protects the earth by depleting carbon dioxide, which in turn prevents too much trapping of heat on the earth—the so-called greenhouse effect. Rainforests once covered 14 percent of the earth's surface; today, they cover 6 percent. The Amazonian rainforest has been depleted by 20 percent and could, were present rates to continue, disappear in 50 years. The cause is largely economic, as the land is harvested for virgin timber (with virtually no capital invested by the landowner) and turned into cattle pastures. Poor peasants, desperate for land, follow highways cut through the forest, slashing and burning the indigenous vegetation before planting their own crops. In recent years, Brazil's booming soy-export industry has been gobbling up land. Heavy rains and flooding quickly wash the soil away after just a few harvests (Raintree Nutrition 2005).

Rainforests are biodiverse. Half the world's species of plants and animals are found in Brazil alone. Some experts think that 50,000 species a year, many of them plants with medicinal promise, are being lost. One drug, Vincristine, derived from the rainforest plant Madagascar periwinkle, has proven important in increasing the survival rate for acute childhood leukemia. Ten million Indigenous people, guardians of knowledge about the forest, once lived in Brazil's rainforest. Today, there are only 200,000 left.

Brazilian environmentalists and sympathetic officials in the federal government have sought to reduce logging, but the country's federal structure and tradition of local rule by *coroneles* have inhibited effective enforcement. Under pressure from international environmentalists, the World Bank and other financial institutions have begun to pressure governments to take action to preserve the forests. In 2003, the Brazilian government signed an agreement with the World Bank and the World Wildlife Fund, a large international nongovernmental organization (NGO), to create an "Amazon Region Protected Areas" program to protect a network of 400 islands in the basin north of the city of Manaus. The area is larger than New York, New Jersey, and Connecticut combined; the ultimate goal of the NGO is to create a preserve the size of California. Lorenzo Carrasco, a fierce critic of such projects, accused the organizations of attempting to keep Brazilians from exploiting the region's mineral and other natural resources (AP 2005).

Loggers, ranchers, and migrant *campesinos* resent having international governmental organizations (IGOs) and NGOs dictate what they can do with land lying within their sovereign borders. They enjoy plenty of economic leverage because they are the key motor behind Brazil's economic growth since 1994. Soy exports are generating crucial foreign reserves needed to pay the debt and could make the country self-sufficient in vegetable oil, a staple of the diet. Many Brazilians ask why their country and other poor countries, deeply in debt, should have to restrict development, while at the same time the most industrialized countries, especially the United States, refuse to cut down on the emission of greenhouse gases.

Not all Brazilians are merely defending an economic interest in resisting limits on exploitation of the rainforest (see Figure 15.7). Many see U.S. policy in the Middle East as a grab for oil and think that the hegemon might eventually turn its attention to their part of the world. General Claudio Barbosa de Figueiredo, Brazilian commander for security in the Amazon, argued in 2005 that behind preservation efforts lies the ultimate goal of "the internationalization of the Amazon." A poll showed that 75 percent of Brazilians believed that their country could be invaded by a foreign power to gain access to its natural resources. "The strategic axis of confrontation has shifted from East–West to North–South," argued Figueiredo. "In other words, the rich countries of the north are confronting the countries that want to develop in the south to impede this in every possible way" (Astor 2005).

FIGURE 15.7   Map of the Amazon Rainforest

Source: © iStockphoto.com/KURL.

Regardless of who is at fault for the disappearance of much of the world's forests, Brazilian environmentalists warn that their own country must face the consequences. Drought conditions have been worsening in recent years, and some believe that the cause is the cutting down of the country's "rain-making machine." Some worry that the rainforest may be reaching the tipping point, when damage is so extensive that it has gained a momentum of its own that will not be easily reversible. Brazilian President Bolsonaro has made things worse, more or less aligning himself with the attitude of General Figueiredo. The Brazilian Amazon lost 3,769 square miles of rainforest between August 2018 and July 2019, according to Brazil's National Space Research Institute. This is the equivalent of one and a half times the size of the state of Delaware in the U.S., up 30 percent from the previous year. The pace of destruction may soon pass a tipping point, past any hope of the forest surviving.

Migration

The migration of Latin American and Caribbean people northward has raised tensions between the United States and its neighbors. Occasionally, migration affects relationships elsewhere as well. Haitians looking for work in the Dominican Republic are frequently rounded up and deported, adversely affecting relationships between those countries. Bolivians and Paraguayans seeking work in Argentina face discrimination. The Mexican government has sought to close its border in the south, quite in contradiction to its complaints about U.S. policy. In 1969 Honduran politicians tried to deport Salvadoran immigrant workers *en masse*, raising tensions that led to the brief "Soccer War"—so called because it was touched off by a riot during a match.

Like iron tailings to a magnet, a relatively rich economy attracts migrants from populations living in poorer conditions nearby. In the case of Mexico and the United States, the developmental gap in terms of GDP per capita is greater than for any other two countries in the world with a common border. Of course, a large portion of the United States is home to descendants of Mexico who lived north of the new border (80,000 in Texas alone, at the time) drawn after the Treaty of Guadalupe ended the Mexican–American War in 1848. It hardly surprises, then, that two-thirds of those who are "Hispanic" (a census designation that includes a small percentage of people of Spanish origin) are descendants of Mexicans. Altogether, in 2002, there were 37.4 million Hispanics in the United States working mostly in the service sector, skilled manufacturing, and transportation. Over one-quarter of the population of western states is Hispanic, and large populations are found in major northern cities. Rates of poverty run high among this community; one-quarter of Hispanic children live in poverty, according to the U.S. Census Population Survey for 2002.

An immediate, pressing issue for advocates of globalization and human rights is the flow of migrants outside established immigration laws, especially to the United States. For some groups, these migrants are criminals and should be called "illegal aliens," the term used by the Colorado Alliance for Immigration Reform (CAIR, http://cairo.org). CAIR denies that its motives are racist and argues that limiting immigration is a method of checking population growth and relieving pressure on resources.

The American Immigration Law Foundation (AILF), on the other hand, uses the term "undocumented workers." The AILF calculated, based on data taken from census reports, that there are approximately nine million undocumented workers in the United States. Of this nine million, approximately six of every ten are Mexicans, and two are from other parts of Latin America (especially Central America). It costs a worker typically US$2,000–US$3,000 to hire a *coyote* to smuggle them across the border. Agents for employers in North America often advance the money to the *coyote*, a practice that turns the immigrants into indentured laborers. Most are men, among whom 96 percent find employment. However, 41 percent are women, of whom 62 percent find wage employment. Women, especially those who are not employed in the wage labor force, hold the new communities together. Although this pool of labor might exert some downward pressure on wages, the jobs taken by these immigrants are usually those that other workers refuse to take, especially in agriculture, services (restaurants, hotels), and construction. Wages may be low, but some jobs that pay US$60 a day in the United States pay only US$5 in Mexico.

The countries that receive the immigrants do find their health and education systems heavily burdened by the influx of undocumented workers, but the net effect on the U.S. economy is positive. A *New York Times* investigative report (Porter 2005) estimates that undocumented workers paid US$7 billion into the Social Security Trust Fund in 2004. In addition, these workers pay sales taxes, and their employers pay into unemployment. The AILF says that in 1990, undocumented workers paid US$547 million in sales taxes in Illinois alone, and their employers paid another US$168 million. Because these workers cannot apply for social security, Medicare, or unemployment insurance, these payments represent a subsidy to these programs.

Estimates are that Mexican immigrants, legal and undocumented, sent US$4 billion to US$6 billion per year home before the 2008 economic crisis, the fourth-largest source of foreign exchange for Mexico. For El Salvador, the dollars emigrants send home constitute that country's largest source of overseas earnings. In June 2005, the Mexican Congress approved legislation making the estimated ten million Mexican citizens living in the United States (half legally, half not, by estimates) eligible to vote, much to the dismay of immigration opponents in the United States who fear the legislation will encourage more migration northward.

Supporters of NAFTA, the FTAA, CAFTA, and bilateral agreements always claim that these accords will bring economic growth and jobs and thus slow the emigration of Latin Americans. Little evidence so far suggests that they are right. In Guatemala and Honduras, land grabbing to grow palm oil for export has amplified violence. Gangs and death squads are employed to force people off the land, especially targeting leaders of environmental, Indigenous, and women's movements. Hundreds of thousands of Central Americans have undertaken the dangerous journey north seeking asylum. In 2018, more than 7,000 of them made a 2,500-mile journey on foot to get to the Mexican border. Throughout 2019 they kept coming, most of them to be turned away. In 2019, the Trump administration managed to convince Guatemala and Honduras to take in refugees sent from the border, ostensibly to await processing of their claims. Under the best of conditions, these poor countries cannot accommodate the migrants, and they are in any case the same areas from which many of them fled.

Venezuela's economic and political crisis has created an unprecedented migration crisis on the continent, that has now been magnified by the coronavirus pandemic. The United Nations Commission on Refugees states that more than 4.6 million Venezuelans have left the country. Many wealthy Venezuelans flew to Europe (especially to Spain) and the United States, with money to pay immigration lawyers. Those middle-class and working-class Venezuelans who sought to emigrate usually have sold all their possessions to buy an airline ticket. Arriving by air results in at least a hearing with an immigration official and temporary residency. Other Venezuelans seeking asylum in the U.S. have joined thousands of others in Mexico awaiting processing, hoping to avoid forcible relocation to Central America. But the crisis is broader, as most Venezuelan migrants have sought refuge in other parts of Latin America, making the journey on foot. Colombia (1.4 million), Ecuador (385,000), and Peru (870,000) have been most affected. Originally, the migrants were treated reasonably well, but that changed as the full dimensions of the crisis became evident.

The roots of the exodus are several, including the mismanagement of the oil boom of 2000 to 2013 and the collapse of oil prices in 2014, but conditions were deliberately made worse by the United States. The Trump administration imposed sanctions in order to exacerbate the crisis and provoke a military coup against President Nicolás Maduro. On February 28, 2020, as the coronavirus was stealing into the Western Hemisphere, the administration announced sanctions on a Russian company that was facilitating exports by the Venezuela state oil company. Venezuela was preparing for a "perfect storm": low oil prices, acute shortages, a devastated healthcare system, and the onset of COVID-19.

To stanch the flow of people across the Mexican border, the United States increased the deployment of technology and personnel along the border. In 2004, Congress passed legislation in the National Intelligence Reform Act (a response to the 9/11 attacks) requiring the Bush administration to add 10,000 more personnel to the Border Patrol. The border has already become highly militarized, and still the immigrants come looking for work. Walls, supplemented by barbed wire, electrified fences, and trenches, now divide populated areas along the border. Then in 2019, the Trump administration began construction of the infamous border "wall."

The militarization of the border and the refusal of Congress to pass legislation to create a guest worker program has become a source of tension between the United States and Mexico. President Vicente Fox was in Washington to discuss this program with President George W. Bush on September 11, 2001, and the events of that day eliminated any prospects for passage of the legislation. Anyone who has crossed the border to enter Mexico from Nogales, Arizona, or San Diego will find little obstruction moving from north to south. U.S. citizens and permanent residents easily cross back, but a long line of pedestrians and cars seeking to enter the United States slowly snakes its way on the Mexican side of the border.

In March 2006, the immigration issue in the United States exploded when Hispanic leaders, joined by other immigrant community leaders, launched massive protests against a law, passed in the House of Representatives, which would have made it a felony to live and work illegally in the United States. If passed by the Senate, the law would have made criminals out of 11 million undocumented workers. The wave of protests shocked national leaders and stalled the proposal. However, a subsequent backlash developed, including a law in Arizona requiring police to check the identification papers of people suspected of being in the United States illegally. A second immigration bill, containing a highly restrictive but still controversial "pathway to citizenship," languished in the U.S. Senate awaiting an uncertain fate in 2013.

It is unlikely that the sovereign power of the U.S. government can cope with the magnetic force that the U.S. economy, as a regional pole of development, exercises on people. At least temporarily, the coronavirus pandemic probably will, as the numbers along the border with Texas diminished in early 2020. But in the United States, the raids by Immigration and

Customs Enforcement (ICE) continue, and few people are at more risk from COVID-19 than immigrants. As *Texas Monthly Magazine* put it (March 21, 2020),

> The coronavirus has effectively turned Texas on its head. Schools have closed, bars and restaurants have been limited to takeout service, and gatherings of more than ten people are prohibited. But inside the walls of the South Texas Detention Complex in Pearsall, it's as if the virus doesn't exist.

Disease and Health: COVID-19 Meets the Supply Chain

Infectious and sexually transmitted diseases are not a new feature of globalization. Many scientists believe that Europeans brought syphilis back to their homeland from the Americas. As we reviewed in chapter 3, after 1492 the Native American population was decimated by diseases brought by the Europeans. This process has hardly ceased. As humans from urban civilizations press further into remote areas of the tropics, the remaining Indigenous populations of the Amazon basin are threatened with diseases they are biologically ill-equipped to resist. For example, in the early 1980s, approximately 450 members of the small Yora Indian population of Peru died after Shell Oil Company workers, loggers, and evangelical missionaries forced contact with the Yora community (Pantone 2008).

Another serious risk that has diminished to a degree but not vanished is from HIV/AIDS. The problem is most acute in the Caribbean, where 1.1 percent of the adult population had AIDS ten years ago (HIV InSite 2008). In the early years of the new century, the population of Haiti actually began to decline, in part because AIDS was afflicting fully 2.2 percent of the adult population (HIV InSite 2007). The exception is Cuba, which has a low rate of infection, in part because of an aggressive testing, education, and treatment program. Cuba's approach started with an ethically questionable decision, partly inspired by homophobia, to forcibly quarantine the infected (approximately 10,000 people between 1986 and 1997) in sanitariums. That practice, good conditions in the sanitaria, and free and good-quality medical care did bring the virus under control and save lives. However, that result probably could have been achieved with voluntary quarantine, given the excellence of care.

No longer are HIV and AIDS patients quarantined, but access to good medical care does help, and voluntary quarantine is encouraged. Today, nearly 60 percent of Caribbean infections are due to unprotected heterosexual sex, whereas drug use and unprotected sex among gay men is the larger cause in other regions of Latin America (Fabbri and Stewart 2019). In 2005, the government finally began to decentralize access to care, although the progress in establishing care through local clinics has been slow because of the cost involved. Remember, Cuba still had not fully recovered from the shock of the collapse of the Eastern European economies.

On the other hand, Cuba has developed and now produces its own drugs for controlling HIV and AIDS. It has established an unusual capacity to deal with the epidemic in comparison to other Latin American states. In 2003, Cuba achieved universal antiretroviral therapy with domestically manufactured antiretroviral drugs for patients meeting international clinical criteria (see Gorry 2005).

The onset of COVID-19 in 2019–2020 generated another health crisis with even greater challenges—to both the sovereign territorial state and the global assembly line. While the global assembly line might react easily enough to increased production of automobiles, diapers, batteries, syringes, etc. in normal times, the coronavirus and associated disease, COVID-19, posed an entirely different set of challenges. Production timelines for test kits, face masks, and ventilators are much longer than the timeframe dictated by the crisis. The urgency was not entirely the making of the virus but of failures of political leadership as well. The urgency could have been reduced had political leaders taken seriously warnings years earlier from epidemiologists and public intellectuals right after the Ebola epidemic of 2013–2015—for example, from Microsoft founder Bill Gates (2015).

As it was, in the state of New York alone only 400 ventilators were available at a time when the governor estimated a need for 30,000 when infections were expected to reach a peak within weeks. At the time, Medtronic, a leading manufacturer of the ventilators, crucial for the survival of people whose lungs were under attack, strained to increase production from 100 to 225 per week. A major contributing factor was that there are 1,500 unique parts that are produced in at least 14 different countries along the global assembly line. Some of those parts makers have their own supply chains to contend with. Ford, General Motors, and 3M corporations are teaming up to use parts from trucks and 3-D printers (another miracle machine predicated on cyber technologies) to produce ventilators, but they also need electronic components from other suppliers (New York Times, March 25, 2020).

As the crisis in China eased, the Chinese turned their attention to the rest of the world—whether for humanitarian or diplomatic reasons. Jack Ma, the founder of Alibaba, the Chinese counterpart to Amazon, tweeted on March 22, 2020, that he would donate emergency medical supplies, including face masks, testing kits, and ventilators, to poor countries, including 24 in Latin America. Argentina, Brazil, Chile, Cuba, Ecuador, the Dominican Republic, and Peru will receive 400,000 testing kits and 104 ventilators. "We will ship long-distance, and we will hurry!" Ma wrote. Generous as the offer was, given the dimensions of the crisis in the region, these numbers were far short of what Latin America has needed.

Even simple face masks, normally less than a dollar to purchase and desperately needed by medical personnel and workers in key areas of the economy (for example, grocery stores, sanitary waste collectors), are produced in supply chains using "just-in-time" inventory management. This means producing only what is needed along each link in the chain in order to lower warehousing costs. In the U.S. alone, the Department of Health and Human Services estimated 3.5 billion masks would be needed. New York Times columnist Farhad Manjoo (March 25, 2020) explained why there was a shortage:

> The answer to why we're running out of protective gear involves a very American set of capitalist pathologies—the rise and inevitable lure of low-cost overseas manufacturing, and a strategic failure . . . to consider seriously the cascading vulnerabilities that flowed from the incentives to reduce costs.

Manjoo might have thought more broadly of what this means for Latin America and the Global South. Global North countries have the power to shift priorities all along the supply chain to meet their needs. Latin America has no such capacity.

According to an engineering newsletter (Henneberry 2020), because surgical masks filter out bacteria better than woven cloth does, most are made from polypropylene, which is a petroleum-based material that is initially processed into plastic pellets. The pellets are melted onto a conveyer and passed through a dye with hundreds of small nozzles and holes that is extruded into a web to make fibers. These are then bonded together by machines into material for masks of varying degrees of filtration. Machines bond the material in layers and attach the strings used to tied them to the face of users. China is by far the largest manufacturer, but Mexico is also a leading producer. According to the U.S. Department of Health and Human Services, 90 percent of the surgical masks sold in the U.S. are manufactured abroad, and the parts are made in a variety of countries, including Colombia and Mexico.

President Trump used his authority under the 1950 Defense Production Act to stop exporting such masks and respirators, crucial to protecting healthcare workers treating COVID-19 patients in the NAFTA countries, which includes Mexico of course, and Colombia, which has a bilateral free trade treaty with the U.S. The transnational company 3M that make N-95 masks used in hospitals warned of "significant humanitarian implications" for healthcare workers in Canada and Latin America. The company said blocking exports could eventually lead to fewer of the masks being available in the U.S. The Trump administration subsequently loosened the blockade (Associated Press, April 6, 2020).

This poses interesting policy questions for Mexico, in particular. As a site of final assembly on the supply line, should its government invoke emergency powers, much like the U.S. has, and reserve masks for its own population? Would its actions be in violation of NAFTA? How would the U.S. respond if it shut down cross-border trade, as Trump has threatened to do on more than one occasion?

Cuba with its long record of sending doctors and medical aid abroad also faces choices on how to respond. The island country has more scientists and health workers per capita than any other country in Latin America, and its command political structures give it some leverage to organize an effective social defense against the spread of the virus. But the tourist industry, the main generator of the economy, has ground to a halt. This may help stop the spread of the virus, but it deprives the country of capacity to import supplies of medicines and food. And as with Venezuela, the decision of the Trump administration has been to further tighten restrictions on flying to the country, reversing the opening of the U.S. to Cuba by the Obama administration. No few observers have recognized that this policy is unconscionably cruel.

In 2020 hopes were rising that vaccines would be approved for distribution early in 2021. But as most of the research, testing, and development of vaccines is being carried out in the wealthier western countries by private companies with government subsidies, it is likely that they will prioritize distribution to their own populations. China might help, but it has one-sixth of the world's population to absorb its production. Russians may seek to gain political favor by distributing vaccines, but their safety and reliability are questionable. Cuba started testing a vaccine in late summer, 2020. It has the experience and scientific institutions capable of generating vaccines, but will need manufacturing partners to mass produce for the hemisphere.

For Review

For each of the following areas—climate change, disease, and migration—what kinds of challenges do Latin American governments face? How do these issues challenge the capacity of individual nation-states to confront them on their own? As this book is written, the full dimensions of the coronavirus were unclear. What were the main challenges facing Latin America as it unfolded?

Can Democracy Exist in a World Without Sovereign States?

We have reviewed powerful forces that seem beyond the power of a nation-state—even one as powerful as the United States—to harness. Though the process of globalization seems inevitable, the particular shape that it takes and the way it affects the prospects for democracy need not necessarily follow a single, inevitable path. Democracy itself will have to become more global, meaning that international organizations will have to be made more responsive to people and their movements and not just to states.

Latin America's social movements have not rejected globalization, but most question the neoliberal version that relies on market forces and competition to generate economic growth, better living standards, and more open, transparent societies. Writers such as Thomas Friedman say globalization as fostered by the WTO, NAFTA, and other trade agreements is beneficial and inevitable. In *The Lexus and the Olive Tree*, he wrote,

> The driving idea behind globalization is free-market capitalism—the more you let market forces rule and the more you open your economy to free trade and competition, the more efficient and flourishing your economy will be. Globalization means the spread of free-market capitalism to virtually every country in the world. Therefore, globalization also has its own set of economic rules—rules that revolve around opening, deregulating and privatizing your economy, in order to make it more competitive and attractive to foreign investment.
>
> (Friedman 2000b: 9)

Those who are known as "anti-globalization activists" think that Friedman and other enthusiasts for free trade and economic integration have spent too much time in luxury hotels or visiting the sterile enterprises of the world's high-tech zones. They have in mind a different form of globalization based on sustainable development, fair trade, and cultural diversity. In other words, these social movements insist that "another world is possible."

This chapter has no pretensions of resolving this debate, and the same can be said for the question of whether globalization will someday completely displace the norm of national sovereignty in world affairs. However, this does not mean we cannot understand the countervailing forces at work. On the other hand, we can see that economic globalization has diversified markets for Latin American exports and sources for imports and investment. It is fair to say that recent growth, social progress, and diversification in its trade and investment partners have given Latin America some leverage in its relationship to the United States and the developed world. However, the control of production of goods and services, the root from which trade and distribution grows, is even more concentrated in the Global North.

Latin American states have struggled to build their own regional diplomatic and economic institutions, which would lessen their political dependence on the hegemonic world power—whether that be Spain and Britain before 1900 or the United States and China in the twentieth century. New cyber technologies may make Latin America even less capable of carving its own path toward a more prosperous location with the networks and chains that make up the globalized world.

Discussion Questions

1. Were you to advise a Latin American government on whether it would be wise to pursue import substitution, liberalization on trade, or some other set of policies to promote economic development, what suggestions might you offer?
2. Would Latin America be better off entering into a NAFTA-like agreement covering the entire hemisphere, or is some other alternative, such as ALBA or Mercosur, preferable?
3. Do you think Latin American countries should give up some sovereign control over their affairs in areas such as human rights and the environment, or should countries be allowed to retain their right to self-determination over these kinds of issues? If you think they should yield on sovereignty, should they do so even if the United States and other wealthy countries refuse to do the same?
4. Do you agree with the Thomas Friedman quote at the end of this chapter, or is your position closer to "another world is possible"?
5. You will be reading this chapter long after the coronavirus pandemic, I hope. How has it impacted globalization and, in particular, Latin America's response to it?

Resources for Further Study

Reading: The Carnegie Endowment tried with some success to make an evenhanded assessment of NAFTA's impact in *NAFTA's Promise and Reality: Lessons From Mexico for the Hemisphere* (2004). Thomas Friedman's *The World Is Flat: A Brief History of the Twenty-First Century* (New York: Farrar, Straus, and Giroux, 2005) offers the strongest pro-globalization argument. Manuel Castells and Roberto Laserna, in "The New Dependency: Technological Change and Socioeconomic Restructuring in Latin America," *Sociological Forum* 4, no. 4 (1980), see technological changes and globalization constraining democracy. Michel Reid, in *Forgotten Continent: The Battle for Latin America's Soul* (New Haven: Yale University Press, 2008), sees globalization as promoting democracy and finds Venezuela's President Chávez to be a threat to progress. William Robinson, in *Latin America and Global Capitalism* (Baltimore: Johns Hopkins Press, 2010), looks at the changing economies of Latin America and also at the resistance to neoliberal globalization.

Video and Film: *Another World Is Possible* (2008) looks at anti-globalization protests at the G8 economic summit in Genoa. *Voices From the Edge: The Favela Goes to the World Social Forum* (2005) is a Brazilian documentary. With an interesting twist on manufacturing and globalization, *The Take*, a documentary by Canadian filmmaker Avi Lewis, captures a movement in Buenos Aires that started with 30 factory workers who would not leave their factory. In protest against Argentina's Carlos Menem (claimed to be "responsible" for a grave economic collapse in 2001) and his powerful company-controlling comrades, these unemployed revolutionaries relied on their slingshots and their value of "shop-floor democracy" in a desperate struggle to get their jobs back. For more on this video, go to www.thetake.org.

On the Internet: The Carnegie study of NAFTA can also be found at http://carnegieen dowment.org/2003/11/09/nafta-s-promise-and-reality-lessons-from-mexico-for- hemisphere. The **World Social Forum** has various sites associated with different coun- tries, conferences, and movements. A prominent portal for the United States can be found at www.ussocialforum.net/. There are no shortages of videos on YouTube where you can hear the views of Thomas Friedman.

16 No One's "Backyard" Anymore?

Focus Questions

► How have the Western Hemisphere's regional and diplomatic systems changed in recent decades?

► How has U.S. intervention in Latin America influenced its politics?

► To what extent has Latin America gained the ability to assert itself diplomatically in world affairs independent of the influence of the United States?

► Is democracy in Latin America being strengthened or weakened by U.S. foreign policy?

O N MAY 30, 2013, Edward Snowden, a contract employee for the National Security Agency, fled the United States for Hong Kong and then traveled on June 23 to Moscow. Snowden had released to news organizations, mainly *The Guardian* (London), detailed information about programs of mass surveillance of citizens in the United States and Britain, as well as embarrassing information about eavesdropping on other citizens of other countries, including European allies and friendly Latin American governments. Before he flew to Moscow, federal prosecutors indicted him on several charges, including espionage. The Kremlin, though unwilling to extradite Snowden, said it would give only temporary asylum and advised him to look elsewhere. His extradition back to the United States became a high priority for Washington, which let governments around the world know that any country granting Snowden asylum would pay a high price for its defiance of the global hegemon on this matter.

Until 2000 it was virtually unthinkable that any Latin American country, other than Cuba (and earlier in the century, perhaps Mexico), would defy the United States on a matter that Washington considered a top priority. However, three countries, Bolivia, Nicaragua, and Venezuela, offered Snowden asylum, and Ecuador said it would consider an application. Ecuador's embassy in London was already sheltering Julian Assange, founder of WikiLeaks, whose publication of sensitive diplomatic documents had embarrassed many governments, including the United States. Although not offering asylum, several expressed sympathy for Snowden, who eventually secured a promise of asylum in Russia until at least 2020.

The swing to the right in both the United States and in several Latin American countries, including Ecuador, seemed in some ways to restore Washington's leverage in the region. But this could easily swing back toward a more assertive Latin American position. China's economic influence (see chapter 15) and Russia's determination to show it is a global power offer Latin America some ballast should it choose to challenge the hegemony of the United

States. In fact, Argentina and Brazil pushed back in 2019 against Washington's attempts to force them to abandon plans to call the Chinese telecommunications transnational, Huawei, to provide them with 5G network capability—all the more remarkable considering that Brazilian President Jair Bolsonaro is an ideological soul mate of Donald Trump.

Much of this chapter outlines the history of and current relations between Latin America and the United States, which remains the dominant power in the hemisphere. Latin America's role in the world is broader than that, as we saw in chapter 15 with China's economic expansion into the region. The turn inward in the way the United States views the world, the aggressive posture assumed by the Trump administration toward Latin America, Russia's revived interest in the region, and the impact of the coronavirus pandemic all suggest that the 2020s will be years of shifts and greater complexity in Latin America's relationship with the world.

■ U.S. Intervention in the "Backyard"

Democracy promotion was less central to the public diplomacy of the United States during the Trump administratin, but it is a long-standing, moralistic component of U.S. foreign policy, closely tied to its liberal ideology. As Greg Grandin (2006) puts it, Latin America served as a "laboratory" for the global role that the United States would assume half a century later, including its policies and actions in Vietnam, Iraq, Afghanistan, and multiple locations in Latin America during the **Cold War**.

By the late 1800s, the United States had survived the Civil War and become an industrial power with formidable economic interests in Latin America. In expanding westward, it displaced its own Indigenous population, a form of territorial colonization justified by the idea of "Manifest Destiny"—the notion that white settlement of the supposedly empty continent was the fulfillment of a God-given imperative. Along the way, the United States clashed with Mexico, annexing half of its territory in the war of 1848. The country's entrepreneurs were already looking in that direction for new markets and investment opportunities. By 1898, the western frontier had largely closed, so the question arose: was Manifest Destiny limited to the west, or should U.S. expansion flow southward? The war against Spain and then the building of a two-ocean navy by President Theodore Roosevelt (1901–1909) afterward settled the question. The United States had become a commercial and military power with imperial ambitions of its own.

In the Caribbean and Central America, some elites encouraged the United States to annex their countries as new states. Elites in that region remembered the lot of their brethren, the slave-owning aristocracy of Haiti who had perished in a slave revolt. They feared the same fate would befall them as Spain's power continued to deteriorate. Before the U.S. Civil War, southern politicians saw the admission of new slave states from this region as a counterweight to the admission of free states as the United States expanded westward. José Martí, the Cuban patriot who initiated the island's final war for independence from Spain, was well aware that the planters in Cuba and the Caribbean put protection of their interests above independence. To keep them supportive of a break from Spain, Martí kept secret his goal of creating a free, democratic Cuba. He was also conscious of the rising power of the United States. He admired its innovative and popular democratic spirit, but like Bolívar he worried about its expansionist tendencies.

Martí had good reason to be concerned. Three years after he died (in 1895) in battle, the United States defeated Spain and "freed" Cuba, Puerto Rico, and other Spanish possessions.

Although freedom fighters had been waging war for decades, the United States occupied Spain's old colonies and negotiated their new status without rebel participation. Cuba was occupied for four years; Puerto Rico remains a territorial possession of the United States to this day. It is considered a "freely associated commonwealth" by the United States, but the United Nations General Assembly considers it a colony. Today, most of the island's population remains relatively evenly divided between those desiring statehood and those wishing to retain the commonwealth status. A small but vigorous independence movement regards the argument as moot, seeing both alternatives as colonialism.

The Spanish–American War of 1898 was a significant watershed in U.S. foreign policy. An explosion and the sinking of the battleship *Maine* in a harbor in Havana touched off the conflict. In the United States, there was a great deal of sympathy for the independence movement, fed by propaganda in the "yellow press," mass-circulation newspapers that had emerged as a new factor in politics. At the same time, Americans held racist stereotypes similar to the ones they held about blacks in the United States; they were transferred to South Americans, Caribbean people, Hawaiian natives, and Filipinos (Johnson 1980). Typical was an editorial cartoon with an image of Uncle Sam smiling contentedly as his "children," all depicted in racist black stereotypes from the era, sleep in bed. Note that the caricature appeared in a Seattle newspaper, far away from the Jim Crow "land of cotton." The image is appalling, but it reflects a historical fact, as well as a practice not entirely purged from the news media today (see, e.g., Said 1981).

CARTOON 16.1 Seattle Post-Intelligencer, 1906. "*The kids are in bed and all is well.*" Central American nations, cast in racist stereotypes and as children, are pacified, bringing prosperity.

Source: Johnson (1980: 199).

U.S. troops withdrew from Cuba in 1903 but only on the condition that Cuba's constitution would recognize the Platt Amendment, passed by the U.S. Senate in 1901. Among its onerous provisions, the amendment prohibited Cuba from acquiring foreign debts and required it to lease lands to the United States for military facilities. Cuba's acquiescent rulers signed a special commercial treaty that gave Washington almost total control over exports of its sugar, the lifeblood of the economy. A U.S. citizen, Tomás Estrada Palma, president of Cuba in 1903, signed a lease giving the United States control "in perpetuity" over Guantánamo Bay, on the eastern tip of the island, for a naval base. After 2001, it became the site for the incarceration of prisoners taken by the United States in its Middle Eastern wars. The Platt Amendment also said, "The Government of Cuba consents that the United States may exercise the right to intervene for the preservation of Cuban independence, the maintenance of a government adequate for the protection of life, property, and individual liberty." This part of the amendment defined a neocolonial relationship that persisted after the amendment was abrogated in 1934.

The (Theodore) Roosevelt Corollary to the Monroe Doctrine, proclaimed in 1904, made this explicit. In his inauguration speech, Roosevelt declared that the United States wished its "neighbors" to be "stable, orderly and prosperous" and that "any country whose people conduct themselves well can count upon our hearty friendship." But, he added,

> chronic wrongdoing, or an impotence which results in a general loosening of the ties of civilized society, may in America, as elsewhere, ultimately require intervention by some civilized nation, and in the Western hemisphere the adherence of the United States to the Monroe Doctrine may force the United States, however reluctantly, in flagrant cases of such wrongdoing or impotence, to the exercise of an international police power.

Roosevelt had risen to fame as the result of his small victory at San Juan Hill in Cuba during the 1898 war, a battle hugely exaggerated by the yellow press. His words were a precursor for the recent justifications of military intervention by the U.S. into "failed states."

Roosevelt's most important direct intervention occurred in 1903, when American forces prevented Colombia's military from responding to the breakaway republic of Panama, then a state within Colombian territory. Roosevelt ordered the action to facilitate the acquisition of the Panama Canal Zone, which was needed to serve American commercial interests and also to facilitate deployment of a two-ocean navy. Colombia had rejected a U.S. proposal to build the canal, so Roosevelt decided to support Panamanian independence. The new government appointed a French businessman to negotiate a treaty. With consultation with Panama, the Frenchman signed an agreement that cut the new country in half, allocating "in perpetuity" a zone of U.S. control five miles wide on either side of the canal, which was completed in 1914. Long-simmering Panamanian nationalism erupted in anti-U.S. protests in 1960. It took 17 more years, but finally Washington signed a new treaty to resolve the issue, returning jurisdiction over the territory to Panama at the end of 1999.

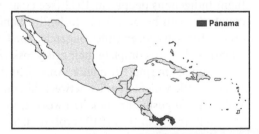

Mexico proved much more difficult to "tame" than other countries in the region. Already heightened by the loss of territory to the United States after the Mexican–American War (1846–1848), Mexican nationalism was reinforced by the revolution of 1910. The United States attempted to manipulate the outcome by backing more conservative factions. Overt military intervention included the shelling of the port of Veracruz in 1914 and the futile pursuit of the rebel Pancho Villa by U.S. troops in Mexico's northern deserts in 1917 (see chapter 8). Villa, angered by U.S. support for his rival, Venustiano Carranza, had staged a minor raid on Columbus, New Mexico, in 1916 in retaliation. His evasion of capture by General Black Jack Pershing's troops helped to make him a larger-than-life symbol of nationalist defiance, a sentiment that continues today in *corridos*, ballads that sometimes depict trafficker and *coyotes* (smugglers of migrants) as heroes not for their crimes but for struggles with authorities. The Mexican case was a precursor of a twentieth-century justification for Washington's intervention in Latin America. The United States came to regard any revolutionary movement as communist-inspired, and any revolution was seen to have a "domino" impact on others in the region. The United States, born of a revolution, had become an antirevolutionary power.

U.S. meddling in Nicaraguan affairs started in the 1800s, when European powers showed interest in the country as a site for a canal. American forces intervened repeatedly to prevent Nicaraguan factions favored by Europeans from gaining power. From a U.S. point of view, the political unrest was chronic and a sign of political immaturity; thus, democracy promotion was welded to national economic and geopolitical interests. In Cuba, the U.S. military (usually the Marines) intervened in 1906–1909, 1911–1912, and 1917–1922; it intervened also in the Dominican Republic (1905, 1916–1924), in Haiti (1915–1934), and in Nicaragua (1909–1933). Rival factions in countries throughout the region came to view the U.S. embassy as a resource in their own intramural disputes. The embassy in effect became a powerful player in the domestic politics of these "sovereign" nations.

The deployment of U.S. forces offshore was often enough to influence the outcome of political conflicts—a tactic known as "gunboat diplomacy." The classic example occurred in 1908. In Venezuela, General Juan Cipriano Castro had seized power in 1899 after a period of civil war. Castro was a maverick nationalist who faced several rebellions financed by foreign interests. When General Juan Vicente Gómez, Castro's second-in-command, moved against his compatriot (who was in Europe for medical treatment), Washington deployed the American fleet offshore, a show of support for Gómez. Gómez would rule with an iron fist for 27 years and preside in the 1920s over Venezuela's first oil boom, distributing the concessions to a small circle of his family and friends who then sold them to foreign companies. Venezuelan presidents Hugo Chávez and Nicolás Maduro often invoked this era in response to Washington's efforts to bring the Bolivarian Revolution (see chapter 8) to an end.

American warships stood by when General Maximiliano Hernández Martínez of El Salvador carried out La Matanza, the massacre of tens of thousands of peasants, most of them Indigenous people, in 1932 (see chapter 9). The American force was deployed in the country's main harbor, ready to lend a hand if the Salvadoran military failed to "restore order." The Salvadoran coffee oligarchy, the Fourteen Families, and the military did not need American help to complete their grisly task (Anderson 1971).

In neighboring Nicaragua, American forces landed multiple times between 1890 and 1928 to settle violent conflict between liberal and conservative elites. One of the liberal generals, José Augusto Sandino, had worked in the Mexican oil fields and absorbed some lessons from that country's 1910 revolution. Sandino was a nationalist and not, like Farabundo

Martí, leader of the Salvadoran revolt of 1934, a communist. He considered the U.S. occupation an affront and organized a peasant army of resistance. The American response set another precedent for Washington's more recent attempts at "state-building" in far-flung parts of the world.

Sandino's army enjoyed popular support and could hide among the people. Between 1927 and 1933, the guerrillas inflicted a mounting toll of casualties that undermined the popularity of the war at home. The occupying force of U.S. Marines was on unfamiliar territory, both geographically and socially; as in Vietnam 40 years later, American soldiers complained they could not distinguish civilians from combatants. Today the operative word for such an enemy is "terrorists"; back then it was "bandits." As in the Vietnam era, some Americans wondered whether it was their place to teach "democracy" to others. The public grew weary of casualty reports, and pressure built for withdrawal. Washington decided its best strategy for stabilizing the country would be to create a professional, politically neutral army. Afterward, the planners thought, Nicaraguan elites would learn to settle disputes through free and fair elections.

With this goal in mind, the Nicaraguan National Guard was created and trained. To command it, the U.S. Marines chose a young liberal businessman, Anastasio Somoza García, who had learned English while at school in Philadelphia. Having "Nicaraguanized" the war, the marines left the country in 1933. The Nicaraguan state for the first time had a well-trained, well-armed force that could keep rival *caudillo* armies at bay. Sandino had said that he would negotiate an end to his resistance once the marines left the country. In 1934, he accepted an invitation to meet with Somoza, who instead ordered the assassination of the guerrilla leader. U.S. aid ended up creating not a neutral, professional army but the basis for a relatively minor *caudillo* to create a family dynasty that lasted 45 years, until the Sandinista revolution of 1979 (Millet 1977).

For Review

What factors influenced the rise of U.S. influence and intervention in Mesoamerica and the Caribbean after the Civil War? What were the economic, geopolitical, and ideological motives at work? How did elites and nationalists respond to American intervention? What precedents were set for U.S. foreign policies in later decades?

▌ Intervention in the Cold War: Covert Operations and Democratic Breakdowns

European missions in the late nineteenth and early twentieth centuries had trained most of the military forces on the South American continent. In the period after World War II, the United States elevated the importance of its own military training and aid missions, extending them beyond the Caribbean region. In South America, the American programs had more to do with modernizing these forces and influencing their doctrines than with creating constabulary forces (e.g., as with the Nicaraguan National Guard). In the Cold War era, an objective of U.S. military aid was to inculcate the strategic doctrine of "national security," the phrase used to justify the creation of a large standing military and other institutions (the CIA, the National Security Agency, etc.; see Schoultz 1987). Throughout the Cold War, national security mainly meant "containment" of communism, though conservatives often argued that the objective should be to roll back rather than merely prevent communism's spread. In the Western Hemisphere, in effect both objectives were pursued after the Cuban Revolution—with "roll back" clearly the objective for Cuba itself.

Cuba, the Bay of Pigs, and the Economic Blockade

One reason that the United States did not invade Cuba with its own troops was the success it had achieved in removing Arbenz in Guatemala in 1954 using proxies (see chapter 9). In 1961, former president Dwight Eisenhower, who had broken relations with Cuba just before John F. Kennedy assumed office in January 1960, bequeathed to the new president a plan hatched by the CIA to emulate its success in Guatemala. Kennedy had doubts, but rather than terminating the operation, he attempted only to reduce U.S. visibility in the project by canceling its air support. On April 17, 1961, about 1,700 Cuban exiles, trained by the CIA in Somoza's Nicaragua, landed on Cuba's south coast, expecting the local population to support them. The population remained loyal; Castro's forces moved decisively—without hindrance from the air—to crush the invasion. Ninety of the invaders were killed, the rest captured.

Invaders captured by the Cuban forces were later ransomed and returned to Miami. They became fierce, implacable enemies of Castro. In their lifetimes, they helped to create an atmosphere of fear and intimidation in Florida that kept any sizable group or institution from opposing relaxation of U.S. pressure on Cuba. Today, the attitudes of Cuban Americans are more varied and complex, but the key power remains in the hands of the first generation and their immediate descendants. The failed invasion at Bay of Pigs greatly enhanced the legitimacy of the communist regime in Cuba and led to closer ties with the Soviet Union. The Soviets installed intermediate-range ballistic missiles, leading to the Cuban Missile Crisis of 1963. The crisis was resolved when the Soviet Union, without seeking advice or consent from Castro, agreed to pull the missiles out in exchange for a promise from Kennedy not to try another invasion and to withdraw some missiles from Turkey.

Roots of the persistently tense relationship between Havana and Washington go back to the war of 1898, the Platt Amendment, and the repetitive intrusion of the United States into the island's internal affairs. Still, when Fidel Castro first came to power in 1959, his relations with Washington were initially good. Some believe that a more enlightened U.S. policy would have prevented Castro from aligning with the Soviet Union and moderated his policies. On the other hand, Castro and his comrades were deeply influenced by the writings of Martí, who—though careful to separate his ideology from Marxism—had warned about the hegemonic pretensions of the United States. If Fidel was not a communist, he was also not a liberal democrat. He was determined not to be one more Latin American leader who abandoned promises of social and economic change to win Washington's support. As Castro began to act to break the neocolonial relationship between Cuba and the United States, things began to spiral out of control (see chapter 9).

The *barbados* mobilized hundreds of thousands of Cubans into a National Revolutionary Militia and the grassroots Committees to Defend the Revolution (CDRs). After the

Bay of Pigs, the likelihood of a counterrevolution diminished considerably, but Washington attempted to sabotage the economy and to assassinate Castro and other leaders. The CIA campaign was code named "Operation Mongoose" and overseen by the notorious U.S. General Edward Landsdale, the model for Ian Fleming's James Bond. Landsdale was known for his innovative and brutal psychological operations campaigns in Southeast Asia. In February 1962, President Kennedy imposed the embargo upon Cuba as punishment for its expropriation of U.S. properties. The sanctions included a travel ban. The ban was loosened briefly during the Carter administration but was reimposed as tensions rose in Central America and with the Soviet invasion of Afghanistan in 1979. Perhaps Cuba's revolutionary path would have led to a one-party state in any event, but U.S. policy reinforced an unhealthy environment for democratic governance in Cuba.

Immigration policy has always been a political football in relations between the two countries. Until January 2013, when the need to get an exit visa to travel was abolished, the Cuban government sought to discourage emigration of its best-educated and most successful athletes and artists. The process of obtaining permission to emigrate was fraught with bureaucratic and political obstacles. The United States for its part sought to embarrass Cuba for restricting the free travel and emigration of its citizens. In reality, Havana was not unhappy to see dissidents and disillusioned people leave. In 1980, after several violent incidents in which Cuban guards prevented would-be asylum seekers from crashing into foreign embassies, Fidel Castro lost patience and announced that any Cubans who wanted to leave could do so through the port of Mariel. Cuban authorities were shocked by the number of Cubans who took advantage.

In an action contradictory to the humanist ideals expressed by Castro himself, the island government rounded up many prisoners and mentally ill patients and sent them out on boats from the port of Mariel. A total of 125,000 Cubans left the island, creating a humanitarian crisis that overwhelmed U.S. authorities. The majority of those leaving, in contrast to the early exiles already established in Miami, were from the lower classes and more likely to be dark-skinned. Upon arrival in the United States via a massive boatlift organized by the Miami exile community, most were imprisoned in refugee camps, some for years.

Neither Cuba nor the United States gained sympathy in the eyes of the international community. Eventually, the Reagan administration negotiated an immigration agreement intended to prevent a repetition of the event. Until 2017, Cubans who sought to leave for the United States, often on rafts or unseaworthy craft, were returned to Cuba if they were intercepted on the high seas, but if they made it to Florida, they were granted special immigrant status, denied to emigrants from all other countries in the region. This was known as the "wet foot, dry foot" policy.

In January 2017, the Obama administration ended the policy as part of agreements with Havana to permit "people to people" tourism, reestablish diplomatic relations, and pursue an end to the unilateral U.S. embargo (which would require congressional legislation). The Trump administration drastically rolled back the policy and ratcheted up economic sanctions. The strategy of the U.S. returned to worsening living conditions with the goal of provoking an uprising against the regime. The Trump administration was under pressure from the Cuban American groups to reinstate the wet foot, dry foot policy, but as of April 2020, the change introduced by Obama was still in place. An estimated 20,000 Cuban migrants were fighting deportation from the U.S. in January 2020 (*Miami Herald*, January 16, 2020).

Because U.S. laws and policy are designed to discourage not only U.S. investors but also foreign investors, the Cubans say the "embargo" is really a blockade, a violation of international law. In 1992, the U.S. Congress enacted legislation to tighten the sanctions by prohibiting branches of American corporations based abroad from doing business in Cuba, which attracted severe criticism from the rest of Latin America. The Helms–Burton Act of 1996 went even further, mandating that the U.S. government deny visas to executives of foreign companies doing business in Cuba. The act also gave Cuban Americans who lost property after the revolution the right to file for restitution in American courts—even if they were not U.S. citizens at the time of the expropriation. Ironically, the Castro government decided to translate and widely distribute the Helms–Burton Act to the Cuban population. I saw Spanish-language copies in the hands of peasants on a cooperative near Holguín in 1994. Why? Because it reinforced concerns in the island's population that Miami Cubans intended to reclaim clinics, schools, cooperatives, and housing that are now part of the fabric of life there.

In April 2009, the new U.S. administration of President Barack Obama lifted sanctions that prohibited Cuban Americans from traveling to visit relatives or sending financial support to them on the island. This initial gesture was welcomed by President Raúl Castro and by many members of the Cuban diaspora. Many of the latter do not share the older generation's bitterness and determination to bring down the communist regime. Economic reforms allowing more room for private enterprise could be an opening for Cubans who, because of the embargo, must stand by as investors from other parts of the world begin to invest. For many Cuban Americans, humanitarian concern for relative and friends on the island surpasses support for policy designed to squeeze the population.

Recent emigrants often leave Cuba for economic opportunity rather than politics (though these are not always easily separable). However, hardline Cuban Americans retain their grip over the politics of Dade County, some other parts of Florida, and parts of northern New Jersey. The political leadership of neither U.S. party has shown much inclination to alienate this powerful lobby that can influence the outcome of presidential elections in two states that have large blocs of votes in the Electoral College. Still, in the 2012 election, Florida voted in the majority for the Democratic presidential candidate. The polls showed that in President Obama's successful bid for the state's electoral votes, he carried a majority of Cuban Americans.

Cuba's foreign policy often consists of a difficult balancing act between support for revolution and a need for normal relations with other countries. Just as revolutionary Mexico was supportive of nationalist movements in Central America in the 1920s, Cuba served that role for revolutionary movements in Latin America in the 1960s. The Soviet Union was less than enthusiastic about Cuban support. Many veteran Latin American communists were reluctant to embrace a strategy that risked the party's significant political influence in established systems, but young communists and leftists throughout the hemisphere embraced Fidelismo. Nowhere were they successful in seizing power. By the 1970s, with Che Guevara killed by American-trained Bolivian commandos in 1967, Cuba had turned its attention to support African liberation movements and to mend fences with other Latin American countries. This diplomatic strategy proved successful in eroding the hemispheric support for U.S. policies.

The close ties between Venezuela in the Chávez years (1999–2013) and its continuing support for Maduro since the death of Chávez were sources of tension in U.S.-Cuban relations, but not enough to deter the opening forged by Obama. That clearly came to an end with the Trump administration.

For Review

What we the original goals of the U.S. embargo/blockade of Cuba? Why has it persisted for 60 years? How did Cuban history shape the attitude of the Castros and their generation of revolutionaries? What changes did the Obama administration introduce? How has it impacted Cuban immigration to the U.S.? Why has the Cuban-American community been mixed in its response?

Send in the Marines?

During World War II, relations between the United States and Latin America were very much shaped by the goal of defeating the Axis powers. Latin America contributed economic resources, as most countries cooperated in holding down prices of raw materials needed for the war effort. Just as they did in World War I, most governments cooperated in monitoring those thought to be sympathetic to the enemy countries of the Allied countries, at times depriving residents of German or Japanese descent (including their own citizens) of rights and property. Especially important was the development of cooperative arrangements among the military establishments of the region. In World War II, Brazil actually contributed troops to the Italian campaign, whereas in other cases branches of the armed forces were provided equipment and training to defend coastlines and important strategic resources.

More formal links between the United States and Latin American militaries were institutionalized in 1947 in the Inter-American Treaty of Reciprocal Assistance (known as the Rio Treaty). The signatories agreed to lend mutual assistance to one another in the event of attack from an outside power. More importantly, the treaty established the basis under which Latin American military officers would be influenced by training both via U.S. military missions in each country and via the attendance of Latin American officers at war colleges and other schools. Probably the best known and most targeted of these programs was the School of the Americas (now called the Western Hemisphere School for Security Cooperation) at Fort Benning, Georgia, founded in 1946. Critics call it the "School for Dictators" because of the large number of its graduates who were later associated with human rights atrocities. Its curriculum at one time included training in torture, ostensibly to train officers to be prepared for what their enemies might practice (Gill 2004).

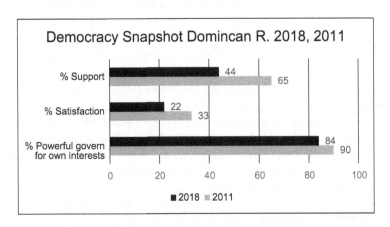

Democracy Snapshot Domincan R. 2018, 2011

% Support — 44 (2018), 65 (2011)
% Satisfaction — 22 (2018), 33 (2011)
% Powerful govern for own interests — 84 (2018), 90 (2011)

■ 2018 ■ 2011

Direct military intervention by U.S. forces became rare in the post–World War II era, but it has happened enough to remind Latin Americans that invasion remains on the table for Washington should circumstances warrant, especially in the Caribbean. The most recent actual invasion took place in the tiny island of Grenada in 1982, but the invasion of the Dominican Republic in 1965 is a better case study of how the United States has often reached for the most risky policy option available—direct military intervention.

The Dominican Republic had suffered a U.S. Marines occupation for eight years early in the century, with U.S. forces leaving behind an American-trained National Guard upon withdrawal in 1924. As in Nicaragua with Somoza and Cuba with Batista, an ambitious young military officer established a dictatorship. Rafael Leónides Trujillo seized power in a coup in 1930 and used the Guard to turn the country into his personal family estate. He gained well-deserved notoriety for his brutality and disdain for democracy. Trujillo's anti-communism played well in the Cold War environment, but Washington was displeased by his attempts to overthrow José Figueres (1948) in Costa Rica and Rómulo Betancourt (1958) in Venezuela, both elected, centrist presidents opposed to communism and friendly to the United States. When Trujillo, after a series of particularly brutal acts of repression in his own country, attempted to assassinate Betancourt, the United States withdrew its support.

In 1961 Trujillo's own army assassinated him, possibly with involvement of the CIA. After a year of uncertainty, Juan Bosch, Trujillo's most important opponent, returned from exile and was elected president in December 1961. Bosch began to implement reforms and develop a friendly relationship with nearby Cuba, alarming Washington, sectors of the Dominican military loyal to the deposed dictator, and the U.S.-based Gulf and Western Corporation, the largest property owner in the sugar-exporting country. In 1963, the army overthrew Bosch, but a countercoup in 1965 sought to restore the constitution and pave the way for his return to power.

President Lyndon Johnson (1963–1968), deeply embroiled in a land war against communist forces in Vietnam, invaded the Dominican Republic with 20,000 U.S. Marines. They installed a compliant transitional regime that paved the way for Joaquín Belaguer, a close associate of Trujillo, to win the presidential election of 1966, heavily stacked in Belaguer's favor. By the time that Bosch finally won an election in 1978, his Dominican Revolutionary Party (PRD) was no longer a revolutionary force. Belaguer remained a powerful influence in Dominican politics until his death in 2002. The invasion ensured that no radical regime would succeed Trujillo, but it committed the United States to the support of a regime notorious for its corruption, presiding over a deeply unjust social structure. In the United States, Johnson sold the invasion as the interdiction of an international communist conspiracy, saying, "The American nations must not, cannot, and will not permit the establishment of another Communist government in the Western Hemisphere." Three years later, leaders of the Soviet Union used a very similar justification for their invasion of Czechoslovakia, putting an end to the Prague Spring (Franck and Weisband 1972). Fidel Castro announced he would support the Soviet action as a "bitter necessity."

The bureaucratic authoritarian regimes of the 1970s and 1980s were not installed by direct U.S. military intervention. However, the United States played a key role in destabilizing elected governments and signaled its support for the founding coups. President Johnson ordered his secretary of defense to do everything possible to help bring down populist João Goulart of Brazil in 1964. In 1976, during Gerald Ford's presidency, Secretary of State Henry Kissinger met with the Argentine foreign minister, Admiral César Augusto Guzetti, at a time when the Argentine military's Dirty War, which took 30,000 lives, was at its peak. Kissinger told Guzetti, "I have an old-fashioned view that friends ought to be supported. What is not understood in the United States is that you have a civil war. We read about human rights problems but not the context. The quicker you succeed, the better" (National Security Archive 2003).

The U.S. involvement in bringing down Salvador Allende in 1973 (see chapter 7) stands out as one of the most egregious cases of antidemocratic intervention by the United States. After Allende finished a close third in the 1958 election, the United States was alarmed that he might win in 1964. With the Cuban Revolution as the background, the Kennedy administration made Chile a prime target of a new hemispheric policy, the Alliance for Progress. The idea was not only to train militaries and prevent a repeat of the collapse of the armed forces—that is, to avoid the kind of collapse that occurred with Batista. The purpose of the Alliance was also to encourage centrist forces to pursue an agenda of reform. One obstacle proved to be the Chilean right, which resisted change, particularly land reform. This dual track of providing military support and encouraging reform was to be practiced again in El Salvador in the 1980s.

The United States spent US$20 million to influence the 1964 vote, $8 per voter and 50 percent of the campaign spending by the winner, Christian Democrat Eduardo Frei (Robinson 1996: 157). As the 1970 elections approached, it was clear that the "threat" of an Allende victory had not been eliminated. Allende narrowly had won the three-way election with 36 percent of the vote. The Chilean constitution called for Congress to choose a president if no candidate secured a majority, and in the past it had always selected the candidate with the most votes. The Nixon–Kissinger administration launched an ambitious plan to sow fear and convince the Chilean Congress to reject Allende. President Nixon ordered the CIA to "make the economy scream" to "prevent Allende from coming to power or to unseat him." Secretly, the CIA shipped weapons and ammunitions for use by a group of military officers who were to kidnap the Chilean military commander, General Rene Schneider, who opposed a coup. The idea was to blame Allende's supporters. Instead, a right-wing military faction linked to the CIA moved first to kidnap Schneider, who was killed in the attempt. In reaction, the military and the country rallied behind Allende's ratification by the Congress (CIA 1970).

After Allende assumed power, the CIA believed that the Chilean military was unlikely to act immediately because of its "apolitical, constitutional" orientation (Robinson 1996: 161). Over the next three years, the U.S. government conducted a coordinated campaign on numerous fronts to bring down Allende. Tactics included subsidizing opposition media and planting false newspaper stories alleging economic shortages—inducing panic buying and real shortages. Another way to create shortages was by funneling funds to striking truck drivers. Right-wing groups were paid to put damaging spikes on highways to discourage drivers willing to work. Striking miners in the copper industry were subsidized with U.S. funds, while Washington effectively sealed off the country from international finance markets and nonmilitary aid programs. At the same time military aid was increased from US$1 million to US$15 million. The size of the U.S. military mission and intelligence activities targeting the military was increased. According to a subsequent U.S. Senate investigation, these activities included compiling names of people who would need to be detained and other contingency plans in the event of coup.

The record does suggest that the United States attempted to keep a distance from planning the actual coup that toppled Allende in 1973. William D. Rogers, who was an assistant secretary of state for inter-American affairs from 1974 to 1976 and later a secretary of state, tried to minimize U.S. involvement. He argued,

> A cursory review of history suggests that had Washington done "all it could" in Chile, it would have attempted an assassination . . . an invasion . . . an armed attack by mercenaries . . . or an attack by the US military . . . Nothing close to such measures was deployed against Allende.
>
> (Rogers 2004)

Here Rogers seems to defend the American role in bringing Pinochet to power by pointing out that assassinations and invasions were not deployed in Chile, though they had been used elsewhere!

Through Operation Condor, U.S. intelligence agencies cooperated with their counterparts in the dictatorships, working together to eliminate leftists. U.S. intelligence agents maintained a close relationship with Chilean general Manuel Contreras and the Chilean secret police, who were the intellectual authors of a car bomb attack that killed Orlando Letelier, a foreign minister in the Allende era, and Ronni Mofitt, his American assistant, on the streets of Washington. Until September 11, 2001, this was the only terrorist attack ever carried out by foreign forces in Washington. When the U.S. ambassador David Popper raised concerns with Pinochet about the country's human rights record, Secretary of State Kissinger reprimanded him: "Tell Popper to cut out the political science lecture" (Bernstein 2008).

Jeane Kirkpatrick, an important official in the administration of President Ronald Reagan (1981–1988), whose academic vita included a book on Argentine politics, justified U.S. support for the military coups that ushered in the bureaucratic authoritarian states and led to the civil wars in Central America in the 1980s. After the Salvadoran army raped and murdered four American missionaries in 1980, Kirkpatrick said, "The nuns were not just nuns, they were political activists, and we should be very clear about that." When challenged to explain how she could justify tolerance of the murderous regimes in Latin America but champion policies to "roll back" communist and leftist regimes, Kirkpatrick (1979) argued that the latter sought to impose their ideology on society permanently. By contrast, she said, "authoritarian regimes" were susceptible in the long run to pressures to democratize. The distinction seemed apt to many in the Cold War, but ten years after Kirkpatrick's assertion, the communist bloc in Eastern Europe began to crumble.

Geopolitical considerations, cultural chauvinism leavened with racism, a notion that Americans had a mission to spread civilization and democracy, and a mindset favorable to expansion (Manifest Destiny) all motivated U.S. intervention in Latin America. However, we should also recognize that many Americans dissented and articulated the country's own heritage of revolution and commitment to self-determination. Furthermore, although their actions are often inconsistent with professed policy, some American presidents have made rights and promotion of democracy a high enough priority to attract criticism from their political opponents. Franklin Roosevelt was president during several interventions, but his Good Neighbor policy showed more respect for Latin America. His New Deal policies to promote economic growth, strengthen labor rights, and institute welfare programs were also admired throughout the hemisphere. Jimmy Carter failed to halt arms shipments to repressive governments in the hemisphere, but his human rights policies were nonetheless welcomed by the budding movements to defend rights in the region.

Both men seem to have personal philosophies that in part motivated their initiatives, but both had other motives as well. Roosevelt thought that the Good Neighbor policy (the phrase was actually first used by his predecessor, Herbert Hoover) would help the United States open doors to increase trade and investment in the region, especially in South America, where European influence was still strong. Carter hoped the U.S. backing of human rights would help restore American prestige and moral leadership, both badly damaged by the Vietnam War, in its global clash with communism. The Reagan administration did not entirely cast human rights and democracy off the agenda. Reagan's own rhetoric, casting the Soviet Union as part of an "evil empire" arrayed against democracy, embraced the selling point—useful at home and abroad—that U.S. policy was fundamentally oriented toward support of human rights and democracy. Obama justified his opening to Cuba on the idea that better relations and commerce with the island would lead to pressure from Cubans for democratization.

We should not assume that Latin American militaries were always pliant tools of U.S. policy. Nationalism is a deeply embedded ethic within the barracks, and it sometimes acts as a source of resistance to U.S. views on the best way to respond to leftist and revolutionary forces in the region. In some cases, such as El Salvador in the 1980s, the brutality of the officer corps (including graduates of the School of the Americas) was seen as counterproductive by their American advisors, but Salvadoran officers were convinced that their way was most effective—just as it had been in 1932. However, there is not much doubt that the formal hemispheric military ties were meant not only to make the military a more effective fighting force but also to gain valuable political allies in a region where military intervention was quite common (Schoultz 1987: 160–190). Not surprisingly, Cuba's rebels decided that quite different doctrines would be necessary to defend the new regime from U.S. intervention. The Sandinistas too began with that assumption, but the Nicaraguan army took on a more conventional role after the defeat of the FSLN in the 1990 elections.

With the shift to the left in the region after 2000, the relationships between the U.S. military and Latin American forces changed, especially where more radical **Pink Tide** leaders ascended to power. Venezuela's radical populist president Hugo Chávez, a former officer, decided in 2005 to change his military's doctrines. Chávez was greatly interested in the theory of **asymmetric warfare**, a military doctrine regarding conflict between two powers that differ both in terms of culture and in terms of overall military strength. He could look to Cuba for an example of successful implementation of the strategy, as it has played a role in discouraging direct invasion by the U.S. military or its proxies. The Pentagon estimated in 1962 that if the United States invaded Cuba, U.S. troops would suffer 18,500 casualties (National Security Archive 2011).

No Latin American country can expect to nearly match the power of the United States. The U.S. military budget exceeded US$748 billion for 2020 (Pentagon, intelligence agencies, other military expenditures). Brazil leads all of Latin America with about $28 billion in the same year. The United States is the only nuclear power in the hemisphere; by treaty, Latin America is a nuclear-free zone. So, Chávez's perspective was that any country seeking to deter possible aggression by the United States must rely on unconventional tactics. His successor, Nicolás Maduro, has maintained the new doctrine.

The Venezuelan high command was dominated by his own appointees, so the new doctrine is officially welcome. In 2020, with President Maduro concerned about an invasion by way of Colombia, the militia drills a lot, but it seems ill-equipped, and many of its members are either elderly or very young. In the long run such a shift may prove controversial within military ranks. The Venezuelan opposition views formation of a militia as a step toward militarization of **civil society** and as the creation of a security institution dedicated to defense of the rule of the Maduro's United Socialist Party of Venezuela, not defense of the nation. It accuses the government of intending to replicate the Cuban model.

Cuba's military and civilians have cooperated in missions (social welfare programs) that have alleviated poverty, but Venezuela's economy, civil society, and military have never undergone the kind of transition, a virtually total reconstruction, that occurred in Cuba after 1959. Chávez himself was a military man with leadership capacity and an ability to connect with ordinary soldiers. Maduro, his successor, came out of the labor movement and does not have the same stature with soldiers as his predecessor had.

For Review

What is the Rio Treaty? What is its stated purpose? How did it influence most Latin American countries' relationship to the U.S.? What is the doctrine of National Security and how does it differ from "asymmetric warfare"? Why might the Cuban militia be more of a deterrent to invasion than the Venezuelan militia?

The Legacy of Cold War Intervention in Latin America

During his eight years in office, President Reagan made it a personal priority to aid the repressive governments of El Salvador and Guatemala as well as the Nicaraguan *contras* in one of the bloodiest regional conflicts of the Cold War. The death toll surpassed 70,000 political killings in El Salvador, 100,000 in Guatemala, and 30,000 in the *contra* war in Nicaragua. Certainly, the Sandinista government and the guerrillas in the other two countries were responsible for some of the violence, but in each country responsibility for a majority of the bloodshed rested with the side supported by the United States (LaFeber 1993). Reagan said of the *contras*, "They are our brothers, these freedom fighters and we owe them our help. They are the moral equal of our founding fathers." The United States continues to maintain that its policies in this decade contributed to the establishment of democracy in the region.

One of the main parts of the American project in Central America in the 1980s was, as in Nicaragua 40 years before, to train a professional army and establish the institutions of **polyarchy**. Organizing "free and fair" elections has as its twin objectives legitimizing the U.S.-supported government and convincing Americans at home to support the war (Herman and Brodhead 1984). To some degree, the strategy was successful. Since the 1980s elections have been held regularly, though whether they are "free and fair" and have established governments responsive to the people is highly questionable (see chapters 8 and 14).

The Central American civil wars came to an end during the administration of President George H. W. Bush (1989–1993). As Reagan's vice president he had held an important role in shaping Central American policies, especially in Honduras, which was used as a forward base of operations by the United States during the conflict. But Bush was more pragmatic than Reagan, and he came to the presidency at the end of the **Cold War**. Cuba appeared (wrongly, it turned out) ripe to fall, with the disappearance of economic aid from the Soviet

Union. European and Latin American leaders were pressuring the United States to end the wars. They took the lead with Europe to media negotiated settlements.

But the legacy of the wars persists to this day. Throughout Central America, refugees from the violence in the countryside swelled the cities. A generation of young (mostly) men had been weaned on violence and were suddenly turned loose into society. This coincided with the emergence of a new source of violence in the form of youth gangs. These bands first emerged among boys who had grown up in refugee families in U.S. cities, especially Los Angeles. It was in Los Angeles that the crack cocaine epidemic, fed in part by drug cartels linked to the *contras* and tolerated by the CIA, took early root (Webb 1999). Widespread passion for guns, alienated young men with little hope for the future, and deepening poverty all accompanied the "successful" installation of democracy in the region.

In June 2005, Amnesty International (AI) published "Guatemala: No Protection, No Justice: Killings of Women in Guatemala." Referring to an epidemic of murders of women, AI said, "According to Guatemalan authorities, 1,188 women and girls were murdered between 2001 and 2004. Many of the victims have been killed in exceptionally brutal circumstances. There is evidence to suggest that sexual violence, particularly rape, is a strong component characterizing many of the killings, but this is often not reflected in official records." The government maintained an attitude of impunity toward the killings. Annual reports by the U.S. State Department recognizing these abuses continue to harshly criticize Guatemala's human rights record, but this did not prevent Washington from supporting Guatemala over Venezuela for a temporary seat on the United Nations Security Council in 2006. Nor has it today stopped Washington from turning away Central Americans seeking asylum from U.S. borders.

For Review

How did democratization and promotion of polyarchy fit into U.S. involvement in Central America's civil wars of the 1980s? Thirty years since the wars ended, around 1930, how has its impact continued to affect both the region and the United States?

Democracy Promotion in the Western Hemisphere

Simón Bolívar had a decidedly mixed view of the United States. He once praised it as a "land of freedom and home of civic virtue." However, in Latin America he is better known for a different quotation. Dismayed by U.S. discouragement of his ambitions, Bolívar wrote in a letter to a British diplomat in Colombia, "The United States appears destined by Providence to plague America with misery in the name of liberty" (Bushnells 1986). Bolívar's political failures had more to do with the attitudes and actions of the Creole elite than with outside intervention by the United States. Still, his prophecy has proven sadly true in many respects.

U.S. troops are less likely these days to engage in an outright invasion, but it is certainly not "off the table," as Washington likes to put it. In 1982, tiny Grenada was the first invasion since the 1965 invasion of the Dominican Republic, as well as the first post–Vietnam War military operation of this type. Another "boots on the ground" intervention took place in Panama, in 1989. The target was Manuel Noriega, a general and power behind the scenes in the country. He was kidnapped and brought back to the United States to stand trial on drug trafficking charges—even though Noriega had been an "asset" working in the employ of the CIA in the 1980s. U.S. forces are more often present in other ways, frequently deployed to train or assist security forces in places such as Colombia, Mexico, and Central America.

More commonly in the post–World War II era, Washington has sought to change regimes in Latin America through destabilizing them. The strategy sometimes relies on funding and training proxies as insurgents, sometimes on undermining a recalcitrant country's economy while bolstering civilian and military opponents, and sometimes both (the "two track strategy"). The flip side of destabilization or overthrow of a government that falls into disfavor with Washington is the attempt to stabilize a new regime. William Robinson (1992, 1996) argues that since the defeat in Vietnam, the United States has placed greater emphasis on state-building to head off revolutionary processes and to shore up regimes installed after episodes of intervention. This has largely taken place through democracy promotion, which Robinson calls "exporting polyarchy" (chapter 1). This strategy is an extension of American **hegemony**—an attempt to construct a world of nation-states whose political systems are based on **polyarchy** and neoliberal economic policies. The editorial cartoons in this chapter show two views of that philosophy from a pro-Sandinista, Nicaraguan newspaper (by the cartoonist Roger) mocking the United States for its sponsorship of elections in the 1980s.

CARTOON 16.2 Nicaraguan cartoonist Roger's view of U.S.-sponsored elections in El Salvador.

Source: From Cartoons from Nicaragua: The Revolutionary Humor of Roger, Managua: Committee of U.S. Citizens Living in Nicaragua (1984: 37).

How Washington Promotes Democratization

Democracy promotion not only includes training and funding for holding elections, but also places stress on building a "civil society" consistent with the principles of a market economy and **pluralist** democracy. This is predicated on the idea that democracy requires the formation of interest groups competing with one another for political influence. One key tool in this effort has been the National Endowment for Democracy (NED, see chapter 13), whose operations, along with those of the Office of Transition Assistance in the State Department and other programs of the U.S. Agency for International Development (AID), reveal much about Washington's approach to influencing Latin American politics in the post–Cold War era. The birth of the NED in 1983 coincided with revolutions that overthrew dictators supported by the United States and that subsequently took a radical turn. Revolutions in Iran in 1978 and in Nicaragua in 1979 had occurred in part because in each case a dictator (Shah Reva Pavlavi and Anastasio Somoza, respectively) had clung to power for too long. The endowment's goals, according to its website (www.NED.org), are "to strengthen democratic institutions around the world through nongovernmental efforts." In its "20th Anniversary Timeline," it listed the following Latin American activities:

- "NED assists the independent Nicaraguan daily newspaper, *La Prensa*, through the purchase of printing supplies without which the paper would have been forced to stop publication." NED proudly cites its success conducting "a wide range of activities supporting the democratic opposition in Nicaragua" in the 1980s. These were parties and politicians aligned with the U.S. financed and trained *contras*.
- "In Chile, urgently needed support is provided by NED to a broad range of political and social forces working for peaceful transition to democracy." The organization takes credit for funding "massive civic education efforts" to encourage a democratic transition in Chile in advance of the 1988 plebiscite.
- In 1990, the NED undertook a mass media voter-education project in Guatemala. In 1994, the NED helped to provide funds to the Civic Alliance for Election Monitoring in Mexico. In 2000, support for the Civic Alliance (see chapter 8) was listed as that year's top priority.
- In 1998, it funded the Center for a Free Cuba and a journal, *Encuentro*, to support dissidents on the island.

In the case of the Civic Alliance in Mexico and support for groups trying to send Pinochet back to the barracks, the NED has made some contribution to making elections cleaner and fairer, but often there is more to that effort than promoting democracy. Chile was a major success for the NED. In the year of its founding, opposition to Pinochet had begun to appear in the streets (see chapter 7). The forces opposing Pinochet, as in Iran and Nicaragua, had different visions of what the new era would look like. Hoping to replicate the success of easing out the dictator Ferdinand Marcos in the Philippines, and also to avoid another revolution in the mold of Iran and Nicaragua, the United States began to pressure the Chilean dictatorship to negotiate with the moderate political opposition. The NED began to fund and train sectors of society to compete with more radical unions, professional associations, women's groups, publishing houses, university associations, and so on (Robinson 1996: 157–175).

As part of its work, the NED funds prominent Latin American, European, and U.S. political scientists to form teams to study "transitions to democracy," always understood as a transition to **polyarchy**. Democracy came to be valued not just for itself but as a system for preventing the radicalization of popular movements, not for empowering them. Routinely, foreign politicians are brought to the United States for workshops where this idea can be reinforced and, in the relevant cases, unity can be promoted. NED funds in Chile were also directed toward inducing unions and other groups in the *barrios*—where Communist Party influence was strong—to participate in the plebiscite.

Between 1984 and 1991, the NED spent US$6.2 million (and the U.S. Agency for International Development spent an additional US$1.2 million) in Chile to help favored groups and encourage the process that led to the plebiscite of 1989 (Robinson 1996: 175). The Chilean opposition was divided on whether to participate in the plebiscite and thereby accept Pinochet's 1981 constitution. U.S. aid helped ensure that the faction favoring acceptance prevailed within opposition ranks (though this seems to have been the majority position in any case). However, NED funds helped offset Pinochet's abuse of incumbency, providing money for polls and training. After victory, most of the "No" (to continuation of Pinochet's rule) forces remained together as the Concertación. The outcome was consonant with U.S. objectives: Pinochet was out of the presidency before pressures for a more revolutionary transition matured, and the Communist Party and other leftist groups were effectively marginalized. The NED also played an important role in the Central American civil wars, notably in Nicaragua, where the NED's support for the opposition helped it defeat the Sandinistas in the 1990 election.

The NED's activities have led some governments around the world to ban foreign funding of nongovernmental organizations. The organization's funding of groups that participated in the short-lived coup against President Hugo Chávez was especially controversial. The NED denies that its aid was directed toward this end, but the Venezuelan government did not see things this way. The incident led Venezuela and several other Pink Tide governments to pass legislation restricting local organizations from accepting foreign funding. This is not unlike the restrictions that the United States places on foreign funding of political parties and the requirement for foreign agents to register. However, such restrictions can be applied with a broad brush against political opponents. Not all organizations that accept funds are disloyal opponents of a government that Washington abjures.

Though the motives for funding are suspect, some organizations receiving NED money have worked in constructive ways on human rights issues and democracy. Mexico's Alianza Cívica (the Civic Alliance), for example, emerged as a genuine movement for clean elections. It was created in 1994 as the result of an innovative campaign to have citizens "adopt" a functionary of the state bureaucracy to audit his or her performance (Avritzer 2002: 124–129). NED monies (e.g., US$52,000 in 2003) continued to fund the Alianza after the election of Vicente Fox in the 2000 presidential election that put an end to 80 years of the PRI's monopoly. Despite this funding, Alianza was harshly critical of the Mexican election campaign of 2006 (see www.alianzacivica.org.mx), in which the U.S.-preferred candidate was victorious. As noted previously, the NED played a role in the Chilean transition from military rule to electoral democracy, supporting opposition to a dictatorship.

The U.S. Department of State also operates a democracy promotion program through the Aid for Transitional Assistance funds, the Human Rights and Democracy Fund, and several separate regional democracy funds. The State Department website stated at that time, "The United States remains committed to expanding upon this legacy until all the citizens of the world have the fundamental right to choose those who govern them through an ongoing civil process that includes free, fair, and transparent elections" (no longer accessible). Funding for these programs for fiscal year 2010, the last year listed on the site, is listed at $210 million. Almost half that amount was designated for Iraq.

Democracy Promotion and the 2002 Coup in Venezuela

In Venezuela, following the electoral victory of Hugo Chávez in December 1998, the NED spent more than US$1 million to support opposition groups in Venezuela between 1999 and 2002. This attempt to strengthen opposition to the popular Chávez was featured as a major accomplishment on the 30th anniversary of the NED's founding (www.NED.org, accessed

December 2012, no longer available). Several of the funded Venezuelan organizations were directly involved in supporting the short-lived coup against Chávez in 2002. Because the Venezuelan media had promoted the coup and prematurely celebrated its success, there exists a visual record of Venezuelans who received NED grants enthusiastically cheering Chávez's fall, which was reversed 48 hours later. The NED was embarrassed but continued to argue that it was working to support a democratic civil society against a government with strong authoritarian tendencies. The NED justified its funding to opposition groups in Venezuela by claiming that it seeks to "level the playing field" because of government support of the Chavista party.

After a solid majority voted "No," not to recall Chávez in 2004, the Venezuelan leader began to crack down on groups accepting NED funding. He charged several organizations with having accepted funds illegally, among them was the group SUMATE ("Join Up"). SUMATE did exercise a constitutional right by gathering signatures to force the 2004 recall; however, its leaders were among the celebrants after the military took control of the presidential palace in the 2002 coup. Afterward, the organization and its leaders were charged with illegally accepting foreign money for the recall. Jorge Vivanco, of Human Rights Watch, criticized the Venezuelan government, claiming that it was persecuting "legitimate electoral activities." The charges were ultimately not pursued. Twelve years later, in 2014, some of the same organizations and leaders were at the forefront of large-scale street demonstrations calling for the ouster of President Nicolás Maduro.

The case raised some important questions about sovereignty, democracy, and civil freedoms. NED-affiliated organizations clearly receive aid from a foreign source. Was SUMATE a party or a group in civil society? The distinction is important because at the time of the recall election of 2004, it was illegal for parties, but not organizations, to accept foreign financial assistance. If it is considered a party, then, as in the United States, it could not receive funds legally. If it is part of **civil society**, as in the United States, it would have to report those contributions, but if it did not operate as a political party, it could legally accept them. SUMATE operated in a gray zone.

In Venezuela, opposition organizations claim that their members are exposed to retribution, and there is evidence that individuals who worked in legal ways to oppose the government were subject to retribution in employment. There can be little doubt, however, that Washington would like to see regime change in oil-rich Venezuela, and its historical track record does not inspire faith in its neutrality in promoting democracy.

The NED's role in U.S. foreign policy is very small in budgetary terms, but it is worth our attention because it demonstrates how democracy conceived as polyarchy (see chapter 1) is central to the exercise of hegemony. The Trump administration has deemphasized democracy promotion. In 2019 it sought unsuccessfully to slash the NED's budget and to cut off NED's relationship to the parties, unions, and business groups that provide the Endowments its directorate. Technically, the NED is a private, not-for-profit institution. While it has been a handmaiden in several cases to American military intervention and foreign policy goals, many of its academic and professional staff have worked with the organization out of a sincere commitment to democratization. This has been an organizational strength that is threatened by the Trump administration's more inward-looking "America First" policies. As of 2020, the NED was still operating, due to strong congressional support, and should the U.S. Democratic Party return to the White House after elections in 2020, democracy promotion will probably return with it as higher priority for U.S. foreign policy.

For Review

How does the NED define its purpose? What does it mean when the NED says it supports civil society? Why do some see it as a tool of U.S. foreign policy? How has democracy promotion fit in with larger U.S. goals in regard to more radical regimes in the hemisphere? How did democracy promotion and specifically the role of the NED come into question in Venezuela during the Chávez era? How did the Chávez government react?

Hemispheric Diplomacy From Chávez to Trump

We are accustomed to hearing North American politicians routinely refer to U.S. support for "free markets and democracy" in the same breath, as though no other combination of political and economic systems makes sense. The United States and Latin American nations pledged themselves to market economies and electoral democracy in a plan of action signed at the first Summit of the Americas in Miami in December 1994. A key plank in the agreement was a commitment to support elected governments threatened by military coups. All heads of state except Fidel Castro of Cuba (who was banned from the summit at U.S. insistence) attended and signed the accords. At the summit, held at the peak of neoliberal influence in the hemisphere, the signatories also agreed to advance **WTO**/GATT trade negotiations and pledged to work for a Free Trade Area of the Americas (see chapters 6 and 15).

However, in this same period, some of the harbingers of change were visible, in part because of global changes. Europeans had taken the lead over the U.S. in negotiating an end to the Central American civil wars. Spain and Portugal had undergone transitions to democracy by 1986 and were members of the (then) European Community. Both, as the "mother countries" of most of Latin America, wished to establish a "special relationship" with the region. A group of Latin American countries (Mexico, Venezuela, Colombia, and Panama) had joined the Europeans, much to the consternation of the Reagan administration, to bring the Central American conflicts to a close. The "backyard" mentality in Washington had not disappeared, but the Caribbean could no longer be considered an American lake.

The nature of "empire" is different today than it was in the era of European dominance. Michael Hardt and Antonio Negri (2000), in their widely read and debated book *Empire*, argue that a new globalized world order has emerged, one that resembles the empires of ancient Greece and Rome. As in the ancient world, the United States is a central political and military power presiding over a vast system of decentralized economic power, diffusing its cultural and political norms throughout the world. On the other hand, despite the changes in the world since the Cold War ended, the United States remains the first or second most important trade partner in the region, with military bases on the South American continent for the first time. With the ascent of Donald Trump and his "America First" ideology, the willingness of the United States to continue exercising power as a hegemon devoted to a liberal world order is in doubt. However, Trump's harsh sanctions against Cuba and Venezuela and his embrace of right-wing authoritarian leaders in Brazil and elsewhere points to the kind of foreign policy of another "America First" president, Teddy Roosevelt, who once said of Panama, "I took the Canal and let congress debate."

Why are different views of "empire" relevant to Latin America's path in the world today? Consider the choice confronting the region's leaders. Should Latin Americans put the emphasis on linking their economies in a trade bloc led by the United States, or should they instead prioritize regional economic integration independent of the United States and diversification of trade and investment with Asia and Europe? Should right-populist governments align with Washington's attempts to overthrow left regimes in Cuba, Venezuela, and Bolivia, or should they embrace China's economic investment and aid, much to the annoyance of Trump's Washington? Does National Security Agency (NSA) surveillance and new forms of cyber warfare represent a threat to the region, or is it part of a shield against the threat of terrorism?

Despite the record of repeated intervention in their internal affairs, most Latin Americans have looked positively at the United States. However, their admiration significantly dropped during the wars in Iraq and Afghanistan, reaching a nadir of 58 percent in the last year of the G. W. Bush administration (2001–2008). The election of the first Afro-descendant president, Barack Obama, seemed to have restored U.S. prestige to more usual levels (see Figures 16.1 and 16.2). What is especially striking is the low levels of confidence expressed by Mexicans. This is hardly a surprise after a campaign in which Donald Trump repeatedly characterized Mexican migrants as criminals, rapists, and murderers. His infamous border wall only antagonizes Mexican public opinion. Nonetheless, President Andrés Miguel López Obrador chose to renegotiate NAFTA at Trump's demand, even though he had been harshly critical of the treaty for years (see chapter 15). His decision is a measure of how much more reluctant he was to deal with an economic crisis (should NAFTA be torn up) than challenge the United States and Trump.

FIGURE 16.1   Percent With Favorable View of U.S.

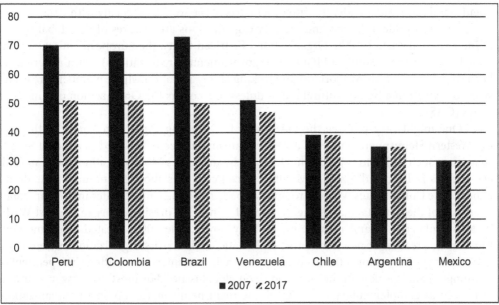

Source: Pew Research Center, Spring 2017 Global Attitudes Survey.

FIGURE 16.2   Percent Expressing Confidence in President Trump, 2017

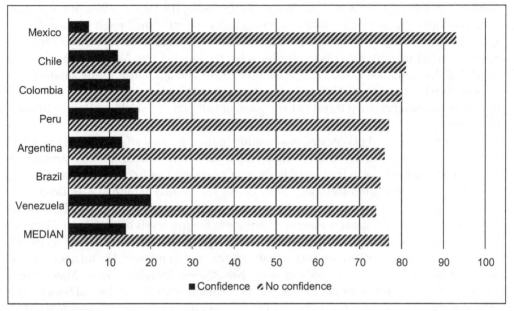

Source: Pew Research Center, Global Attitudes Survey, Spring 2017.

However, in the 2000s Latin American countries became much more proactive in their diplomacy. Each country's interactions with the United States remained the single most important of its bilateral relations, but Latin America was beginning to interact more frequently and more independently with other parts of the world, especially with Asia.

Regional trade, military, and security organizations are features of the global system of international relations. The Organization of African Unity, the European Union, and the Arab League are all examples of IGOs (intergovernmental organizations). Latin America has been the only major Third World region lacking an organization whose members are exclusively drawn from a broad cultural area—unless one counts the Organization of American States (OAS).

One might very well see the OAS as an IGO uniting "American states" or those in the Western Hemisphere; indeed, Pan-Americanism has been expressed as an ideal by U.S. statesmen, such as Thomas Jefferson, Henry Clay, and James Monroe. Latin American leaders, such as Bolívar and Martí, have often voiced concerns about falling under the dominance of the United States. While strongly sympathetic to the United States in the immediate aftermath of the criminal mass slaughter of 9/11, Pink Tide presidents began to resist Washington's unilateralism and reliance on military power. The 2000s created some momentum for the creation of new economic, diplomatic, and security organizations where Latin Americans could act more effectively to resolve their own interstate conflicts independent of Washington and speak with their own voice on global issues. For most, the new institutions were seen as complementary to the OAS, the main hemispheric diplomatic organization. However, more radical Pink Tide leaders had greater ambitions.

The OAS and the Attempt to Form Alternatives

In 1948, one year after the signing of the Rio Treaty creating a military cooperation between the United States and most of Latin America, the countries of the region founded the Organization of American States, which replaced a looser association, the Pan-American Union. Bolívar's notion of Pan-Americanism envisioned Latin American unity as a bulwark against domination by the United States. The OAS, headquartered in Washington, is a hemispheric organization that is cynically called "the office of the colonies" by some Latin Americans. In 1962, the OAS adopted a resolution expelling Cuba (formally, Cuba remains a member, but without representation) and in doing so defined any state that identified itself with Marxism–Leninism as unqualified for membership. By 2010, Latin American governments were ready to readmit Cuba, but Havana expressed no interest. The Obama administration opposed the move, but it did not act (for example, by threatening to withdraw funding) to prevent the OAS from changing its posture on Cuba.

On several occasions the OAS has provided diplomatic cover for U.S. intervention, including the 1954 intervention in Guatemala against the elected president, Jacobo Arbenz. The OAS reacted ambiguously to the U.S. invasion of the Dominican Republic in 1965. It supervised the election in 1962 that brought the leftist Juan Bosch to power—much to the displeasure of the United States—touching off the crisis that eventually led to the U.S. Marines invasion of 1965. Many Latin American countries objected, but faced with a *fait accompli*, the OAS decided to provide a multinational force to replace the U.S. occupation force, paving the way for elections in which Bosch was defeated. Similarly, the organization condemned the coup that removed President Manuel Zelaya in Honduras in 2009, but in 2010 it endorsed elections to replace him.

The OAS has not always conformed to Washington's lead. For example, it refused to endorse the *contra* war in Nicaragua in the 1980s, and it condemned (though belatedly) the 2002 coup endorsed by Washington in Venezuela. The organization played an important role in bringing an end to the 1980s civil wars in Central America, one not welcomed by the Reagan administration (1981–1988). In 1989 the OAS took a stance against the U.S. invasion of Panama. Though it did not condemn the invasion, it expressed "deep regret" for the U.S. action and called for a withdrawal of troops. Two of its autonomous units, the Inter-American Commission on Human Rights and the Inter-American Court on Human Rights, have taken on an important role in adjudicating human rights disputes brought by individuals and groups of citizens against governments in the region that are signatories to the Convention on Human Rights. OAS observer missions have played key roles in highly polarized political situations—for example, in Nicaragua in 1984 and 1990 and in Venezuela in 2004.

In 2005, Latin Americans seemed to have dealt U.S. diplomacy a severe setback by rejecting the U.S.-backed (Mexican) candidate to become the OAS secretary general, selecting instead Chilean José Miguel Insulza. So, it could not have come entirely as a surprise when in June 2009, the United States was set back again when member states voted to readmit Cuba—though under some conditions. The OAS and the Commission found they had vocal and powerful critics from another source as well. In Washington, Republican conservatives who have threatened to cut funding for the organization unless it implemented sanctions against nations that, according to the Republican right, are in violation of the Inter-American Democratic Charter. This document, signed by most of the region's states in 2001, incorporated the plan of action into a formal treaty. Cuba and Venezuela were what the conservatives had in mind. The charter was signed in the waning moments of the Washington Consensus, and most Latin American countries, and a few years later the Pink Tide governments, were not enthusiastic about its narrow liberal focus.

In the United States, the new generation of conservatives is suspicious of any concessions that Washington might make to international organizations. Foreign aid, which includes money for the OAS, is on their agenda for deep cuts, if not elimination. At times the OAS is under pressure from its members (and not just ALBA) to put the United States under the same scrutiny on human rights and democracy as other member states. There was a possibility—a hope in some eyes, a threat in others—that the impressive OAS building in Washington, an architectural masterpiece incorporating cultural elements from all the member nations, would become merely an impressive art museum.

Contrary to U.S. concerns, Insulza became a thorn in the side of Venezuela, which was leading an attempt to form alternative Latin American organizations that would offer the United States no more than observer status. The **ALBA** (**Bolivarian Alliance for the Americas**) under Chávez's leadership proposed a radically alternative concept of economic integration (see chapter 15). It also served as a diplomatic forum for Latin American and Caribbean governments, mostly left of center. Many of these governments saw the OAS as too closely influenced by Washington. In addition, many were favorably disposed toward Venezuela, whose petrodiplomacy provided social aid and money for development projects. Two fledgling alternatives to the OAS emerged—CELAC and UNASUR.

CELAC, the Community of Latin American and Caribbean States, was founded in December 2011. The organization's member nations in January 2013 formulated a plan of action, shaped in part by social movements meeting separately and by international organizations, such as the United Nations Economic Commission for Latin America. The invited movement organizations suggested free health care and education, as well as the creation of a CELAC television channel. However, the summit did not address funding for such projects, nor was it resolved at the subsequent January 2014 summit.

UNASUR, the Union of South American Nations, was founded on May 23, 2008, at a summit of heads of state of the continental countries. UNASUR was envisioned to fulfill a variety of functions. Among its subsidiary councils is an Electoral Council, charged with electoral observation, an alternative of OAS delegations that many Latin American states saw as biased toward Washington. However, the most important innovation of UNASUR was that for the first time the countries on the continent sought to establish a pan-continental diplomatic organization with the capacity to address regional problems and mediate conflicts without the participation of the United States. This potential was demonstrated when UNASUR mediated the conflict that threatened to bring about interstate war between Colombia on one side and Venezuela and Ecuador on the other. Despite Colombia's close relationship to the United States and the role of the U.S. military advisors, bases, and funding in its conflict with the FARC (see chapter 10), Colombia agreed (under prodding from Brazil) to UNASUR's mediation.

Of these initiatives, UNASUR probably advanced the furthest institutionally. It managed to establish a South American Defense Council. Colombia initially was reticent to join because of its close military ties to the United States, but it joined in 2008, the year before the crisis with Venezuela and Ecuador. Although Venezuela took the lead originally in proposing UNASUR, the support of Brazil was indispensable to its success. Furthermore, President Bachelet of Chile, a more centrist leader of the Latin American left and daughter of a general, took the lead in organizing the Defense Council's plans and first meetings. The Defense Council represented a significant departure from the security system established by the Rio Treaty, with its clear reliance on U.S. military doctrine and training. It has also laid the basis for increased cooperation on a range of technical, social, and economic matters.

In contrast to the OAS, UNASUR refused to recognize the legitimacy of elections organized by the new government after the 2009 Honduran coup, directly at odds with U.S. policy. UNASUR also expelled Paraguay from membership (as did Mercosur) for a year after the irregular removal of elected President Lugo from power by that country's parliament. UNASUR, in contrast to the United States, characterized his ousting as a coup. It also condemned a police rebellion against leftist President Rafael Correa as a coup attempt.

UNASUR never developed in its short life the institutional bureaucracy that the OAS had at its disposal or the institutional memory. For example, UNASUR's South American Electoral Council was to be made up of officials from the electoral institutions of each member nation, but it did not have a permanent institution comparable to the OAS's Department for Cooperation and Electoral Observation. Similarly, in the area of human rights, in January 2013 the organization committed itself to establishing a permanent human rights organization, but nothing comparable to the Inter-American Commission on Human Rights and the Inter-American Court on Human Rights was created.

Creating alternatives for the IACHR was perhaps the most important item that the ALBA countries had on the agenda for CELAC. Leaders of the ALBA countries complain that the commission is biased by institutions to influenced by the United States (see chapter 14). Venezuela claims that the IACHR was particularly tepid in reacting to the short-lived coup against Chávez in 2002, a claim the commission denies (see Emersberger 2010; IACHR 2010). In September 2012, Venezuela formally withdrew from the convention, which it had ratified in 1977. The withdrawal allowed Venezuela to deny the IACHR jurisdiction over issues in the country after September 2013. The IACHR claims Venezuela remains obligated to the convention because of its membership in the OAS; the IACHR has not made the same claim about the United States, which never ratified the hemispheric human rights charter.

By 2020, after the coup against Evo Morales in Bolivia and the shift to the right by Ecuadorean President Lenín Moreno, ALBA had been reduced to Venezuela, Nicaragua, Cuba, and several smaller Caribbean nations. UNASUR had almost entirely disappeared, as 12 nations had already withdrawn and Brazil's Bolsonaro announced in 2019 that Brazil would withdraw. Uruguay withdrew in 2020. Brazil's support for UNASUR and Venezuela's other initiatives for integration were indispensable to their establishment and survival. Unless there is a rapid shift back toward the left in the hemisphere, the integration initiatives of the Pink Tide era are likely to disappear entirely. In fact, Chile's conservative president, Sebastian Piñera, took the lead in 2019 to announce the establishment of an alternative to UNASUR called PROSUR, but it has not reached the level of **institutionalization** that either ALBA or UNASUR reached for a brief time. Another regional group, the Lima Group, has formed as a coalition of conservative states supportive of the claim of former president of the Venezuelan National Assembly Juan Guaidó to have legitimately replaced Maduro as president.

The posture of the OAS has tilted, as it often does, toward the U.S. agenda. But that could change. Conservative presidents in Brazil, Ecuador, and Chile are all under tremendous pressure from people dissatisfied with their performance. Mexico and Argentina saw right-wing presidents replaced by leftist presidents in 2019. In Bolivia, polls showed strong support for exiled President Evo Morales's MAS party for new elections in May, subsequently postponed. The massive problems arising from climate change, migration, and environmental degradation are not going away and cannot be solved by individual nation-states. The United States may proclaim its support for "democracy" in Venezuela and Cuba, but its attempt to foment a coup by making living conditions worse in the midst of a health crisis can only reduce whatever moral authority it has left in the region.

The coronavirus pandemic, if not met effectively, is likely to further erode confidence in the ability of ruling elites. Certainly, it is difficult to see how neoliberal economic policies can cope with the enormous challenges of overwhelmed healthcare systems and extreme drops in demand and prices for the region's exports. Jair Bolsonaro was facing a middle-class uprising, with daily, noisy *cacerolazas* (banging of pots and pans at an appointed hour) as a result of his continued insistence that there was no need for people to self-isolate. However, the left governments have not always responded more effectively than those on the right. AMLO initially recommended people try to live normally and trust in the mystical power of two amulets he held up as his "protective shields." Daniel Ortega of Nicaragua counseled against social isolation, although he himself disappeared from public view.

Although it has less influence than before, the Pink Tide has not entirely left the diplomatic scene. Leftist governments were angered by the OAS's failure to condemn the coup in Bolivia. OAS Secretary General Luis Amalgro endorsed an OAS election observer team's harsh criticism of the 2019 presidential election in Bolivia. The controversial report claimed that Bolivia's electoral authority had manipulated the count to declare Morales the winner in the first round (OAS 2019). The report thereby lent support for the coup that forced Morales to flee the country. At the heart of the report's allegation was that the preliminary announced results were inconsistent with the final tally the next day, which showed that Morales had won a sufficient plurality (more than 40 percent) to avoid a second round. Two follow-up analyses, one by academics at M.I.T.'s Election Data and Science Lab and the other by the Center for Economic Policy Research in Washington, argued that the official tally was fully consistent with the preliminary figures. The earlier totals, showing Morales short on what he needed, were based largely on the earliest returns in cities. The vote totals that came in overnight were largely from more remote areas that are strongholds of Morales's support among Indigenous groups.

It is not likely the Pink Tide experiments in alternative economic integration and diplomacy will revive quickly, but the OAS may also find it difficult to bridge the divide between Latin America's neoliberal elites and the populists that draw political strength from Caribbean and Latin American people facing rising precarity from the economic and biological ravages of a pandemic.

For Review

What is the Organization of American States? In terms of membership and scope, how does it differ from ALBA, CELAC, and UNASUR? What challenges has the OAS faced from its own members and at times from the United States government? Why has the outlook for success of the new organizations for regional cooperation darkened?

◼ The Foreign Policy of Latin American States: Issues and Examples

Most of this chapter has examined how U.S. foreign policy has influenced Latin America, with some emphasis on the ramifications for democracy in the region. Despite signs of some decline in U.S. influence and the expansion of economic and political ties between Latin America and other parts of the world, the gravitational weight between Latin America and the United States remains strongly pitched toward Washington. However, the relationship is not static, and each country in Latin America has foreign relations issues with its neighbors and with other parts of the world on its agenda.

Latin American nations enjoy the good fortune of having little threat of war with one another. The last large, full-scale war, the Chaco War (1932 and 1935), occurred between Bolivia and Paraguay. They disputed the Chaco region, a wilderness area but one thought (correctly, as it turned out 80 years later) to have significant energy resources. The conflict cost 100,000 lives for two of the poorest countries in the world. Smaller-scale, shorter border conflicts have taken place and left some bitterness between the contending nations. In 1969, Honduras and El Salvador fought a five-day "Soccer War." The immediate catalyst was a riot at a soccer match between the two countries, but the tensions had built up over border issues, especially undocumented migration of Salvadorans into their less populated neighbor. Fighting broke out briefly in 1995 between Peru and Ecuador over a border dispute dating back to the independence era, but the conflict led to a settlement of the dispute three years later. There remain simmering conflicts among several other neighbors on the continent, but at present none seem to threaten war, and the emergence of new regional diplomatic forums provides enhanced opportunity to mediate these kinds of disputes.

What follows is a broad summary of foreign policy issues for selected countries. In each case we review briefly the country's relationship with Washington and the main issues on its agenda in relations with, respectively, other parts of Latin America and the world.

Brazil

Without a doubt, Brazil's large population, landmass, and economic resources make it the most influential country in the region. It borders on every South American nation except Chile and Ecuador. Many of those borders are ill-defined; indeed, insofar as they are marked by rivers subject to periodically heavy rains, they may shift. Whether governed by the military, by conservative, moderate, or leftist presidents, Brazil has seen itself as a potential world power. Between 2000 and 2014 it was counted among the rising BRICS countries (Brazil, Russia, India, China, and South Africa) expected not only to develop but to work together diplomatically to defend the interests of the Global South. Brazil's weight in hemispheric affairs is expressed in the fact that press reports sometimes use the phrase "according to Itamaraty," referring to the modernesque building in Brasília where the Ministry of External Relations is located. As one analyst (Burges 2012) put it, "Brazil is a position to now be more of a rule maker than a rule taker."

During the years (2003–2016) of two presidents of the left Workers Party, ALBA countries tended to take a more aggressive stance than Brazil did in challenging Washington and advancing new hemispheric diplomatic and economic initiatives. In some ways, Brazil welcomed this posture, led by Venezuela's Chávez, as it opened space for Itamaraty to advance its own agenda, especially on economic issues involving intellectual property (Brazil wants more technology transfer). Venezuela took the most militant position on relations with Iran, permitting Brazil to more quietly and steadily assert its right as a sovereign nation to carry out economic and political relations with the Islamic regime that Washington regards as a pariah.

Revelations that the U.S. had spied on President Dilma Rousseff shook U.S. relations with Brazil. For the first time a Latin American leader, Rousseff, canceled a planned visit to Washington. Not only did the U.S. National Security Agency eavesdrop on her communications, but also the Obama administration refused to assure her it would not happen in the future. On the other hand, Brazil made it clear very early on that it would not offer asylum to Snowden.

Brazil's relationships with neighboring countries tend to be normal, if not cordial in most respects. At times tensions emerge over economic relations with Argentina, especially when Brazil's robust currency increases its strong and consistent trade surplus with its Mercosur partner. Probably its tensest relations were with Bolivia, despite that both Lula and Morales were part of the Pink Tide, over that country's 2006 nationalization of natural gas fields being exploited by Petrobras. A solution was negotiated because Bolivia needs investment from Petrobras, and Brazil needs energy for São Paulo and the rest of its dynamic southern states.

Brazil tends to criticize the imposition of sanctions by the United States on Iran. It has conducted its own negotiation on nuclear issues with the Islamic republic, much to the consternation of the United States. President Bolsonaro angered Iran by expressing support for U.S. goals of forcing Iran to abandon its nuclear capability, but the Brazilian president is reluctant to break close commercial ties with the Islamic Republic, his country's largest importer of its corn. On the other hand, Bolsonaro's contacts with Trump's inner circle of advisers proved useful in convincing Trump to roll back his plan to raise the tariff on Brazilian steel exports.

Brazil was a supporter of UNASUR and CELAC, in part because a portion of the Venezuelan-led integration project included a regional development bank that, with Brazilian backing, would extend its economic influence. As just noted, Brazil's withdrawal from UNASUR probably will prove the death of the diplomatic experiment. Brazil has harshly criticized Venezuela and at times spoken as though Brazil would cooperate in a military effort to oust Maduro. However, Brazil's military has shown little enthusiasm for going to war with its brothers in arms to the north.

Besides its geopolitical and economic weight, Brazil's advantage over every other Latin American state is the well-trained core of experienced diplomats who are trained and work at Itamaraty. Some analysts (e.g., Burges 2012) think that the institution is too conservative in the sense that it defines its mission narrowly as advancing Brazilian national sovereignty, causing it to underestimate the need to seek multilateral solutions on, for example, climate issues. Itamaraty's support for multilateralism may be pragmatic, used to advance its own autonomy, not embraced as a principle.

Venezuela

Venezuela's self-identity has long been linked to advancing the ideal of Pan-Americanism found in Bolívar's writings. It also has had pretensions to exert influence over the Caribbean region. Under President Hugo Chávez, Venezuela assumed a much more assertive role in hemispheric affairs, rivaling Cuba as, from Washington's perspective, the most troublesome regime in the region. Chávez took the lead in the creation of UNASUR and CELAC, though, as previously mentioned, Brazilian support was the crucial factor in their initial (but temporary) success.

Venezuela's main leverage in hemispheric affairs came from the petrodollars at its disposal. Between 2000 and 2014, it used its financial resources to fund oil-discount programs (PetroCaribe, PetroSur) and a continental satellite network, Telesur. Through its CITGO subsidiary, Venezuela even provided discounted oil to a number of poor communities in the northern United States, a reversal of the usual flow of foreign aid. In its early years, the country's ability to carry out foreign policy initiatives was hamstrung by the attitudes of its professional foreign service corps, made up mostly of individuals ideologically aligned with the policies of the Punto Fijo era. A former ambassador to Washington told me that the content of confidential meetings held in the embassy would often find its way into the opposition media back home.

Like so many other facets of government under Chávez, control over foreign policy remained firmly in the grasp of the president. This meant that on important and lesser matters alike (whether to issue a visa, for example, for a visit by a dignitary), foreign ministry officials would not act before hearing from the president. Chávez was also criticized by friends, not just opponents, for verbal blasts at rival countries, in particular the United States, often employing highly sexist language toward Secretary of State Condoleezza Rice. On the other hand, Chávez showed himself to be quite pragmatic on several key issues, even to the point of extraditing members of FARC to Colombia in the face of criticism from his supporters.

In the region, Venezuela's thorniest relations have been with Colombia. Tensions have periodically flared between the two countries for decades over demarcation of the boundary waters north and west of Lake Maracaibo, but Chávez never made that a high priority. Instead, it is Colombia's long-standing civil war, especially its conflict with the FARC, that has been at the center of at times highly tense relations between the two neighbors. Colombia, especially under President Álvaro Uribe (2002–2010), charged that Venezuela was aiding the rebels and providing shelter for them in its territory. Chávez denied the allegations.

Whatever the actual relations between the Bolivarian government and the FARC, it is clear that Chávez's own sympathy for the FARC waned over time. That fact became obvious when Manuel Santos, Uribe's defense minister and successor to the Colombian presidency, sought out a more cooperative relationship. Venezuela still resents Colombia's allowing the United States to maintain seven "forward operating locations" (a euphemism for "military bases") in the country.

President Nicolás Maduro served as foreign minister before being elevated to the vice presidency in the closing months of Chávez's life. He took an especially forward role in the Middle East (and not just with oil-exporting countries) and Africa. The country has staunchly asserted its right to maintain economic and political relations with Iran, including its right to carry out economic relations in defiance of the sanctions imposed by the United States. Chávez sought to mediate early in the conflicts in Libya and Syria and accused the United States of seeking the overthrow of regimes rather than seeking a negotiated resolution. His embrace (literally) of former president Mahmoud Ahmadinejad, despite the Iranian politician's anti-Semitic utterances, was especially controversial. The deterioration of Libya and Syria into civil war, along with the threat that these countries might become havens for terrorist organizations, suggests that Chávez's intuitions on the conflicts were more prescient than those of Washington.

Should Maduro fall, whether by elections or otherwise, to the opposition, certainly Venezuela's economic support for Cuba (already faltering because of low oil prices) would come to an end. Maduro himself has moved to scale back Chávez's nationalist oil policies, which included strong support for OPEC, an organization that Venezuela helped found. In its severely weak political and economic position, Venezuela's Bolivarian government has made it clear it is willing to revise policies and make deals very favorable to transnational oil companies, whatever their home country (including China) (Hellinger 2017). Venezuela has an enduring, antagonistic relationship with oil companies that will reassert itself in the long run. Venezuelans see the oil as the nation's property, and as the sovereign owner of the subsoil wealth it is likely someday to seek to redress the arrangements made today. However, that day is not imminent, regardless of whether Maduro or the opposition prevails politically.

Bolivia

Under President Evo Morales, Bolivia acquired an outsized influence in international forums because of the global welcome given to the Americas' first Indigenous president. He joined Ecuador's President Rafael Correa and Venezuela's Chávez as the most outspoken critics of Washington. Morales's stature enabled him to assume a strong position of advocacy in international forums on global warming, although his own policies on expansion of mining did not always live up to his rhetoric. His warnings of an environmental "holocaust" and demand that countries take immediate measures to limit warming to no more than one degree (centigrade) shook up the December 2009 climate change summit in Copenhagen.

Bolivia has a long-standing concern with the fate of Bolivian immigrants in Argentina, where they have suffered discrimination and harassment. It also has a long-standing, bitter dispute with Chile over the loss to that country of its outlet to the sea, a consequence of the War of the Pacific (1879–1883). Nationalist resentment toward Chile was a factor in the successful popular resistance in 2003 to increased natural gas extraction through foreign investment, with the gas to be sent through the disputed region for export. President Morales has refused to negotiate bilaterally with Chile, as urged by the OAS, and instead opted to take the dispute to international forums.

Bolivia is not likely to maintain these postures, except on the issues with Chile, if the right-wing political movements that fomented the November 2019 coup keep their grip on the country. However, the awakening of Indigenous political movements in the Andes is nothing ephemeral. This change represents a significant new domestic force that will shape Bolivian foreign policy at some point—sooner if the MAS party wins back power. More likely, however, Bolivia is entering a highly conflictive domestic era of politics as its conservative, Euro-descendent elites attempt to roll back Indigenous influence.

Mexico

"So far from God, so close to the United States" is a sentence Mexicans often mutter. Mexico has attempted to balance defense of national autonomy on some issues (restrictions on foreign investment in oil; relations with Cuba; rights of Mexican immigrants in the United States, etc.) against the reality of having a land border with a superpower in both economic and military terms. The country also benefits from a developed university system and intellectual establishment that provides key advisors for the president and candidates for its foreign service school. However, even by Latin American standards (and in contrast to Brazil), Mexican foreign policy is concentrated in the presidency.

The return in 2012 of the PRI to control of the presidency initially meant some shifting on what has become one of the country's two most contentious foreign policy issues, cooperation with the United States in the drug war and emigration. President Nieto showed wariness about allowing the U.S. security forces to actively take part in the government's efforts to subdue the drug cartels. He appointed a foreign minister who was a well-known critic of President Calderón's drug war policies. One of Mexico's concerns is that many of the guns fueling the drug violence are purchased in the United States, where gun control is lax. Nonetheless, as the violence continued, Peña Nieto continued to rely on U.S. security forces for aid in antidrug enforcement.

Like any Mexican president might be expected to do, Peña Nieto expressed indignation at Donald Trump's racist rants toward Mexican immigrants during the 2016 presidential campaign. He caught flak from his political opponents, including López Obrador. But when AMLO became president, he too had to face the reality of the hegemon on his northern border. As mentioned earlier, the longtime critic of NAFTA renegotiated the deal, as Trump demanded, and signed the United States–Mexico–Canada Agreement. AMLO retreated from an initial policy of reducing persecution of the antidrug war as well, although he continued in early 2020 to reject increased U.S. involvement in persecuting it. López Obrador also agreed to cooperate on holding tens of thousands of migrants seeking asylum in the U.S., most of them from violence-wracked Central America, in border camps.

Mexico has had numerous conflicts over trade with the United States. For example, under NAFTA, Mexican trucks were to have full access to U.S. highways, but Washington refused to implement the treaty provision. In 2009 Mexico retaliated with some tariffs. Finally, in 2011, the two countries negotiated an agreement whereby Mexico would lift the tariffs but accept regulations and inspections. Mexico has also attempted to integrate Central America more deeply into its sphere of influence with Plan Puebla Panama, oriented toward integrating nine southern Mexican states with all of Mesoamerica and Colombia in a NAFTA-like association.

Backyard, Front Porch, or Neighbors

The section just concluded is not meant to be anything like a full survey of the long- and short-term foreign policy agenda in Latin America. It is meant more to provide a survey of the diversity of challenges it faces in finding its own path in world affairs. The United States seems to be drawing inward in most parts of the world but simultaneously becoming more aggressive in reasserting its "manifest" role as the hemispheric hegemon. Undoubtedly, how the coronavirus pandemic plays out politically and economically in the coming years will have some influence on how that challenge is confronted.

Overall, in the second decade of the twenty-first century, one could see countervailing pulls on Latin America. New diplomatic and economic organizations seemed promising in giving the region a more unified voice and some capacity to resolve intraregional conflicts without relying on the United States. The diversification of trade and investment, reductions in poverty in many countries, and lack of defined policy on the part of Washington are all forces encouraging regional autonomy.

Relations among Latin American countries and between Latin America and the rest of the world are likely to be in flux. Diversification of the region's trade partners and sources of investment probably mean that there will be competition for access to Latin America's natural wealth, opening leverage for Latin America. At the same time, they sometimes pull the countries in different directions—the northern tier toward the United States, the western regions toward Asia, and the eastern side of the continent toward Europe. Latin Americans themselves are likely going to be pulled in different directions politically as they confront questions about the wisdom of continuing to rely on extraction of natural resources and reliance on global assembly line labor.

In April 2013, Secretary of State John Kerry spoke to a committee of the House of Representatives about how the United States had been neglecting Latin America. He said that President Obama would soon make a trip through the region. Whatever good intentions the secretary may have had in mind, he undermined them in his testimony by telling Congress, "The Western Hemisphere is our backyard." Perhaps it was a slip of the tongue, but perhaps it reveals what seems to be constantly in the back of the mind of most citizens of the United States.

Our review of the history of U.S. intervention in Latin America certainly gives reason to suspect the motives and consistency of Washington's policies toward Latin America, yet we should be cautious about simply thinking that the United States has always supported dictatorship. Most Latin Americans, rather than reject the United States' expression of support for democracy, would simply prefer that the United States not assume it has a monopoly on what kind of politics and economic system best meets Latin American needs. Despite the resentment engendered by Washington's continued view of the region as a "backyard" and by repeated intervention in the region's internal affairs, most Latin Americans still look positively at the United States, even if they have a low opinion of Donald Trump.

It is unlikely that the United States can simply restore its diminished hegemony to what it was in the Cold War, but it is also unrealistic and undesirable to think that the gravitational pull of the United States, which remains a colossus in military terms and the preeminent economic power in the region, will simply disappear. The era of bold innovations in Latin American diplomacy, ones associated with the leadership of Chávez and his promotion of "twenty-first-century socialism," are at an end. But it is unlikely that the pendulum in the hemisphere will swing to the right any more than it did to the left in the Pink Tide era. What we can say is that Latin Americans are likely to return sooner or later to the search for a collective voice in world affairs. It is part of the unfulfilled legacy of Bolívar and Martí. The receding Pink Tide changed the picture considerably after 2010.

Discussion Questions

1. What has motivated U.S. foreign policy on democracy and human rights? Are democracy and human rights goals in and of themselves, or are there more imperial motives behind democracy promotion?
2. What do you think would be the most intelligent policy for the United States to take toward Cuba today? What goals would you set for that policy?

3. Do we tend to give the United States too much credit or blame for what happens in Latin America? If you had to quantify it, how much of the course of events—for better or worse—in Latin America should be ascribed to U.S. policy? None? Ten percent? Fifty percent? More? Why?
4. Would it be a good or bad development for democracy if some regional organization, such as CELAC or UNASUR, were to displace or even exist along with the OAS?
5. Would it be better if the United States was to recommit to promoting liberal democracy in Latin America, or should the matter of democracy be left up to each country in the region?

Resources for Further Study

Reading: Larry Diamond, editor of the *Journal of Democracy* and collaborator with the U.S.-funded National Endowment for Democracy, defends pluralist democratization and worries about recent tendencies in *The Spirit of Democracy* (New York: Times Books, 2008). A critique of "transitionology" is William Robinson's *Promoting Polyarchy: Globalization, US Intervention, and Hegemony* (New York: Cambridge University Press, 1996). The editorial caricatures in this chapter are among many analyzed by John J. Johnson in *Latin America in Caricature* (Austin: University of Texas Press, 1980). Christopher Sabatini does not endorse U.S. hegemony in the past, but he does think it brought some benefits and at times strengthened democracy. See his article "Will Latin America Miss U.S. Hegemony?" *Journal of International Affairs* 66, no. 2 (Spring/Summer 2013): 1–14. For a U.S. government justification of democracy programs, see *Foreign Assistance: U.S. Democracy Programs in Six Latin American Countries Have Yielded Modest Results*, GAO-03–358 (March 8, 2003). It is based on case studies of U.S. policy toward Bolivia, Colombia, El Salvador, Guatemala, Nicaragua, and Peru. NED funding of the opposition to Chávez, including groups engaged in the 2002 coup, is documented by Eva Gollinger and Saul Landau in *The Chávez Code: Cracking US Intervention in Venezuela* (Olive Branch Press, 2006).

Film and Video: A list of films (and literature) about the Guatemalan case can be found at http://depts.washington.edu/hrights/guatbib.html. *When the Mountains Tremble* (1983), about Nobel Prize winner Rigoberta Menchú, remains a classic of the genre. *Missing* (1982) is about the political disillusionment of an American father, played by Jack Lemmon, as he tries to find the truth behind the disappearance of his son in Chile during the 1973 coup. Another film, *State of Siege* (1973), by the same director, Costa Gavras, looks at American involvement in the destabilization of Uruguay. Obie Benz's *Americas in Transition* (1981) is a short, Oscar-nominated documentary describing U.S. relations with several Latin American countries in the 1970s and 1980s, including Chile, El Salvador, Guatemala, and Nicaragua.

On the Internet: The Americas Program (http://americas.irc-online.org) at the Washington-based Center for International Policy is a valuable resource for a variety of progressive organizations' views on U.S. policy toward Latin America. The National Security Archive (www2.gwu.edu/~nsarchiv) at George Washington University is a trove of primary source material on U.S. security programs and intervention. Try searching for "death of Che Guevara."

PUNTO DE VISTA: WHERE DOES DEMOCRACY RANK IN U.S. FOREIGN POLICY PRIORITIES FOR LATIN AMERICA?

What follows is a thought experiment. Imagine a simple matrix (see Table 16.1) presenting two stark choices on each axis: democracy versus dictatorship and capitalism versus socialism. Before you read on, review the choices and rank-order the four possibilities in the matrix.

You might find the question hard to answer. What kind of democracy are we talking about in the matrix? Assume polyarchy— the pluralist variant described throughout this book. What is socialism? Indeed, socialism has many variations; so also does capitalism, which may take the form of an unregulated, free-market system or may be heavily influenced by the government, as it was in the import substitution era. You might not be sure whether a system with a strong welfare system is socialist or just a more humanistic form of capitalism. We have also seen that dictatorships can vary enormously in their degree of harshness and popularity. You have discovered what comparativists have long known: that classification risks oversimplifying reality.

Do the best you can. At the end of this chapter, return to the exercise and see whether your views have been reinforced or changed. In the Afterword, a brief conclusion to this book, I'll discuss my own views of U.S. preferences. (I generally find that many of my students do not share my answer.) What follows are some perspectives for you to consider as you decide on how to rank the outcomes.

Some radical critics contend that capitalist dictatorship is the preferred objective because dictatorships more harshly repress labor and are friendlier toward American investments. War hero General Smedley Butler saw his military service in the Caribbean and Central America as little more than gendarmerie for business interests. In 1933, he wrote,

> I spent thirty-three years and four months in active military service as a member of this country's most agile military force, the Marine Corps. I served in all commissioned ranks from Second Lieutenant to Major-General. And during that period, I spent most of my time being a high class muscle-man for Big Business, for Wall Street, and for the Bankers. In short, I was a racketeer for capitalism.

He went on,

> I helped make Mexico, especially Tampico, safe for American oil interests in 1914. I helped make Haiti and Cuba a decent place for the National City Bank boys to collect revenues in. I helped in the raping of half a dozen Central American republics for the benefits of Wall Street. The record of racketeering is long. I helped purify Nicaragua for the international banking house of Brown Brothers in 1909–1912 . . . I brought light to the Dominican Republic for American sugar interests in 1916. In China I helped to see to it that Standard Oil went its way unmolested.
> (www.fas.org/man/smedley.htm, accessed July 7, 2005)

TABLE 16.1 Preferred Political and Economic Outcomes in U.S. Foreign Policy

	Capitalism	Socialism
Democracy	Capitalist Democracy	Socialist Democracy
Dictatorship	Capitalist Dictatorship	Socialist Dictatorship

On the other hand, we have seen that foreign investment in Latin America began to increase in the late twentieth century only after the transitions to democracy took place—Chile being a key example here. Is the objective of U.S. foreign policy in the era of globalization mainly defense of American business interests, or is U.S. policy more oriented toward defense of capitalism as a global system? If the latter, what kind of system is best, dictatorship or democracy?

Point/Counterpoint

Based on the history and present policies of the United States, what regime, in your opinion, is the most preferred, what is the least preferred, from the U.S. perspective?

If you placed support for democracy ahead of support for capitalism, how do you respond to claims that dictatorships are friendlier to big foreign corporations, restricting worker rights and remaining lax on environmental standards?

If you placed defense of capitalism ahead of democracy, how do you respond to those who point out that the United States supported the transitions to democracy in the most recent era of military dictatorship?

For More Information

Walter LaFeber, *Inevitable Revolutions: The United States in Central America*, 2nd ed. (New York: Norton, 1993), looks closely at American policy toward many of the countries that were occupied by General Butler's forces. See also Greg Grandin, *Empire's Workshop: Latin America, the United States and the Rise of the New Imperialism* (New York: Metropolitan Books, 2006). Julia Sweig is the senior advisor for Latin America for the Council on Foreign Relations. Her task force report *Friendly Fire: Losing Friends and Making Enemies in the Anti-American Century* (New York: Public Affairs, 2006) looks at Latin America and the United States during the Cold War.

Afterword

Tentative Answers to Frequently Asked Questions About Democracy in Latin America

Focus Question

▶ Can democracy last in Latin America?

WHEN MOST POLITICAL scientists and political leaders in North America speak of "democracy," they mean something like Dahl's conception of **polyarchy**, what we more variously call "liberal," "representative," or "electoral" democracy. In fact, most of us simply say "democracy" when referring to what really is only one framework, one way of doing democracy. I say "doing" because democracy is not a thing but a set of relationships among people, a way of making decisions that affect an entire community that gives everybody voice and impacts upon what emerges from democratic processes.

In the Introduction I argued that liberal democracy is weak if political equality is not complemented by social and economic equality and by strong civic participation. Rather than replace liberal democracy with some other form of state, my argument is that we need to expand the scope of decisions on which we have the right, even the duty as citizens, to speak and act freely. Another reason is that we can see in Latin America why the rights and freedoms of representative democracy should not be cavalierly disparaged. Given the brutality and atrocities committed by the military dictatorships that ruled most of Latin America in the 1970s, few people who live in that region would take lightly the rights they have under liberal democracy. If polyarchies did not deliver the kinds of social and economic progress that Latin Americans hoped for when the transitions to democracy occurred, that does not mean the solution lies in military or populist dictatorships.

For a quarter century, since the 1980s at least, optimistic comparativists saw a **third wave** of democracy arising out of the forces of **neoliberal** globalization. After 2010, many of the same voices began warning of a lapse back into authoritarianism, that a "third wave of authoritarianism" was taking shape. The motor force, they claimed, was a rise of populist leaders who were loosening the "guardrails" on democracy. Latin American examples were prominent in this diagnosis, which makes a compelling case for using the tools of comparison to assess the origins, character, and consequences of Latin America's experience with democracy. Having seemed finally, at the turn of the millennium, to be on the verge of consolidating democracy after a history punctuated by coups, civil warfare, military rule, dictatorships, foreign interventions, and instability, Latin America today seems to have joined most of the rest of the world in a retreat from liberal democracy. However limited and flawed polyarchy may be, it is "really existing democracy"—the only one we have at the moment. That is why the subtitle of this textbook has changed from "Democracy as Last?" to "Can Democracy Last?"

The pluralist view tends to see strong government as the enemy of a strong civil society. However, some pluralists, such as Benjamin Barber (1984) and Robert Putnam (2002), present a somewhat different formula: A strong civil society reinforces a strong democracy. This version of pluralist thought is less hostile to the state and more skeptical about the democratic benefits of free-market capitalism. It tends to value participation more than the traditional pluralism espoused by Dahl and the "transition to democracy" theorists. In the end, the role of parties should not be to control participation but to institutionalize rule by the people. So far, other institutions—for example, the military and mass media—have not proven more capable than parties in meeting this task.

While my own concerns are with the shortcoming of pluralist orthodoxy in political science, I would be remiss in suggesting that any other school of thought has all the answers. While some political scientists think that democratic institutions are easily overloaded when too many people participate and make demands upon the political system, other pluralists insist that participation, especially voting, speaking out, and organizing, are essential to make liberal democracy work. Some pluralists see social and economic equality as a condition favorable to democracy; others see it as something democracy tends to produce. These are among many questions that comparative political science tries to address, and that is why this text of Latin America tries to integrate comparative theory and methodology into an introduction of the region's politics.

Few pluralists would say that equality and participation are irrelevant to democracy. Just about any book on democracy includes some discussion about electoral turnout and the need to ensure that voting is accessible to everyone and ballots are fairly counted. But few advocate, as I do in this book, that these criteria should be expanded, that participation should penetrate the workplace and social life, and that social and economic equality should be used as direct measures of how close a country comes to the democratic ideal.

In Latin America and many other parts of the world, representative democracy has come to be questioned because it seems unable to address inequalities so serious that large portions of the population seem to be excluded from any hope of attaining decent, dignified living conditions. The concentrations of wealth at both global and national levels have intensified feelings of exclusion. The reactions to these conditions can be profoundly democratic or profoundly threatening to democracy. While the Pink Tide governments of the 2000s and 2010s fell short of their goals, they also were experimental laboratories for experiments in participatory democracy, in contrast to the authoritarian socialism of the twentieth century. Consider some of the innovations and developments in Latin America in the last 25 years: Participatory budgeting, new branches of government, workers seizing and running factories that owners shut down, vigorous neighborhood organizations, egalitarian new religious philosophy, Indigenous and Afro-descendent people as well as women rising to highest places in government, and well-established human rights organizations.

For some radical critics, these experiments insufficiently break from neoliberalism and capitalist globalization. Some say that they merely attempt to humanize capitalism—as though such an effort might not be itself worthy or a step toward constructing alternatives to twentieth-century capitalism. Adam Smith observed that the tendency to "truck and barter," that is, engage in market activities, is a human characteristic. In many ways, the democratic experiments in Latin America sought to subordinate the market and entrepreneurism to society, breaking from neoliberalism that would subordinate society to the market.

The coronavirus pandemic, which had not even reached its pinnacle in the United States and Latin America as I wrote, has dramatized the urgency of rethinking how to do democracy—as though that urgency should not have been clear already from the consequences on our lives of climate change, migrations, financial speculation, unprecedented concentrations of wealth, and destructiveness of modern warfare. By the time this book reaches your hands or your screen, we will have a better idea of how the epidemic has shaped the coming decade. As of May 26, 2020, overall South American infections had reached nearly 655,000, with over 25,000 deaths. Brazil alone was expected to reach 88,000 deaths from COVID-19 by August. Peru and Ecuador were among the hardest-hit countries on the continent. Mexico, Central America, and the Caribbean together had reported nearly 98,732 infections, with nearly 9,000 deaths. Mexico, Panama, Guatemala, and Honduras had been hardest hit. COVID-19 infections in Latin America still had not reached their peak. Updates and analysis of the pandemic is available on the eResource site that accompanies this text.

Can Democracy Last?

How the United States responds to Latin America's search for its own path in the 2020s will have an impact on how these tendencies unfold. In response to the "Punto" question in chapter 16, I would argue that United States' foreign policy prefers capitalist democracy to all other forms of political economy. Although many U.S. diplomats and officials sincerely profess that Washington's main goal is supporting democracy, history suggests that concern for capitalism has trumped support for democracy whenever the two conflict. The destabilizations or invasions of the elected governments of the Dominican Republic, Guatemala, Chile, and Nicaragua are just a few cases supporting my claim. U.S. pressure on Cuba contributes to maintenance of a siege mentality that is hardly conducive to democratic rule of any type.

Democracy is experienced by people in different ways. In Latin America, we have a rich laboratory of experimentation underway, sometimes at the level of local rather than national politics. By way of conclusion, let me suggest some very tentative answers about democracy's future in Latin America.

1. *How likely is it that Latin America will lapse again into outright authoritarianism?* Given the developments of the 2010s, no one should be confident of the answer, "not very likely," commonly given to this question 20 years ago. However, not all factors are aligned in favor of the "third wave of authoritarianism." Democracy remains a norm of the international system, which is one reason that aspiring authoritarian leaders still seek legitimacy through the ballot. More importantly, people's movements are now linked globally into networks that allow them to exchange experiences and support one another's democratic struggles.
2. *Is the U.S. model the best form of democracy for all?* The people of the United States can take pride in our own democratic traditions, but there is much hubris in our certainty that others should adopt our political ways. We welcome delegations to study our traditions or our local governments or election system, but increasingly we take little interest in our own government and show little knowledge of political affairs. Over the past 50 years, Latin Americans have had to struggle for freedom and democracy, and these struggles have generated experiences from which we in the north should learn.

3.   *Is globalization the enemy or a friend of democracy in Latin America?* Neither one—and both! Across cultures, around the world, there is evidence that most people feel that government and control over the economic forces that most shape their lives have receded from their influence. However, Latin Americans have shown a resilience in drawing on their past to invent ways of recovering control—that is, democracy-building.

4.   *How will the coronavirus pandemic affect democracy's prospects in Latin America?* You will be in a better position than I am to answer this question, seated in front of my computer at home in October 2020. For many reasons the outbreak is likely to be even more devastating on Latin America, especially on its healthcare providers, than it is shaping up to be in the Global North. I would rather pose a few questions to ask when the crisis has subsided. Has the crisis reinforced a tendency to fear migrants and put national responses ahead of global solutions? Or, has it made us all more sensitive to the need for a global collective approach to wealth and income inequality, climate change, and epidemics? The pandemic has dramatized the growing **precarity** (see chapter 2) of life everywhere in our globalized world. It is likely to be felt more widely and deeply in Latin America and throughout the Global South.

The Oscar-winning Korean film of 2019, *Parasite*, portrayed how working people providing the basis for wealthy families' well-appointed lifestyle are relegated into fighting one another for economic scraps. The film demonstrates that the lives of both the wealthy and the poor intersect in ways that dehumanize and lead to tragedy for both. It is a morality tale for our times, conceived just before the coronavirus epidemic demonstrated vividly how the fates of those living more precariously—economically vulnerable, older, less healthy—are tied to the more fortunate.

We need to approach understanding Latin American politics with a degree of humility about our own democratic shortcomings, particularly our high rate of voter abstention, the persistence of gender and racial discrimination, and the growing inequality between rich and poor. The promised land of democracy, whatever it looks like, is not yet visible, but I do think all of us, including Latin Americans, will not find it without recognizing our intertwined fates and learning from our successes and failures.

Discussion Question

Choice, participation, and equality: Now that you are concluding this book, and probably also your classes, if you were evaluating the condition of democracy for each country of the world, what would you consider? How would you want to measure them, either quantitatively or qualitatively? Is that exercise worthwhile? Why or why not?

ALBA—Bolivarian Alliance for the Americas, an alternative economic integration alliance promoted by Venezuela, which embraced Nicaragua, Bolivia, Ecuador, and several smaller Caribbean states as of 2014.

Afro-descendent—Refers to Latin Americans of African ancestry, especially those whose genealogy can be traced to the transatlantic slave trade.

anarchism (-ist)—a philosophy that rejects the necessity of the state, seeing all forms of government as inherently repressive, by definition; mutualist anarchists stress worker democracy in the form of direct worker management of enterprises.

apartheid—state policy of white supremacy and separating the races in South Africa for most of the twentieth century.

area studies—interdisciplinary research and teaching devoted to understand cultural, social, economic, and political aspects of particular countries and geographic regions.

asymmetric warfare—a military doctrine whereby a weaker power concentrates resources and develops strategies to exploit the political and military weaknesses of the larger power—for example, by preparing civilian militias, taking advantage of terrain, inflicting casualties to wear down political support for war in the strong power, and so forth.

barrio—neighborhood; usually poor neighborhood.

blandos—refers to "soft-liners" among military and civilian officials negotiating a transition to democracy, blando meaning "soft" in Spanish. See ***duros*** for hardliners.

Bolivarian—name adopted by Venezuela's Hugo Chávez for his own and his movement's political philosophy, which was to be based on the life and writings of the country's great independence hero, Simón Bolívar.

bourgeoisie—a French term meaning "town dwellers" that Marx used to describe the capitalist economic class as it arose out of feudalism and struggled with the landed aristocracy. Depending on the context, it can refer to capitalists, but it often is used as well to refer to the middle class in general.

Brandt Report—a 1980 report of a commission headed by former West German chancellor and social democrat Willy Brandt, calling for a series of measures to reduce the gap between rich and poor nations in the world; it was shortly afterward superseded by the rise of neoliberal leaders, such as Ronald Reagan and Margaret Thatcher, who successfully restored the primacy of a more market-oriented approach to the global economy.

breakdown (of democracy)—the process by which populist-era democracies collapsed as a result of political polarization and inability of political elites to compromise.

BRICS—mnemonic popular between 1990 and 2010 for Brazil, Russia, India, China, and South Africa, all of which were showing signs of sustainable economic growth at the time. The five countries have continued to informally meet to plan strategies before important international meetings.

broadening of democracy—the idea that democracy ought to be extended to more spheres of life beyond the affairs of government.

bureaucratic authoritarianism—a term coined by political scientist Guillermo O'Donnell to describe the type of military rule that emerged in the Southern Cone and Brazil, combining harsh military rule designed to suppress all political participation with economic policy-making by civilian technocrats.

cacerolazo—form of protest, usually by women, characterized by mass banging of empty pots.

cacique—literally, "chief." The term originally pertained to the head of an Indigenous village, community, or nation but became more generally used in reference to a political strongman.

capitalism—a social and economic system characterized by private ownership of the "means of production" (factories, farms, offices, technology, etc.), allocation of goods and services by the market, and the great majority of the employees working for wages or salaries.

catch-all party—a political party that seeks to obtain votes across class lines, as opposed to class-based parties that mobilize primarily from the working class and poor.

caudillo (-ism)—a form of personalism; literally, "man on horseback," an allusion to the strongmen who achieved regional or national leadership as a result of their fighting ability and leadership qualities during the violent, anarchic nineteenth century.

charisma, charismatic—referring to authority, based on a highly personalist style by which a leader appeals to masses of people, who in turn project upon the leader the qualities of a messiah who can address their needs and desires.

checks and balances—the constitutional principle that in a democracy the danger of concentrated power can be minimized by separating and dividing power among branches of government, much like James Madison promoted and accomplished in the Constitution of the United States.

Chicago Boys—economists that, following the teachings of Milton Friedman (an economist at the University of Chicago), advocated **laissez-faire** policies to dramatically roll back the state's role in the economy.

Christian democrats—parties that emerged after World War II as centrist parties espousing capitalism humanized by Christian social justice doctrines.

civil society—that sphere of group activity occupying associational space between the individual and family, on one hand, and government and the state on the other. In Anglo-American thought, the marketplace is often seen as friendly or even part of civil society; in Latin America, many social movements see the market as corrosive of the social solidarity needed for a strong civil society. Alternatively, civil society is seen as the network of social and economic organizations and social movements seeking to advance the interests of different groups and to influence the political attitudes of others.

clientelism—practice on the part of politicians of exchanging material benefits for support, such as votes.

cocaleros—mostly Indigenous movement of peasant cultivators of the coca plant in the Andes. More specifically, the movement led originally by Evo Morales, elected president of Bolivia in 2006.

Cold War—an ideological battle in which two global, nuclear superpowers, the United States and the Soviet Union, attempted between 1945 (the end of World War II) and 1991 (with the fall of communism in Eastern Europe) to promote or impose their particular political and economic system on other countries. In many Latin American countries, dictatorships justified their seizure of or continuing in power with a "national security" argument based on the notion that communism was an alien threat.

commodity—a good produced to be sold on the market, not consumed by its maker, but also, and as used in this book, agricultural and mining products, as distinct from manufactured products.

communism, communists, or Communist Party—political parties that formed, usually as a faction of socialists, in the aftermath of the Russian Revolution of 1917. Communists tended to be strongest where workers, urban or rural, were paid wages. Often, they had success organizing in key sectors of the export economy. Most communist parties lost members and supporters at the end of the Cold War. The Communist Party is the governing party in Cuba today.

communitarianism—a social philosophy and/or way of life, prevalent among many Indigenous peoples, though not exclusive to them, based on the idea of common ownership of property, especially the land, and sharing in both producing and distributing economic goods.

compadrazgo—the Catholic practice of assigning "godparents" to children, often used in Latin America as a way for a powerful or wealthy individual, such as a landowner, to bestow special favor on the son of a subordinate, such as the child of a peasant or employee. A form of patronage, part of a system of clientelism.

comparative advantage—an economic theory associated with the British classical economist David Ricardo, who argued in the early 1800s that **free trade** benefits both partners, even when one country could produce something imported more cheaply, because by freely trading what each most efficiently (the "advantages") produces, both sides benefit.

comparative politics—a subfield in political science where comparison is utilized as a way to generate theories of politics; more generally associated with the study of politics in cultures different from our own.

comparativists—those in different fields of study (history, economics, literature, etc.) who specialize in the study of other cultures and use comparison (see **comparative politics**) to do so.

constituent assembly—a people's congress empowered to rewrite and reform the constitution and institute regime change.

constituent power—the assertion of a democratic right of "constituents" to exercise their power to make such changes over the resistance of elites who are not trust to reform the prevailing regime.

core nations—rich capitalist countries that have developed economies and, according to world systems theory, exploit the nations of the periphery.

coronel—Portuguese term used in a similar way to *caudillo*.

corporatism, corporatist—(1) a theory about the relationship between state and society that emphasizes a tendency for social organizations to develop a privileged relationship with government bureaucracies, undermining a central tenet of pluralism—that is, the idea that individuals can freely join and leave organizations; (2) an ideology that an activist state has a responsibility to mediate competition among social classes and groups, defending the interests of the weakest groups and looking out for the welfare of the community as a whole.

criollo **(also, Creole)**—the colonial upper class that over time became resistant to rule by the Spanish and Portuguese authorities. When used sociologically, "Creole" has not only class but also race overtones because Creoles considered themselves white. However, because independence leaders, such as Bolívar, were usually Creoles, the term is sometimes used as a synonym for "national"—as in *comida criolla* or "national food."

crisis of representation—a situation in which the relationship between the masses of people in society and the political elite grows so distant that the latter lose legitimacy in the eyes of the former. Often an important indication of weakness in a **polyarchy**.

debt crisis—associated with the inability of Latin American governments to make service and interest payments in dollars on loans; first became visible in 1982, when Mexico announced it did not have sufficient dollar reserves to make its payments.

deepening of democracy—the idea that besides extension of voting and citizenship rights, a strong democracy is evidenced by growing respect for rights, tolerance, rule of law, and so on.

delegative democracy—term coined by Argentine political scientist Guillermo O'Donnell to refer to the tendency of citizens to invest power in a single elected leader, leaving other aspects of democracy superficial, such as the rule of law.

deliberative democracy—a form of democracy characterized by a high degree of citizen formulation of policies, debate, and even legislation.

dependency, dependency theory (theorists)—argues that Latin American economic development has been decisively and negatively shaped by the way it is integrated into the global economy; more narrowly, it refers to the theory that Latin America has been chronically disadvantaged by its export of raw materials, said to be undervalued compared with imported manufactured goods.

devaluation—when a government weakens the national currency against others (e.g., requires more pesos to purchase each dollar) or allows the currency to weaken by removing the prior fixed rate of exchange and allowing it to float.

developmentalism, developmentalist—referring to economic views (and those who held them) that advocate state policies designed to produce economic growth through industrialization.

Dirty War—fierce repression unleashed by the Argentine military junta in 1976 against the civilian population, especially the left.

discourse—a term used in many different ways, but mainly in this book we refer to the way that language is utilized in public arguments, discussions, political advertising and campaigns, and other social settings to mobilize or convince others to rally behind a leader or political cause.

duros—military and civilian official, the "hardliners" (*duro* meaning "hard" in Spanish) most opposed to a negotiated transition to democracy. See **blandos** for so-called soft-liners.

ECLAC (CEPAL in Spanish)—the United Nations Economic Commission on Latin America and the Caribbean, which developed a "structural" analysis of obstacles to development and diagnosed a chronic unfavorable balance of trade between exported raw materials and imported manufactured goods.

ejido—traditional, community- or municipality-owned land in Mexico.

encomienda—the system by which the Spanish Crown granted conquistadors and early Creole landed elites the right to work mines and land with labor owed to them by Indigenous peoples. The Indians were "entrusted" (as *encomendados*) to the elites, who were expected to Christianize them and care for their souls, a responsibility taken much more seriously by the Church than by the colonial landed elite.

Estado Nôvo—literally, the "new state," the name given by Brazilian leader Getulio Vargas (1937–1945) to the corporatist state erected on the basis of the constitution he wrote in 1937 in an attempt to enlist labor, capital, and government in a common alliance for economic development. (See **corporatism**).

ethnic cleansing—a type of genocide in which an ethnic group is targeted for destruction and/or removal from territory it occupies.

excluded sector, exclusion—similar in meaning to "marginal" (see later entry) but implies that marginality is created by social and economic policies and processes and is not simply a condition generated by overpopulation.

fascism—often loosely attached to any repressive regime; historically, in Europe fascism was associated with hypernationalism, strong corporatist tendencies, militarism, and scapegoating of communists, Jews, and other minorities.

favela—poor urban neighborhood in Brazil.

federalism—division of sovereign authority between the central government and lower jurisdictions (e.g., states). Examples include Brazil and the United States.

free trade—the goal of most recent trade treaties; the idea here is to reduce various subsidies and protectionist measures that inhibit the free flow of goods and services across national borders in accordance with supply and demand in the global market (see comparative advantage).

Free Trade Area of the Americas (FTAA)—an attempt fostered by the United States to create a hemispheric free trade area based mostly upon the North American Free Trade Agreement (NAFTA) among Canada, Mexico, and the United States.

Gini coefficient—a measure of the equality of either wealth or income. Zero represents perfect equality, where all individuals or households have the same income or wealth; 1 equals perfect inequality, where one individual or household has all of the income or wealth.

global assembly line—a more popular term referring to the way in which production of final consumer goods can be traced back through multiple stages, much in the way that assembly lines built automobiles, but now across many different national boundaries. See also **supply chain**.

Global South—referring to poorer countries tending to lie futher south on the globe and the wealthy countries that tend to lie in the Northern sectors of the globe.

globalization—broad international tendency toward free flows of trade and communication among nations; especially associated with the changes in production of goods and services made possible by the information revolution.

governance—the ability to carry out the routine tasks of government efficiently and impartially; the ability to reach decisions accepted by society in a timely, effective manner.

Great Depression—a global economic crisis that began with the collapse of the New York Stock Exchange in 1929, spread throughout the world, and did not finally end until the conclusion of World War II in 1945.

haciendas—large, traditional landed estates worked by peasants, also called *latifundia*.

hegemon, hegemonic, hegemony—referring to a form of leadership in which force is always present but usually secondary to cultural and economic power. The Italian thinker Antonio Gramsci summed it up as force plus consent. Can also be applied to dominance of a social class or group within a society or to the dominance of a country or bloc of countries in world politics.

huasipongo—semifeudal system of control over peasants in Ecuador, where into the mid-twentieth century land could be sold along with the labor of the peasants living on it.

hybrid regimes—political systems that have emerged from authoritarianism and have not completely discarded past patterns but that do show many hallmarks of pluralism; also pertains to democracies that have decayed but show many of these hallmarks. See also **illiberal democracy**.

hyperurbanization—the tendency for the population growth of cities to outstrip the services (education, transportation, sewerage, etc.) needed to support decent living conditions.

illiberal democracy—phrase coined to describe political systems with popularly elected presidents who concentrate great power around themselves and effectively limit opposition by restricting civil freedoms.

IMF—see **International Monetary Fund**.

import substitution industrialization (ISI)—a set of policies, including tariffs on imports and subsidies, designed to encourage domestic production of manufactured goods. Typical development strategy in the populist era.

informal sector—that part of the economy in which workers are not covered by labor laws and often scrape by on day-to-day temporary employment. Typical of this sector are the armies of small vendors who eke out a living selling toys, cosmetics, used books, DVDs, and so forth on the streets and sidewalks.

institutionalism—branch of comparative politics that emphasizes and promotes the study of constitutional arrangements, as opposed to giving primacy to cultural, social, and economic processes in understanding politics.

institutionalize, institutionalization—the process by which a political arrangement or organization becomes valued in and of itself and not just for whatever specific benefit or outcome it produces.

International Monetary Fund (IMF)—founded after World War II to provide stability for the world monetary market, the IMF took on the role as key negotiator on behalf of international banks during the debt crisis of the 1980s, insisting that indebted governments adopt a package of neoliberal policies in exchange for new loans.

ISI—see **import substitution industrialization**.

junta—literally, a "council." Usually refers to a collective leadership of military leaders who have installed themselves via a coup.

la raza—"the race," often meaning "new race," often equivalent to *mestizaje*.

laissez-faire—French for "let do," an economic doctrine advocating minimum government regulation of the market. Stands in contrast to the philosophy of state-led development or "state capitalism" practiced in Latin America before 1980.

latifundia—see *haciendas*.

Lava Jato—a car wash near Rio de Janeiro which served as a drop-off point for political bribes associated with Petrobras, the state-owned oil company. The scandal enveloped former President da Silva (Lula) in 2017, when he was convicted in a trial with serious irregularities. At the time of his conviction, da Silva was leading in polls for the 2018 presidential election.

legitimacy—the quality of ruling through consent and lawful authorization rather than force.

LGBTQ+—one of several terms used by groups of people who do not consider themselves heterosexual, meaning here lesbian, gay, bisexual, transgender and others, including intersex and questioning. Adopted for use in this book from Boulder County, Colorado, Family Services www.bouldercounty.org/families/lgbtiq/lgbtiq-definitions.

liberal democracy—based on the theories of John Locke and Thomas Jefferson and to some extent J. J. Rousseau, a form of democracy based on the idea of free individuals consenting to form a government based on individual freedom and rights, including the individual right to property, consent of the governed, and limited ability of government to intervene in economic affairs.

liberalism—a political ideology that privileges individual choices and rights over those of communities or the state; defines individual choice as the essence of freedom; prefers the market over government as the preferred way of resolving economic conflict; views property rights as natural rights and an extension of individual rights; and circumscribes government power with constitutional limits and with checks and balances.

liberal modernization—referring to the period, roughly 1850–1920, when most of Latin America underwent a period of state- and nation-building, usually including the development of new export sectors stimulated by rising demand for raw materials in foreign markets; building of railroads, ports, and other facilities with foreign loans; and professionalization of the armed forces. Often overseen by liberal parties or *caudillos*.

liberation theology (theology of liberation)—a Marxist-influenced religious philosophy that emerged in Latin America in the aftermath of Vatican II (1962) as a reflection on the practice of clergy committed to implementing a "preferential option for the poor."

libertarian—an advocate for maximum free play of market forces and minimal government regulation, subsidies, and welfare. Closely identified with the Chicago School of Economics.

lost decade—the 1980s, when overwhelming debt and a global recession led to a period of low and sometimes negative economic growth rates.

machismo—hypermasculinity; a tendency among men to attempt to show sexual prowess through various forms of speech and behavior.

macroeconomic—pertaining to the major processes and systems that make up national and economic systems, as opposed to microeconomics, where the "firm" (company) is the unit of analysis. Gross domestic product (GDP), inflation, balance of trade, and rates of monetary exchange are examples of measures often used to study the macroeconomic situation of a country.

maquila—labor-intensive, export-oriented factories originally set up in Mexico along the border with the United States, now commonly found in the Caribbean and Central America.

marginal—see "**informal sector**." People in this sector are often excluded, not by choice, from mainstream social and economic life.

marianismo—political appeal, often stereotyped, of women as nurturers, mother figures, and reconcilers in times of conflict.

Marxism (-ist)—very broad school of thought, with many branches, associated with Karl Marx, a German philosopher who argued that ultimate political power resides in the hands of those who control the means of production (land, factories, machines, etc.) and argued that true democracy could come only after those who had to sell their labor to these owners revolted and established common ownership ("communism") of these means.

mass organizations—usually associated with revolutionary regimes, these are usually officially sanctioned as the only legitimate channels of representation. Defenders see them as instruments of participatory democracy; critics see them as instruments of corporatist control. Defenders and critics alike see them as alternatives to voluntary organizations associated with pluralism.

means of production—land, machinery, buildings, and so on used to produce other goods and services.

mensalão—a common practice in Brazil of paying a monthly stipend, in effect a bribe, to secure votes needed to pass national legislation through a Congress severely broken into small factions, often from the highly autonomous states of the federation. Also the name of the scandal that enveloped high offices linked closely to President Luiz Inácio Lula da Silva (Lula) in 2005.

Mesoamerica—literally, "between the Americas" (i.e., between North and South America). Usually thought to include Panama, the countries of Central America, and Mexico, though Panama is often considered part of South America, because it was once a province of Colombia, and Mexico is often categorized as part of North America.

mestizo, mestizaje—people of mixed racial stock, mainly Indian and Hispanic. *Mestizaje* refers more broadly to the notion that Latin Americans are a "new race" with a distinct national identity.

minifundio—a small plot of land insufficient to support a family, whose members therefore seek to support themselves by working on nearby *latifundia*.

modernization—a general framework for understanding economic and political development as involving the transformation of traditional society and culture into a social system based on valuing individual treatment, separating religious authority from political authority, professionalizing bureaucracies, and establishing the political authority of all citizens.

modernization, modernization theory—as used in political science, especially in studies of development, modernization refers to the idea of inducing social, economic and political changes that advance a nation toward the supposed countries of the world that have already passed through this process, often through "stages" in historical progress. Usually associated with the idea of "advancement" toward Western "developed" countries, with an emphaisis on changes in cultural values associated with the passage from feudalism to capitalism.

monoculture—technically refers to repeated planting of a single crop in one area. More specifically, it refers to a pattern of economic dependency whereby many colonies were forced into specializing in the production of a particular commodity (rubber, cotton, sugar, hemp, coffee, etc.) for export, reducing diversity and making the population more dependent on imported goods purchased by earnings from exports.

mulato, **mulatto**—people of mixed racial stock, many African with Hispanic and/or Indian heritage.

multilateral—refers to political and economic agreements that involve more than two countries (bilateral).

NAFTA, North American Free Trade Agreement—Free trade agreement among Canada, the U.S., and Mexico, 1994–2019. Renegotiated and replaced with the United States–Mexico–Canada Agreement (see **USMCA**).

National Endowment for Democracy (NED)—quasi-private association of organizations linked to U.S. unions and business organizations and to political parties, funded by Congress for the ostensible purpose of supporting democracy and a strong civil society overseas, accused of intervening in support of U.S. interests abroad.

nationalism—a sense of shared identity of people in a given territory or state, built around one or more commonalities in history, language, ethnicity, religion, culture, and so on; embodied in symbols such as a flag, anthem, and literature.

national liberation—a term that was widely adopted by African and Asian leaders in anticolonial struggles in the twentieth century. Although most of Latin America was independent at the time, post–World War II revolutionary movements adopted the term to denote their goal of achieving economic and cultural and not just political independence.

nation-state—the main political unit in the international system that reached its apogee in the post–World War II era. Presumes the right to sovereignty is based on a people's claim to be a nation, in turn based on the idea of a shared birthright.

neocolonialism—a "new" (neo) form of colonialism where the dominated society retains formal sovereign status.

neo-extractivism—"extractivism" refers to the historical dependence of Latin American economies on exports of raw materials "extracted" from natural resources; neo-extractivism refers to the continuation of this tendency since 1990, but often under the administration of leftist governments that have reformed the terms under which extraction takes place and the uses of the profits. However, overall the economies remain highly dependent on extractive industries.

neoliberal (-ism)—a "new" (neo) form of nineteenth-century liberalism; neoliberalism advocates a reduced role of the state in guiding economic life and increased reliance on laissez-faire. Generally, neoliberal economic philosophy is associated with structural adjustment packages mandated by the International Monetary Fund and with the Washington Consensus.

new institutionalism (-ists)—(1) school of thought among economists, focused on the importance of political institutions in fostering economic development; (2) comparative political scientists who argue for more attention to constitutions, laws, and formal political processes in regions, such as Latin America.

nongovernmental organizations (NGOs)—formally organized groups in civil society, domestic or international in nature; many domestic organizations are networked or partially funded by foreign NGOs or states.

OAS, Organization of American States—hemispheric diplomatic organization formally founded in 1948, with roots in previous organizations dating to 1889, headquartered in Washington D.C., and including all states (including Cuba, with membership suspended) in North and South America and the Caribbean.

Obredecht—a huge Brazilian construction company that was discovered to have paid over $788 million in bribes to Latin American politicians all over the region between 2001 and 2016.

oligarchy—a ruling class made up of a tight-knit group of wealthy elites.

organic law—a law, distinctive to the French system and influential in Latin America, that is seen as a direct outgrowth of the constitution and can be modified only by an extraordinary majority (typically three-fifths or two-thirds).

pacts—formal and informal agreements among elites to limit democracies founded after periods of authoritarian rule or at the end of severe political crisis.

Panama Papers—11.5 million leaked documents from a Panamanian law firm that specialized in offshore havens for funds, licit or illicit, revealing money laundering and tax-avoidance machinations by wealthy global elites, including many from Latin America.

Pan-Americanism—referring to the idea that all Latin Americans share a common national "American" identity that transcends the boundaries of countries.

pardo—a term used in Venezuela and some other countries, referring to people of mixed race; very similar in meaning to *mulato*.

party system—the way that parties interact with one another and with civil society, especially in regard to the way they structure political competition.

patriarchy—a condition, which few societies have escaped, in which men hold greater power than women and also on balance hold power over women.

patrimonialism (patrimonial state)—tendency to use state resources to secure the loyalty of citizens; the exchange of material resources for loyalty.

patronage—the practice whereby politicians use their influence over government to help their friends and supporters, often thereby showing favoritism against the interests of supporters of opponents.

peon, peonage—referring to the system of forced labor whereby a peasant is perpetually exploited by a landowner through the former's perpetual indebtedness to the latter.

periphery—those countries that historically were integrated into the world system as providers of primary commodities produced by hyperexploited labor; those parts of the world that have relatively little power compared with the wealthy, core nations.

personalism—tendency in political culture to look to a strong leader, often associated with charismatic authority and **clientelism**.

Pink Tide—the wave of victories by leftist parties and leaders that began in December 1998 with President Hugo Chávez in Venezuela. Called "pink" to distinguish these leaders and parties from "red" communists and to indicate a diversity of associated programs and social bases.

plebiscite—an election called to express the popular will on a significant issue, such as whether an existing state or constitution is legitimate or whether a particular ruler should be allowed to stay in power.

pluralist, pluralism—referring to a school of thought in political science that argues for the study of group behavior and competition among elites. Pluralism is both an empirical theory about how politics works in all societies, even dictatorships, and a normative theory about the form democracy should take (see **polyarchy**).

plurinational state—a state that recognizes not one national identity but several; recognized nations share governance and autonomy within a constitutional framework allowing for cultural diversity.

political opportunity structures—political sociologist Sidney Tarrow's concept of the degree to which social and political conditions steer the course of social movements and shape their possibility of success in achieving change.

polyarchy—term coined by Robert Dahl to describe his theory (see **pluralism**) of democracy, arguing that instead of viewing societies as one pyramidal system with elites at the apex, we ought to see multiple (poly) hierarchies in society, with competing elites at the surface. Polyarchies are characterized by several features associated with liberal democracy, most importantly constitutions requiring elites to compete for power through elections.

popular sector—refers loosely to those social classes that do not include the wealthiest strata of society. The popular sector always includes workers, peasants, and the **informal** or **excluded** population; whether this includes the middle class depends on who is using the term and what audience is being addressed.

populism (-ist)—the political practice of appealing for mass support by championing the cause of ordinary people against powerful elites. The period between 1930 and 1980 is considered an era of populism in Latin America, epitomized by leaders such as Juan Perón of Argentina and Getúlio Vargas of Brazil, as well as populist parties such as Venezuela's Democratic Action party and Peru's APRA.

positivism—a social philosophy that advocates use of scientific method to test theories and research human behavior, with the purpose of applying results to promote social progress.

precarity—a felt state of insecurity common to all humans as biological creatures in need of adequate security from violence, access to health care, nutrition, and other basic requirements for physical survival. Studies of mass mobilizations have in recent years seen precarity as having grown in the era of neoliberalism.

preferential option for the poor—a principle enunciated by the leader of the Jesuit order of priests in 1968, arguing that because Latin America is poor and the home of a majority of the world's Roman Catholics, the Church has a responsibility to take the side of the poor in struggles for social and economic justice. Heavily criticized by conservative sectors of Catholicism, who say it violated the principle of a "catholic" Church that equally regards all the faithful.

proletariat—wage workers; those who sell their labor to make a living; a synonym for the "working class" in Marxist tradition, which developed in an era when most wage earners were factory workers.

proportional representation—a system of allocating seats in a legislature to parties, in principle according to the percentage of votes received in an election. Requires that seats be distributed based on results nationally or in multimember districts (i.e., more than one representative elected per district).

regime, regime change—a change in regime goes beyond the state itself, a change in the "order of things," including the relationship between state and society and in the rules of the game by which political elites compete; a regime change may be revolutionary but usually is not as deep or broad as a revolution.

rent-seeking—a tendency for private actors to seek wealth through their connections to government.

republic, republicans—from the Latin, "res-publicae," things pertaining to the publically constituted state, as opposed to an emperor or monarch. Republics are theoretically states rooted in the authority of citizens. As not all republics have universal, equal citizenship, republics are not necessarily democratic.

royalty—a fee paid by a company or individual to the state for the right to explore for, mine, or drill for minerals under the surface of the land. So called because originally it was the "king's share" of such extraction.

rule of law—the condition that all citizens are treated the same under the law and can rely on the state to guarantee both justice and security for persons and property.

secularism—belief in the necessity of separating church and state, championed by Liberals against Conservatives in the nineteenth century, rarely fully implemented, the major exception being Mexico in the decades after the 1910 revolution.

social debt—the term used by some groups in Latin America to suggest that governments have as much responsibility to honor promises to finance programs that help the poor as they do to pay the debt owed to foreign banks.

social movement—loosely associated individuals or organizations that take action in resistance to common problems, in defense of common interests, or in the quest to force the government or other social actors to respond to widely supported demands.

Southern Cone—looking at a map of South America, the southernmost regions spread out wider on an east-west axis, within which one finds Argentina, Chile, southern Brazil, Paraguay, Uruguay, and (some would say) southern Bolivia. These countries are considered the Southern Cone.

state capitalism—often associated with import substitution, a set of policies associated with the idea that development requires active state intervention to guide and regulate market forces, even promoting state ownership of key industries in some crucial sectors.

structural adjustment—a package of policies that the International Monetary Fund typically requires of governments before granting loans (known as "special drawn rights"), including cuts in the budget, restraint on money supply, reduction of tariff protection to domestic industries, great emphasis on export, and other measures associated with neoliberal economics.

supply chain—the sequence by which most manufacturing and agro-industrial commodities are produced through a kind of assembly line, but not in one country alone, passing through many stages across several countries. See also **global assembly line**.

technocrats—ministers, advisors, and other officials in the government bureaucracy chosen for their expertise and regarded, for that reason, as being apolitical.

technopols—economic and technical experts who, like **technocrats**, are influential because of their expertise but are much more overtly political in publicly advocating for their ideas.

third wave—a theory advanced by political scientist Samuel Huntington that for the third time in history (the first being in the 1800s, the other just after World War II) international forces are at work to reinforce a worldwide movement toward liberal democracy.

Third World—during the Cold War, the label for countries who sought to assert independence from either bloc; today refers in general to countries that have had a colonial or neocolonial past and remain underdeveloped. Always a vague term, it is believed to be obsolete by some.

totalitarianism—often seen as the opposite of democracy, this term applies to ideologies, including fascism and communism, that **pluralists** say result in an all-powerful dictatorship and eliminate the boundary between the state and **civil society**.

transition to democracy—the process of moving from dictatorship to polyarchy. Applies to many regimes in different parts of the world, but most strongly associated with the reestablishment of polyarchies in the Southern Cone and Brazil after 1980.

transnational, transnational corporations—any organization or group that not only has memberships that are multinational but consists of networks that cross national boundaries in how they operate and are governed or managed. Early use of this term was intended to contest the idea of a "multinational corporation," one with no loyalty to any particular nation-state. Increasingly, the terms are interchangeable, but "transnational corporations" not only operate or have branches in different countries, but have interlocking ownership, directorates, and high-level executive managements crossing national boundaries. "Transnational corporations" is often associated with the idea that a "transnational" capitalist class has emerged.

twenty-first-century socialism—a concept promoted by Mexican thinker Heinz Dieterich, rejecting the idea of a vanguard and critical of actual existing socialism in the twentieth century, advocating socialism based on more "horizontal" relations among social movements.

twenty-first-century socialism—see **socialism of the twenty-first century**.

underdeveloped, underdevelopment—referring to countries that are generally poor, have not historically passed through industrialization, and generally have lower standards on various measures of human welfare (education, health, etc.). The term usually implies that countries pass through common stages in a transition to a "developed" status, though this idea is vigorously debated among comparative political specialists.

uninominal representation—a system of electing representatives, one to each district. Also known as "single-member district."

United Nations Commission on Trade and Development (UNCTAD)—originally founded as an organization to promote stability in the prices of commodities exported by Third World nations; this organization evolved in the 1980s to promote free trade and policies favorable to foreign investment.

USMCA, United States–Mexico–Canada Agreement—see **NAFTA** as well. Renegotiated trade accord replacing NAFTA, with modest strengthening of minimum labor and environmental standards and requirements for increased value-added (proportion of manufacturing done in Mexico for export to the U.S.).

value chains—a term commonly used in business and management discourse in reference to the way the global economy is organized. The final product before it reaches the consumer passes through a series of stages, from extraction of raw materials used to produce and transport it, through multiple sites in many different countries where other workers and factories refine, process, and assemble components. This process sometimes is called the "global assembly line."

Washington Consensus—refers to a widespread understanding among Latin American governments (excepting Cuba) that the only acceptable regime type is a pluralist democracy coupled with a free-market economy. Although various versions exist, the main features were outlined in 1990 in a speech by John Williamson, a researcher at the Institute for International Economics in Washington, DC. By 2000, the consensus was being widely questioned.

World Bank—formally, the International Bank for Reconstruction and Development (IBRD), founded after World War II to finance the reconstruction of Europe and Japan, and in more recent decades a credit agency for Third World development projects too large or risky to attract private capital.

World Social Forum—annual gatherings of representatives of social movements to discuss alternatives to neoliberal globalization; originated in Porto Alegre, Brazil.

world systems theory—a broad theory about the development of the global economy associated with the theorist Immanuel Wallerstein. World systems theory categorizes nations into the wealthy nation-states of the core, or center, and those poor ones of the periphery, with a semideveloped group categorized as part of the semiperiphery. The core exploits the periphery, and this accounts in large measure for the latter's underdevelopment. However, unlike the dependency approach, world systems theory does see the possibility of nation-states moving from one category to another over time. The theory also divides world history into stages according to which nation of the core enjoys global hegemony, with general agreement that Spain dominated the 1500s, England the 1800s, and the United States the twentieth century.

World Trade Organization (WTO)—headquartered in Geneva, Switzerland; the WTO is an international organization responsible for enforcing existing global free trade pacts and promoting an open world trade system.

References

Introduction

Albright, Madeleine. 2018. *Fascism: A Warning*. New York: Harper.

Almojuela, Maria. 2012. "Deepening Democracy Means Looking Beyond Elections," *Oxpol, the Oxford University Politics Blog* (blog.politics.ox.ac.uk, November 28, accessed November 1, 2019).

Borón, Atilio. 2005. "Guardianes de la democracia," *Agencia Latinoamericana de Información* (www.alainet.org, accessed July 22, 2010).

Castañeda, Jorge. 1993. *Utopia Unarmed*. New York: Vintage Books.

Castañeda, Jorge. 2006. "Latin America's Left Turn," *Foreign Affairs* (May/June, www.foreignaffairs.com/articles/61702/jorge-g-castaneda/latin-americas-left-turn).

ECLAC (UN Economic Commission for Latin America and the Caribbean). 2012. "Poverty Continues to Fall in Latin America but Still Affects 167 Million People," Press Release, August 12.

Ellner, Steve. 2012. "The Distinguishing Features of Latin America's New Left in Power: The Governments of Hugo Chávez, Evo Morales, and Rafael Correa," *Latin American Perspectives*, 39.96 (December): 96–114.

Green, James. 2012. "'Who Is the Macho Who Wants to Kill Me?' Male Homosexuality, Revolutionary Masculinity, and the Brazilian Armed Struggle of the 1960s," *Hispanic American Historical Review*, 92.3 (August): 437–469.

Lagos, María. 2019. *El fin de la tercera ola de democracias*. Santiago: Corporación Latinobarómetro (www.latinobarometro.org/lat.jsp).

LASA. 1984. *The Electoral Process in Nicaragua: Domestic and International Influences: The Report of the Latin American Studies Association Delegation to Observe the Nicaraguan General Election of November 4, 1984*. November 19.

Latinobarómetro. 2009, 2013, 2019. *Informe Latinobarómetro 2013 (Latin Barometer Report)*. Santiago: Corporación Latinobarómetro (www.latinobarometro.org).

Levitsky, Steven and Daniel Ziblatt. 2018. *How Democracies Die*. New York: Crown.

Lewis, Martin W. and Karen Wigen. 1997. *The Myth of Continents: A Critique of Metageography*. Berkeley: University of California Press.

Shifter, Michael. 2011. "Latin America: A Surge to the Center," *Journal of Democracy*, 22.1 (January): 107–121.

Chapter 1

Anria, Santiago. 2016. "More Inclusion, Less Liberalism in Bolivia," *Journal of Democracy*, 27.3 (July): 99–108.

Borge, Tomás. 1992. "Interview with Fidel Castro," *El Nuevo Diario* (Managua, June 4).

Buxton, Julia. 2001. *The Failure of Political Reform in Venezuela*. Aldershot: Ashgate.

Castañeda, Jorge. 1993. *Utopia Unarmed: The Latin American Left after the Cold War*. New York: Alfred Knopf.

Center for Systemic Peace. 2019. *The Polity Project* (www.systemicpeace.org/polityproject.htm, accessed November 13, 2019).

Ceresole, Norberto. 1999. *Caudillo, ejército, pueblo. El modelo venezolano o la posdemocracia (Leader, Army, People: The Venezuelan Model or Post-Democracy)*. Archived in *Venezuela Analytica* (www.analitica.com/bitblio/ceresole/caudillo.asp, accessed December 27, 2010).

Chalmers, Douglas, M. do Carmo Campello de Souza and Atilio A. Borón (editors). 1992. *The Right and Democracy in Latin America*. New York: Praeger.

Collier, David. 1995. "'Corporatism' in Latin American Politics," in Peter Smith (editor), *Latin America in Comparative Perspective: New Approaches to Methods and Analysis*. Boulder, CO: Westview Press.

Dahl, Robert. 1971. *Polyarchy: Participation and Opposition*. New Haven, CT: Yale University Press.

De Soto, Hernando. 1989. *The Other Path: The Invisible Revolution in the Third World*. New York: Harper and Row.

Domhoff, G. William. 1967. *Who Rules America?* Englewood Cliffs, NJ: Prentice-Hall.

Evangelii Guadium. 2013 (www.vatican.va/holy_father/francesco/apost_exhortations/documents).

Farthing, Linda. 2010. "Controlling State Power: An Interview with Vice President Álvaro García Linera," *Latin American Perspectives*, 37.4 (July): 30–33.

Fukuyama, Francis. 1992. *The End of History and the Last Man*. New York: The Free Press.

García-Guadilla, María Pilar. 2011. "Urban Land Committees: Co-Optation, Autonomy, and Protagonism," in David Smide and Daniel Hellinger (editors), *Venezuela's Bolivarian Democracy: Participation, Politics, and Culture under Chávez*, pp. 58–79. Durham, NC: Duke University Press.

Guillermoprieto, Alma. 2000. "Letter from Mexico: Enter Harpo," *New Yorker* (July 24): 30.

Hellinger, Daniel. 1991. *Venezuela: Tarnished Democracy*. Boulder, CO: Westview Press.

Huntington, Samuel. 1991. *The Third Wave: Democratization in the Late Twentieth Century*. Norman: University of Oklahoma Press.

Inglehart, Ronald and Christian Welzel. 2005. *Modernization, Cultural Change and Democracy: The Human Development Sequence*. Cambridge: Cambridge University Press.

Kane, Richard F. 2005. "Brazil's Neoliberal Marxist," *Brazil Magazine* (June 15, www.brazzil.com, accessed January 31, 2007).

Lanz, Laureano Ballenilla. 1919. *Cesarismo Democrática: Estudios sobre las bases sociológicas de la constitución efectiva de Venezuela (Democratic Caesarism: Studies of the Sociological Bases of the Actual Venezuelan Constitution)* (edition of 1990). Caracas: Monte Avila.

La Ramée, Pierre M. and Erica G. Polakoff. 1997. "The Evolution of the Popular Organizations in Nicaragua," in Gary Prevost and Harry E. Vanden (editors), *The Undermining of the Sandinista Revolution*. London: Macmillan Press.

Lewis, Norman. 1989. *God Against the Indians*. New York: McGraw-Hill.

Linz, Juan J. and Alfred Stepan (editors). 1978. *The Breakdown of Democratic Regimes*. Baltimore, MD: Johns Hopkins University Press.

Linz, Juan J. and Alfred Stepan (editors). 1996. *Problems of Democratic Transition and Consolidation: Southern Europe, South America and Post-Communist Europe*. Baltimore, MD: Johns Hopkins University Press.

Linz, Juan J. and Arturo Valenzuela (editors). 1994. *The Failure of Presidential Democracy: The Case of Latin America*. Baltimore, MD: Johns Hopkins University Press.

Lührmann, Anna and Staffan I. Lindberg. 2019. "A Third Wave of Autocratization Is Here: What Is New about It?" *Democratization*, 26.7 (March): 1095–1113.

MacNeil, Robert. 1985. "Fidel Castro Interview, Part 2," *The MacNeil/Lehrer Newshour* (February 11).

MacPherson, C. B. 1972. *The Real World of Democracy*. New York: Oxford University Press.

Mainwaring, Scott and Timothy Scully (editors). 1995. *Building Democratic Institutions in Latin America*. Stanford, CA: Stanford University Press.

Mainwaring, Scott and M. Soberg Shugart (editors). 1997. *Presidentialism and Democracy in Latin America*. Cambridge: Cambridge University Press.

Mark, Jason. 2001. "Brazil's MST: Taking Back the Land," *Winning Campaigns*, 22: 1 and 2.

Michels, Robert. 1915. *Political Parties: A Sociological Study of the Oligarchical Tendencies of Modern Democracy*. Trans. Eden and Cedar Paul. Glencoe, IL: The Free Press.

Mills, C. Wright. 1956. *The Power Elite*. Oxford: Oxford University Press.

Munck, Gerardo L. 2004. "Democratic Politics in Latin America: New Debates and Research Frontiers," *Annual Review of Political Science*, 7: 437–462.

O'Donnell, Guillermo. 1994. "Delegative Democracy," *Journal of Democracy*, 5.1: 55–69.

O'Donnell, Guillermo, Philippe C. Schmitter and Laurence Whitehead (editors). 1986. *Transitions From Authoritarian Rule: Tentative Conclusions about Uncertain Democracies*. Baltimore, MD: Johns Hopkins University Press.

Perón, Juan. 1950. "Mensaje a la Asamblea Legislativa," *Discursos de Juan Domingo Perón*. Partido Justicialista, Provincia de Buenos Aires (www.pjbonaerense.org.ar/Peron_Discursos_01051950.aspx).

Perone, Jim. 2000. "Is the Pope Capitalist?" *Laissez Faire City Times*, 4.1 (January 3, www.zolatimes.com, accessed January 21, 2002).

Philip, George. 1996. "Institutions and Democratic Consolidation in Latin America," in Julia Buxton and Nicola Phillips (editors), *Developments in Latin American Political Economy: States, Markets and Actors*. Manchester: University of Manchester Press.

Prevost, Gary and Harry E. Vanden (editors). 1997. *The Undermining of the Sandinista Revolution*. London: Macmillan Press.

Raby, Diane. 2006. *Democracy and Revolution: Latin America and Socialism Today*. London: Verso.

Robinson, William I. 1992. *A Faustian Bargain: U.S. Intervention in the Nicaraguan Elections and American Foreign Policy in the Post-Cold War Era*. Boulder, CO: Westview Press.

Robinson, William I. 1996. *Promoting Polyarchy: Globalization, US Intervention, and Hegemony*. Cambridge: Cambridge University Press.

Romero, Aníbal. 1999. "Democracias de jugete en América Latina," *Venezuela Analytica* (July 25, www.analitica.com/hispanica/8252042.asp, accessed December 9, 2010).

Ruchwarger, Gary. 1985. "The Sandinista Mass Organizations and the Revolutionary Process," in Richard Harris and Carlos Vilas (editors), *Nicaragua under Siege*. London: Zed Books.

Schiller, Naomi. 2011. "Catia Sees You: Community Television, Clientelism, and the State in the Chávez Era," in David Smide and Daniel Hellinger (editors), *Venezuela's Bolivarian Democracy: Participation, Politics, and Culture under Chávez*, pp. 104–130. Durham, NC: Duke University Press.

Schmitter, Philippe. 1974. "Still the Century of Corporatism?" in Schmitter and Gerhard Lembruch (editors), *Trends Toward Corporatist Intermediation*. Beverly Hills, CA: Sage.

Stavenhagen, Rodolfo. 1966–1967. "Seven Erroneous Theses about Latin America," *New University Thought*, 4.4 (Winter): 25–37.

Stavenhagen, Rodolfo. 1974. "Dependency Theory: A Reassessment," *Latin American Perspectives*, 1.1 (Spring): 124–148.

Tangeman, Michael. 1995. *Mexico at the Crossroads: Politics, the Church, and the Poor*. New York: Orbis Books.

Vilas, Carlos. 1993. "The Hour of Civil Society," *NACLA Report on the Americas*, 37 (September–October): 38–42.

Wiarda, Howard. 1981. *Corporatism and National Development in Latin America*. Boulder, CO: Westview Press.

Williamson, John. 2002. "Did the Washington Consensus Fail?" *Outline of Speech at the Center for Strategic & International Studies*, Washington, DC, November 6.

Womack, John Jr. 1968. *Zapata and the Mexican Revolution*. New York: Vintage Books.

Zakaria, Fareed. 1997. "The Rise of Illiberal Democracy," *Foreign Affairs*, 76.6 (November–December): 22–43.

Chapter 2

Barbados Group. 1993. "Barbados III: On Democracy and Diversity," originally in *Abya Yala News* (www.nativeweb.org/papers/statements/state/barbados3.php, accessed December 9, 2010).

Barker, Ernest (editor, translator). 1962. *The Politics of Aristotle*. New York: Oxford University Press.

Butler, Judith. 2011. "For and Against Precarity," *Tidal. Occupy Theory, Occupy Strategy*, number 1 (December, www.e-flux.com/wp-content/uploads/2013/05/7.-Butler_Precarity.pdf?b8c429, accessed December 6, 2019).

Declaration of Quito. 1990 (www.nativeweb.org/papers/statements/quincentennial/quito.php, accessed December 9, 2010).

ECLAC (United Nations Economic Commission on Latin America and the Caribbean). 2019a. *Region Has Underestimated Inequality* (www.cepal.org/en/pressreleases/eclac-region-has-underestimated-inequality, accessed December 11, 2019).

ECLAC (United Nations Economic Commission on Latin America and the Caribbean). 2019b. *Social Panorama of Latin America, 2018*. Santiago, CL: ECLAC.

Gender Equality Observatory. 2019. *United Nations Economic Commission on Latin America and the Caribbean* (https://oig.cepal.org/en, accessed December 11, 2019).

Global Finance Magazine. 2018. Wealth Distribution and Income Inequality. 2018 (www.gfmag.com/global-data/economic-data/wealth-distribution-income-inequality).

Gurr, Robert Ted. 1970. *Why Men Rebel*. Princeton, NJ: Princeton University Press.

International Labor Office (ILO). 2018. *Global Wage Report*. Geneva: International Labor Office (ILO).

Johnson, John J. 1958. *The Emergence of the Middle Sectors*. Stanford, CA: Stanford University Press.

Lorey, Isabell. 2015. *State of Insecurity: Government of the Precarious*. London: Verso.

Lustig, Nora (editor). 1998. *Coping with Austerity: Poverty and Inequality in Latin America*. Washington, DC: Brookings Institution.

Melguizo, Angel and Nora Lustig. 2015. "How Middle Class Are Middle-income Households in Latin America?" *Organization of Economically Developed Countries* (May 20, www.oecd.org/dev/development-posts-how-middle-class-are-middle-income.htm, accessed December 15, 2019).

Monreal. 1999. "Sea Changes: The New Cuban Economy," *NACLA Report on the Americas*, 32, 5: 21–29.

Morrison, Judith. 2007. "Race and Poverty in Latin America: Addressing the Development Needs of African Descendants," *UN Chronicle*, 44.3 (September).

Nun, José. 1967. "The Middle Class Military Coup," in Claudio Veliz (editor), *The Politics of Conformity in Latin America*, pp. 66–218. London: Oxford University Press.

O'Donnell, Guillermo. 1999. *Counterpoints: Selected Essays on Authoritarianism and Democratization.* South Bend, IN: University of Notre Dame.

Pertierra, Ana Cristina. 2008. "En Casa: Women and Households in Post-Soviet Cuba," *Journal of Latin American Studies*, 40: 743–767.

Sosa Pietri, A. 1998. "Venezuela, el 'Tercermundismo' y la OPEP" ("Venezuela: 'Third Worldism' and OPEC"), *Venezuela Analytica* (October; website no longer available on-line).

United Nations. 2019. *Human Development Report*. New York (http://hdr.undp.org/sites/default/files/hdr2019.pdf, accessed September 14, 2020)

United Nations. 1999. *Human Development Report*. New York: Oxford University Press.

United Nations. 2008. *Permanent Forum on Indigenous* (www.un.org/esa/socdev/unpfii/, accessed December 11, 2019).

Van der Hoeven, Rolph. 2000. *Poverty and Structural Adjustment: Some Remarks on Tradeoffs Between Equity and Growth*. Geneva: International Labour Organization.

Chapter 3

Achtenberg, Emily. 2012. "Bolivia: End of the Road for TIPNIS Consulta," *NACLA Blog* (December 13, www.nacla.org/blog/2012/12/13/bolivia-end-road-tipnis-consulta).

Anderson, Benedict. 1983. *Imagined Communities: Reflections on the Origins and Spread of Nationalism.* London: Verso Press.

Anria, Santiago. 2016. "More Inclusion, Less Liberalism in Bolivia," *Journal of Democracy*, 27.3 (July): 99–108.

Bowman, Bryan. 2019. "Was Bolivia's Presidential Election Fraudulent After All?" *Global Post* (December 17, theglobepost.com/2019/12/17/bolivia-oas-election, accessed December 18, 2019).

Catholic News Services. 2012. "Bolivian Census to Allow Citizens to Register as Indigenous," (November 17, www.catholicsentinel.org/Main.asp?SectionID=2&SubSectionID=34&ArticleID=19873).

Crosby, Alfred, Jr. 1991. "The Biological Consequences of 1492," *NACLA Report on the Americas* (September): 6–13.

Diamond, Jared. 1997. *Guns, Germs and Steel: The Fates of Human Societies*. New York: Norton.

Dore, Elizabeth. 1991. "Open Wounds," *NACLA Report on the Americas* (September): 14–21.

Galeano, Eduardo. 2001. *The Open Veins of Latin America: Five Centuries of the Pillage of a Continent*. New York: Monthly Review Press.

Holloway, Joseph E. n.d. "Slave Resistances in Latin America," *The Slave Rebellion Website* (http://slaverebellion.org/index.php?page=slave-resistances-in-latin-america-2, accessed April 1, 2014).

Holston, James. 2008. *Insurgent Citizenship: Disjunctions of Democracy and Modernity in Brazil*. Princeton, NJ: Princeton University Press.

Hylton, Forrest and Sinclair Thomson. 2004. "The Roots of Rebellion: Insurgent Bolivia," *NACLA Report on the Americas*, 38.3 (November–December): 15–19.

Keen, Benjamin and Keith Haynes. 2000. *A History of Latin America* (sixth edition). Boston: Houghton Mifflin.

Lazar, Sian. 2008. *El Alto, Rebel City: Self and Citizenship in Andean Bolivia*. Durham, NC: Duke University Press.

Mann, Charles C. 2005. *1491: New Revelations of the Americas before Columbus*. New York: Alfred Knopf.

Manzano, Juan. 1996. *Autobiography of a Slave*. Detroit, MI: Wayne State University Press.

Mörner, Magnus. 1967. *Race Mixture in the History of Latin America*. Boston: Little, Brown.

Pilcher, Jeffrey M. 1998. *¡Que vivan los tamales! Food and the Making of Mexican Identity*. Albuquerque: University of New Mexico Press.

Rostow, Walt W. 1960. *The Stages of Growth: A Non-Communist Manifesto*. Cambridge: Cambridge University Press.

Schroeder, Susan. 2000. "The Mexico that Spain Encountered," in Michael C. Meyer and William H. Breezley (editors), *The Oxford History of Mexico*. New York: Oxford University Press.

Schwartz, Stuart. 2000. *Victors and Vanquished: Spanish and Nahua Views of the Conquest of Mexico*. Boston: Bedford/St. Martins.

Selverston-Scher, Melina. 2001. *Ethnopolitics in Ecuador: Indigenous Rights and the Strengthening of Democracy*. Miami, FL: North-South Center, University of Miami.

Silverblatt, Irene. 1987. *Moon, Sun and Witches*. Princeton, NJ: Princeton University Press.

Stolle-McAllister, John. 2005. "What Does Democracy Look Like?" *Latin American Perspectives*, 32.4 (July): 15–35.

Wallerstein, Immanuel. 1974. *The Modern World System: Capitalist Agriculture and the Origins of the European World Economy in the Sixteenth Century*. New York: Academic Press.

Williams, Eric. 1970. *From Columbus to Castro: The History of the Caribbean*. New York: Harper and Row.

Wilpert, Greg. 2004. "Racism and Racial Divides in Venezuela," *Venezuelanalysis.com* (January 21).

Chapter 4

Anderson, Benedict. 1983. *Imagined Communities: Reflections on the Origins and Spread of Nationalism*. London: Verso Press.

Burns, E. Bradford. 1996. *Latin America: A Concise Interpretive History* (sixth edition). Englewood Cliffs, NJ: Prentice-Hall.

de Tocqueville, Alexis. 1835/2000. *Democracy in America*. Trans. George Lawrence. Ed. J. P. Mayer. New York: Perennial Classics.

Keen, Benjamin and Keith Haynes. 2000. *A History of Latin America* (sixth edition). Boston: Houghton Mifflin Company.

Levine, R. M. 1995. *Vale of Tears: Revisiting the Canudos Massacre in Northeastern Brazil, 1893–1897*. Berkeley: University of California Press.

Loveman, Brian. 1999. *For La Patria: Politics and the Armed Forces in Latin America*. Wilmington, DE: Scholarly Resources.

Soares, José Celso de Macedo. 2009. "Coronelismo, enxada e voto," *Diario do Pernambuco* (June 18): 13B.

Ugalde, Luis. 1978. *Venezuela Republicana: Siglo XIX*. Caracas: Centro Gumilla.

Williams, Robert G. 1994. *States and Social Evolution: Coffee and the Rise of National Governments in Central America*. Chapel Hill: University of North Carolina Press.

Chapter 5

Bergquist, Charles. 1986. *Labor in Latin America: Comparative Essays on Chile, Argentina, Venezuela, and Colombia*. Palo Alto, CA: Stanford University Press.

Burns, E. Bradford. 1993. *A History of Brazil*. New York: Columbia University Press.

Cardoso, Fernando Henrique and Enzo Faletto. 1979. *Dependency and Development in Latin America*. Berkeley: University of California Press.

Corradi, Juan. 1985. *The Fitful Republic: Economy, Society and Politics in Argentina*. Boulder, CO: Westview Press.

Daly Hayes, Margaret. 1988/1989. "The U.S. and Latin America: A Lost Decade?" *Foreign Affairs*, 68 (No. 1, America and the World): 180–198.

Drake, Paul W. 1978. *Socialism and Populism in Chile: 1932–52*. Urbana: University of Illinois Press.

Fraser, Nicholas and Marysa Navarro. 1980. *Eva Perón*. New York: Norton.

Hodges, Donald. 1976. *Argentina 1943–1976: The National Revolution and Resistance*. Albuquerque: University of New Mexico Press.

Hoogvest, Ankie. 1991. *Globalization and the Post Colonial World: The New Political Economy of Development* (second edition). Baltimore, MD: The John Hopkins University Press.

Huntington, Samuel. 1968. *Political Order in Changing Societies*. New Haven, CT: Yale University Press.

Johnson, John. 1958. *Political Change in Latin America: The Emergence of the Middle Sectors*. Palo Alto, CA: Stanford University Press.

Karl, Terry. 1994. *The Paradox of Plenty: Oil Booms and Petro-States*. Berkeley: University of California Press.

Laclau, Ernesto. 2005. *On Populist Reason*. London: Verso.

Levitsky, Steven and Daniel Ziblatt. 2018. *How Democracies Die*. New York: Crown.

Lowy, Michael. 1987. *Notebooks for Study and Research*, vol. 6. Amsterdam: International Institute for Research and Education.

Nun, José. 1976. "The Middle Class Military Coup Revisited," in Abraham Lowenthal (editor), *Armies and Politics in Latin America*. New York: Holmes & Meier.

Page, Joseph. 1983. *Perón: A Biography*. New York: Random House.

Perón, Juan. 1950. *Mensaje al inaugurar el Congreso nacional May 1, 1950 (Message for the Inaugural National Congress)* (http://lanic.utexas.edu/larrp/pm/sample2/argentin/peron/500679t.html, accessed July 28, 2009).

Rostow, Walt W. 1960. *The Stages of Growth, a Non-Communist Manifesto*. Cambridge: Cambridge University Press.

Stavenhagen, Rodolfo. 1974. "Dependency Theory: A Reassessment," *Latin American Perspectives*, 1.1 (Spring): 124–148.

Vilas, Carlos M. 1987. "Populism as a Strategy for Accumulation: Latin America," in Michel Lowy (editor), *Notebooks for Study and Research*, vol. 6. Amsterdam: International Institute for Research and Education.

Weber, Maximillian. 1947. *Max Weber: The Theory of Social and Economic Organization*. Trans. A. M. Henderson and Talcott Parsons. New York: The Free Press.

Chapter 6

Amin, Samir. 1977. *Imperialism and Unequal Development*. New York: Monthly Review Press.

Armijo, Leslie Elliott and Phillippe Faucher. 2000. "We Have a Consensus: Explaining Political Support for Market Reforms in Latin America," Paper prepared for delivery at the *96th Annual Meeting of the American Political Science Association*, Washington, DC, August 31–September 2.

Armstrong, Robert and Janet Shenk. 1982. *El Salvador: The Face of Revolution*. Boston: South End Press.

Cardoso, Fernando Henrique. 1977. "The Consumption of Dependency Theory in the United States," *Latin American Research Review*, 12.3: 7–24.

Cardoso, Fernando Henrique and Enzo Faletto. 1979. *Dependency and Development in Latin America*. Berkeley: University of California Press.

Cueva, Agustín. 2003 (originally 1976). "Problems of Dependency Theory," in Ronald H. Chilcote (editor), *Development in Theory and Practice*. Trans. J. Villamil and C. Fortín. New York: Rowman and Littlefield.

da Costa, Ana Nicolaci. 2008. "In Brazil Middle Class Dreams Built on Credit," *Reuters* (July 15, www.reuters.com/article/idUSN0827980620080716, accessed December 9, 2010).

Deutsch, Karl W. 1961. "Social Mobilization and Political Development," *American Political Science Review*, 55.3 (September): 493–514.

Dos Santos, Theotonio. 1974. "Brazil: The Origins of a Crisis," in Ronald Chilcote and Joel Edelstein (editors), *Latin America: The Struggle with Dependency and Beyond*. New York: Schenkman.

Drake, Paul W. 1978. *Socialism and Populism in Chile 1932–52*. Urbana: University of Illinois Press.

Dussel, Enrique. 1980. "Philosophy and Praxis" (Provisional Thesis for a Philosophy of Liberation), in John B. Brough et al. (editors), *Philosophical Knowledge*. Washington, DC: Catholic University of America (www.ifil.org/Biblioteca/dussel/textos/c/1980-115.pdf, accessed July 15, 2008).

ECLAC (United Nations Economic Commission on Latin America and the Caribbean). 2019a. *Foreign Direct Investment in Latin America and the Caribbean*. New York: United Nations Press.

ECLAC (United Nations Economic Commission on Latin America and the Caribbean). 2019b. *Region Has Underestimated Inequality* (www.cepal.org/en/pressreleases/eclac-region-has-underestimated-inequality, accessed December 11, 2019).

Frank, Andre Gunder. 1967. *Latin America: Underdevelopment or Revolution*. New York: Monthly Review Press.

Franko, Patrice. 1999. *The Puzzle of Latin American Economic Development*. Lanham, MD: Rowman and Littlefield.

Furtado, Celso. 1971. *La economiía latinomericana: formación histórica y problemas contemporaneous (The Latin American Economy: Historical Formation and Contemporary Character)*. Mexico City: Siglo Veintiuno Editores.

Galeano, Eduardo. 1997. *The Open Veins of Latin America*. New York: Monthly Review Press.

Gardy, Alison. 1994. "Mexico's Political Reforms Must Begin in the Streets," *Wall Street Journal* (November 18): A19.

Hanson, Simon. 1951. *Economic Development in Latin America*. Washington, DC: Inter-American Affairs Press.

Hellinger, Daniel. 1991. *Venezuela: Tarnished Democracy*. Boulder, CO: Westview Press.

Hudson, Michael. 2003. *Super Imperialism: The Origins and Fundamentals of U.S. World Dominance* (second edition). London: Pluto Press (https://libcom.org/files).

Huntington, Samuel. 1968. *Political Order in Changing Societies*. New Haven, CT: Yale University Press.

Karl, Terry. 1994. *The Paradox of Plenty: Oil Booms and Petro-States*. Berkeley: University of California Press.

Kaufman, Robert R., Harry Chernotsky and Daniel Geller. 1975. "A Preliminary Test of the Theory of Dependency," *Comparative Politics*, 7.3 (April): 303–330.

Lipset, Seymour Martin. 1960. *Political Man*. New York: Doubleday.

Martínez-Piedra, Alberto and Lorenzo L. Pérez. 1996. "External Debt Problems and the Principle of Solidarity: The Cuba Case," in *Cuba in Transition*, vol. 6. Proceedings of the Fifth Annual Meeting of the Association for the Study of the Cuban Economy (ASCE), University of Miami, Miami, FL, August 8–10.

Marx, Karl and Friedrich Engels. 1848/1948. *The Communist Manifesto*. Moscow: International Publishers.

Moguel, Julio. 1994. "Salinas' Failed War on Poverty" (interview), *NACLA Report on the Americas*, 28 (July): 38.

Osava, Mario. 2004. "Brazil's Shrinking Middle Class," *IPSNews.net* (September 21, http://ipsnews.net/africa/interna.asp?idnews=25559, accessed December 9, 2010).

Pérez, Mamerto, Sergio Schlesinger and Timothy A. Wise. 2008. *The Promise and Perils of Agricultural Trade Liberalization: Lessons from Latin America*. Washington, DC: Washington Office on Latin America.

Petras, James. 1980. *Critical Perspectives on Imperialism and Social Class in the Third World*. New York: Monthly Review Press.

Potter, Georgia Anne. 2000. *Deeper than Debt: Globalization and the Poor*. Bloomfield, CT: Kumarian Press.

Remmer, Karen. 1998. "The Politics of Neo-Liberal Economic Reform in South America, 1980–1994," *Studies in Comparative International Development*, 33.2: 3–29.

Rostow, Walt W. 1960. *The Stages of Growth, a Non-Communist Manifesto*. Cambridge: Cambridge University Press.

Schumpeter, Joseph. 1947. *Capitalism, Socialism and Democracy*. New York: Harper.

Wachtel, Howard. 1977. "A Decade of International Debt," *Theory and Society*, 9.3: 504–518.

Wallerstein, Immanuel. 2004. *World-Systems Analysis: An Introduction*. Durham, NC: Duke University Press.

Weber, Max. 2002 (original 1905). *In the Protestant Revolution and the Spirit of Capitalism and Other Writings*, edited by Peter Baehr and Gordon C. Wells. New York: Penguin Classics.

World Bank. 1996. *World Debt Tables 1994–1995*. Washington, DC: World Bank.

Chapter 7

Albright, Madeleine. 2018. *Fascism: A Warning*. New York: William Collins.

Allende, Salvador. 1973. "Last Words to the Nation" (www.marxists.org/archive/allende/1973/september/11.htm, accessed April 13, 2020).

Andersen, Martin Edwin. 1993. *Dossier Secreto: Argentina's Desaparecidos and the Myth of the Dirty War*. Boulder, CO: Westview Press.

Avritzer, Leonardo. 2002. *Democracy and the Public Space in Latin America*. Princeton, NJ: Princeton University Press.

Castañeda, Jorge. 1993. *Utopia Unarmed: The Latin American Left after the Cold War*. New York: Alfred Knopf.

Cockroft, James. 1996. *Latin America: History, Politics and U.S. Policy* (second edition). Chicago, IL: Nelson-Hall.

Dos Santos, Theotonio. 1974. "Brazil: The Origins of a Crisis," in Ronald Chilcote and Joel Edelstein (editors), *Latin America: The Struggle with Dependency and Beyond*. New York: Schenkman.

Drake, Paul W. 1978. *Socialism and Populism in Chile 1932–52*. Urbana: University of Illinois Press.

Friedman, Elizabeth. 2000. *Unfinished Transitions: Women and the Gendered Development of Democracy in Venezuela*. University Park, PA: Penn State Press.

Garretón, Manuel. 1986. "The Political Evolution of the Chilean Military Regime and Problems in the Transition to Democracy," in Guillermo O'Donnell, Philippe C. Schmitter and Laurence Whitehead (editors), *Transitions from Authoritarian Rule: Latin America*. Baltimore, MD: Johns Hopkins University Press.

Huntington, Samuel. 1968. *Political Order in Changing Societies*. New Haven, CT: Yale University Press.

Huntington, Samuel. 1991. *The Third Wave: Democratization in the Late Twentieth Century*. Norman: University of Oklahoma Press.

Kaufman, Robert R. 1972. *The Politics of Latin Reform in Chile, 1950–1970: Public Policy, Political Institutions, and Social Change*. Cambridge, MA: Harvard University Press.

Keck, Margaret. 1992. *The Workers' Party and Democratization in Brazil*. New Haven, CT: Yale University Press.

Kornbluth, Peter. 2013. *The Pinochet File: A Declassified Dossier on Atrocity and Accountability*. New York: The New Press.

Latinobarómetro. 2018. *Informe Latinobarómetro 2013 (Latin Barometer Report)*. Santiago: Corporación Latinobarómetro (www.latinobarometro.org.)

Levitsky, Steven and Daniel Ziblatt. 2018. *How Democracies Die*. New York: Crown.

Linz, Juan J. and Alfred Stepan (editors). 1978. *The Breakdown of Democratic Regimes* (4 vols.). Baltimore, MD: Johns Hopkins University Press.

Mallinder, Louise. 2009. *Uruguay's Evolving Experience of Amnesty and Civil Society's Response*. Belfast: Queen's University, Institute of Criminology and Criminal Justice.

Moulian, Tomás. 2002. *Chile Actual: Anatomía de un mito (Chile Today: Anatomy of a Myth)*. Santiago: LOM Ediciones.

Nun, José. 1967. "The Middle Class Military Coup," in Claudio Veliz (editor), *The Politics of Conformity in Latin America*, pp. 66–218. London: Oxford University Press.

Nun, José. 1976. "The Middle Class Military Coup Revisited," in Abraham Lowenthal (editor), *Armies and Politics in Latin America*. New York: Holmes & Meier.

O'Donnell, Guillermo. 1973. *Modernization and Bureaucratic-Authoritarianism: Studies in South American Politics*. Berkeley, CA: University of California.

O'Donnell, Guillermo. 1978. "Modernization and Military Coups: Theory, Comparisons, and the Argentine Case," in Abraham Lowenthal (editor), *Armies and Politics in Latin America*, pp. 197–143. Teaneck, NJ: Holmes and Meier.

O'Donnell, Guillermo and Philippe C. Schmitter. 1986. *Transitions From Authoritarian Rule: Tentative Conclusions about Uncertain Democracies*. Baltimore, MD: Johns Hopkins University Press.

O'Donnell, Guillermo, Philippe C. Schmitter and Laurence Whitehead (editors). 1986a. *Authoritarian Rule: Comparative Perspectives*. Baltimore, MD: Johns Hopkins University Press.

O'Donnell, Guillermo, Philippe C. Schmitter and Laurence Whitehead (editors). 1986b. *Transitions From Authoritarian Rule: Latin America*. Baltimore, MD: Johns Hopkins University Press.

O'Donnell, Guillermo, Philippe C. Schmitter and Laurence Whitehead (editors). 1986c. *Transitions From Authoritarian Rule: Southern Europe*. Baltimore, MD: Johns Hopkins University Press.

Oppenheim, Lois Hecht. 1993. *Politics in Chile: Democracy, Authoritarianism, and the Search for Development*. Boulder, CO: Westview Press.

Osava, Mario. 2004. "The Struggle to Pry Open Brazil's Military Archives" (www.antiwar.com/ips/osava.php?articleid=3859, accessed August 12, 2004).

Przeworski, Adam. 1986. "Some Problems in the Study of the Transition to Democracy," in Guillermo O'Donnell, Philippe C. Schmitter and Laurence Whitehead (editors), *Transitions From Authoritarian Rule: Comparative Perspectives*. Baltimore, MD: Johns Hopkins University Press.

Rettig Commission. 2000. "Report of the Chilean National Commission on Truth and Reconciliation" (www.usip.org/sites/default/files/resources/collections/truth_commissions/Chile90-Report/Chile90-Report.pdf).

Robinson, William I. 1996. *Promoting Polyarchy: Globalization, US Intervention, and Hegemony*. Cambridge: Cambridge University Press.

Roxborough, Ian, Phil O'Brien and Jackie Roddick. 1977. *Chile: The State and Revolution*. London: Macmillan Press.

Sartori, Giovanni and Giacomo Sani. 1983. "Polarization, Fragmentation, and Competition in Western Democracies," in Hans Daalder and Peter Mair (editors), *Western European Party Systems: Continuity and Change*. Berkeley, CA: Sage Publications.

Sigmund, Paul E. (editor). 1970. *Models of Political Change in Latin America*. New York: Praeger.

Stepan, Alfred. 1971. *The Military in Politics: Changing Patterns in Brazil*. Princeton, NJ: Princeton University Press.

Stepan, Alfred. 1978. "Political Leadership and Regime Breakdown: Brazil," in Juan J. Linz and Alfred Stepan (editors), *The Breakdown of Democratic Regimes in Latin America*. Baltimore: Johns Hopkins University Press.

Trigona, Marie. 2006. "Recuperated Factories in Argentina: Reversing the Logic of Capitalism," *Znet* (March 27).

Valenzuela, Arturo. 1978. *The Breakdown of Democratic Regimes: Chile*. Baltimore, MD: Johns Hopkins University Press.

Welzel, Christian. 2009. "Theories of Democratization," in Christian Haerpfern et al. (editors), *Democratization*. New York: Oxford University Press (www.worldvaluessurvey.org/wvs/articles/folder_published/publication_579/files/OUP_Ch06.pdf).

Winn, Peter. 1989. *Weavers of Revolution: The Yarur Workers and Chile's Road to Socialism*. New York: Oxford University Press.

Zenteño, Raúl Benítez (editor). 1977. *Clases sociales y crisis política en américa latina* (*Social Classes and Political Crisis in Latin America*). Mexico City: Siglo Veintiuno.

Chapter 8

Albright, Madeleine. 2018. *Fascism: A Warning*. New York: Harper.

Avritzer, Leonardo. 2002. *Democracy and the Public Space in Latin America*. Princeton, NJ: Princeton University Press.

Burns, E. Bradford and Julie A. Charlip. 2002. *Latin America: A Concise Interpretive History* (seventh edition). Upper Saddle River, NJ: Prentice Hall.

Camp, Roderic Ai. 1999. *Politics in Mexico: The Decline of Authoritarianism*. New York: Oxford University Press.

Collier, George A. (with Elizabeth Lowery Quaratiello). 1999. *Land and the Zapatistas: Rebellion in Chiapas* (second edition). Oakland, CA: Food First.

Coronil, Fernando. 1997. *The Magical State: Nature, Money and Modernity in Venezuela*. Chicago, IL: University of Chicago Press.

Crozier, Michel, Samuel Huntington and Joji Watanuki. 1975. *The Crisis of Democracy*. New York: The Trilateral Commission.

Cyr, Jennifer. 2013. "Political Parties and the State in Post-Collapse Venezuela and Bolivia," Paper delivered at the *XXXI International Congress of the Latin American Studies Association*, Washington, DC, May 29–June 1.

Ellner, Steve and Daniel Hellinger (editors). 2003. *Venezuelan Politics in the Chávez Era: Class Polarization and Conflict*. Boulder, CO: Lynne Rienner.

Foweracker, Joe and Ann Craig (editors). 1990. *Popular Movements and Political Change in Mexico*. Boulder, CO: Lynne Rienner.

Handelman, Howard. 1997. *Mexican Politics: The Dynamics of Change*. New York: St. Martin's Press.

Hellinger, Daniel. 1991. *Venezuela: Tarnished Democracy*. Boulder, CO: Westview Press.

Hellinger, Daniel. 2003. "Political Overview: The Breakdown of Puntofijismo," in Steve Ellner and Daniel Hellinger (editors), *Venezuelan Politics in the Chávez Era*. Boulder, CO: Lynne Rienner.

Huntington, Samuel. 1968. *Political Order in Changing Societies*. New Haven, CT: Yale University Press.

Jones, Bart. 2007. *Hugo! The Hugo Chávez Story from Mud Hut to Perpetual Revolution*. Hanover, NH: Steerforth Press.

Karl, Terry Lynn. 1986. "Petroleum and Political Pacts: The Transition to Democracy in Venezuela," in Guillermo O'Donnell, Philippe Schmitter and Laurence Whitehead (editors), *Transitions From Authoritarian Rule: Latin America*. Baltimore, MD: Johns Hopkins University Press.

Karl, Terry Lynn. 1997. *The Paradox of Plenty: Oil Booms and Petrostates*. Berkeley, CA: University of California Press.

La Botz, Dan. 1995. *Democracy in Mexico: Peasant Rebellion and Political Reform*. Boston: South End Press.

Langston, Joy. 2006. "The Birth and Transformation of the Dedazo in Mexico," in Gretchen Helmke and Steven Levitsky (editors), *Informal Institutions and Democracy: Lessons from Latin America*. Baltimore, MD: Johns Hopkins University Press.

Levine, Daniel. 1978. "Venezuela Since 1958: The Consolidation of Democratic Politics," in Juan J. Linz and Alfred Stepan (editors), *The Breakdown of Democratic Regimes: Latin America*, pp. 82–109. Baltimore, MD: Johns Hopkins University Press.

Levitsky, Steven and Daniel Ziblatt. 2018. *How Democracies Die*. New York: Crown.

Levy, Daniel and Gabriel Székely. 1983. *Mexico: Paradoxes of Stability and Change*. Boulder, CO: Westview.

McCoy, Jennifer and David Myers (editors). 2006. *The Unraveling of Democracy in Venezuela*. Baltimore, MD: Johns Hopkins University Press.

Merrill, Tim and Ramón Miró (editors). 1996. *Mexico: A Country Study*. Washington, DC: GPO for the Library of Congress (http://countrystudies.us/mexico/).

Meyer, Jean. 2006. *The Cristero Rebellion: The Mexican People Between Church and State 1926-1929*. Cambridge: Cambridge University Press.

Meyer, Michael C. and William H. Beezley (editors). 2000. *The Oxford History of Mexico*. New York: Oxford University Press.

Middlebrook, Kevin J. 1986. "Political Liberalization in an Authoritarian Regime," in Guillermo O'Donnell, Philippe C. Schmitter and Laurence Whitehead (editors), *Transitions From Authoritarian Rule: Latin America*, pp. 123–147. Baltimore, MD: Johns Hopkins University Press.

Mommer, Bernard. 1988. *La cuestión petrolera*. Caracas: Universidad Central de Venezuela-TROPYKOS.

Mommer, Bernard. 2002. *Global Oil and the Nation State*. Oxford: Oxford Institute for Energy Studies.

Murphy, James. 2019. *Saints and Sinners in the Cristero War: Stories of Martyrdom from Mexico*. San Francisco: Ignatius Press.

NACLA (North American Congress on Latin America). 1994. *Mexico Out of Balance*, 38.1 (July–August).

Orme, William A. Jr. 1996. *Understanding NAFTA: Mexico, Free Trade and the New North America*. Austin: University of Texas Press.

Padgett, L. Vincent. 1966. *The Mexican Political System*. Boulder: University of Colorado.

Pilcher, Jeffrey M. 1998. *¡Que vivan los tamales! Food and the Making of Mexican Identity*. Albuquerque: University of New Mexico Press.

Przeworski, Adam. 1986. "Some Problems in the Study of the Transition to Democracy," in Guillermo O'Donnell, Philippe C. Schmitter and Laurence Whitehead (editors), *Transitions From Authoritarian Rule: Comparative Perspectives*. Baltimore, MD: Johns Hopkins University Press.

Rey, Juan Carlos. 1972. "El sistema de partidos venezolanos (The Venezuelan Party System)," *Politeia*, 1: 135–175.

Ruiz, Ramón Eduardo. 2000. *On the Rime of Mexico: Encounters of the Rich and Poor*. Boulder, CO: Westview Press.

Shirk, David A. 2005. *Mexico's New Politics: The PAN and Democratic Change*. Boulder, CO: Lynne Rienner.

Tinker-Salas, Miguel. 2009. *The Enduring Legacy: Oil, Culture, and Society in Venezuela*. Durham, NC: Duke University Press.

Uslar Pietri, Arturo. 1936. "Sembrar el Petróleo" (https://hemerotecavirtualsembrarpetroleo.blogspot.com, accessed January 25, 2020).

Velasco, Antonio. 2015. *Barrio Rising: Urban Popular Politics and the Making of Modern Venezuela*. Berkeley, CA: University of California Press.

Womack, John Jr. 1968. *Zapata and the Mexican Revolution*. New York: Vintage Books.

Chapter 9

Anderson, Thomas P. 1971. *Matanza: El Salvador's Communist Revolt of 1932*. Lincoln: University of Nebraska Press.

Arendt, Hannah. 1963. *On Revolution*. New York: Viking Press.

Armstrong, Robert and Janet Shenk. 1982. *El Salvador: The Face of Revolution*. Boston: South End Press.

Barry, Tom and Deb Preusch. 1986. *The Central America Fact Book*. New York: Grove Press.

Borge, Tomás. n.d. "My Personal Revenge" (www.geocities.com/~thinkink/war/justice.htm#books, accessed July 28, 2009).

Brenner, Philip, William M. LeoGrande, Dona Rich and Daniel Siegel. 1989. *The Cuba Reader: The Making of a Revolutionary Society*. New York: Grove Press.

Cabezas, Omar. 1985. *Fire on the Mountain*. New York: Crown Publishing.

Debray, Regis. 1967. *Revolution in the Revolution*. London: Penguin Books.

De la Fuente, Alejandro. 2001. *A Nation for All: Race, Inequality, and Politics in Twentieth-Century Cuba*. Chapel Hall: University of North Carolina Press.

Doyle, Kate and Michael Kornbluth. 1997. "CIA and Assassinations: The Guatemala 1954 Documents," *National Security Electronic Archive Briefing Book*, no. 4 (www.gwu.edu/~nsarchiv/NSAEBB/NSAEBB4/, accessed December 9, 2010).

Echeverría, Dayma, Albert Gabriele, Sara Romano and Francesco Schettino. 2019. "Wealth Distribution in Cuba (2006–2014), a First Assessment Using Microdata," *Cambridge Journal of Economics*, 43: 361–383.

Goldstone, Jack A., Ted Robert Gurr and Farrokh Moshini. 1991. *Revolutions of the Late Twentieth Century*. Boulder, CO: Westview Press.

Hinckle, Warren and William Turner. 1981. *The Fish Is Red: The Story of the Secret War Against Castro*. New York: HarperCollins.

Jonas, Susanne. 1991. *The Battle for Guatemala: Rebels, Death Squads and U.S. Power*. Boulder, CO: Westview Press.

Lauria-Santiago, Aldo. 1999. *An Agrarian Republic: Commercial Agriculture and the Politics of Peasant Communities in El Salvador*. Pittsburgh, PA: University of Pittsburgh Press.

Machiavelli, Niccolo. 1947. *The Prince*. Ed. T. G. Bergin. New York: Appleton Century Crofts.

Martí, José. 1999. "Letter to Manuel Mercado," in Deborah Schoonaka and Mirta Muñiz (editors), *The José Martí Reader*. New York: Ocean Press.

Matthews, Herbert. 1957. "Before the Year Ended, He Said, He Would Be a Hero or a Martyr. Interview with Fidel Castro," *New York Times* (February 24): 1A.

Millet, Richard. 1977. *Guardians of the Dynasty*. New York: Orbis Books.

Pérez, Louis A. 1988. *Cuba: Between Revolution and Reform*. New York: Oxford University Press.

Prevost, Gary and Harry E. Vanden (editors). 1996. *The Undermining of the Sandinista Revolution*. London: Macmillan Press.

Robinson, William. 1992. *A Faustian Bargain: U.S. Intervention in the Nicaraguan Elections and American Foreign Policy in the Post-Cold War Era*. Boulder, CO: Westview Press.

Roman, Peter. 2003. *People's Power: Cuba's Experience with Representative Government*. Lanham, MD: Rowman and Littlefield.

Chapter 10

Albright, Madeleine. 2019. *Fascism: A Warning*. New York: HarperCollins.

Alpert, Megan. 2016. "15 Years and $10 Billion Later, U.S. Efforts to Curb Colombia's Cocaine Trade Have Failed," *Foreign Policy* (February 8, foreignpolicy.com, accessed February 7, 2020).

Becker, Marc. 2006. "Mariátegui, the Comintern, and the Indigenous Question in Latin America," *Science & Society*, 70.4 (October): 450–479.

Brenes Castro, Arnoldo and Kevin Casas Zamora. 2003. "Soldiers as Businesspeople: The Central American Militaries," in Jörn Brömmelster and Wolf Christian Paes (editors), *The Military as an Economic Actor: Soldiers in Business*, pp. 52–87. New York: Palgrave-MacMillan.

Brömmelster, Jörn and Wolf Christian Paes. 2003. *The Military as an Economic Actor: Soldiers in Business*. New York: Palgrave-MacMillan.

Colombia Human Rights Network (CHRN). 2001. 2001 Report (http://colhrnet.igc.org/, temporarily suspended for development, accessed September 14, 2020).

Diamint, Rut. 2002. "Civilians and the Military in Latin American Democracies," *Disarmament Forum*, 2: 15–24.

Dominguez, Jorge and Abraham F. Lowenthal (editors). 1996. *Constructing Democratic Governance in Latin America*. Baltimore, MD: Johns Hopkins University Press.

Dugas, John. 2016. "Colombia," in Harry E. Vanden and Gary Prevost (editors), *Politics in Latin America: The Power Game*, pp. 433–458. New York: Oxford University Press.

Ellner, Steve. 2019. "Introduction: Pink Tide Governments," *Latin American Perspectives*, 46.224 (January): 4–22.

Gorriti, Gustavo. 1999. *The Shining Path: A History of the Millenarian War in Peru*. Chapel Hill: University of North Carolina Press.

Huntington, Samuel. 1968. *Political Order in Changing Societies*. New Haven, CT: Yale University Press.

Huntington, Samuel. 1991. *The Third Wave: Democratization in the Late Twentieth Century*. Norman: University of Oklahoma Press.

Janowitz, Morris. 1960. *The Professional Soldier: A Social and Political Portrait*. Glencoe, IL: The Free Press.

Lasswell, Harold. 1936. *Politics: Who Gets What, When and How*. Reprint 1950. New York: McGraw-Hill.

Levitsky, Steven and Daniel Ziblatt. 2018. *How Democracies Die*. New York: Crown Press.

Loveman, Brian. 1999. *For La Patria: Politics and the Armed Forces in Latin America*. Lanham, MD: Rowman and Littlefield.

Loveman, Brian and Thomas M. Davies Jr. (editors) 1997. *The Politics of Antipolitics: The Military in Latin America*. Lanham MD: Rowman and Littlefield.

Lührmann, Anna and Staffan I. Lindberg. 2019. "A Third Wave of Autocratization Is Here: What Is New about It?" *Democratization*, 26.7 (March): 1095–1113.

Millet, Richard. 1977. *Guardians of the Dynasty*. New York: Orbis Books.

Mounk, Yascha. 2018. *The People vs. Democracy: Why Our Freedom Is in Danger and How to Save It*. Cambridge, MA: Harvard University Press.

National Security Archive. 2004. "U.S. Intelligence Listed Colombian President Uribe among 'Important Colombian Narco-Traffickers' in 1991" (August 2, nsarchive2.gwu.edu/NSAEBB/NSAEBB131, accessed February 7, 2020).

National Security Archive. 2018. "The Colombia Project" (https://nsarchive.gwu.edu/project/colombia-project, accessed April 13, 2020).

Norden, Deborah L. 2003. "Democracy in Uniform: Chávez and the Venezuelan Armed Forces," in Steve Ellner and Daniel Hellinger (editors), *Venezuelan Politics in the Chávez Era: Class, Polarization and Conflict*, pp. 93–112. Boulder, CO: Lynne Rienner.

Nordlinger, Eric. 1976. *Soldiers and Politics: Military Coups and Governments*. New York: Pearson.

Nun, José. 1967. "The Middle Class Military Coup," in Claudio Veliz (editor), *The Politics of Conformity in Latin America*, pp. 66–218. London: Oxford University Press.

Painter, James. 1987. *Guatemala: False Hope False Freedom*. London: Catholic Institute for International Relations.

Perlmutter, Amos. 1977. *The Military and Politics in Modern Times: On Professionals, Praetorians, and Revolutionary Soldiers in Modern Times*. New Haven, CT: Yale University Press.

Pion-Berlin, David and Rafael Martínez. 2017. *Soldiers, Politicians, and Civilians Reforming Civil-Military Relations in Democratic Latin America*. New York: Cambridge University Press.

Robinson, William I. 1996. *Promoting Polyarchy: Globalization, US Intervention, and Hegemony*. Cambridge: University of Cambridge Press.

Sánchez, Alex. 2011. "Costa Rica: An Army-less Nation in a Problem-Prone Region," Council on Hemispheric Affairs (June 2, https://www.coha.org/costa-rica-an-army-less-nation-in-a-problem-prone-region/#:~:text=Costa%20Rica-,Costa%20Rica%3A%20An%20Army%2Dless%20Nation,in%20a%20Problem%2DProne%20Region&text=The%20combination%20of%20rising%20criminal,tackle%20growing%20security%2Drelated%20issues, accessed September 14, 2020).

Sartori, Giovanni and Giacomo Sani. 1983. "Polarization, Fragmentation, and Competition in Western Democracies," in Hans Daalder and Peter Mair (editors), *Western European Party Systems: Continuity and Change*. Berkeley, CA: Sage Publications.

Senem, Aydin-Düzgit et al. 2019. "Post–Cold War Democratic Declines: The Third Wave of Autocratization," *Carnegie-Europe* (https://carnegieeurope.eu/2019/06/27/post-cold-war-democratic-declines-third-wave-of-autocratization-pub-79378, accessed February 5, 2020).

Stepan, Alfred. 1971. *The Military in Politics: Changing Patterns in Brazil*. Princeton, NJ: Princeton University Press.

Stepan, Alfred. 1978. "Political Leadership and Regime Breakdown: Brazil," in Juan J. Linz and Alfred Stepan (editors), *The Breakdown of Democratic Regimes in Latin America*. Baltimore: Johns Hopkins University Press.

Sunstein, Cass R. (editor). 2018. *Can It Happen Here? Authoritarianism in America*. New York: William Morrow.

Tuft, Eva Irene. 1997. *Democracy and Violence: The Colombian Paradox*. Bergen, Norway: Chr. Michelson Institute (https://open.cmi.no, accessed January 30, 2020).

Weber, Max. 2013. Reprint of 1916 edition. *Politics as a Vocation*. Atlanta, GA: Isha Books.

Chapter 11

Alexander, Robin and Dan La Botz. 2014. "A Workers' Defeat—For Now," *NACLA Report on the Americas* (Spring): 49–53.

Azicri, Max. 2000. *Cuba Today and Tomorrow: Reinventing Socialism*. Gainesville: University of Florida Press.

Barber, Benjamin. 1969. "Conceptual Foundations of Totalitarianism," in Benjamin R. Barber, Michael
    Curtis and Carl Friedrich (editors), *Totalitarianism in Perspective*, pp. 3–52. New York: Praeger.
Barry, Tom and Deb Preusch. 1986. *The Central America Fact Book*. New York: Grove Press.
Bergquist, Charles. 1986. *Labor in Latin America: Comparative Essays on Chile, Argentina, Venezuela, and
    Colombia*. Stanford, CA: Stanford University Press.
Berins Collier, Ruth and David Collier. 1991. *Shaping the Political Arena*. Princeton, NJ: Princeton University
    Press.
The Brazil Business. 2016. "Social Classes in Brazil" (https://thebrazilbusiness.com/, accessed February 21,
    2020).
Brigida, Anna-Catherine. 2018. "Latin America Has Become an Unlikely Leader in LGBT Rights," *Quartz*
    (qz.com, accessed February 26, 2020).
Burbach, Roger. 2002. "'Throw Them All Out': Argentina's Grassroots Rebellion," *NACLA Report on the
    Americas*, 34.1: xxx.
Conaghan, Catherine. 2011. "Rafael Correa and the Citizens' Revolution," in Steve Levitsky and Kenneth
    M. Roberts (editors), *The Resurgence of the Latin American Left*, pp. 260–282. Baltimore, MD: Johns
    Hopkins University Press.
Crozier, Michael, Samuel Huntington and Joji Watanabi. 1975. *The Crisis of Democracy*. New York: New
    York University Press.
Cusicanqui, Silvia Rivera. 2004. "The Roots of Rebellion: Reclaiming the Nation," *NACLA Report on the
    Americas*, 38.3 (November–December): 19–23.
Cypher, James M. 2014. "Energy Privatized: The Ultimate Neoliberal Triumph," *NACLA Report on the
    Americas* (Spring): 27–31.
De Soto, Hernando. 1989. *The Other Path: The Invisible Revolution in the Third World*. New York: Harper
    and Row.
Dinegro Martinez, Alejandra. 2019. "App Capitalism," *NACLA Report on the Americas*, 51:3 (Fall):
    236–241.
Friedman, Elizabeth. 2000. *Unfinished Transitions: Women and the Gendered Development of Democracy in
    Venezuela*. University Park, PA: Penn State Press.
Hellinger, Daniel. 1996. "Venezuelan Democracy and the Challenge of the *Nuevo Sindicalismo*," *Latin
    American Perspectives*, 23 (Summer): 110–131.
Holmes, Jennifer and Sheila Amin Gutiérrez de Piñeres. 2006. "The Illegal Drug Industry, Violence and
    the Colombian Economy: A Department Level Analysis," *Bulletin of Latin American Research*, 25.1
    (January): 104–118.
Hylton, Forest and Sinclair Thomson. 2003. "The Roots of Rebellion: I. Insurgent Bolivia," *NACLA Report
    on the Americas*, 38 (November–December): 15–19.
Ikawa, Daniela. 2009. "The Right to Affirmative Action in Brazilian Universities," *The Equal Rights Review*,
    3: 28–37.
InSight Crime. 2016. *Honduran Elites and Organized Crime*. Washington, DC: InSight Crime.
Keck, Margaret. 1992. *The Workers' Party and Democratization in Brazil*. New Haven, CT: Yale University
    Press.
LaFeber, Walter. 1993. *Inevitable Revolutions: The United States in Central America*. New York: Norton.
Mallen, Ana L. and María Pilar García-Guadilla. 2017. *Venezuela's Polarized Politics: The Paradox of Partic-
    ipatory Politics under Chávez*. Boulder, CO: First Forum Press.
May, Channing. 2017. *Transnational Crime and the Developing World*. Washington, DC: Global Financial
    Integrity (gfintegrity.org, accessed February 25, 2020).
Portes, Alejandro and Kelly Hoffman. 2003. "Latin American Class Structures: Their Composition and
    Change During the Neoliberal Era," *Latin American Research Review*, 38.1 (February): 41–77.
Rodríguez, Roberto. 1996. "Before Canseco—Early History of Latinos in Baseball Full of Hits and Runs
    around the Colorline," *Black Issues in Higher Education* (April 18): 18–19.
Roman, Peter. 2003. *People's Power: Cuba's Experience with Representative Government*. Lanham, MD:
    Rowman and Littlefield.
Rosenburg, Tina. 1987. "Death Watch in Mexico: Labor Boss Fidel Velazquez," *The Nation*, 24 (April 18).
Sagas, Ernesto. 1993. "A Case of Mistaken Identity: Antihaitianismo in Dominican Culture," *Latinameri-
    canist*, 29.1: 1–5.
Schneider, Ben Ross. 2004. *Business Politics and the State in Twentieth-Century Latin America*. Cambridge:
    Cambridge University Press.
Senzek, Alva. 1997. "Entrepreneurs Who Become Radicals," *NACLA Report on the Americas*, 30.4 (January–
    February): 28.

Smith, Adam. 1776. *Inquiry into the Nature and Causes of the Wealth of Nations*. London: Methuen (www.bibliomania.com/2/1/65/112/frameset.html, accessed December 10, 2010).

Swanger, Joanna. 2007. "Feminist Community Building in Ciudad Juarez: A Local Cultural Alternative to the Structural Violence of Globalization," *Latin American Perspectives*, 34.2 (March): 108–123.

Tarrow, Sidney. 1994. *Power in Movement*. Cambridge: Cambridge University Press.

Thompson, E. P. 1966. *The Making of the English Working Class*. New York: Vintage Books.

Tilly, Charles. 1978. *From Mobilization to Revolution*. Reading, MA: Addison-Wesley.

United Nations Office on Drugs and Crime. 2008. *Elementos Orientados para las Políticas Públicas sobre Drogas en la Subregión*. Lima, Peru (www.unodc.org/documents/peru/ElementosOrientadores-Peru-June08.pdf).

U.S. Senate. 1975. "Covert Action in Chile, 1963–1973," *Staff Report of the Senate Select Committee on Intelligence Activities*. Washington, DC: U.S. Government Printing Office.

Chapter 12

Alcoñiz, Isabella and Melissa Scheier. 2007. "The MTL Piqueteros and the Communist Party in Argentina," *Latin American Perspectives*, 34.2: 157–171.

Castañeda, Jorge. 2006. "Latin America's Left Turn," *Foreign Affairs*, 85.3 (May–June): 28–43.

Dalton-Acton, Lord John. 1907. "Letter to Bishop Mandell Creighton, April 5, 1887, Transcript of," in J. N. Figgis and R. V. Laurence (editors), *Historical Essays and Studies*. London: Macmillan (available at https://history.hanover.edu/courses/excerpts/165acton.html, accessed September 14, 2020).

Domínguez, Jorge. 1997. *Technopols: Freeing Politics and Markets in Latin America*. University Park, PA: Pennsylvania State University Press.

Duverger, Maurice. 1972. *Party Politics and Pressure Groups: A Comparative Introduction*. New York: Thomas Crowell.

Elbaum, Jorge. 2019. "El documental de Netflix sobre Cambridge Analytica y el fraude electoral en Argentina," *Centro Latinoamericano de Análisis Estratégico* (August 8, estrategia.la, accessed March 5, 2020).

Encarnación, Omar G. 2018. "The Trumpification of the Latin American Right," *Foreign Policy* (April 16, foreignpolicy.com/2018/04/16/the-trumpification-of-the-latin-american-right, accessed March 2, 2020).

Gottberg, Luis Duno. 2011. "The Color of Mobs: Racial Politics, Ethnopopulism, and Representation in the Chávez Era," in David Smilde and Daniel Hellinger (editors), *Venezuela's Bolivarian Democracy: Participation, Politics and Culture under Chávez*, pp. 271–297. Durham, NC: Duke University Press.

Gramsci, Antonio. 1971. *Selections from the Prison Notebooks*. Trans. Quinton Hoare and Geoffrey Nowell Smith. New York: International Publishers.

Harris, Richard. 1993. "The Nicaragua Revolution: A Postmortem," *Latin America Research Review*, 28.3: 197–213.

Hellinger, Daniel. 2005. "When 'No' Means 'Yes': Electoral Politics in Bolivarian Venezuela," *Latin American Perspectives*, 32.3: 8–32.

Landi, Oscar. 1995. "Outsiders, Nuevos Caudillos y Media Polítics," in Perelli et al. (editors), *Partidos y Clase Política en América Latina en los 90 (Parties and Political Class in Latin America in the 90s)*. Costa Rica: Instituto Interamericano de Derechos Humanos.

Levitsky, Steven and Lucan Way. 2002. "The Rise of Competitive Authoritarianism," *Journal of Democracy*, 13.2 (April): 51–69.

Lustig, Nathan. 2018. "Latin America's Growing Mobile Market" (April 5, nathanlustig.com, accessed March 4, 2020).

Mainwaring, Scott. 1995. "Brazil: Weak Parties, Feckless Democracy," in Scott Mainwaring and Tim Scully (editors), *Building Democratic Institutions: Party Systems in Latin America*. Stanford, CA: Stanford University Press.

O'Hara, Michael. 2018. "A Look at the Mobile Ecosystem in Latin America," *IGC Connect* (January 23, igcconnect.com, accessed March 4, 2020).

PBS (Public Broadcast System). 2001. *The Commanding Heights: The Battle for the World Economy*. New York: A Touchstone Book.

Pecci, Gioacchino. 1981. *Rerum Novarum*. Vatican City: Papal Encyclical.

Prevost, Gary and Harry E. Vanden (editors). 1997. *The Undermining of the Sandinista Revolution*. London: Macmillan Press.

Quandt, Midge. 2007. "The Left in Latin America Today" (www.quandt.com, accessed April 22, 2007).

Rial, Juan. 1995. "Percepciones sobre las instituciones democràticas y los medios de comunicación" ("Perceptions about Democratic Institutions and the Means of Communication"), in Perelli et al. (editors), *Partidos y Clase Política en América Latina en los 90* (*Parties and Political Class in Latin America in the 90s*). Costa Rica: Instituto Interamericano de Derechos Humanos.

Roberts, Kenneth. 2018. "Political Parties in Latin America's Second Wave of Incorporation," in Eduardo Silva and Federico M. Rossi (editors), *Shaping the Political Arena in Latin America*. Pittsburgh, PA: University of Pittsburgh Press.

Rodríguez, Pablo. 2019. "Argentina, Cambiemos and Cambridge Analytical," *Buenos Aires Times* (September 14, betimes.com.ar, accessed March 5, 2020).

Rogers, Katie. 2020. "Trump's Rally Recipe: Just Add Data, Money, Entertainment and Grievance," *New York Times* (February 28).

Tamayo, G. 2012. "La derecho, facebook y el odio a Chávez: Visión crítica de una marcha contra Hugo Chávez convocada en Facebook [sic]," Thesis, Universidad Andina Simón Bolívar, Ecuador (www.alainet.org/es/articulo/204620, accessed March 5, 2020).

Thompson, Stuart A. and Charlie Warzel. 2019. "One Nation, Tracked," *New Your Times* (December 19).

Zamora, Rubén. 1997. "Democratic Transition or Modernization? The Case of El Salvador Since 1979," in Jorge Domínguez and Marc Lindenberg (editors), *Democratic Transitions in Central America*. Gainesville: University of Florida Press.

Chapter 13

Ames, Barry. 2002. *The Deadlock of Democracy in Brazil*. Ann Arbor: University of Michigan Press.

Astor, Michael. 2008. "Brazil's President Says G-8 No Longer Relevant," *Associated Press* (November 16).

Avritzer, Leonardo. 2002. *Democracy and the Public Space in Latin America*. Princeton, NJ: Princeton University Press.

Broadman, H. G. and F. Recanatini. 1999. *Seeds of Corruption: Do Market Institutions Matter?* Washington, DC: World Bank. Working Paper 2368.

Buxton, Julia. 2001. *The Failure of Political Reform in Venezuela*. Aldershot: Ashgate.

Cameron, Maxwell A., Eric Hershberg and Kenneth E. Sharpe (editors). 2012. *New Institutions for Participatory Democracy in Latin America: Voice and Consequence*. New York: Palgrave-MacMillan.

Cary, John. 2002. "Parties, Coalitions and the Chilean Congress in the 1990s," in Scott Morgenstern and Benito Nacif (editors), *Legislative Politics in Latin America*, pp. 222–253. Cambridge: Cambridge University Press.

Coppedge, Michael. 1994. *Strong Parties and Lame Ducks: Presidential Partyarchy and Factionalism in Venezuela*. Stanford, CA: Stanford University Press.

Crisp, Brian. 2000. *Democratic Institutional Design: The Powers and Incentives of Venezuelan Politicians and Interest Groups*. Palo Alto, CA: Stanford University Press.

Diamond, Larry. 2005. "The State of Democratization at the Beginning of the 21st Century," *Journal of Diplomacy*, 6 (Winter–Spring): 13–18.

Dilla Alfonso, Haroldo. 2006. "Cuban Civil Society: Future Directions and Challenges," *NACLA Report on the Americas*, 39.4: 37–42.

Global Development Research Center. n.d. "Understanding the Concept of Governance" (www.gdrc.org/u-gov/governance-understand.html, accessed July 28, 2009).

Hammergren, Lynn. 2008. "Twenty-Five Years of Latin American Judicial Reforms: Achievements, Disappointments, and Emerging Issues," *Whitehead Journal of Diplomacy and International Relations*, 9.1 (Winter–Spring): 89–104.

Herman, Edward S. and Frank Brodhead. 1984. *Demonstration Elections: U.S.-Staged Elections in the Dominican Republic, Vietnam, and El Salvador*. Boston: South End Press.

Huntington, Samuel. 1968. *Political Order in Changing Societies*. New Haven, CT: Yale University Press.

La Botz, Dan. 2012. "Mexico's Labor Movement after the Elections: A House Still Divided," *NACLA Report on the Americas*, 45.1 (Winter): 34–37.

LASA (Latin American Studies Association). 1984. *Report of the Latin American Studies Association Delegation to Observe the Nicaraguan General Election of November 4, 1984. LASA Forum* (Fall). Latin American Studies Association.

Levitsky, Steven. 2000. "The 'Normalization' of Argentine Politics," *Journal of Democracy*, 11.2: 56–69.

Maher, Stephen. 2012. "Elections, Imperialism, Socialism, and Democracy: Coups and Social Change in Latin America," *NACLA Report on the Americas*, 45.1 (Winter): 56–58.

Mainwaring, Scott and M. Soberg Shugart (editors). 1997. *Presidentialism and Democracy in Latin America*. Cambridge: Cambridge University Press.

McCarthy, Michael M. 2012. "The Possibilities and Limits of Politicized Participation: Community Councils, Coproduction, and *Poder Popular* in Chávez's Venezuela," in Maxwell A. Cameron, Eric Hershberg and Kenneth E. Sharpe (editors), *New Institutions for Participatory Democracy in Latin America: Voice and Consequence*, pp. 123–148. New York: Palgrave-MacMillan.

Morgenstern, Scott and Benito Nacif (editors). 2002. *Legislative Politics in Latin America*. Cambridge: Cambridge University Press.

Munck, Gerardo L. 2004. "Democratic Politics in Latin America: New Debates and Research Frontiers," *Annual Review of Political Science*, 7: 437–462.

Mustapic, Ana Maria. 2002. "Oscillating Relations: President and Congress in Argentina," in Scott Morgenstern and Benito Nacif (editors), *Legislative Politics in Latin America*, pp. 23–47. Cambridge: Cambridge University Press.

Neto, Octavio Amorim. 2002. "Presidential Cabinets, Electoral Cycles and Coalition Discipline," in Scott Morgenstern and Benito Necif (editors), *Legislative Politics in Latin America*. Cambridge: Cambridge University Press.

O'Donnell, Guillermo. 1994. "Delegative Democracy," *Journal of Democracy*, 5.1: 55–69.

Roman, Peter. 2003. *People's Power: Cuba's Experience with Representative Government*. Lanham, MD: Rowman and Littlefield.

Saney, Isaac. 2004. *Cuba: A Revolution in Motion*. London: Zed Books.

Von Mettenheim, Kurt and James Malloy (editors). 1998. *Deepening Democracy in Latin America*. Pittsburgh, PA: University of Pittsburgh Press.

Wei, Pan. 2006. "Toward a Consultative Rule of Law Regime in China," in Suisheng Zhao (editor), *Debating Political Reform in China: Rule of Law vs. Democratization*. Armonk, NY: M. E. Sharpe.

WikiLeaks. 2009. "Paraguayan Pols Plot Parliamentary Pusch" (March 28, https://wikileaks.org/plusd/cables/09ASUNCION189_a.html, accessed September 14, 2020).

Chapter 14

Amnesty International. 2002. "El Salvador: 10th Anniversary of Peace Accords, Still No Justice," AI Index: AMR 29/001/2002 (January 16, www.amnestyusa.org).

Amnesty International. 2006. "Mexico: Killings and Abductions of Women in Ciudad Juarez and the City of Chihuahua—The Struggle for Justice Goes On," AI Index: AMR 41/012/2006 (February 20, www.amnestyusa.org, accessed August 28, 2007).

Barry, Tom. 2005. "Southcom Generals Say 'Not in Our Backyard,'" *Updater*, Americas Program, International Relations Resource Center (www.americaspolicy.org, accessed June 20, 2006).

Bass, Hyatt. 2016. "Soffiyah Elijah: Lessons from Cuba's Incarceration Model" (Interview), *Guernica Magazine* (March 21, www.guernicamag.com, accessed March 17, 2020).

Bremer, Catherine. 2007. "Once Quiet Towns Engulfed by Mexican Drugs War," *Reuters* (July 18).

CIP (Center for International Policy). 2006. "Plan Colombia: Six Years Later," *International Policy Report* (www.ciponline.org/colombia/0611ipr.pdf, accessed July 28, 2009).

COHA (Council on Hemispheric Affairs). 2005a. *Too Close for Comfort: El Salvador Ratchets Up Its U.S. Ties*. Washington, DC: Council on Hemispheric Affairs, July 19.

COHA (Council on Hemispheric Affairs). 2005b. *Washington Secures Long-Sought Hemispheric Outpost, Perhaps at the Expense of Regional Sovereignty*. Washington, DC: Council on Hemispheric Affairs, July 20.

Cruz, José Miguel. 2010. "Police Misconduct and Democracy in Latin America," *AmericasBarometer Insights*, 33.

Emersberger, Joe. 2010. "IACHR Rehashes Debunked Claims about Venezuela," *Venezuelanalysis.com* (May 6, http://venezuelanalysis.com/analysis/5337, accessed August 10, 2013).

Gender Equality Observatory. 2012. *Annual Report 2012*. New York: United Nations Economic Commission on Latin America.

IACHR. 2010. "Democracy and Human Rights in Venezuela," *Inter-American Commission on Human Rights* (www.cidh.oas.org/countryrep/Venezuela2009eng/VE09CHAPIENG.htm, accessed August 10).

ICEFI (Instituto Centromericano de Estudios Fiscales). 2019. *Costa Rica: Recomendaciones al proyecto de presupuesto 2020* (icefi.org, accessed April 13, 2020).

Issa, Daniela. 2007. "Praxis of Empowerment: *Mística* and Mobilization in Brazil's Landless Rural Workers' Movement," *Latin American Perspectives*, 34.2 (March): 124–138.

Kaufman, Robert. 1972. *The Politics of Land Reform in Chile 1950–1970: Public Policy, Political Institutions, and Social Change*. Cambridge, MA: Harvard University Press.

Kawell, JoAnn. 2002. "Drug Economies of the Americas," *NACLA Report on the Americas*, 36.2 (September–October): 25–26.

Kruger, Mark H. 2007. "Community Based Crime-Control in Cuba," *Contemporary Justice Review*, 10.1 (March): 101–114.

Lacey, Marc. 2007. "Drug Gangs Use Violence to Sway Guatemala Vote," *New York Times* (August 4): A1.

Latinobarómetro. 2006. *Informe Latinobarómetro 2005 (Latinobarometer Report)*. Santiago: Corporación Latinobarómetro (www.latinobarometro.org).

Latinobarómetro. 2013. *Informe Latinobarómetro 2012 (Latin Barometer Report)*. Santiago: Corporación Latinobarómetro (www.latinobarometro.org).

Lauria-Santiago, Aldo. 1999. *An Agrarian Republic: Commercial Agriculture and the Politics of Peasant Communities in El Salvador*. Pittsburgh, PA: University of Pittsburgh Press.

Mackey, Danielle and Ciara Eisner. 2019. "Inside the Plot to Murder Honduran Activist Berta Cáceres," *The Intercept* (December 21, https://theintercept.com/2019/12/21/berta-caceres-murder-plot-honduras, accessed March 14, 2020).

Miller, Jamie. 2003. *The Intellectual, Economic, Ludicrous Whisperings of God*. Mennonite Central Committee (www.mcc.org/globalizationconsultations/latin_america/miller.html, accessed June 1, 2007).

Miller, John. 2005. "Free, Free at Last," *Dollars and Sense* (www.dollarsandsense.org/archives/2005/0305miller.html, accessed October 4, 2008).

National Security Archive. 2009. "'Body Count Mentalities', Colombia's 'False Positives' Scandal, Declassified," *The Colombia Project* (January 7, nsarchive2.gwu.edu/NSAEBB/NSAEBB266/index.htm, accessed April 7, 2020).

O'Donnell, Guillermo. 1998. "Polyarchies and the (Un)Rule of Law in Latin America," in Juan Méndez, Guillermo A. O'Donnell and Paulo Sérgio Pinheiro (editors), *The Rule of Law and the Underprivileged in Latin America*. Notre Dame, IN: University of Notre Dame Press (www.march.es/ceacs/publicaciones/working/archivos/1998_125.pdf, accessed December 9, 2010).

Pérez-Liñán, Aníbal and Andrea Castagnola. 2019. "The Perils of Judicial Reform," *AulaBlog.net* (July 9, accessed March 17, 2020).

Phillips, Tom. 2006. "Blood Simple," *Observer* (London, September 17): 27.

Putnam, Robert. 1993. *Making Democracy Work: Civic Traditions in Modern Italy*. Princeton, NJ: Princeton University Press.

Quirós, Ludmila. 2019. "Latin America: Growing Threat from Brazil's PCC," *AulaBog.net* (February 2, 2020).

Schor, Miguel. 2003. "The Rule of Law and Democratic Consolidation in Latin America," Paper prepared for delivery at the *2003 Meeting of the Latin American Studies Association*, Dallas, TX, March 27–29.

Thompson, Theresa and Anwar Shah. 2005. "Transparency International's Corruption Perceptions Index: Whose Perceptions Are They Anyway?" Discussion Draft Revised March 2005, World Bank (http://siteresources.worldbank.org/INTWBIGOVANTCOR/Resources/TransparencyInternationalCorruptionIndex.pdf, accessed March 10, 2020).

Transparency International. 2005. *Global Corruption Barometer 2004* (www.globalcorruptionreport.org/gcr, accessed December 9, 2010).

UNCTAD. 2019. *Trade and Development Report 2019*. New York: United Nations Publications.

UNDP. 2012. *Anticorruption Programs in Latin America and the Caribbean*. New York: United Nations Development Programme.

UNODC. 2019. Criminal and Criminal Justice Statistics (https://www.unodc.org/unodc/en/data-and-analysis/statistics.html, accessed September 14, 2020).

U.S. Department of State. 2004. *Country Reports on Human Rights Activities*. Washington, DC: U.S. Department of State.

Webb, Gary. 1999. *Dark Alliance: The CIA, the Contras and the Crack Cocaine Explosion*. New York: Seven Stories Press.

Witherspoon Institute. 2020. "Abortion The 17+ Women in El Salvador: A Case of Infanticide Impunity in the Name of Abortion Rights," *Public Discourse* (February 9, www.thepublicdiscourse.com/2020/02/59850, accessed March 12, 2020).

WOLA (Washington Office on Latin America). 2020. *Beyond the Narcostate Narrative: What U.S. Drug Trade Monitoring Data Says About Venezuela*. Washington, DC (www.wola.org/wp-content/uploads/2020/03/Narcostate-Venezuela-Drug-Trafficking-Ramsey-Smilde.pdf, accessed March 14, 2020).

World Prison Brief. 2017, 2018. *World Prison Population List*. Institute for Crime & Justice Policy Research (www.prisonstudies.org, accessed March 11, 2020).

Chapter 15

Aguilar, Julián. 2012. "Twenty Years Later NAFTA Remains a Source of Tension," *New York Times* (December 7).

Angosto-Ferrández, Luis Fernanda. 2015. *Venezuela Reframed: Bolivarianism, Indigenous Peoples, and Socialisms of the 21st Century*. London: Zed Books.

AP (Associated Press). 2005. "Stealing the Rainforest," *Associated Press* (July 4).

Astor, Michael. 2005. "Brazilians Suspect Foreigners Covet Amazon Rainforest," *Associated Press* (May 18).

Bacon, David. 2004. *The Children of NAFTA: Labor Wars on the U.S./Mexican Border*. Berkeley: University of California Press.

Barkin, David. 2006. "Building a Future for Rural Mexico," *Latin American Perspectives*, 33.2 (March): 132–140.

Benson, Todd. 2005. "Brazil Says Deal on Drug Isn't Assured," *New York Times* (July 16): B13.

Birns, Larry and Sarah Schaffer. 2005. "CAFTA and Its Discontents," *Council on Hemispheric Affairs* (May 31, www.coha.org/2005/05/31/cafta-and-its-discontents, accessed July 22, 2007).

Boué, Juan Carlos. 2013. *Enforcing Pacta Sun Servanda? Conoco-Phillips and Exxon-Mobil Versus the Bolivarian Republic of Venezuela and Petróleos de Venezuela*. Working Papers Series 2, No. 1. Centre of Latin American Studies, University of Cambridge.

Defense Advisory Board. 2019. *The 5G Ecosystem: Risks and Opportunities for DoD* (media.defense.gov, accessed March 25, 2020).

Deitz, Henry and James Street (editors). 1989. *Latin America's Economic Development and Structuralist Perspectives*. Boulder CO: Lynne Rienner.

Delp, Linda, Marisol Arriaga, Guadalupe Palma, Haydee Urita and Abel Valenzuela. 2004. *NAFTA's Side Agreement: Fading into Oblivion?* Los Angeles, CA: UCLA Center for Labor Research and Education.

ECEN. 2005. *Report. European Christian Environmental Network* (No longer online).

ECLAC (United Nations Economic Commission on Latin America and the Caribbean). 2019. *Foreign Direct Investment in Latin America and the Caribbean*. New York: United Nations Press.

Enloe, Cynthia. 2000. *Bananas, Beaches, and Bases: Making Feminist Sense of International Politics*. Berkeley: University of California Press.

Esquival, Gerardo. 2011. "The Dynamics of Income Inequality in Mexico since NAFTA," *Economía*, 12.1 (Fall): 155–179.

Fabbri, Morris and Kearsley A. Stewart. 2019. "Cuba Quarantined People with HIV," *Tampa Bay Times* (November 29).

Friedman, Thomas. 2000a. "The Coalition to Keep the World's Poor People Poor," *New York Times* (April 14).

Friedman, Thomas. 2000b. *The Lexus and the Olive Tree: Understanding Globalization*. New York: Farrar, Straus, and Giroux.

Friedman, Thomas. 2005. *The World Is Flat: A Brief History of the Twenty-First Century*. New York: Farrar, Straus, and Giroux.

Gardini, Gian Luca. 2009. *Latin America in the 21st Century: Nations, Regionalism, Globalization*. London: Zed Books.

Gates, Bill. 2015. "The Next Outbreak; We're Not Ready," *Ted Talks* (www.ted.com/talks/bill_gates_the_next_outbreak_we_re_not_ready?, accessed March 25, 2020).

Gorry, Connor. 2005. "Cuba's National HIV/AIDS Program," *MEDICC Review*, 13 (April 2011): 5–8.

Gray, Lorraine (director). 1985. *The Global Assembly Line* (motion picture). New Day Films.

Henneberry, Brittany. 2020. "How Surgical Masks Are Made," *Thomas* (www.thomasnet.com/articles/other/how-surgical-masks-are-made, accessed March 25, 2020).

HIV InSite. 2007. "Haiti," University of California, San Francisco (http://hivinsite.ucsf.edu/global?page=cr02-ha-00, accessed April 23, 2009).

HIV InSite. 2008. "Caribbean," University of California, San Francisco (hivinsite.ucsf.edu/global?page=cr02-00-00, accessed April 23, 2009).

Jawara, Fatoumata and Aileen Kwa. 2002. *Behind the Scenes at the WTO: The Real World of International Trade Negotiations*. London: Zed Books.

Johnson, Tim. 2012. "Mexico's 'Maquiladora' Labor System Keeps Most Mexicans in Poverty," *McClatchy DC* (June 17, www.mcclatchydc.com/2012/06/17/152220/mexicos-maquiladora-labor-system.html, accessed October 25, 2013).

Lama, Abraham. 1999. "Glacial Snow Disappearing in the Andes," *InterPress Service*, July 24 (ipsnews.net, accessed December 10, 2010).

Mumme, Stephen. 1999. "NAFTA's Environmental Side Agreement: Almost Green?," *Borderlines*, 9 (www.irc-online.org, accessed April 26, 2006).

New, William. 2012. "Brazil HIV Drug Patent Ruling Allows Generics, Sends Pipeline Process into Doubt," *Intellectual Property Watch* (March 21, www.ip-watch.org/2012/03/21/brazil-hiv-drug-patent-ruling-allows-generics-sends-pipeline-process-into-doubt).

Newzoo. 2019. *Newzoo Mobile Market Report* (https://newzoo.com/products/reports/global-mobile-market-report, accessed April 13, 2020).

Pantone, Dan James. 2008. "Uncontacted Amazon Indians in Peru" (www.amazon-indians.org/Uncontacted-Amazon-Indians-Peru.html, accessed July 28, 2009).

Papademetriou, Demetrios, John Audley, Sandra Polaski and Scott Vaughan. 2003. *NAFTA's Promise and Reality: Lessons for the Hemisphere*. Washington, DC: Carnegie Endowment for International Peace.

Porter, Eduardo. 2005. "Illegal Immigrants Are Bolstering Social Security with Billions," *New York Times* (April 5): xx.

Raintree Nutrition. 2005. "Welcome to the Rainforest" (www.rain-tree.com, accessed July 28, 2009).

Robinson, William I. 2004. *A Theory of Global Capitalism: Production, Class, and State in a Transnational World*. Baltimore, MD: The Johns Hopkins Press.

Schurman, Rachel. 2003. "Fish and Flexibility: Working in the New Chile," *NACLA Report on the Americas*, 37.1: 36–37.

Scott, Robert. 2003. *The High Price of Free Trade*. Washington, DC: Economic Policy Institute. Briefing Paper No. 147.

Silberman, Jonathan, Martín Koppel and Mary-Alice Waters. 2004. "Radical Reorganization and Cutback of Cuba's Sugar Industry," *The Militant*, 68.5 (February 9, www.themilitant.com/2004/6805/680550.html, accessed December 10, 2010).

Smith, Adam. 1766. *Inquiry into the Nature and Causes of the Wealth of Nations*. London: Methuen (www.bibliomania.com/2/1/65/112/frameset.html, accessed December 10, 2010).

Strange, Susan. 1996. *The Retreat of the State: The Diffusion of Power in the World Economy*. Cambridge: Cambridge University Press.

USTR. 2004. *NAFTA: A Decade of Success*. Washington, DC: Office of the U.S. Trade Representative (www.ustr.gov/Document_Library/Fact_Sheets/2004/NAFTA_A_Decade_of_Success.html, accessed November 2, 2009).

USTR. 2005. *CAFTA: Facts*. Washington, DC: Office of the U.S. Trade Representative.

World Bank. 1996. *A Mining Strategy for Latin America and the Caribbean*. Washington, DC: World Bank. Technical Paper No. 345.

Chapter 16

Anderson, Thomas. 1971. *Matanza: El Salvador's Communist Revolt of 1932*. Lincoln: University of Nebraska Press.

Avritzer, Leonardo. 2002. *Democracy and the Public Space in Latin America*. Princeton, NJ: Princeton University Press.

Bernstein, Adam. 2008. "Obituary: David Potter, 95; Ambassador to Chile During Pinochet Era," *Washington Post* (July 31): B7.

Burges, Sean. 2012. "Is Itamaraty a Problem for Brazilian Foreign Policy?" *Política Externa*, 21.3: 133–148 (in English at http://anclasblog.files.wordpress.com/2013/01/2012-2013-english-seria-o-itamaraty-um-problema-para-a-policc81tica-externa-brasileira.pdf).

Bushnells, David. 1986. "Simón Bolívar and the United States: A Study in Ambivalence," *Air Force Review* (July–August, www.airpower.maxwell.af.mil/airchronicles/aureview/1986/jul-aug/bushnell.html, accessed December 27, 2010).

CIA (U.S. Central Intelligence Agency). 1970. *Report of CIA Chilean Task Force Activities, 15 September to 3 November 1970*. National Security Archives (November 18, www.gwu.edu/~nsarchiv/NSAEBB/NSAEBB8/ch01-01.htm, accessed April 27, 2009).

Emersberger, Joe. 2010. "IACHR Rehashes Debunked Claims about Venezuela," *Venezuelanalysis.com* (May 6, http://venezuelanalysis.com/analysis/5337, accessed August 10, 2013).

Franck, Thomas and Edward Weisband. 1972. *Word Politics: Verbal Strategy Among the Superpowers*. New York: Oxford University Press.

Gill, Leslie. 2004. *The School of the Americas: Military Training and Violence in the Americas*. Durham, NC: Duke University Press.

Grandin, Greg. 2006. *Empire's Workshop: Latin America, the United States and the Rise of the New Imperialism*. New York: Metropolitan Books.

Hardt, Michael and Antonio Negri. 2000. *Empire*. Cambridge, MA: Harvard University Press.

Hellinger, Daniel. 2017. "Oil and the Chavez Legacy," *Latin American Perspectives*, 212.44 (January): 54–77.

Herman, Edward S. and Frank Brodhead. 1984. *Demonstration Elections: U.S.-Staged Elections in the Dominican Republic, Vietnam, and El Salvador*. Boston: South End Press.

IACHR. 2010. *Democracy and Human Rights in Venezuela*. Inter-American Commission on Human Rights (www.cidh.oas.org/countryrep/Venezuela2009eng/VE09CHAPIENG.htm, accessed August 10).

Johnson, John J. 1980. *Latin America in Caricature*. Austin: University of Texas Press.

Kirkpatrick, Jeane. 1979. "Dictatorships and Double Standards," *Commentary Magazine*, 68.5 (November): 34–45.

LaFeber, Walter. 1993. *Inevitable Revolutions: The United States in Central America*. New York: W.W. Norton.

Millet, Richard. 1977. *Guardians of the Dynasty*. New York: Orbis Books.

National Security Archives. 2003. *Electronic Briefing Book No. 104*. Washington, DC: George Washington University (www2.gwu.edu/~nsarchiv/NSAEBB/NSAEBB104, accessed March 26, 2020).

National Security Archives. 2011. *Operation Desert Storm: Ten Years Later*. Washington, DC: George Washington University (www.gwu.edu/~nsarchiv/NSAEBB/NSAEBB39, accessed March 26, 2020).

OAS (Organization of American States). 2019. *Final Report of the Audit of the Elections in Bolivia: Intentional Manipulation and Serious Irregularities Made It Impossible to Validate the Results*. Washington, DC: Organization of American States.

Robinson, William I. 1992. *A Faustian Bargain: U.S. Intervention in the Nicaraguan Elections and American Foreign Policy in the Post-Cold War Era*. Boulder, CO: Westview Press.

Robinson, William I. 1996. *Promoting Polyarchy: Globalization, US Intervention, and Hegemony*. Cambridge: Cambridge University Press.

Rogers, William. 2004. "Fleeing the Chilean Coup: The Debate Over U.S. Complicity," *Foreign Affairs*, 83.1 (January–February): 160–165.

Said, Edward W. 1981. *Covering Islam*. New York: Pantheon.

Schoultz, Lars. 1987. *National Security and United States Policy toward Latin America*. Princeton, NJ: Princeton University Press.

Webb, Gary. 1999. *Dark Alliance: The CIA, the Contras and the Crack Cocaine Explosion*. New York: Seven Stories Press.

Afterword

Barber, Benjamin. 1984. *Strong Democracy: Participatory Politics for a New Age*. Berkeley: University of California Press.

Putnam, Robert D. (editor). 2002. *Democracies in Flux: The Evolution of Social Capital in Contemporary Society*. New York: Oxford University Press.

Index

Note: Numbers in **bold** indicate a table. Numbers in *italics* indicate a figure.